HAMMER

HAMMER

Armand Hammer

with Neil Lyndon

A PERIGEE BOOK

Perigee Books
are published by
The Putnam Publishing Group
200 Madison Avenue
New York, NY 10016

First Perigee Edition 1988

The author gratefully acknowledges permission from
Frederick Fell Publishers, Inc., to reprint material
from *The 14-Karat Trailer* by Myron Zobel,
copyright © 1955 by Myron Zobel.

Library of Congress Cataloging-in-Publication Data

Hammer, Armand, date.
    Hammer / Armand Hammer, with Neil Lyndon.—1st Perigee ed.
      p.   cm.
Includes index.
    ISBN 0-399-51441-4
    1. Hammer, Armand, date.   2. Businessmen—United States—
Biography.   3. Capitalists and financiers—United States—
Biography.   4. Statesmen—United States—Biography.   5. United
States—Relations—Soviet Union.   6. Soviet Union—Relations—United
States.   I. Lyndon, Neil.   II. Title.
HC102.5.H35 1988   88-4161 CIP
338′.092′4—dc19
[B]

Printed in the United States of America
1   2   3   4   5   6   7   8   9   10

Acknowledgments

_____

_____

_____

_____

This book could not have been composed and would not now be completed but for the efforts of a very large number of people to whom I offer my heartfelt thanks.

The staff of my office at Occidental Petroleum in Los Angeles took on innumerable extra tasks to assist me in researching and checking my story. Special thanks go to Richard Jacobs, Florence Ajamian, Patricia Claytor, Cathy Kosak and Claude Jones.

Patricia Hall worked for a very long time to assemble an immense archive of my papers and worked with tireless cheerfulness to assist Neil Lyndon, my collaborator.

Paul Hebner, Secretary of the corporation, and his assistant, Linda Granito, combed the early records of Occidental to help me assemble that vital section of this book.

Frank Ashley and his staff at Oxy provided invaluable research assistance with exemplary efficiency. John Bryson has photographed many of the incidents described here. At the Washington office of Occidental International, the President, William McSweeny and his staff—notably Eleanor Connors, Bob McGee and Galina Sullivan—gave unstintingly of their time to fill in missing details and refresh my memory with good stories. They also read the manuscript and commented wisely upon it. In New York, Benedict Lissim and Fran McClure were always ready to help me. In London, Sir Ranulph Fiennes and Alex Blake-Milton helped when called upon. In Moscow, Michael Bruk and Nina Vlassova were ever receptive to render assistance.

Dennis Gould and Martha Wade Kaufman provided valuable advice for the pages in this book concerning my interest in art. Also my deep thanks to Dr. Maury Leibovitz, who contributed to my recollections of the Knoedler acquisition, as well as my early days with Occidental.

Yechiel Kadishai, the loyal friend and assistant to Menachem Begin, and Dr. Zvi Dinstein, Chairman of the Israel Institute of Petroleum and Energy, provided invaluable assistance in reconstructing the chronology of my activities with Israel.

John Tigrett and George Williamson, long-time friends and colleagues, assisted in recollections of the early days of Occidental's overseas activities.

My dear friends Louis Nizer, Arthur Groman, Irving Stone and Mrs. Morton Phillips (Dear Abby) also read the manuscript with great care and gave much helpful advice. Louis deserves my special gratitude for generously allowing me to profit at length from his own writings on some of the incidents described in this book.

Phyllis Grann, President of The Putnam Publishing Group, brought the keenest of critical eyes to bear upon the book, and her Editor in Chief, Neil Nyren, shaped the finished work with extraordinary deftness and speed.

My wife, Frances, tolerated my absorption in this project with the same grace and humor that she has brought to all our ventures together in the last quarter century. This book would not exist without her and neither would I.

The full list of those who assisted in the preparation of this book would fill many pages. My apologies go with my thanks to those I have omitted. Everybody who helped me added strengths and benefits to the book: its weaknesses and whatever mistakes it may contain are solely my own responsibility.

In memory of my beloved parents,
Julius and Rose Hammer,
and my beloved brothers,
Harry and Victor

Contents

Photographs follow pages 192 and 352.

HAMMER

Prologue

————————————————

————————————————

————————————————

————————————————

————————————————

I have never been much occupied with my past; it has never held my deepest interest. I have always cared most for the present and the future, for the work that I can do today and the opportunities that it will bring tomorrow. I have no time to spare for yesterday: let it rest in peace.

Raking over the past and sifting its dust is an occupation for the idle or the elderly retired. I may be elderly—at the time of this writing I am eighty-eight—but I have not retired and I hope never to be idle.

This is a strange start to an autobiography, in which I hope to tell the full story of my life so far. But I want to explain that I care more for the whole meaning of the story than for the particular events and scenes which make it up. *What* I have done does not interest me so much as *why* I did it.

Mine has been a life of hectic action and endeavor, rather than of quiet contemplation. I have always felt that the highest human expression comes in our creative endeavors, those which draw upon all of our powers of imagination, intelligence and understanding; and throughout my life I have tried to bring all my energy and all my wit to every working day. Jimmy Stewart expressed the same attitude, but less piously, in the film *Shenandoah:* "If we don't try, we don't do. And if we don't do . . . what are we on this earth for?"

As a child, I composed a personal creed, which I would repeat to myself at bedtime. Though I was not raised in a religious home, my creed was a kind of prayer to God, the unknown spirit of life which can inspire us and charge our being. I asked God, then, that I might be given the strength to help deserving people as much as I was able.

I have never prayed for power or fame or riches, though I have enjoyed them all in abundance. I hope that I have never been greedy. If my main motive had been to make myself rich, I could have been numbered among the multibillionaires of the world. I am not. All my life I have given away a large part of my fortune, more money than I could ever count. Fortunately, I have always had the ability to make money, leaving me with plenty to share. My childhood creed has always been my guide.

My life spans the present century and it has sometimes precariously bridged the greatest cultural and political divide in history—the ideological gulf between the capitalist countries of the West and the socialist countries of the East. My work has carried me to every corner of the world and into the company of the leaders and rulers of nations. In all my time and in all my actions, I have tried to accomplish something of lasting benefit to the world; to add what I can to the riches of the planet and to share with all people the beauty and the delight of life.

This is the story of my odyssey.

1

Chernobyl, Nicholas Daniloff and David Goldfarb

This book was almost finished when I had to start it again.

In the late spring and early summer of 1986, while I was working on the last chapters of these memoirs, three incidents occurred in quick succession which opened a new chapter in my life—and one of the most important to date. Two of them—the Chernobyl catastrophe and the release of Nicholas Daniloff, clearing the way for the Reykjavik Summit—were of lasting significance for the world. One of them—the release of David Goldfarb—closely affected the life of only one man and his family. Yet they all, in their various dimensions, show the efforts that I have been trying to make, throughout my long life, to bring understanding to relations between East and West.

In an eerie way, the calamitous explosion at the nuclear reactor in Chernobyl, eighty miles from Kiev in the Soviet Union, connected me with my past and completed a circle of my adult life. I found myself supplying medical aid to relieve a disaster in Russia, exactly as I had when I first entered that country in July 1921.

As a newly qualified young doctor, I went to Russia in 1921 to work in the Urals among the victims of famine and an epidemic of typhus. For supplying much-needed grain to the starving Russians, I was personally thanked by Lenin, who took me under the wing of his patronage.

Sixty-five years later, in May 1986, I was able to help the Russians with medical assistance after their dreadful and ominous disaster at Chernobyl. For arranging to send them four of the Western world's most brilliant doctors, and for supplying them with about a million dollars' worth of medical supplies, I was invited to see General Secretary Mikhail Gorbachev, who thanked me and the doctors on behalf of the Russian people.

The symmetry of these events stuns me.

It began on Monday, April 28, 1986. I was in Washington for the opening festivities of an exhibition of Soviet-owned Impressionist and Post-Impressionist masterpieces at the National Gallery. It was an exhibition I had helped to arrange—the first major cultural exchange after the Reagan/Gorbachev Geneva Summit Conference of November 1985.

First slowly, and then as a flood, stories began coming from Europe that day of a nuclear disaster in the Ukraine. The news was confusing and incomplete. We began to hear of the dreaded possibility of a "meltdown," and it soon became clear that a major catastrophe had occurred.

On Tuesday morning, April 29, I received a call in my hotel suite. Dr. Robert Gale was urgently trying to reach me.

I knew Bob Gale very well, both personally and for his outstanding reputation in the field of bone-marrow transplants for the treatment of leukemia. As Chairman of the President's Cancer Panel, I knew that Dr. Gale directs the bone-marrow-transplant unit at UCLA and is Chairman of the International Bone Marrow Transplant Registry in Milwaukee—an organization which holds computer records of potential donors of bone marrow for 128 centers around the world.

I called him immediately.

Bob Gale wastes no words. He quickly explained to me that bone-marrow transplantation might offer the only chance of survival for victims of radiation at Chernobyl. One of the purposes of the International Bone Marrow Transplant Registry is to respond to precisely such a disaster. They have access to lists of names of some fifty to a hundred thousand volunteer donors, most of them living in the United States, Western Europe and Scandinavia.

Massive radiation exposure, he went on, destroys the victims' ability to manufacture blood cells in their bone marrow. "Individuals who received high doses and were not killed outright will die within two to four weeks because of bone-marrow failure," he said. "The way to save them is by identifying them and doing transplants."

Bob wanted to place himself and the resources of the Registry at the Russians' disposal. He knew that the United States government had offered the Russians any form of assistance they needed, but that offer, as well as offers by other governments, had been turned down. With my contacts in the USSR, might I be able to help?

I said I would give it my best effort. I knew Gorbachev and I would transmit Bob Gale's offer to him.

I immediately composed a letter to Gorbachev in Moscow and sent it to Oleg Sokolov, the Acting Ambassador at the Soviet Embassy in Washington. I also sent it by telex to my good friend Anatoliy Dobrynin, formerly Ambassador to Washington and now a Secretary of the Central Committee of the Communist Party in the Kremlin. I asked both men to relay my letter to Mr. Gorbachev as quickly as they could.

After explaining the importance of the transplants and the circumstances of Dr. Gale's offer, I wrote:

> *Dr. Gale is prepared to come immediately to the Soviet Union to meet with Soviet nuclear scientists and hematologists to assess the situation and decide on the optimal course of action with the hope of saving the lives of those at risk. Dr. Gale can take a flight from Los Angeles tomorrow at 3:00 P.M. (Wednesday, 30 April) which would arrive in Moscow at 6:00 P.M. on Thursday, 1 May. I will bear all costs for his efforts, which can be so important to saving the lives of those citizens who have been exposed.*

Just prior to sending this letter, I put in calls to high-level friends of mine in the State Department to make sure that they knew about my offer and that I wasn't crossing any lines with them. They were very enthusiastic and told me that I should go ahead as fast as I could.

The first response came very quickly. That evening I received a call from Yuri Dubinin, the man who would be the new Soviet Ambassador to the US. Acting in his capacity as Soviet Ambassador to the UN, he called me from New York to express support for our proposal. Also that day, at a previously arranged meeting, I told Senators Ted Stevens, Richard Lugar, Claiborne Pell and Albert Gore, Jr.—four of the Senators on the Observer Group which periodically visits the Geneva arms talks—of my efforts, and they not only wholeheartedly endorsed the plan, but the next morning would send a letter of their own to Acting Secretary of State John Whitehead encouraging his support.

Time passed. After Dubinin's call, there was no further response. I could only wait. On the evening of April 30, I sat next to Mr. Whitehead at the opening celebration of the Soviet exhibition at the National Gallery, and he told me he supported the effort. Victor Isakov, the ranking Soviet Embassy official, came up to me, warmly encouraging. But still no word.

The opening ceremonies were far overshadowed by the news from Chernobyl: everyone in Washington—everybody in the world—was wondering fearfully what the next news bulletin would contain. We all felt helpless in the face of a catastrophe so remote and yet so immediate in its effects for the whole world.

Finally, forty-eight hours after my letter left, on the morning of May 1, a reply came. Oleg Sokolov called me at my home in Los Angeles: the Soviet government welcomed the offer and wanted to take it up immediately.

"Of course we'll reimburse you for all the money you have to lay out," he said.

"Let's talk about that later," I replied.

Sokolov also telephoned Dr. Gale. "What will I do about a visa?" Dr. Gale asked me.

"Don't worry about a visa," I told him. "It will be waiting for you at the airport." Anybody familiar with Russian ways and their endemic delays will understand the extreme exception that the Soviets were making in this emergency.

My personal staff got to work with Lufthansa representatives to speed Bob Gale's departure. He would fly from Los Angeles to Frankfurt and make the connection there for the flight to Moscow. By three P.M. he had gone.

I had given Bob Gale all my telephone numbers, including my unlisted numbers at home, and had asked him to call me, day or night, if he needed anything. He said, "I'd like to do that, but I understand it takes up to twelve hours to place a call from Moscow to America."

"Use the phones in my Moscow office," I said. "You can dial direct from there, and I'll instruct the staff to make the telephones available to you twenty-four hours a day; and they will give you any other help you need with transportation and translation."

He also had a complete set of numbers for Richard Jacobs, Vice President of Occidental Petroleum and my executive assistant. The switchboard at Occidental Petroleum, which is open twenty-four hours a day, was instructed to patch calls from Dr. Gale through to us, wherever we might be, whenever they might come. My home is connected to the office by a direct line, and our WATS system is capable of hooking up a call to any receiver in the United States.

In the weeks to come, some Los Angeles hostesses were to be very startled when their telephones rang in the middle of the evening and they were asked if Rick or I were available to take a call from Moscow.

The first call came as soon as Bob got into his room at the Sovietskaya Hotel. It was early morning in Los Angeles, and I was working on a late chapter of these memoirs when the call was put through to the library at my home.

Not knowing what to expect, Bob had feared that he might be treated with reserve or suspicion. At the very least, he expected some difficulties with language and communication. But his fears had been unfounded. Bob said that he had been welcomed with open arms by officials of the Ministry of Health and had immediately been taken to Moscow's Hospital No. 6. This one-thousand-bed general hospital contained a large ward devoted exclusively to leukemia patients. Three hundred victims of radiation from Chernobyl had been admitted there. Bob found little difficulty in communicating with the Russian doctors, many of whom spoke English, and whose working vocabulary of specialist terms was largely identical to our own.

By the time he spoke to me, Bob had been able to assess the situation and the necessary next steps.

The three hundred people at Hospital No. 6 had suffered the earliest effects of radiation from the explosion of the reactor at Chernobyl. Thirty-five were in critical condition, and, of these, thirteen needed bone-marrow transplants. Many of the remaining twenty-two had suffered such extensive injuries that not even transplants could help them.

The job was enormous and there was no time to lose. "I really need some help out here," Bob said. "Top people."

"Just tell me their names and we'll send them out," I said.

In short order we had contacted Dr. Paul Terasaki, the world-renowned expert on tissue-typing from UCLA; Dr. Richard Champlin, Bob Gale's associate in transplant operations at UCLA; and Dr. Yair Reisner, an Israeli scientist from Weizmann Institute in Rehovot who was on loan to the Memorial Sloan-Kettering Cancer Center in New York. They agreed to go to Moscow immediately. Again, I told them: "Don't worry about visas. They will be waiting for you at the airport when you arrive."

Purchasing their tickets with Lufthansa, Rick Jacobs charged nearly eight thousand dollars to his American Express card, a transaction which took forty minutes to be cleared.

Dr. Reisner, a specialist in cleaning bone marrow to make it acceptable to the recipient, was understandably apprehensive about his journey. He may be the only Israeli ever to have embarked on a flight to Moscow without a visa! All his fears were allayed, however, by the warmth of the reception he got from his Russian colleagues.

Bob Gale also asked for a long list of medical supplies, which we arranged to gather from fifteen different countries and fly to Moscow. The biggest items were three machines for separating blood cells and one for counting blood cells. Lufthansa cooperated magnificently in getting the supplies to Moscow on their first available flights. The doctors were ready to begin work.

For two weeks the four Americans and their Russian colleagues operated night and day on the patients who had been chosen for transplants. Nothing on such a scale had ever been attempted before. Bob

Gale himself performed all thirteen transplants, assisted by Dr. Champlin and the Russians—a remarkable number considering that in his normal working week he rarely performed more than two to four.

Since the Russians possessed inadequate facilities for tissue-typing on such a scale, Dr. Terasaki set up a laboratory with the equipment we had sent and taught the Russians how to use it. He also found some of his former UCLA students at Moscow hospitals and recruited them for the emergency.

Every day, when he called me or Rick Jacobs, Bob Gale had a new list of requests. His calls frequently came in the small hours of the night or just around dawn. Since we were also trying to cover our normal work, Rick and I were working treble time in those weeks. We were lucky if we got three and a half or four hours' sleep a night.

Some of his requests were personal. He asked that his wife, Tamar, be sent out to keep him company; she traveled on an Israeli passport. Mrs. Gale left for Moscow on the day Bob made his request. He also asked for some simple home comforts. The American doctors had been frustrated by their Soviet colleagues' habit of taking a very long lunch, and they quickly opted to take lunches with them to the hospital. But they all had a yearning for bagels and ale. Rick arranged for a crateful of their choices to be sent by our office in London.

On May 12, I went to Moscow. My art collection, Five Centuries of Masterpieces, had gone to Russia in March and had been exhibited at the Hermitage in Leningrad, as part of the American exchange for the Soviet works now on display at the National Gallery in Washington; now my collection was about to transfer to Moscow's new State Museum of Art. I had a long-standing commitment to attend the new opening—but it was also an excellent opportunity to see if there was anything more I could do to help Bob Gale and his hardworking team.

Crates of medical supplies were loaded into the holds of my plane—a customized Boeing 727 with long-range fuel tanks which flies under the call sign Oxy One. Squads of reporters and batteries of TV crews turned up at our private hangar at Los Angeles Airport to see us off.

The reporters all wanted to press me for news about the catastrophe, very few details of which had emerged from the Soviet Union. I knew little more than they. I could only say that I hoped our efforts to help the victims might do something to improve relations between the US and the USSR. The Chernobyl disaster vividly underlined the need for cooperation and understanding between our countries. It was vital, I stressed, that President Reagan and Mr. Gorbachev should meet again in another summit conference and revive "the spirit of Geneva" which they had created in their "fireside chat" during their first summit meeting in November 1985. I hoped that our medical aid might soothe some of the bad temper which had flared between the two countries in 1986.

But the main thing was simply to do something to help people in trouble. If there was something I could do to provide relief after a disaster, I felt that I should do it. That's all.

In Moscow I wanted to go straight to Hospital No. 6 to greet the American doctors and visit their patients, but the Soviet officials were very negative. They frowned and shook their heads. They seemed to be afraid that I might catch some disease from the victims or absorb radiation from them, which can sometimes happen.

"You will understand, Doctor Hammer," they said. "It is quite impossible."

No officialdom in the world can beat Soviet officialdom when it puts on its full regalia of stubborn and willful opposition. Fortunately I have an advantage: during nearly ten years of business life in Moscow in the twenties, I learned how to beat or circumvent the Russian bureaucratic system decades before most of today's officials were conceived. I know all the devices and all the strategies, from blandishment and flattery to threat and bluster. Sometimes the only way to deal with Soviet bureaucracy is to lock horns with it and wrestle it to the ground.

This was one of those times.

"If you won't let me in the hospital," I said, "I'm going to go down there and sit outside the gates until you do."

That cut some ice, as did another move. One of the quickest ways through Soviet red tape is to make a successful appeal over the\heads of the junior apparatchiks. I asked my friend Anatoliy Dobrynin to help me out. That did the trick. When I was taken to Hospital No. 6, the Deputy Minister of Health himself, Mr. Oleg Shchepin, was waiting to accompany me into the building.

The Director of the hospital, a matronly physician named Mrs. Angeline Guskova, reached out and embraced me and we established an immediate rapport. Dr. Baranov, Professor of Hematology, fitted me with a sterile outfit—mask, cap, gown and booties—and conducted me through the ward and the separate rooms. The hospital was immaculate and surprisingly well equipped, but what drew my attention immediately was the patients.

Most of them were men—guards and employees of the nuclear plant at Chernobyl. Some were firemen who had tried to fight the fire and control the accident. One was a physician who had risked his life volunteering to help the victims on the site of the disaster as soon as it occurred.

Some of them didn't appear to be in too bad a shape, but others looked terrible, heartbreaking. Speaking in Russian, I tried to cheer them up and give them heart. I told them that we were from the United

States and they were getting the best medical care in the world. Some of them pleaded with me and held on to my hand, and I told them courage, courage—everything that could be done to help them was being done and would be done—but still they wouldn't let go. Knowing that some of these victims would not survive, despite the heroic efforts of the doctors, I could hardly control the tears. I had to turn away from them and walk out of the room.

On May 14 Mikhail Gorbachev spoke in public for the first time about the Chernobyl disaster, in a full-scale television address to the Soviet people. After describing details of the accident and the measures which had been taken to control it, he continued:

> We express our kind feelings to foreign scientists and specialists who showed readiness to come up with assistance in overcoming the consequences of the accident. I would like to note the participation of the American medics Robert Gale and Paul Terasaki in the treatment of the affected persons and to express gratitude to the business circles of those countries which promptly reacted to our request for the purchase of certain types of equipment, materials and medicines. . . . We highly appreciate the sympathy of all those who treated our trouble and our problems with an open heart.

It was very gratifying—but then he turned the guns of his rhetoric on Western governments and gave a broadside to the American media for having "launched an unrestrained anti-Soviet campaign. It is difficult to believe what was said and written," he said, recalling headlines in American papers such as THOUSANDS OF CASUALTIES, MASS GRAVES FOR THE DEAD, DESOLATE KIEV, ENTIRE UKRAINE POISONED, and so on.

Listening to these salvos whistling across the world's airwaves, I felt very unhappy. The war of words between Russia and America was pushing toward new frontiers of acrimony and suspicion. Mr. Gorbachev obviously had a case against the Western media, but the West had a case against the Soviets, too. The Politburo had undeniably been slow to alert the world to the potential dangers of the Chernobyl catastrophe.

However, the world gained nothing from machine-gun exchanges of insults and accusations fired from entrenched positions of prejudice and hostility. The world itself is menaced by what might be called the Chernobyl syndrome, not least because the accident there could have occurred anywhere in any country with nuclear power stations. The problem of rogue nuclear power plants, like the menace of nuclear weapons, required cooperation, not insults.

Upon my arrival in Moscow I had sent Mr. Gorbachev a note,

through Anatoliy Dobrynin, hoping for an interview. An answer soon came from one of his assistants that, given the short notice of my request and Mr. Gorbachev's extremely busy schedule, he was sorry that he would be unable to fit me in.

On May 15, however, Dr. Bob Gale and I were holding a press conference at the Foreign Ministry Press Center before four hundred media representatives from around the globe. This was the first time Bob would be speaking in public since his arrival in Moscow.

During the conference, I was handed a note: Mr. Aleksander Bessmertnykh, Deputy Foreign Minister, wanted to speak to me on the telephone. I left the podium and took the call. Gorbachev had changed his mind: the General Secretary wanted to see me that day at five P.M. —and he asked that I bring Dr. Gale with me. Returning to the podium, I passed a note to Bob Gale, who announced the invitation to the press.

Bob spoke with a moving and sober composure at this conference, which must have been an ordeal for him, exhausted as he was and unused to facing television klieg lights and battalions of reporters. He announced agreement with Soviet officials that details of the injuries and treatment of the victims of Chernobyl should be published in medical journals to help scientists learn from the experience. And he made a point of chilling significance: "We are very hard pressed," he said, "to deal with the three hundred victims of a nuclear reactor accident. I think it should be very evident now how inadequate would be any response to a nuclear attack or thermonuclear war."

When it was my turn, I was asked to tell the story of my involvement in the aid and how much it had cost. I said that the Soviet government had offered to reimburse all my expenses, but that I wanted to waive that offer as a gift to the Russian people.

Bob Gale and I went from the news conference to the opening of my art collection and from there to the Kremlin. We rode in Anatoliy Dobrynin's official ZIL limousine, Bob Gale and I in the back seat and Secretary Dobrynin in the front. A follow car with plainclothes police handled the traffic for us. All of the streets were blocked to any other traffic as we headed directly for the Kremlin.

Punctually at five P.M. we arrived at the Kremlin, but we were made a moment late by a very slow elevator which has been in use since the time of Lenin—I know that for a fact: I'd taken it many times. We went directly to Mr. Gorbachev's fourth-floor office, where we were greeted by the General Secretary. As we had met before and knew each other, he welcomed me first and then Dr. Gale. We all took seats at the long table in his room.

Speaking through an interpreter, Mr. Gorbachev thanked Dr. Gale and me and said the Soviet Union would find some way to acknowledge the efforts made by Bob and his team. Then, though he never raised his voice, his tone grew darker. His face became red. For about five minutes, without notes, Mr. Gorbachev spoke very swiftly and powerfully. Anger made him fluent.

He asked, rhetorically, what kind of people the Western governments and media were to take advantage of a human tragedy on the scale of Chernobyl. "What is your administration trying to do?" he said. "Are they trying to separate me from my people? Drive a wedge between me and my people? I'm being criticized because I didn't announce the accident immediately. I didn't know myself how serious it was until I got a report from the commission I sent there. The local people were not giving me full information and they'll be punished for it. As soon as I got the information, I immediately gave everyone the facts."

He said he had just returned from the Politburo meeting where they had discussed the Chernobyl problem. "My briefcase is full of letters and telegrams from Russians all over the country offering to help and sending money. Some offered to donate their salaries to help or to take victims into their homes. I've even got two letters here from Americans."

He opened his briefcase and showed us two letters. Both had bills clipped to them. One was from an older woman in New York who enclosed a five-dollar bill; the second was from another woman who enclosed a ten-dollar bill.

Mr. Gorbachev smiled and said, "Apparently she is richer than the first lady," adding, "but neither one is as rich as you are, Doctor Hammer."

Then he turned to the lessons of Chernobyl. "This disaster underlines the dangers of nuclear war and the dangers of extending nuclear weapons into space," he said, referring to the issue of the Strategic Defense Initiative (SDI), commonly known as Star Wars, which so occupies Soviet anxieties. He said that a Chernobyl in space would be "unthinkable" and that if America put up these kinds of weapons in space they would be followed by the Soviets putting up more weapons. "The world would become an insane asylum," he said.

I had listened quietly to this lengthy speech. Having spent time with Mr. Gorbachev before, I know the strength of his mind and his opinions and I could see that he had a lot of steam to let off. Now I saw an opportunity to divert his mind from his obvious anger over the media treatment of Chernobyl. "Surely," I said, "the Chernobyl incident opens the way to reconvene a summit meeting?"

Mr. Gorbachev reminded us that he and Reagan had met in Geneva. One meeting to "get acquainted" was important, he said, but there must now be something productive and substantial produced from a further summit. Each leader must be able to take home something positive.

He listed the items that could form the basis for a summit:

1. A nuclear test ban.

2. Ratification of SALT II.

3. A 50-percent reduction in nuclear armaments immediately.

"Chernobyl is the opportunity," I told him. I said, as I had said to him before, that Ronald Reagan was himself a good man who wanted to go down in history as a successful President. He could do this only by assuring a lasting peace with the Soviets. However, he was surrounded by a number of people who did not want a summit.

I told Mr. Gorbachev that he had to get past these people and address himself directly to Reagan. "He is the force in American politics," I said. I painted a picture of Gorbachev and Reagan walking alone together at Camp David, working out the issues directly between them. I also envisioned Mr. Gorbachev making a speech before Congress, where he would be warmly received.

He answered that the American administration "is acting as though I must come to Washington for a summit, no matter what. This is simply not the case." He said he was prepared to wait. I urged him to arrange a meeting between Secretary George Shultz and Soviet Foreign Minister Eduard Shevardnadze, leading to a meeting between Reagan and himself. "What could be more appropriate," I asked, "than a meeting on Thanksgiving, the day all Americans associate with peace?"

Bob Gale backed me up. He said that the tragedy of Chernobyl and the potential destructiveness of nuclear weapons had impressed itself upon every human being in the world. Therefore this moment might be opportune to press forward with a strong initiative for peace before we all forgot the potential lessons to be learned from Chernobyl.

We were all speaking emotionally now. I added a closing note: "Mr. General Secretary," I said, "I have two great hopes for the remaining years of my life: to see a cure for cancer—which, as Chairman of the President's Cancer Panel, I believe is not far off—and world peace. If I can do anything to assist the consummation of these goals, I shall feel that my life has been worth something."

Mr. Gorbachev smiled warmly and said, "You are an eternal optimist, Doctor Hammer. I too hope that these achievements will occur in your lifetime."

He wished us farewell and thanked us again. The meeting had lasted an hour and five minutes. I stayed behind to talk privately to

Gorbachev and Dobrynin while Bob Gale and the others left. I brought up the need to increase the rights of Jews to emigrate, and referred to a letter on the subject my friend Guilford Glazer had written to Dobrynin. Gorbachev conferred with Dobrynin about giving attention to humanitarian cases. He assured me action would be taken. Later, the Soviet Union granted exit visas to 117 members of divided families (those with spouses or relatives in the West). About one-third of these were Jews.

Before we left Moscow on the morning of Friday, May 16, Bob Gale went again to Hospital No. 6 to say goodbye. The Russian doctors there embraced him with all the warmth of true colleagues who had battled and worked together. Tears filled their eyes. As he was leaving the hospital, he told me he turned to look up for the last time and saw, through the windows of the ward for the Chernobyl victims, the machines we had sent, still working to save their lives.

We all collapsed on Oxy One. Frances and I were joined by Bob and Tamar Gale, Yair Reisner and my staff. Dick Champlin remained in Moscow to finish his work. En route to London, we shared the celebration of my eighty-eighth birthday with caviar, Stolichnaya vodka and birthday cake.

Tremendous press interest attended our arrival in Los Angeles. Local television stations covered the event on live transmission. Bob Gale, by now becoming seasoned in handling the media, repeatedly emphasized that the outstanding lesson of Chernobyl was that the peoples of the world must come together to prevent similar disasters in the future.

It was a lesson we were able to press home again a week later. On May 23 Bob Gale, Paul Terasaki, Richard Champlin and I flew to Washington to see Secretary of State George Shultz, who warmly thanked us for our efforts but was disappointed, he said, that the Russians had refused help from the government. He knew that Bob Gale was returning to Moscow shortly to continue his work with the victims of Chernobyl and that I was hoping soon to see Mr. Gorbachev again. He asked us to carry a message to the Soviets: they needed to understand, he said, that the American government does not control the American press. If the Russians were angry about coverage of the Chernobyl disaster in American media, they should not suppose that the newspapers were speaking with the authority of the government.

"They really must make this distinction," he said. "They don't seem to realize that we don't control the media."

Photographs were taken and then the doctors left. I stayed behind to talk for a while with George Shultz and Mark Palmer, who was the Deputy Assistant Secretary specializing in Soviet Affairs and is now US Ambassdor to Hungary.

I told them more about my conversation with Gorbachev, relaying the terms which he had outlined for a summit agenda. George Shultz said that he very much wanted Gorbachev to set up a meeting such as I had suggested between himself and Shevardnadze to agree on an agenda for a fall summit. Again, I pressed the need for a discussion of the lessons of Chernobyl. Only international cooperation, led by the USA and the USSR, could help to ensure that there would be no repetition of the catastrophe at any one of the hundreds of nuclear plants around the world. Mark Palmer expressed regret that President Reagan could not receive us. Later I learned that Admiral John Poindexter, the National Security Advisor, turned down George Shultz's request for us to see the President. Why he rebuffed the Secretary of State I will never know, but this may hint toward some of the friction between the two men which surfaced a few months earlier.

As we flew home on Oxy One, there was more champagne and caviar. In part we were still celebrating my birthday, but the cause for joy was greater than that. In the month of May, while the terrifying clouds of nuclear fallout hung above the world, we had done something to show that, when people can act toward each other with human understanding, suffering can be relieved and the great problems facing humanity can be overcome.

In the overall context of US/USSR relations, the work of Bob Gale's team in Moscow's Hospital No. 6 may have been only a small step toward peace—but it was a step; lives which would have been lost were saved; Russians and Americans worked side by side in a collaboration which resulted in mutual esteem and affection. The foundations were set for an exchange of scientific and medical information which may help us to understand and avoid any similar nightmarish calamity.

In addition we had shown that individuals can make a difference on the world stage. The initial reactions and counterreactions to Chernobyl were filled with fear and anger. In the face of near-universal criticism, the Soviets could have refused to divulge specific information about the accident—but, following Gorbachev's acceptance of our offer to have Dr. Gale fly in, the mood of the Soviet leadership began to shift. They realized that they had to tell the entire story, both for their own and for the world's sake, and later that summer they held an unprecedented international review of the accident in Vienna. Had they not received an outstretched hand from the West, they might never have decided to be so open with the world.

In June 1986 Bob Gale returned to Moscow to check on the progress of his patients, four of whom are, at the time of this writing, still alive. This is about a 35-percent survival rate, which Bob considers good, especially considering the delay in the operations, the difficulty in finding suitable donors on such short notice and the fact that the

Russians selected the patients to be operated on. He also visited Chernobyl and Kiev and signed an agreement for the setting up of a private foundation, which has been named the Armand Hammer Center for Advanced Studies in Nuclear Energy and Health, to be directed by himself and me, with a board of distinguished scientists in the fields of epidemiology and high-dose radiation effects, which would study the incidence of cancer and other sicknesses, during their lifetimes, of the hundreds of thousands of people who were exposed to radiation in the Chernobyl disaster. The foundation received the blessing of the State Department, and we invited government agencies, as well as the National Academy of Sciences, to join with us in the endeavor, which my foundation agreed to fund. The first meeting of the advisory group of scientists from various parts of the world was held in my office on July 8, 1986, and it was a great success.

In mid-July I too visited Chernobyl. I wanted to see the devastation for myself. Two scenes from that trip will always live in my memory. One was the view from the helicopter as we approached the Chernobyl reactor—a rubblized frame which reminded me of nothing so much as a collapsed bomb site. The second was what we saw next, as we continued to the nearby city of Pripyat. There we saw enormous apartment houses standing guard over a ghost town. There was no sign of any life whatever. There was laundry on the line, hay in the fields and automobiles in the street, but no one to use them. No dogs or cats roamed the streets. Mr. Anatoliy Efimovich Romanenko, Minister of Health of the Ukraine, who was with Bob Gale and me, told me that this had once been a rich farm area replete with livestock. Yet below us was the eerie stillness of a lifeless plain.

I could think only of the results of the neutron bomb, that "miracle" weapon designed to eliminate life yet retain architecture. This represents man's greatest folly, and I can only hope that Chernobyl's Pripyat stands as a monument to what must never be.

The effort to avoid the unthinkable devastations of nuclear war has been my chief preoccupation in recent years, during which I have dedicated my life to encouraging human understanding toward the goal of peace. Uppermost in my mind during the years since the collapse of détente has been the necessity for regular summit meetings between the leaders of the US and the USSR. This book contains many stories of my efforts toward that end. In the late summer of 1986 I was able to play a small part in facilitating the mini-summit in Reykjavik between Reagan and Gorbachev, when I helped to resolve the crisis over the American journalist Nicholas Daniloff.

What did I do? I talked; I visited; I sent letters; I went back and forth between Moscow and Washington; I did what I could and I did what I do best—seeking a solution by compromise. I believe that it is one of the higher refinements of civilized behavior for opposing parties to settle their differences by compromise for the sake of a mutually desirable outcome. That, after all, is what I've been doing all my life.

I happened to be in Russia when news broke of the arrest on August 30 of the American journalist Nicholas Daniloff, Moscow correspondent of *U.S. News and World Report.* Mr Daniloff's arrest followed the arrest in New York on August 23 of the Soviet spy Gennady Zakharov, and it was so obviously a tit-for-tat formality that it seemed to cause very little excitement in Moscow. It was not at all clear then whether Mr. Daniloff would be detained or brought to trial. The story was muddy and insubstantial. The arrest was not even mentioned during my three-hour meeting on September 2 with Prime Minister Nikolai Ryzkhov in his Kremlin office. However, Mr. Ryzkhov said something that day which was to assume a larger significance in my later efforts over the Daniloff/Zakharov case. He began our meeting by saying:

"I applaud what you did to help us with the Chernobyl disaster. Your efforts did much to normalize the situation." These words were very heartening to me. I took them to mean that the Soviets had learned that they might be more open in their dealings with America, and that the exaggerations of the American media do not necessarily reflect the attitudes and intentions of the administration. This was to become a key point, as we shall see.

Only when I returned to New York, in the first week of September, did it become clear to me how seriously threatening the Daniloff case might become. On arriving in New York, I read an article in the *New York Times* which spoke very ominously of the damage the affair was causing to the vital negotiations between Secretary Shultz and Foreign Minister Shevardnadze in their preparations for a summit agenda. Shultz and Shevardnadze were supposed to be announcing a date for a summit. It was now clear that there would be no summit while the Daniloff case was unresolved.

Also, at that moment, I became aware for the first time that a powerful aroma of skulduggery overhung the crisis. The arrests of the two men seemed to have been conducted behind the backs of the two leaders, and it looked as if somebody might be trying to spoil the chances for a summit. On the day Mr. Zakharov had been arrested, the President had been on vacation in California and George Shultz had been staying at the Bohemian Grove, the exclusive businessmen's retreat in northern California. Therefore the decision to make the arrest had been taken at an operational level of the FBI without reference to the highest authority. That looked suspicious, and it was matched by an equally suspicious circumstance connected with Mr. Daniloff's arrest: Mr. Gorbachev had himself been out of Moscow when Daniloff had been picked up by the KGB. It looked as though the hard-liners on both sides who opposed a summit meeting were doing their best to stir the pot.

They were succeeding. The American media were working themselves into a lather about the detention of their brother journalist in Moscow, and the administration had reacted intemperately, thrusting Mr. Reagan and Mr. Shultz straight into the front lines with the highest profile of belligerence.

In reaction, Mr. Gorbachev had entered the fray, declaring that Mr. Daniloff had been caught "red-handed" receiving secret documents and that he would be brought to trial in Moscow.

All this became clear to me during the evening of September 4, while I was attending the opening at the Metropolitan Museum in New York of the Soviet Impressionist and Post-Impressionist Collection. In the great gathering there of Ambassadors and senior administration officials, I got a clear picture of the menacing scale of the crisis.

At my house in Greenwich Village, I stayed up most of the night, trying to figure out a way to help resolve this crisis. By morning it was clear what I should do.

I had had previous experience in helping to resolve a very similar crisis. During the summer of 1978, in retaliation for the arrest of two Soviet spies in New York, the Soviets had arrested an American businessman named Francis Crawford on alleged black market charges. At that time, at the request of the Carter administration, I had flown to Yalta to see General Secretary Leonid Brezhnev to urge Crawford's release. I had suggested that Mr. Crawford be brought quickly to trial and then be expelled from the country rather than be imprisoned in Russia. In exchange the Soviet spies would be expelled from the USA and some dissidents would be allowed to emigrate.

Mr. Brezhnev bought this proposal in 1978 and the crisis was smoothly resolved. (The full story of this incident is described in chapter 23, "Business with Brezhnev.")

During my long night awake in New York I realized that a similar deal could settle the Daniloff/Zakharov crisis. First thing next day I contacted John Whitehead, Deputy Secretary of State (then acting as Secretary), offering my assistance in any way and outlining my proposal. I told him that I intended to make connections at the highest level in Moscow to push the same proposal. He urged me to go ahead.

The next day, Friday, while I was at lunch at the Lotos Club in New York, I telephoned Anatoliy Dobrynin, reaching him at his country dacha outside Moscow. He and I have been friends for more than two decades and, having been through many crises together, we speak now with complete openness and informality.

"Anatoliy," I said, "I believe you may not realize the seriousness of this problem. The administration and the American media are taking a very hard line on the Daniloff case. Unless it's resolved quickly, it could blow apart the chances for a summit. I think I may have a solution and I want to write a letter to General Secretary Gorbachev to explain it."

Dobrynin told me to write my letter and assured me that he would bring it to Mr. Gorbachev's attention.

After outlining the story of my 1978 mission to Yalta, I wrote:

I believe this case could be quickly resolved in the same fashion as the Crawford case. The details could be worked out by Secretary Dobrynin, working with the US Chargé d'Affaires Mr. Combs, or by dealing with Acting Secretary of State Whitehead, or Under Secretary Armacost, through your Ambassador, Mr. Dubinin.

With this unnecessary irritant removed from the front pages of the Western press, we could then proceed with the serious matters between our two countries at a summit meeting between yourself and President Reagan at which something concrete could be accomplished.

On Anatoliy Dobrynin's recommendation, I sent this letter to Mr. Dubinin at the Soviet Embassy, asking him to relay it to Mr. Gorbachev in Moscow through diplomatic channels. Meanwhile I sent a copy to John Whitehead.

After another restless night I decided that more immediate action was required. Letters alone would not do the job. I called John Whitehead and said, "Why don't we go to Moscow together and get this thing sorted out?"

John was all for the idea, said he'd like to go, but he'd have to think about it. Within a few hours John called me back to say that my plan was a nonstarter. The President had decisively entered the picture, sending a personal letter to Mr. Gorbachev vouching that Nicholas Daniloff was not a spy and calling for his immediate and unconditional release. With such an absolute demand having been issued, the chances for a compromise settlement were greatly diminished. The administration was obviously determined to lock horns with the Soviets, and the press was full of rhetoric about eyeball-to-eyeball confrontations and speculations as to who would blink first. This language dates, of course, from the Cuban missile crisis of the early sixties, when the world came closer than at any other moment to nuclear war. It struck me as exceedingly inappropriate that such language should be used to stoke up antagonisms over the Daniloff/Zakharov affair.

However, the die was cast and I could only stand in the wings and observe the deadlock, which endured throughout the middle weeks of September. This restraint frustrated me very much, and by September

21, no advance or change having occurred in the crisis, I had had enough. I decided that if I obtained the President's blessing, I would go to Moscow on my own initiative.

During those September days of frustration, I had refined my own proposals. I wanted to suggest that Mr. Daniloff should be brought to trial in Moscow on a lesser charge than espionage. The Soviets had announced that they had found some undeclared property among his possessions and that he was suspected of smuggling (the suspicious items were apparently pieces of family jewelry which Daniloff admitted he had failed to declare on his entry customs declaration). I wanted to suggest that he be tried only on this minor charge, for which it would be very normal to fine him and expel him from the country.

The issue, already overheated, was being fired up unnecessarily by a further complication. The US administration was demanding the withdrawal of twenty-five Soviet employees from the UN on allegations that they were spies. I wanted to propose that this demand be shelved for a while, at least until the Daniloff/Zakharov dispute was settled. The affair was plainly getting wildly out of hand and some sensible restraint was essential.

On the evening of September 21 I saw President Reagan in Washington at a reception at the White House. We talked, one-on-one, for a few minutes. His mood was unmistakably serious when he said, "I told Shevardnadze that I have put everything on hold until this Daniloff affair is solved"—meaning that the meetings between Shultz and Shevardnadze would definitely not result in a date for the summit. I said, "I want to go to Moscow immediately to see if I can be of help at the highest level. Nothing must be allowed to stand in the way of the summit." The President encouraged me to do whatever I could to help the situation.

Next day I went to New York to hear Mr. Reagan's address to the General Assembly of the United Nations, and I took the opportunity to have a brief meeting with my old friend Shimon Peres, then Prime Minister of Israel. I asked him for a list of Jewish dissidents whom the Israelis wanted the Soviets to release. I told him that I hoped I might be able to encourage a settlement in Moscow which could effect the release of some dissidents as well as Nicholas Daniloff. He quickly gave me several names.

Later that day I met with Soviet Ambassador Dubinin and Foreign Minister Shevardnadze at the Soviet Mission in New York. I had to enter the building through a back door to avoid the swarming herd of reporters outside the front door. My staff was keeping absolutely locked secrecy about my intended flight to Moscow.

I talked with Dubinin and Shevardnadze at great length. The Foreign Minister liked my idea of separating the question of the twenty-five Soviet UN employees by asking Shultz to postpone his October 1 deadline for their departure. Both men encouraged me to go to Moscow. Ambassador Dubinin had personally issued instructions for visas to be made out for me and my party and that formality—normally the work of weeks—was completed immediately.

I flew out that day and arrived in Moscow in the late afternoon of September 23. Secretary Dobrynin had sent his top aide to meet me at the airport, a mark of the high seriousness with which he viewed my visit. That same evening I was taken to see Dobrynin in his office at the Central Committee building. We got right down to business. "There has got to be," I told him, "a rational solution to this. I really believe an arrangement can be worked out to suit both sides."

Dobrynin repeated to me the same thought which Eduard Shevardnadze had spoken in New York: the question of the twenty-five Soviet employees at the UN really had to be separated from the Daniloff/Zakharov case, he said, and deferred until that more important case was settled.

I said I felt confident that this uncoupling could be effected and that the Soviets could conclude a deal, confident in the Americans' good faith. I made it clear that Daniloff had to be freed without condition. I also suggested that Louis Nizer, one of the most prominent attorneys in America and my old friend, be consulted to advise on a solution to the legal problem. I suggested that I write another letter to General Secretary Gorbachev, detailing my proposals. Dobrynin said he would make sure that it went straight onto Mr. Gorbachev's desk.

I wrote the letter. Next day Dobrynin called me at my Moscow apartment to say that Mikhail Gorbachev had read my letter and "warmly appreciated it." Apparently it helped to resolve the situation, because Dobrynin said to me, "You now can go home." Then he added that Gorbachev had remarked to him, "Where does Hammer get his energy?" I agreed with Dobrynin that I would get back to New York and try to continue my efforts to bring the two sides closer together.

Arriving back in New York thirty-six hours after I had left the USA, I consulted Louis Nizer, who came up with a legalistic alternative to a plea bargain for Zakharov. Louis said that a plea of *nolo contendere*—effectively neither an admission nor a denial of guilt—might satisfy both sides and unblock the legal jam over Zakharov's position. I forwarded this proposal to Ambassador Dubinin in a letter.

At this moment, unfortunately, the news of my Moscow mission leaked to the press. The *New York Times* had heard about my trip and was going to publish a story. To keep the record straight I issued a brief statement describing my recent meetings with high-level Soviet officials in the hope of helping to find a quick resolution of the Daniloff affair.

During the following weekend, the last in September, I began to hear that a solution was emerging. It was announced by George Shultz on the morning of September 30. Daniloff was on a plane out of Moscow at that moment, he said, having been released without trial. Zakharov was in court in New York, pleading *nolo contendere* to espionage. He would be expelled from the country and, directly thereafter, dissidents Dr. and Mrs. Yuri Orlov would be granted permission to leave the USSR.

The crisis was over. Mr. Reagan then announced that he had accepted General Secretary Gorbachev's offer to meet in Reykjavik, Iceland, ten days later.

The American media were immediately up in arms, complaining that President Reagan had been weak, that he had done a bad deal, that he had "blinked." Dan Rather contacted me in Boston, where I was chairing a meeting of the President's Cancer Panel, to ask my opinion for inclusion on *The CBS Evening News*.

"I don't think that either one lost," I said. "I think they both won. . . . Mr. Gorbachev got what he wanted. Mr. Reagan got what he wanted. And I think that the result is going to be good for the world. . . . The President has shown statesmanship. Mr. Gorbachev has shown statesmanship. The stakes are much greater than the personal ego of either one."

Thus the storm blew over. The summit meeting was fixed and went ahead. I don't claim full credit for solving the Daniloff affair, though the *Chicago Tribune* of October 23, 1986, quoted Ruth Daniloff, Nick's wife, as "telling friends that Armand Hammer played a major behind-the-scenes role in the release of her husband. The role may have been the crucial element in Daniloff's release." I do feel some satisfaction, however, at having kept open the lines of communication by which a deal could be made. Those lines had threatened to close like sclerotic arteries, blocking the summit. That they remained open owes something, I suspect, to the "normalization" which Premier Ryzkhov described after Chernobyl. Despite all their innate suspicion and distrust, the Soviets did eventually believe that a resolution could be achieved. As long as that belief survives, we have reason to hope for better relations between the superpowers.

The case of David Goldfarb, the renowned Soviet geneticist, was curiously intertwined with the Daniloff story, and it is certain that Dr. Goldfarb would not have been allowed to leave Russia with me, to join his son in New York, if the Daniloff crisis had not been settled.

From all points of view the Goldfarb story is one of the happier events of my life, and I think it shows how much more relaxed the Soviets have become in their dealings with the West since Chernobyl.

The release of David Goldfarb was also one occasion when I was able to use my contacts in Moscow, simply and quickly, to effect a clean-cut solution to a human problem.

It began, however, with an unhappy mixup. Alex Goldfarb, the geneticist's son, sent me a letter which I did not receive.

Alex, a microbiologist, was allowed to leave his native Russia when he was twenty-eight and he has lived since 1975 in New York. There, by strange chance, he became an assistant professor at the Julius and Armand Hammer Health Sciences Center at Columbia University. We did not know each other, but, on July 23, 1986, he wrote me a letter asking me to help save his father's life.

David Goldfarb is not only a world-famous geneticist; he is also a Hero of the Soviet Union, a former member of the Communist Party there and a military hero, having lost a leg in the siege of Stalingrad. After he retired in 1979, he was told that if he wanted to he would be allowed to leave the USSR. He applied for permission to go. It was not forthcoming.

In 1984 his fate became entangled with that of his friend Nicholas Daniloff: the KGB approached Goldfarb to cooperate in a plot to plant documents on the reporter. David Goldfarb refused. His life in Moscow immediately became much less enjoyable and comfortable.

His health was very poor. He suffered multiple ailments, including failing eyesight and diabetes. By the time Alex Goldfarb wrote to me, his father was suffering from gangrene in his remaining leg; one of his toes had been amputated and it seemed likely that he would lose the leg. The standard of his medical care seemed inadequate to save his life.

Alex's letter explained the perilous state of his father's health and asked me to help to get his father out before he died.

I didn't get the letter.

Alex had found out that I was in Moscow and sent his letter to me by telex at my Moscow office. It arrived after I left Moscow. Because I was traveling, I knew nothing about the letter until *The Wall Street Journal* printed an Open Letter to me from Alex Goldfarb, under the headline TO RUSSIA WITH HOPE: A PLEA FOR ARMAND HAMMER'S HELP. I got in touch with him immediately and offered to do everything I could to help his father.

My first opportunity to help arose when I saw Anatoliy Dobrynin in Moscow on September 3. I told him about David Goldfarb's case and he said, "I'll look into it."

Back in New York I telephoned Alex Goldfarb and informed him of my meeting with Dobrynin, advising him to "try to be patient. These things take time with the Russians." Alex Goldfarb replied that some changes seemed to be occurring already. The day after my meeting with Dobrynin, he said, his father had been visited by Boris Petrovsky, ex-Minister of Health, and a medical commission of some thirty doctors who had examined his medical record and evaluated the standard of his hospital care. Alex was sure that this inspection—and the consequent dramatic improvement in his father's medical care, which had now become comparable with the care that a member of the Central Committee might receive—must have resulted from my interview with Dobrynin.

Next I received a letter from Nicholas Daniloff himself, asking me to do what I could to help his friend David Goldfarb. At the moment I received the letter, the Daniloff crisis was at its height, but Nick Daniloff had written the letter before his arrest in late August. It had taken more than a month to reach me.

On October 12 I again arrived in Moscow for business meetings. In my meeting with Anatoliy Dobrynin on October 13, I again raised Dr. Goldfarb's name and said, "I would like to take him back to America with me tomorrow, on my plane, to join his son."

Dobrynin said, "Really, it's impossible."

I replied, "I'm accustomed to doing the impossible. Let's give it a try."

Dobrynin said that he would get back to me.

In the afternoon I was at a meeting in the Kremlin with Deputy Prime Minister Vladimir Kamentsev when Dobrynin duly called.

"Armand," he said, "you can take Dr. Goldfarb with you to America tomorrow if he wants to go and if his doctors will permit him to travel." I immediately asked Dobrynin for permission to visit Dr. Goldfarb in the hospital and he acceded.

I was inexpressibly jubilant. A short time later a call came from Sergei Chetverikov, Acting Deputy Minister for Foreign Affairs (signifying that the Soviets were dealing with this matter at the highest level), with instructions on where to go. I could see Dr. Goldfarb, Mr. Chetverikov said, at the Vishnevsky Institute for Surgery. I should be there at six forty-five P.M.

I was there. The Director of the Institute, Dr. Mikhail Ilyitch Kuzin, a distinguished surgeon, met me, and after a half-hour consultation in which he agreed that Dr. Goldfarb would be fit to travel, he guided me through the hospital to David Goldfarb's ward.

We found him sharing a room with three other men, all seriously ill. They were under intensive care, with many pipes and drips attached to their bodies. Dr. Goldfarb, lying in the bed by the window, looked forlorn, although in somewhat better shape than any of them.

I took his hand and said, in English, "I have come here to take you to America in my plane to be reunited with your son."

He seemed strangely unbelieving. He replied, very calmly, in English, saying, "This is my dream."

Obviously he did not immediately understand that I was offering to reunite him with his son the very next day!

Dr. Kuzin intervened, speaking in Russian: "Doctor Goldfarb," he said, "you must understand that Doctor Hammer's offer is perfectly genuine. The authorities have granted permission for you to leave tomorrow on Doctor Hammer's plane."

David Goldfarb seemed to need a moment to absorb this information. Then, speaking very calmly again, he said, "Of course I would love to go. But I cannot leave without my wife."

I said I was sure this too could be arranged. I asked him to give me her address and telephone number. He tried to write the information, but his sight failed him and he had to dictate the words to the doctor. I sat beside him, holding his hand and trying to reassure him, saying, "You will be better in America. You're going to be all right."

I spoke to Mrs. Goldfarb on the telephone and told her I was coming to visit her that evening in her apartment. When she let me into her modest but comfortable three-small-room apartment and sat me in the chair beside her desk, I tried to explain that she could come with me to America the next day. She replied: "Certainly I would like to go, but what about my job at the Polyclinic?"

"Mrs. Goldfarb, you won't need a job," I answered. "You are going to America. Your son will look after you. I will write a note to your employer and everything will be all right." I arranged to meet her the following morning at nine-thirty, when we would go together to the OVIR (the government visa office) to obtain her visa. She handed over their passports, which I took, little realizing that they were merely internal passports, entitling the bearer to travel only within the USSR. Mrs. Goldfarb then began to occupy herself with packing a small bag for her husband and seemed to become preoccupied with the problem of which of his coats to take. This was her only sign of mental turmoil, and she debated with herself briefly before choosing a black leather coat. "I must go and see David," she said. "Will you give me a ride to the Metro?"

During that evening I placed urgent telephone calls to tie up the loose ends. Speaking from his dacha, Anatoliy Dobrynin reassuringly said that he saw no problem in Mrs. Goldfarb's position. "I am certain that she can leave if she wants to," he said.

I put in a call to Tom Simons, Deputy Assistant Secretary of State who had succeded Mark Palmer, to tell him the news and to ask that entry visas be granted for the Goldfarbs. I told him that it was "ninety-percent certain" that the Goldfarbs could leave Moscow with me the next day.

I urged the necessity for absolute secrecy. The Soviets had emphasized that there was to be no publicity before my plane had left Soviet
airspace.

Then I had to cancel my scheduled engagements in Russia. I had
planned to go to Kiev to attend the opening of my art exhibition there
and a concert in aid of Chernobyl victims which I had arranged, at
which John Denver was to perform. I asked Bob Gale to stand in for
me at the exhibition, and I apologized to John Denver. To both men I
had to say, "I can't tell you why I can't come with you but you'll soon
know and you'll realize how important it is that I go back to America
immediately."

It was a busy night.

Next morning, when I arrived at her apartment, Mrs. Goldfarb
was ready to go, sitting quietly among the nineteen suitcases she had
packed with the help of her daughter and son-in-law. That sounds like a
lot of luggage, but when you consider that she was leaving behind a
lifetime, and all her possessions, to which she she would probably never
return, she had been remarkably modest in her packing.

We drove together to the OVIR offices where the business of
issuing the new emigration passports was conducted by a three-star
General of the MVD (the internal police) and an official from the US
desk of the Soviet Ministry of Foreign Affairs. All the work of preparing the documents had been completed by the time we arrived, and the
formalities were dispatched with astonishing speed. Anatoliy Dobrynin
had obviously swung all of his clout. Within fifteen minutes we were
back in our cars and on the way to the hospital.

During the drive Mrs. Goldfarb looked constantly out the window
at her native Moscow. She kept speaking the names of the passing
buildings, as if she were bidding them farewell. "There is the Bolshoi,"
she said, "and there is Detski Mir [Children's World—the largest toy
store in Moscow]." I did not interrupt her soliloquy, which was obviously private.

A large group of well-wishers—including the Goldfarbs' daughter
and her husband, their two children and many friends—had gathered
in the hospital grounds around an ambulance which was waiting to take
Dr. Goldfarb to the airport and my plane. Their moods were mixed.
They knew that they were seeing the Goldfarbs for the last time and
were sad. Yet they were also glad to know that the Goldfarbs would at
last be reunited with their son Alex (whom they had not seen for eleven
years) and that David Goldfarb would receive the best possible treatment in American hospitals.

Mrs. Goldfarb walked resolutely through the hospital to her husband's ward, the movements of her tiny, stocky body displaying no
urgency, no unsteadiness. He was lying on his bed, ready for us,

dressed in a blue warm-up suit. He was lifted into a wheelchair and then he quietly took his leave of those other patients in the ward who were conscious. The stoical dignity of the Goldfarbs in these moments was very moving.

Even at the ambulance, taking leave of their family, they kept their composure, though the grandchildren shed many tears and were barely consolable. Then Mrs. Goldfarb joined her husband in the ambulance and we wheeled out of the hospital grounds in a long convoy, led by my Chaika limousine with its headlights blazing. A series of Volga cars and taxis followed, carrying the daughter's family and the friends.

These taxis caused a rumpus at the airport. Arrangements had been made to allow us to drive directly onto the tarmac and up to the steps of my plane, avoiding the customary delays of baggage and document examination at the airport. The airport Director didn't mind my Chaika or the ambulance enjoying this exceptional privilege, but he objected to the humble Volgas and taxis, as if the dignity of his airport were diminished by their intrusion on the tarmac. It took some time to soothe his ruffled feathers.

Then there was a further delay while I had to convince the border guards that the Goldfarbs really could depart for the United States without entry visas. "Their visas will be waiting for them in New York," I said. This claim obviously strained the guards' credulity to the breaking point, and they had to make many urgent calls on their radios before they could accept that a fast one was not being pulled on them.

Then at last we were clear to go.

Dr. and Mrs. Goldfarb were accommodated in the office in my suite of staterooms on the plane. My wife, Frances, prepared a bed for Dr. Goldfarb on my couch and made Mrs. Goldfarb comfortable in a reclining chair. I sat beside him, holding his hand. Now he began to show some emotion. Once we were airborne, he seemed truly to believe, for the first time, that he would see his son. "It is a miracle," he kept repeating to me, "truly a miracle."

We asked if he would like something to eat and drink and, perhaps, to watch a movie. He was eager for everything. Thus, when I called his son Alex in New York from the aircraft's telephone, I was able to say, "Your father has just finished a hearty meal. He is feeling great. He's sitting up, drinking champagne and watching *My Fair Lady*."

When the plane stopped to refuel in Iceland, I called my people in Washington and New York and told them that they were now free to break the news and meet us when we landed at Newark.

I have hardly ever seen such a massive group of media representatives as those gathered to meet us when we landed. In addition there were many members of the Goldfarb family, representatives of the State Department, and the family physician, Dr. Kenneth Prager, who came aboard the plane to examine David Goldfarb. Nicholas Daniloff was there, too. It was a long time—a long, joyous time—before we were ready to bring David Goldfarb off the plane on a stretcher.

He was lifted to face the barrage of microphones and he and I spoke briefly to the press. Speaking in Russian, which his son translated, he said, "I haven't seen my son for eleven years. I have waited for eight years for this day. I thought it would never come. And then a miracle happened and Doctor Hammer appeared at my bedside and said, 'I want to take you on my plane to America.'" The word "miracle" was much on David Goldfarb's lips that evening.

Then he sped off to Columbia Presbyterian Hospital and I went to my Greenwich Village home.

And that was that: it was done. I have to admit I could hardly believe it myself—everything had happened so quickly; all the expected obstructions of the Soviet bureaucracy had dissolved so instantly.

I wasn't the only one who couldn't quite believe it. The President wrote to me from Air Force One to say:

Dear Armand,
I don't know how you did it, but a big thank you from your countrymen on bringing the Goldfarbs out of the Soviet Union. It was a truly humanitarian deed and we are proud to have them in our country, reunited with their family.
Ron.

Viewed in a longer perspective, the most encouraging aspect of the Goldfarb story may be the portents that it carries for future dealings between America and the USSR. I feel sure that the release of David and Cecilia Goldfarb, without any conditions, could have happened only with the approval of General Secretary Gorbachev. It speaks volumes of Gorbachev's power and his decisiveness . As I conclude this chapter, I have just viewed an uncensored interview with Andrei Sakharov, the most eminent dissident in the Soviet Union, on CBS-TV. Gorbachev himself phoned Sakharov to tell him that he and his wife could return to their home in Moscow after his several years in exile. Sakharov was welcomed at his former position at the Science Institute with great applause. If, therefore, the Soviet system under Gorbachev can respond so readily to a humanitarian problem and reunite parents with their son, and grant release to Sakharov to return to his home with his wife and speak freely, then we may have hope that a new relationship is possible.

I have been looking for that new relationship all my adult life, battling to bring better understanding, greater tolerance and easier trust between East and West.

That story now follows.

2

My People

I was born on May 21, 1898, in a tiny cold-water apartment at 406 Cherry Street, right in the middle of the Lower East Side of New York, near to the heart of the Jewish ghetto in Hester Street. The date of my birth was so long ago that even I find it hard to cast my mind across the gulf of time.

When I was born, the United States had just gone to war with Spain. The main headline in the *New York Times* of that day read: SPAIN'S FLEET RUNS AWAY? reporting that Admiral Sampson's ships were trying to intercept the Spanish Fleet, which had disappeared from Santiago de Cuba. William McKinley, soon to be assassinated, was President. The economic order of capitalism was attaining its zenith in America, making astronomical fortunes for men with names like Rockefeller, Vanderbilt and Morgan. Meanwhile, Czar Nicholas II was on the throne in Russia, and the young V. I. Lenin was serving an exile in Siberia for his subversive activities. On May 21, 1898, the *Times* of London was mostly filled with obituaries and articles about the death, some days before, of William Ewart Gladstone, who had been five times Prime Minister in the reign of Queen Victoria and who had entered the House of Commons at about the time of the Great Reform Act of 1832. In the whole of America, in the year of my birth, only one thousand motorcars were produced. That's how long ago it was.

In his autobiography, diplomat and political sage George Kennan, who is nearly the same age as I am, observed that old men today are probably further removed from their earliest experiences than old men of previous generations who lived when the pace of social change was less precipitate.

I am sure he is right. I feel certain that when my own grandfather was old, he must have felt nearer in memory to his childhood than I do now. My grandfather experienced enormous changes in his own life and fortunes, moving all over Europe from Russia to Paris and then to America, but the overall pattern of life, and the external appearance of social life in general, remained recognizably similar throughout his time.

He was born in the age of the horse-drawn cart and he lived to see the coming of the age of the motorcar. My earliest journeys were made in horse-drawn buggies; but I have lived to travel by supersonic aircraft and to see men on the moon. I was born just as the military age of the cavalry charge was passing into history; but I have lived to witness the creation of the Doomsday machine so long foretold by our forebears.

As for my own forebears, they came from Russia, and before that from Israel. According to a family legend, repeated to me by my grandfather Jacob Hammer, my people were descended from the Maccabees of Israel. Judah Maccabee, also called Judah the Hammer, led the Maccabean rebellion of the Jews against the armies of the Seleucid dynasty, and in 164 B.C. his guerrilla fighters defeated the Seleucids near the fortress of Beth-Zur and opened the way to Jerusalem. They entered in December of that year and there cleansed and rededicated the Temple, a victory that has been commemorated ever since in the winter festival of Hanukkah.

As far as I know, my ancestors took the name Hammer with them when they migrated to Russia, though God alone knows who they were or when they arrived in their new land.

My grandfather Jacob was the son of a wealthy shipbuilder in the town of Kherson, on the north bank of the Dnieper River, but most of the fortune that Jacob inherited was washed away while he was still a boy. Relatives who administered his inheritance in trust had invested all the money in salt, which was then reckoned to be as safe an investment as government bonds today. Jacob's salt was piled on the shores of the Caspian Sea when one day a freak typhoon struck the area and gusted the sea ashore. Almost all of my grandfather's fortune was carried away in the waves.

Poor Jacob was something of a lightning rod for calamity; misfortune descended on his head almost as often as on Job's. He lost his first wife in appalling circumstances, sometime around the year 1865. She was trampled to death in mob panic when fire broke out in the synagogue in Odessa, where Jacob had settled after his father's death. The stampeding congregation shunted Jacob out of the doors and he was unable to fight his way back to her.

Jacob was soon remarried to my grandmother Victoria and took with him his sons by his first marriage, William and Alfred. Victoria was the daughter of a very prosperous merchant from Elizabethgrad—today called Kirovgrad—a young widow with a daughter named Anniuta from her first marriage. Jacob and Victoria's marriage was always stormy, racked both by my grandfather's possessive jealousies and by political disagreements. My grandmother was an idealistic revolutionary; my grandfather was deeply conservative and pro-establishment. I don't think my grandmother was much affected then by the Marxist ideas of revolution which were sweeping Europe; she was simply anti-czarist and republican. Anyway, my grandparents never could see eye to eye on any political question, and they could seldom agree to disagree, so their battles raged for the better part of forty years.

Jacob tried to do his best in business ventures, but he was just never very successful. One scheme after another would be launched, always to founder just off the slipway in the financial shallows. He once went to Poland to purchase a vast load of goose feathers, intending to make quilts for the beds of the middle classes. It was probably a sound enough idea, but Jacob ended up stuck with a warehouse full of feathers.

My father Julius was born in Odessa on October 3, 1874. Less than a year later, in 1875, my grandparents traveled with three of their four children to America. My grandmother was afraid of the pogroms, and she was also in some danger of arrest for her political views. There's no doubt, also, that the family was hard up and they were driven to travel abroad in search of prosperity. Anniuta was left in Elizabethgrad with Victoria's well-to-do parents.

The new arrivals didn't find much fortune in the land of promise. I don't know where they lived then or what my grandfather attempted in America. I must guess that success again eluded him because, after three years, the family was on its way back to Europe, where they were to remain for a further twelve years. However, my grandfather had had the good sense to become an American citizen, which enabled him to travel throughout Europe and Russia without hindrance.

Again, my grandfather tried to turn his hand to a variety of business projects both in Paris and Odessa, but only one—a machine that printed business cards while you waited—had more than a moderate success.

Some unexpected good fortune did come the family's way, however, when Anniuta married a very wealthy entrepreneur named Alexander Gomberg, who lived in Paris and in Odessa. This Alexander Gomberg, my uncle, who was later to play an important role in my own early business efforts in Russia, had the ill luck to have a name which sounded like that of a firebrand Bolshevik revolutionary named Alexander Gumberg, who lived in New York and attracted the worried attentions of the authorities during the years around the time of the Russian Revolution.

Whenever he came to America, my uncle was subject to interrogation and close scrutiny by government agents who supposed that *he* was the one who wanted to tear down capitalism and make a workers' paradise. Nothing could have been further from Uncle Alexander's intentions. He was as devout and dedicated a capitalist as ever set foot on the floor of the Bourse, proud of his wealth and his possessions, and it was a source of great irritation to him to be mistaken for a revolutionary!

Alexander Gomberg (the capitalist) helped my grandfather to set up yet another of his enterprises in Paris, where Jacob established a business selling art and antiques. This proved to be the last of his European undertakings, however. The single outstanding benefit to the Hammer family of Jacob's peripatetic wanderings in search of a good living was that all the children were multilingual from their earliest days. However, English was about to become the family's tongue. In 1889 Jacob set forth on his last voyage back to America, taking with him a good part of the stock from his antiques business, which was to furnish his homes for the rest of his life.

When my grandparents settled in Branford, Connecticut, adjoining New Haven on the north shore of Long Island Sound, they were poorer than they had ever been. For a time Jacob was unable to make much of a living at all, and all the boys had difficulties finding work except for odd jobs. My father, Julius, who was only fifteen, temporarily gave up his education to work in the town's steel mill as the family's principal provider.

Like Jacob his father, Julius was well-built, tall and husky. The long hours he spent swinging a sledgehammer in the inferno of the foundry, being paid by piecework, added thick ropes and planks of muscle to his frame; he became so immensely strong that he could bend a railroad spike in his bare hands. Despite his youth, he became a dominant figure among the workingmen at the mill and he took a lead in organizing them into a trade union when he was recruited as a member of the Socialist Labor Party.

Throughout his life, my father was warmly emotional and sentimental, easily moved to anger and pity by the sufferings of the poor and the cruel labors of the underprivileged masses of that time. The socialism which he adopted, as a working adolescent, was a simplistic mix of idealism and Marxist dogma, forged in the heat of feeling rather than systematically acquired through practical analysis.

The ground of his socialist attachment had also been prepared by his mother, Victoria, who had carried to America the radical beliefs and antiestablishment passions of her Russian upbringing.

Julius might easily have traveled the opposite political road. My grandfather, Jacob, remained staunchly conservative: practically his first act when he finally settled in America was to join the Republican Party. But Victoria, who was highly intellectual and looked very much like Queen Victoria, with her squat body and her proud head (and was even more like the old Queen in her firm beliefs and powerful presence), usually had the upper hand in the political wranglings which shook their house. Julius naturally saw the living confirmation and proof of his mother's beliefs in the conditions of work at the mill and the grueling lives of his workmates, many of whom were already active socialists. Socialism was very widespread among the working classes of the East Coast at that time, and my father was not at all peculiar or exceptional in becoming a member of the Socialist Labor Party.

My grandfather was not, however, entirely without influence over his son. Julius shared his father's interest in business and was undaunted by his father's lack of success. Julius wanted to improve the family's standard of living. To do so, he realized that he must earn more than his laborer's wages. He urged his parents to move with him from Branford to New York City, where he could learn a business and provide for the resumption of his education. He prevailed and the family moved, sometime around 1892, when my father was about nineteen years old.

They went to live on the Lower East Side of Manhattan, among the crowded hordes of new immigrants—mainly Russian and Irish—who had congregated there, making the area a ghetto as restrictive and enclosed in its way as anything they had left behind in Europe.

Looking for a job, my father answered a want ad from a drugstore at Number 6 Bowery, for a clerk who could speak Italian. The druggist's first question was, "When did you learn to speak Italian?"

"I don't speak Italian," my father replied, and the man immediately tried to turn him away, explaining that most of the store's customers spoke only Italian, no English. My father was desperate for any work and he pulled a bold stunt. He said to the druggist, "I will learn Italian in two weeks, and if I don't speak it fluently by then, you don't have to pay me anything."

The druggist gave my father a trial. Within two weeks, Julius had learned the language to the druggist's satisfaction and surprise. He had lived twenty years in the Bowery without knowing more than a few words of Italian.

My father was always an exceptionally hard worker and, being very intelligent and resourceful, he quickly familiarized himself with the business, got himself registered as a pharmacist and, after a few years, had saved enough from his salary to buy out the owner. One of the clerks in the drugstore who now worked for my father was called Joseph Schenck and he asked my father to join with him and his brother Nick in an idea they had to create a chain of theaters for the new moving pictures.

My father turned the offer down, chiefly because he had spotted an opening for himself in the wholesale pharmaceuticals market, which he thought more dependable than the movies. Nick and Joe Schenck then went on to make great fortunes for themselves through the Loews chain of theaters; and they both became heads of studios—Nick ran MGM and Joe had Twentieth Century–Fox.

Like Jacob, Julius wasn't the world's greatest businessman.

He wasn't entirely wrong about pharmaceuticals, however. Working as a pharmacist, he had realized that standard remedies produced by the big drug companies were made of very cheap ingredients on which the companies were making exorbitant profits. He thought he could wholesale the goods at considerably lower prices, so he acquired an abandoned loft on the Upper East Side, turned it into a small pharmaceuticals plant and sold some of the products in his own store.

He did well enough out of this business to buy more drugstores, one for himself on Rivington Street, in the heart of the ghetto, and one for each of his half brothers, William and Alfred. He set them up as partners and managers in stores, William on the Lower West Side and Alfred in Brooklyn. The little chain traded as Hammer Drug Stores.

In this way, the young socialist revolutionary became a junior-league capitalist, without ever, I think, being troubled by the contradiction and certainly without ever losing a scrap of his political convictions. If anything, his socialist beliefs strengthened during his years when he lived with his parents on the Lower East Side.

Life in the family home must have been less than tranquil: the occupants were riven by extreme political differences. My grandmother, Victoria, had, by now, herself taken up the banner of the Socialist Labor Party, and she accompanied her son to party meetings and rallies. My grandfather, meanwhile, was going to Republican gatherings and had become passionately patriotic for the American way of business and democracy.

It must have been during this period that my father first fell under the influence of Daniel De Leon, the leader of the Socialist Labor Party, whose faithful follower my father remained to the end of De Leon's days.

De Leon was a very exceptional character who has been described as the first and probably the only man who occupied the position of the traditional political boss in the socialist movement of America. He was a small, full-bearded man, about 5′5″, always dressed in an opera cloak. His movements and features were very quick and he had the piercing, staring eyes which are, to me, the universal mark of the fanatic. These eyes come in all shades, but in De Leon they were black. He had, too, the personal power of the fanatic, a magnetic persuasiveness which made all his followers feel that they were basking in pure light, while those he rejected were made to feel that they had been cast into outer darkness. He was ruthless in his dealings with people: in his mind, you were either for him or against him, and it followed that you were either absolutely good or absolutely bad.

De Leon carried my father away with him. My opinion has always been that De Leon effectively brainwashed my father. It is hard for me otherwise to make sense of my father's opinions, which I found so unreal, so incongruous, so unfitting both to his own social position and to the realities of life in America as they became obvious to me. I always thought that he and his friends were living in the old world of the pogrom, that they didn't understand the new world of America. Throughout our lives, he was as perplexed by my views as I was by his. Though we were never angry with each other, we never came close to a mutual understanding, and we had many arguments, particularly when I discovered that, without my knowledge or approval, he had made an application for me to join the Communist Party! Needless to say, I never became a member of or contributor to that or any Communist front organization. In some ways my father was one of the most intelligent men I ever knew, but he was always, essentially, a naive and unworldly man. In his political opinions, his head was governed by his heart—and De Leon had seized his heart and held it tight, as if in talons.

My grandmother's influence on my father was not limited to politics. She wanted her son to become a doctor; she felt that the life of a businessman was not a fitting occupation for him. Intelligent and exceptionally well read, especially in the classics, she venerated learning. She wanted to see my father resume his formal education and acquire a medical degree. Once my father had set himself up with a good income from his drugstores and his pharmaceutical business, he felt that he was ready to take on the immense additional strain of medical studies. But, before his enrollment at medical school came his meeting with my mother; and me.

My parents met in 1897 at a socialist outing which was probably held on a Sunday at a park in Brooklyn, or the Bronx, both largely rural areas in those days. My father was twenty-three years old and the girl he met told him she was twenty-one. She was probably at least twenty-four at the time. Throughout her life, even in old age, when people usually boast about their years, she habitually fibbed about her age and regularly snipped off a few years. Her married name was Rose Lifschitz; later and forever she was to be known as Mama Rose.

She had been married to a much older man who had died of a heart attack, leaving her a poor widow with a small son, Harry, who was then three years old. She was working as a sewing machine operator in a garment factory on the Lower East Side, and her minimal wages supported not only herself and her child but also her own mother, who had emigrated from Vitebsk in Byelorussia in 1890, and her younger sister Sadie and younger brothers Willie and Eddie. They also contributed their meager earnings from occasional small jobs.

My mother Rose never cared much for or about politics. I suppose that she went on the socialist outing that day to have a cheap day out away from the sweatshop and the pandemonium of the Lower East Side; and perhaps she was hoping to find an eligible man as a husband for herself. The attraction she felt for my father, Julius, can't have been from the meeting of political soulmates. I think she fell for his looks and charm and, above all, his self-confidence and courage—qualities which she also had in plenty.

My parents were married in 1897 and went to live in that tiny cold-water apartment at 406 Cherry Street. And then I came along.

My Early Life

My father named me Armand after Armand Duval, the romantic hero in Dumas's *La Dame aux Camélias,* or so he said. It is fairly obvious that he must also have had in mind the symbol of the Socialist Labor Party—an arm and a hammer.

I have had more fun out of the constant confusion of my name with the baking soda which is sold all over America. In about 1950, on a whim, I decided that I would like to buy the Arm and Hammer Baking Soda Company. I was then, with my brother Harry, in the whiskey and alcohol distilling business.

As a joke, I had designed an ensign with an arm and a hammer for my yacht. Whenever the yacht appeared in American waters, people would come up to me saying, "Ah, you must be the baking soda king." I grew a little tired of denying any connection until my brother Harry suggested we buy the company so that my reply could be, "Yes, I am indeed." Harry looked into the possibility and came back with a report which wiped the smiles off our faces. Arm and Hammer Baking Soda was owned by the Church & Dwight Company and was a private family concern founded in 1836 and run by two nice old brothers in their seventies. Their company was sound as a bell. The brothers had been mildly surprised and not thoroughly delighted that anybody should have thought of trying to buy them out. They told Harry sharply that their company was not for sale. Our interest had, in any case, waned: Harry guessed that the deal would have cost at least forty million dollars, rather more than any whim was worth. At that price, I decided, it was cheaper to be known as the baking soda king for nothing.

Recently, however, by one of those strange sequences of events that I am always experiencing in the business world, Occidental became one of the largest individual shareholders in Church & Dwight. This came about as a result of Occidental's acquisition of an Alabama potassium carbonate plant in an entirely unrelated deal. Church & Dwight was a major consumer of the output of the plant, and a joint venture was formed between Oxy and Church & Dwight called Armand Products Co., and I was elected to Church & Dwight's board of directors. The two brothers have passed away, but the family members and management own more than 50 percent in the aggregate, while Oxy owns 5 percent, besides a 50-percent share of Armand Products. It was both a good business deal for Occidental and a chance to fulfill my wish, at least in part. Henceforth, I can answer truthfully, "Yes, I am the baking soda king."

My first years were spent in my parents' little flat in Cherry Street, from which we moved when I was about two and a half, to not much more luxurious accommodations in an apartment over one of my father's drugstores at 304 Rivington Street, still in the middle of the Lower East Side. My father had first enrolled as a medical student at Columbia College of Physicians and Surgeons in the fall of 1896, but he withdrew that same year: as a twenty-two-year-old bachelor, he must have found it beyond his powers to combine his businesses with his studies. In 1898, four months after I was born, he tried again and this time, helped no doubt by my mother and the stability of his new marriage, he was able to stick to his herculean task.

I am glad to say I have never suffered from extreme poverty, from not knowing where the next meal would come from or how the bills would be paid. My parents were far from wealthy when my father was a medical student and I was a baby, but, by his great efforts with his debt-burdened stores and his pharmaceuticals business, he contrived, even when we were living in cold-water flats in the Lower East Side, to provide us and his parents with modest comforts of home and a reasonable standard of living. He even found money to spare to help support my mother's family.

The example of what my father accomplished in those years has influenced me very deeply, encouraging me to believe that almost any ambition can be achieved with sufficient initiative, resourcefulness, application and effort. To put it more simply, my father worked like a dog to meet his responsibilities to his family and to improve himself; and he was fortunate to find himself in a country and at a time which stimulated and rewarded such efforts.

My first memory is of an accident which nearly ended my life when I was only about two and a half years old. I was playing alone in the sitting room of my parents' flat, tinkering with a toy coffee-grinder made of tin. I fell awkwardly and a corner of the toy punctured my scalp. I remember my horror at the flood of blood which gushed down my face and, echoing in my memory, I can hear my own cries of panic as I called for my mother. She ran from the kitchen, stanched the blood with a towel pressed to my temple, scooped me up in her arms and fled with me to a nearby doctor who stitched up the wound.

The operation was done without anesthetic, and I can still feel the needle piercing my skin and the stitches tugging at the wound. The doctor told my mother that I had been very lucky; another few millimeters and the tin toy would have punctured my brain and that would have been the end of my story. Instead, I have sported a scar like a canyon above my right temple all my days.

In my mind's eye I can compose sketchily a picture of the Lower East Side as it appeared to me in my earliest days. I can see the narrow streets packed with pushcarts and the tall houses whose fire escapes were laden with laundry and household goods of every description. Whole families lived, cooked and slept outside on those fire escapes during the fiery months of summer. The strong smells of the streets are still with me—the powerful odors from the fish carts mingling with the stands selling hot chestnuts and the extremely primitive sanitation of the area.

Many hard lines have been written about the conditions of life on the Lower East Side; and there's no doubt that, in the desperate fight for survival, crime and prostitution and all forms of degradation flourished there. I was unaware of all that. The place seemed to me warm and vibrant and full of delicious surprise and I was bitterly disappointed when my parents decided, mainly for the sake of the children, that they should move to a more tranquil neighborhood.

My father's MD was conferred upon him on June 11, 1902. He had already moved his family to the Bronx, in preparation for the beginning of his new career. To provide working capital for his practice and to help establish the family in our new home, he sold his two drugstores to his clerks, accepting notes so that they could pay him out of their earnings. He also liquidated his small wholesale pharmaceuticals business.

In all, his capital could have been only just enough to fix up his new office and provide for his family for a year or so while he built up his medical practice. It took a lot of courage to make that move, but one of the traits I most admired in my father was his courage. I hope that I inherited some of that quality from him.

Our new home—a walk-up flat on Webster Avenue—was separated by less than five miles and the East River from the little apartment we had left in Rivington Street, but our surroundings could not have been more different if we had moved a thousand miles. Nobody who knows the terrible desolation and ruin of the Bronx as it is today would believe that the place we moved to was then barely developed countryside, newly connected with Manhattan by the arrival of the elevated railroad—the Third Avenue El. Unmade roads meandered around large private houses set in their own extensive and tidy gardens. Only a few newly constructed tenement houses were to be seen.

We had exchanged the pandemonium and rough-and-tumble of the Lower East Side for quiet spaces where people strolled about their business, and children, for the most part, knew their places. I can't say that I was very thrilled by the contrast, at first, but I learned to adjust.

Very shortly after our arrival in the Bronx, my brother Victor was born and I well remember Harry's and my excitement at the prospect of a new brother or sister and the urgent hushings with which my father tried to quiet us while my mother, attended by a midwife, labored to give birth.

From the moment of his birth, I felt a deep protective instinct toward Victor and I continued to feel this throughout our lives, until the day my kid brother died in 1985, aged eighty-three. For some reason I always felt more worldly than he and better equipped to take and give the rough treatment that you have to expect in life. I recall my mother saying she gave Victor so much attention because "Armand can take care of himself and everyone else as well."

Be that as it may, after a couple of moves, when I was seven we settled in a house at 1488 Washington Avenue. It was a two-story frame house, with a detached garage and a well-kept garden full of roses and peonies which I could pick to put in my blouse and give to my best girl of the moment.

With one extended interruption, 1488 Washington Avenue was to be my home. Not much remains today of the house that I so fondly recall; it has been wiped out in the general devastation of the South Bronx. Where it stood, there is now a vacant lot of rough ground in which the broken foundations of the old house can still be seen. There used to be a drugstore on the corner, next door to our house, from which we would buy our penny candies and fruit drinks. That shop is now a dilapidated liquor store.

We Hammer boys all went to school nearby, at Public School 4, where I can't say that any of us shone brightly as stars of scholarship, though my brothers had, in abundance, other qualities which can be very useful to small schoolboys. Harry was a demon incarnate with his fists; nobody could lick him; he could take on schoolyard bullies in twos and threes and emerge triumphant. No talent could have been more desirable in an older brother; the words "I'll sic my brother Harry on you" struck terror into the heart of any boy who threatened me and Victor.

Victor, always small and wiry, had learned that a good joke can be as disarming as a left hook; and he had begun to compile the collection of one-liners and shaggy-dog stories to which he added all his life. He was always on the lookout for new comic turns to add to his repertoire. One of his greatest triumphs was in performance with Dollie the Collie, the Dog Who Could Count.

Dollie had been given to my father by a grateful impoverished patient in lieu of payment for Dad's services. She could do any arithmetical problem—addition, subtraction, multiplication—nothing was too hard for her. Victor would lead Dollie into the schoolyard and, to the astonishment of his schoolmates, the performance would begin.

"Now, Dollie," Victor would say, "what's two plus three?"

Dollie would bark exactly five times.

"Three minus two, Dollie."

A single bark.

"Now, here's a hard one, Dollie: you'll have to concentrate. Divide eighteen by six."

A pause while the dog computed the answer, and then—amazing—three crisp barks.

Dollie was a figure of majestic mystery whose secret was never discovered by Victor's admiring friends. The trick was simple. The dog had learned to bark for as long as Victor stared her in the eye; she stopped barking the instant he looked away. It never failed.

Even before we moved into 1488 Washington Avenue, my father had become a prominent and greatly loved figure in the area. Everybody knew him. It was an almost ecstatic experience for me to ride with him when he went on his doctor's rounds in his horse-drawn two-seater buggy. People on the street and patients at their doors greeted him with such warmth that waves of pride and honor would surge in me to find myself the son of such a father, a man so obviously good, so obviously deserving of the affection he received.

Naturally, I wanted to be like him, to earn his love and to share the love he got from other people. As soon as I was able to understand that my father was a doctor, I wanted to be a doctor too. Medicine was obviously the best and noblest of callings, and my dream of boyhood was to grow up to become my father's partner. In the bottom of my heart I still feel some sorrow that this dream never came true.

My father's practice, which he conducted from offices and a surgery on the first floor of our house, grew large and thriving and he prospered. He could have made himself many times richer, however, if he had insisted on collecting all his bills; or if he could have restrained himself from giving money away; but then he would not have been the man he was.

I realize that there is a danger here of making my father sound too good to be true, but I have seen, in his office, drawers full of unpaid bills for which he refused to demand payment because he knew the difficult circumstances of the patients. And I heard innumerable stories from patients about his leaving money behind to pay for the prescriptions he had written when he visited people who were too poor to eat, let alone pay the doctor.

My mother took a brisker view of my father's patients. Casting her eye around the patients in my father's waiting room, she would pick out the obvious malingerers and firmly advise them to go home and take a little bicarb of soda.

It must have been the example of my father's goodness which first inspired me to compose an early version of my personal creed, which I mentioned in the Prologue and which I have tried to live by all my life. Ours was not a religious household, but from the age of about six, I found that I wanted to address myself to and get strength from the divine spirit of life. In my bed at night, I would ask to be as good as I could be and to give as much help as I could to others. I found that I liked myself best when I was helping other people—and I wanted to like myself.

As my father's practice grew, he had to take on a full-time assistant. Quite soon, despite his generosity with money, he had the means to help most of the members of his and my mother's families and set them up in their own homes in the immediate neighborhood. Something like a Hammer family compound came into being in houses around 1488 Washington Avenue.

My father's parents, Victoria and Jacob, after more than a quarter of a century of disharmony, had finally agreed to live apart; and they took separate apartments near our house. Jacob moved into a ground-floor apartment directly across the street from us and, having recently become an agent for the Equitable Life Assurance Company, he put up in his windows the sign of his new business, of which he was fiercely proud. I often walked across the street to my grandfather's rooms and he spent countless hours patiently talking to me. He showed me the furniture he had brought with him from his Paris antiques business and told me the history and the special qualities of every piece. He would take down and open for me the massive books he had inherited from his father on the science of shipbuilding. And he told me, in great detail, the stories of our family history which I have related.

No religious feasts or festivals were ever celebrated in our house. There was a synagogue next door, but none of the members of my family ever attended services there. Jewish observances had gradually ebbed out of my family's life by the time I was born; and my parents had, in fact, become members of the Unitarian Church.

Unitarians share an eclectic gnosticism and general openness toward all spiritual faiths, with favor for none. My father found these attitudes compatible with his socialist humanism and I, too, have frequently attended Unitarian gatherings all through my life.

During my childhood we usually went to New Jersey for the Christmas holiday to stay with my parents' friends Malka and Mendel Kornblatt on their farm at Metuchen. Everything they ate—meat, vegetables, eggs, butter, cheeses—they had raised, killed, cured or made with their own hands.

Through Mendel Kornblatt I had my first introduction to the economics of the marketplace and made my first forays into trade. He took me with him when he went to market in Jersey City and I would help him to sell the produce from his farm. I suppose I must have been about seven or eight years old at the time.

We left the farm in Mendel's horse-drawn cart very late at night, about eleven or twelve. We had to be at the market in the small hours, long before dawn, and the journey must have been nearly thirty miles. Mendel made a bed of straw for me in the back of the cart and I would be rocked to sleep among the boxes of fruits and vegetables as the cart swayed and the horse plodded through the night.

At the market I helped Mendel prepare and display his produce, shining up the fruit, washing the vegetables, carefully placing all the best pieces at the front and on the top. I was very interested in comparing his prices with his competitors' and I went walking round the market asking the price of a pound of this, a bushel of that. Then I returned to Mendel with a market report, telling him that he was overpricing here or selling himself short there. After the market, when Mendel wanted to go home lest I be exhausted, I encouraged him to go around the shops in Jersey City and Newark with his unsold goods and offer them at bargain prices. I could see that he would be carrying a dead loss if he took any of it home.

These were the moments when my fascination with business began; and how appropriate that it should have happened in the marketplace, where all the economic laws of trade are laid bare and made obvious for anybody with eyes to see. I was instantly charmed and thrilled by the harmony, in business, of theory *in* practice; and I seemed to recognize by instinct the immutable laws of supply and demand, the importance of good products and the advantage of intelligent salesmanship over dumb optimism.

The semi-rural idyll of my childhood was not to last. We were living, after all, on the fringe of the fastest-growing metropolis in the world, and New York City came roaring over the East River and consumed the open spaces of the Bronx. The roads were surfaced; buildings were constructed on every foot of land and whole streets of new shops came into being. By 1908 our house on Washington Avenue had become tightly hemmed-in by blocks and ranks of tenement buildings for working- and lower-middle-class people.

These refugees from the overcrowded ghettos of Manhattan promptly overcrowded the Bronx, and the area very soon became as undesirable a place in which to raise young children as the Lower East Side itself. In fact, the Bronx became worse, if anything, because it lacked the social cohesiveness, the warm sense of community, which had held the people of the Lower East Side together, however tough their circumstances.

Packs of youths began to rove our streets looking for trouble. There was something like open warfare between gangs of young Jews and their anti-Semitic Irish counterparts.

This fighting had been a regular and established feature of life in the Lower East Side, but down there the gangs were at least separated by a strict territorial demarcation—some streets were known to be Irish while others were Jewish, and each made a no-go area for the other side. Lacking such boundaries, the Bronx became an open battlefield for adolescent hostilities.

They touched me directly only once. I was riding on the Third Avenue El with my mother, Victor and Harry, when some Irish boys got into our car. We were alone with them. There were three or four of them and I suppose that their average age must have been about fifteen. I was about eleven years old at this time, and Harry fifteen. The Irish boys began to insult us all, calling us anti-Semitic names and making a very unpleasant scene. Harry told them to stop and they made the big mistake of asking him who he thought could make them.

Harry took them all on and, using all his boxing expertise, he started laying them out left and right while my mother pleaded with them all to put down their fists and be gentlemen. Once Harry got into a scrap, however, there was no holding him, and he went on pulverizing those Irish boys until the train drew into a station and they all fled. I think they must have been mighty glad to get out alive.

My parents began to worry seriously about the bad influences to which we boys were now exposed. They decided to act when they discovered that I had played hooky from school one day in Palisades Amusement Park in New Jersey. Clearly it was time for a healthier environment.

They contacted old friends of my father's from his days in Connecticut and made arrangements for Harry to go to the house of Rabbi Wellington in Waterbury; and me to the house of the George Rose family in Meriden. Harry was then sixteen and I was twelve. At only eight years of age, Victor was too young to be separated from our parents. Two more years were to pass before he was sent to stay in Daniel De Leon's house in Pleasantville, New York.

George Rose had been a fellow worker of my father's at the steel mill in Branford, Connecticut, and a fellow member of the Socialist Labor Party. When I went to live with his family, he had abandoned his socialism and was working as an engraver.

The Roses were very good, decent people whose home was as comfortable as their very modest means allowed. Their little two-story cottage on Bronson Avenue was literally on the wrong side of the tracks. The small town of Meriden, the population of which was then about thirty-two thousand, was divided by the railroad, and the homes of most of the well-to-do were on the east side while the working people were all grouped together on the west.

I can't remember often feeling homesick or unhappy while I was staying with the Roses. They were such kind and hospitable people that they made me feel at home, and I made periodic visits to my parents during the summer holidays. I *was* lonely when I was sent to summer camp and my parents—as often happened—were too busy to visit me on weekends. Then, when other boys and girls were having happy reunions with their parents, I would go off by myself, feeling very morose and neglected.

One of Meriden's most appealing aspects was the face of Dorothy King. She was the most beautiful girl I had ever seen—well-formed, with shining blond hair and lovely blue eyes. She snared my heart from the moment I set eyes on her at school. Before I could pluck up the nerve to approach her, I spent a long, tortured time admiring her from afar—literally from afar, since Dorothy was distinctly a creature from the other side of the tracks. A large part of Meriden seemed to be named after her family, including King Street School, which we attended, and, obviously, King Street itself.

When Christmas came, I spent the whole of my week's allowance—one dollar—on a box of candy for her and, all my nerves quivering, went to her house to present it. For days I had been rehearsing the speech I would make when I put the box into Dorothy's hands, and, being overrehearsed and overwrought, the walk to her house felt to me like the last steps of the condemned man. A maid answered the door and found me too bashful even to ask to see Dorothy. I stuck the box in the maid's hands and fled.

The gift worked despite my bashfulness. Dorothy thanked me very charmingly, giving me the chance to ask for her company on my Flexible Flyer. That was an invitation no girl of spirit could refuse. The Flexible Flyer was the last word in factory-made sleds, a Porsche among toboggans, and I had saved hard to get mine. All the sacrifices I had made were forgotten one moonlit night, when I slid on my Flexible Flyer from the top to the bottom of a snowy King Street, with Dorothy King seated behind me, her arms around my waist.

Many decades later I asked my friend Senator Styles Bridges to recommend a lawyer to represent me in a tax litigation. Bridges proposed former Senator John Danaher and introduced him to me over the telephone. "Hammer?" said Danaher. "Is your first name Armand?" I said it was. He said, "That's interesting. I'm married to Dorothy King. She's never forgotten you. She's still got a snapshot she took of you in your short pants and button shoes." That information and the photograph which he sent me gave me a thrill even after all those years.

Finally we were to meet again when Dorothy and her husband were my guests at the opening of the Julius and Armand Hammer Health Center at Columbia University, which I endowed in 1978. And then, to complete the circle, their son, who was a former district attorney in Hartford, became one of my attorneys when he entered private practice: Occidental still employs his services whenever we have business in Connecticut.

It was during the long quiet evenings in Meriden that I first read the stories of Horatio Alger and found myself stirred by the portraits in those stories of poor young boys who got ahead by their own efforts. Those fictions led me to the true stories of the lives of great American entrepreneurs like Rockefeller, Carnegie, Vanderbilt and Huntington; and I began to see plainly that the American system made it possible for individuals to do great things, to create lasting business enterprises which gave employment to millions and improved the living standards of everybody. I was particularly impressed with the charitable endowments of these vastly rich men—the colleges, libraries, art galleries and medical facilities. I began to work harder at school to impress Dorothy King. Quite suddenly my marks in class went from a mediocre average to the very top and I started to get straight As.

My parents were pleased with my progress. After I had been in Meriden for four years and at Meriden High for two years, they decided that my head was now level enough not to be turned by any evil influences in the Bronx. They took me home and I was enrolled in the junior class at Morris High in the Bronx. Not even the loss of Dorothy King lessened the pleasure of my homecoming.

I was now fifteen years old. Many of my attitudes and habits of mind had been formed in outline and my personality had largely been shaped. I plainly recognize my adult self in the person I was then. In 1914, soon after the first reports began to be published of the dreadful carnage in the trenches of the First World War, I made a speech at Morris High which I called "The Last War of Mankind." Except for its high-flown style and some of its more elaborate rhetorical devices, I could make much the same speech today.

I spoke of the horror and futility of war. I said that the scientific advances of mankind had made wars between nations capable of eliminating entire generations of young men. I called upon my audience to promise themselves that, at the end of the war in Europe, they would do everything in their power to make sure that there was never another. I remember that I went for a note of high emotion, exclaiming "Did they raise their son that his torn and bloody body should lie rotting on the battlefield?" I must have come close to bringing this line off, because the judges awarded me the school's gold medal for oratory.

Quite soon after returning to the Bronx, I did my very first big business deal. Walking on Broadway, I had seen a used 1910 Hupmobile roadster which I wanted for my own as only a sixteen-year-old can want a car, or anything. The price on the car was $185, about as much as some people earned in six months then. I knew that it would be pointless to ask my parents for the money, they would have told me that I was too young to drive and that other, poorer people could make far better use of $185. True, of course, but no help to me.

I decided to ask my brother Harry to help. He was then twenty years old and working as a pharmacist in Liggetts' Drug Store in the Bronx. Harry had the cash, all right, but he took some persuading.

"How do you expect to pay me back?" he asked.

"I'll get a job," I said.

Harry looked down his nose at me. I was still at school, and any job that I could expect to get would pay pennies. Nonetheless, Harry lent me the money, with the proviso that he could use the car whenever he wanted.

I already knew where I was going to get the money. Christmas was coming and a candy manufacturer, Page and Shaw, was advertising for men with cars to help them deliver their Christmas specials. The pay was twenty dollars a day, big money for the time.

As soon as I had got the Hupmobile, I took it to Page and Shaw's plant where, a small youth in a very small car, I joined a long line of big cars driven by big men. The man who was hiring the drivers looked at me. And then he looked at the car. And then he looked at me again and said, "Where do you think you're going to put the candy in that thing?"

Inspiration came upon me. I said, "I'm going to take out the seats and sit on a box. There'll be plenty of room for the candy."

The man was obviously going to turn me down. In desperation, I made him an offer. I said, "If I don't make as many deliveries as the big cars, you don't have to pay me anything." We shook hands on the deal and I got to work.

Within two weeks, with the help of my schoolmate Maxie Rosenzweig, I had earned enough to repay Harry in full and get outright ownership of the car, and I still had quite a bag of money left for myself. I haven't done many deals which have given me more pleasure than that. I took very much to heart this early lesson that you can get most things you want if you plan the right strategy, make the right deal and work your socks off.

But I still wanted to be a doctor like my father. In my last years at Morris High I worked with absolute determination to prepare myself for medical school. When I graduated from Morris, I knew in my bones that I was on my way to Columbia, treading in my father's footsteps. It was one of the happiest and proudest days of my life when in 1917, after two years of premedical at Columbia Heights for my MBS degree, I presented my application at Physicians' and Surgeons' Medical School at Fifty-ninth Street and Ninth Avenue and the registrar looked at me and said: "You're Julius Hammer's son, aren't you? Well, I processed his application in 1898, the year you were born."

4

The Student Millionaire

In 1917, when I enrolled at Columbia Physicians' and Surgeons', known as P&S, all quarters of my life felt settled and squared and my career seemed to be moving on well-grooved routines toward a predictable and happy outcome. No sign was detectable on this smooth surface of the eruptions which were about to jolt my family to its foundations and transform my life forever.

My father's half brothers were doing well with their drugstores. My mother's brother Willie had become a prosperous ladies' hat salesman, and her brother Eddie was a great favorite in the family because he had become a junior Barnum and Bailey, running his own successful traveling circus. Mother's sister, Sadie, had made a good marriage, and all in all, it looked as if all the hardships and difficulties of our families were set in the past. The twentieth century seemed to beckon fair.

The first disturbance in the picture came from far away. The Great War in Europe reached even into Washington Avenue in the Bronx. When the United States entered the war, Harry immediately enlisted and, with his experience as a pharmacist, he was sent to France to serve in Mount Sinai Base Hospital Number 3 right on the front line in the Marne.

Harry was plucked away at the precise moment my father needed him most. During the summer of 1917, my father became ill with a heart condition, which forced him to make a radical reorganization of his working life. If Harry had been available, my father would certainly have turned to him first for help. In Harry's absence, my father had no choice but to come to me.

My father's illness—an arterial occlusion which could probably be cured today by a simple bypass operation—had undoubtedly been brought on by the strains of his work, and he had probably suffered a mild heart attack. During the middle years of that decade, he had been exhausting himself fighting the polio epidemics which swept through New York City in successive waves of destruction and misery, killing, twisting and mutilating hundreds upon hundreds of children, especially in the poorer areas of the city.

The dreadful scourge of this disease distressed my father beyond words. I remember seeing him come home to 1488 Washington Avenue late one night after he had been out on his rounds tending afflicted children. He came into the living room and threw himself on the sofa, near tears with pain and frustration at the pitiful suffering he had just seen. "This disease is such a mystery," he said. "We don't understand anything about it and I don't believe we'll ever find a cure."

Quack remedies of all kinds abounded for "infantile paralysis," as it was called. Desperate parents were advised to try any kind of pointless exercise to help their suffering children, such as bathing them daily in seawater. This fad caused many people to move their homes out to Coney Island, leaving their work, their friends and families, to be closer to the wholly unhelpful sea.

While my father was so deeply troubled by the polio epidemics, he was also in difficulties with his business. Since 1915 he had been involved in a company called Good Laboratories, a little venture in pharmaceuticals manufacturing like the one he had started while he was still a druggist and medical student, and later sold.

He had been brought into this business by a small-scale accountant named Henry Fingerhood. My father supplied the company with his medical and pharmaceutical knowledge, and Fingerhood was the business manager. The two men had made an agreement that if either of them wanted to withdraw from the partnership, he had to offer his share to the other for the same price he was willing to pay.

My father came to see me one day in the summer of 1917 while I was attending summer classes in my pre-med course and living on campus. He was in poor health but he set out his position to me with great force and clarity.

It was obvious to him, he said, that Fingerhood was deliberately running down the company, trying to force my father to sell his interest. The company was taking a considerable trading loss and was on the verge of insolvency. Knowing my father to be under pressure because of his ill health, Fingerhood had delivered him an ultimatum: accept twenty thousand dollars to get out of the mess or put up the same figure himself to buy Fingerhood out.

My father knew for sure that, although the company was tiny, it was essentially sound and there was a good market for its products. He was certain that its fortunes could be reversed if Fingerhood were ousted and the company was properly managed. With his health in such a poor state, the job was too much for my father, especially as he wanted to continue his medical practice. He was determined to buy Fingerhood out and install me as the Chief Executive of the company.

In so many words, my father told me that I might have to leave medical school, at least for a while, to run the business. He was apologetic about this turn of events, but he was expecting no more of me than he had achieved himself when he was a young medical student running his drugstores. He suggested I could stay at medical school and try to combine the business with my studies, and he said, "I did it, son, and you can do it too."

His apologies were all unnecessary: I didn't resist at all. In fact, I was thrilled by the challenge. Could I run the company? Could I turn it around? Would I be able to manage the staff? How would I combine the business with my studies? Far from feeling intimidated by these questions, I felt excited by this opportunity to prove myself and do something genuinely useful for the parents who had been so generous to me. So far my life had been comfortable, cosseted and quiet. My parents had wanted to make sure that their children would not suffer the hardships of their own young days, and they had succeeded. Now, however, I had a chance to show that I was more than a soft child of privilege—that I had the mettle to enter the grown-up world of business and hold my own with experienced adults.

The immediate first necessity was to raise the twenty thousand dollars to buy out my father's partner. We arranged to borrow the money, on my father's signature, from a bank in the Bronx. Then we went together to see Fingerhood and, to his amazement, presented him with completely turned tables. Having offered to buy out my father for twenty thousand dollars, he was now obliged to accept my father's offer of the same money for his share in the company. Ours was a very brief meeting. Seeing that he had been outmaneuvered and routed, Fingerhood quickly resigned his position, signed a general release terminating all his interests in the company and pocketed my father's check.

Having dealt with him, my next pressing problem was to make arrangements for my medical studies. Obviously, if I was going to be running a business most of the day, I could not attend all my lectures and classes. I needed a stand-in, a kind of amanuensis.

One of the brightest men in my year was Daniel Mishell, a very hardworking and hard-up student. I hit on a plan to help us both. I had rented an apartment on the ground floor of a brownstone house at 168 West Seventy-seventh Street, between Columbus and Amsterdam. I offered my spare room to Dan, rent-free, if he would take down full notes of all the lectures and give them to me to study in the evenings.

Now I was all set. I had a free hand in control of the company and I was covered at Columbia: I could turn all my attention to the business, for my father's sake and my own.

The company was then based in a small store with a rear workshop on Third Avenue in uptown Manhattan. About two dozen women were employed filling bottles with medicines and one or two men ran machines which made pills. The company's only trading advantage over its well-established brand-name rivals was in its prices: it charged a good deal less for products which contained the same ingredients as the more flashily packaged bottles and boxes of the others.

The difficulty was drawing the attention of prescribing doctors to the particular benefits of our products, bombarded as they were by blandishments and samples from all the major producers. I had to offer them some advantage that they would be foolish to ignore or reject.

The key, it was obvious to me, lay in the samples distributed by drug company salesmen. These samples were always tiny quantities of the drug being offered for sale. The doctors dumped the samples on their back shelves or in their wastebaskets. I decided to make the samples full-size bottles and packets, which they would never throw away. I guessed that they would give the samples to their patients, for treatment, and that when the sample was used up, the patient would ask for more of the same at his local drugstore.

My father and Fingerhood had renamed the company, giving it the more imposing-sounding name of Allied Drug and Chemical Company. I thoroughly reorganized the sales force by putting a lot more men in the field at greatly increased rates of commission. I didn't need anybody to tell me a cardinal rule of business practice: if you want somebody to work for you, you'd better make it well worth their while. People will always work harder if they're getting well paid and if they're afraid of losing a job which they know will be hard to equal. As is well known, if you pay peanuts, you get monkeys.

The company expanded very quickly as our sales increased and the work force grew from dozens to hundreds. Less than a year after I had taken control, I moved the company's headquarters from Third Avenue to a much bigger plant on the Harlem River in the Bronx. We were getting orders faster than we could fill them and my day was extremely exacting. I would arrive home at my apartment bushed from my day's work, only to face four or five hours' concentrated study on the notes which Dan Mishell had prepared for me.

As soon as the company started making good profits, Henry Fingerhood resurfaced.

He claimed that my father and I had swindled him and he began a million-dollar suit against us. This was the first time that I discovered how much I enjoyed legal combat when I felt right was on my side.

After asking friends for the name of the best commercial trial lawyer in New York, I went to see Max Steuer, who was then at the height of his powers and fame. I put my dilemma to him and he said: "Well, young man, I am willing to represent you, but I must warn you that I think this case may go to court and my fees for court appearances are one thousand dollars a day."

I said, "I don't believe this man will go to court. He signed a general release. I think he's bluffing. I want you to write a stern letter to show him that I mean to fight. I propose that I should pay you a thousand dollars for writing that letter. What do you say?"

Steuer agreed to these terms in writing, and then he wrote the letter, which I practically dictated. As I had guessed, Fingerhood—whose complaint was a tissue of lies—was scared stiff when he got a letter from the famed Max Steuer and he immediately backed off and dropped his suit.

As soon as he heard this, Max Steuer sent me a letter claiming the credit for my victory and enclosing a bill for ten thousand dollars. I wrote back reminding him of our original terms and sending him a copy of our agreement. Steuer then himself backed off and conceded defeat. I was flattered to hear some years later that Max Steuer told a mutual friend, "Armand Hammer is the only man who ever outsmarted me."

After about a year of grueling work, I realized that I needed some expert help on the executive side of the company. I installed Alfred Van Horn as President and Chief Executive Officer and gave my brother Harry the title of Vice President and Treasurer, while I assumed the title of Secretary. Mr. Van Horn had previously sold his own pharmaceutical manufacturing company, called Van Horn and Sawtelle, to Johnson & Johnson. It was about this time that my father made a gift to me of all his stock in the company and I became the outright owner.

One of the fastest-growing items on our order books was, at first, a complete mystery to me and the company's executives.

Between 1918 and 1919 we discovered to our bewilderment that orders for cases of bottled tincture of ginger had risen by some thousandfold. We were getting immense orders from the most improbable places, especially the states of the Deep South and the Midwest, and we were considering making special arrangements to produce and deliver our hugely increased orders.

I couldn't imagine what was going on. Finally, to try to get to the bottom of the business, I went to see a customer of ours, a druggist in Richmond, Virginia, whose own orders of tincture of ginger had enormously increased.

The man gave me a long, slow, worldly look and said, "You really mean to say you don't know anything about this?" Even though I felt that I was looking like a fool, I swore my innocence.

"Come with me," he said, and led me into a back room of his drugstore. There he took out a glass, a bottle of ginger ale and a quantity of tincture of ginger, and combined the lot with a few ice cubes in a fizzing potion.

"Here, taste this," he said.

I drank and was immediately jolted by the mule kick of a really powerful ginger-ale highball. The kick came from the tincture of ginger, which was laden with alcohol. The taste was something less than pure ambrosia, but there was no denying that the drink carried a belt.

My customer explained that, in these Volstead Act days, people were going wild for any drink which had the properties of alcohol but which was legal, within the strict limits of the Prohibition laws.

He didn't need to paint the picture for me in oils. I could see that my little company was sitting on a gold mine in its tincture of ginger supplies. I could also see that if I didn't get hold of some more, fast, somebody else would. In fact I learned, on making inquiries, that some of the largest drug manufacturing companies were already active in the tincture of ginger business.

I went immediately to our bankers and obtained letters of credit for a million dollars or more. By this time, Allied Drug and Chemical was in solid good fortune and the banks were very eager to lend us money. As everybody knows, they are most apt to lend it when you've already got plenty of it.

Then I checked with the US Department of Commerce to find out which countries were shipping exports of ginger, and I hired agents, through help-wanted ads in the newspapers, to go to all those countries of the world from which ginger originated—chiefly India, Nigeria and Fiji—and buy up all of the future production of ginger there.

In this way Allied Drug and Chemical Laboratories effectively cornered a world monopoly in ginger and, consequently, in the production of tincture of ginger in the United States. All the major drug houses, which had been sharing in the bonanza, now had to get their supplies from us.

The results were astonishing. Our order book became almost unmanageable. We had to install special bottling lines at the plant to handle production, and we were shipping out truckloads every day, especially to the dry states of the South. The total work force at our plant grew to nearly one thousand five hundred employees.

Quite suddenly I became a very rich young man. It was an extremely complicated exercise every day to balance my checkbook. Some days I was depositing up to $30,000. Not even Gloria Swanson herself—whose Hollywood contract for $1,000 a day had amazed the nation—could match earnings on that scale. Average income in the United States in 1919 was about $625 a year. In that year my personal income was over $1 million net.

I hear that legend today has it that I made my first fortune as a bootlegger. Well, I've been called plenty worse things and they've been untrue too. Bootlegging was illegal: there was nothing illegal about the tincture of ginger trade—not until the federal government changed the law, anyway. At that point, as I'll describe in a moment, Allied Drug and Chemical got out of the business: there wasn't much choice.

What with the demands of my business life and the difficulties of keeping up with my studies at Columbia, I was bound to neglect some aspects of my personal life. The main victim was my girlfriend.

"Bennie," whom I had met through Daniel Mishell, was a beautiful nurse and I was in love with her. She was a Quaker, very devout and very demure. The combination of her looks and the obvious purity of her character had been irresistible to me and, in my mind, I had raised her onto a pedestal of unsullied womanhood, thinking her almost too good for me. I was completely infatuated with her and had serious thoughts of proposing marriage, but while I was so busy, barely able to spare the time to see her, it was obviously pointless to make any definite plans for a wedding.

One day my friend Maxie Rosenzweig went to my apartment to collect some medical books for me and bring them to my office. I gave him my key. When he returned, he hesitantly stammered out a story which shocked me so much that I almost collapsed.

Opening the front door, he said, he glimpsed a naked form darting from Dan's bedroom to the bathroom. It was Bennie, my intended bride, running from the bed she had been sharing with Dan Mishell, my roommate.

I was thunderstruck with astonishment and rage. I went straight to the apartment, where Dan was now alone, and a fearful scene ensued in which I really felt for some moments that I might kill Dan. It ended when I told Dan to pack his things and clear out.

I like to laugh about this drama now, but it was far from funny at the time: the young don't tend to see much comedy in sex.

Some weeks later Daniel Mishell came to see me when I was in Mount Sinai Hospital having my tonsils removed, and we made up our friendship. He told me that I was better off without Bennie because she had been distributing her favors very widely among the interns at the hospital, and he had felt that in joining the list of her lovers he wasn't committing an original sin. I can't say that I was much consoled by this news.

To cheer myself up I gave myself a new house, a Steinway grand piano and a car. I've still got the piano and the house: a charming place in Greenwich Village which had been a carriage house and now had one huge living room more than two and a half stories high, capped by a skylight. On the first floor was a balcony which led to a bedroom and a bathroom. Perfect for a young bachelor. The surrounding streets were filled with noisy restaurants and shops and, night and day, the place hummed with music and gaiety.

In his autobiography *As I See It,* J. Paul Getty described the days when he first had plenty of money of his own, in Los Angeles during the years of the Great War. By his own account, Paul had a hectic initiation into the pleasures of female companionship which gave him a lifelong taste for more of the same. Paul very comically described the chagrin he saw on the face of Hugh Hefner sixty years later, when he told Hefner all about his sexual escapades in Malibu in 1916. Paul said it was as though Hefner liked to believe that absolute chastity had been the unbroken rule of life until the so-called sexual revolution of the fifties and sixties in which Hefner had had such a notorious role. Getty had to assure Hefner that young men and women had fully enjoyed each other long before Hefner started his own sexual song and dance.

As it was in Getty's experience on the West Coast, so it was in mine in New York.

In my living room I installed an immense couch, like a Middle Eastern potentate's throne. It was mounted on a wooden platform above a step about eight inches high. A thick, soft mattress, covered with a sumptuous counterpane, rested on the platform, and colorful pillows were strewn on top. The whole effect was extremely sensual and voluptuous. My guests could drape themselves on and around my throne and lie back and enjoy themselves while my friend Phil Baker— one of the stars of George White's *Scandals,* one of the biggest Broadway hits in town—who used to MC these occasions, played the accordion and cracked jokes.

When I married my third and last wife, Frances, with whom I at last found the contentment which I had been seeking all my life, practically her first act was to give orders for the removal of that huge couch: she could have made no clearer sign that with her arrival a new order had begun, to which I acceded with only a suppressed sigh of nostalgia for the delights that couch had borne.

It was never difficult for me to obtain liquor for my parties. Allied Drug and Chemical was trading in bonded liquor, legally sold with doctors' prescriptions for medicinal purposes, so my contacts in the trade were very good. Naturally enough, some fairly serious drinking got done at these parties: but I'm sure that I'm not deluding myself when I say that I was never drunk myself. I have always known when I've had enough and, at that moment, I have put down my glass. I can't remember ever having had a hangover in my life, which is a somewhat surprising thing to say for a man who became, in his middle life, one of the biggest producers of distilled spirits in the United States.

When I lived in Russia in the twenties, I learned to follow the Russian habit of taking a small bite of food with every glass of vodka, and this practice, which I have followed ever since, has helped to keep me sober (though there is a limit even to the effectiveness of this safeguard). For about the last twenty years I have hardly taken any drink at all, just an occasional glass of wine with a meal, and every now and then some sherry or a glass of my favorite champagne. I need my wits to be as clear and sharp as I can keep them if I am going to accomplish everything I want to do in the life remaining to me. There simply isn't time to be befuddled.

The fortunes piling up in the accounts of Allied Drug and Chemical benefited all the members of my family: we all shared in the company's success. Victor had completed his freshman year at Colgate and had switched to Princeton to study art history and acting. Now he found himself with plenty of money just at the moment when he was ripening to enjoy it; and he would motor down to my parties with his college friends.

My mother loved my little house in the Village, and never having been slow herself to get into the swing of a party, she liked to stop by my house and check out the action. "Live dangerously carefully," was one of my mother's favorite mottos, and I could say that it has been my watchword as well.

Harry had come back from the war just at the beginning of 1919 and had plunged straight into the business as Treasurer of our corporation. With his help and the highly competent and responsible work of Alfred Van Horn, the executive structure of the company was secure and tight and I could afford more time for my medical studies which, as I advanced toward graduation, were becoming so demanding that I couldn't possibly spare a full working day, every day, to run the company.

Some deft executive footwork was called for when the federal government changed the regulations governing the sale of tincture of ginger, to scotch (forgive the pun) our lucrative trade.

The new rules required the alcohol, which was the main ingredient of the product, to be "denatured," which meant making it unpalatable by the addition of bitter chemicals. The bottom dropped out of the market as if it had been drilled by a laser. For a short time, we tried marketing a hair tonic fortified with the "denatured" alcohol, but it failed to find many customers—except among those few who like to drink hair tonic—and was quickly abandoned.

We needed to find another trade, another market, and we decided on a bold step. The conventional wisdom of the day in the pharmaceuticals industry was that the ending of the war would cause a slump in trade because of canceled military and government contracts. I believed the opposite. I reckoned that a general boom of consumption was more likely to follow the war as the men came home and wartime restrictions on spending were lifted.

With the very substantial liquid resources at our disposal, largely from the tincture of ginger trade, we decided to gamble on my instinct and invest heavily in buying government surplus stocks of drugs and chemicals. The quantities we bought were huge and the prices were a steal. Our competitors, the major drug producers, all of whom were cutting production and discounting stock, thought we were crazy and riding for a terrible fall.

They were wrong. I was right. There *was* a postwar boom, led by consumer spending. Demand expanded very quickly and we were able to set very profitable prices on the supplies which we had so cheaply obtained.

One of our smaller customers—for such drugs as chloroform, morphine, codeine and the like—was Ludwig Martens, head of the unofficial diplomatic mission in New York of the new Bolshevik revolutionary government in the new Soviet Union.

It has been alleged that Allied Drug and Chemical, under my father's direction, became a front organization for the Bolsheviks, obtaining foreign exchange for Moscow and laundering funds for the American Communist Party, of which my father had become a founding member in 1919. Nothing could be further from the truth: first, because my father no longer had any control over the company; second, because rock-ribbed Republican Alfred Van Horn would have died rather than allow company funds to be diverted to the American Communist Party or the laundering of currency for the Kremlin; and third, because that simply wasn't the kind of business we were in.

My father did have a close connection with Ludwig Martens and was an unofficial trade adviser to the unrecognized Russian diplomatic mission in New York—the United States and USSR would not establish full relations until 1933. Obviously, my father's prominence in the American Communist Party gave him a special interest in helping the Russians, who were at that moment fighting a civil war at home and an economic blockade from the West.

But that was my father's interest only. Allied Drug and Chemical entered into business with Martens not for reasons of political sentiment but for profit, and we competed against other American companies eager for the business for the same pecuniary reasons. The total volume of business we did with them did not exceed one hundred fifty thousand dollars, of which about half was for an oil-well machinery order, and even *that* money went uncollected when Martens and his delegation were suddenly expelled from the United States in 1921. At that time our company's annual turnover was several million dollars.

The clouds of innuendo haunted my father, though, and the consequences were very grave. The small trade our company conducted with the Russians may have contributed to an attack upon him which had the most painful repercussions and brought about one of the most unhappy episodes of my life.

My father's radical socialist beliefs and activities had always, and not surprisingly, made him a marked man. During the middle years of the decade, however, he was never seriously troubled by the authorities, chiefly, I would guess, because they did not regard him as an actual menace, as indeed he was not.

All that changed in 1919, as the first serious Red Scare in the United States got under way and my father became the subject of hostile scrutiny. As Stephen Birmingham writes in *The Rest of Us:*

> 1919 became the year of the zealot, an era of revenge against domestic foes, real or imagined. The Hun had been brought to his knees, but now it seemed that there were other heads to be bloodied.
> In 1919, the anarchists Emma Goldman and Alexander Berkman were released from prison and deported to Soviet Russia, along with more than 200 other "traitors." An additional 249 Russian "undesirables" were shipped out aboard the SS *Buford*. A young special assistant to Attorney General Alexander Palmer—the chief executioner of this red scare—was 24-year-old John Edgar Hoover, whose job it was to handle deportation cases involving alleged Communist revolutionaries.

America was divided between the majority which viewed the new Bolshevik regime in Russia with alarm and the minority which greeted it with joy. The Jews of New York were also divided. Generally speaking, Jewish immigrants from Russia were pro-Soviet while Jews who had come from Germany were anti-Soviet. To quote Stephen Birmingham again:

> The Russians had arrived with their souls afire with socialism, with the stirrings of the Bolshevist movement, and were already struggling to form trade guilds and unions to do battle with "the bosses." But the Germans by now were contented capitalists, conservative supporters of President Theodore Roosevelt. The Russians appeared to pose a real threat to the American way of life as the Germans had

learned to enjoy it, and it seemed essential that this Jewish radicalism be nipped in the bud, that the Russians be retrained in the "proper way of American political thinking."

There were German Jews involved in what happened next. They were not alone, of course; my father had offended many powerful interests. His socialism was a thorn in the flesh of the Tammany Hall Democrats who had the lucrative unions and city contracts in their pockets. There were plenty of people out to get him after the war, and in 1919 they got him. My beloved father was arrested and charged with manslaughter.

5

The Decisive Moment

The experience of seeing a parent tried and imprisoned can hardly be imagined. As a trauma of human life it must compare with bereavement or the loss of love. All of us are, at some moment, bereaved, and most of us have survived broken love affairs. Relatively few people have to endure the sight of a beloved parent in the dock or in prison uniform, but I think it's true to say that those of us who share this nightmare never fully get over it. Charles Dickens was scarred forever by his father's imprisonment when he was a child, though it is also possible that the experience was one of the foundation stones of his genius. As for myself, I was not a child when my father was arrested, but the passage of many decades has done little to ease the pain I felt when I saw my father led away to the cells.

I have hardly ever spoken about this experience in any detail and I bring myself to the task of describing it now with considerable reluctance and deep feelings of unease.

In mid-July 1919 two detectives from the Bronx District Attorney's office called at my father's offices on Washington Avenue. For some reason which I have never understood, my father did not see them. There must have been some mix-up, some misunderstanding. I think my father sent a message through the maids that he was busy and asked the men to come back another time. Anyway, they seem to have gone off in a bad temper, feeling that proper respect had not been shown to their office.

They had wanted to question my father about the death, early in July 1919, of one of his patients, a Mrs. Marie Oganesoff. She had died following a dilation and curettage my father had performed to effect a therapeutic abortion. Mrs. Oganesoff was the wife of a former attaché at the Russian Embassy—the Czarist Embassy in Washington, not Martens's unofficial Soviet diplomatic mission.

The men from the DA's office had brought with them bottles of influenza medicine which my father had prescribed for the woman and they wanted an explanation of the prescriptions. The question of the woman's influenza was later to become vital in the case; if my father had seen the DA's men that day, and taken the opportunity to make a full statement, he might have cleared himself without further ado.

The first I knew of this case was when my father was arrested in August 1919, charged with manslaughter in the first degree and released on bail of five thousand dollars. Naturally, the family immediately gathered round my father to support him; and then I heard his story.

The facts of the case, from my father's side, seemed straightforward. Mrs. Oganesoff was a patient with a long history of nephritis—progressive kidney failure—and heart trouble. Both in Europe some seven or eight years before and in the US more recently she had been told by her doctors that she must never have more children because pregnancy would kill her. She had undergone numerous abortions, even effecting some with her own hands, using knitting needles.

During the year that she had been my father's patient, he had already aborted one of her pregnancies by dilation and curettage of her uterus. On that occasion she had been accompanied to my father's surgery by her husband, who knew all about the peril of her medical history but went on impregnating her just the same. Since there was no urgency in her case at that time, my father had sent her home after performing the simple operation, in the presence of another physician, as the law required.

This time Mrs. Oganesoff had contacted my father by telephone, begging for an appointment to see him at his office on Saturday, July 5, 1919; my father was staying the weekend in the country at Edgemere on Long Island and he returned to the Bronx especially to see Mrs. Oganesoff.

She was pregnant again. Her menstrual period was nine days late. She had already tried to abort herself, using a darning needle dipped in iodine, but she had merely damaged herself internally and made herself bleed. She was extremely unhappy, frightened and desperate.

She begged my father to act there and then. She said, according to my father's memory: "There is no use persuading me to leave it go. You know my history. You know I cannot leave it go. It is a question, will you relieve me now or will you keep me in misery for a few weeks and then I will have to have it done anyway?"

My father reproached her for having tried to abort herself, saying, "When you bring an instrument into your uterus, you are taking a chance on infection." She replied, "Well, then how can you talk to me about postponing the case when you have said to me yourself that I might have infected myself, and in such a case every hour may count?" (I am taking these words from the transcript of evidence heard in the court, but they fit exactly with the account my father gave me when I first heard this story.)

The woman was also suffering from headaches, sore throat and slight fever, consistent with the onset of influenza, an epidemic of which was then sweeping New York. Influenza was a far more serious illness then than it is today, as witness the fact that ten million people died in the worldwide Spanish influenza epidemic of 1918.

My father was in a quandary. He felt that he didn't want to perform the operation, but Mrs. Oganesoff's plight was obviously extreme and he had to consider the risk that in her desperation she might inflict even more serious injuries upon herself. Her character was very high-strung and, as her previous actions showed, she was capable of doing anything to herself.

My father summoned his young assistant, Dr. Benjamin Diamond, to come into the examination room and give a second opinion.

Dr. Diamond had only about eighteen months' experience as a practicing physician, but he was very talented and my father rated his opinion very highly. Having explained the case and the patient's history, my father put on surgical gloves and conducted an internal examination which showed that the woman was hemorrhaging heavily, *not* discharging menstrual blood. It was impossible to determine whether she was pregnant: they had to take her word for that.

"What would you do in these circumstances?" my father asked his partner.

"Well, she may be infected and, therefore, she may have trouble in spite of a curettage, but I think she'd have a better chance if you curetted her right here and now," Dr. Diamond said.

My father decided to conduct the operation after thoroughly sterilizing his curettage instruments.

At that moment he may have acted imprudently, without a proper regard for his own safety. The laws of New York were extremely strict concerning abortion, and the medical fraternity had been complaining for many years that unless they were reformed, some honorable physician, acting to save his patient's life, would inadvertently find himself breaking the law and risking twenty years' imprisonment. He could have disregarded the woman's pleading and sent her home or to a hospital. Then he would have been safe, though her life would have been endangered by the delay.

Later on he blamed himself bitterly for his imprudence; but he had truly felt that Mrs. Oganesoff's life was in danger and he believed it was his duty to save her.

After the operation he prescribed some medicines for her influenza and sent her home with her maid in her chauffeur-driven car.

No money changed hands, neither did my father issue a bill for his services, which has always seemed to me to be a clinching fact. Abortionists always charge for their services in cash in advance. The absence of any payment makes it obvious that my father was not conducting an illegal, back-street abortion practice—which is, effectively, what was alleged against him.

Having returned to her home, Marie Oganessoff deteriorated rapidly. On the Sunday evening following the previous day's operation, Mr. Oganesoff summoned my father to his wife's bedside. She had a temperature of 103 degrees Fahrenheit. My father told the husband that she was suffering from flu and advised him to look after her, following the normal procedures.

During the next days, she became very seriously ill, too sick to be moved from her bed to a hospital. Her influenza was aggravated by the onset of peritonitis almost certainly caused by her attempts to abort herself using the darning needle. Toward the end of the week, Mr. Oganesoff brought in another doctor whose first diagnosis was that she had typhoid fever. When she died on the following Friday, he certified that the cause of death was peritonitis resulting from an abortion.

My father believed that the primary cause of her death was intestinal influenza, and that the peritonitis was the result of her self-inflicted injuries.

Mr. Oganesoff began a private action against my father for malpractice. Maybe he was sincere, but I have always wondered about his motives. He was a rabid anti-Bolshevik, not least because the change of government in Moscow had cost him his job. He may also have thought that he would win a big settlement from my father in damages; and, perhaps, he was transferring to my father some of the guilt he may have felt himself since it was he who had repeatedly made his wife pregnant when he knew that her life was in danger. His private action led to the police inquiry, to the investigation, arrest and trial.

The case immediately attracted a storm of publicity, much of it damaging to my father's chances for a fair trial. The main headline in the *Bronx Home News* was MILLIONAIRE DOCTOR ARRESTED—which would have been funny if my father's case hadn't been so perilous. *I* was the millionaire in the family.

My father could not continue his practice while criminal proceedings were outstanding and, in the long interlude of almost a year between his arrest and the beginning of his trial, he sold his practice and the family home at 1488 Washington Avenue to his assistant, Dr. Diamond. It was a very sad decision, but there was no avoiding it.

On my advice, and mainly at my expense, my parents moved to the Ansonia Hotel at Broadway and Seventy-third Street in Manhattan, where they remained until the end of the trial and where my mother continued to live until 1923.

There, my father spent his time preparing his defense.

My father was never shrewd or self-centered. He could never be bothered to concentrate on calculating his interests. His unselfishness was very endearing most of the time, but in assembling his defense for the most important ordeal of his life, when he was facing a possible sentence of twenty years in prison—which would have been the remainder of his life—his lack of care was almost foolhardy and it was to have disastrous consequences.

He turned for advice to an old friend named Henry Kunz, who had been a very prominent lawyer in New York until he himself had run into trouble with the law for advising a bankrupt client how to hide his assets, and had served a term of imprisonment. When he had been released, in about 1918, and was not allowed to resume his law practice, my father had induced me to give him a job with Allied Drug and Chemical.

Henry offered to look after the management and direction of my father's defense, the hiring and instructing of the lawyers. The trouble was that Henry Kunz was a scoundrel. In choosing my father's lawyers, his first concern was for his own interests. He hired the former Assistant District Attorney, James W. Osborne, Jr., who had prosecuted him, in the hope that the man would help him to get a pardon, and as the principal trial lawyer, he hired a friend of his, Herbert Smyth, who had never defended a criminal case—but who I believe kicked back a percentage of his fees to Kunz.

I know Kunz was a crook because, months after my father's trial, I caught him cheating our company as well. I found he was taking bribes from our suppliers—one of them, for instance, a bottle manufacturer, added 10 percent to his price for Kunz's benefit, as shown by a letter addressed to him which I opened accidentally.

Kunz's choices were catastrophic: both lawyers were incompetent—and one was a hopeless drunk.

On many evenings during the trial, I saw Osborne, collapsed on the bar of a nearby restaurant or being supported to his car. I would wonder, "How on earth can that man sober up enough to do his work properly in the morning?" He couldn't.

Herbert Smyth, on the other hand, was a famous Wall Street lawyer who had made himself immensely rich conducting boardroom disputes and corporate business. He had never fought a criminal case in his life. He was a character straight out of the pages of Dickens, his disorganized mind concealed with grand manners of speech and an imposing bearing. Wearing a frock coat and sporting a monocle, he turned up at court every day in a chauffeured Rolls-Royce. No appearance could have done more to provoke the hostility of the crowds of poor people who thronged the streets outside the Bronx County Court every day; and I expect the effect was the same on the jurors, who were people of a similar background.

This music hall duo made a shambles of my father's case. I longed to fire them on the spot and get better men—and I did, in fact, retain a Bronx lawyer named John Kadel to assist them—but it was too late to bring in an entirely new team of lawyers.

Some key elements of the prosecution's case supported my father's position, but these potential advantages were neglected by his lawyers. Called as a witness for the prosecution, Mr. Oganesoff acknowledged that his wife had a history of kidney disease, that she had had many previous abortions in Europe and that he had been warned that she might die if she had more children. This testimony alone ought to have been enough to clear my father, since it established beyond question that the woman's life was endangered by her pregnancy. The lawyers ignored the point.

The vital question in the case was whether it had been necessary to perform the curettage to preserve the life of the patient. If that could have been proven, my father's actions would have been entirely legal. Despite all the testimony available to them, from Dr. Diamond and from many other physicians, the lawyers simply botched this defense. They failed even to introduce the material evidence of the prescriptions my father had written for Mrs. Oganesoff's influenza. The absence of this proof reduced to mere hearsay my father's claim that the woman was already ill with flu when she came to his offices and that he had tried to treat her responsibly.

Mr. Oganesoff also testified that his wife had developed a high fever within two hours of returning to their home from my father's offices. If that fever marked the onset of the peritonitis which had killed her, as the prosecution claimed, it could not have been the result of the curettage my father had performed. Peritonitis does not set in within two hours. It could have been the result of only one thing: her own efforts with the darning needle.

These failures were damaging enough. Worse yet was the hopelessly feeble cross-examination of the principal witness for the prosecution, Dr. Benjamin Schwartz, the Assistant Medical Examiner.

In answer to a hypothetical question, and basing his answer solely upon the autopsy which he had conducted on Mrs. Oganesoff, Dr. Schwartz gave his opinion that the cause of death had been the abortion conducted by my father. Schwartz swore that the patient's heart and other organs had been normal, though no test of the heart or valves had been conducted at the autopsy and no microscopic examination of the kidney had been made.

As insubstantial as it was, the evidence went unchallenged. To the jury, understandably enough, Schwartz's testimony alone was enough to convict my father—his own lawyers didn't question it very hard, so why should they?

But something else was at work here as well.

The men who tried and prosecuted my father represented an exact cross-section of the powerful groups my father had offended. The District Attorney, Francis Martin, was an Irish Catholic who was very strongly against abortion of any kind for any purpose, besides being a declared anti-Communist. The Assistant District Attorney, Albert Cohn,* and the judge, Louis D. Gibbs, were both anti-Communist Jews. All three men shared open hostilities toward my father's political beliefs.

In addition, Dr. Benjamin Schwartz was not all that he appeared. A few years after my father's trial he was himself arrested on charges of criminal conspiracy and convicted in the federal courts as the leader of a ring of thieves who had robbed insurance companies by giving patients drugs to simulate heart conditions. Did Schwartz give testimony against my father to ingratiate himself with the district attorney? I have always believed so.

It was on the uncorroborated evidence of this man that my father was found guilty.

Before the jury returned with their verdict, there was to be one more dramatic twist in the story which, again, must have counted against my father. On Thursday, June 24, a juror called Joseph Maher complained to a New York newspaper called the *World* that he had been offered a bribe of ten thousand dollars to bring in a not guilty verdict. The judge then interviewed Mr. Maher in his chambers and the complaint was discussed in open court. Immediately, of course, public suspicion determined that my family, supplied by my wealth, had been up to no good.

The judge was convinced that the offer of the bribe had not come

---

*By a strange turn of fate, Albert Cohn was the father of Roy Cohn, who was disbarred in 1986 for nonethical practice of law and then died, reportedly of AIDS.

directly or indirectly from the defendant, but meanwhile the newspaper story had been circulated in the jury room and read by all the jurors, and instead of immediately applying for a mistrial, my father's lawyers congratulated the judge on preserving "the rights of our client." Mr. Maher's complaint in court was bound to have prejudiced the minds of the jurors.

Four days after the jury returned its verdict, the Bronx grand jury investigating the bribe attempt indicted a suspect. He was described in the indictment as Thomas Sheehan of 744 East 168th Street, Tammany District Captain of the Fourth Assembly District, the Bronx.

Mr. Sheehan's affiliations made it abundantly clear from which quarter the imbroglio had emerged. He was never brought to trial— Tammany was very powerful in those days.

Sheehan's identity became known too late to help my father. At one o'clock in the morning on June 26, 1920, after four and a half hours of deliberation, the jury returned with a verdict of guilty to the charge of manslaughter in the first degree. My father was taken into custody to await sentence. I still can't convey my feelings of pain and shock at that moment.

The verdict unleashed a barrage of publicity and protest. We were besieged, night and day, by newspaper reporters and friends and sympathizers. The medical fraternity was horrified by the verdict and, before his sentencing on June 30, four hundred New York physicians and surgeons signed a petition deploring the verdict and calling for an amendment of the law. Very few of the signatories knew my father personally. As Dr. Abraham Goldman, President of the Bronx County Hospital Association, explained to the *New York Times:*

> The Dr. Hammer incident is but an example of what the medical profession today has to contend with. Every reputable physician in this state is laboring under the fear that he himself will be the next victim of a law which not only should have been taken off the statute books years ago, but which is resulting greatly in handicapping the medical profession.
>
> The conviction of Dr. Hammer is a blow to the profession as a whole. Under the present law, it was inevitable that sooner or later some reputable physician would fall victim to it. For years we have fought to remedy this evil whereby a jury of laymen can declare an operation unjustified despite the expert opinion of many members of our profession.

The petitioners' wisdom had no influence upon the judge. He sentenced my father to jail in State's Prison at Sing-Sing for not less than three and a half and not more than fifteen years.

In the first week of August, on the first day when we were allowed, we visited my father in Sing-Sing and saw him in prison uniform, surrounded by thieves, murderers, rapists and gangsters. My father, typically, had already begun to see his sentence as an opportunity to help needy people and he was quite cheerful. In time, he became secretary of the prisoners' mutual benefit association and was very active in trying to improve their conditions; he also spent a lot of his time giving medical advice and general counsel to his fellow prisoners.

He was never bitter about his imprisonment. He believed, certainly, that he had been the victim of a great injustice, but he stoically accepted his fate. He never once railed against the United States or blamed his country for the injustice he was suffering. My father, although a socialist, had enjoyed his life in America, with his prosperous practice and his comfortable home, and he was not going to surrender those advantages lightly.

I took it upon myself to manage the preparation of my father's appeal, one of my earliest experiences in combining a public relations campaign with a legal fight. It was obviously important for my father's case that the physicians and surgeons who had petitioned the court in his support should also lend their weight to his appeal. Two hundred of them put their names to a brief *amicus curiae* which ran to well over forty pages. The guiding principle of this brief was expressed in a paragraph annexed to the petition, in which the physicians declared:

> We intend as far as possible to acquaint the Court with numerous experiences of a similar nature which most of the undersigned have had, and if it is to be a fact that a physician, able to judge the imperative need of an immediate curettage, must always have present the picture of a possible conviction for manslaughter in the first degree if his patient shall die through any cause, directly or indirectly connected with the curettage, the practice of curetting in order to save life will be abandoned, with the result that hundreds and thousands of unfortunate women needing immediate curettage because of medical necessity, especially in neighborhoods of the poorer classes, will be the sufferers and will undoubtedly die.

The drunk and the monocle-wearer were not retained to fight the appeal before the appellate court. In their place I engaged William Fallon, a brilliant trial lawyer but too addicted to liquor to do the thorough job needed. Searching for a replacement, I hit upon Maurice Wormser. Wormser was one of the best-known lawyers in America, editor of *The New York Law Journal* and one of the few Jews ever to have been appointed as a full professor to the faculty of the Jesuit Fordham Law School.

Wormser was a very brilliant man who, in my opinion, might have made the Supreme Court if he could have overcome one disadvantage.

He was as deaf as a post, but his vanity would not allow him to wear a hearing aid. Actually, his deafness was not an unmitigated disadvantage: he could use it with great skill when it suited him—when, for instance, a judge or an opposing counselor tried to interrupt while he was making a speech. Wormser would just keep right on speaking and there wasn't much anybody could do to stop him. As a matter of fact, he could read lips clear across a courtroom, but he never let anybody know.

He wrote a masterful brief for my father's appeal and he told me that if I wanted to get the best man to argue it in court I should retain a former member of the Appellate Division of the Supreme Court, Judge Francis M. Scott. That wasn't so easy to accomplish: Judge Scott had never conducted a criminal case and he was very reluctant to accept the job. I managed to persuade him. I encouraged him to see that he had it in his hands to right a terrible injustice.

Despite the brilliance of these lawyers, my father lost his appeal on January 14, 1921. It was a close thing. Two judges dissented from the decision, which made a majority of only one vote against my father. Again, the testimony of Schwartz was decisive. The court decided there were not sufficient errors of law to reverse the jury's verdict.

Nothing remained to be done to help my father. He simply had to serve out his time until he could apply for parole and we had to get on with our lives as well as we could. It was a very sad and depressing time, but we had to try to make the best of it. It was very important that I should finish my medical studies and graduate—that was my main task. Nothing could have been worse for my father's morale than if I had dropped out or flunked my exams.

In my senior year, something happened which almost finished off my medical career before it had properly begun. Seniors had to put their obstetrical studies to test by delivering several babies. We were required to take up residence in the New York Nursery and Child's Hospital for Women, adjoining the medical school, where we could treat women as outpatients during their pregnancies and ultimately deliver their babies.

One night, very late, a nurse woke me and gave me a card directing me to a woman in labor at Sixtieth Street and Tenth Avenue, a few blocks from the hospital. I took my bag of instruments and rushed away for my first delivery. I found the family's apartment high in a tenement in the poor Italian neighborhood and was led to the woman's bedside by a distraught husband. I had been told to expect a normal labor. The woman was screaming in agony. It was a breech delivery. I had missed the lecture on breech deliveries. I knew enough, however, to realize the imminent danger to mother and child if the baby's feet were delivered first and the head was not immediately released. The baby would strangle and the mother's abdomen would have to be cut open in an emergency cesarean section. They both could die.

I had packed the standard textbook, Cragin's *Obstetrics,* in my bag. I now rushed to the bathroom to read it and memorize the illustrations on technique.

Dashing back to the woman, I found that meconium (feces) were being released, which meant that there were only minutes to save them both.

Following Cragin's instructions, I inserted the index and middle fingers of my right hand into the womb and the child's mouth, rotating and sliding the head cautiously in one direction, then the other, until I swiveled it out of the womb. I cut the umbilical cord and brought the baby to life with a little slap; and nearly collapsed on the spot with relief.

The father and neighbors who had gathered around burst into applause as we gave the child to the exhausted mother. Then they set about creating a vast celebratory breakfast, which I was mighty glad to join, and some copious quantities of wine were drunk.

Later that morning at Columbia, I was summoned out of class to see the Dean, Dr. Samuel Lambert, in his office. Word had spread through the school that I had successfully made a breech delivery and I supposed that Dr. Lambert wanted to congratulate me.

On entering the Dean's office I was slightly puzzled to find that many senior members of the faculty were sitting with him. Surely I didn't deserve such lavish and formal praise. I was even more disconcerted by Dr. Lambert's opening words: "Mr. Hammer, you have been summoned here to answer why you should not be expelled."

"Expelled!" I gasped.

"You risked the lives of a child and its mother in a dangerous situation. You should have called for a staff doctor or a member of the faculty. How dared you undertake a breech delivery without any experience?"

I was so dazed that I could barely reply. I managed to say, "The diagnosis and treatment card given to me gave no indication that this was not a normal pregnancy."

Dr. Lambert's answer was prompt and curt: "When you discovered it was a breech, you should have called for help immediately."

I protested. "There was no telephone in the house. Besides, I realized there was not time. The child would have strangled before anybody could have arrived." This cut no ice with Dr. Lambert.

"You could have found out much sooner that this was a breech case. Then you would have had time to call for an experienced obstetrician." The injustice of this attack angered me and I answered back.

"Doctor Lambert, this woman was treated by your staff here for months. If they couldn't discover that the baby was in an abnormal position during this long period, how do you expect a novice like me to do so on a moment's notice?"

Now I had turned the tables and put the Dean and his faculty on the defensive. They were forced to recognize the weakness of their position. They dismissed the case against me and sent me back to my class. I left the room shaken by the inquisition, but glad that, for once, my belligerent character had given me voice when I needed it.

Though I was to make election to Alpha Omega Alpha, the Phi Beta Kappa of medical schools, the last months of my studies were a very hard grind. On top of the distractions of business, I now had the added burden of making the journey to visit my father in Sing-Sing, upstate in Ossining. Freeways and fast cars have reduced this trip today to about one and a half hours from central Manhattan. In 1921 the round trip took most of a day.

My visits to my father in prison did, in fact, almost cause me to fail my final exams, which would have meant the complete destruction of my hopes for a medical career.

One class I had to skip because it fell on visiting day was Dr. Loeb's class in pharmacology. Dr. Loeb was lame in one leg, very crotchety and tough on his students. His final examinations were expected to be the most difficult of all. I worked as hard as I could preparing for his exam, but I had to depend on the textbooks.

When the question paper was distributed in the examination room, I ran my eye down the list of questions, trying to suppress a rising panic. I was aghast to find that I couldn't answer a single question. Not one. Loeb had set them all from one of his latest lectures, which I had cut.

What was I to do? I was faced with the certainty of flunking the paper: I would have returned a complete zero, an F.

I sat at my desk pondering this quandary for some minutes and then I closed my book and left the room. I walked into Central Park, dragging my feet in misery. It was a glorious summer's day, as every day always is in the examination season. I found a big rock, climbed to the top and lay down to think about my problem: that rock is still there and I look at it with mixed feelings every time I drive by.

Finally I decided what I should do. Next morning I went to see Dr. Loeb in his laboratory. He was there alone, grading papers from the previous day's examination. "I'm putting my future in your hands," I said to him. Then I told him the whole truth—that I had missed the vital lecture because I had been visiting my father in Sing-Sing.

He heard me out without saying a word. Then he suddenly turned and picked up an examination book, gave it to me and said, "Here. Take this and go over there and sit down and write out your answers to the questions."

Overnight, I had looked up all the answers to the questions in the paper and I was ready to write. I sat down and completed the paper very quickly, gave it to Dr. Loeb and departed. He awarded me an A in pharmacology. By his actions, he did more than simply save my student career. Who can guess what the long-term consequences would have been if I had failed my final examinations? I am not sure how I would have been able to bear that disappointment.

The final exams included one other tricky moment. I completed the paper in ophthalmology quite easily. Daniel Mishell's notes had been comprehensive and I had memorized the complete syllabus, so there was no difficulty with the paper itself. The trouble came once I had finished.

Candidates were asked to write the name of the professor who had given the course on the outside page of their examination books. Never having been to any of the lectures, I didn't know the professor's name. I got out of my chair and approached the proctors who were standing at the back of the hall, wearing their black gowns and overseeing the exam. "Could you please tell me the name of the professor who has given this course?" I asked one of them. The proctor looked at me very strangely and then he spoke a name. I went back to my desk, wrote the name on my book and left the hall.

But the proctor's odd look puzzled me. I walked up to some of my classmates outside the examination room and said, "Tell me, who was that proctor standing at the back of the room? What's his name?" They told me his name. It was the same name I had written on my book. I had asked the professor of ophthalmology for the name of the professor of ophthalmology!

My marks for my four years as a medical student included one C— in surgery, where I had had to miss very many operations. Otherwise I got mostly As and a few Bs. Dr. Morris Dinnerstein, a distinguished member of the faculty, named me as the graduating class's "most promising student."

I was offered a medical internship at Bellevue Hospital to specialize in bacteriology and immunology, which was my particular interest.

A Bellevue internship was the most sought after and cherished reward open to new graduates of Columbia's P&S. Only two internships were available every year—one in surgery and one in medicine—and it was a tremendous honor to be chosen. I was very surprised to find my name listed for one of the spots, but I had done everything possible to win this prize.

The internships were the gift of the head of Bellevue Hospital, a professor of medicine named Dr. Van Horn Norrie, a renowned diagnostician. He was also famous for his collection of etchings which he had bought with the very large inheritance he had received from his family.

I decided that I would make Dr. Norrie aware of me: I wanted to make sure that he would remember my name. I did some extensive research on him and found out that his etchings were by far his greatest passion.

Taking books from the library, I studied everything I could find about etchings. When I was finally sure that I knew my ground, I was bold enough to approach him on one of his hospital rounds.

"I understand that you're a great collector of etchings, Doctor," I said.

"How did you know that?" he said.

"Well, I'm very interested myself in art, especially etchings, and I've frequently come across your name in the literature as one of the great collectors."

He warmed considerably to me.

"I'd love to see your collection some day," I said.

"Why don't you come to my home on Sunday afternoon and I'll be glad to show you the whole collection."

Sunday came around and I went to his home. We walked through his elegant house, every room of which was hung with his etchings. Here I recognized a Rembrandt, there a Dürer. "Oh, that's your famous Rembrandt," I would say. "And that must be your extraordinary Dürer." I knew the names of most of them, which impressed him no end. He invited me to stay for tea and we talked on and on.

After that, of course, he knew exactly who I was. I've always wondered if, in awarding the internship, he was influenced less by my examination marks than by having found in me, or so he thought, a brother collector. In truth, I never had an etching.

The internship was to be taken up in January 1922. I graduated in June 1921. I had nearly six months on my hands and I had decided to retire from business and devote myself to research medicine. All my life I had wanted to become a doctor. Since my early boyhood I had dreamed of joining my father as his partner.

I couldn't think how else I should occupy myself, until an inspired thought entered my mind and made it absolutely clear what I should do and where I should go.

The news of that year's appalling famine in Russia had just startled the world, news exaggerated by wild newspaper stories of revolt and pitiless repression, of madness and despair which were supposed to be racking Russia. It was unmistakably true, however, that hundreds of thousands of famine refugees were streaming into the Volga towns from their fields burned barren by eight weeks' drought; and that an epidemic of typhus was running through this multitude.

Reading one such newspaper report, I had the thought which was to be the most important of my life. It truly was the decisive moment of my young life and the turning point of my life as a whole. Everything that went before this moment is one story, everything which comes after is another.

I would go to Russia. I would practice my medicine among the victims of the typhus epidemic. Perhaps I might even be able to collect the hundred and fifty thousand dollars still owed to Allied Drug and Chemical for the medicines and oil well machinery shipped there.

I also felt that it would please my father if I visited Russia—the country of his birth and, since the Revolution, the land which figured so vividly in his political dreams. I could be his eyes and ears there, and I could send him letters, to his cell in Sing-Sing, to describe the condition of the country.

In Russia I could gain valuable experience in fighting the typhus epidemic and I could give myself a breathing space in which to decide the next step in my career. The land of my fathers, that unknown land of future promise and past and present woe, beckoned me. I was twenty-three years old. My youth was done.

6

A Russian Business Romance

Though my journey to Russia was my first trip abroad, my leave-taking of New York was not the celebratory affair usual when a youngster, newly graduated from college, takes his first independent steps into the big world. No parties, no bands playing on the dock to send me on my way. All that would have been inappropriate in view of my father's circumstances. Instead, my arrangements were made quickly and soberly. Within a month of graduating, I was on my way.

From the Surplus Stores department of the War Department, I bought an entire field hospital, fully stocked with tents, camp beds, operating tables, generators, surgical instruments, uniforms and a hundred and one other items. The complete hospital was a vast creation, capable of tending the needs of hundreds of patients at one time, and it filled many trucks when it was loaded for shipment. Its original cost was $60,000. With packing and shipping expenses, it cost me over $100,000. I intended to present it to the Soviets as a gift, and that's what I did.

I also bought a brand-new ambulance and fully stocked it with drugs and all the latest equipment, at a cost of about $15,000. This too I intended as a gift to the Soviets, but on the side of the ambulance I painted the words AMERICAN MEDICAL MISSION TO MOSCOW. I wanted to make sure everybody knew where the help came from.

The field hospital and the ambulance were loaded into a freighter and shipped directly to the Baltic port of Riga, from whence the cargo would go to Moscow by rail. I boarded the *Aquitania,* then the flagship of the Cunard Line, for the crossing to Southampton, on the south coast of England. In London, I was going to meet Boris Mishell, the European agent of our company and the uncle of my former flatmate, Dan Mishell, who would guide me across Europe on the final stage of my journey.

In my later years I came to love the sea, but I certainly didn't enjoy it that time. Even though I was making the crossing at the best time of year and in the most luxurious ship of the day, I quickly found myself to be no match for the Atlantic rollers. It was impossible for me to stay on my feet: within moments of standing up, waves of nausea engulfed me. The only solution was to stay in my cabin, flat-out in bed and motionless. I was transported to Europe like an Egyptian mummy, regularly tended by solicitous stewards who tipped light liquids and foods into me and then patiently mopped them up again. I had brought a portable Edison gramophone with me and several boxes of records. The machine was placed within reach of my feeble hands so that I could wind it up from time to time as I played through my collection of John McCormack's Irish ballads and Caruso's operas. When the ship finally sailed into the sheltered waters of the Solent, leading to the docks of Southampton, the relief from my miseries felt like a rebirth.

Almost at the moment of my arrival in Europe, I was caught in the net of intrigue and mystery which is Russia's poison—and her charm.

On that fine July morning when the *Aquitania* was being nosed against the Southampton quay by a swarm of tugs like ants pushing a huge beetle, I stood on the deck among the crowd, my heart singing with excitement. A curt word of command and the railings slid aside for the long gangway with its corrugated footpath. There was a moment's bustle as the harbor officials and porters came aboard, then I pressed forward with the rest.

Suddenly I felt a touch upon the arm. "Doctor Armand Hammer, I believe?" said a cultured English voice.

A slim blond stranger smartly dressed in gray tweed clothes, with gloves and cane, stood at my side.

"Good staff work in the London office," I thought to myself. "How nice of Boris to send down someone to welcome me."

"Yes," I replied smiling, with outstretched hand. "I suppose you've come to meet me."

The stranger looked somewhat taken aback. Without shaking hands he said, "Yes, I have, but—er—in fact, Doctor Hammer, I am a representative of Scotland Yard, and I am instructed to inform you that you will not be allowed to land—not at least until you've satisfied us with regard to certain matters."

Today, I suppose, I would take a thing like that more coolly. Even

ten years later, I would have been more in command of myself, after
my experiences in Russia and the Border States where one becomes
accustomed to the unexpected. But at that moment I was absolutely
flabbergasted.

"What?" I gasped. "Not land? Scotland Yard? Why, what on
earth's the matter?"

I've realized since that I couldn't have made a better reply. My
bewilderment was obviously sincere. He answered quietly that I must
stand aside; when the rest of the passengers had left the ship, he would
discuss the matter further. I was completely dazed. I had done nothing;
my passport was entirely in order; I would only be in England for a few
days; what could be wrong? The detective questioned me for fully ten
minutes before I realized the cause of all the trouble.

What was the purpose of my visit to England, he asked, and whom
should I see there, and how long did I propose to stay? I said I was just
traveling through, but expected to see my London agents and some of
the sights.

"Through to where?" he asked sharply. "Perhaps to Russia?"

"I hope so," I answered confidently. "You see, I'm a doctor, and
we have business, and the famine—"

"I know all about that," he said, writing fast in his notebook.
"Very well, you will stay in your cabin until further notice, and I warn
you that I am empowered to examine your person and baggage."

Then suddenly the truth flashed upon me. Before I had left New
York, Charles Recht, the New York attorney employed by the unofficial Soviet Mission, had suggested that Ludwig Martens might be
amused to see the film that had been taken of his deportation on the
celebrated "Soviet Ark" a year before. So public had the occasion been
that it never entered my head to refuse to carry the film: who could
possibly think it a secret or subversive document? I had yet to learn that
many things connected with Russia, both outside the Soviet Union and
within, are capable of varied interpretation and that almost invariably
both sides assume the worst.

Already, instead of a medical volunteer, I had become a political
suspect.

In the midst of my dismay, however, I have to admit I was terribly
thrilled. Here I was arrested—or something mighty near it—by
Scotland Yard itself. The most lurid detective fiction had nothing on
me, as I sat in my cabin that long, hot morning, with a "guard," a
smiling sailor (what a pity he hadn't a bayonet and a sinister scowl) at
my door, wondering what in heaven's name to do.

I soon puzzled out how my name must have come to the Yard's
attention. I had sent a cable from New York to the Berlin representative of the Soviets saying I was coming, hoped to go to Moscow, and

was bringing the Recht film for Martens. I had some kind of idea that this would smooth the way for me a little. There were such dreadful stories about the difficulties of traveling in Russia and how they took everything from you at the frontier save an extra suit of clothes and shirt and shoes and underwear, and maybe, if you were lucky, a loaf of bread and a Dutch cheese.

But why Scotland Yard should intercept that innocent message or imagine it was a plot against the British Empire, I am still at a loss to understand. Of course they'd just had a big coal strike in England and there was a lot of talk about mysterious "Bolshevik agents." Indeed, plenty of people, Churchill among them, had believed in 1919 that Great Britain was on the verge of a revolutionary insurrection.

Even so, my position seemed absurd. I sat and thought about it until my brain knocked on all four cylinders, but I couldn't see any sense in it.

Rimmer, my cabin steward, provided a welcome diversion. At one P.M., just as I was getting hungry, he arrived with a tray of food and goggling eyes. The "guard" seemed to have vanished. Hitherto I had been no more than the average young American tourist to this steward, part of his job and a potential source of tips. Now I was something different, a "suspicious character." Perhaps, he remarked eagerly, in his Lancashire accent, I was "'anging oonder t' shaader of t' scaffowd."

My steward hoarsely whispered his readiness to serve me. A letter, or—his eyes gleamed—a message, he was mine to command. My first instinct was suspicion, but then I thought again. After all, there could be no harm in explaining my plight to the American consul and my London agents. It was a ridiculous contretemps, but there was nothing to worry about.

I nodded assent, to Rimmer's evident delight. "When I bring yer tea," he muttered in a thoroughly conspiratorial manner, "you pass me t' stoof"—did he think I was smuggling diamonds?—"an' aall 'aand it on."

Looking back, it seems rather childish, but I wasn't much more than a kid, after all, and the crisis had come upon me suddenly. Anyhow, the faithful Rimmer took my letters ashore and fed me like Elijah's ravens. I suppose, too, Scotland Yard gave itself a private view of my film and found there was nothing in it to distress King George (though I never got it back and Martens never saw it).

After two days I was suddenly released by the detective, who apologized for the inconvenience caused me and said I could get my papers back by calling at headquarters. As soon as I reached London, I took a cab to Scotland Yard and was immediately ushered into the private office of an important-looking official who apologized very effusively in a refined manner, saying that "It was just a misunderstanding."

Apparently he thought his gray-tinged hair gave him the authority to warn me in a fatherly tone of the lack of wisdom in trying to do business with the "Bolshies." He said knowingly: "I have been in Russia during the Kerensky regime and the Bolshevik Revolution, and I can assure you that any businessman who is insane enough to send his goods into Russia will have them seized by the Bolsheviks and will certainly never be paid for them."

As I left his office to return to my hotel, the Savoy on the Strand, the newsboys were shouting, "Extra! Extra! British Delegation of Businessmen Leaving For Russia!" And the newspaper's headline was: BUSINESS COMMENCING UNDER NEW ANGLO-RUSSIAN TRADE AGREEMENT. "That's teamwork for you," I thought. "Scotland Yard ever trying to serve British interests and eliminate foreign competition".

(Seven years later, while sitting in the visitors' gallery of the British Houses of Parliament, I had the satisfaction of hearing a speech by a Cabinet Minister who was not too friendly to the Soviet regime. He said: "We know of no incident in the trading transactions between our merchants and the London representatives of the Soviet government where the latter has not met its obligations fully and promptly." My Scotland Yard official proved to be a very poor prophet.)

Instead of becoming disheartened by my experiences of the past few days, I was now more determined than ever to visit Russia, and hurriedly made my preparations to leave for Berlin.

Boris Mishell certainly came into his own during these last days in London. He knew where the best of everything was to be had, and his name was like a magic password among storekeepers and suppliers. Boris—who was a very robust fellow with plenty of energy and a huge laugh—prided himself on being a man of the world with an irresistible attraction for ladies. He really did have one in every town upon whom he could count for a warm reception. He went full-out to show me a good time in London, introducing me to the Prince of Wales's tailors, who fitted me out in the finest English tweeds, taking me to restaurants and theaters and keeping me up late at night. After a few days of that I was glad to resume my travels just to be able to get some rest.

As my train wound down through Holland and Germany to Berlin, I wish I could say that I was alertly observing the passing scene from the window and taking notice of my first moments on the soil of mainland Europe. But most of the time, I was out cold in a corner of our compartment, trying to recover from the excesses inflicted by Boris Mishell.

Arriving at last in Berlin at the Friedrichstrasse Bahnhof, I went to stay in the Adlon Hotel on the Unter den Linden, that splendid and spacious street which in those days presented so curious a contrast of opulence and misery. Rich "Schiebers" (speculators) flaunted the furs and jewels bought with their easy money, while beside them, people once comfortably off—professors, government employees, ex-Army officers and the middle class generally—wore shabby clothes and had pinched, pale faces. There were scores of beggars, too, many of them mutilated soldiers. I was startled. I had always heard of Berlin as the most orderly of cities, where everything was trim and tidy, yet here on the Linden itself there was poverty and suffering. I began to realize how terrible had been the pressure of war and blockade upon the German people.

So extremely depressed was the German mark that it was possible to make huge profits in all kinds of speculations, especially if they could be negotiated in foreign currencies. I couldn't resist a small speculation of my own. Walking on the Linden with Boris Mishell, I passed a showroom in which a magnificent Mercedes-Benz sedan was displayed, marked with an absurd price in German marks of the equivalent of about fifteen hundred dollars. We knew, on sight, that the car was worth at least five thousand dollars abroad and I decided on the spot to buy it and make arrangements to have it exported to America when I returned from Russia in the planned six months.

As it happened, I never took delivery of the Mercedes. It remained with the dealers for some months until, when it became obvious that my stay in Russia was going to become so protracted that I might never use the car, I made arrangements for it to be sold in Berlin at considerable profit.

After this speculative diversion, I hurried at once to the International Sleeping Car office and reserved a place on the train to Riga for the following day. Then I went around to the Soviet Delegation to get my visa, where an unkempt youth confronted me with sheaves of paper. I must fill in these forms, he said, and produce three photographs, and then my application would be considered. I brushed him aside airily—too airily. "I want to see your chief," I said. "My visa must already be here. I am leaving Berlin tomorrow." The youth snickered. He led me into a small, bare room where a Soviet official, the first real Bolshevik I had ever met, received me courteously.

I explained my business, producing my passport, and said, "I shall be glad if you can fix the visa immediately as I propose to leave tomorrow and have a good deal of business to do here." He smiled wearily. "Have you filled in your application forms?" he asked.

"No," I said. "Is that necessary? You see, I am in rather a hurry."

The official sat up straight. "When do you wish to go to Russia?" he asked. "I mean to say, if you are in a great hurry, it might perhaps be arranged in two or three weeks, but of course first of all you must fill in the application forms."

"What?" I gasped. "Three weeks? But I have reserved my place on the train tomorrow. Why, in America—"

The official's smile broadened. "My dear Doctor Hammer," he said. "You Americans are so impetuous—and so persistent. One of your countrymen applied for a visa three months ago, and would you believe it, he comes in every day to ask me why the permit has not arrived."

"Oh," I said. "Indeed. But I understood that a visa was awaiting me here, and . . ."

"He said the same thing," replied the official urbanely. "Well, never mind, just file your application and perhaps in two or three weeks . . ."

I went back to the Adlon feeling rather sunk. I asked advice from various friends of Boris Mishell and decided to send a cable to the Foreign Office in Moscow, explaining that I was a medical doctor and a friend of Charles Recht, and at his suggestion had purchased a field hospital to do work in the famine area. I hoped that that might unblock the bureaucratic congestion. Then I packed up my troubles and some sports clothes and went off to seek solace in the mountain resort of Garmisch-Partenkirchen in the Bavarian Alps, leaving a forwarding address with the hotel in case a miracle should emerge from Moscow.

Ten days later I received a cable, relayed from Berlin, stating, YOUR VISA GRANTED. LITVINOV. I am sure that the Foreign Office in Moscow must have checked the contents of my cable with Ludwig Martens; and he, having been helped in the United States by my father, must have spoken for me.

In great excitement I extricated Boris from the bars he had been habituating, flung our luggage in the car and directed the driver to return to Berlin with all speed, where I examined timetables. The best way to go was by boat from Stettin (now Szczecin in Poland) to Riga in Latvia, then an independent state.

Nobody warned me about a crossing of the Baltic: no words could have conveyed its horror.

Like some hell-bound crate out of the pages of Conrad, the rusty little steamer which worked that voyage strained all its plates and nearly burst its boiler to make the crossing. Turning, twisting, lunging and climbing into the teeth of the storm, it worked its way to the top of titanic waves to slither into the gulf beyond. Every descent seemed certain to be our last. I clung to my bunk, racked with nausea and resigned to my death, which must surely come at any moment when the pounding sea finally smashed through the ship's flimsy hull.

Meanwhile that oaf Mishell was sitting at the Captain's table, filling his stomach and swapping filthy jokes with his new friend, the Captain. They had the restaurant entirely to themselves. Anyone of less than the coarsest composition was groaning in the last extremes of misery and trying to settle final accounts with the Maker.

It took three days to reach Riga. If you look at the map, you'll see that you could almost walk from Stettin to Riga in three days.

Riga had once been the greatest Western emporium of Russian trade, with nearly three-quarters of a million inhabitants; now, like Vienna, it had become the impoverished capital of a tiny state whose magnificent buildings and well-planned streets housed less than three hundred thousand people.

Latvia, of course, was not then part of Russia. Under the terms of the Treaty of Versailles, its independence had been guaranteed, though that was to count for nothing in 1940 when Stalin occupied the country, along with Estonia and Lithuania.

Riga provided me, however, with my first insight into the ways of the old Czarist Empire. There was some difficulty about my baggage in the customhouse. "Slip him something," whispered Boris Mishell, ever wise in the ways of the world. I handed the customs officer a dollar bill. He gave me a severe look and ignored it. For a moment I felt anxious: you must remember that this was my very first trip to Europe, and I innocently supposed that bribing officials was a crime.

"Not enough," whispered Mishell. I tried ten dollars. My baggage was passed in two minutes, with smiles and bows, the customs officers themselves carrying it out of the customhouse and loading it into a waiting cab, much to the annoyance of some stolid-looking Latvians who were thus delayed with their own baggage examination. I learned later that I had touched two extremes—the recognized rate for American visitors was five dollars.

Riga was a splendid city, but its leading hotel at that time, the Rome, was far from a splendid hotel. It had only one bath, which no one seemed to use, and when I saw it, I understood why.

But when word went around that I was on my way to Russia, I suddenly found that every waiter in the place showed the most flattering eagerness to serve me. I was ushered to the best tables and attended with great ceremony, my every wish instantly gratified. At first I was puzzled, but the secret was revealed on my second evening.

The headwaiter, a distinguished man with a short gray goatee, approached me and said in a confidential whisper, "You are going to Russia?"

"Yes," I said, "what about it?"

He hesitated for a moment, then hissed dramatically, "It is *death*!"

Before I could reply, he plunged into a long and confused account of his escape from the "Red Terror." He had been pursued, it seemed, by human wolves, or maybe they were real wolves, I couldn't quite understand which. Anyway, he had a terrible experience, and escaped only by a miracle. With great emphasis of words and gestures, he urged me to turn back while there was yet time. I was still young, he said, and life spread fair before me. "Why court death?" he added on the same tragic note as he began. "Because it *is* death."

I didn't sleep very well that night. I don't often remember my dreams, but I do remember that I dreamed that night that I was being chased across a trackless steppe by a pack of wolves, all with the headwaiter's fat, pasty face and small goatee. The nightmare recurred all night and receded only with the dawn; slightly shaken and unnerved, I went out to buy provisions for the trip to Moscow.

No one could tell me how long the journey would take. One left Riga, it appeared, late at night, and in the course of a day or two—they didn't even seem sure about that—arrived at Sebesh, the Russian frontier station. After that, they said, with luck, one reached Moscow some days later. And without luck, I wondered, what happened? That apparently was a thought upon which it was not wise to dwell.

I bought cheese, butter, jam, sardines, bread and biscuits—enough to fill a packing case. Then I piled all my baggage on three cabs and drove to the station.

It was nearly midnight; the station was dark and gloomier still. But the passengers, a mere handful, who were risking the adventure into the unknown Red Russia, were gloomiest of all. Suddenly Boris Mishell, who earlier had expressed regret he could not accompany me but now seemed quite cheerful about it, gave a sharp cry. "Great heavens," he said, "I've forgotten your candles!"

"Candles?" I repeated stupidly. "Why do I need . . ." But already he was chasing down the platform as if all the wolves of Russia were after him, leaving me alone with an enormous pile of baggage and a stolid Lettish porter who understood no word of any language known to me.

The train was due to leave at eleven forty-five. As the minutes passed, I grew anxious, but nothing seemed to happen. The train was still dark and the little groups on the platform, huddled timidly together, showed no sign of wishing to enter it. At eleven forty-five, a bell rang but still nothing happened and no one moved. I felt detached from the world as if in a dream. The only real thing was the square dark face of my Lettish porter. I continued to wait.

At the stroke of midnight Mishell reappeared, breathless, with two candles in either hand. Just as I sighted him, the bell rang twice.

"I knew there was time," he puffed. "You'd have been lost without the candles. You know there are no lights on the train."

"Oh," I said. "Is that so? Did you bring matches, too?"

He hadn't, but we got a box of bad ones from the Lettish porter who finally piled all my baggage into a compartment, dark as pitch, with bare wooden benches, and not overly clean.

"You're lucky," said Mishell. "The upholstered cars are full of vermin and typhus germs, but here you'll be quite comfortable."

We stood a candle up in a pool of its own grease on the window ledge where many other candles had stood before. Then the bell rang again, three times. It was twelve-twenty. Boris bounded from the train. "Good luck," he shouted. "Good luck! I will cable your folks at once if anything happens to you."

With these parting words of encouragement, I began the last stage of my journey to Russia . . .

Not even the moment when the detective tapped me on the arm at Southampton gave me such a thrill as when our train halted just beyond the frontier between Latvia and Soviet Russia, beside a tiny hut over which floated a red flag, and a patrol of Red Army soldiers clambered aboard.

Here, at last, was the Red Army, of which I had heard so much, with their strange peaked caps. The caps had been resuscitated by the Bolshevik warlord, Trotsky, from the ancient history of Russia, and were modeled after the headgear of the Scythian archers who more than two thousand years previously had driven back the hosts of Darius, the Persian King of Kings.

Their Commander, a good-looking young fellow, neat and clean-shaven, passed through the train collecting our passports. He spoke only Russian, but I understood the meaning of the word "pass" when he spoke it.

Then we came to Sebesh, and husky porters with white aprons lifted out the baggage for customs examinations. The dreaded Bolshevik customs proved quite simple. An official who spoke excellent English seemed to know all about me and the purpose of my journey. He hardly allowed me to open my trunks. "That's quite all right, citizen," he said.

That was the first time I'd heard the word, pronounced *grazhdenin,* which had but recently replaced the term *tovarish,* or comrade, nowadays usually used to and by members of the Communist Party. The officer continued, "I will tell the porter to put your things on the Moscow train."

"When does it leave?" I asked.

He waved his hand and replied vaguely. "Soon."

"Have I time to get something to eat?" I asked.

"Oh, yes, citizen, you have time."

I had, indeed, because the train didn't leave until seven hours later.

It was a repetition of the journey from Riga. Unlighted compartments save for my candle. Wooden benches and an atmosphere that was not clean. At each station there was a little hut marked KIPYATOK, hot water, in big letters where everyone ran with kettles to get water for their tea.

"There is much cholera and typhoid," said one of my companions, "so we have boiled water at every station. It is good, *nicht wahr*?"

Finally—I'd lost count of time, it probably wasn't more than eighty hours after leaving Riga—my companion caught my arm and pointed eastward. Far off in the distance an enormous gold dome glittered in the sun's rays. "Moscow!" he cried. "The great Cathedral, built to commemorate Napoleon's defeat. Moscow, our Red Moscow!"

Was he more proud of Red Moscow or the victory over Europe's conqueror? This was my first meeting with the contrast between national and revolutionary pride which was, at that moment, a paradox even more acute than it is today. But I did not think of it then. I was not so much concerned with abstract paradox as with the fact that I had reached Moscow at last!

7

A Revolution in Tatters

Today, even in Russia itself, scarcely anybody survives with adult memories of Moscow as it was in the early summer of 1921, when the earth-shaking eruptions of the Revolution and the exhaustions of the civil war were still fresh in their effects; and when the doomed experiment of the first Communist society on earth was reaching its final days. Not more than a handful of Westerners are alive who visited Russia at that moment, and I am sure that I am alone in having acquired, then and in the years which followed, an intimate working acquaintance with the Soviet Union in its transition from War Communism to State Socialism. Others, like George Kennan, came later and stayed longer; or, like the late Averell Harriman, came later and left sooner. Nobody else that I know of can give a firsthand account of that decisive summer of 1921 when Lenin, the father of Communism, dramatically reversed the course of the Revolution and ensured that the Soviet Union, as we have come to know it throughout this century, would survive. My memories of that time have the hard clarity which the mind is capable of only when it is completely absorbed in and thrilled by the moment. As Wordsworth said of the French Revolution: "Bliss was it in that dawn to be alive, But to be young was very Heaven." Moscow then was very far from heaven, but surely there was no more interesting place on earth to be at that moment.

At Moscow's Riga Station, I was met by a man named Leo Wolff, a representative of the Anglo-American department of the Soviet Foreign Office. He told me that his chief, Gregory Weinstein, had received a letter about my coming from Charles Recht, and that Weinstein would be glad to see me.

Wolff, a cheerful little fellow with rosy cheeks, helped me pile my baggage on a dilapidated auto-truck in which he had come to meet me. We took our seats on top of the pile, and with a loud grinding of gears set off, rattling through the streets at a brisk pace.

If there were evidences of poverty and suffering in Berlin, Moscow was utter desolation. The streets were almost deserted, and great holes yawned in the roadway and sidewalks. The houses looked ready to fall to pieces, unpainted, many with patches of plaster falling away, and roofs half stripped of tiles. On many streets the walls and fronts of the houses were scarred by bullets of rifle and machine-gun fire. From nearly every window protruded the end of a tin stovepipe whose smoke had made an ugly black flare on the wall. The stores were all empty, their windows broken or their fronts hidden by boarding.

As we neared the center of the town, there were more people, but little traffic save for an occasional wagon and a shabby cab. The people seemed clad in rags; hardly any wore stockings or shoes, but had wrappings of dirty cloth around their feet and legs; others wore felt boots; the children were all barefoot. No one seemed to smile, everyone looked dirty and dejected. Here and there one saw a neater figure in a military uniform or in the black leather coat and breeches and high boots worn by Communist officials, but they too seemed pale and careworn. I wondered if Wolff was the only man in Moscow who looked cheerful and had pink cheeks.

In the Bolshoi Theater square, whose neglected garden was full of pallid children, we swung round a big low building, formerly Moscow's leading hotel—the Metropole—now dilapidated and shabby as the rest. We halted before its annex which, Wolff told me, was occupied by the Foreign Office, or *Narkomindel,* as it was called, a compound word of the first syllables of four Russian words meaning People's Commissariat of Foreign Affairs.

It was about one o'clock in the afternoon, but neither Mr. Weinstein nor his assistant, Mr. Samuel Cagan, was in his office. "They probably won't be here till later," Wolff explained, adding with a smile, "You see, Comrade Chicherin, the Foreign Commissar, prefers to work at night, so of course his staff has to sleep in the daytime."

"What?" I said, thinking that he was joking. "Work at night? But surely you don't mean he receives visitors, foreign diplomats, and that sort of thing at night, too?"

"Yes, of course," said Wolff. "Sometimes he sees people in the daytime, but his usual time for appointments is between one and four A.M."

He suggested that while I was waiting I take a walk about the city. Unfortunately he couldn't accompany me, but he assured me that I would be all right, and if I did get lost I had only to ask for the Metropole. So I set off a little doubtfully. Before I left Wolff, he took me around to the Government Treasury Department—there were no banks then—to change my money. In exchange for my dollars they gave me a big broad sheet of what looked like coupons. Wolff explained with pride that this was a new Soviet device to save trouble and printing costs.

One simply cut off a coupon each time one wanted to buy anything. If I remember rightly they were worth about ten cents apiece. A pair of scissors was a handy thing to have about you.

As I walked through the streets, I couldn't for the life of me see what there was to buy—except trumpery stuff like buttons and lace, or apples sold by hawkers on the curb—as all the stores were boarded up, empty. Oh yes, and there were shoeshines. I think the thing that struck me most that day was the fact that there was a Georgian or Armenian shoe shiner at nearly every corner. Most of them hadn't any polish, but they'd spit on your shoe and rub it hard with a rag til it nearly shone, and for this service I saw the coupons passed.

The streetcars were still free, free transport having been one of the promises of the Revolution. There seemed to be very few of them trundling slowly along, each one with people hanging on to it or to each other, in a cluster, like flies on a lump of sugar. Every now and then one would fall off, pick himself up, and run after the car to catch on again. It was a curious thing to watch.

The horse-drawn cabs called *izvoschiki,* however, one paid for, and I found later it was necessary to bargain with the driver, who always asked at least twice what he expected to get. I made my first attempt to haggle a few weeks after I arrived in Moscow, while my grasp of the language was still as elementary as it could be. I asked a driver how much it would cost to go to a certain hotel. *"Piatorka,"* he replied—a slang word meaning "a fiver." I thought he was saying fifteen rubles, so I held up the fingers of both hands and said, "Ten." He said: "Okay. Please step in." All the way to the hotel he kept grumbling to himself under his breath. When I had sat down to my lunch, I asked my friends what might have been wrong with the driver. They explained that, having offered the man twice the price he was asking, I had deprived him of the opportunity to haggle, which he regarded as an essential part of his working day.

These working practices, by the way, hold true right up to the present time. Russian cabmen are a conservative folk—most of them didn't hesitate to speak their mind about the Revolution in unkind terms—and when everything else was nationalized they somehow managed to retain their independence and the right to work for money.

When I returned after my walk, Mr. Weinstein was in his office, where he received me very kindly. He was a slim figure of about fifty years with a goatee and eyes that crossed. He had been the editor of a workers' socialist paper in New York before the Revolution. He said he hoped in a few days to put me in touch with the Health Department which, he assured me, would be delighted to accept my offer of equipping a medical unit to work in the famine area. He then telephoned the Savoy Hotel and asked Wolff to take me around and get me settled in my room.

Never in my life have I seen a hotel less worthy of the name Savoy. We staggered under our burden up dirty stone stairs along a grimy passage into a filthy room. A bedstead and mattress but no sheets or blankets, a grease-stained table with a cloth top and two rickety chairs and a cupboard; otherwise the room was bare. The wooden floor was uncarpeted and paper was hanging in damp strips from the walls. On the table, however, was a Swedish telephone apparatus of the latest type, in good working order.

Although I did not know it, this room was to be my home for the next ten days, and never, I can assure you, was home less sweet. There was not only dirt, but rats and mice and smaller vermin in prodigious quantities, which fled in droves to their corners when I entered the room.

When Wolff had gone I made a hurried meal from my Riga supply. He had told me that no food was served in the hotel, but that in a day or two the Foreign Office would get me a *payok,* or ticket, entitling me to receive bread and meat and vegetables, if there were any, in one of the state food depots.

I rang the bell and after a long interval a slatternly girl appeared. I made signs to her to try and clean up the room, especially the horrible-looking mattress, and put on the sheets and blankets I had brought with me. She stared at me. I offered her money—a row of coupons—but she shook her head. Suddenly she caught sight of some cakes of soap in my open bag and burst into a flood of Russian. I gathered that soap was better currency than Soviet paper and made signs that she would receive a cake of it if she fixed the room as I wanted her to.

Well, she did her best, which wasn't much, and went off triumphantly with the soap. Gradually, in the next few days, by the same means I got the room cleaned up a little and some more furniture was brought in, but it was still pretty terrible—especially the bedbugs. Another foreigner staying in the hotel told me he had thrown away his old mattress and sprayed all the iron works of the bed with kerosene, put his own bedding on it and moved it away from the wall, standing each of the four legs in a saucer of kerosene. He thought he was safe. "But the little devils climbed up onto the ceiling and bombed me from the air, never missing once!" he said. He was Raymond Gram Swing, the highly respected American writer and commentator. We became lifelong friends and, twenty years later, joined forces in New York in the fight against the Nazis.

There was the ruin of a bathroom attached to my room—that was where most of the rats lived—but, of course, no water. One could, however, get hot water from a stove in a little sort of kitchen space at the end of the corridor where some of the guests used to cook on small portable kerosene stoves, or *primus*. But each person was allowed only one kettleful with which to make tea or maybe to shave, if he had the soap and a razor. I now understood why the people of Moscow looked so dirty.

After three or four days, the diet of sardines and cheese (without bread) which I had brought from Riga upset my stomach and I became quite sick. I didn't go out anymore, just stayed in that dreadful room, learning by heart a hundred Russian words each day.

My grandfather having forbidden any language but English in our family home in America, I had arrived in Russia not knowing a single word of the language. I had learned French and German at school and was reasonably competent in those languages, but learning Russian presented quite a different order of difficulty. The more I learned, the more horrified I became by the magnitude of the task. Russian is a very deceptive language, because it looks easy at first: it's like setting out for a gentle stroll and realizing that you've committed yourself to scaling Himalayan peaks.

I had to struggle very laboriously with an English-Russian dictionary which gave pronunciations in phonetics. I would write the English word on one side of a piece of paper and the Russian on the other side and keep turning it over and over until I had got a word in my head. By this haphazard method, I came to know some Russian words by their approximate sound before I could decipher the alphabet.

The third day, my friends at the Foreign Office became anxious, as they hadn't seen me around, and came to inquire. They found a doctor, who managed to secure some milk and fresh meat and vegetables on a prescription for me, and then, when I was better, they gave me the promised *payok*.

I took it around to the food depot to find a line of about one hundred people waiting. That wasn't encouraging, so I strolled up to the front of the line to see what they were getting. A hunk of black bread that looked as if it was made out of mud and sawdust, and a handful of moldy potatoes; that was all. Most of the people in line were women, shabbily dressed, some with babies in their arms, others with children holding to their skirts.

When I saw how these people were eyeing me, in my newly made London tweeds, I decided I would rather starve than deprive a single one of them of the precious handful of food which was so far from adequate for their daily needs. Hiding my *payok* ticket from view, I retraced my steps to the Metropole.

I don't know what I would have done if I hadn't noticed that one of my new friends in the Foreign Office, named Gayov, who had charge of stamping passports, looked fat and well-fed. He always went off by himself somewhere at the lunch hour instead of sitting down with the rest of them to the meager ration provided by the Foreign Office. (One thing I must say about Moscow in those days, it was share and share alike for all. If the public went hungry, so did the Communist officials, and the latter worked much harder into the bargain.)

So I trailed this Gayov one day, at a discreet distance, and followed him up two flights of stairs to what looked like a private apartment. As the door closed behind him, a savory smell came forth that made my mouth water. I waited an hour till he had gone away, because I didn't want him to think I had been trailing him, then I tried my luck.

It worked! The place was like a small private restaurant—I found later there were quite a number of them in Moscow, where one could buy meals in the ordinary way. Theoretically they were illegal, but they were tolerated if they didn't become too well known—like speakeasies in New York.

This speakeasy-in-food was run by a lady bootlegger who spoke German and was willing to take a chance with a foreigner even though she did not know him. I had my first real meal in more than a week. Hot soup and *piroshki* (little Russian pies filled with meat, cheese or cabbage), also roast duck and stewed apples, bread and butter. Of course, no liquor, nothing but tea. It cost about twenty cents in American money, but I wouldn't have missed it if it had been two hundred dollars.

After that, Moscow looked brighter and I felt that I could bear it. Three days later, Mr. Weinstein was as good as his word and arranged for me to see Dr. Nicholas Semashko, the Commissar or Minister of Public Health, who was very affable and thanked me warmly for my offer of aid. He spoke of the great need of medical supplies in Russia, and by way of illustration told me that major operations in some parts of Russia had to be performed without anesthetics, owing to the absence of ether or chloroform.

He explained that it would take considerable time before Russia could make good the deficiencies in such supplies caused by the Allied blockade and the stoppage of imports. I replied that I was aware of this shortage from the fact that the Martens mission had purchased supplies of chloroform and ether from the Allied Drug and Chemical Corporation. My hospital was stocked with a good supply. Semashko brightened visibly at this news.

"We are so poor," he said, "that when a patient leaves our hospital all his cotton bandages are collected and used over again—after being sterilized, of course."

He then referred me to one of his subordinates who was in charge of their foreign department. Now, I thought, I could really get some action, but the official in question was out of town and would not be back for a month or so. My hopes were dashed again.

At this point I began to think of going home. It seemed impossible to do anything in Russia. Then I was informed by Mr. Weinstein, who had continued to show a friendly interest in me, that a special inspection train was being sent to the Ural Mountains to investigate conditions in the industrial regions there, and that I could go along if I wanted to while waiting for my own plans to materialize. The inspection team was to be led by my father's old friend Ludwig Martens.

Of course I jumped at the chance, and for three nights in succession drove over with my baggage and food chest to a station on the other side of town, only to be told each time that the train's departure was "postponed until tomorrow" owing to some defects in the running gear that needed repair. Railroads, it appeared, shared the prevailing demoralization, and it was the utmost they could do to keep some sort of suburban service running and an occasional mail train on the main line.

Finally, on the fourth day, I received a telephone message saying we would positively leave at five P.M. Once more I drove over to the station, arriving there at four-thirty. By this time my enforced study of Russian was bearing fruit and I was able to make inquiries. There was, it appeared, a train, yes; it would leave tonight but when or from what platform was uncertain. Then other members of the party gradually arrived, some of whom spoke English.

At eight o'clock the train backed into the platform and I secured an upholstered bunk in a private car—formerly the property of some high dignitary in the Czar's government—and planted my candle on the window ledge. At last, at eleven, we pulled out slowly, with much wheezing of the engine, on a trip that lasted nearly a month and was to be, for me, of the most absorbing interest and abiding consequence.

That journey, begun early in the month of August 1921 and so lightly undertaken, changed my whole future in Russia. Had I not taken it, it is probable that after some weeks' more delay I would have been attached to one of the Russian relief units, would have worked there for a few months with my hospital and then gone home to take up my internship at Bellevue Hospital. But fate ruled otherwise. It is to this journey that I owe my first start in Russian business, which later proved so successful; and the still greater privilege, as I shall describe in a moment, of a personal acquaintance with Lenin.

Ludwig Martens, the chief of our expedition, was now in charge of the Soviet metallurgic industry. He had taken along with him several of his assistants, mostly engineers. Besides myself there were two other Americans in our party: A. A. Heller, a wealthy socialist writer who had become active in the American Communist movement after the Russian Revolution, and Miss Lucy Branum, a plucky little social worker and former suffragist who was also much taken with the ideals of the Revolution. Both these people were typical of the Western visitors who later came to be known, collectively, as fellow travelers— bemused idealists who had a great deal of emotional and intellectual difficulty squaring their romantic expectations of the Soviet Union with the exceedingly grim realities.

Our train was drawn by a wood-burning locomotive of czarist vintage. It consisted of three or four cars, each of which contained compartments furnished with softly upholstered couches. These were made up into beds at night by the soldiers who staffed the train. Each car also included its own toilet facilities, so we were traveling in exceptional comfort—though slowly.

For three days and nights the train rumbled slowly eastward until, as we neared the Volga, we came into a region of parched fields and sunburnt crops. As far as the eye could see were grainfields, which should now have been ripening with golden stalks standing four feet high, ready to harvest. Instead there was nothing but dry, stringy grasses, or so they looked, only eight or ten inches tall above the cracked, dry earth.

At Ekaterinburg—where the Czar and his family had been executed in July 1918—we got our first sight of the famine. At this time the peasants in what was later known as the "famine area" were barely existing, at a level slightly above starvation. The scanty stocks they had kept from the year before were almost exhausted, and, as it was evident that the present crop had completely failed and that they had nothing to sustain them through the winter, they fled from their desolate fields as from the plague. While the Communist aspirations of the Bolshevik Revolution were still being applied, however weakly and ineffectually, travel on the railroads was free—if one could find a place.

By tens and hundreds of thousands, the unhappy peasants flocked to the nearest railroad and boarded what trains they could, crowding into freight cars in the hope that they might find some livelihood, however meager, in the urban centers. Disease—cholera, typhus and all the epidemics of childhood—was rife among them.

I had imagined that my professional training as a physician had steeled me against human suffering, but my first vision of a "refugee" train in Ekaterinburg struck me cold with horror.

I learned there had been a thousand persons—men, women and children—aboard the train when it had left Samara in the Volga region. When it pulled into Ekaterinburg, after several days' travel, not more than two hundred of the strongest were living. Some, of course, had actually died of hunger, but disease had claimed most of the victims.

During our twenty-four hours' stay in the station yard of Ekaterinburg, I received direct eyewitness knowledge of what a Russian famine meant. Children with their limbs shriveled to the size of sticks and their bellies horribly bloated by eating grass and herbs, which they were unable to digest, clustered round our windows, begging piteously for bread—for life itself—in a dreadful ceaseless whine. We could not help them. Here and there it was possible to give one youngster a meal, but if we had distributed every scrap of food on our train, it would have been as nothing to feed this multitude.

I was to see many dreadful sights in the famine region, but the memory of that Ekaterinburg station is burnt deep into my memory. Two things stand out in that vision of horror: the busy stretcher-bearers carrying the dead into one of the waiting rooms where they were stacked up in tiers like the carcasses of animals to await the carts that would take them to burial in a nameless grave. And the black ravens circling ceaselessly above.

As the winter came on, there were to be worse horrors in store than any I had seen. It became impossible to bury the dead in the hard-frozen ground, and corpses stripped naked, because their clothes were too precious to waste, lay in heaps in cemeteries to which the death carts had brought them. The carrion crows and vagrant dogs fared well in those dreadful days. To complete the tragic picture, there were grim tales of cannibalism, of mothers driven frantic, killing one child to keep the rest alive, and worse still, of butchers selling human flesh for profit.

Shaken, stunned by what we had seen in Ekaterinburg, we went on through the Ural Mountains, where our train was visited by scores of delegations from the mining and industrial sections, asking for help. These people were of a higher caliber than the Volga peasants and had not fled from their homes, but they too knew that unless relief reached them in time they could not survive the winter.

Everywhere we went we met the same condition—tremendous mills, factories and mine works standing idle and the workers hanging about, hungry and despairing. Even if the mills and factories could be put into operation, there was no market for their products, owing to the economic stagnation of the entire country. In several of these places I saw considerable stocks of valuable material—platinum, mineral products, Ural emeralds and semiprecious stones—and in Ekaterinburg I had seen stores of furs deposited there by hunters and trappers who were still continuing to try to earn their livelihood under the Soviets exactly as they had under the Czar.

I asked some of my friends on the train why they didn't export some of this stuff abroad and buy grain in return. "It is impossible," they cried. "The European blockade against us has just been lifted. It would take us too long to organize the sale of these goods and the purchase of food in return."

Then there came to me the single proposition which most dramatically changed my life. "Why," I said, "I can arrange it for you, if you like, through a concern owned by me and my family in New York. We can also buy foodstuffs for you. Is there anyone here with authority to make a contract?"

A meeting of the Ekaterinburg Soviet, chaired by the Secretary of the local Communist Party, was hastily convened. Martens invited me to attend this meeting and explain my proposal.

It was explained to me that about a million bushels of wheat were needed to save the Ural population from starvation and tide them over until the next harvest. The US had a bumper crop that year and grain was selling for a dollar a bushel. When it fell below a dollar, the farmers preferred to burn it rather than to bring it to market. "I have a million dollars," I said. "I will ship you a million dollars' worth of grain on credit, providing that each ship bringing a cargo of grain is reloaded for its return trip with a cargo of goods." Would they agree? The members of the Soviet looked at me with smiles. My answer was the sending of a lengthy cable to New York, addressed to my brother Harry and to Alfred Van Horn, the President of Allied Drug and Chemical, explaining the nature of the transaction and requesting that they charter the first available vessels and load them with grain for Petrograd.

I informed them that these ships would be loaded for the return journey with an approximately equivalent value of furs, hides and other goods. We were to get a 5-percent commission on both sides of the transaction, but my heart had been so wrung by what I had seen that the thought of doing business and making a profit did not enter my head at that time. All I wanted was to convince my business associates at home that they could send food to Russia without serious loss and to show the Russians how to utilize the raw materials they had on hand in such abundance to save the Ural population from starving. I cabled Harry to assure Mr. Van Horn that I accepted full responsibility that the Russians would carry out their contract.

When it became known that "the American," as I was called, had cabled New York to send grain immediately to Russia for reshipment to the Urals, the populace at the stations wherever our train stopped hailed me as their savior. At one town the local Soviet called a meeting and asked me to make a speech. Now, I said to myself, I will reap some benefit from those long hours of toil in Moscow when I memorized a hundred Russian words every day.

I made my speech and the applause was deafening. I sat down feeling pretty good and said to Ludwig Martens, who was sitting beside me: "I am grateful to your countrymen assembled here for their kind indulgence in not laughing at my incorrect pronunciation and mistakes, and I'm glad they understand that we are going to help them."

"Understand?" he laughed. "They understood nothing! They thought you were speaking in English." To add to my embarrassment, there came requests from the audience for an English-speaking comrade to "translate" my speech!

It was with the greatest difficulty that I assumed an unconcerned air, as I sat there and heard my first "Russian" speech translated into real Russian by Ludwig Martens.

During the weeks I spent in the Urals I visited, among other properties, some asbestos deposits in the neighborhood of Alapayevsk, where a number of the Czar's relatives and some high dignitaries were executed in the summer of 1918 and their bodies thrown into one of the shafts. It was suggested to me that these asbestos deposits, which had formerly belonged to the state railroads, might interest American investors on a concession basis.

The whole outfit, building and plant, was pretty much as it had been left after the Revolution. The property was not being worked, but I could see for myself that it had great possibilities, and might easily be developed. It was an open-pit mine and the long, valuable asbestos fibers were in seams visible to the naked eye, with very little overburden.

One of my friends on the train, a Russian mining engineer who had formerly worked in the neighborhood, explained to me how valuable this property might become with proper development, and I must admit his facts and figures interested me considerably. But I was still thinking about doing famine relief work and I simply earmarked his information as of possible interest to business people in America.

We continued our trip through the Urals at the same slow speed as we had come, amid the same scenes of suffering and desolation. One day, I remember, the train stopped at a small wayside station. Glad of the opportunity to stretch our legs, several of us took a walk along the dusty road leading to a village two or three miles away.

Halfway between the station and the village we found a lonely little hut and in the yard an old man with a gray beard, a typical Russian peasant, laboriously sawing pine wood into planks.

"What are you doing, little uncle?" said one of my friends.

"Sawing wood," replied the ancient laconically.

"But why make planks?" we asked. "What are you going to make?"

The old man gave us a strange, dumb look like a hurt animal. "My coffin," he said. "I am all alone, you understand, and I have food for three more weeks only, then I must die. But before that I will have made my coffin and will lie in it to await death so that I shall not be buried like a dog in the bare ground."

He was an old man and probably would not have lived much longer anyway, but this scene was more painful to me than any of the terrible things that I had seen before. Such complete resignation before such certain death seemed to typify the Russian people of that time.

It seemed a labyrinthine paradox. Here in the Urals lay the greatest treasures of the world—the richest mines of platinum, emeralds, asbestos, copper and almost every known mineral—yet the people were unable to utilize them even to provide themselves with the barest necessities of life and were starving to death.

Our trip would have been prolonged further, but that day we were all greatly excited to learn that Lenin himself wished to talk to Ludwig Martens. In those days there was no telephone service from Moscow to the provinces, but "conversation" was carried on by telegraph. Martens invited Heller and me to be present in the telegraph office of a small railroad station while Lenin "talked" to him.

Lenin asked Martens various questions about the state of affairs in the Urals and the possibilities of work there. Then to my amazement the tape unrolled a message about me.

"WHAT IS THIS WE HEAR FROM THE EKATERINBURG ROSTA [telegraph agency] ABOUT A YOUNG AMERICAN CHARTERING GRAIN SHIPS FOR THE RELIEF OF FAMINE IN THE URALS?"

"IT IS CORRECT," Martens replied. "DR. ARMAND HAMMER HAS INSTRUCTED HIS ASSOCIATES IN NEW YORK TO SEND GRAIN IMMEDIATELY TO PETROGRAD ON THE UNDERSTANDING, WHICH HAS BEEN APPROVED BY THE EKATERINBURG SOVIET, THAT A RETURN CARGO OF FURS AND OTHER GOODS WOULD BE TAKEN BACK TO COVER THE COST OF THE GRAIN SHIPMENT."

"DO YOU PERSONALLY APPROVE THIS?" Lenin asked.

"YES," said Martens, smiling at me. "I HIGHLY RECOMMEND IT."

"VERY GOOD," was Lenin's answer. "I SHALL INSTRUCT THE FOREIGN TRADE MONOPOLY DEPARTMENT TO CONFIRM THE TRANSACTION.

"PLEASE RETURN TO MOSCOW IMMEDIATELY."

8

Lenin

It was nearing the end of August 1921, when I returned to Moscow. I had been away less than a month, but short as the time was, I rubbed my eyes in astonishment. Was this Moscow, the city of squalor and sadness that I had left? Now the streets that had been so deserted were thronged with people. Everyone seemed in a hurry, full of purpose, with eager faces. Everywhere one saw workmen tearing down the boarding from the fronts of stores, repairing broken windows, painting, plastering. From high-piled wagons goods were being unloaded into the stores. Everywhere one heard the sound of hammering.

My fellow passengers, no less surprised than I, made inquiries. "NEP, NEP," was the answer. This was the New Economic Policy which had just been introduced by Lenin, despite considerable opposition from some of his associates. Only Lenin himself could have initiated this policy, which marked one of the most dramatic and decisive changes in the history of our century; and Lenin had to call upon all the immense reserves of loyalty felt toward him and all his mesmeric powers of persuasion to convince his comrades. If the NEP had been proposed by anybody else, he would certainly have been shot as a traitor to the Revolution.

The decree inaugurating NEP had been published in Moscow on August 9. It seemed as if it meant nothing less than the abandonment of Communism and the restoration of capitalist methods. As Lenin said at the time, and as events were later to prove, NEP was not the acknowledgment of complete failure which the enemies and critics of the Soviet called it. It provided for State Socialism rather than Communism, and maintained the control of the state over industry and business. It did, however, open the door to private initiative and allow people to work and do business in the old-fashioned way—for money—and to be paid accordingly, instead of the moneyless ticket system that had been tried previously.

Its immediate effect was to bring forth untold quantities of goods of every variety which suddenly appeared as if by magic. The shelves of formerly empty stores were overloaded with articles which had not been seen since the days of the Bolshevik Revolution four years before. In addition to a great variety of food products and delicacies, one could buy the choicest French wines, liqueurs and the best of Havana cigars. The finest English cloth lay side by side with the most expensive French perfumes.

It took the magic of the NEP to bring forth these goods from their hiding places in cellars, barns and secret hoards. In its early days, too, NEP offered a wider latitude to private storekeepers than would subsequently be the case, and it is not too much to say that this eleventh-hour measure gave the first impetus to the economic rehabilitation of Russia. In one fell swoop, Lenin saved the Revolution.

Fifty-five years later, Janos Kadar was to introduce very similar measures to revive the Hungarian economy and society, and the new modernization policies of the Chinese government today bear very striking marks of similarity as well. (Kadar, incidentally, does not refer to his economic policies as "restoring capitalism," but, he explained to me, as "allowing for human nature"!)

Along with the benefits of this new vigor came prostitution, gambling and illicit trades of all kinds. Those who profited from these trades caused great offense with the ostentatiousness of their wealth. A rash of new jokes about the hated "NEP men," as the profiteers were called, began to circulate in Moscow (the Muscovite taste for sharp political jokes flourishes even today). One of the jokes I remember dated from the time the philanthropist and explorer Fridtjof Nansen was missing in the frozen north of Russia in 1922 and, for a few days, all the telegraph lines were kept open free of charge exclusively for news of him.

One NEP man cables another and says: "HAVE YOU ANY NEWS OF NANSEN?"

The other replies: "NO. HAVE YOU?"

"NO," comes the answer. "BUT I'VE GOT SIX CASES OF COGNAC WHICH MIGHT INTEREST YOU."

(Incidentally, I got to know Dr. Nansen, the most modest of great men, during his long stay in Moscow. He, too, had come to Russia to fight the famine and had done great work, especially for children. One day he said to me, "What a splendid fur coat you are wearing! Where did you get a coat like that?" I replied that I'd bought it from the Trade Department and Dr. Nansen said no more.

A day or two later I met Nansen, all smiles. The Trade Department had sent him a magnificent coat. When he asked what it cost, they told him proudly, "The Soviet government is not so poor that it cannot make a small present to the man who has saved so many of its children's lives." They refused to accept a cent.)

The day after my return to Moscow I was summoned urgently to the Foreign Office. They had received a telephone message from Lenin's office saying he wished to see me at once. I could barely control my excitement. At the age of twenty-three, I was to meet the leader of the Revolution, the man who had come to exert more power over the Russian people even than the Czars he had deposed.

I was accompanied to my interview with Lenin by Boris Reinstein, an American Communist of Russian origin who was attached to the Foreign Office and to the Communist International Trade Union movement, the Profintern. Reinstein had been a druggist in Buffalo and he knew my father well, since they were both members of the Socialist Labor Party. He was well-known to Lenin and he had, in fact, furnished Lenin with the writings of Daniel De Leon. I have always understood that Lenin got some of his ideas from De Leon, with whom he was fully in accord.

We walked together to the Troitski Gate of the Kremlin, which is a curious little round white tower connected with the main body of the fortress by a bridge over gardens where once there was a moat. At the gate they said that they had been advised by telephone from Lenin's office to admit me. Reinstein showed his Communist Party card, which was sufficient as a pass, while the guards verified my passport and took it away from me. I was a little disquieted, but they told me they would give it back to me when I returned, and meanwhile they gave me a pink ticket or pass on which was written my name. I passed several guards of sentries, each of whom demanded that I produce my pass before permitting me to proceed farther.

Passing under the big archway, I found myself in a large square courtyard flanked by cannons captured from Napoleon, still to be seen in the same place today. I called the Kremlin a fortress, but in reality it is more than that. It is a sort of central town within a town, the citadel of Moscow guarded by enormous walls and towers. There are churches in it of great antiquity and beauty, decorated with priceless icons, some painted by the greatest of all icon masters, Andrei Rublev, and containing the funeral casks of the Imperial families over many centuries. The area is crowded with palaces and barracks—some new, some old— and streets of buildings, formerly occupied by members of the Czar's court, now used by Communist officials. Lenin's office was on the second floor of a large modern building on the central square. Forty years later I was to take the same walk to meet Khrushchev in the very same building and, later, his successors Leonid Brezhnev and Mikhail Gorbachev.

I passed a sentry before I entered the building and there was another sentry at the door of the corner rooms which the Soviet leader occupied. Since that August day in 1918 when the Social Revolutionary Dora Kaplan shot Lenin as he was leaving a workers' meeting in Moscow—which, though not fatal, undoubtedly shortened his life—he had been guarded from assassination by every possible precaution.

I passed through a large room, full of people working busily on rolltop desks, like the outer office of any big American businessman, and was conducted to the double door of Lenin's private office by his secretary, Maria Ignatierna Glasser, a little hunchbacked girl. She shared the innermost secrets of the Red Dictator, possessed his full confidence and never, on any occasion, used her position for her own advantage or that of her friends.

Lenin rose from his desk and came to meet us at the door. He was smaller than I had expected—a stocky little man about five feet three, with a large, dome-shaped head and auburn beard, wearing a dark gray sack suit, white soft collar and black tie. His eyes twinkled with friendly warmth as he shook hands and led me to a leather-cushioned chair beside his big flat desk. We sat so close that our knees almost touched.

The room was very small and unpretentious, full of books, magazines and newspapers in half a dozen languages. They were everywhere, on shelves, on chairs, piled up in heaps on the desk itself, save for a clear space occupied by a battery of telephones. There was a piece of gold-bearing quartz used as a paperweight, and ivory and bronze statuettes which had been sent to Lenin as presents by peasants' and workers' organizations. In one corner stood a large potted palm.

All this I saw at the first glance, but to this day I cannot recall more about what the room was like or whether there were pictures on the walls. During the hour or more our conversation lasted, I was completely absorbed by Lenin's personality. His powers of concentration were tremendous. When he talked to you, he made you feel you were the most important person in his life. He had a way of holding his face close to yours, his left eye squinting, but his right eye transfixing you as if it were trying to pierce your innermost soul. By the time we were through, I felt embraced, enveloped, as if I could trust him completely.

He began by giving me a quick glance sideways, as if to probe me with those sharp brown eyes. There seemed to be a trace of laughter in them.

"Shall we speak in Russian or English?" he began.

I replied that I would prefer English since he spoke so perfectly.

"Oh, far from perfect," he answered. "I suppose you find Russian a very difficult language to learn. Most foreigners do."

I replied that I was working hard to learn it and that I had been trying to master a hundred words a day.

Lenin gave me a smile of great sweetness and charm. "I used the same method myself when I was in London," he said. "Then I used to visit the reading room in the British Museum and read books to see how much I could remember. At first it is not so bad, but the more you learn, the more difficult it is to retain."

He spoke eagerly and emphatically in English, without many gestures save for a quick cutting movement of the hand to drive home his point. I afterward noticed that this was also one of his characteristics in public speaking. Occasionally he paused for a word, but for the most part his English was easy and fluent.

Our two countries, the United States and Russia, Lenin explained, were complementary. Russia was a backward land with enormous treasures in the form of undeveloped resources. The United States could find here raw materials and a market for machines, and later for manufactured goods. Above all, Russia needed American technology and methods, American machines, engineers and instructors. Lenin picked up a copy of *Scientific American*.

"Look here," he said, running rapidly through the pages, "this is what your people have done. This is what progress means: buildings, inventions, machines, development of mechanical aids to human hands. Russia today is like your country was during the pioneer stage. We need the knowledge and spirit that has made America what she is today."

Several times during our conversation there were interruptions by secretaries with documents. Lenin waved them aside.

"You have traveled in Russia?" he asked abruptly.

I replied that I had just spent almost a month in the Urals and the famine region.

His face changed, the eager interest faded from his eyes and his expression grew infinitely sad. In that moment I realized what a weight lay upon the shoulders of this man.

"Yes," he said slowly, "the famine . . . I heard you wanted to do medical relief work. . . . Yes. . . . It is good and greatly needed, but . . . we have plenty of doctors. What we want here is American businessmen who can do things as you are doing. Your sending us ships with grain means saving the lives of men, women and little children who would otherwise helplessly perish this winter. To the gratitude of these agonized people, I add my humble thanks on behalf of my government." Lenin stopped abruptly—apparently to control the tears which gathered in his eyes.

"What we really need," his voice rang stronger and his eyes brightened again, "is American capital and technical aid to get our wheels turning once more. Is it not so?" he asked Reinstein, who had been silent during most of the interview. Reinstein nodded approvingly.

I said that from what I had seen in the Urals there was plenty of available material and manpower; that many factories were in much better shape than I had expected.

Lenin nodded. "Yes," he said, "that's it. The civil war slowed everything down and now we must start in afresh. The New Economic Policy demands a fresh development of our economic possibilities. We hope to accelerate the process by a system of industrial and commercial concessions to foreigners. It will give great opportunities to the United States. Have you thought of that at all?"

I said that one of the friends on the train, a mining engineer, had wished to interest me in an asbestos mine in Alapayevsk which seemed to have a most hopeful future. I added a few words about my own affairs being insignificant.

Lenin checked me. "Not at all," he said, "that is not the point. Someone must break the ice. Why don't you take this asbestos concession yourself?"

I was astounded and aware, in that moment, of the historic opportunity Lenin was offering me. I was also instinctively skeptical that it could be made to work. From what I had seen of Russian methods, it looked as if the preliminaries of such a deal might last for months. I said something to that effect.

Lenin caught my meaning in a flash. "Bureaucracy," he said, "this is one of our curses. I am telling them so all the time. Now here is what I'll do. I'll appoint a special committee of two men, one of whom will be connected with the Peasant and Workers' Inspection Commissariat, and the other with the All-Russian Extraordinary Commissions [commonly called the Cheka] to deal with this matter and give you all the help they can. You may rest assured that they will act promptly. It shall be done at once."

Thus in my presence was created the embryo of what later was to grow into the Concessions Committee of the Soviet Union.

"You will make your arrangements with them," Lenin continued rapidly, "and when you have reached some sort of tentative agreement, you will let me know. We understand that we must ensure conditions that will allow concessionaires to make money in Russia. Businessmen are not philanthropists, and unless they are sure of making money they would be fools to invest their capital in Russia."

I told Lenin there was a doubt in my mind as to the possibility of working without friction with Russian labor, especially since they had become accustomed to look upon the "capitalist" as their enemy. "Can the Russian government assure me of no labor troubles?" I asked.

Lenin answered in that quick manner of his. "Our workers will be happy to get employment and good wages and it would be foolish for them to cut away the limb of the tree on which they are sitting. While our government cannot give orders to a trade union, still, as a workers' government, we have sufficient influence to ensure that the unions will carry out fully the terms of their collective contracts with you. Above all, it is essential that you become thoroughly familiar with our labor laws. If you obey these laws you will have the full protection of our government." Finally he said, "Do not worry too much about details, I shall see that you receive fair treatment. If there is anything you want, write and tell me.

"When you have made a provisional contract," he went on, "we shall approve it in the Council of Commissars without delay. What we decide goes, you understand," and again he made that decisive cutting gesture with his right hand. "In fact, if necessary, I won't even wait for the council to meet. A matter like that can easily be arranged by telephone."

Lenin was as good as his word. In an incredibly short time I was to find myself the first American concessionaire, obligated to begin the reconstruction of an industry with which I was wholly unfamiliar.

In looking back over the years at this memorable interview, I have tried my hardest to recollect the most striking feature of it all. I think it is this—that before entering Lenin's room I had been so greatly impressed by the terrific veneration which he aroused among his followers that I somehow expected to meet a superman, a strange and terrible figure, aloof and distant from mankind.

Instead it was just the opposite. To talk with Lenin was like talking with a trusted friend, a friend who understood. His infectious smile and colloquial speech, his sincerity and natural ways, put me completely at my ease.

Lenin had been called ruthless and fanatical, cruel and cold. I refuse to believe it. It was his intense human sympathy, his warm personal magnetism and utter lack of self-assertion or self-interest, that made him great and enabled him successfully to hold together and produce the best from the strong and conflicting wills of his associates.

I realize, of course, that there are critics of the Soviets who would say that Lenin displayed his ruthlessness by signing the order which permitted the Ekaterinburg Soviet to execute the Czar and his family. I think it has to be remembered that at that moment Russia was engaged in a desperate civil war and, if the White Russian Army had been able to rescue the Czar—as it so nearly did—it would have reinstated him and destroyed the Revolution. Lenin also had a personal reason to hate the Czar's family: the Czar's father, Alexander III, had given orders for the execution of his older brother, Alexander, for an assassination plot on Alexander III. I have always believed that this act, more than anything else, was the reason that Lenin became such an ardent revolutionary.

I have one more reflection on this interview with Lenin, a thought which has gathered strength in my mind over the sixty-five years since that memorable day in the Kremlin.

I am frequently asked which person, of all the great world leaders I have met in my life, I have most admired. There is no doubt about the answer. The greatest man was Franklin Delano Roosevelt, who was, of all the men of my time, my great hero. In FDR were combined, to an unparalleled degree, all the most desirable qualities of the great statesman. Nobody could equal the speed of his mind, the warmth of his character and the charm of his personality, and to these attributes was added an unmatched capacity for decisive executive action. FDR was the consummate "can-do" President, who would brook no delay in the execution of an idea or policy once it had passed scrutiny in the fine mesh of his mind.

I have often been asked to compare Lenin with FDR. They shared many qualities—not the least of which was that they were both approachable, unintimidating men who did not stand for a moment on the dignity of their office. In the presence of both men I felt the same captivating excitement and the same alertness. No half-baked idea, no vagueness could be risked with either man: they would spot it in a flash and dismiss it.

They both had a strong sense of humor, though Lenin did not laugh as much as FDR, who loved nothing more than a joke and who was always on the lookout for the ridiculous and the absurd; but then Lenin did not have much to laugh about. The condition of the Soviet Union and the colossal strains of his work did not leave much room for humor.

They did share, however, one characteristic of mind—and this is the thought with which I want to conclude this chapter. Like FDR, Lenin was capable of dazzling intellectual flexibility. Being the father of the Russian Revolution, Lenin is usually portrayed as a rigid theoretician who strictly inflicted the dogma of Marxism on the Soviet Union. However true this picture may be of Stalin—who succeeded Lenin and who unquestionably ground that country into a pitiless subjection to his own peculiar and byzantine theories of socialism—it does not apply to Lenin. The record of this interview with Lenin shows his true character.

People I meet today, especially journalists who interview me, are astonished to hear that Lenin told me, in effect, that Communism was not working and that the Revolution needed American capital and technical aid.

The world has largely forgotten how deeply the Bolsheviks admired the industrial achievements of America and how common it was to hear them say that they wanted to make Russia a "socialist United States." Lenin was greatly responsible for promoting that attitude, and it is not appreciated how pragmatic and realistic was the cast of his mind. Perhaps I can best convey this by saying that my own father—who in many ways typified the idealistic Communist sympathizer of those times—was far more romantic in his socialism than Lenin. It remains one of the ironies of my life that I found the father of world Communism to be less pure as a Communist and more pragmatic than my own father.

9

Trotsky and the American Capitalist

I clearly remember every step I took as I entered the Kremlin for my interview with Lenin: I can remember almost nothing of my departure. I left his office in a state of such excitement, my brain swarming with questions and ideas, that I noticed nothing of my surroundings before I found myself back in my squalid hotel room. Never in my young life had I needed so much to be alone in order to settle my mind.

I knew, without doubt or question, that my interview with Lenin had diverted the course of my life and opened a new world before me. Only rarely is it possible to know, at the time, when a major change is occurring in life: most change occurs imperceptibly and the significance of a moment is apparent only in retrospect. At that moment in Moscow, however, I could see clearly that, by lightly resting his hand for a moment on my life, Lenin had caused a polar shift in my world, altering the axis of my life forever. Great leaders can do such things.

I felt almost as if I had been taken up to the top of a mountain, from which all Russia could be seen below, and Lenin had said, "Take your pick." This immense country, with its inestimable wealth of natural resources, its vast reserves of labor and its almost untouched potential, had been laid open to me by its leader, who was probably the single most powerful man in the world at that moment. My breath was almost taken away by the panorama of opportunity that lay before me.

With Lenin's protection and patronage I could add an incalculable fortune to my present wealth by developing new enterprises in Russia. My previous accomplishments were as nothing compared with what I might achieve: my business activities in New York now seemed like very small potatoes indeed, though they had made me a very rich young man by normal standards. There was not a single moment's doubt in my mind that I must seize this opportunity and follow it wherever it led. The beginning of my medical career would obviously have to be postponed indefinitely. I wasn't going to forsake the chance to do such great things in Russia even for an internship at Bellevue. I wrote immediately to Dr. Van Horn Norrie at Columbia to explain my position and present my apologies.

(I later found out that Dr. Norrie carried my letter in his wallet for a long time, because nobody had ever turned down one of his prized Bellevue medical internships. Hans Zinsser, the renowned bacteriologist with whom I had intended to conduct research work in bacteriology and immunology, was so amazed by my decision that he made a special detour to Moscow while he was en route to India in 1923 to try to get me to change my mind.)

Then, having burned my bridges, I tried to concentrate on the steps necessary to take full advantage of my new opportunity. I didn't get very far with it, but spent a restless time tossing and turning in my bed—not, for once, because I was being pursued by a battalion of insects, but because my mind was overwhelmed by legions of thoughts.

If I had not known before what Lenin meant to Soviet Russia, I would have found it out the day following my interview with him.

As usual I went to the Metropole Annex in the morning to see my friends there, and as usual when they asked me how I was I had some remarks to make about conditions at the "Hotel" Savoy, which seemed to get worse instead of better. This time Mr. Weinstein was all concern.

"My dear Doctor Hammer," he cried, "why didn't you tell us sooner? I shall make different arrangements at once!" He jumped to the telephone and within half an hour I was sitting with my baggage in a big limousine on my way to the Government Guest House across the river, opposite the Kremlin.

This mansion, the Sugar King's Palace as it was generally called, had formerly been the property of Haritonenko, a Ukrainian of humble origin who had acquired control of the beet-sugar industry and who, when the Revolution occurred, was reputed to have been worth a quarter of a billion dollars.

His house was furnished gorgeously but without taste. The walls were covered with pictures, some the merest daubs; others, especially a lovely Corot, fit to adorn any gallery in the world. The pride of Haritonenko's heart was a huge stained-glass window overlooking the wide oak staircase and oak-paneled hall where suits of armor and a big stuffed bear formed incongruous neighbors to a large piece of modern Japanese bronze statuary, incredibly ugly and grotesque. After the Revolution the house had been retained by the government as a place to entertain foreign visitors, and its furniture and fittings were unchanged. Today it is the residence of the British Ambassador.

However, I was not inclined to criticize the aesthetic imperfections of the former owner. I had been living in a verminous room, with no service, no meals or restaurant, nothing save a little hot water. Suddenly I found myself in a palatial suite with bathroom attached—and hot and cold water actually on tap—neat as a pin, and, wonder of wonders, containing a large comfortable bed with real sheets and blankets. There were well-trained servants, an excellent cuisine, and if need be, a bottle of old French wine from the well-stocked cellar. I could hardly believe it was real. Such was the magic of Lenin's name and of my new status as a potential concessionaire.

My suite had been occupied not long before by the well-known English financier Leslie Urquhart, whose "Russo-Asiatic" corporation had been the greatest foreign enterprise in Czarist Russia. Its interests included valuable copper mines and other minerals, tracts of timberland of almost unlimited extent, and mining and oil rights over the richest section of western Siberia.

Urquhart had tried to renew with the Bolsheviks the concession contract he had been granted by the Czar, but his terms were so stiff, and his claim for alleged damages so exorbitant, that he left Moscow without reaching an agreement. In 1922 he was more successful—or less insistent—and actually signed a preliminary contract with Leonid Krassin in London. It was vetoed by Lenin, however, in the spring of 1923 because the British Fleet at Constantinople insisted upon the right to search Russian vessels passing through the Dardanelles. Urquhart thereupon became a bitter enemy of the Soviet state.

The apartment next to mine had been used by the Anglo-American writer Clare Sheridan, during her stay in Moscow. The adventurer Washington Vanderlip, who had so narrowly missed obtaining a concession for the Kamchatka oil field, had a suite across the corridor.

In 1919 Washington Vanderlip had come to Moscow, traveling on nothing more than his nerve. When the Russians asked him whether he was actually Frank Vanderlip, then a power in the National City Bank, or a near relative, he just smiled mysteriously and said: "Hush, we American financial magnates do not like personal questions." In fact, he had no connection.

Vanderlip was received by Lenin and did actually obtain concession rights to some of the most valuable sections of the Kamchatka fields. He might, perhaps, have found backing to exploit them had he not talked rather too much to the newspapers before his return to America. I am not sure of this, but at any rate, his plans fell through and the concession lapsed.

After the finest (and most needed) bath I ever had in my life, and a hearty meal, I returned to the foreign office to ask about a visa for Boris Mishell, who had returned to Berlin from Riga and was patiently waiting for news from me. "It shall be cabled immediately," they assured me.

I went out of the foreign office walking on air and cabled Boris: VISA GRANTED. COME AT ONCE VIA RIGA.

A little later I remembered the fine Mercedes-Benz auto I had bought in Berlin, so I sent another cable: COME WITH AUTO QUICKLY AS POSSIBLE.

In the course of the afternoon I received information that my asbestos concession was being rushed through as Lenin had promised, and it became clear to me that I needed the advice of my manager without delay.

So that night I sent a third cable: IF POSSIBLE ARRANGE COME DIRECT BY AIRPLANE. Then I went to bed feeling I'd fixed things splendidly.

Unfortunately Mishell received the second cable first and took it to mean that I was telling him to drive by auto right through to Moscow, risking his neck by running across the Russian border without a visa. He thought I had gone crazy.

Within an hour he received my message about the airplane and then—he told me afterward—he knew I was either mad or delirious. He sat for some time in deep distress and perplexity, wondering how best to help me and how to break the news to my folks at home.

This, after all, was the first time he had heard from me since I entered Russia. Then my first cable reached him and he began to understand. But he didn't worry about autos or airplanes, he just took the train for Riga, which perhaps was the wisest thing he could have done.

I met him at the station with a high-powered Foreign Office car so newly arrived from abroad that it positively sparkled. The worthy Boris had evidently heard worse stories about the famine in Russia than I had. His compartment was absolutely crammed with foodstuffs. Sausages in packets, tens upon tens of cans of fish and meat and vegetables, loaves of bread in piles, in short, enough food to feed an army.

With the help of two strong porters we moved his supplies over to the auto. When he saw it, his jaw dropped.

"Good God," he gasped. "Is this yours?"

I just smiled. "I think," I said, "it would be a good idea to distribute some of this stock of yours to the poor people around the station—those sausages, for instance, which are bursting out from the packet."

"Don't we need them?" he said.

"Not with me you don't," I replied, as calmly as if I hadn't felt exactly the way he did about six weeks before. "But these people do: so step on it and start handing them out."

I managed to keep a grave face, but it was hard work. He'd been told that food in Moscow was life itself, yet here was I, an "old inhabitant," casually telling him to get rid of his precious cargo. If it hadn't been for the auto I bet he'd have refused, but that was something concrete. So the local urchins reaped a rich harvest and we drove off at last amid loud cheers for America.

When we reached the Sugar King's Palace, I took our Boris, who had been silent and thoughtful during the ride, to the room adjoining mine.

"Perhaps you'd like a hot bath before dinner," I said nonchalantly. "I'll tell them to get it ready and then you'll find dinner in the sitting room. Would you prefer Johannesburg wine or Burgundy?"

As I have said, Mishell was a man of the world who had traveled far and wide and prided himself on never being at a loss. This time he was simply dumbfounded. "So this is Moscow," he stammered. While he stared at me like a child who is being told something beyond its understanding, I rang the bell. I asked the servant in Russian to prepare the bath and then I ordered dinner. Mishell still stared. After a time he found his voice and said weakly, "You seem to be comfortable here."

My control finally gave way and I roared with laughter. "I don't know how you did this," he said, "and I don't care, but I'll say you've done it all right. Bring on your Burgundy! It's just what I need after all this."

After Mishell arrived we had daily conferences with the authorities about the new concession. We found the Russians most ready to meet us halfway, but just before the final concession contract was signed I happened to mention that Lenin had told me that if there was anything I wanted, to be sure and let him know.

"What?" cried Boris. "He told you that?"

"Yes," I said. "But I don't think we need it."

"Like hell we don't," he said, hastily winding a sheet of paper into his Corona typewriter.

"I can think of lots of things," he said. "First of all, what about offices? I don't know that anything yet has been said in regard to that. And then the question of transportation. How are we going to get out to the Urals, have you thought of that?"

So together we drafted the following memorandum, which we headed Amendments to the Asbestos Concession Agreement:

1. We are entitled to receive from the Government: offices, warehouses, etc., wherever we consider it necessary. The Soviet Government undertakes whenever needed to supply us with soldiers (militia) to protect our property.

2. The Government grants the right to our employees to travel freely about Russia and to enter and leave the country at will. This, of course, pertains only to American citizens.

3. The Government radio and telegraph stations are placed at our disposal for the prompt transmission of our telegrams.

4. The Government renders us every possible assistance in the prompt movement of our freight cars and also places at our disposal private cars to transport our employees throughout Russia.

5. To avoid all red tape, delays and hindrances, the Government undertakes to appoint a committee of two persons, one from the Workers' and Peasants' Organization and one from the "Cheka" to whom in case of misunderstanding we can refer as competent authority to settle all disputes without loss of time.

"I guess that's about all," said Boris. So we telephoned to Lenin's office and in ten minutes a courier arrived by bicycle to fetch our memorandum. This document was to play an important role in our future business activities in Russia. When our concession agreement was finally signed, we found our memorandum was attached to it, countersigned by the President of the Council of the Peoples' Commissars, Alexander Tsyurupa, acting for Lenin and the secretaries of the President of the Council of Commissars. The document was like an official decree. Not a word of it had been changed, nor an addition made by the Soviet Premier. His approval was unqualified and the document proved of enormous value.

Among other things it gave us the right to attach freight cars containing supplies for our workers at the asbestos mines to any passenger train. In those days, when traffic was still in a state of disorganization, this was a great privilege.

Our contract, the first American concession which actually came into being, was signed in the Foreign Office on October 28, 1921, with all the ceremony of a peace treaty. On behalf of the government the

Vice Commissar of Foreign Affairs, Mr. Maxim Litvinov, affixed his signature to the document, which was adorned with a huge red seal truly as large as a saucer. It was also signed by Peter A. Bogdanov, then chairman of the Supreme Council of Peoples' Commissars and later President of the Amtorg Trading Corporation—the official representative of the Soviet Trading Monopoly in the United States which was set up in 1925.

Our next task was to find suitable offices. At that time there were scores of empty business premises in Moscow. Armed with the concession agreement, Mishell and I proceeded to the headquarters of the Moscow Housing Department, where they showed the utmost readiness to help and sent us out at once with an official to look at some buildings. He promptly led us to a large, square marble building, four stories high, in the center of the town. I believe it had formerly been a bank and it was really a noble edifice.

"How would this suit you?" he asked. "It is in pretty good repair, though it might be a little bit difficult to heat at first. But I think we can arrange that. I hope it will be big enough."

"What?" I gasped. "The whole building? What about the rent?"

"Oh, a nominal sum," he smiled and mentioned the equivalent of about thirty dollars a month.

I was startled, not having realized that in those days there were so many empty places of business that the authorities were glad to have them occupied simply for the sake of maintenance.

I did, however, say it was too large and finally selected a good office on the first floor overlooking the intersection of the two principal business streets in Moscow—what would correspond, one might say, to Times Square. The address was Kuznetski Most 4. The building had previously belonged to the former Court Jeweler, Carl Fabergé, in whose work I was to become intensely interested, both from an artistic and from a business point of view. The rent on the building was around twelve dollars a month. Later on, when our activities had expanded and our demand for office space had greatly increased, we exchanged these quarters for others in a street near to the Savoy Hotel, again on most advantageous terms.

One of the points mentioned in our letter was about the question of guards for our property and goods. When I spoke about it at the Foreign Office, they suggested that I had better get in touch with Leon Trotsky, the Commissar of War. I naturally jumped at the chance of meeting this other outstanding figure of the Revolution, and two days later I was informed that he would receive me in his office at four o'clock.

The War Office was situated in a large building with white columns outside the Kremlin. The moment I entered it, I was struck by its great difference from all of the other Soviet administrative offices I had visited. The place was scrupulously clean and tidy. There were no chatting groups of comrades in the corridors, no cigarette stubs on the floors, no tea glasses in saucers on the desks.

The sentry at the door examined my credentials and directed me to an anteroom upstairs. At three minutes to four, in came a snappy young aide in khaki uniform with a Sam Browne belt and a heavy revolver at his hip. "Comrade Trotsky is waiting for you," he said curtly. "Will you please come with me?"

He led me through rooms filled with diligent workers. The place was a hive of industry. We passed other sentries, and it struck me that the Red Warlord was guarded more closely than Lenin himself. Of course, Lenin lived in the Kremlin—a fortress in itself—but from the attack upon Lenin and the campaign of assassination undertaken by the Social Revolutionaries in the summer of 1918, the Bolsheviks had learned to leave no stone unturned in order to protect their leaders.

Not that anyone ever questioned Trotsky's personal courage. Indeed, on one occasion he showed the rarest kind of bravery in facing a mob howling for his blood. It occurred in Leningrad during the early days of the Revolution. There was a scandal in high Communist circles. Pavel Dybenko, the idol of the Red Fleet, a handsome young noncommissioned officer who had brought the cruiser *Aurora* up the river from Kronstadt to shell the Winter Palace and drive Kerensky's government out in panic, had suddenly left Petrograd for the Crimea with Madame Alexandra Kollontai, who then occupied a prominent position in the Communist Party. It was a sort of unofficial honeymoon. The more austere of their comrades regarded it as nothing less than desertion in time of war and demanded, quite seriously, that the couple be made an example of—that they should both be shot.

Trotsky, in particular, had pressed for their execution. The fact became known to the sailors of the Red Fleet, and one morning a body of them, several hundred strong, appeared in the courtyard of the building where he worked, shouting threats of vengeance. A terrified secretary ran into Trotsky's room.

"The sailors have come to kill you, Comrade," he cried. "Save yourself immediately by the back staircase while there is time. They have defied the guards and swear they will hang you on the lamppost in the courtyard."

Trotsky leaped to his feet, ran down the front staircase, out into the courtyard. "You want Trotsky," he shouted, "here I am!" Without waiting an instant, he burst into speech. Instead of weakening, he maintained his denunciation of Dybenko and justified it in the most vigorous language.

Such was the magic of his personality and oratorical power that within ten minutes the sailors were carrying him around the courtyard in triumph.

Lenin disposed of the Dybenko-Kollontai affair in a characteristic way. At a meeting of the Central Committee of the Communist Party to decide finally what punishment should be inflicted, Lenin waited till the rest had finished speaking, then said quietly, with tongue in cheek, "Comrades, you are right. Their offense is most serious, and the penalty should be exemplary. Personally, I think shooting is far too good for them. I propose, therefore, a fate more terrible still. Let it be resolved that our erring comrades be condemned to mutual fidelity for the space of five years."

Kollontai's bigness of heart was notorious, and Dybenko was not a dashing young hero of the Red Navy for nothing. The council received Lenin's suggestion with uproarious laughter and the incident was closed. But reports whispered that Madame Kollontai never quite forgave Lenin.

Heavy curtains shrouded the door of Trotsky's office and the big room was in semidarkness as I came into it, although it was afternoon of an early autumn day. The shades were drawn over the windows, shutting out all daylight. Trotsky sat at a big flat desk on the far side of the room under an electric light, the only illumination in the place, like the spotlight of a theater. He always had a strong sense of dramatic values. I learned afterward that a steel netting protected the windows outside from a possible grenade or bomb. This network had been installed in the summer of 1919, when a couple of anarchists killed some twenty members of the Moscow Communist Committee by hurling a heavy bomb into the room where they were holding a meeting.

The Red Warlord wore khaki breeches, a plain tunic buttoned up to his neck, and glasses. His face was angular, his eyes were blue, and though he greeted me quite cordially, his glance was cold and piercing, very different from Lenin's human and friendly attitude. Never once during the meeting did he smile. We talked in German, which he spoke perfectly. He knew all about our concession and the contract I had made before to supply foodstuffs to the Urals in exchange for goods. He spoke of the unlimited possibilities of that region. In his opinion its mineral resources had hardly yet been scratched. He had just returned, he told me, from an inspection trip through the Urals and was convinced that it offered great possibilities to American capital.

He asked what I thought about it. Did the financial circles of the United States regard Russia as a desirable field for investment? I replied cautiously that I wasn't quite sure. It was too early as yet to give an opinion. Perhaps later. . . .

Trotsky came back with a somewhat curious argument. Inasmuch, he said, as Russia had had its Revolution, capital was really safer there than anywhere else because, of course, "whatever should happen abroad, the Soviet would adhere to any agreements it might make.

"Suppose," he continued, "one of your Americans invests money in Russia. When the Revolution comes to America, his property will of course be nationalized, but his agreement with us will hold good and he will thus be in a much more favorable position than the rest of his fellow capitalists."

I stared at him in surprise for a moment, wondering whether he was serious. Then I realized that he was wholly sincere and that he really believed a Bolshevik revolution in America was only a question of time. I did not attempt to contradict him.

Trotsky readily agreed to supply the guards we required and I left him after an interview of about half an hour with the feeling that this was a man of remarkable but imperious character, with great ability and unflinching will, but a degree of fanaticism of which Lenin had given me no sign.

It is irresistibly fascinating to speculate today, sixty-six years after I met Trotsky, on the might-have-beens for Russia and the world if his character had been different. Say, for instance, that he had been a warmer personality, less absolute in his intellectual rigor, more diplomatic and accommodating toward those who took a different line from his own.

Then he might easily have been able to succeed to the leadership on Lenin's death, instead of his adversary, Stalin.

The Soviet Union would then have shown quite a different face to the world from the icy and forbidding countenance of Stalin's Russia— though it might even have been more actively dangerous. Trotsky would have tried harder to foment revolution in other countries, especially in Europe; and such a policy would undoubtedly have led to war with those countries, the eventual military defeat and overthrow of the Soviet Union and the restoration of a Kerensky-like regime. Stalin, while believing in the ultimate overthrow of capitalism, was more pragmatic. He wanted to prove that socialism worked in Russia before he attempted to conquer the world, as Trotsky would have tried to do immediately.

10

Doing Business Under NEP

The day after my meeting with Trotsky we put an advertisement in the papers for office furniture, as the premises we had taken were almost bare. Three or four people had come to see us in response with desks and tables to sell, when in came a young girl, neatly but poorly dressed. She said that she had no furniture but, seeing our advertisement, she figured we would require help as well, so she had come along to seek a job. That sounded more like the American spirit than I had been used to among Russians. I engaged her services on the spot and she proved a valuable member of our staff until she left us some years later to be married.

The girl, Anna Ivanovna, had had an unusual career. When she was eighteen years old, her parents had been killed by the Whites—whereupon, having no brothers, she dressed herself in boy's clothes and enlisted in the Red Army to serve throughout the civil war without anyone becoming aware of her sex.

While we were in the midst of all the bustle of opening an office, the porter we had hired—an ex-aristocrat, a most dignified gentleman with a long gray beard—came in and told me nervously that a detachment of soldiers had arrived, demanding that the place be shut at once.

"What?" I said. "You're crazy. There must be some mistake."

He insisted, and a moment later brought the two officers in charge into my office. Sure enough, they declared that the place must be closed, as we had not received a "patent" from the Moscow Soviet (city council) to open an office. They were quite polite but equally categorical: everyone had to be arrested, they said, and they would place seals on the doors.

I tried to argue. They would not listen. Then I produced the amendment to our concession signed by Tsyurupa and their attitude changed a bit. However, they were still suspicious, as if the document might be a fake. Seeing this, the resourceful Boris, who had come into the room, picked up the telephone on my desk and said to the operator, "The Kremlin, please; I wish to speak to Comrade Lenin."

At the mention of this name, the officers grew pale. Lenin's secretary, Fotyeva, answered the phone and, when the matter was explained to her, requested that one of the officers come to the instrument.

Knowing nothing of what she said to him, we could only surmise by the trembling voice of the officer, who was visibly shaking and stammering into the transmitter, "*Da, da*"—meaning "Yes, yes."

When he had hung up the receiver and composed himself, he said: "Ah, that makes a difference. It was doubtless merely an oversight on your part. The formality can be arranged quite easily."

He promised to arrange it himself without delay, and the soldiers withdrew. Sure enough, I obtained my patent the following morning, but the incident had taught me a valuable lesson. I gave instructions to have the memorandum which Lenin had approved put in a large frame and displayed in a prominent place on the office wall. It did prove invaluable to us in many difficult situations that arose later. Mishell and I carried photographic copies of the document with us wherever we went and frequently produced them when we encountered any kind of obstruction: the effect was always magical, the obstruction invariably evaporating as if it had never existed.

Early in December 1921 the first boatload of grain from America to fulfill the barter contract I had made with the Ekaterinburg Soviet reached Russian waters. The delay in shipping the grain was unavoidable, as this was the first shipment and the whole transaction was so unusual. The port of Petrograd, as it was still called—now Leningrad— was already frozen, so the shipment was routed to Revel (Talinn), the Baltic port of Estonia.

I had already been to inspect the goods sent from Ekaterinburg to pay for our grain which, owing to the difficulties of transport, had not reached Moscow until the beginning of November. They consisted largely of furs and hides, but there was something else, too. In casual conversation with an official in the Moscow Trade Department, whose duty it was to furnish export licenses, I had said jokingly, "Well, why don't you send some caviar? We've not had any in New York for a long time and it ought to sell like hot cakes."

This officer had taken me at my word. He produced nearly a ton of caviar in fifty-pound wooden kegs and, sure enough, when it reached

New York, it sold at fancy prices—ten dollars a pound or more. Nowadays, of course, ten dollars will scarcely buy you an ounce of the best Russian caviar.

We obtained an order to have all the goods transferred to Revel and I went there to supervise the work of unloading and loading the steamer.

At that time, Revel was one of the depots for Russian business, but most of the stuff that reached it from Russia came by contraband channels—art treasures, jewels, platinum and heaven knows what, smuggled across the border in exchange for foodstuffs. In the winter of 1921, however, there was also an office of the Russian Foreign Trade Department in the city, buying goods abroad for delivery in Revel against payments in gold bullion.

I found the Soviet Foreign Trade Office in Revel very angry about America. It appeared they had bought a large stock, I believe over a million pairs, of American Army boots, which were part of the war stocks sold in Europe after the armistice. The boots looked good but, as it turned out, their soles were made of paper. The price of leather was extremely high during the First World War and it is possible that the Army authorities had approved this papier-mâché substitute for soles. On the dusty roads of France, in summer, the soles might have stood up quite well, but they simply went to pulp in the slush of a Russian winter.

The Russians in Revel were furious and complained that they had been robbed. I believe they actually received a refund for the boots, but be that as it may, the incident did not redound to the credit of American business and it certainly added to my difficulties.

It was no picnic trying to conduct a business anywhere in Russia at that time. The Foreign Trade Office in Petrograd looked upon our activities with suspicion and did everything possible to cause us difficulties and delays in carrying out our program. The position became so bad that I wrote a note of complaint to Lenin's first assistant, Gorbunov. Evidently he showed the note to Reinstein, who forwarded it to Lenin himself, with explosive results. Lenin dashed off a handwritten note to Zinoviev, the head of the Petrograd Communist Party. He wrote:

Comrade Zinoviev!
    Today Reinstein showed me a letter from Armand Hammer, about whom I have already written to you (an American, son of a millionaire, among the first to take a concession from us—extremely profitable for us).
    He writes that in spite of my letter, his colleague Mishell (colleague of Hammer) bitterly complains about the rudeness and bureau-

*cracy of Begge [head of the Foreign Trade Office], who received him
in Petrograd.*

*I will complain about Begge's conduct to the Central Committee.
This is an outrage. In spite of my letter to you and your deputy, things
were done just the opposite.*

*And nobody informed me about this, neither about disagreeing
with me, or anything.*

I ask you to verify this and give this matter special attention.

*Was my letter (my telephonogram) to you or your deputy brought
to the attention of Begge? If so, Begge is responsible. If not, your
secretary or somebody is.*

*Who is responsible? It is necessary to find out. Can you bring
pressure on Begge and clean up the matter?*

Lenin

All the vital components of Lenin's character and his genius are in
this note—the feverish activity, the remorseless attention to detail, the
impatient urgency of his drive to break through the cobwebs of bureaucracy and red tape which were clogging the wheels of the Russian
economy. I don't know where he got the idea that my father, not I, was
the American millionaire—perhaps from Reinstein, who had returned
to Russia before he knew that my father had made a gift of his pharmaceutical company shares to me—but it became stuck fast in his mind
and he repeated the same mistake in another of his notes about me.

Like all of Lenin's acts, the writing of this note had an instantaneous effect. The obstructions which were blocking us in Petrograd
miraculously vanished.

I was able to arrange the reloading of our vessel satisfactorily, and
when the Russian goods reached New York, my brother Harry and our
business associate in America had an agreeable surprise.

Far from being less than the value of the grain shipment, they
proved to be nearly a hundred and fifty percent greater; and although
we were operating only on a commission basis, the surplus value established confidence hitherto lacking. Subsequent shipments of American
grain were continued without delay.

The shipment I had dispatched was the first Soviet goods to be sent
direct to the New York market, although I believe that a year or more
after the Bolshevik Revolution Russian goods were reaching America
from Vladivostok, which did not become part of the Soviet Union until
the Japanese evacuation in 1922.

By this time things were developing so fast that it seemed desirable
that I should return to America to discuss the details of future business.

In New York I began to think of the possibilities which had been
offered me as Moscow agent for American machinery and equipment. I
knew that the Soviet government was strongly supporting a campaign

for the mechanization of agriculture. Tractors were needed in large quantities.

Before the war, my uncle Alexander Gomberg had held a Ford agency in southern Russia. I asked him whether he thought Henry Ford would be interested in renewing connections with the Russian market. He told me frankly that Mr. Ford's attitude toward the Bolsheviks was not friendly, but offered, if I wished, to arrange for me to meet him.

I went alone by train to Detroit, where I was met by Mr. Charles Sorenson, one of the Ford executives, who drove me out to Dearborn. There, in the office of the *Dearborn Independent,* the newspaper owned by Henry Ford, I met Mr. Cameron, the editor, and a few minutes later Henry Ford himself entered the office. He was very tall, slim and gangling, simply and casually dressed in a soft shirt with a plain tie and flannel trousers. In everything—dress, manner and expression—he reminded me a lot of Will Rogers.

Ford began by saying curtly that although the Russian market had undoubted possibilities, he would prefer to wait for a change of regime before doing business with Russia. I was not long out of college, and like most youngsters, I regarded Henry Ford as a great and marvelous figure in American industry, but I found the courage to reply.

"Well, Mr. Ford," I said, "if you're waiting for a change of regime in Russia, you won't do any business there for a long time."

He gave me a keen glance. "You seem very sure," he said. "Why do you say that?" I explained as best I could that Lenin had given the land to the peasants and the factories to the workers and that, since most of the nobility and the middle class had fled the country, there was hardly anybody left who might want to revolt against the Bolsheviks. Although Ford obviously didn't agree with me, he seemed interested and asked me to have lunch with him.

Ford told me an amusing story of Russia in the prewar days. He had been reading a lot about nihilists and bombs when, one day, a large round box arrived from Russia addressed to him personally. He wanted to open it at once, but his wife and son advised caution; it might be an infernal machine—why not consult the police headquarters? So an expert came from the bomb squad and examined the package suspiciously.

"You have done wisely to call me in," he declared. "This package has an ominous look and a most peculiar shape."

He bent down close to it and listened. "It does not tick," he said, "but perhaps the mechanism has stopped." He examined the package again, then turned to Henry Ford and said solemnly: "Have you a concrete cellar with strong walls?" That brave man took the package down to the cellar and gradually, nick by nick, removed the paper wrapping. Then he began to chip away the wooden sides of the box.

Ford waited anxiously, wondering whether his house would be blown up. Suddenly the police officer appeared with a sheepish grin. "It's all right, Mr. Ford," he said. "It's only a cake," and he produced the *koolich* which every Russian family makes for Easter. The dangerous "infernal machine" was just a little present from my uncle Alexander Gomberg. "And a mighty good cake it was," concluded Henry Ford. "I wouldn't share it with anyone and used to take a big hunk with me to work every morning until it was finished."

We lunched together in a little white cottage near the experimental works where Ford was then spending most of his time on the problem of simplifying and perfecting the Fordson tractor. After my conversations with Lenin and Trotsky, it was most interesting to meet this giant of American industry.

Henry Ford had more in common with Lenin than with Trotsky. Like Lenin, he cared nothing for outward appearance or dress; like Lenin, he was human and friendly and shrewd; like Lenin, he had the prestige of success and his wealth gave him power as Lenin had power. What is more, and of this I am convinced, both men were honestly trying, according to their lights, to accomplish something which would benefit large numbers of their fellow men. Fundamentally, both were interested in achievement. Both of them, Ford in his first little workshop and Lenin in his exile in Switzerland, had been mocked as dreamers. Both had the strength of character to burn through to their goal.

There the parallel ends. What Ford achieved brought him vast wealth. Lenin died as poor as he had lived. Lenin looked at the world from the standpoint of a world leader. He combined acute political statecraft with knowledge of history and peoples and a profound insight into the principles of international policy. So too, Trotsky, with his superfine brain and linguistic knowledge.

As I talked with Ford, it was obvious that he was no match for Lenin and Trotsky in international affairs, but there rang through every word he said something of the same quality of genuineness which had so impressed me in my talk with Lenin. Here too, in such different circumstances, was a man who believed in humanity and progress.

I told Ford that the Russians were more interested in tractors than in automobiles. He frowned and thought for a moment. "Tractors are all right," he said, "and I shall never rest until I have proved to the world that animal traction on a farm is out of date. But the automobile is progress. If Russia is to develop, it must have mechanical transportation."

I replied that the Russian roads were impossible. "That's one of the great mistakes," said Ford, with a quick gesture of the hand which reminded me, strangely enough, of Lenin. "Cars must come before roads. If you get the cars, the roads will follow automatically. That's been true in America. It must apply to Russia also."

He went on to speak in general terms about the question of roads and motor transportation, and I listened, entranced. Here, at least, Henry Ford was as good as the Russian leaders. But to Lenin and Trotsky the whole world was an intellectual banquet. They could talk as easily about Germany or France or England or America as about their own Russia; whereas some of Ford's ideas about Russia were clearly the result of misinformation; they were so utterly remote from the truth.

"What you must tell your Russian friends," he said, "is that automobiles are not a luxury, but a means of service required by modern conditions."

He turned with a smile to Mr. Sorenson. "Do you think the American public regards our autos as a luxury?" he asked.

Sorenson grinned. "Of course not," he said. "A necessity, not a luxury. It's only when they get rich that people buy a luxury car in this country."

Ford turned back to me. "You see what I mean," he said. "That's what you've got to tell the Russians. But anyway, how many tractors do they want?"

"Millions," I replied. "If they can afford to pay for them."

"Ah," said Ford, "that's the trouble. You know, Doctor Hammer, we are losing money on every tractor we produce. When the plans for our tractor output were being made, my financial department told me that I would lose money on every tractor until I was selling a thousand a day. We haven't got to that yet, but we will, and I reckon"—again that whimsical smile—"I can afford to lose it."

After lunch Ford took me over his model farm, where everything was mechanized. "This is what they ought to have in Russia," he said. "If the Soviet state is as stable and powerful as you say, why can't they do it? Because," he answered his own question, "from what you tell me, I judge they are starting from the ground up and trying to jump right away from the late Middle Ages to the twentieth century." He rubbed the back of his head thoughtfully. "No reason why they shouldn't, as far as I can see," he said, "if they are as good as you say."

I told him that the Bolsheviks did want to do just that, but that they were terribly handicapped by lack of technical knowledge and trained engineers.

"You know, Mr. Ford," I added, "you may not believe it, but in Russia they think you're one of the most wonderful people in America: you and Edison. You see, putting all questions of Communism and capitalism aside, they know that you and Edison have done something here they want to do in their country, and they are eager to learn how. Would you be willing, if I could arrange it, to let some young Russians come here and learn your methods—and all about tractors and autos too—so as to teach people when they return home?"

"Don't see why not," said Ford. "We'd be glad to have them."

On my return to Russia four months later, I did arrange to send a number of our young Russian employees to Detroit to work and study in the Ford factory and on the Ford farm.

I arranged to take a number of models of the Ford car and Fordson tractor back with me to Moscow. I was also provided with hundreds of meters of film depicting the Ford works. Last but not least, I obtained the agency for all Ford products in Soviet Russia.

Spurred by this success, I made arrangements with several other manufacturers to represent them in Russia and obtained their approval of the same suggestion I had made to Mr. Ford—that they would allow Russian engineers to study in their works and then attach them to our staff in Moscow as demonstrators. I made contracts to represent thirty-seven American companies in Russia—among them were Allis-Chalmers, U.S. Rubber, Underwood Typewriters and Parker Pens. As a consequence of all these deals, all the trade between the United States and the Soviet Union was to pass through my hands for several years.

I then began to make plans to return to Moscow in the spring of 1922.

I decided that I had to concentrate exclusively on my Russian businesses and arranged to sell Allied Drug and Chemical. It was bought out by Alfred Van Horn and a number of other company executives who paid me more than a million dollars in cash and settled the balance of the sale with promissory notes. My brother Harry resigned from the company and joined the board of the corporation I registered in Delaware to handle our Russian trade. It was called Allied American Corporation. Harry joined as Secretary and Treasurer.

Victor returned with me to Moscow.

Victor was then twenty-one and by his own rueful admission, he had never been much of a student, just getting along.

He had always had real talent as an entertainer; even as a five-year-old he had worked up an act which would have the whole family rocking with laughter—a recital of "Mary Had a Little Lamb" in multiple dialects with assorted quick changes. At Colgate and Princeton he had spent all his spare time in college theatricals, though the snobbishness, and perhaps the anti-Semitism, of some of his fellow students held him back in the drama societies. When I arrived in New York I discovered that he had definitely decided to follow a career on the stage, had applied to the American Academy of Dramatic Arts and won a scholarship.

We were all proud that his talent had been recognized and rewarded, but my mother was uneasy. She didn't feel that the vagaries of
the stage were quite as desirable for one of her boys as the practice of
medicine or even a life of business. She prevailed on me to see if I
might influence my kid brother.

I tackled him. I said, "We all know you've got talent and we think
you might go a long way, but let's face facts: the chances of your being
a great success on the stage are a thousand to one. Nobody doubts that
you've got the dedication, ability, discipline and so on, but luck is the
most important factor. Why don't you come back with me to Moscow
and you can study at the Moscow Art Theater."

"The Moscow Art Theater?" he said. "Wow! That's a dream."

"Yes," I said, "but in the meanwhile, since I'm not going back for
several months, you could make yourself useful to me, get some commercial skills. There's a Miller's School of Shorthand and Typewriting
here in New York where in one month they'll teach you everything.
You get done there and you'll be able to be my assistant."

Victor would always do anything to help the family and, knowing
how tough things were for me while our father was in prison, he signed
up directly at the secretarial school, where he was a quick and diligent
pupil (though he claimed in later years to have expunged every line of
shorthand from his memory: he said that if I thought he could still do it,
I would still have been giving him dictation when we were in our
eighties).

On my way to Moscow through London I stopped to browse in
Leonard Partridge's antique shop. Leonard was not as famous as his
brother, Frank, who was purveyor to the Royal Family. In Leonard's
window I was taken with a small item which I decided to buy as a gift
for Lenin.

It was a bronze monkey, contemplating a human skull. The
monkey was seated on a stack of sculptured books, one of which was
Charles Darwin's *Origin of Species*. I was able to present it to Lenin
when I saw him for a brief moment with Reinstein in May 1922. Lenin
was very intrigued by the symbolism of the little statuette and he made
an extraordinarily clairvoyant remark: with the weapons of war becoming more and more destructive, he said, civilization might be destroyed
if humanity didn't learn to live in peace. The time might come, he went
on, when a monkey would pick up a human skull and wonder where it
came from. He was speaking twenty-three years before the first detona-
tion of a nuclear weapon ushered us into the age when his prediction
might come true. Lenin gave orders that the bronze was not to be
removed from his desk and it is still there today, in his Kremlin office,
which is now a national museum.

In Berlin I met our mining engineers, who had come from Russia with plans for the technical equipment of the asbestos mine, and after consultation with them, the necessary orders were passed on to America. This time, however, there was no delay or trouble about my visa, and, after a tedious journey from Riga, I found myself back in my palatial quarters at the Sugar King's Palace opposite the Kremlin. As I looked out of my window at this fortress which had housed the Romanovs for so many centuries, I could not help reflecting on the strangeness of fate, which had so suddenly stripped everything from those once all-powerful rulers who treated all Russia as their playground and their treasure house.

Fate was now beckoning me on to seek my fortune in this land of such unpredictable promise, of such immense reward and cruel penalty.

11

Red Czars, Commissars and the Death of Lenin

My first task was to attend to the shipment of machinery and supplies to the mines which were situated near Alapayevsk, some one hundred miles north of Ekaterinburg, now called Sverdlovsk. In order to see that everything was running smoothly, Boris Mishell and I made a trip to Alapayevsk in June 1922. To our dismay we found our workers so discontented that they were near to revolt.

Leo Wolff, whom I had appointed manager, met us looking pale and anxious. When I asked what was wrong, he told me bluntly, "We promised them food, but they are still hungry. The food has not come and they say we have tricked them. The position is dangerous and threats have been made against me. A mob of hungry men surrounded my house and I had to draw my revolver before they would leave. I've cabled a dozen times to Petrograd for explanations about the grain shipments without avail and, unless the food comes soon, some will die of starvation and I cannot answer for the consequences."

I was horrified. The cars with grain had left Petrograd sealed, with guards, routed direct to Alapayevsk. They ought to have arrived at least a fortnight earlier. Without waiting a moment, we returned to Sverdlovsk. Sure enough, the shipment had arrived there intact and safe some time before and had been dispatched northward. Accompanied by an official of the railroad administration, Wolff, Mishell and I retraced our steps and, about halfway to Alapayevsk, found twenty-five cars, the first shipment, waiting on a siding. The seals were unbroken and the guards reported nothing unusual, but the station commandant was holding them because, he alleged, a bridge a little way north of the station was unsafe.

"Why didn't you send them over in small lots if that is true?" he was asked.

His reply was unsatisfactory. Finally, when he saw an opportunity, he called Wolff aside and said in a low tone, "You are a businessman. Give me five hundred bushels of grain [equivalent to half a carload] and your cars will move." Wolff told him he would think it over.

There followed an exchange of cables between Wolff and the Soviet officials in Sverdlovsk, and within two hours the cars were on their way. Wolff later told us that the station commandant was recalled at once to Sverdlovsk and, after a brief trial, he was shot. Justice was rough and peremptory on that revolutionary frontier.

That remarkable and sinister man, Felix Dzerzinsky—who had created the Cheka, the forerunner of the KGB—had just been put in charge of state railroads by Lenin and given a free hand to reorganize them by any means he saw fit. Inefficiency and graft were rampant, but within a year Dzerzinsky succeeded in bringing order out of chaos. It soon became known on the railroads that attempts to steal foodstuffs on the part of officials would mean death.

Walter Duranty, the *New York Times* correspondent in Moscow, once told me a dramatic story about Dzerzinsky's methods involving an affair at Omsk in 1922. At that time the Volga famine was at its height and, although there was plenty of grain in Siberia, none of it was being shipped through to starving Volga. Dzerzinsky personally went to Omsk to investigate. He held a meeting of all the railroad executives and minutely examined every detail of their work.

Everything seemed in order, so he hitched his private car to an eastbound train and rode for a day across the steppe. At a small way station some two hundred miles from Omsk, he ordered his car unhitched. The train went on and the Commissar was left to confront a startled station commandant who thought his last hour had come.

"It's all right, Comrade," Dzerzinsky reassured him. "I simply want to try a small experiment. You have, I see, some loaded grain cars waiting here in your station. Why are they not sent on westward?"

The commandant answered, "I've cabled to Omsk several times, but there is no reply."

"Aha," said Dzerzinsky. "Just as I thought. Well, cable again saying that there is a wagon here listed 'urgent shipment to Omsk' and see what happens."

There was no reply the next morning, so Dzerzinsky ordered that a second message should be sent, stating that the private car of an important government official had been sidetracked there and that it was necessary to make arrangements to route him on.

Twelve more hours passed without reply and Dzerzinsky began to get annoyed. His time, he said, was too valuable to waste, even in experiments.

"Cable them," he said, "that I, Dzerzinsky, demand an engine be sent immediately with clear right-of-way along the whole route to fetch me back to Omsk at once. Make your message as strong as possible."

There was still silence and Dzerzinsky was actually forced to cool his heels in that little station for another twenty-four hours before he could flag a westbound train. On arrival, he again called a meeting of the office personnel from high to low. "He did not raise his voice, and there were no signs of anger in his face," said Duranty's informant, who was present at the meeting, "but his eyes were terrible."

"What I want to know," Dzerzinsky concluded, "is what became of those cables and why they were not answered."

For a moment his hearers stared at him in dismay and at the two big Cheka guards in full uniform behind him. Then one of the least important officials replied in quavering tones that he had received and pigeonholed the cables.

"Why?" demanded Dzerzinsky.

There was no reply, but it was quite clear that this was the usual procedure. The Omsk headquarters evidently declined to bother about little things like that.

"Very good," said Dzerzinsky finally. "I understand the state of affairs here and it is going to be changed." He turned abruptly to the official chief of the department. "Step forward," he said. "And you too," pointing to the principal assistant. "It is you who are to blame for this," he said. "You are responsible for this office, and it is you who will now be punished for the failure to supply food to our starving countrymen in the Volga. Take them out into the courtyard," he said to his guards, "and shoot them."

"Now," concluded Dzerzinsky, as the shots rang out in a dreadful silence, "let this be a lesson and a warning to the rest of you. You will never know in the future that a cable regarding a sidetracked freight car may not come from me or one of my assistants."

Within a week Siberian grain had begun to flow into the Volga.

On my return to Moscow I decided to make a trip through the south to organize business, particularly in regard to tractors.

I visited Kharkov and the Ukraine, Rostov and the rich north Caucasian grain region; Baku, the great oil center, and Tiflis (now called Tbilisi), the ancient capital of Georgia. The economic revival was now well under way, and during my trip I obtained quite large orders for as many as a hundred or two hundred American tractors at a time, particularly the less expensive Fordsons. In the meantime we had started the training of mechanics, so that we were able to meet the shipment with a full complement of drivers. Finally, I received a cable stating that the first shipment of fifty tractors was due to arrive at the Black Sea port of Novorossisk.

We had the crates unpacked on the dock, inspected the machines and filled them up with gas and oil. I mounted the first tractor, Boris Mishell got behind the wheel of the second, and then we set off in a procession for the center of the city.

Our appearance created a terrible panic. The population was convinced that an invasion of American or English tanks had begun. Alarm bells were rung, the garrison and Communist Guard called out and the local Soviet met in haste to take measures against the enemy.

When they discovered the truth, their military plans were hastily changed into a glorious welcome. Our procession was greeted with tumultuous applause; I don't believe that any victorious general ever entered a city with more éclat.

A few days later we drove the whole fleet of tractors as a demonstration from Novorossisk to Rostov, about a hundred miles. Most of the peasants along the route had never seen anything like our machines and, the word having spread by this time, they flocked in thousands to view the new marvel from America. The roads were densely lined with spectators all the way, though our procession must have been barely visible in the storm of dust which our wheels kicked up from the unmade roads.

At Rostov a big field had been provided where the tractors were put through their paces, showing how they could be used for pumping, sawing wood and driving electric-light plants, as well as plowing. The demonstration was a tremendous success. We took orders for hundreds of machines. All those orders, of course, were placed by party functionaries on behalf of collective farms. Not a single tractor was sold to a private peasant.

On this occasion I met three very interesting personalities. The first was Bill Shatoff, a former Chicago anarchist who had come to Russia in 1918 but now, to my amazement—and, I believe, his own— was President of the newly created Industrial Bank of Rostov, which was financing the tractor purchases for the district. Although he was not a member of the Communist Party, he was fully trusted by the Bolsheviks and was afterward put in charge of the construction of the "Turk-Sib" Railroad, which was to link the cotton fields of Turkestan with the food-producing regions of Siberia.

The second personality was Kliment Voroshilov, at that time Commander of the southeastern section of the Red Army, whose headquarters were at Rostov. A clean-cut, modest officer, who would have thought then that within five years he would have taken the place of

Trotsky as Commissar of the Army and Navy, and as a member of the Politburo of the Communist Party?

Voroshilov's rise was to continue to the highest ranks of Soviet military and civic power. He made himself an immortal hero of the Russians when he directed the operations that finally broke the Nazis' siege of Leningrad in 1943, and he was President of the USSR from 1953 to 1960.

The third man was Anastas Mikoyan, then Secretary of the local Communist Party. He was a strikingly clever young fellow, very quick and astute, half Georgian and half Armenian. He too rose like a rocket and soon became Commissar of Home and Foreign Trade and one of the leading officials of the Communist Party. If I had been asked in those days to bet on which of the young Bolsheviks I thought most likely to have a successful political career, I would have backed Mikoyan. His restless, nervous manner disclosed a fierce and cunning sense of self-interest, which would help him to survive. God knows what horrors Mikoyan tolerated or turned his back upon during Stalin's years, but, as I would have predicted, there he was, close to the summit of influence as Khrushchev's Deputy Prime Minister, when I returned to Moscow—for the first time in over thirty years—in 1961.

I have always believed that it was Mikoyan, together with Suslov, who engineered the plot which overthrew Khrushchev. Mikoyan learned that Khrushchev wanted to get rid of him as Deputy Prime Minister after Mikoyan had criticized Khrushchev for his handling of the Cuban missile crisis. Khrushchev's excuse for wanting to remove Mikoyan was that he was "too old." As he proved, he was not too old to look after himself in a power struggle.

At dinner one evening during the spring of 1922, I met Lenin's brain specialist, Professor Foerster. Lenin's state of health and the danger of his suffering a fatal stroke was always the talk of Moscow at the time. Professor Foerster did not speak too hopefully of his patient and emphasized Lenin's reluctance to allow himself the complete rest his condition required.

"He always tells me," said the professor sadly, "'I have so much to do, and the time is so short.'" The words were all too prophetic. I have always felt sure that if Lenin had worked less he might have lived for many years longer.

Through Professor Foerster I was able to follow the course of Lenin's illness. During the summer of 1922 he gradually recovered and was able to resume work in the autumn. He made several speeches in public and seemed to be quite himself again. The professor returned to Germany for a holiday and it was the general impression in Moscow that the Soviet leader was cured. But the relentless malady of hypertension or high blood pressure associated with arteriosclerosis which had killed his father, at almost the same age as Lenin, could be averted, as the professor had said, only by absolute rest and calm.

In the winter of 1922 he suffered first a tiny brain lesion. There soon followed a graver stroke. This time Lenin's right side and hand were paralyzed.

He was moved to Gorki, a country house thirty miles from Moscow which had formerly belonged to the textile multimillionaire Savva Morosov. It was a charming Italian-style mansion with slim marble columns set in beautiful surroundings. Morosov had been one of Czarist Russia's leading collectors of French Impressionist paintings. By one of those peculiar coincidences which lock up the circles of my life, some of the pictures originally collected by Morosov were included in the exhibition I arranged at Washington's National Gallery in July 1986.

Beautiful as Gorki was, it was also a house of ill omen. Here Morosov, so rich and successful, had died by his own hand, no one knew why, but Muscovites suspected that he feared the madness which was said to run in his family.

At Gorki, Lenin fought with death. "There is so much work for me to do," he kept repeating. Stricken with almost complete aphasia, he forced himself to learn to speak again, helped by his devoted wife, Krupskaya, and his sister, Maria Ulianova. Unable to move his right hand, he learned to write with his left.

Eminent physicians from all over the world were summoned to Lenin's bedside. There was little they could do. Professor Foerster, caught by Lenin's personality, would not leave him. "I saw myself," he told me once, "as his second in a terrible duel. My science told me that the case was hopeless, but it seemed to me incredible that Lenin should die." And once again his patient rallied and grew better.

It brings a lump into my throat to remember that Lenin, in his deep illness, thought of me and sent me a message through Professor Foerster. "Tell young Hammer," he gasped painfully, "I have not forgotten him and wish him well. If he has difficulties, tell him to be sure and let me know."

Lenin needs no praise from me. History will give him his place among the great of the world, but for myself, I am proud to think that I talked with him, that I was able to earn even a small measure of his approval and that he took my hand in friendship.

By Christmas of 1923 Lenin was sufficiently recovered to attend a hunting party, sitting propped with pillows on a sleigh. He talked more easily now and the drawn grimace on the right side of his face had almost vanished. On Christmas Day he gave a party in the big house for the children of estate employees and the nearby village. There was a Christmas tree, of course, and lighted candles and gifts for all. "Outworn superstition," say the Bolsheviks of a later day and try to banish Christmas from their children's hearts. Lenin was more tolerant.

Three weeks later, on January 21, 1924, death struck him, suddenly and without pain. As they bore him from the house at Gorki, to the greatest pageantry of mourning modern Russia had ever known, the Christmas tree, with its tinsel and guttered candles, standing in the large hall looked down upon his passing.

Professor Foerster brought us the news of Lenin's death late at night. He was all broken up; the end had been so sudden and he had hoped against hope until the last.

Lenin's funeral ceremonies will never be forgotten in Russia. I am one of the very few people left alive who witnessed them, which makes me the object of the deepest curiosity and reverence in Russia today. People everywhere want to shake my hand because I shook Lenin's hand and saw him laid to rest in Red Square.

I doubt whether there was ever anything so simple yet so tremendously impressive as those ceremonies for Lenin. In quick succession, from 1982 to 1985, I attended the funeral ceremonies in Red Square for Leonid Brezhnev, Yuri Andropov and Konstantin Chernenko. Moving and solemn as those funereal pageants were, they did not begin to approach the massive outpouring of grief which attended Lenin's passing.

A group of Lenin's nearest associates met the train bringing his coffin at a station on the outskirts of Moscow and carried it for five and a half miles through the streets on their own shoulders, changing relays every half mile. An artillery gun carriage had been provided, with six superb black horses. Lenin's friends waved it aside—they and only they should bear their leader's body.

He was laid in state in the many-columned hall of what had formerly been the Nobles' Club of Moscow and was now the headquarters of the Union of Labor Federations. I was to see the bodies of Brezhnev, Andropov and Chernenko lying in state in this same building sixty years later. Here, as if sleeping, Lenin lay for seventy-two hours, with four motionless watchers standing at the corners of his bier. They were changed every quarter of an hour, so many and eager were those who wished to share that deathwatch. Meanwhile, in endless procession, day and night, the people of Moscow filed through the hall to pay their final tribute. Three-quarters of a million men, women and children formed that silent river, flowing through without a break.

It was a period of intense cold, between thirty and forty below zero Fahrenheit. The average time of waiting outside before the public could enter the hall was five hours. The long lines extended for miles, moving forward at slow intervals. Great wood fires burned every hundred meters, and at night it was a weird and striking spectacle: the dark masses of people, whose breath rose up like fog, the lurid flames and the drifting clouds of smoke. From villages fifty miles away, peasants came on foot, to pay homage to the man who had given them the land for which they had hungered for centuries. From the distant cities of Russia, those in authority came speeding in special trains, cursing each delay for fear they might not arrive in time.

No king or emperor or pope ever received such final homage. Strangely enough, those Bolsheviks who professed to believe neither in God nor resurrection followed the old Russian belief that saints remain indestructible until the Judgment Day. They had Lenin's body embalmed and placed it in a small but beautiful mausoleum at the foot of the great red-brown walls of the Kremlin in Red Square.

The mausoleum was built in two and a half days, with constant shifts of workmen toiling day and night. On the morning of the funeral, a Sunday, Lenin's body was placed in the mausoleum. On the top of this strange building, part Egyptian pyramid, part dream of Cubist architecture, was a small gallery where Soviet leaders took their places during the funeral. The massive and forbidding edifice which dominates the square today, and upon the top of which the members of the Politburo always appear on great occasions of state, was not erected until some years after Lenin's death. There Lenin still lies, as if asleep, guarded by soldiers with fixed bayonets at the head and foot of his bier, while pilgrims pass through to see him, thousands every day, including those from the farthest boundaries of Russia.

The day of the funeral, after Lenin's body had been borne by his dearest friends to its last resting place, the garrison of Moscow and the organized masses of the workers marched through the square in dense ranks. I pictured Trotsky, still Warlord of the Red Army, standing in the little group on the mausoleum gallery. As his legions roared salute, his face would have lit with pride. There was a man who had given of his best to defend the Revolution, who had done more than any other to make the Red Army a victorious fighting force. But he lacked Lenin's selfless absorption in the cause. Although devoid of the least trace of personal greed, Trotsky was a man consumed by ambition. He always wanted to play a big role and be a shining figure.

On the same occasion here was another man standing amid the little group on the mausoleum. He made no speeches, received no salutes; he was quiet and unobtrusive, but his eyes were keen and watchful. His name was Joseph Dzhugashvili, whom the world came to know under his Bolshevik pseudonym of Stalin.

I would never have believed at that time that I would see the day when this unassuming man, who continually avoided the spotlight of publicity, would become the most powerful leader of Russia. Meanwhile, of course, the Warlord Trotsky, deprived of his power and position, would be sent out of the country into exile—eventually to be assassinated in Mexico on the orders, it is said, of that same slight and unassuming figure, one of the most terrible of all the tyrants of Russian history.

12

Big Business and the Soviet

In *As I See It,* John Paul Getty tells a story about me. Like everybody who is reputed to be wealthy, Paul was constantly besieged by people who wanted to snatch a piece of his fortune for themselves, or to learn "the magic formula" for instant riches. It made him impatient to be nagged by people who insisted that there must be some "secret" by which he had made his fortune—rather than the more obvious qualities of hard work, ingenuity, resourcefulness and care.

Paul remembered that I had once been approached at a party by somebody who had asked me the "tell-me-the-secret-of-making-millions" question.

According to his version, I furrowed my brow and said, "Actually, there's nothing to it. You merely wait for a revolution in Russia. Then you pack all your warm clothes and go there. Once you've arrived, you start making the rounds of the government bureaus that are concerned with trade, with buying and selling. There probably won't be more than two or three hundred of them. . . ." At this point my questioner angrily muttered something and turned away.

My answer was not entirely a joke. The nine years I spent in Russia in the twenties were packed with the most strenuous and taxing efforts, with a dozen and one business ventures which, like all businesses, had their ups and downs and their successes and failures. I have gathered together here a chapter of stories about my business activities and experiences in that time. Dull it wasn't.

In the winter of 1922 I made a second visit to the mines at Alapayevsk, accompanied by my brother Victor. At that time trains ran only every three or four days between the mainline stations of Ekaterinburg and Alapayevsk, one hundred miles to the north. We arrived in Ekaterinburg to find that we had just missed a connection, so I decided to make the trip by sleigh and we engaged three sleighs with two horses each. A wonderful journey ensued, traveling day and night through the snowbound forests, with three relays of horses en route. Often there was no regular track, and the sleepy driver left it to the horses to find their own way.

The driver sat in front and we lay back, swathed in furs on a couch of hay. Night traveling was a weird business. The forests echoed with the howling of wolves, and from time to time we could see their eyes gleaming as they kept pace with us among the trees.

Like so many American boys, I gained my first knowledge of Russia from a story that I had read in a primer about a pack of wolves pursuing a Russian family driving in their sleigh through the woods. As the wolves grew more daring and leaped up at the horses' throats, the unhappy father threw first one child, then another, to the ferocious pack, thus finally saving his own life and that of his wife and his eldest son. That story came back to me as I saw the fiery eyes of the wolves in the forest and occasionally glimpsed a dark shape slinking between the trees.

Suddenly Victor grabbed my arm.

"Where is our driver?" he cried.

I looked up. The driver's seat was empty and the reins were hanging limply on the trotting horses' backs. We turned the sleigh around and retraced our steps. The wolves, it seemed to my anxious imagination, were closing in upon us. A few hundred yards back we found our driver, a Tartar, who had evidently gone to sleep and fallen from his seat when the sleigh struck a root. He was the most terrified Tartar you ever saw, quite certain that the wolves were going to eat him. He leaped back into his seat with cries of thankfulness and lashed the horses to a gallop.

Some years later, in Moscow, I met the Managing Director of a New York fur corporation who had spent twenty years of his life in Alaska and northern Siberia. As we were speaking of furs and pelts, the conversation turned to wolves and I told him of that dreadful night ride through the Ural forests. He grinned sarcastically.

"So I suppose they ate you," he said. "Or maybe you threw them the Tartar?"

"Well," I said defensively, "it was a close call."

He laughed aloud. "In all my experience," he said, "I've never known a case where wolves attacked human beings unless they were wounded or dying. And mind you, I'm not speaking of your little wolves in European Russia, but the grey Alaskan or Siberian wolves, which sometimes are as big as a Shetland pony. They are, all of them, cowardly, and all these stories are bunk. Neither you nor your Tartar were in the slightest danger at any moment."

I was rather indignant. "The Tartar was scared enough," I said, "and he ought to know. He had lived in those parts all his life."

"Tartars," the fur man jeered. "They don't know anything. I tell you all those stories of wolves attacking sleighs are nonsense. Of course, a mad wolf—and they do go mad sometimes—is as dangerous as a mad dog, or worse, but that's all. What's more, wolves *don't* hunt in packs—never more than four or five together, and then it's just the sire and dam and the pups of the last litter."

Whether or not he was right about wolves, I certainly met something extremely dangerous on that trip—namely, *samogon,* real Russian firewater, a sixty-proof spirit distilled from grain or potatoes by peasants to replace vodka, which was, for a brief time, forbidden after the war. *Samogon* is not clear like vodka, but a pale, cloudy fluid with the kick of a mule. When we stopped to change horses they gave it to us "to keep the cold out." It certainly did that job. It went down like liquid fire and made me gasp for breath. "White lightning" is a reasonably apt name for this demonic potion. I haven't come across *samogon* in Russia for sixty years, but I'll bet it's still being distilled out in the backwoods.

The Ural town of Alapayevsk, near which our asbestos concession was situated, was previously known to me only as the scene of a tragedy where a number of the highest figures of the Romanov regime met a terrible death during the worst "terror" period in the summer of 1918. They included at least two members of the Romanov family and a number of nobles formerly connected with the court. As with the Czar and his family, the reason for their execution was the rapid advance of the Siberian White forces westward. Their bodies were found in the same deserted mine which we had taken over, by the Whites, who gave them a public funeral at Ekaterinburg, exacting terrible reprisals from the local population.

Our concession included a large area of wood and meadowland covering several hundred acres. There was excellent fishing in streams and lakes and hunting in the woods. The asbestos mine was a large open hole about one thousand feet in diameter, graded in terraces down to the bottom, which was about one hundred feet below the surface.

Never in my life have I seen anything so old-fashioned as the way this property was worked. The workers used to pick away at the ore with cumbersome hand drills, usually taking about three days to bore a hole deep enough for a dynamite charge. Then the fragments of ore would be carried up in baskets on the men's backs to a higher terrace, where they would sit in rows with little hammers, chipping away to remove the stone from the ore. When the ore was cleaned it was transported by peasant carts to the railroad station, ten miles away. Of course, during the time when the peasants were busy or bad weather made the roads impassable, the ore was not transported but just piled up at the mine.

Labor conditions, prior to the Revolution, had been atrocious. The workers were herded in filthy barracks, like animals. They worked twelve hours a day six days a week, for an average wage of fifteen rubles a month, then about seven dollars. The foreman used whips to drive these "cattle," and cases of violent assault or even murder were not uncommon. On Sundays everyone got drunk! That was the only relaxation.

In prewar days the mine had been a government property, and under the tariff conditions then in force ought to have been most profitable. In point of fact, a privately owned competing enterprise in the same neighborhood had arranged by a little judicious bribery to prevent the exploitation of the richest ore. Thus, buildings were erected over one vein so that it could not be worked, and another equally rich section was chosen as a dump for the waste stones and hidden by hundreds of tons of debris.

The mechanical methods we introduced were a nine-day wonder. Peasants came from fifty miles away to see our compressed-air drills at work, but the greatest success was our power-driver sawmill. Until it arrived, local people had laboriously sawed planks by hand from a tree; it took two men a full day to make a single plank. Our four-bladed automatic saws cut a tree into planks in a few minutes. That sawmill proved a godsend to the whole neighborhood. Peasants would haul logs from miles around, although they could have bought the planks direct from us at a trifling cost, just for the pleasure of seeing them sliced, as one put it, "like a knife cuts butter."

We installed electric power and light for the whole community, which caused a sensation since none of the local people had ever seen an electric bulb before. At first, they tried to light their fires with bulbs unscrewed from their fittings and were totally mystified to get no result. Other people journeyed from hundreds of miles to see this modern miracle.

We quickly substituted mechanical crushers for the old system of nicking away stone from the ore with little hammers and put in a narrow-gauge railroad to transport the ore from the mine. According to the terms of our contract, we were required to build houses for the workers, provide schools and a hospital and dispensary and certain other facilities.

I have explained how we brought in food for the workers, but there was another item hardly less important—clothing. Our workers had to endure the rigors of the local climate with rags and tatters on their backs and sometimes on their feet, too; or they were shod with the poorest and flimsiest boots. We had to do something to help them.

In New York my brother Harry purchased a large quantity of American war stocks that were sold after the armistice, and he sent them to us in Alapayevsk, with the most comical results. There, in the heart of Soviet Russia, a visitor would find one man dressed in a full uniform of the Marine Corps; another would have an American tunic above his baggy Russian breeches and felt boots; a third would wear an American Army cap that contrasted strangely with his sheepskin coat. They even cut up coats and made them into clothes for the children, and although much of the material would not have been considered first quality in the United States, it made a tremendous impression in Alapayevsk, where everyone thought the American Army must all be millionaires if they could wear clothes like that.

Victor remained at the mine when I returned to Moscow. I told him that I wanted him to learn all about the business and be my main contact there. In fact, my main motive was to keep him out of the clutches of "the Black Panther," a Moscow woman for whom he had fallen head over heels, regardless of her well-known ability to eat boys like him before breakfast. Victor labored duly hard at the mine and put up with his exile without too much complaint for about eighteen months. While he was there, not long after Lenin's death, a reporter from *Pravda* visited the mine, interviewed Victor and Leo Wolff and wrote a long and vitriolic attack on us, bitterly portraying us as rapacious American capitalists. The reporter might have made a convincing case if he had gotten a few facts straight. For a start, he thought Victor was me! *Pravda* would never have dared to print this attack while our patron, Lenin, lived. Its appearance shows how much more difficult our position became after Lenin's death.

The asbestos proposition did not prove as successful as we had hoped. There was a big fall in world prices of asbestos, owing to overproduction in Canada, whose mines had been greatly developed during and immediately after the war. As business conditions in Russia improved, however, the demand for low-grade asbestos as insulating material for boilers, pipes and refrigerating plants and for fireproofing generally began to grow, so that by the end of 1925 our concession, which covered a period of twenty-five years, did at last begin to show a profit.

I also had something less than a success when I purchased an export bank in Revel, Estonia, to handle the accounts of our asbestos concession and other trade with the Soviet Union. I believed that it would be a good way to avoid the complications of handling our business through American and European banks, and would allow us to avoid the stigma of being represented by Soviet banking institutions.

The bank was called the Harju Bank. I put my uncle, Alexander Gomberg, in charge of it. He was an excellent businessman but he had no previous experience of banking. He didn't notice when officers of the bank colluded with some of its customers to make loans of the bank's money.

I wasn't able to keep an eye on the bank's business day to day, and it rapidly got out of hand. By May 1925 we were faced with a considerable emergency, with a raft of bad loans drifting helplessly in a financial tempest of embezzlement and misappropriation. The only recourse was to take the loss and close the bank.

Corruption was always rampant in Russia. Greasing palms and scratching backs was part of the daily routine of life in Czarist Russia. Even after the Revolution, especially after Lenin's introduction of NEP, one of the worst aspects of the corruption was dishonesty and the readiness to accept bribes on the part of some state officials and businessmen. As a relatively naive and inexperienced young man, I was rather surprised and perplexed when I first came across corruption among certain civil servants. After a short time I developed a nose for graft which was as sure and reliable as a hound dog's.

In the spring of 1923, for instance, a state trading department called the *Gostorg* was organized, and we, as importers of American machinery, had close relations with the department. We also suffered from its constant obstructiveness and an endless succession of difficulties, often on the most trivial pretext. I decided to get to the root of the matter and made an appointment for Boris Mishell and myself to see the Director of the *Gostorg,* whose name was Cagan.

He kept us waiting for nearly an hour in his anteroom, but finally received us quite affably, and instead of proceeding to business began to talk about the difficulty of getting things from abroad, and the fact that I or some of our people were constantly crossing the frontier.

"My father-in-law is a doctor," he said, "but he can't get rubber gloves for operating. Can you have a few pairs brought in?"

"Why, yes," I said. "That's easy enough. We will be happy to help you."

This seemed to me a simple courtesy, but he at once began to hint pretty strongly that our difficulties would vanish if we showed ourselves "a little more accommodating" in other respects.

"Hello," I thought, "this smells like graft." So I replied vaguely to Mr. Cagan, as if I had failed to understand him, and he did not press the subject further. Our difficulties continued, however, and I knew that we had gained nothing by our interview. I wrote letters and tried to get satisfaction but without success.

Then one day I heard that Cagan had been arrested by the OGPU, the Secret Political Police, and his apartment searched. I was told they found no less than a hundred thousand pounds in English currency. In addition to his work in the *Gostorg,* Cagan had had power to charter freight cars for the transport of goods. He had, it appeared, run a regular business of moving freight for private speculators at a time when transportation was urgently needed to bring food supplies to the hungry populace; hence his wealth.

Investigation showed that he had arranged to "visit" Germany on a purchasing mission for the *Gostorg,* where he would have been able to settle and live comfortably on his ill-gotten gains. He was tried on a charge of treason under an article of the Soviet penal code concerned with abuse of position for personal profit by state officials, and he was condemned to be shot. When it was known that his appeal for clemency had been refused, and while he was waiting for the sentence to be carried out, his wife was allowed to visit him in prison. She brought him poison and he cheated the firing squad.

In those days, perhaps even more than now, it was necessary to watch your step most carefully if you were doing business in Russia. Another story illustrates this point. One day in the summer of 1923, a rather well dressed young man, speaking excellent English, came into my office in Moscow with a letter of introduction to suggest that we interest ourselves in building houses in the city or repairing damaged buildings.

He said that his brother, who was the President of the new Commercial and Industrial Bank, would supply credit for this scheme at nominal rates so that it would not be necessary to bring in *valuta*— foreign exchange—from abroad.

The plan sounded fine; he gave facts and figures to show a large annual profit, but there was something about him and his project which did not seem quite right to me and, after some consideration, we refused. Two or three years later he and his brother were arrested on a charge of misuse of funds and condemned to five and three years' imprisonment respectively. We had been lucky.

The brother of the man I met had made quite a success of his banking operations; the charge on which he was convicted was mainly of a technical nature. What he had done was to lend money at a nominal rate of interest for such building operations as had been proposed to me.

If he had lent to a state or even a foreign organization at such rates, he would not have committed a crime, but to have benefited his brother in this way was a punishable offense. Moreover, the man was a Communist and had behaved in a way which shocked the "moral conscience of the party." He had a nice villa in the country, valuable horses and a carriage which had formerly belonged to a nobleman, and gave parties where pretty ladies from the ballet were very much in evidence.

In any Western country this kind of behavior is far from a crime, but in Russia Communists were and are supposed to set an example of modesty and propriety—although party officials have always been permitted to indulge their tastes for luxuries as long as they do it discreetly and don't exceed the level of "perks" permitted for their particular station.

The banker was also the subject of unfounded rumors that as a member of the Moscow Commission, which in those days determined the rate of exchange for Soviet currency, he might have let his brother know what the rate would be so that he could speculate on the "black bourse."

This black bourse was one of the most curious phenomena in Moscow. Theoretically, private dealing in exchange was forbidden, but actually one of the passages in the big GUM department store buildings on Red Square was reserved for money changers. It was done quite openly—there were even soldiers to guard the large sums being exchanged. My brother Victor was our representative on the black bourse. He would offer stacks of new bills in all denominations in exchange for the rubles that we needed for our current operating expenses. There was always a better rate for a new hundred-dollar bill, probably because it was less bulky than smaller bills and easier to hide.

A man would have a bag of gold coins, for instance, perhaps three hundred pieces worth ten rubles each. Without any attempt at secrecy he would offer to sell them for Soviet rubles or American dollars or English pounds. Representatives of the State Bank used to attend these meetings and buy or sell their own and foreign currency as the occasion demanded. The area in the passage where they conducted these operations was barred off by a sort of fence from the public, and one had to pay the equivalent of fifty cents to enter. The woman who sat at the little wicker gate, selling the entrance tickets, used to keep a loaded revolver lying on the table in front of her. In those days the possession of money was still dangerous in Moscow.

The black bourse actually served a valuable purpose in the stabilization of Soviet currency which, although the world may not realize it, was one of the miracles of modern finance. It is customary to talk about the recovery of the mark after its slump in the twenties as an exceptional achievement—but Germany was a modern industrial country and enjoyed the all-powerful aid of American banks, whereas Russia accomplished her stabilization alone.

The credit is due to two men: Mr. Grigori Sokolnikov, then Minister of Finance, who later became head of the All-Russian Oil Syndicate; and Mr. Shineman, then President of the State Bank.

In the winter of 1921, after our asbestos concession had been signed, I went to see Mr. Shineman, who had just been appointed to his position as head of the newly formed bank. I found him in a small room in a building on the Kusnetzky Most. The place was being reconstructed and I had to pick my way carefully through wheelbarrows of bricks and mortar. In these modest circumstances Mr. Shineman was busy engaging personnel for what later became a truly gigantic enterprise.

He seemed surprisingly young for such a post, but impressed me greatly by his optimism. We talked for a time about the possibilities of transferring funds from America to Russia. Then he said, smiling, "I heard, Doctor Hammer, you are the first American concessionaire in Russia. Don't you think you would also like to be the first depositor in the Soviet State Bank?"

It so happened that I was just beginning to feel the need of Soviet currency, so I produced my letter of credit and opened an account in dollars—I forget how many millions of rubles my first deposit of five thousand dollars was worth—and received a passbook numbered "I."

At that time the total value of Soviet currency, which was depreciating rapidly, could not have been worth much more than thirty million dollars in terms of foreign *valuta*. By an ingenious system of buying and selling on the black bourse, in addition, of course, to the rapid growth of prosperity which followed NEP, the State Bank was able by the middle of 1924 to replace *sovesnaks*, as the depreciated notes were termed, by an issue of *chervonetz*, gold rubles, worth the prewar figure of fifty-two American cents. By the end of 1928 the total currency issue was approximately 1800 million rubles with a value in *valuta* of more than 900 million dollars.

On my next trip to America I arrived in New York aboard the White Star liner *Majestic*, on June 13, 1923, to be greeted by newspaper reporters who had heard of my dealings with Lenin. They gathered round me in a very excited crush, shouting questions and talking over one another, like the great fraternity of journalists the whole world over. I wasn't accustomed then, as I am today, to facing the babble of the news media and I had to make an effort to control my nerves and try to speak calmly. Looking today at the report of this press conference, which was carried in the *New York Times* the following day, I don't think I did too badly for one who had just turned twenty-four.

I said to the reporters: "When I conferred with officials of the Soviet government, I told them that I was a capitalist, that I was out to make money, but entertained no idea of grabbing their land or their empire. They said, in effect, 'We understand you didn't come here for love. As long as you do not mix in our politics, we will give you our help.' And that is the basis on which I conducted negotiations."

It is curious for me to read these words today and see that I have been explaining myself, in exactly the same terms, in answer to the same kinds of questions for over sixty years. Western reporters are always asking me how I describe myself in Russia, and I always reply that I tell the Russians that I am a capitalist, that I believe our system is better than theirs and that I want us to coexist peacefully in order that history may decide which of our systems is better. If my words haven't changed much over sixty years, neither have the reporters.

In the summer of 1923 a great Agricultural Exposition was held in Moscow, in the grounds of what had formerly been the Sans Souci palace which Catherine the Great had given to her lover, Count Orlov. Our company made a great effort at this exposition and I am proud to remember that the American flag floated over our pavilion. By this time we had arranged to represent a considerable number of American firms, in addition to the Ford agency, so we displayed all kinds of American-made machinery as well as the Fordson tractors and Ford cars.

There had been some trouble about our Ford cars in connection with Henry Ford's allegedly anti-Soviet attitudes and the strongly anti-Semitic tone adopted by his *Dearborn Independent* newspaper. A shipment of two hundred cars intended for our company was held up at Riga as the Soviet officials declined to give permits routing it to Moscow. The reason they gave was that the cars were not made strongly enough to stand up to Russian roads.

Since these cars were consigned to the War Department, I appealed to Trotsky to help us. He immediately gave instructions to have the shipment released and said curtly that whatever might be Henry Ford's attitude with regard to the Bolshevik question in general, and anti-Semitism in particular, no true Marxist would allow sentiment to interfere with business. His words startled me at the time, but they wouldn't surprise me today. Throughout my many years of dealing with top politicians around the world, I have usually found that the ones who are supposed to be prisoners of a rigid ideology are the most flexible and coolly pragmatic in their judgments—a very strange paradox, but a fact nonetheless.

Sometime later in America I told Ford himself about this incident, and he very firmly declared that he had no anti-Semitic prejudice.

"I have lots of excellent Jewish workers and some of my best agents are Jews," he said. "But I have the strongest feelings against a certain group of Jewish bankers who tried to take advantage of me when they thought I was in need of their assistance. I do not like bankers as a class, but this particular group of bankers I abhor. That is the true story of my so-called anti-Semitism."

His reply contains an unpleasant echo of the standard anti-Semite's line: "Some of my best friends are Jews, but . . ." All I can say is that he always dealt straightforwardly with me, and with my uncle Alexander Gomberg, and leave it at that.

On July 14, 1923, we signed a concession contract for Allied American Corporation with Mr. Frumkin, Acting Commissar of the Foreign Trade Monopoly Department. The Commissar, Leonid Krassin, had told me that I could obtain the contract on condition that I guaranteed to export from Russia the equivalent of our annual imports from America. The minimum sum of export and import which we guaranteed was $1,200,000, making a total turnover of $2,400,000 per annum. The contract was yearly with a clause providing for renewal.

In the two years, 1923–1925, we had a total turnover of $12,500,000. Imports chiefly consisted of machinery, automobiles, tractors and other means of production. Our exports included a great variety of products, but our main trade was in furs. We established a network of fur-gathering stations across huge areas of the Urals and Siberia and conducted a trade which was like the old days of the West and the Hudson's Bay Company.

Trappers and hunters came to our stations in the late fall to collect advances in credit for their work, which were paid in the form of food, clothing, rifles and bullets. In the spring the hunters returned to the station with their haul of pelts and negotiated the balance of their settlement in cash. In this way we acquired vast stores of beaver, mink and sable, which eventually found their way onto the backs of the elegant ladies of New York, Paris and London.

Something changed in 1925, however. Before the termination of the second year of our agreement, I went again to see Leonid Krassin in his office on the Ilinka. He explained to me, cordially but quite firmly, that the development of Soviet trade abroad through their own agencies such as *Arcos* and the newly formed *Amtorg* made it henceforth undesirable to do business through foreigners. However, he added, that did not mean that the Soviet authorities were blind to the great services we had been able to render in building up Russian-American trade during the difficult period of organization. He expressed the hope that we would find other but no less profitable fields of enterprise in Russia.

Krassin's main target was my contract with Henry Ford. He wanted me to step aside so that the Soviets could deal with Ford directly. They had already approached Henry Ford with this suggestion and he had turned them down, saying: "Do all my business with Armand Hammer. He is my authorized agent."

Now Krassin was determined to get me out of the way. He expressed his determination in the form of a blandishment. "You can have any concession you desire," he said, "if you will surrender the Ford agency."

I said that we had been approached by an English shipbuilding corporation with a view to the sale of shipping to the Soviet.

Krassin frowned. "No," he said. "We hope to build our own ships at home. What is needed now, Doctor Hammer, in this country, is industrial production.

"Why don't you interest yourselves in industry?" he went on. "There are many articles which we have to import from abroad that ought to be produced here." I said that I would consider the suggestion and let him know as soon as possible if I had any proposal to make.

I gave the question a lot of thought but I found it difficult to make up my mind. The problem was soon solved by an accident. I went into a stationery store to buy an indelible pencil. The salesman showed me an ordinary lead pencil that would have cost 2 or 3 cents in America and, to my astonishment, he said the price was fifty kopeks—26 cents.

"Oh! But I want an indelible pencil," I said.

At first he shook his head, then he appeared to relent.

"As you are a foreigner, I will let you have one, but our stock is so limited that as a rule we sell them only to regular customers who buy paper and copybooks as well." He went to the stockroom and came back with the simplest type of indelible pencil. The price was a ruble, then worth 52 cents.

I made further inquiries and discovered that there was an immense shortage of pencils in Russia, as they all had to be imported from Germany. Before the war there had been a small pencil factory in Moscow run by some Germans, but it had ceased production. Plans had been made to remodel and enlarge it as a state pencil factory of the Soviet but, at that time, in the summer of 1925, they had not advanced beyond the project stage.

I decided that here was my opportunity. I arranged an interview with Yoffe, Vice President of the Central Concessions Committee under Trotsky, who by that time had already been removed as Commissar of War because of his opposition to Stalin. Yoffe was one of the ablest of the Bolshevik leaders. He had been a close personal friend of Trotsky's for many years and was trusted by Lenin. Poor Yoffe! His fate was perhaps the most tragic of any of the Soviet leaders.

As the struggle between Trotsky and Stalin intensified, Yoffe's attachment to Trotsky brought him increasing trouble and distress, which preyed upon his health. In the autumn of 1927 he made an appeal to the authorities for money to allow him and his wife to go to Germany for further treatment. His request was denied, though he was offered treatment in a Kremlin hospital. The expulsion of Trotsky from the Communist Party proved the final blow to Yoffe's nerves, already shattered by months of terrible suffering which not even morphine could alleviate.

In November he shot himself, leaving a pathetic letter to Trotsky, which was seized by the authorities but afterward published in the monthly *Bolshevik*. One of his friends told me that he chose that moment for his suicide to enable Trotsky's group to make speeches at his funeral and thus get access to public opinion which was denied them in the official press. Stalin was too clever. Although Yoffe was buried with military honors, the hour chosen was twelve o'clock the day after his death, when the people of Moscow were at work. Although Trotsky, Kamenev and other opposition leaders were allowed to make speeches, there were no more than a few hundred people present, nearly all of them confirmed oppositionists already.

All of that lay two years ahead when I met Yoffe, who was a short, thickset man with keen dark eyes and one of the quickest minds I ever came across. He most warmly welcomed my suggestion for a pencil factory, but asked at once whether pencil-making was not largely a German monopoly and whether I would not have difficulty getting the business started. I said cheerfully that I would cross that bridge when I came to it, but in the meantime I wished to work out with him details of a concession.

I said that we were prepared to put up a cash deposit of fifty thousand dollars as a guarantee that we would begin production within twelve months after signature of the contract, if the Concessions Committee would agree to our conditions. Further, we would obligate ourselves to produce a million dollars' worth of pencils in the first operating year. Yoffe looked rather surprised, but he said that on that basis we could be assured of the most sincere cooperation on the part of the Concessions Committee.

He was as good as his word. The concession agreement was worked out in the record time for Russia of three and a half months (a concession for the development of the Lena goldfields took nearly two years to negotiate; and the Japanese fisheries concession in Far Eastern Soviet waters required almost as long).

Our deal was done despite great opposition from the Russian state pencil concern—the one which had failed to get started in the factory previously owned by the Germans. They inaugurated a press campaign against "foreign capitalists who try to exploit Russia's wealth." I paid no attention to it, beyond reminding the concessions committee of our cash guarantee and asserting that despite the big start the state concern had over us we would be first into large-scale production.

In October 1925 the agreement was signed by Litvinov for the

Commissariat of Foreign Affairs and Piatikov, who later became President of the State Bank, on behalf of the Concessions Committee. Our promise of a fifty-thousand-dollar cash guarantee became a clause in the agreement, and the money was duly deposited in the State Bank. Then, at the beginning of November 1925, I left Moscow for Germany.

I had obtained an important and, as events were to prove, a most profitable concession contract, but I did not know the first thing about manufacturing pencils, so I went to Nuremberg, the heart of the German pencil industry, to learn.

Nuremberg, which was also known in those days as the town "where the toys come from," was like a picture in an ancient book. It was a medieval town with many-gabled houses and narrow winding streets. From old-fashioned inns hung painted signs that had been new when America was discovered. Over the central town behind its old-world battlements there brooded an atmosphere of peace and rest, and the stillness of great age. Yet Nuremberg was the center of the modern pencil industry, which had been developed from modest beginnings by the Faber family, in whose hands it still remained.

More than two hundred and fifty years ago, the first Johann Faber made the first lead pencil in Nuremberg. By 1925 the little town had become surrounded by up-to-date pencil factories, all owned by the Faber family or its offshoots and connections. Largest of all was the factory of A. W. Faber, direct descendant of Johann, at a little town named Fürth, a few miles outside Nuremberg.

No prince or feudal baron ever ruled his estates more completely than the firm A. W. Faber ruled Fürth. Its word was law and everything—municipality, police, public utilities—was under its control.

Many years before I ever saw Fürth, the firm had decided that a railroad, or even trolley cars, might bring in undesirables, might make its workers discontented and interfere with the even tenor of their services to the House of Faber; so the railroad passed Fürth by and the stranger who went within its gates had to come by carriage or auto or on foot.

The other pencil factories in the area were strongholds, too. Most jobs within them had been held by the same families for generations, passed from father to son in a long line of patient craftsmen, each perfect in his job. In their jealous eagerness to retain the monopoly of pencil-making, the Fabers had been careful never to let any of their subordinates know more than one part of their complicated organization; knowledge of the whole was reserved for members of the family and a few trusted adherents.

After I had spent a week in Nuremberg, I knew no more of the pencil business than on the day of my arrival, except that I had begun to realize the difficulties I was up against. If I could have canceled my concession at that moment, I think I would have been ready to do so. Just when it seemed completely hopeless, a lucky chance opened the door for me.

Through a letter of introduction to one of the local bankers, I hired an engineer named George Baier, who held an important position in the Nuremberg affiliate of Eberhard Faber USA, one of the principal local pencil factories. When young, he had learned the pencil-manufacturing business in one of Nuremberg's factories, but being of an adventurous disposition, he had accepted an offer to build a pencil factory in Russia. That was shortly before the war. When the war began, he was trapped in Russia and interned, then released, but he had not been permitted to return to Germany, so he had married a Russian wife and found other employment in Russia until the conclusion of hostilities allowed him to return home.

But he was not welcomed back. His former employers said that he had been disloyal to them! For years the man could not obtain a job, and, finally, when they thought he had learned his lesson, the boycott was lifted and he was allowed once more to work. Such treatment may sound incredible in this day and age, but in Nuremberg it was common practice. I discovered the case of one foreman who, after twenty-five years of service, accepted an offer to go to South America to work in a newly opened pencil factory. He obtained a passport to leave Germany, but his departure was actually forbidden by the Nuremberg police! For ten long years he remained in Nuremberg, unable to get a job in the one trade he knew.

This tyranny backfired against those who exercised it and worked in my favor. I found plenty of men eager to exchange their old bondage for a freer life. In the course of two months I was able to engage the staff I needed. I offered them the opportunity to earn far more money than they would ever have accumulated in Fürth. George Baier was to receive a salary of ten thousand dollars a year plus a bonus of a few cents for every gross of pencils we produced. Not long after we began production, that bonus was running at several times his salary. I struck similar deals with the other men for pay based on performance.

Hiring the men was not the end of my difficulties. It proved necessary to secure their passports in Berlin, where the Faber influence was not great enough to cause trouble. Then we had to engage in an elaborate charade to obtain Russian visas for the men we had hired: they could not be issued in Berlin without word getting to Faber. We took the men and their families to Finland, ostensibly on holiday, and got the visas issued in Helsinki. Our workers then journeyed directly to Moscow.

In the meantime I placed orders for the needed machines and prepared a program for our factory-to-be. Many of the men I hired were married, with families, so I had to promise them homes with gardens such as they had had in Nuremberg, schools for their children and the comforts of German life which they feared (reasonably enough) might be lacking in Moscow.

I even agreed to supply them with good German beer, but fortunately they found Russian beer sufficiently to their liking.

Then I went to Birmingham, England, to make similar arrangements for the pen department of our factory. Originally we had not thought of manufacturing anything but pencils, but the concession committee was so insistent that we should also manufacture steel pens that we finally agreed to do so.

To my astonishment I found much the same state of affairs in Birmingham as in Nuremberg. There too, it was a closed industry, with most of its workers trained from childhood under semifeudal conditions. In Birmingham, however, I had more success among the younger men, many of whom had been disturbed in their routine of life by the war and were willing to seek new adventures abroad.

Taught by experience, I began my reconnaissance in Birmingham with an advertisement in the local newspapers for an engineer and, after picking my man, I was able to engage my skilled workers through him. After ordering machinery, I left for Moscow, where I arrived early in 1926, less than three months after the concession had been signed. At least I felt we had made a good beginning.

The next job was to find a suitable location for our factory. Two or three years earlier I could have secured a modern factory with ease, at a nominal cost, but the stimulus given to industry by the New Economic Policy, and the stabilization of the Soviet currency on a gold basis, had brought about a very different state of affairs. After an exhaustive search, I heard of an abandoned soap works on the outskirts of the city, near the Moscow River. From every point of view except buildings, it was an admirable site. It included more than a square mile of land, with ample space for the houses, gardens and schools I had agreed to build, and enough room for any developments we might later contemplate. However, the buildings were mere shells without roofs or floors, little better than ruins.

Within a week I had secured a ten-year lease—that was the duration of our concession—and set a thousand men to work. The buildings were rapidly repaired and a steam-heating plant ordered from Germany was installed. By April it was possible to begin setting up the machinery that was now arriving from abroad. Meanwhile, we built cottages for the German and English workers and laid out their gardens.

We built a clubhouse, a school, a restaurant and a first aid station, later to be transformed into a hospital. It was a regular little city. The school I built is still in use today, laboring under the unwieldy nomenclature of "The 647 Kindergarten and Creche of the Moscow Writing Appliances Plant."

With regard to the machinery, I had taken the precaution of insisting that each firm send its own experts to attend to the setting up of the machines. Each piece was numbered and the whole program had been worked out beforehand to the minutest detail. This was an indispensable factor in Russia, where foreign machinery of the latest type was always a sealed book to Russian workers and engineers. The Soviet government lost countless hundreds of thousands, one might almost say millions, of dollars by attempting to install foreign machinery without proper technical advice, and by expecting it to function on a hundred-percent scale with only Russian workmen to handle it.

(In those days, the Russians were often negligent in following even the simplest maintenance routines to keep their expensive foreign machinery in good running order. After we handed over our pencil factory to the Soviet authorities in 1930, all oiling of machines ceased, and there was a catastrophic explosion in the hydraulic lead-forming division of the plant in 1931 which killed a large number of workers.)

By the first of May, almost exactly six months after the signing of our contract, the factory was a going concern and the first pencils had been produced to salute the great Soviet holiday.

We had agreed to produce pencils within twelve months, and had given a bond of fifty thousand dollars to back our pledge. We had done the work in six months, to the amazement of the Concessions Committee and—be it said—of the Soviet organization which had opposed our concession on the ground that it would soon be producing pencils without need of foreign help. Many months were to elapse before our rivals were able to justify their boast. In the meantime our deposit was returned with thanks and congratulations and we were able to secure a predominant position in the Soviet market.

Most of our German specialists were wholly unfamiliar with Russia, indeed many of them had never been outside of their native Bavaria. Imagine then my anxiety when one evening soon after the workers arrived I received a message from the factory that a German had gone for a walk before supper and had not returned.

It was then about ten o'clock, and I immediately phoned the militia headquarters, asking them to instruct their local stations to look out for a middle-aged man who spoke no Russian and who had doubtless lost his way.

At midnight there was no word of the missing man. By this time his wife was so frightened that I went over to the factory myself. I found the entire German group on the verge of panic: only a few days in Moscow and already one of their number had mysteriously disappeared! No doubt, they said, he had been shot or fallen prey to bandits in this terrible country. Some of them were talking of returning home.

I consoled them as best I could but I, too, had begun to feel really anxious. I phoned the militia two or three times more during the night, but they had no news.

When I reached the factory in the morning, the Germans were in a terrible state of distress. I was trying, without much success, to make the best of things, when suddenly a big auto drove up and out jumped our missing specialist, all smiles, followed by a Red Army officer in uniform. He had a remarkable story to tell.

He had gone for a walk in the city and had come to a huge and splendid building surrounded by a battlement wall and lofty towers. How was he to know that he had come to the boundary of the Kremlin itself? Seeing people enter through one of the gates, he had followed them, without let or hindrance, and had enjoyed walking about the streets and courts of the fortress, examining the beautiful old buildings, the cannon captured from Napoleon and other things of interest.

At this point the Army officer, who belonged to the Kremlin Guard, took up the story. "About nine last night," he said, "a man was observed wandering about the Kremlin in a strange and suspicious manner. He was followed at a discreet distance and finally made his way to one of the gates. Here he was challenged by the sentry who demanded his pass to enter the Kremlin. He replied in an unintelligible manner and was unable to produce a pass. He was accordingly arrested and confined in the guardroom for the night. Once the door was barred upon him he began to raise a terrific uproar, something no one could understand, and beating and kicking at the door. At last the Commandant was summoned, who procured an interpreter and found the man was a German mechanic employed by you.

"He protested most loudly against his imprisonment, saying that he was a peaceful German worker who had done no harm to anyone. The documents in his possession seemed to substantiate this, so we asked him how he had obtained access to the Kremlin past the guards at the gate. 'I just walked in,' he replied. 'Others were going that way, so I followed them. No one tried to stop me.'

"This also proved correct," the officer concluded. "Apparently the sentry had thought that he must be a delegate to the session of the Central Executive Committee meeting in the Kremlin and, when he walked boldly by, had not thought to challenge him. It was then too late to send him home, so we kept him till morning, and we hope he is none the worse for his adventure."

On the contrary, our man Schultz felt himself a hero. Once the misunderstanding had been explained, he told us, the Commandant had treated him most kindly. He'd been given a good meal and the

assurance that whenever he wished to visit the Kremlin in a more
regular fashion he had only to ask the Commandant and he would
receive a pass and a guide to show him around. All the Germans were
wreathed in smiles to welcome back their lost colleague and all talk of
flight to Fürth was forgotten.

As I very shortly found out, a manufacturer's problem in Soviet
Russia was not principally one of sales, as it was in America, but almost
wholly one of production. Since the Revolution, the shortage of manufactured goods had been so severe in comparison with the steadily
growing demand that any article of general use or consumption produced inside the country at anything like a reasonable price was effectively pre-sold. It is hardly too much to say that in the 1920s there was
no sales problem in Russia at all.

Production, on the other hand, was a terrible headache. It was
always hard to obtain raw materials, especially when most materials
had to be brought in from outside of Russia, as was the case with us at
first. Efficient workers were very hard to find, and their slackness and
indiscipline, especially in timekeeping and sticking to the job, was a
startling eye-opener for me, accustomed as I had become to the punc-
tual habits and hard work of our labor force in New York. From the
outset, therefore, I found myself up against the problem of producing
more and more pencils to meet demand. Beginning with one shift, I
soon found it necessary to employ two, and in some departments,
three.

In the early days, although the regular daily wage our people
received was above the Moscow average, their slowness and general
laxity nearly drove our German foremen to distraction. Men would idle
about gossiping and smoking cigarettes instead of working. I was near
to despair when I conceived the idea of putting them on piecework and
the scene changed immediately, almost as if by magic. Under the spur
of piecework, it was a common thing to see men coming into their shop
half an hour before the whistle blew in the morning to tune up their
machines, so as to start work at full speed "right off the gun."

My brother Victor was pressed into service as a guinea pig to help
us estimate the rate at which it would be reasonable to expect the other
workers to perform. He did every job in the place and he drove up the
work rates so hard that the workers began to complain that he never
took time out to go to the bathroom.

It surprises many people to learn that it was possible to introduce
piecework in a Moscow factory in 1925. In fact, piecework was ex-
pressly permitted in the terms of the NEP, though I'm not sure how
widespread the practice was before it transformed our plant.

Now our German foremen were able to report that instead of

lagging far behind the production rates they had known at home, most of our Russian workers were beating German records. Wages, of course, advanced correspondingly, but so did profits, and we never had cause to regret the introduction of piecework.

News of the large sums to be earned at the Hammer factory soon spread through the city and we were literally besieged with applications for jobs. For many months letters came in by the sackload from all over the country.

Finally, to avoid the trouble of handling these countless applications, we agreed with the Central Trade Union Bureau to hire all our help through the state labor exchange, which we notified whenever we wished to take on new employees, stating precisely what we wanted. The exchange then would send us applicants in the order in which they were listed on its books, but if for any reason we did not think a candidate was suitable we could refuse him and pick a second or third. In this connection, I remember a rather curious incident which illustrates Soviet conditions in an unusual way.

Shortly after we had reached the agreement with the labor exchange, a young woman came into my office with a most sad story.

Her husband had died suddenly and she had been left almost penniless, with two small children to support: would I take pity on her and give her a job? I would have been glad to help her, but was forced to explain that we had signed an agreement to hire everyone exclusively through the labor exchange: I suggested that she apply there immediately. If they sent her around to us, I promised I would see that she was taken on.

When she reached the exchange she found that her name would be placed at the bottom of the very long list of those who had already applied and were waiting for jobs, whereupon she took her courage in both hands and wrote a letter to Kalinin, the peasant President of the Soviet Union, telling him her desperate position and begging him to help her. Kalinin must have received thousands of such appeals every day, but it was his boast that none of them was too humble for his attention and he maintained a separate bureau to investigate and deal with such cases. Within a week the widow was notified that Kalinin had intervened on her behalf at the labor exchange and that her name had been put at the top of the list. A few days later she appeared at the factory, in reply to our request for additional help, and was given a job.

Soviet labor laws are extremely complicated, as many a foreigner attempting to do business in Russia has learned to his sorrow. We employed a legal expert whose sole duty it was to deal with labor questions.

Of course, we had to make an agreement with the trade union to which our workers belonged, and this required lengthy and detailed negotiation. However, the great power and influence of the trade unions was not without its advantages to the employer of labor in Russia. Once the employer had signed a collective agreement with the union branch, there was little risk of strikes or similar trouble. Both sides were equally bound by the agreement set down in black and white, and the union was strong enough to prevent any infringement by the employees.

The agreement included a code of rules, worked out in minute detail, to which both workers and employer were compelled by law to adhere. It thus became a safeguard for the employer no less than for the workers.

For instance, should a worker prove unsatisfactory or commit any breach of discipline, he was given a warning. A second misdemeanor, a second warning, after which he could be fired. He still had the right of appeal to the special labor courts, but they usually judged cases fairly on their merits.

We had fifty such cases go before the labor court in one year, of which we lost only three. Twenty-seven were complete victories for us and twenty were partial victories. The Soviet labor code required that a man so dismissed should be placed at the bottom of the list at the labor exchange, which meant he would find it extremely difficult to secure another job.

For grave misconduct or theft, of course, the culprit could be dismissed without the double warning. This did not usually apply to petty theft, however, where the goods stolen were worth less than two and a half dollars. On one occasion, not long after we had begun work, I was informed that our pencils were being sold on the Moscow markets, which clearly pointed to a leakage somewhere. I applied to the police, who put a couple of detectives into the factory, ostensibly as workers. After a few days' investigation, they brought a worker into my office and ordered him to take off his boots. His high leather boots carried a good cargo of pencils.

Subsequently, by agreement with the trade union, the duty of preventing petty theft was laid upon the workers' factory committee, which assigned a group of employees as vigilantes. The measure worked very well, and in the two years that followed we had no further trouble on this score.

With the greatest difficulty and effort, we steadily forced production upward. During the first year, instead of the million dollars' worth of pencils we were pledged by our concession agreement to produce, we managed to turn out two and a half millions' worth. In the second year we increased it to four million. In the first year we cut the retail price of pencils from 50 cents to 5, and import was henceforth forbidden, which gave us a further stimulus, as we were enjoying a virtual monopoly. The greater part of our output was taken by state organizations and cooperatives, but we were not precluded from doing business with private dealers, whose number, however, had been continually diminishing under the burden of taxation and other restrictions.

Our production in the year 1927 increased from the previous year's from 51 million pencils to 72 million, and production of steel pens rose from 10 million to 95 million. The number of employees mounted from 450 to 800, and the average monthly wage from 122 rubles to 154 rubles (about $77). By the end of our time in Moscow, in 1930, we were producing nearly half a million pencils a day and employing a thousand workers. We were not only able to supply the entire pencil and steel pen requirements of the Soviet Union, but also exported about 20 percent of our production to England, Turkey, Persia, China and the Far East.

Our pencils and pens were used in every school and educational institution in the Soviet Union, and the name Hammer, stamped on each one, became familiar to every Russian. Our stationery and promotional papers were emblazoned with the Statue of Liberty, and our most popular brand of pencils was called "Diamond" and was distributed in green boxes marked A. HAMMER—AMERICAN INDUSTRIAL CONCESSION. They were tremendously prized objects. When I met Nikita Khrushchev in 1961 he told me with great glee that he had learned to write using our pencils, and the same story has been told to me by a succession of Soviet leaders, including Leonid Brezhnev and Konstantin Chernenko.

I still regularly receive letters from old people all over the Soviet Union who tell me how they received a Hammer pencil on their first day in school sixty years ago.

We suddenly found ourselves eulogized in the Soviet press. In two years we had turned Russia into an exporter of a manufactured product, one which even before the war had been imported for millions of gold rubles. We received daily visits from workers' delegations, student classes in engineering schools and government commissions. Each visitor went away enthusing about the efficiency of the "Amerikanski" methods.

However, we came in for our share of criticism and abuse as well as praise. When our balance sheet was published in the newspapers and it was shown that our net earnings after tax for the first year were over two million rubles—one million dollars—articles appeared in the local press stating that our prices were too high and calling on the government to do something to develop their own pencil industry and prevent the foreign capitalists from pumping so much gold out of the country.

I was somewhat disheartened by these attacks, and it was some time before an event occurred which helped me to take them more philosophically.

In 1928 a delegation of American college Presidents and professors, headed by Professor John Dewey, was visiting Russia. Many of them were my guests during their stay in Moscow. One evening at dinner the Minister of Education, Anatoliy Lunacharsky, leaned over and whispered in my ear, "I have been following the attacks on you in the newspapers; don't pay any attention to them. You know, some of the comrades have to let off steam periodically and since they haven't local capitalists to train their guns on, you have to be the goat. Why," said Lunacharsky, "haven't you seen the way the newspapers have been attacking me? Even we Bolshevik Ministers get plenty of abuse in our own press."

Nevertheless, we took the hint and reduced our prices, although thanks to increased production and efficiency, our profits in the succeeding years remained the same or more.

By the end of 1929 we had expanded into so many different branches of industry that our single pencil factory had become one of a group of five factories, manufacturing metal articles, celluloid and allied products. With this expansion and the increasing need for credit by our customers, our own need for credit increased, but the foreign situation was unfavorable for any financing. The best solution seemed to be to sell out to the Russian government. That suited them because their five-year plan provided for the purchase of our concession before its expiration. We entered into negotiations with Kamenev, then the President of the Main Concessions Committee. After lengthy negotiations, a fair price was agreed upon, payable over a period of eighteen months. The Russians met their obligations promptly and final settlement was made in August 1931.

I say that "the foreign situation was unfavorable." What I really mean is: Stalin was exercising his power and trying to bring about Socialism by force. At that very moment he was stepping up his apparatus of terror and repression, and the Soviet Union was moving into the darkest decades of its existence to date. The forced collectivization of the farms was beginning, as were the massive, farcical and terrible show-trials of Stalin's political opponents. The forced labor camps of the Gulag were receiving their early victims, with millions to come.

None of that was clear to me or to many other observers in the last years of the twenties. Stalin's preoccupations in those years were chiefly with his political struggles with Trotsky—struggles which were mostly hidden from the public. Stalin's character and his intentions were not to be fully revealed until after I had left Moscow, though I heard enough about him and read enough between the lines of the newspapers to perturb me and make me think that we should leave his orbit.

I never met Stalin—I never had any desire to do so—and I never had any dealings with him. However, it was perfectly clear to me in 1930 that Stalin was not a man with whom you could do business. Stalin believed that the state was capable of running everything, without the support of foreign concessionaires and private enterprise. That was the main reason I left Moscow: I could see that I would soon be unable to do business there and, since business was my sole reason to be there, my time was up.

Moscow Days and Nights

The twenties of the twentieth century were also my twenties. The decade's roar of hedonism from Chicago and New York was heard as not much more than a faint sigh in Moscow; nonetheless, Moscow had its moments and some of them were mine. I was a maturing young man with plenty of money in my pocket, an eye for a pretty woman and a developing taste for good things. Moscow was not overflowing with opportunities for indulgence, but a resourceful young man could always find a corner of pleasure somewhere in that harsh landscape.

One of the most unusual and unexpected of those pleasures was Brown House.

The Brown House was a substantial mansion with about thirty rooms at Sadovaya-Samotechnaya 14. In the early twenties it had been occupied by Colonel Haskell, the Director in Moscow of Herbert Hoover's American Relief Association. When Colonel Haskell vacated the house in 1924, the Russian authorities suggested that I should take it, at an irresistibly modest rent. I was then seeking a suitable house for my parents, and my business interests had expanded so much that, luxurious as the accommodation was at the Sugar King's Palace, I needed a large permanent residence in which to entertain my clients and the growing numbers of American and European visitors who wanted to see us. The Brown House seemed perfect. The trouble was that it contained not a stick of furniture, not a carpet or a picture.

I asked my brother Victor to come from Alapayevsk, where he had been looking after the asbestos concern, and help me out. Thus began our interest in collecting and trading in works of art and antiques which developed into a major business and a lifelong passion.

Having studied art history at college, Victor had a fairly sound beginner's knowledge with which to begin touring the sales and markets of Moscow in search of furnishings for the Brown House. Neither of us had any idea of the fabulous treasure which was waiting to be snapped up. As soon as we realized, we became very excited and embarked on a frenzied crash course to educate ourselves.

The light broke when we bought a fine porcelain plate from a stall selling junk in the Flea Market. It was priced at a few rubles, but we knew on sight that it was a valuable piece. It turned out to be part of one of the Czarist collections, made in the Imperial Porcelain Works which had been created by Elizabeth, daughter of Peter the Great, and greatly expanded by Catherine the Great. The works produced porcelain exclusively for the royal household—none of it was ever sold to the public while the Czars were on the throne—and vast quantities of its production had been strewn to the winds after the Revolution and was now turning up in all kinds of unlikely places.

For instance, in a hotel in Petrograd, where Victor and I were having lunch one day, we came across a complete banquet setting of dishes dated 1825 which had been made for Czar Nicholas I. This immensely valuable set was being used in the hotel's routine business and the manager didn't think very highly of it. "The dishwashers complain that the plates break too easily," he told us. We offered to take it off his hands in exchange for a complete set of new crockery, and he was delighted to make the deal.

The monogram and crown of the Czar was burned into the bottom of each piece. The painting of the Imperial china was often done gratis by famous Russian artists who considered it a privilege to give their services to the Emperor. The stupendous nature of their labor may be conceived, for instance, when one reflects that the famous Bird Set of Nicholas II, originally consisting of six thousand pieces, carried three different bird motifs on each piece. It took six years to complete the decoration of this one service.

During the Imperial epoch, collectors would pay as high as 500 rubles ($250) to bribe a servant to steal a single plate from the royal household.

Glassware of the finest quality was also made in the Imperial Factory. Among the articles which Victor and I gathered together was a wine service with the royal coat of arms in gold and enamel placed underneath the surface between two layers of glass. The man who executed this work died at the turn of the century, carrying the secret with him, and to this day it remains a lost art.

I kept a very small part of the Imperial china I acquired in Russia in my personal possession and I have it still. When I revisited Moscow in 1961, for the first time in thirty-one years, I went to see Lenin's modest quarters in the Kremlin with my wife, Frances. When the guide opened a cupboard door, Frances seized my arm and whispered, "Look, Armand, they've got some plates from our dinner service." The rest of Lenin's apartment, by contrast, was furnished as roughly and simply as a common laborer's home.

The same magnificent tableware may recently have played a small role in the unfolding of Soviet history. The former Politburo member Grigori Romanov apparently borrowed glassware and china from the Catherine the Great collection for the wedding of his daughter. In the riotous party, a large quantity of the priceless collection was smashed, causing such offense among Romanov's colleagues that his reputation was seriously damaged.

The scandal was not forgotten when the question of the leadership came to be settled after the death of Konstantin Chernenko. Romanov was excluded and the victor, Mikhail Gorbachev, quite quickly removed him altogether from the Politburo.

Realizing that we had stumbled on an Aladdin's cave of booty, Victor enlisted the advice and guidance of an expert connoisseur, a composer friend of ours named Benedictov. Victor became his pupil and spent day after day with him, visiting markets and auction rooms. Benedictov was a great expert on icons, and he had an uncanny eye for an ancient work which had been covered over with new paint. He taught Victor how to clean the icons, exposing the centuries-old original images. Victor bought them in dozens.

The old Russians had great reverence for icons, continually crossing themselves before the images. These icons were used in the home as well as in the church, and the average orthodox Russian would have at least one in every room, usually hanging in the corner with a light burning under it. For the illiterate it was the only means of studying the Bible. Some of the icons depicted entire Biblical stories, others represented the various saints or the patron saint of the owner.

I was rather amused when, on a hunting trip in Siberia, I entered a peasant's hut to get a little hot water for tea and found, in one corner of the room, an icon of his patron saint with the eternal candle burning under it, while in the opposite corner was a portrait of the Bolshevik leader, Lenin, with a candle burning under it as well.

Our fellow collectors were very few. The most important were the French Ambassador, Ebert, and the German Ambassador, Count Brockdorff-Rantzau, who, on account of their diplomatic privileges, had no difficulty in sending their possessions out of Russia.

Whenever something of value turned up in Moscow's commission stores, we would be sure to meet the French Ambassador or his wife, who would appear on the scene, magnifying glass in hand. The German Ambassador rarely appeared in person. He depended more on his agents. They returned empty-handed to him so often, having been dispatched to make a purchase only to find that the object bore a label saying SOLD TO MR. HAMMER, that the Count became intensely displeased and made an official and bitter complaint about us. The Russians merely shrugged. They knew the rules of competition even if the Count didn't.

Our home in Moscow very quickly became a virtual museum, filled with relics of the Romanov dynasty (though not, as someone has recently claimed, the Imperial crown jewels—those were a bit beyond my means!). From china, icons, antique furniture and objets d'art, we moved rapidly on to the collection of paintings. Benedictov explained to us that the market in fine art in Moscow at that moment presented a unique opportunity without precedent in the civilized world.

The Russian nobility and aristocracy had always been renowned for the quality of their collections of paintings. From the time of Peter the Great, when Russia first began to look westward and to see itself as a European state, many of the finest works of art had been acquired to decorate the great houses and castles of Russia. From Titian to Picasso, the canvases of the masters had been sucked into Russia like snow-flakes in a blizzard. After the Revolution, when the aristocracy fled the country with little more than the clothes they stood up in, nearly all their collections had been left behind.

Though the Soviet authorities were trying hard to bring the collections together for public exhibition in museums, hundreds upon hundreds of great pictures had fallen into private hands and were now available for sale, either officially or on the black market.

I knew next to nothing about art at that time, and I have to admit that my first interest in assembling our collection in Moscow was monetary and material: besides being able to furnish and decorate the Brown House with good things at bargain-basement prices, I saw that we had lit upon a sound investment for the mountains of rubles which were growing in our accounts and for which there was very little to buy in Russia. It was always in the forefront of my mind that a good collection of treasures from the Imperial palaces and paintings and drawings by famous masters might make a fluidly convertible commodity in the West if we could manage to get it out of Russia.

Very quickly, however, I found myself seduced by and wedded to art. Studying the lives of the painters and the genesis of their works led me into the mainstream of European history and was an education in itself—but I was also moved and stirred by paintings as only music had previously affected me. A universe of sensation and thought truly had opened to me. I felt as if I had been living all my life in three wings of a mansion, unaware that a fourth existed; and, the doors having been flung open, I entered rooms full of light and color and beauty.

Victor got hold of an almanac of pictures and prices, a kind of dealers' guide called *Bénézit* which listed the prices at which works had changed hands in the past. It became his Bible as he raced around Moscow bidding on pictures. Right from the start, he made stunning purchases at crazy prices. The first pictures he bought were a Caspar Netscher, a Gerard Dou and a Terborch, all at a fraction of their value on the international market. None of these works was a masterpiece, but they were all good pictures of soundly proven provenance and we were very thrilled with ourselves and our luck.

Naturally, as raw beginners, we were bound to make some mistakes and we offered a tempting target for the con men who can always be found hanging on to the art world. We made our biggest and most salutary error over *The Circumcision of Christ* by Rembrandt. In the process, we found ourselves enmeshed in one of the most extraordinary art frauds of all time, and one which, as far as I know, has never been revealed.

One of Rembrandt's *Circumcision of Christ* paintings—he did several—was one of the lost masterpieces of the world. It had vanished in the nineteenth century, never to be heard of again. One day Victor came dashing into the Brown House in a tremendous state of breathless excitement, saying that he had been offered the chance to buy the lost Rembrandt.

We had been giving some work to an old picture restorer who had been employed at the Hermitage in Leningrad before the Revolution. He had just told Victor that he knew what had happened to the Rembrandt and where it was to be found. He said that it had been owned for some generations by a noble Russian family and that the present owner, with whom he was in contact, was living in secret in Moscow, needed money and was willing to sell. The asking price was 50,000 gold rubles, equivalent to about $25,000—a steal.

We let the man know that we were very interested and after a few days he came to see us with a parcel under his arm, bound in brown paper and string. In a scene like the unveiling of the Maltese Falcon, we hung over him while he cut away the wrappings and revealed the exquisite picture. It was small, only about 24″ x 30″, mounted on a wooden panel without a frame. It had a beautiful old patina and was unmistakably the work of the great master himself: no two ways about it.

We gave the picture restorer cash on the spot and practically hugged each other at having acquired not only our first Rembrandt, but one of the most sought-after pictures in the world. It was almost too good to be true, but we didn't dwell on that thought.

A couple of months later Victor was going to Germany on business and we agreed that he should take our Rembrandt with him to show to Professor Max Friedländer, the Director of the Berlin Museum, who was one of the outstanding art authorities in the world. We were so proud of our picture and we wanted to show it off.

Friedländer was tremendously excited to see the picture; almost beside himself. He summoned all the members of his staff into his room to see it and started to give them a long lecture about its history and its special qualities. He was treating it as one of the major art finds of the century.

While he was talking, one of his assistants took a little piece of cotton wool soaked in alcohol and started rubbing at a corner of the picture. To his horror, the paint immediately started to dissolve. He interrupted Friedländer.

"Look at this, sir," he said. "The paint is coming away."

"What!" said Friedländer, spinning around to look at the picture. "My God, it's a fake. A patent fake." He swore violently and then he said, "But it's a brilliant forgery: the man who painted this is the equal of Rembrandt."

Victor was very down-in-the-mouth when he got back to Moscow. I asked him, "What did Professor Friedländer say about our Rembrandt?"

"He said, 'Our Rembrandt is no Rembrandt,' that's what he said," Victor replied.

What were we to do? My first instinct was to report the matter to the police. But I was reluctant to ruin the picture restorer, who was a poor old man, and, not believing that he could possibly be the author of such a consummate swindle, I wanted to get to the bottom of it.

We summoned the man and told him that the jig was up, that we knew the Rembrandt was a fake. I gave him a choice: either he could tell us everything he knew or we would go straight to the police. He was very scared. He started talking. His story was amazing.

The picture had been painted, he said, by a man whose name was very well known to us and to all Moscow—M. Yakovlev, the Director of one of Moscow's state museums, who was also quite a well-known painter in his own right, having had a number of exhibitions in Moscow galleries. He was a highly respected figure. I was flabbergasted. It was like being told that the Director of the National Gallery in Washington was faking old masters.

Apparently Yakovlev and the picture restorer were running a regular and highly profitable trade in fake pictures, with Yakovlev as the forger and the picture restorer as the front man.

"Right," I said. "Let's go. We're going to get our money back."

Carrying our "Rembrandt" and practically dragging the wretched picture restorer, we went to Yakovlev's house. His face drained of all color when he saw us and I noticed that his knees actually shook. He confessed immediately and begged us not to turn him in, since besides getting a very lengthy term of imprisonment, his career would be utterly destroyed.

I was mainly interested in getting our money back. Much of it had already been spent. Yakovlev had bought a grand piano for his wife and had wasted a lot of money on drinking and gambling. Only about five thousand dollars of our money was left, but that was better than nothing. To make up the balance, he offered to paint portraits of our whole family, but I preferred to take off his walls some of his own very good pictures. Once we had settled this compensation, he relaxed a little and he told us his story.

As a very young man, he said, he had been an extremely promising painter and had traveled to Paris, Rome, Berlin and Amsterdam to study. He had tried to improve his own technique by copying great masters and he had found that his copies were almost indistinguishable from the originals.

When he returned to Moscow, he had a long struggle with poverty because his own works weren't selling. That was when he began to forge lost masterpieces. He would study engravings in catalogues of known pictures which had disappeared, and then he would mount his forgeries on wood panels of minor paintings which were authentically of the period.

It was some consolation to Victor and me to discover that we weren't the only ones to have been duped. Yakovlev took us into his studio and showed us catalogues from some of the museums of Europe.

"See that Frans Hals," he said, pointing at a page of the catalogue from a German museum. "That's mine. And"—he turned to another catalogue—"this Rubens—mine too." Curators all over Europe had bought and hung some of his forgeries. As far as I know, Yakovlev's fakes are still in place, still attracting the admiration of scholars and art lovers.

I kept our fake Rembrandt for many years as a salutary reminder of how easily a collector of art can be duped. I found that it emitted a strong silent warning to be cautious whenever I got overexcited about the opportunity to acquire a rare picture.

It hung in my office in the Hammer Galleries in New York throughout the thirties. Our great friend and partner Morris Gest—of whom I shall have plenty to say later—was always fascinated by the picture and, because I loved to tease him, I never told him the truth about it. The fact that Christ was a Jew and was seen undergoing the Jewish ritual of circumcision enthralled Morris as a paradox. Finally he implored me to sell it to him: he wanted to give it to his father-in-law, the great Broadway producer David Belasco.

Belasco, born a Jew, had converted to Protestantism: in fact, he always wore his collar back to front like a clergyman—whether as a joke or because he had actually studied to be a minister, I don't know. Anyway, when Belasco fell terminally ill and was in the hospital, Morris wanted to give him the Rembrandt to cheer him up.

I told Morris the true story of the picture and I said, "I won't sell it to you. Take it. You can give it to your father-in-law, but you must tell him that it's a fake," which Morris duly did.

That might have been the end of the story, but there was one more twist. When David Belasco died, his estate was inherited by his daughter, Mrs. Morris Gest. When she died, her pictures—including, apparently, *The Circumcision of Christ* by Rembrandt"—were sold by a small dealer. The picture then disappeared again. Many, many years later, Victor and I were in a small museum in this country when he seized my arm and hissed, "Look, Armand, look!" There was our "Rembrandt": the museum was very proud of it.

I am not going to name that little museum or any of the others in which Yakovlev told me that his pictures were hanging. If his forgeries are going to be unmasked, somebody else will have to do the job.

Moscow wasn't only a repository for great art in those strange days; anything could be had for a price. As I have said, the magic of Lenin's NEP produced a flood of consumer goods from all quarters: restaurants and bars began opening up all over town and some of the entertainments of city night life appeared. Beneath its grim and sullen exterior, behind its shabby façade and its forbiddingly locked doors, Moscow began to enjoy a secret life of pleasure.

Parker pens gave us a key to unlock closed doors or get a smile from a frosty maître d'. Our contract with Parker gave us an unlimited supply of those big fat orange-red fountain pens with black tops which the company produced in those days. Ownership of one of those pens—a commonplace in America—was a mark of the highest social achievement in Moscow. Men would display them on the *outside* of their coats. Our supplies of Parker pens opened any number of doors for Victor and me. Any recalcitrant official or dealer would treat us like kings the moment we made them a present of a Parker.

No shortages of food affected the Hammer household, since the black market was always thriving and bulging with produce from farmers who brought their goods to be sold under the counter. Anything could be had for a price, but for those without the price, there were always lines—as there still are, though no shortages today stand comparison with the deprivations of those days. Lines would form for the simplest necessities—bread, meat, clothes. A Muscovite might wait in line for a whole morning to get a little saucepan or a couple of rolls of toilet paper of the coarsest quality. The rule in Moscow then was, if you saw a line forming, you'd better get in it, otherwise you would miss a chance which might not come again for weeks or months.

Once, with his ever-eager eye for a joke, Victor and a friend stood, one behind the other, at the door of a disused warehouse. Within half an hour a long line had formed behind them, though nobody in the line had any idea what they were supposed to be waiting for. Victor and his friend eventually slipped away to enjoy their joke: the line continued to grow.

For a short time in 1921 I was the only man in Moscow who owned a private automobile—a Model T Ford, one of the first to arrive in the first consignment from Detroit. This distinction made me a very desirable friend and companion for the young ladies of Moscow, since it was an immeasurable mark of status to be seen riding in or descending from a car rather than a hired horse-drawn taxi or sled.

Today, more than a million cars a year are being built in Russia and half of them go into private hands. This means, I have always said, that half a million new capitalists are made every year in Russia, because when a person gets a car he gets an important article of private property which he will want to protect for its value. To own a car, or even to get a share in one, remains the dream of a lifetime for many Russians. It is still common for a Russian to save for as long as ten years to fulfill this dream.

I have always liked the Russian joke about the widowed lady who advertised in a lonely hearts column for a mate and added that he must be able to drive an automobile. Among the many replies she received was one from an ardent suitor who wrote, "Am extremely interested in your advertisement. Enclosed is my photograph. Please send me a photo of your car."

It was so unusual to see a car in Moscow in the twenties that people would stop and stare when one passed, and a parked car would always draw an inquisitive crowd. Nearly all of the cars belonged to foreign embassies and were occupied by prominent embassy officials. In fact, an official's standing was judged, in the first place, by whether or not he had the use of a car and, secondly, by how fast it was driven—the higher the official's position, the faster it went. This is still the case today. If you're standing in Red Square and a ZIL or Chaika comes zooming across the square, scattering pedestrians and cutting across the traffic, while the police frantically whistle and gesticulate to make way for it, you can be pretty sure that a high member of the party has just crossed your path. If a Moskvitch, the Russian version of a Volkswagen, comes chugging out and has to wait its turn for a gap in the traffic, the passenger can be reckoned to be no-account.

Almost all the official cars in the early days—and still today—were fitted with curtains which were always drawn, ostensibly to prevent assassinations—though it always seemed more likely to me that the assassin's attention would be attracted by drawn curtains.

Not all the cars in Moscow belonged to embassies: on returning home from the theater at midnight it was not an uncommon sight to see the glaring headlights and hear the thundering noise of a magnificent open Rolls-Royce touring car dashing through the deserted streets with Trotsky seated next to the driver.

I, too, had a driver—Grishayev, whom we called Grisha. He had formerly worked for a prominent Commissar and he had come to us from Colonel Haskell when we acquired the Brown House. He seemed to feel that he had come down a big notch in the world and he couldn't get it out of his head that we were not representatives of government or of an official organization, but were plain American businessmen. One day I noticed that a little flag, marked in red letters with the name ALAMERICO, was fluttering from the radiator of my Model T.

"What's that for?" I asked him.

He smiled shyly. "You'll see," he said.

We drove away to cross central Moscow. At a junction, a policeman put up his club to signal us to stop, but Grisha took no notice and drove straight ahead. The policeman's whistle shrilled behind us.

We stopped and the officer strode up to the car, obviously ready to give us a scolding and perhaps a summons. Grisha calmly pointed to the flag on the radiator and said, *"Amerikanski Missi"* (American Mission). The policeman smartly saluted, apologized and waved us on our way.

Grisha was disgusted with me when I made him stop around the first corner and remove the pennant. I didn't want to risk displeasing the authorities by sailing under false colors. Grisha shook his head in despair.

With the advent of NEP and the spread of wealth—much of it ill-gotten—more private cars appeared on the streets. They were easy to distinguish, because the authorities had made a rule requiring all private cars to be marked with a yellow stripe around the entire body: this came to be known as the "Moscow Ticket." The tax collectors took a keen interest in any car marked with the Moscow Ticket and followed it closely, wanting to know how a private person could afford a car.

Having served the minimum term of his prison sentence, my father was released from Sing-Sing on parole in 1923, and he joined my mother in her apartment at the Ansonia Hotel. Naturally, I had seen both my parents during my visits to America, and I had encouraged them to come to Moscow and live with me when my father was released.

While my father was in prison, I personally arranged to sell all of the stocks in which he had invested and put the proceeds in his bank account. My father was not a gambler, but he had a weakness for the stock exchange and I was determined to protect the modest capital he had assembled in his working life. Thereafter, he never risked his savings on the stock exchange, with the result that they were protected and he was unaffected by the great crash at the end of the decade.

In addition to the forfeiture of his other civic rights on his release from prison, he was forbidden to practice as a physician. Since he wanted to work, having had enough of enforced idleness, I asked him to represent me and Allied American, our import-export concession, with some of our American clients.

In this capacity he went to see Henry Ford in Dearborn to propose the idea that Ford should build a factory in Russia, manned with Russian workers but supervised by Ford foremen and technicians from Detroit. Henry Ford toyed with the idea for most of the decade and finally, in 1929, he did sign an agreement to cooperate with the Russians in building a plant for cars and trucks on the Volga at Nizhniy-Novgorod, now called Gorky. During the thirties, this plant was to produce upward of one hundred thousand units a year. Henry Ford received thirty million dollars for his side of the deal and the Russians paid the cost of equipping and building the factory.

All the friends and medical colleagues who had supported my father when he had appealed against his sentence and conviction now rallied round to help him again in a campaign to obtain a pardon and the restoration of his citizenship. Governor Al Smith of New York finally granted this pardon on November 12, 1924.

By that time he and my mother were already in Moscow. By strange chance they arrived in Moscow on May Day, 1923. My father was hugely thrilled to arrive in the land of his socialist dreams on this, the greatest festival day in the Communist calendar: it took some time to persuade him that Moscow was not always so festive or welcoming.

My father's presence in Moscow did not significantly add to or alter my business endeavors there. As a mark of courtesy to him, to give him a title and an official role in our enterprises, I made him Chairman of the Moscow board of our joint-venture export-import contract with the Soviet Trade Monopoly, which used the trade name Alamerico, but he was not overly active and he did not take an executive lead in our affairs: that remained in my hands. Though he was delighted to be in Russia, he never gave up his American passport and he had no desire to end his days there. In fact, though his belief in socialism never wavered, he became increasingly disillusioned about

Communism while he lived there and, in the end—witnessing the growth of Stalin's terror—he began saying that he did not intend to be used as fertilizer for the next generation.

At first, however, both my parents took to their new lives with great pleasure. They loved the Brown House, which by this time was filling up with exotic and lovely furnishings and decorations, and my mother got straight into the party life of Moscow which Victor and I had been discovering. I sometimes think that my mother would have gone to a party in Ulan Bator if she had heard of one: nothing would keep her away from a good time. A story which completely typifies my mother was told to me by Professor John Dewey, who stayed with us for a while in the Brown House when, in 1928, he led a delegation of professors on a tour of Russia.

One morning he came down to breakfast to find my mother seated at the table spooning caviar onto her plate and washing it down with little glasses of clear liquid.

"May I ask what you're drinking?" he said.

"Vodka," she said.

"Vodka for breakfast?"

"Why not?" she replied. "It's made out of cereals, isn't it?"

The Brown House became a haven for visitors to Moscow from the West, particularly for visiting Americans who treated it almost as an unofficial embassy and the most reliable place in town to get a good meal. Visitors and guests poured in over the years of our occupancy. Unfortunately, I was out of the country on business when Douglas Fairbanks and Mary Pickford came to visit, but my parents were very proud of having entertained the two most famous movie stars of the time. I was in Moscow, however, when Will Rogers came as one of our most entertaining and memorable guests.

He arrived, completely unannounced and unexpected, on one of those afternoons at the pencil factory when everything was going wrong. My secretary called me on the telephone and said, "There's a man called Will Rogers here to see you." "Will Rogers?" I said, with my jaw dropping. "Did you say *Will Rogers*?"

My younger readers probably can't imagine how stupendous this news was. At the time, Will Rogers was probably the most famous man in America, after the President. When George Bernard Shaw visited America in 1929 he said of Will Rogers, "I had no idea, until I came here, how important he is: he's almost as important as I am."

The first thing he said to Victor and me when he came into our office was, "What on earth are you two fellows doing in this place? Why don't you go home?" Victor quickly assured him that nothing was further from our minds.

He was looking for Walter Duranty of the *New York Times* and he'd heard that we might know where to find him: Duranty was the Dean of foreign correspondents and a close personal friend of mine. We offered to drive him across to the other side of the Moscow River. It was a hot July day. As we crossed the bridge, Will let out an Indian war whoop. "What's the matter?" we said. "Don't you see what I see?" he said. "There are women bathing stark naked down there and men right alongside them." We explained to him that there wasn't a bathing suit to be had in all of Russia. So that's where he got the title for the book he wrote about his trip, called *There Isn't a Bathing Suit in Russia* (to which he added the line that if there was one, somebody was probably using it as an overcoat).

He stayed in Moscow for a short while, writing his articles about Russia, and no man was ever better company or better-natured. He made us laugh all the time. He had a lovely, simple way of putting things. After he'd been in Moscow for a while, trying to get to understand Communism, he finally decided what he thought of it: "Communism's like Prohibition," he drawled in that Okie accent. "It's a fine idea, but it won't work." He was right.

Will was given an early clue about the likely outcome of the developing power struggle between Stalin and Trotsky when he went to see Trotsky but was put off with the chilling statement that Trotsky was no longer of any importance.

Not long after my parents arrived in Moscow, there was another addition to our household, when I met my first wife.

In the summer of 1925 I went with some friends on a holiday to Yalta in the Crimea. One night they took me to a concert of gypsy songs featuring a famous singer, Olga Vadina. We had seats in the front row because my friends were friends of hers. The moment I saw her, I felt as if I'd been struck by a bolt of lightning; she knocked me out. She had an extraordinary combination of dark skin and light blue eyes, with honey-blond hair and a glorious figure. Was I smitten! All through her performance I sat with my mouth opening and closing like a fish out of water. While she sang romantic gypsy ballads in a low, sexy voice, she stared straight back into my eyes and her smile was like fire. I just had to meet her.

Our friends played Cupid. After the show they took me backstage to meet Olga in her dressing room and, though I felt tongue-tied for once in my life, I managed to get out the words in my garbled Russian to invite her to join us for supper. After that, we were inseparable.

Olga was married to her manager—he was in Moscow at the time—but nothing was going to get in our way. In a matter of days she decided to divorce her husband and marry me. When we went to the station to take the Moscow train, our friends gave us a send-off as if we had already married and were setting off on our honeymoon. Our compartment was filled with carnations, which we both loved: they were strewn in piles across the cushions and woven around the luggage racks and couches.

Olga's story was like something out of a novel. She was a baroness, the daughter of a general, Baron von Root, whose Junker ancestors had been brought from Germany to join the armies of Peter the Great. Educated at the Smolny Institute in Petrograd, she had had a childhood and upbringing of the greatest luxury and privilege. Her mother's maiden name was Kosciusko and she was descended from the famous Polish general who had helped George Washington defeat the British in the American Revolutionary War.

When the Russian Revolution broke out, her father had commanded White Russian troops in the civil war and had moved his family from Moscow to Kiev, in the middle of the battle zone.

Olga went to work singing her gypsy songs in cabaret clubs to support her mother and young sister and brother. Kiev was constantly changing hands as the war surged back and forth, and one day, while the city was in the hands of the Bolsheviks, Olga was caught in a roundup of suspected White Russian sympathizers and sentenced to be shot by a firing squad. She was actually in the line waiting to be led to the wall, hearing the fusillades of execution, when she was spotted by a Bolshevik colonel who had heard her sing and decided to rescue her.

He took her to her home, only to find that he also had to rescue the rest of her family. A Bolshevik search party had been working through the building where the family was living and had just arrived at Olga's mother's apartment. In her panic the mother had mistaken them for White Russians and, to show where the family's sympathies lay, she had pulled out a photograph of her husband, the Baron, in one of his dress uniforms, all glittering with Czarist decorations. The Bolshevik soldiers had decided to execute the whole family on the spot.

Again, the Colonel interceded, dismissing the soldiers, and then offered to help save Olga's father. He sent him a message to say that if he would defect to the Red side, he would be granted an amnesty. The father made his way across the lines and was given a job as an instructor in the Soviet Military Academy in Kiev when it finally became a permanent part of Soviet territory.

By the time I met her, Olga had become one of the biggest stars in Russia. She sang with a throaty, smoky voice like Dietrich, and she looked quite like Garbo, though she radiated a lot more passion and vivacity than either of them. Like many Russian women, she was as temperamentally volatile as a racehorse, a real prima donna; but I wasn't complaining. I knew that I had taken on a very exceptional woman.

Somebody recently suggested that Olga might have been an agent of Dzerzinsky's secret police. Heaven knows where this idea got started, but it certainly made me laugh. The police force hasn't been made yet which could contain and discipline a character like Olga. She could no more have been an agent than she could have sat at home working on a needlepoint tapestry!

I set Olga up in an apartment with her mother, and she and I lived together as common-law man and wife. My experiences with Bennie, the nurse who had deceived me, had soured me on marriage. Then, one day, recognizing that I was in love with Olga, I realized that I would regret it bitterly if anything happened to her after I left Russia. I decided that the best protection I could give her was marriage.

We were married on March 14, 1927.

The reception party at the Brown House was an absolutely typical Russian affair. It began with vodka and it ended with vodka. There were about three hundred people in the house when the party began at six in the evening, and at least the same number—maybe more—were still in the house when we left the party at five in the morning. Gangs of Olga's friends from the theater came to the party and they sang and danced all night. One thing you've got to say for Russians: they know how to toast a wedding.

We were both eager to have a child as soon as possible. Months turned into years, and still Olga did not conceive. I consulted a specialist in Moscow who said I was okay. We became very concerned and, at length, Olga went to Switzerland to consult an eminent specialist. He reassured her that nothing was wrong with her and advised her to take a month's rest in Switzerland, and then have me join her and try again. His counsel was very sound: within a month of our return to Moscow, Olga had conceived, and our son Julian was born on May 7, 1929.

By that time I had built a new house for us, close to the Sugar King's Palace, opposite the Kremlin. Surrounded by a high wall to give us complete privacy, the house was on a good piece of ground with a lovely garden and space for the blue chow and the poodle we kept. My parents stayed on at the Brown House.

Ours had not been the first Moscow wedding in the family, and Julian was not the first Hammer boy to be born there. Victor had a family of his own. About the time that I met Olga, Victor met Varvara, whom we called Vava. She was also a singer of gypsy songs—such women seemed to have a fatal attraction for us—and also a divorcée— very glamorous and sensuous. After their wedding they lived together in a very handsome apartment, filled with antiques and pictures, and their house became a favorite meeting place for Moscow's artistic and literary set. When their son was born, they named him Armand. He was always known as Armasha, a pet name for Armand.

Armasha still lives in Moscow, the victim of a very sad chain of events. Victor's marriage was to end very unpleasantly. While he was away from Moscow on business in 1928, his wife was caught *in flagrante delicto* with one of his best friends. It was Vava's own mother, Victor's mother-in-law, who discovered the adultery and, being very fond of Victor and unhappy for him, she reported the affair to him and to me. Victor was dreadfully broken up, and his first reaction was that he wanted to get out of Moscow and put Vava far behind him. Fate was about to present us with an opportunity which speeded his departure.

One evening in June 1928 we were joined for dinner at the Brown House by Emery Sakho, an American dealer who represented a New York company called Peasant Art Importing Company of 677 Lexington Avenue and 14 East Thirty-eighth Street. Sakho, a Hungarian, traded in antiques, works of art and, chiefly, in embroidered fabrics. He had been having a very hard time doing business with the Soviet authorities, who had become very well aware of the value of their art treasures, and, desperately in need of foreign exchange, they were driving very hard bargains with any foreign dealer. Sakho was near to despair when he came to our house, and when we took him on a tour of the rooms, he threw up his hands in amazement.

"My God," he said, "this place is like a museum. It's fantastic!"

He went from room to room, from picture to picture, from object to object, demanding, "What did you pay for this?" and exclaiming "My God!" in disbelief every time we told him. During dinner he put a proposition to us: he would take us as full partners in his business if we would supply him with similar art works for resale in America.

I was very enthusiastic and a deal was done. Sakho's proposition seemed to offer the ideal opportunity to put the collection on sale in the US and get the best benefit from it. The arrangement would also give Victor an ideal chance to get out of Moscow, since he was obviously the one who could best look after our side of the partnership in New York. A year later, when we were negotiating with Kamenev for the sale of our factories, we made it a condition of the sale that there should be a clause permitting us to take out of Russia all our household effects, including our collection of antiques and works of art. By that time it had expanded to fill several warehouses. Although we were never sure that we would get permission to export everything we had acquired, we believed that the art market offered such bargains that, especially in view of the falling ruble, we were better off to have our money in art.

In July 1928 we directed our New York lawyers to incorporate a company to handle this business. Registered in Delaware, it was called Antique Importers, Inc., and it was owned 50 percent by Sakho and 50 percent by me. In November 1928 we changed the name to Importers of Antique Art, Inc., and took offices in that name at 14–16 East Thirty-eighth Street in New York.

We applied to the museum authorities for a license to export our works of art. Depending on the quality of each item, we were charged an export tax of between 15 and 35 percent of its cost. We immediately began packing and shipping those works of art to our New York company, and Victor redoubled his efforts to buy suitable treasures.

Our partnership with Sakho ran into trouble from the start.

Sakho could not live up to his promise to handle the selling side of our partnership. Most of his efforts resulted in a farce. He concentrated solely on the conventional auction rooms, like the small auction houses in New York, and did nothing to draw special attention to the unique qualities of our collection: the extraordinary romance of the Imperial connection was left unpublicized. The sales were a flop.

Soon after we entered into the partnership, Sakho had to withdraw from it. His limited fortune had been invested in stocks, and he had speculated on the market in the lunatic fever of speculation which infected America in the late twenties. He was constantly being called for margin and he was desperately short of cash. Sakho had not been especially stupid or bad: he had simply, along with millions of Americans, succumbed to the collective fantasy of easy fortunes to be gained by nothing more than a timely call to an astute Wall Street broker. The crash of 1929 wiped Sakho out. He went to Harry and asked him to tell me that he was no longer able to continue his side of the deal; in fact, he pleaded with us to buy him out.

We didn't seem to have a lot of choice. Such a substantial part of our profits from our years in Moscow was invested in pictures, Fabergé eggs, objets d'art, fabrics, jewels and antiques that we had to find a way to negotiate their sale, even if it meant becoming full-time professionals in a trade in which we had previously acted only as enthusiastic amateurs.

At that point, Mr. Morris Gest—theatrical impresario, friend and rogue—took a hand in our affairs and, as was his way, shook them by the scruff of the neck and turned them upside down. He stepped in to buy Sakho's share of the business, acquiring a 50-percent interest. We were very glad to have his cash, and he was very glad to have ours.

Morris Gest and I set up a gallery to exhibit and sell our collection and called it L'Ermitage. It was located at 3 East Fifty-second Street, and Harry and Victor were to manage it. Morris's participation didn't greatly improve the trading position of the company, which rapidly went from bad to worse. Poor Sakho had been only one of a legion of lemmings who had gone hurtling into Wall Street's abyss. I received an unending stream of cables from Harry and Victor telling me how impossible they found their task, in one of which Harry said, HOW CAN

WE BE EXPECTED TO SELL FABERGÉ EGGS AND CZARIST TREASURES
WHEN STOCKBROKERS ARE JUMPING OUT OF WINDOWS AND FORMER
CHAIRMEN OF CORPORATIONS ARE SELLING APPLES ON STREET COR-
NERS???

By ingenious and energetic salesmanship, some items were sold,
but when I examined the trading records my brothers sent me, I found
no cash returned to the company for these sales. When I asked my
brothers the meaning of these entries, they replied, "Oh, that's Morris." That explained everything. Morris Gest was as inventive in finding
ways not to hand cash over as he was in making it.

Morris Gest had first zoomed into my orbit in Moscow, when he
visited me with Sol Hurok, one of the greatest of the American im-
presarios who took Russian productions to America, a business in
which Morris himself was very interested. I was immediately taken with
Morris, his boundless energy and sense of fun. I loved to see him
whenever I visited New York and he always showed me off to anybody
we met, insisting that I tell them the story of my Russian experiences—
he once roped me into a press conference he was giving in St. Paul,
Minnesota, where he was drumming up a stage show, and I found
myself splashed across the pages of local newspapers as "Morris Gest's
friend, the pencil king of Russia." When Morris became a partner in
the L'Ermitage venture, he offered to sell items of Czarist treasure
from the gallery to friends and acquaintances.

Morris's approach was a typically simple combination of guile and
browbeating. Visiting friends for dinner or for the weekend, he would
compliment the hosts on the refinement of their taste and the beauties
of their home. Then he would spot a small flaw or gap and say: "I know
exactly the picture/fabric/objet d'art/bauble which would fill that gap
and complete this room. Trust me. Let me bring it to you. If you don't
like it, I'll be amazed. I've got access to a store of the greatest Czarist
treasures the world has ever seen."

Morris was turning a handsome little sideline in this trade. He
would have been a very valuable partner in the enterprise if only he
ever let us have the proceeds of his sales. Getting cash out of Morris
was harder work than breaking rocks: it wasn't that he was actually
dishonest or desperately poor. On the contrary, Morris had substantial
personal means. The trouble was that he also had a hundred and one
schemes going on for which he always needed ready money.

Most of Morris's bigger speculations were not on Wall Street, but
on that other thoroughfare of a million broken dreams, Broadway. He
was like a kid about big shows, and he was never happier than when he
was bringing on a new production.

Over the years he had had some spectacular successes such as *Chu
Chin Chow, Mecca* and *Aphrodite;* and he had been the first to bring to

America the Bolshoi Ballet, the Moscow Art Theater, Eleonora Duse and Fokine. But he had some titanic failures, too—the most monumental of which was his Passion Play.

Victor loved Morris, as did we all, and they often went to the theater together. One day Morris persuaded Victor to go with him to a town in the Midwest to see an open-air production of a Passion Play. Now, Morris's education had been a very informal affair, mostly gathered in the world's school of hard knocks, and—while he knew a good show when he saw one—his critical faculties were not oversupplied with historical or literary learning.

After the first act, Morris was in rapture over the Passion Play— the acting, the script, the production, all entranced him. He made up his mind right then that he would buy up the show and transfer it to a big theater on Broadway. He only stayed for the first act; that was all he needed to see to make up his mind.

He didn't know what happened at the end of the play. He had been brought up as a Jew: how should he know that the climax of every Passion Play is the crucifixion of Christ, with Pilate and the Jews getting the blame?

When the play opened on Broadway, it was picketed by hundreds of New York's outraged Jews. The theater was empty. The production closed in a week and Morris lost his shirt. I don't like to think how many of his sales of our works of art contributed to that fiasco. It certainly strapped him for cash, and we had to make repeated demands of him, some of which stopped only just short of formal action. He kept promising to repay us out of the proceeds of his next show, for which he had typically astronomical expectations. It was called *The Miracle,* and he was developing it in theaters out of town. "When *The Miracle* comes to Broadway," he said, "I'll repay you twice over, you'll see." The miracle never happened. But it was impossible to be cross with Morris for long. He was so charming in his roguishness that we never seriously fell out with each other and always remained good friends.

Comical misfortune was always dogging Morris's heels; his life was a catalogue of bizarre reversals which he overcame with irrepressible sense of humor. The story of his parents' plight in Russia was typical.

Born in a village in the Ukraine, Morris had made his own way to America as a youth. When he began to achieve some success in business, he started planning to have his parents join him, but the Bolshevik Revolution made it much more difficult for them to leave Russia and they were effectively cut off.

All the stories about famine and typhus in the Urals and Ukraine in the early twenties drove Morris nearly crazy. He pictured his elderly parents starving, sick, close to death. He made everybody share this picture. At this time it was possible to send food parcels to Russia

Mama Rose and me, aged two.

The suntanned Hammers: Harry, the tallest, then me and Victor with Mama Rose, about 1906.

Dr. Julius Hammer and Rose Hammer, 1910.

Little Grandma and Willie Robinson.

Victoria Hammer, about 1909.

Jacob Hammer, about 1909.

Rose Hammer with her father,
taken in Russia, about 1912.

Seventeen years old, at Morris High School.

Nineteen twenty-one, just graduated from medical school and ready to practice medicine in Russia.

Touring the famine region of Russia—a trip of great consequence for my future. American social worker Lucy Branum and two Russian members of my staff are to the right.

The portrait Lenin gave me on November 10, 1921.

First Alamerico office, Kusnetskiy Most #4, 1921—originally the Fabergé works.

Boris Mishell and me in the Alamerico Corporation office, Moscow—
Lenin's picture and decree are on the wall behind us.

Workers at the asbestos mine, our first concession, 1922.

Our first shipment of Fordson tractors being unloaded at Novorossisk, February 1923.

The first tractor field demonstration. Facing the camera on the left with beard and mustache is a young Soviet official named Anastas Mikoyan. To his left is Voroshilov and then Bill Shatov. Boris Mishell is behind Voroshilov. I am peering over the shoulder of the tractor driver.

Rose Hammer with
"My Son the Asbestos King"
in the Urals, 1923.

Working hard in my office
at the pencil factory, 1925.

With Julian,
Paris 1930.

With brother Harry—
two boulevardiers—
Paris 1931.

Portrait of Olga ▼ and Olga dressed
as a gypsy singer, Paris 1930.

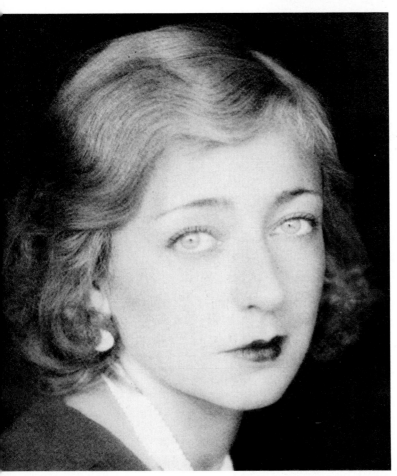

Three of the Russian treasures sold by the
Hammer Galleries: an icon of the Madonna
and Child; a ruby, emerald, and pearl gold
quill pen (now owned by Frances Hammer);
Napoleonic jeweled egg by Fabergé.

The Hammer Galleries, New York City
in the late thirties. ▶

ineteen forty-five. By now I'd
dded distilling to my list of
rofessions.

My new offices on the 78th floor of the Empire State Building—the three-hundred-year old Treaty Room of Uxbridge served as my private office; the Council Chamber from the last of the Medici palaces was my boardroom.

Julius and Rose Hammer, 1940.

Barrels of J. W. Dant Kentucky bourbon, 1948.

The Hammer brothers—(left to right) Armand, Victor, Harry—in 1951.

My yacht, the *Shadow Isle*.

Prince Eric, the pride of Shadow Isle Farms, with farm manager John Frenzel, Angela, and me, 1951.

Frances and me in front of our first
oil well, Mountain View, California, 1956.

Eleanor Roosevelt and Rose Hammer in
1959 outside the Hammer home, formerly
the Roosevelt cottage, at Campobello Island,
purchased by the Hammers and later
donated to the Canadian and American
governments.

With Alexei Kosygin on the left and And
Gromyko on the right, in Russia, 1964,

With Nikita Khrushchev, Moscow 1961—back
to Russia for the first time in thirty-one years.
Autographed to "the man who knew Lenin."

and with Anastas Mikoyan, forty-one yea
after that tractor demonstration.

through the American Relief Association (ARA). Morris would get hold of everybody he met and say, "Please, I implore you, send an ARA food parcel to my people in the Ukraine who are starving, and may be dying for all I know." A lot of parcels got sent. Meanwhile, Morris befriended Herbert Hoover himself, the Director of the ARA. "Please," he said, "you've got to help my poor old parents who can't get out of Russia and are in desperate trouble there."

Hoover took pity on Morris and made arrangements for the Gest parents to be brought home to America on a United States Navy warship which was specially sent on its mercy errand; and Hoover got a special exemption and pass for Morris's parents from the Soviet authorities.

The battleship's captain and one of his lieutenants duly traveled to the Ukrainian village where the parents still lived. When Morris's father came to the door, the Captain said, "On the orders of Herbert Hoover himself and due to your son Morris's efforts on your behalf, I bring you great news. You are saved. We are here to take you back with us to America."

The old man looked at the Captain in silent amazement for a moment, then he said, "Take us where?"

"To America, sir. Your troubles are over."

"Troubles, what troubles? Are you crazy? We're not going anywhere, and you can tell that to Morris and Herbert Hoover, whoever he is."

"No, but sir, you don't understand . . ."

"*You* don't understand, young man," said the father. "We've got a wonderful business here: you'd have to kill me before I'd leave it. Look here."

He led the Captain into the front room of the house, which had been made into a simple shop. The shelves were groaning with tins and packets of food. They were selling, at fabulous prices, all the food parcels which had come from America, dispatched by Morris's sympathetic friends. They'd never been so well off in their lives.

In our last years in Moscow, while we were feverishly buying works for resale in New York, we were obliged to register every work of art we possessed with the Museum Administration of Moscow, which periodically came to our house to "take inventory." They had the right to retain any of our purchases, if they chose, for the Museum, and nothing could be removed without their permission. Fortunately they wanted very few items, and, thanks to our contract with the government for the sale of our factories, the necessary permission for export was granted for the bulk of the collection, although not without a blizzard of red tape, and only after we had paid that heavy "export duty" based on the Museum Committee's valuation.

We *were* invited to be commission agents in one of the most amazing art transactions of all time. Our clients were not the Soviet government though, as some have thought, but prominent Americans seeking to do business with the Russians—who, as they showed, were very well able to look after themselves without any help from me.

In 1928, in order to relieve their desperate need for foreign exchange, the Soviets decided they would offer for sale part of the stupendous collection of pictures at the Hermitage in Leningrad. A group of more than twenty masterpieces was offered, including some of the most famous pictures in the world—such as Raphael's *Alba Madonna,* van Eyck's *Last Judgment,* Velázquez's *Innocent X* and Botticelli's *Adoration of the Magi.* Also put up for sale was perhaps the greatest of all paintings by Leonardo da Vinci, the *Benois Madonna,* which was said to be even finer than the *Mona Lisa* hanging in the Louvre. At that time there was not a Leonardo in the United States, and the offer of the *Madonna* aroused huge excitement in this country and drew a flurry of bids from the wealthiest and most powerful collectors.

I had no intention of personally entering bids for any of the pictures on sale. At that time I was not a collector of the greatest works of art and, to speak candidly, I needed my cash for my business. Any one of the pictures in that sale could be expected to fetch many hundreds of thousands of dollars even then, and I couldn't possibly have contemplated investing so large a part of my fortune in such works. In any case, my main personal interest in the art business was to get Victor out of Russia and away from his disastrous marriage.

I did, however, become involved in the sale. A mysterious letter arrived from Max Steuer, the famous New York lawyer who had helped me and my father when we had been threatened with an action by Henry Fingerhood, my father's original partner in Good Laboratories and Allied Drug. Max wrote, asking Victor and me to act as his agents in acquiring a small group of the Hermitage pictures, to include the Leonardo. He was willing, he said, to pay five million rubles—two and a half million dollars—for the group. He offered us a commission of 10 percent on the purchase price in the event that the deal was successfully concluded.

My suspicions were immediately aroused. Max Steuer was indisputably one of the most successful, and therefore one of the richest, lawyers in New York, but I found it hard to believe that he had become so very prosperous as to be able to bid millions of dollars for works of art. Moreover, I knew that Max had recently begun to collect pictures in a small way, but it didn't make sense that he should now be going up against the most prestigious collectors in the world, like Andrew Mellon, to acquire the greatest masterpiece in existence. On the face of it, he ought to have been in no better position to enter this sale than I was myself. I guessed that he must be acting for another party, presumably one of the great collectors who wished to preserve his anonymity.

Nonetheless, Max's offer was obviously good and we stood to make a hefty commission, so I approached Anastas Mikoyan, who was in charge of the Foreign Trade Ministry, the agency conducting the sale. Mikoyan, who knew the price of a button let alone a Leonardo, dismissed the bid out of hand, calling it ridiculous. "The Leonardo alone is worth two and a half million dollars," he said. He had already received an offer of six million dollars for the group Max Steuer wanted, excluding the Leonardo.

I sent cables and letters to Max Steuer, giving him Mikoyan's reply and warning him that if he didn't make his offer more realistic there was a real danger that the Russians would simply withdraw the Leonardo from sale. He replied, asking me to offer two million dollars for the Leonardo alone, not a cent more.

We went back to Mikoyan with Steuer's offer, which he considered with better grace. After a time, we heard that Steuer's bid might be accepted if it was increased by two hundred thousand dollars, to discharge the 10-percent export duty which would be imposed on the picture.

We relayed this information to Steuer. By this time we had heard from our brother Harry in New York that Steuer was definitely acting for a third party and, having tired of indulging him in his pretense that he was acting on his own behalf, we advised him to tell his client— whose name was still unknown to us—that the Russians would not budge from their price.

Max's reply let the cat out of the bag. His client, he said, would go no higher than two million dollars, but, if the bid should be accepted, he would open an irrevocable letter of credit with a New York bank and send Bernard Berenson to Moscow to seal the picture for its journey to America.

Once we heard Berenson's name, we knew that Max Steuer must be acting on behalf of Sir Joseph Duveen, the most famous art dealer in history. Bernard Berenson was on Duveen's payroll and the only man in the world whose opinions on art Duveen respected more than his own. Berenson had been an unofficial tutor to such influential figures as Marcel Proust; Kenneth (later Lord) Clark; John Walker, the distinguished Chief Curator, now Director Emeritus, of the National Gallery in Washington; and Carter Brown, the current Director of the National Gallery. If Berenson was willing to come to Moscow at the behest of Max Steuer's client, that client had to be Duveen.

Duveen had also, we suspected, separately instructed other agents in Moscow to bid for the Leonardo. I think he wanted to confirm that the price we were relaying from Mikoyan was genuine and that we were not misleading him. Negotiations were further muddled and obscured by the intervention of Morris Gest, who acted as an unofficial intermediary between us and Max Steuer. Harry had frequent cause to complain that Morris's energetic mouth made it impossible to do business quietly and discreetly, and heated letters were exchanged between Moscow and New York urging Morris to can it.

All of Duveen's labyrinthine maneuvers over the Leonardo *Madonna* came to nothing, however, because—as I had predicted— the Russians were not to be moved from their price, and they ultimately withdrew the picture altogether from sale.

Thus Sir Joseph lost the Leonardo he coveted so much *for the second time*. Before the Revolution, the picture had been offered to Duveen by its then-owner, a female relative of the actor Peter Ustinov. Duveen called in Berenson, who confirmed the picture's genuineness and told Duveen that he must buy it without fail. Under Russian law, however, the owner was required to offer the picture to the Czar for the Hermitage Museum for the same price. To Duveen's measureless chagrin, the Czar bought it. Thus Peter Ustinov's relative got a Berenson verification of her Leonardo for free.

The bulk of the Hermitage Collection was, of course, acquired by Knoedler Galleries in New York on behalf of Andrew Mellon, and became the most outstanding acquisitions in one of the greatest personal collections of the century. It was bequeathed to the National Gallery, where it is presently housed. By one of the chances with which my life is filled, my connection with that historic sale was renewed, thirty years later, when the Hammer Galleries acquired the Knoedler Galleries, the oldest and one of the most respected art houses in America, suppliers of masterpieces to every important collector in the country from Mellon to Frick to Rockefeller. By the time we acquired the Knoedler Galleries, I had a few masterpieces in my own collection. Back then in 1929, however, I was content with lesser artistic ambitions and glad to be competing with Knoedler using somebody else's money.

The possessions in our Moscow collection which had most enthused Sakho when he asked to go into partnership with us were not our pictures, but our objects of art and precious rarities. Among the articles in our collection were very many bales of eighteenth-century fabrics, shimmering with genuine gold and silver threads, formerly used for copes and chasubles in the private chapels of the Czar. Victor had come across these fabrics one day when he was foraging in the basements of the Winter Palace in Leningrad.

A gang of workers was ripping through a mountain of the fabrics, stripping them of their glittering threads and burning the vestments. He told me about it, and I bought the whole pile for sixty thousand dollars, little more than the gold and silver value of the threads. Later, in America, these fabrics were to return several million dollars to us when they were made up into evening wraps, piano throws, handbags and exotic evening slippers.

Among the priceless jeweled articles we had been able to obtain by paying little more than their intrinsic value in precious stones and gold was a collection of fabulous Easter eggs. These had all formerly belonged to members of the Imperial family, who had commissioned them and exchanged them as gifts. They had been ordered from the Court Jeweler, Carl Fabergé, who was rightly known as the "Cellini of the North," and many of them had been executed by his foremost master, Perchin. They were among the most refined and exotic possessions of the richest and, you might say, the most self-indulgent royal family in the world, and I suppose it is one of the minor paradoxes of the century that they should have ended up in the hands of a young man from the Bronx.

The Romanov family's habit of exchanging these beguiling and wonderful eggs seems to have begun in 1885, when Fabergé proposed to Czar Alexander III that for the next Easter gift for the Empress Maria Feodorovna he should make an egg containing a surprise.

Fabergé produced what was, to all appearances, an ordinary hen's egg—but one made of gold, enameled opaque white. It opened to reveal the yolk, also of gold. The yolk itself opened and inside was a chicken of gold in different shades. Within the chicken was a model of the Imperial crown, identical in all respects to Catherine the Great's stupendous original. And inside the crown hung a tiny ruby egg. Some surprise!

Alexander was so delighted that Fabergé received a standing order for an egg every Eastertide, and a bargain was struck between Emperor and craftsman: Fabergé was given carte blanche to make whatever took his fancy and the Czar was to ask no questions, on condition that each egg should contain some unprecedented surprise. Alexander's son, Czar Nicholas II, continued the bargain and the tradition, adding to it by commissioning two eggs every year—one for his wife, the Empress Alexandra Feodorovna, and the other for his mother, Maria Feodorovna. By the time of the Revolution, Fabergé had produced some fifty Imperial Easter eggs in gold, enamel and precious stones which, for ingenuity, beauty and craftsmanship of design, were fit to be compared with the greatest treasures of ancient civilizations.

Carl Fabergé kept the bargain he had made with Alexander III, even in the very last dying moments of the Imperial regime. He made two Easter eggs for 1917 but, taking them for delivery to the Czar at Tsarskoe Selo, he was told that his patron could not receive them. The Czar was a prisoner in the palace.

Late in 1929 Victor heard from the Soviet agency *Antiquariat,*
which had been established to sell art treasures, that a number of
Fabergé eggs could be bought if the price were right. Seven or eight of
them were on offer at first, for an average price of about fifty thousand
dollars each. I had no hesitation in purchasing every one we were
offered and, eventually, we were able to acquire fifteen.

One of these eggs was a gift on Easter morning, 1895, from Nicholas II to his mother, the Dowager Empress Maria Feodorovna. It was
of solid gold and rose-colored enamel. Perchin had spent several years
making it. It was profusely decorated with rose diamonds and emeralds, the top of the egg surmounted by a beautifully shaped star sap-
phire. The inside was lined with a fine red velvet and had a pocket
containing a folding screen of ten miniatures painted on mother-of-
pearl, the frames carried out in the same superb workmanship as the
rest of the egg.

The miniatures, which were the crowning beauty of that work of
art, were painted by the famous Russian miniaturist Krijitski, and depicted the various Danish abodes and palaces of the Empress, formerly
Princess Dagmar of Denmark. It was known as the Danish Egg.

This same egg would now sell for more than one million dollars,
twenty times what I paid for it.

A second egg, even more lavish, was the famous Diamond and
Lapis Egg. It was made of the finest lapis with gold mountings. The
design included several double-headed eagles, each surmounted by a
crown. The top had a rectangular flat diamond which showed the initials AF surmounted by a crown and the date 1912. Those were the
initials of Alexandra Feodorovna. The bottom was also set with a large
diamond. Inside the egg was the double-headed Russian Imperial Eagle, entirely set with diamonds and mounted on a lapis lazuli base. On
the breast of the eagle under the crown was a miniature of Czarevich
Alexis in a sailor suit, showing both front and back view. Nicholas II
had presented this egg to his wife, Czarina Alexandra, on Easter morning of 1912. It was also signed by Fabergé, who had spent three years
making this little intricate gift which was found in the collection of
crown jewels in the Alexander Palace.

These eggs were to form the dazzling centerpiece of the exhibitions
and sales which we mounted in America. Many years later, a large
group of these fabulous Easter eggs was acquired by Malcolm Forbes,
some at million-dollar prices, and are now housed in the Forbes Museum at the publishing headquarters of *Forbes* magazine in New York.

Thus I began one of the most unusual and interesting episodes of
my business career, as an art dealer and supersalesman in department
stores. That story is for another chapter—another decade, another
continent and, after nine years, home at last.

Home Free

As the train which bore me and my family away from Moscow in the early fall of 1930 slowly clattered over the points outside the station and then pulled onto the tracks, bound for Warsaw and Paris, I leaned my head against the cushions and closed my eyes. I did not see Moscow as it slipped away.

I had reason to be relieved. I found myself home free. My ambitions had been realized, despite the gathering difficulties of recent years which had threatened to thwart them. Ever since the death of Lenin, I had felt Stalin's oppressive hand tighten its grip on the country, promising to squeeze the life out of my business endeavors. By following Stalin's activities in the press and in conversations, I had seen clearly that he meant to undo Lenin's NEP and rid the country of foreign concessionaires. I had taken my leave just in the nick of time.

My parents were to remain at the Brown House to ensure issuance of the notes and transfer of the cash due to us under our final settlement. They would also supervise shipment to New York of our works of art. Otherwise, few tangible marks were left of my long sojourn in Moscow. Not even the name of our pencil factory remained: on our departure, the Soviets promptly renamed it after Sacco and Vanzetti, the anarchist martyrs of the Red scare in America in the late twenties— and it still bears their names today. No longer would the catalogue of the factory bear the symbol of the Statue of Liberty. Hereafter it would be the hammer and sickle.

Paris seemed to invite me with the rich promise of everything that had been missing from my life for the previous nine years—comfort, elegance and ease: the dignity of a business career in a society which honored business and, most appealing of all perhaps, a release at last from the incessant suspiciousness and secretiveness of Communist Russia.

Olga was almost beside herself with happiness to be leaving Moscow. In Paris she could expect to resume the life which had been hers in Moscow before the Revolution—a life filled with parties, fine clothes, servants, good food and entertainment. Olga also had very definite bohemian tastes. In Moscow she had surrounded herself with the young artists and writers who had briefly—until the iron-handed philistinism of Stalin's "Soviet Realism" descended—made Moscow a vibrant center of the living arts; but the magnet for all the artists of the day was still the Paris of Hemingway, Joyce, Fitzgerald, Pound, Gertrude Stein and Picasso, to which we were heading.

Olga couldn't wait to plunge into this society. She was like an exotic tropical bird who had been confined for years in a cage, muted and clipped, and was now suddenly released, soaring and singing. She was to give several concerts in Paris which were well-received by the Parisian public and critics.

Olga had an Aunt Tanya in Paris who was married to a member of the French cabinet. Through these people, we were immediately well-placed in the city, an array of introductions open to us at the most influential levels. We looked for a house and soon found a lovely villa at Garches, up a steep and winding hill about fifteen miles from the center of Paris and overlooking the whole city. The villa had previously belonged to a very well known dress designer named Mlle. Barth, and it was duly exquisite. Furnished with authentic Louis XVI pieces and fin-de-siècle pictures, it had a dining room walled with windows which opened upon the view of the city and the River Seine; and it became our delight to give dinner parties there with all Paris stretched below us in a glittering vista. After dinner we liked to take our guests out to walk in its lovely rose garden, which was delicately formal. I have rarely been happier than I was in that house.

I had left Moscow knowing exactly what I intended to do in Paris. In Russia I had met a wide circle of Western businessmen who had traded with the Russians and had accepted payment half in cash and half in promissory notes for the goods and services they supplied. Among them were former partners of Averell Harriman who had had an ill-fated manganese concession. They had no confidence in these notes: they did not believe the Russians would pay. They figured that the behavior of the Soviets over the international debts of the Czarist regime—debts which the Bolsheviks had refused to honor—was a bad omen for the promissory notes which the new government had issued against their own debts. I believed the opposite.

My attitude toward the Soviets was based upon my business experience. I had invariably found that whenever a company supplying me had gone bust, been liquidated and then re-formed, the new management always paid its debts promptly and in full, being desperate to establish a good name with its customers. I viewed the Russians in the same light. Having (justifiably, I believe) refused to pay the Czar's debts, the Soviets were now anxious to prove their own reliability in trade. I was certain that they would not default. They couldn't afford not to pay: in revenge, the world would have denied them every scrap of the trade which they were still seeking.

Harriman's associates offered me their three-year promissory notes at the going rate of 2-percent discount per month (I didn't find out until years later, when Averell himself told me that he had sold none of his own promissory notes: he hung on and got paid in full). I was thus able to discount these notes at up to 72 percent over their full three years, and was able to borrow money on my own credit at 6 percent per annum to pay for them. Since, as I had anticipated, the Russians paid every note and met every obligation, my profits were very great indeed—it's hard to put a figure on them now, but they were well into several million dollars.

I was, in a small way, a gentleman merchant banker. I followed only the one single activity—acquiring Russian promissory notes—and the establishment I needed was, consequently, very small. Just a suite of offices at 34 rue Tronchet and a staff of a few secretaries and a bookkeeper. After the frenzy and pandemonium of the pencil factory, with its hundreds of workers and its incessant bedlam of production, my life in Paris was as sedate and placid as the Seine itself.

So calm, in fact, was this life that I took to napping in my office—a habit which I have practiced ever since. I kept a pillow, an alarm clock, a hairbrush and a bottle of hair tonic in a safe in my room. After one of the long, lavish and lovely lunches which are the particular bonus of a businessman's life in Paris, I would return to my office and tell my secretaries that I was not to be disturbed. Then I would draw the drapes, take my pillow out of the safe and lie on the sofa for half an hour of deep slumber. When the clock woke me, I tidied my hair, put on my coat, replaced the pillow in the safe and told the secretaries that I was ready for my next appointment.

Paris was paradise. I felt there that I had entered fully bloomed into life as a mature man. I was happily married to a most beautiful and exciting woman. Our son Julian was then at that entrancing age between babyhood and boyhood when his every word and deed was an original act, freshly minted from a mind exploding with curiosity. I had cultivated the interests of my early life and added to them during my years in Russia, and now I knew my tastes very well and had extensive means with which to indulge them. Music, art, business and family life absorbed me completely and filled me every day with pleasure. I felt that I had paid my dues during the foregoing thirteen years, since I had taken over my father's ailing company, and now the rewards were coming to me in full flood: it would have been graceless of me not to relish them. I could have lived in Paris indefinitely. I was to be there in full-time residence for little more than a year.

Our venture in selling Czarist art treasures was giving me cause for serious concern. L'Ermitage, the gallery we had opened, was losing money in alarming amounts. The only successes in selling our collection had been racked up by Morris Gest and, as I have said, his efforts were about as profitable to us as throwing our treasures in the East River. The letters and cables I received from Harry and Victor were unremittingly gloomy and despairing: they couldn't see any way for us to make a success of our undertaking.

Through the winter of 1930–1931, I sat in my office in Paris reading these dispiriting communications and hoping for the best. My replies to Harry and Victor encouraged them to be optimistic: the crisis couldn't last, I told them; rich people always manage to hang on to some of their wealth and the stock market was bound to pick up. But as the figures for the gallery continued to show no trade to speak of, I became seriously worried and, by the early spring, I had made up my mind that I should go to New York myself and take the business in hand.

Meanwhile, still in Paris, my path crossed briefly, and for the first time, the shining comet's tail which Franklin Roosevelt was to burn upon the history of the twentieth century. I count myself privileged to have lived in his era, and I shall always be proud that he and his wife, Eleanor, called me their friend and acknowledged the small efforts I made to support their great work.

FDR was still Governor of New York at that moment, and his close friend, former US Senator Henry French Hollis of New Hampshire, had opened a legal practice in Paris. Henry became my own lawyer in Paris and a good friend as well. He was intensely interested in my experiences in Moscow and encouraged me to think that I could give useful counsel to FDR, who was then running hard for the White House. If elected, FDR intended to normalize diplomatic relations with the USSR and grant the formal recognition which the United States had always refused.

Of course I believed such a plan was of paramount importance— anything that might retard or reverse Russia's retreat into the wintry isolationism which Stalin favored was greatly to be encouraged. I thought, even then, that it was terribly dangerous for the world that so vital a state as Soviet Russia should be disconnected from the community of trading nations; and in the forefront of my mind—as it has never been far from it—was Benjamin Franklin's aphorism that trading nations seldom make war.

Roosevelt's rational and healthy attitude to the matter would have been enough on its own to earn my support, but there was so much more which drew and held my admiration. In him was everything noble and good about American liberalism. FDR believed with every atom in the American system and defended it passionately, but at the same time he understood that the wealth of America needed to be harnessed and directed not only for the good of all Americans but for the good of the world. He never questioned that America was and could be a force for the betterment of all humans: that was the meaning and the impulse of the New Deal which he offered with such eloquence, wit, glamour and compassion.

If it sounds as if I was star-struck, I was. Roosevelt seemed to me to have arrived on the world stage at exactly the moment when only he could give the leadership the world so desperately needed.

Henry Hollis urged me to contribute to FDR's campaign and to lobby other businessmen in France to do likewise. I didn't need much urging.

On July 28, 1932, I sent a cable to Governor Roosevelt, heartily favoring the recognition of the Russian government, based upon my nine years' business experience in Russia as an American citizen. Two days before that, I wrote a letter to Henry Hollis, strongly declaring my support for FDR, and he in turn forwarded it to Louis McHenry Howe, confidential adviser, unofficial "campaign manager" and close friend to Roosevelt. With it, he enclosed a letter of his own, enthusiastically describing my credentials and background, and graciously referring to me as "one of the most remarkable men I have ever known. The advice of Dr. Hammer," he went on, "regarding affairs in Russia and the best way to deal with the present government would be extremely valuable."

As it turned out, I didn't have time to do much more for Roosevelt in 1932 than donate money to the campaign and encourage my friends to do the same—though Roosevelt's path and mine were to cross many times in the years to come. Throughout that summer—and for many summers to come—I was up to my armpits in the extraordinary work of selling Czarist art treasures to the Middle America whose prosperity Roosevelt did so much to revive.

When I landed in New York, after yet another of those Atlantic crossings I had come to dread so deeply, Victor and Harry met me with very long faces and a gloomy outlook.

There was no point in continuing to try to sell our treasures through L'Ermitage, they said. We should close the gallery, take the choicest pieces from our collection for our own personal enjoyment and store the rest until such time as the economy picked up and people began to spend money again.

Looking at the full records of their work over the previous year, I saw their pessimism confirmed. They had managed to sell next to nothing. Most of our property was still unpacked from the boxes and crates in which it had been shipped from Russia, and was running up a big dead loss in storage expenses in a warehouse on the Upper East Side, where it filled many rooms.

However, Morris Gest's successes in selling our Czarist treasures proved that there was at least some demand for it; we just needed to find a more efficient and cost-effective way to reach our market (Morris's was the kind of success which no business can afford). I told my brothers that we weren't just going to lie down and take a beating. After all, an investment worth several million dollars was locked up in these works of art and we needed to find a way of unlocking it.

"Listen," I said to Victor and Harry, "not everybody can have lost their money in the Crash. There will always be people who will like the idea of owning something which belonged to royalty and having it in their homes."

I couldn't see why the art business should be any different from any other: if you had something to sell which other people wanted, and if you made them aware of your product and offered it at a good price, how could you go wrong? What was so special about art? I've always said, "There is no such thing as a bad business, just bad businessmen."

Our first task obviously was to inventory our collection: at that moment we didn't even have a complete list of all the objects filling the warehouse. How could we offer it for sale when we didn't know exactly what it was?

Victor set to work and drew up a detailed inventory in a very short time, putting a price on every object he catalogued—for the most part, he was guessing. There was no established market for the goods we had to sell. Who could say, for example, what a housewife in Poughkeepsie might pay for a pair of nineteenth-century Russian candlesticks which had formerly belonged to the Czar?

The solution to our marketing problem came to me by chance, but, then, chance is not entirely a matter of chance. If you work hard and concentrate on your problem and pay attention to any possible solution, you can make your own luck to a large extent. My luck came when I heeded the wisdom of a very intelligent man named S. L. Hoffman.

Samuel Hoffman was an immensely wealthy dress manufacturer. An entirely self-made man, he—like so many other American entrepreneurs of that age—had been born in Russia and had fought his way out of New York's Lower East Side. He made his greatest fortune during the Depression, when the garment trade as a whole was taking a terrific beating. Recognizing that people had to have clothes, no matter how adverse the economy, Hoffman hit on a way to sell ladies' dresses for one dollar apiece. He installed huge machines in his factories capable of cutting and sewing the shapes for scores of dresses in simple movements. Then he supplied the garments to department stores all across the nation. His one-dollar dresses were among the most famous marks of that desperate economic time.

Samuel Hoffman and I were both clients of the same lawyer in New York, Jacob Schapiro. Schapiro introduced us, and I told Sam about my difficulties with our Czarist art. "Department stores," he answered. "Try the department stores."

He made a perfectly logical case. The department stores, he said, were always looking for some fresh attraction to draw in the customers, and they were particularly good at mounting special promotions. "You've got a wonderful story to tell with this Czarist art, all about its provenance and history and how you came by it," he said. "The department stores love a good story. They'll help you to display your collection to its best advantage."

I jumped at this idea. It had all the hallmarks of the perfect solution. I decided, straightaway, that I would write a personal letter to all the heads of all the country's major department stores, telling them my story and offering them the Czarist art. Samuel Hoffman kindly offered to help me.

I worked hard on the composition of the letter, making the proposition as enticing and intriguing as I could. I gave a brief account of my time in Russia and my business experiences there, and explained how I had become interested in Russian art "because of the falling ruble and my desire to convert my rubles into something tangible." I went on, "We are not art dealers, as such. But we were (and are) interested in disposing of this art."

I offered the treasures to the stores at a discount of 40 percent from the listed retail price. I hired a printer to make up a batch of price tags embossed with the double-headed eagle crest of the Imperial family, below which was printed a brief history of the object. Then I sat back to await the flood of offers which I felt sure would come. Nothing happened. The answers from the stores which bothered to reply were very dismissive and discouraging. I was beginning to feel that S. L. Hoffman had led me into a blind alley when a telegram arrived from St. Louis, from a Mr. Joseph Laurie, Vice President of Scruggs-Vandervoort-Barney.

COME IMMEDIATELY, said the telegram. I called him on the telephone and he was very enthusiastic. He said that he would give us a good space in the store and put on a big promotion. Right away, Victor and I went out of the office, over to Sixth Avenue where I had heard that a theatrical company which had gone broke was selling its traveling trunks in a liquidation sale. We bought every trunk they had, had them sent up to the warehouse, packed up a good selection of our treasures and put them on a train to St. Louis.

Leaving Harry in New York, Victor and I went on the train with our trunks filling the luggage cars—a friendly railroad conductor let us check them on our personal tickets, so we got free haulage. In St. Louis I met Mr. Laurie and said that I believed the success of the venture depended on getting good coverage in the newspapers. I wanted them to treat our exhibition not as just another department store promotion, but as a solid news story. I told Mr. Laurie that I wanted to meet the publishers and editors of the local newspapers and I asked him to go with me to make introductions. Naturally, no newspaper likes to give free advertising space to a department store or any other regular adver-tiser, but I felt that our story might get their journalistic juices flowing.

The editors saw the news value of our story. I gave them pictures of our fabulous Fabergé eggs and various other treasures and told them the full story of my years in Russia. The story was prominently carried in both of St. Louis's daily papers.

Next day, about five thousand people were lining the sidewalk, waiting to get into the store. They swarmed all over our exhibition, snapping up bargains as quickly as the sales slips could be written out. During the first week of the promotion, our special display room was visited by an average of two thousand people a day, and sales soared into hundreds of thousands of dollars. It turned out that Victor's pric-ing had been pretty astute. Some quirk or fancy had put it in his mind, whenever he was unsure of a price, to round it up to the nearest dollar or hundred and deduct one unit—so he priced a bead at $9.99 and a bangle at $99. As far as I know, that marketing device had never been employed before in the selling of art; and I have yet to come across a Rubens offered on the conventional market for $999,999.

Our show was a smash. Before the end of our first week, Mr. Laurie was writing to me at my hotel in St. Louis, asking me to extend the exhibition for another week and get fresh supplies from Harry in New York. The trunks were duly freighted back to the warehouse and refilled from our stocks, shipped back to St. Louis and emptied onto our tables and counters in time for Monday morning's opening of the new week.

As part of the promotion, Victor had agreed to give a lecture in Scruggs-Vandervoort-Barney's music hall, introducing our collection and giving some stories of our experiences in Russia.

It was a typically knockabout performance and, in front of his biggest-ever audience, Victor was in his element. His talk was such a hit that Mr. Laurie wrote specially to me "to arrange to have Mr. Victor Hammer deliver another lecture in our music hall because so many have expressed great disappointment at not hearing him today [February 2, 1932]."

As soon as they read about our success, the other big department stores came running. Marshall Field's in Chicago, which had not bothered to answer my original letter, sent a vice president named Ray Schaeffer posthaste to check us out, and he wrote such an enthusiastic report that the store booked us in for a three-week appearance after our stay in St. Louis.

In Chicago I made the same approach to the local newspapers, with even more spectacular results. The store was literally jammed, day after day, with eager customers. The three-week booking at Marshall Field turned into three months, and I had to leave Victor there to run the main show while I took a smaller traveling exhibition on the road to Bullock's Wilshire in Los Angeles, Halle's in Cleveland, J. L. Hudson in Detroit, the Emporium in San Francisco, Kaufman's in Pittsburgh, Hutzler's in Baltimore, Woodward and Lothrop's in Washington and so on and on backwards and forwards across the nation.

In the fifteen months between February 1932 and June 1933, we staged twenty-three exhibitions and sales in different cities. I got to know every attendant on every sleeping car on all the great trains of the time. I covered almost as many miles by rail that year as I do by jet today.

I loved every aspect and detail of our new business: it was such a refreshing change from all my earlier ventures. Manufacturing businesses are intensely absorbing, but the management of large staffs of workers with all their labor problems and the difficulties of arranging distribution of the products, to say nothing of the complexities of dealing with state bureaucracies and labor unions, can exhaust even the keenest enthusiasm after a time.

Our new art business had all the razzmatazz and immediacy of a traveling circus. Having arrived in a city, we put up our tent, figuratively speaking, in a department store, laid out the wares, sent out the publicity and waited for the paying customers to arrive. If they didn't like what they saw, they didn't pay. My job was simple: I had to make the show captivating and irresistible. I was the circus barker and ringmaster. I couldn't get enough of it.

I particularly enjoyed writing the copy for our advertisements, which I did without professional help of any kind. Getting across the special excitement of our collection called for a style of writing which, I found, was like writing a telegram, where every word had to do the work of ten because it cost so much.

Being completely in charge of press and public relations for the business, I quickly discovered that an inch of editorial copy in a newspaper was worth a foot of paid advertising, and that a photograph on editorial pages was almost beyond price. When our exhibition arrived at William Hengerer's department store in Buffalo, a local photographer had the bright idea of photographing a couple of young society ladies posing in the Czarist robes and chasubles from our collection. Since the girls were well-known stars of Buffalo society, the picture made the front page and brought in crowds of customers. I took this lesson to heart and, from then on, I made sure that some local celebrity was invited to pose with articles of the collection wherever it traveled. The pictures always got a good show in the papers.

At Marshall Field's in Chicago, we had a terrific stroke of luck when a niece of the dead Czar Nicholas II came in to see the exhibits and touch the possessions of her lost family. I couldn't have prayed for a better piece of publicity.

During one of his talks, Victor was asked about the Anastasia affair, which was then enthralling the world. Along with the rest of the Imperial family, Anastasia, youngest daughter of Czar Nicholas II, had been presumed shot dead in the cellar at Ekaterinburg where they all perished. However, in the early thirties, a woman appeared in America who claimed to be Anastasia herself.

Her story was that she had been protected from the executioners' bullets by the body of one of her relations and that, pretending to be dead, she had received a blow on the head from one of the soldiers who went among the bodies, clubbing them with rifle butts. When she regained consciousness, she said, she was helped to escape by one of the soldiers who was guarding the cellar; and then she made her way to the White Russian armies and was spirited out of Russia, first to Rumania and then to America. Along the way, she had acquired a confusing multiplicity of identities, assuming first the name of a Polish girl, Franziska Schanzkowski, and then, having married an American, calling herself Mrs. Anderson.

The so-called Anastasia was under the protection and tutelage of a wealthy American woman who claimed to be certain of her credentials and was seeking formal recognition of her birthrights. A vast fortune might have awaited Mrs. Anderson if she could prove herself to be the living heir to the countless millions said to be on deposit in Romanov accounts throughout Europe.

Well, Victor was asked his opinion of the matter and he, quick as ever on his toes, replied, "I don't doubt that a blow on the head might render a person unconscious and cause loss of memory; or that, on recovering, that person might have been able to escape. But I can't imagine a blow, no matter how severe, which would cause a native-born Russian to speak the language with a Polish accent—as this woman does."

The enigma of Anastasia/Mrs. Anderson was never satisfactorily resolved, though Victor's skepticism seemed to me to be the most accurate comment on the affair.

It was at that time that Ray Schaeffer of Marshall Field's told me I should write a book about my experiences in Russia to help promote our treasures. In three weeks during the summer of 1932, drawing from memory and from incomplete notes in a diary I had kept during the twenties, I wrote *The Quest of the Romanoff Treasure* (the publisher, Paisley Press, gave the book the title). The writing streamed onto the page with hardly a break or hesitation. I was painfully aware of the inevitable shortcomings of a book written at such speed—the finished manuscript seemed patchy and incomplete—but the book received favorable reviews and various of my friends, such as Walter Duranty, said that I had missed my calling and that I should have been a journalist. Some people might take this as an insult, but I knew they meant to be kind.

In January 1933 Lord & Taylor in New York invited us to open a short engagement with our collection, inaugurating an association which was to last two and a half years. Lord & Taylor was run by probably the only woman managing a major department store at that time, a brilliant executive named Dorothy Shaver. When I went to see her in the winter of 1932, and told her all about our success around the country, she immediately offered to give us a three-week exhibition. The sales of that show were so tremendous, and the promotion brought so many people into the store, that she said, "Why don't you stay here indefinitely?"

On April 5, 1933, Lord & Taylor opened an icon gallery on the seventh floor of the store, entirely supplied with our collection from the Winter Palace and other Imperial palaces. It was, without question, the biggest single exhibition for sale of Russian icons in New York since the Russian Revolution, and it brought us attention from serious art critics around the world. One of the most eminent men to visit the gallery was Professor Paul Muratoff, who lived in Paris, had lectured at Oxford, Cambridge and the Courtauld Institute in London, and was recognized as the world's leading authority on icons.

Professor Muratoff made a thrilling discovery at our gallery. One of our icons turned out to be a major masterpiece by Stroganov, one of the greatest of all icon painters.

It was a field altar or camp's church from the private chapel of the Winter Palace, and it had last belonged to Czar Nicholas II. It depicted the Trinity, the favorite saints of Russia and the miracles of the New Testament. We had acquired it believing it to be an eighteenth-century work, and it was displayed thus in our collection.

Muratoff scrutinized this icon minutely, returning to it over and over again. Finally he declared his belief that it had been repainted—as many icons were during the reign of Peter the Great—and was much older than we supposed. He offered to supervise cleaning the icon and we readily agreed. The process revealed the accuracy of the professor's instincts and the glories of the original work—a depth and warmth of color and a fineness of line which had been obscured in the repainting. Muratoff triumphantly declared in a written statement that it was "one of the 16th-century *Stroganov* masterpieces. Its date is about 1580."

The gallery on the seventh floor wasn't enough for Dorothy Shaver. She believed that our unique collection could support an independent venture. She knew of a vacant store on the southeast corner of the Waldorf-Astoria at Park Avenue and Fiftieth Street, and suggested that we go into partnership with Lord & Taylor to open a branch there. It was an inspired idea: with Lord & Taylor's support in promotions, the branch prospered very vigorously and was responsible for a vast volume of trade until we decided, in 1935, that we were strong enough to go completely independent, and opened our own Hammer Galleries at 682 Fifth Avenue.

Once the branch was established at the Waldorf-Astoria, it was no longer necessary for us to be on the road with our show and, with great relief and some millions of dollars of profit, we ended our travels.

By that time, having disposed of at least 90 percent of all the art treasures which we had originally collected in Russia, we had several times replenished our stocks. Victor made a number of extended visits to Berlin to deal with the agency the Soviets had created to oversee its art exports. He found himself in a very strong position to acquire the best possible goods and terms, since we were now of course paying the Russians in the dollars for which they were so desperate.

Victor also wanted to go to Moscow to visit his son Armasha, and to renew his efforts to get the boy an exit visa so that he could come to live in America. As long as Stalin was in power, the Russians always refused.

Meanwhile, my parents, having left Russia, continued to act on our behalf as purchasing agents. They spread their activities wide across Europe, and traveled often, especially to the south of France, in search of Czarist antiquities for our gallery. On one of these trips, early in 1932, my father found himself briefly in a German jail.

It was an appalling incident. Though he was still robust and strong, my father was now in his late fifties. Jails are never holiday camps, but European prisons in those days were very nasty places. My father found himself in circumstances which compared unfavorably even with the conditions he had endured in Sing-Sing. He took his brief detention in his usual philosophical stride, waiting patiently until I could make arrangements to have him cleared from the charge. I was not so calm. Tied up to my neck with the business of selling our Russian art treasures in America, I went nearly frantic in New York while my father was in prison in Erfurt.

It was a sorry story of swindle and corruption on the part of one of our employees, with my father the victim.

He'd been left behind in Moscow to complete the deal with the Main Concessions Committee for the sale of my pencil concession. The conclusion of the deal called for extensive auditing to establish the book value of the business, and the Soviets, naturally, were in no hurry to complete that process because they were so short of currency. In the meantime the pencil factory continued its business, and the Concessions Committee was bound to pay our creditors, including all foreign suppliers, who had to be paid in foreign currency. To establish the extent of each demand, my father called a meeting in Moscow of all the company's creditors and signed agreements with each of them, determining the amount of their claim, based upon the government audit.

One of these creditors was a German named Bach who had supplied slats of impregnated synthetic cedar and was in litigation with us because we had rejected an inferior consignment. At the creditors' meeting in Moscow, Bach took a cut in the amount of his claim and signed an agreement.

Meanwhile the office in Berlin which handled our business with German suppliers was still open and functioning, and on one of his trips there, my father took an employee from our Moscow accounting office named Georg Schonzwit. My father trusted Schonzwit far enough to give him access to letters my father had foolishly signed in blank to be used for settling debts with small creditors.

One day while my father was away from Berlin, Schonzwit took some of those letters from the safe, wrote out a fictitious claim, forged a check on one of our German banks and split the proceeds with one of his friends.

Returning to Berlin, my father discovered the swindle and threatened to turn Schonzwit over to the police unless he and his friend returned the money. Almost immediately, my father received a call from our supplier Bach, who wanted to meet him in Erfurt. When my father got there, he was arrested. Bach had sworn out a complaint, using an affidavit obtained from Schonzwit. The complaint alleged that my father had received full settlement from the Soviet Concessions Committee of Bach's disputed claim against our company. Schonzwit's affidavit declared that my father had defrauded Bach, giving him only his reduced claim and pocketing the difference. Bach had told the police that my father was going to Switzerland to deposit his money there.

The affidavit had been cooked up between Schonzwit and Bach, of course, but Bach had very skillfully arranged to attack my father on home turf. He prevailed on a friendly judge first to issue the warrant for Father's arrest and then to lock him away. At first the judge refused my father bail altogether, then he set a prohibitive amount, and finally the only way to get my father free was to get the case out of the judge's jurisdiction, which we did, to Berlin.

Schonzwit then disappeared. After I threatened Bach with prosecution for perjury, he agreed to drop his case. The case was settled, with each side paying attorneys' fees. Bach got his payment from the Concessions Committee and the case was closed.

Through it all, my father never showed any sign of distress, though he did once say to me, "German jails aren't exactly a picnic, I've discovered." I was so angry I could have boiled Bach in oil. My father thought the incident was little more than a nuisance, which he quickly forgot.

During the rest of the thirties my parents stayed in Europe, making occasional visits to New York to see us. They were not to return to New York to live until near the end of the decade, when war in Europe had become inevitable and the great dictators, Hitler and Stalin, were shaping up for their apocalyptic clash.

The life of my own little family had been pitched and tossed by the events of the previous few years. The happiness of our life in Paris had lasted only a year, and sadly but inevitably, my marriage to Olga and my relationship with our son Julian suffered from our prolonged separations while I was looking after the art business.

Olga and Julian remained in Paris when I returned to New York in 1931, and I went back to live in my little studio house in Greenwich Village. Ten years had passed since I had last lived there full-time and I was very happy to be back.

In 1932 I tried to straighten out my family affairs by bringing Olga and Julian over from Paris. Olga was eager to come, but she made one absolutely inflexible condition: she must bring the Russian nanny who had been with us since Julian's birth in Moscow. This apparently simple demand involved me in a set of maneuvers which required as much ingenuity as a major takeover.

The nanny, named Xenia Parousine, had been Olga's own nurse in her childhood. She was now about seventy years old. She was wonderfully loyal and loving, and Olga was devoted to her. Having been born in a peasant family, she spoke only Russian, which she could neither read nor write. In any and all language, she was a total illiterate.

By 1932 United States immigration laws had become very tough. It was an unyielding rule that all prospective immigrants should either speak English or have a basic literacy in their own language.

I knew that I was in plenty of trouble. If I wanted my family to be with me in New York, I had to find a way to get the nanny through the immigration net. If she was refused entry and sent back to France, Olga would go straight back with her. No question.

At first I tried to get the immigration authorities to bend a little on their rules. This is an old lady, I said, and she can't be expected to master her ABCs at the age of seventy. No dice.

I sent a cable to Olga to explain the position, saying, WASHINGTON REFUSED INTERFERE STOP DECISION PARIS CONSUL FINAL STOP VERY STRICT OWING UNEMPLOYMENT CRISIS STOP AM TERRIBLY LONESOME WANT TO SEE YOU BOTH TELEGRAPH YOUR DECISION.

Olga's reply said, in effect, this is your problem, you solve it. She said, HAVE OBTAINED VISA NURSE UP TO NEW YORK WITHOUT PERMISSION TO LAND STOP TRY TO ARRANGE STOP.

I went to meet the *Aquitania* with a heavy heart. I hadn't been able to solve the problem. I had one last avenue to explore.

I had arranged to go out to the ship on the pilot's cutter. I sat quietly behind the immigration officers in the ship's saloon while they administered the literacy test to newly arrived immigrants. They had a big book, pages of which were written in all the major European languages: each new immigrant had to read the page in his or her own native language.

I listened closely while the test was administered to a Russian immigrant. The text, it turned out, was the story of Goldilocks and the Three Bears. I memorized the exact form and language in which the story was written and hurried away to find the nanny.

"You know the story of Goldilocks and the Three Bears, don't you?" I said in Russian.

"Of course I do," she said.

"All right. That's what they're going to get you to read," I told her. "And this is how it goes."

"I know how it goes," she said.

"Listen. Memorize these words." I repeated the words on the page, down to the end of the first paragraph, which was my limit.

When her turn came for the test, Xenia put on an Oscar-winning performance. Donning her spectacles, she peered studiously at the page and then fluently repeated the words she had memorized.

A Russian-speaking assistant stood beside the immigration officer who was supervising the test. After Xenia had flawlessly rattled off a couple of sentences in Russian, the assistant interrupted and said, "She's all right." Thus my family passed safely and intact into the

United States and we had time for a proper and joyous reunion.

Unfortunately Olga didn't take a happy view of the accommodations I had prepared for them. She took one look at my little house in Greenwich Village and uttered the Russian equivalent of "Armand, you must be kidding. We can't live in a doll's house." So we took a large apartment on Fifth Avenue not far from the Metropolitan Museum.

That was more to Olga's liking, but it didn't make her happy. Unable to speak English, she was lonely in New York City, especially when I was away—as I was most of the time. Her difficulties made things worse between us and seemed to bring into focus the fact that we had very little in common. She wasn't interested in business; I didn't care much for the kind of light entertainment that was her passion— big-band music, for instance. She, quite naturally, wanted to spend a lot of her time with the expatriate Russian community in New York, talking about the old days, and often went to the Russian restaurants and nightclubs. The incessant nostalgic talk in those places bored me. I was interested in the America of the day. We began, slowly and without great rancor, to drift apart. Effectively, we separated.

Olga decided that she would be happier in a house in the country and we bought a spread up in Highland Mills, a suburb of Monroe in upper New York State, where there was quite a large group of Russian expatriates. It was a lovely house, with nice grounds and a menagerie of pets, but I was only rarely able to get there and, within a couple of hours of arriving, I would be bored out of my mind, drumming my fingers with nothing to do, eager to get back to my work.

Things between us picked up a bit when the Hammer Galleries opened a branch in Palm Beach and Olga and I took a villa down there. Since Palm Beach was one of the hottest spots of personal disposable wealth in the world, and since the goods we had to offer were luxury items with a particular appeal to the rich, Palm Beach seemed like an obvious place for us to try our luck. On a seasonal basis, from January to March or April of every year from 1934, we rented a store in the Everglades Club on Worth Avenue, the snootiest address in the snootiest street of that most class-conscious of all towns in America. Our biggest trade there was in trinkets to be given as gifts. A guest would present his host with a cigarette case made by Fabergé for the Czarina for which we would charge him $300; as a birthday present, one society lady would send another a little Romanov snuffbox, price $175. These prices should be multiplied by ten for today's values.

A name in every society column and a face in every newspaper picture of Palm Beach parties those days was Prince Mikhail Gounduroff. He lent (or rather, we hired) his princely tone to our business, acting as a noble presence in our store and attending openings of our traveling exhibits.

Prince Mikhail had swept into our New York galleries one day, ostensibly to look at our Czarist treasures, but actually hoping to pick up a crust or two. His family was distantly related to the Romanov Imperial family and lived, it seemed, in a castle in Germany. Mikhail, however, being the second or third son, did not stand to inherit any of his family wealth and, despite the grandeur of his connections, he was looking for a job.

He was doing his best to cut a dashing figure in New York, impressing hostesses and eating as many free dinners as he could, but he was hampered by being stone broke. I thought that a genuine Russian Prince might add a certain éclat to our ventures and I gave him a nominal function at a modest salary. He didn't have to do much more than hang around looking princely and give an occasional word of advice to potential customers, and these duties he performed with an exquisite sense of dramatic opportunity.

When we sent him to Chicago for one of our shows at Marshall Field's, we arranged to have him met at the station by a squad of police motorcyclists who gave him escort, sirens wailing, to the store. With a true professional's eye for a good headline, Mikhail halted the cavalcade en route when he spotted a hot dog stand. He explained to the panting reporters that his chief delight in America was a good hot dog and that he could never pass one by. They loved that.

Having Mikhail's name connected with the business also helped to dilute some of the hostility we encountered from other aristocratic Russian emigrés in New York. Some of them were scandalized to see the former possessions of their Imperial family openly on sale in a gallery and exhibited in department stores. They thought it was a terrible act of lèse-majesté and they were always complaining to newspapers.

A couple of times in the mid-thirties our galleries were burglarized and items of particular sentimental meaning to White Russians were stolen. During the night of March 24, 1934, a thief smashed our windows and took the gold-hilted, jeweled sword which had formerly belonged to Grand Duke Vladimir, uncle of the last Czar. On the hilt of this three-foot-long sword, studded with diamonds, rubies and sapphires, were the words "For Bravery" and the Imperial crown, inlaid with gold. In October 1937 a smash-and-grab robber took from our windows a diamond and gold snuffbox, worth five thousand dollars, which had been given to Czarina Marie by the Shah of Persia, Nasr-ed-Deen.

The White Russian emigrés plainly thought that mere businessmen from the Bronx had no right to handle the sacred property of the Imperial family. Having Prince Mikhail's presence in the gallery—suavely assuring customers that the items were genuine—helped to blunt their criticism.

Mikhail was most in his element in Palm Beach where he was an immense smash with the society hostesses. Olga and Palm Beach were made for each other, too, and we were happy when we were together there. She loved the parties and her name appeared regularly in the society columns of the local papers, especially after she was named as the best-dressed woman in Palm Beach. But the gulf between us was widening.

And my attentions were wandering. On my many evenings alone in New York and around the country, I began to date other women and I suppose that, from about 1934, I was really looking for another wife. For quite a long time, I had a big crush on Helen Hayes.

It never amounted to much. I was married and, therefore, circumspect in my approaches to her. She too was married.

I first saw her in 1934, when she was appearing as Mary, Queen of Scots. I thought she was so splendid in the role that I wanted to send her a token of my admiration.

In the Imperial Collection at our gallery, I found a little morocco-bound book embossed in gold with the monogram and crown of the former owner, the Dowager Empress of Russia, Maria Feodorovna. It was a glamorously told historical novel, by an anonymous author, and its subject was Mary, Queen of Scots. I sent it over to Helen Hayes at the theater, with a note saying how much I had enjoyed her performance.

Helen's manager thought the gift might make a useful line of publicity for the star, and he asked me to go over in person and present it to her in her dressing room for the sake of newspaper pictures. There I was, shaking the hand of the outstanding female genius of the American stage at that time, entranced by her lovely, open, laughing manner. She made a very striking impression on me in that brief moment and she stuck in my thoughts.

A few months later I found another book on Mary, Queen of Scots in the Imperial Collection, with an even more romantic history than the first. This volume had been presented to Czar Alexander I in about 1860 by the celebrated actress Adelaide Ristori, one of the foremost Italian tragediennes of the nineteenth century, who had made her reputation playing Lady Macbeth, Queen Elizabeth and Mary Stuart. The book was marked with the bookplate of the Czar himself and the text was in Italian and French.

I sent this book to Helen Hayes, too, who replied with a very warm note inviting me to see her again. We arranged to meet on the evening of March 11, 1936, after one of her performances as Queen Victoria in *Victoria Regina*. The following day I wrote an account of our date in my diary—an unusual thing for me to have done, since my diary was not kept regularly and was mainly a record of business negotiations.

That diary entry makes an unusual period piece and I want to reproduce it here:

I went about my work at the office mechanically all day with but one thought in my mind—would my illusions of Helen Hayes be shattered when I met her?

In order to be at my best, it was my intention to get a few hours' rest before leaving for the theater. However, some last-minute business detained me in the office and all I could do was to get a sleepless half hour. At last, I was on my way to the theater, resplendent in my tails and opera hat.

Even the drizzling rain could not dampen my excited, buoyant spirits. My seat was in the second row on the aisle, affording me an excellent opportunity to study every expression and line in Miss Hayes's face. What impressed me especially was her tired appearance and the heavy lines in her face and neck. It was as if premature age was setting in as a result of strain and hard work. Her performance, however, was flawless and exactly what one would expect of a finished artist. You forgot yourself and you forgot that you were in a theater seeing Helen Hayes. It was Victoria herself who was appearing before you and you were carried along with this courageous little figure, enjoying her naivete, delighted by her piquancy and charm.

Now and then, Helen Hayes's eyes scanned the faces of her audience in the first few rows and I found myself secretly hoping that I was the object of that search which seemed to end when her eyes rested on mine. The scene with Disraeli proved my undoing. It was so full of tenderness and beauty that the tears just seemed naturally to roll down my cheeks. A work of art was being created in which two great souls drew out the best that was in each other.

Disraeli and Victoria adored each other and worshipped each other but their love and devotion was on a higher plane than amatory passion. Each had been bereft of a mate whose loving memory was still the dominating thought, coloring the remaining few years of life.

After the performance, I sent my card backstage with the attendant at the stage door. An efficient young lady quickly appeared and ushered me into the darkened, mysterious passages behind the scenes and to one side of the stage. Would I mind waiting a few minutes while Miss Hayes was taking off her makeup? I found myself in a little group with about six others waiting to say hello or to introduce some friends from out of town.

Finally, the door of the tiny, unpretentious dressing room opened and Miss Hayes appeared in a short plaid mannish-looking dressing gown evidently worn for comfort and warmth rather than for beauty.

Below the edge of the robe could be seen the "schoolgirl legs" so vividly named by Ashton Stevens [a well-known critic], still covered by the black cotton stockings which Victoria had worn in the last act. A pair of house slippers and disheveled head of hair completed the picture. While Miss Hayes exchanged pleasantries with her guests, I tried to keep out of range, not wishing to intrude until her guests departed. However I was spied and a pleasant, warm voice called out, "Won't you come in, Dr. Hammer? I will be ready soon."

I was introduced to some of the visitors—acquaintances from London—who lingered. After a few minutes they departed and I was seated behind the flimsy curtain, on the other side of which Miss Hayes was dressing. She kept up a delightful conversation regardless of the curtain dividing us. "Thank you for the orchids: they're the most beautiful I've ever seen! And the roses, too! Let me see how you're dressed," she said and the robe-covered figure suddenly appeared from behind the curtain.

Eyeing me in my waistcoat, she exclaimed, "White tie! And I have to wear a frock that covers my throat. You see, I have a cold and really am in no condition for going out. My stomach has been upset all evening and I 'upjammed' after the performance. I was out with Paul Chavahavadze [a Southern Russian prince] and his wife last night and must have eaten something which disagreed with me."

I expressed my sympathy and suggested that we postpone the appointment to some other evening. She would not hear of it. "I'll be all right, although I'll be poor company for you, as it will have to be nothing but Perrier water for me: that's the only thing I can take."

Unfortunately the entry in my diary ends there, but I vividly remember the rest of the evening and my memory is not at fault when I say that Miss Hayes was able to manage something stronger than Perrier water. I took her for dinner at the Maisonette Russe in the St. Regis Hotel, where we put away a lot of champagne and were serenaded by gypsy violinists until the early hours of the morning.

The next day I was worried that I might have made her suffer with too much champagne. I sent her an apologetic note and one of the evening bags which had been made up for our gallery out of the eighteenth-century fabrics woven with gold and silver threads which we saved from the Hermitage. She wrote back to say, "I have wanted one ever since I used to stand like an urchin outside your window at Fiftieth and Park Avenue admiring your treasures." She said that, far from harming her, the champagne had made her "wake up next morning feeling all brand new."

That was the last time I saw her. We exchanged notes for a time in a formal and polite correspondence. The faint heart did not catch the fair lady. The crush waned, as crushes often do, leaving only the mildest memory of a charming and very exceptional woman.

Through my art business, another lady's path briefly crossed mine. Though I saw her only for a week, she stayed in my mind forever and she was to become the most important woman in my life and my most durable and happy love.

When our main exhibition and sale was at Marshall Field's in Chicago in 1933, a beautiful and wealthy young woman named Mrs. Frances Tolman bought a number of the choicest items from Victor, with whom she struck up an acquaintance. Later, in 1934, she loaned us her purchases when we mounted an exhibition at our gallery, and came to New York as our guest. I met her then.

Frances was the wife of Elmer Tolman, a rich and prominent citizen of Chicago, the son of a banker from whom he had inherited several million dollars. They lived in Mundelein, Illinois, near Lake Forest, about an hour from Chicago on a spread so big that it included a one-hundred-acre lake and an eighteen-hole golf course. Frances was his second wife. His first had preferred living in the glamorous society circles of Europe, and their daughter had committed suicide after several unsuccessful marriages to titled European gigolos. Elmer was much older than Frances and, despite all her efforts to restrain him, he spent most of his time drinking.

By the time she came to New York to visit our show, she had been married for several years and was becoming increasingly unhappy. She was very fond of Elmer, who was good and generous to her, but he wanted no more children and his drinking problem was very severe. She once said to me, "Elmer couldn't pass by a bar without going in to get a snootful the same way you can't pass by a telephone booth without going in to make a call. I'm not sure which addiction is more of a trial to live with."

We met when Victor took Frances and a friend to a nightclub and then brought them down to my studio house in the Village. Frances fell in love with the house. And we fell in love with each other. During the week that followed, we saw a lot of each other. I was effectively separated from Olga, who was living up in Highland Mills, and I wanted Frances to leave her husband and marry me. She was deeply torn. She was tortured by the idea of hurting Elmer, but she wanted to be with me.

At the end of the week she went back to Chicago, not knowing what to do. She talked to her family there, turning over her problem while I waited in New York in an agony of suspense for her decision. Her family advised her to forget me and make the best of her marriage with Elmer, however unsatisfactory it was. In the end she decided to follow their advice. She wrote me a letter, full of the most touching and tender pain, to tell me of her decision.

Though we decided that it would be better not to see each other again, she continued writing to me. I sent my replies to a box number in Chicago.

I recently found two of these letters between the pages of an old diary, and the heart-searching pain of Frances's words took me straight back to some of the most poignant moments of my life.

The first of these letters dated from 1937. She wrote endlessly of her difficulties in living with Elmer when her heart was with me. She felt terrible guilt, but she could not resist adding the line "I love you," even though she wrote it upside down. The second letter was written in 1940, when Frances was readying to fight the Nazis if they landed in Mundelein. She had just returned from a trip to Florida with Elmer and she complained that there had been too many bars there and that her tolerance had been strained to its limits.

The correspondence went on, spasmodically, for years. Meanwhile, Harry and Victor became very close friends with the Tolmans, and Harry accompanied Elmer on a hunting trip to Mexico. Frances settled down to her life with Elmer, traveling with him in the winter, first to California where they rented houses and then around the world. I never ceased to hope that fate might sometime make it possible for us to be together.

Among the houses Frances and Elmer rented in Los Angeles was one which they later bought—a charming shaded villa with a lovely rose garden in the Holmby Hills area between Westwood and Bel Air. It had been the property of movie actress Gene Tierney and her husband Oleg Cassini. That house was to be the one Frances and I would share for thirty years! All the items which Frances Tolman bought from our show in Chicago are now shared by us in our beloved home.

Twenty years after our first fleeting encounter in New York, we were to meet again—in circumstances which I will recount in a later chapter—and this time, I determined that nothing would stand in the way of Frances Tolman becoming the third and last Mrs. Armand Hammer.

We continued to mount lavish displays of Russian art all around the country, and to deal with an ever-growing stream of wealthy and powerful customers. Of all the extraordinary customers served by the Hammer Galleries in the thirties and forties, however, none were stranger than Harry Clifton and King Farouk of Egypt. I became enmeshed in the business affairs of both these men, and odder days of work I have never done than attending to their quixotic interests and demands.

My office on the mezzanine floor of the Hammer Galleries had a spy-hole drilled in the wall, through which I could keep an eye on the shop. One day in 1934 I looked through the spy-hole and was aghast to see Victor piling treasures on the counter and apparently about to hand them over to a young tramp. About fifteen thousand dollars' worth of jewels and precious objets d'art were stacked in front of a man whose arms were sticking out of the coat-sleeves of his disheveled suit, who wore no tie and whose wild hair looked as if a porcupine had run through it. Unlike today, it was unusual in the mid-thirties for someone to go out shopping for jewels and works of art looking as if he'd slept in a hedge. I buzzed through urgently to Victor and told him to come and see me and leave somebody to keep an eye on the man and our treasures.

"What on earth are you doing?" I said. "That man doesn't look as if he could afford the price of a subway ticket."

"I know," Victor replied, "but he says he's an Englishman called Harry Clifton, that he's staying at the St. Regis Hotel and he'd like his purchases delivered to him there."

"Did he give any references?" I said.

"Yes. He gave the name of Marcus and Company across the street." A very prominent Fifth Avenue jeweler.

"Well," I decided, "tell him there will be a delay while we have his things packed for him, and meanwhile I'll check him out."

The tramp left the gallery and I called Mr. Marcus.

"Do you know a Mr. Harry Clifton?" I said.

"We certainly do," he said.

"Well, he's just bought about fifteen thousand dollars' worth of goods here and I would like to know if his credit is good."

"Is Harry Clifton's credit *good*?" Incredulity vibrated down the telephone line. "He's good for everything you've got in your store and everything in ours as well. He's one of the richest men in England. His family owned the whole city of Blackpool, and he has tremendous holdings in real estate on which he gets an income of ten thousand dollars a day or more."

"Ah," I said, trying to conceal my amazement. "Well, that rather alters the picture. I'm much obliged to you."

I told Victor to get Mr. Clifton's purchases packed up without delay and we hurried together to the St. Regis Hotel to deliver them personally, along with a few other items which we hoped might interest him. Harry bought the lot with scarcely a second look. Then he got interested in the story of our Russian experiences and we stayed talking with him and struck up the beginnings of a good friendship.

After that he invited us often to lunch with him at his favorite Chinese restaurant, where he would consider his investments between courses. His style of decision-making was about as random as a one-armed bandit. After he had marked out a few stocks, he would summon the Chinese waiter and say, "Waiter. Should I buy or should I sell?"

The mystified Chinaman, who could hardly speak English, would gaze uncomprehendingly at Harry.

"Just tell me," Harry would insist. "Buy or sell."

The man would finally give it his best shot. "Buy," he guessed.

"All right," said Harry, and he would go to the telephone and call his broker and say, "I want you to buy ten thousand of this stock and ten thousand of that."

That was Harry's normal way of conducting his investments, and it caused dismay on Wall Street: some of the stocks he picked out had never traded that much in a whole year. The authorities suspected that some fiendish criminal mind was working a dastardly system, and the SEC investigated Harry's dealings. When they discovered the truth about Harry's methods, they were dumbfounded.

Harry used to place his orders through a brokerage house called Carl Loeb Rhoades, which kept a small office in the St. Regis. Harry took to one of the salesmen there so much that he offered to buy him a seat on the New York Stock Exchange on Wall Street, an offer worth half a million dollars today. The poor man, whose career expectations were those of a modest salesman, didn't know what to say in reply, and he felt that he should get the permission of his firm. By the time he had got the answer, Harry had changed his mind and had moved on to the pleasure fields of San Francisco and Los Angeles. I am told that the man almost went berserk thinking of the fortune which he had lost by his procrastination.

Harry wasn't exactly careless with his fortune. He felt that he should look after it, but it didn't greatly interest him. He was only in his mid-twenties when we met. His father had died only a few years before, leaving Harry his huge fortune. Harry wanted to see America and the world and to enjoy himself. Before he left New York for the West Coast, he decided to appoint me his financial agent. He said, "I'm notifying my banks that if any checks come through for large amounts, they are to ask you before they pay out, to make sure that there are no forgeries." Taking power of attorney to one of the richest men in England was no stranger than any other of Harry's commissions, and I accepted it unquestioningly.

The most trying side of the job was attempting to keep track of Harry. We hardly knew where he was at any particular moment and he certainly never knew where he was going next. It was completely fruitless to bother to write to him, because he always threw all his letters, unopened, into a suitcase. From time to time he would send the suitcase to his secretary for the letters to be dealt with: she would find months-old unopened correspondence and letters which she had sent to him in the first place. Tracking him down by telephone was like trying to follow the White Rabbit through its burrows.

One day the Chase Manhattan bank called me to say, "We have a check here, drawn on Mr. Harry Clifton's account, for one hundred fifty thousand dollars, which we have just certified because the signature is genuine and there are more than sufficient funds on deposit. However, we have misgivings about the check, because it is written out to a Mr. Brice, whose name and reputation you may know."

I certainly did know Mr. Brice's name. He was the brother of Fanny Brice, the great comic actress, and he had a terrible reputation as a cardsharp who played with marked cards. I said to the bank, "Don't pay out until I have spoken to Mr. Clifton."

I had to do the work of a Pinkerton man to trace Harry, who had been meandering aimlessly around California. I finally tracked him down in Los Angeles at the house of a lady mystic and gospel tub-thumper named Violet Greener, for whom he was building a temple called Abageg Temple—why, I never knew. He seemed to be having too good a time to be bothered over a check for $150,000. His first response was to tell me to authorize the payment and quit worrying. Finally I caught his attention.

"Did you know that this man Brice has a reputation as a cardsharp?" I said.

"Well, no, I didn't know that," he said. "And I did lose this money to him in some games of cards. I met him on the ship coming over from England and I ran into him again here where he invited me to join his game. Nonetheless, Armand, it is a debt of honor and I have to pay it."

"I don't believe you do, Harry," I said. "This man is renowned for running crooked games. And he has been playing with IOUs which he could never have paid because he hasn't got any money. I think you've been defrauded. My advice is not to pay."

"Well, Armand," he said airily, "I'll leave it all up to you. You do whatever you think best."

I notified the Los Angeles police of my suspicions. They raided Brice's game, caught him red-handed with marked cards and arrested him. I told the bank to withhold payment on the check.

At first the bank refused. They had never before stopped payment on a certified check. I told them that I would hold them responsible for my client's losses and I gave them the alternative of being liable for the $150,000 or accepting my indemnification if Mr. Brice ever sued them. Of course he did not.

The next time Harry Clifton was in New York, he strolled into my office and walked up to a little picture by Frans Hals which was hanging on my wall. He asked if it was for sale. I said that the price was $100,000.

Then he spotted a small Rubens priced at $50,000. "I'll take them both," he said.

I would gladly have cut the prices substantially for a serious buyer. I had owned the pictures for some time and had never had a serious bid for either of them. I said, "I'm more than willing to give you a discount, Harry."

"I offered you one hundred and fifty thousand. If you won't sell it to me for the price I'm offering, I shall never speak to you again."

I apologized. Harry wrote out his check for $150,000, made a crack about having it certified, took the Frans Hals and the Rubens off the wall, put them under his arm and strolled out of the galleries. No man ever carried the burden of a great fortune with more charm or less anxiety.

Personal charm was not one of King Farouk's outstanding characteristics, but, like Harry Clifton, he was not racked with guilt and anxiety about his fortune. In fact, Farouk of Egypt was of a type which the world may be glad to have seen the last of—the absolute monarch who treated the world as his personal nursery and all the things in it as his toys. It was my peculiar fate to become chief supplier of toys to the King.

The parade of customers passing through the doors of the Hammer Galleries was so exotic and flamboyant that I grew blasé about the extraordinary transactions I often glimpsed through the peephole in my office wall. Even so, I was intrigued, one day in 1939, when I glanced through and saw Victor showing some of our Fabergé pieces to a small, slender man of Arabian appearance, impeccably dressed in starched linen, sober suit and gleaming shoes. Among the articles Victor was demonstrating was perhaps the most valuable piece in the gallery at that moment—Fabergé's Swan Egg in which a diamond-encrusted swan swam by clockwork on a smooth surface like a lake, flapped its wings and arched its neck. The egg was priced at $100,000, and was not usually taken out of its showcase for the interest of casual visitors who were simply window-shopping.

As soon as I could get Victor's attention, I took him aside and asked him about this mysterious character.

"He is an aide to King Farouk of Egypt," Victor said, "and he is in town for the World's Fair to buy anything he thinks the King might like."

"Did he say what kind of things the King likes?" I asked.

"Just about anything expensive, it seems," Victor laughed.

"Ah," I said. "Well, I should think we might be able to help him there."

We made a big fuss over the aide and took him down into our basement, which had been furnished and decorated like one of the Czar's rooms in the Kremlin. We displayed all of our treasures to him and gave him photographs and full descriptions which he could take back to Farouk for his approval.

We didn't hear from Cairo for some weeks. The war was on, the Nazis were beginning their advance across North Africa and the world was in chaos. Then came the message from the Abdin Palace, which amounted to: "His Majesty desires to purchase the Swan Egg. Please deliver same and anything similar you might recommend."

We were eager to comply, but Egypt was not the easiest place in the world to reach at that moment. Rommel's blitzkrieg was bearing down on the borders of the country, and the Germans were blockading sea routes in the Atlantic and Mediterranean with their U-boats. I couldn't possibly leave my businesses for a trip of indeterminate length, but Victor thought it would be fun to see a King in his palace—especially as I had done some research and discovered that Farouk had a passion for tricks, magical illusions and practical jokes. He seemed like a customer tailor-made for Victor. We went up and down Broadway together, visiting joke shops and buying mechanical tricks. Then we loaded Victor up with a satchelful of these tricks and another satchelful of jewelry, which I told him never to take off his shoulder. He set off on his hazardous journey by seaplane.

When he arrived in Cairo, he was greeted by an aide and a squadron of troops drawn up in his honor for his inspection, like a visiting head of state. He was also presented with a solid gold hammer lying in a velvet-lined case and inscribed, *Welcome to Cairo, Mr. Hammer.*

At the Abdin Palace, he was quickly brought into the presence of the King. Farouk fell on the contents of Victor's two satchels with cries of delight, like a child on Christmas Day. The trashy tricks from Broadway thrilled him as much as the jewels from the Romanov palaces. Farouk particularly liked to play with the palming tricks Victor had brought and to mesmerize his fawning courtiers with "hunt the pea." Victor's stock with Farouk shot up like a missile.

Victor was never a shrewd businessman, but he was one of the most naturally gifted salesmen I ever met. He just naturally charmed the socks off every potential customer with his wit and warmth, and Farouk was no exception. As a mark of his special affection, Farouk even allowed Victor to see a secret room in the palace which was the King's furtive delight: it was filled with pornography, erotic pictures and sculptures and an array of instruments for sexual perversion; many of them baffled Victor completely and he was unable even to guess at a function for them. Farouk also had a workshop filled with armor and cannons, in which he liked to tinker. I don't suppose a more immature man than Farouk ever occupied the throne of any nation. The wonder is that he lasted as long as he did.

Victor was such a big hit with Farouk that soon after his return to New York I got a letter dated February 26, 1940, from a Mr. Mourad Hohsen, Administrator General of the Private Effects of the King, which began:

> *Sir:*
>
> *I have the honor to inform you that His Majesty the King, my August Master and Sovereign, has been pleased, in His great benevolence, to accord you the title of "Supplier to His Majesty the King."*
>
> *I am pleased, in consequence, to send you the Royal Escutcheon and the Brevet establishing the title granted to you, as well as the conditions governing the use of this title which you are requested to sign and return.*

We added the King's coat of arms to our stationery, opened a special bank account with a princely advance which Farouk sent and prepared to serve his requests. They rained upon us like leaves in an autumn wind, a never-ending succession of bizarre demands, which were always delivered in the grave tones of courtly address, no matter how absurd.

For example, I have a letter from the King's private secretary, dated March 26, 1940, which speaks of the "high consideration His Majesty has been graciously pleased to give" to a descriptive note we had sent concerning a collection of watches which Farouk now wanted to buy. The watches were titillating creations whose workings featured round-the-clock copulations.

Another letter from the Abdin Palace speaks in detail of Farouk's difficulties in mastering a contraption he had ordered and which we sent: "The motor of the 'Universal Health Builder' [the secretary wrote] is adaptable only to a 60 periods electric current. But as the current in use at the Palace does not exceed 40 periods (110 volts), it will not be possible to use the apparatus unless the motor could be changed—or the whole apparatus if necessary. Would you kindly see to that?"

Mercifully, time has erased the memory of the "Universal Health Builder" and I can no longer guess which of Farouk's vanities it was meant to satisfy. Neither can I now imagine what kink of the regal mind caused him to inquire about "the new experiments made on cotton to find new uses for it—in particular 'cotton roads' and 'cotton ice cream'"—except to note that cotton was Egypt's main cash crop.

Of all the purchases I made on Farouk's behalf, none was more absurd than the Continental Clipper. This incident was so ridiculous that I would hardly expect to be believed in telling it. Fortunately, the whole story is recorded in a book called *The 14-Karat Trailer* by Myron Zobel, the creator of the Clipper, and skeptics can check the record in his pages.

Myron Zobel was a man possessed of a vision. Where other men on the verge of retirement dream of oceangoing yachts or sleepy farms on which to spend their declining years, Zobel, a former advertising executive, was obsessed with plans for a Land Yacht—a trailer to end all trailers, in which he and his wife could travel majestically across America.

Zobel's fevered imagination ran riot on his plans. He conceived of a palace on wheels which would be drawn by a truck, driven by a uniformed crew. Zobel would communicate with the crew by intercom from the flying bridge of his Clipper. He also intended to be in contact with the whole world by shortwave radio. The trailer was to have accommodations like a suite in a luxury hotel: master bedroom with bathroom, lounge, galley, bar with wine cellar—no luxury was to be spared.

Zobel originally committed $2500 to a draftsman's rendition of his dream. By the time the blueprints were finished, he had already spent $6500. The final cost would have been $200,000 in today's money and he had created a monster. It was forty-six feet long, and it weighed more than fifteen thousand pounds standing at the curbside before any passengers entered.

The Continental Clipper was the *Spruce Goose* of the road—a disaster. Its array of tires overheated and exploded as soon as the contraption was in motion. The vast demands of the electrical circuits drained the batteries in minutes. Lights blew. The shortwave radio never worked well enough for Zobel to communicate with his drivers in the truck, let alone with the rest of the world. Whenever the Clipper took a bend, bottles and glasses in the bar would be smashed to smithereens. The plumbing system sprang more leaks than the Pentagon.

After some years of exhausting and expensive efforts, Zobel decided to throw in the towel and sell his dream machine, which had become his personal nightmare. The trouble was finding a purchaser who would be dope enough to take it on. The only people who answered Zobel's advertisements in *Fortune* magazine were cranks and rubberneckers curious to see one of the great follies of the modern world.

One dignified elderly gentleman who was obviously very rich did seem like a serious prospect, but when he inspected the Clipper, he shook his head. "Young man," he told Zobel, "I have a fishing lodge in Maine, a shooting box in Scotland and an island of my own in the Florida Keys. But I'll be damned if I can afford this thing."

Zobel became reconciled to his loss and left the Clipper to rot on a vacant parking lot in Manhattan. However, he had not reckoned with the five months that were to elapse before his advertisements reached Cairo and came beneath the all-devouring eye of Farouk. The King scoured the editorial pages and advertisements of sheaves of American publications in search of novelties, and he sprang into action as soon as he saw Zobel's advertisement and its illustration of the Land Yacht. He decided that he had to have the Clipper as a mobile palace in which he could flee Cairo if Rommel succeeded in breaking down the British Eighth Army and entered Egypt. I received a curt instruction to acquire the Clipper at the advertised price. I will now hand the story over to Myron Zobel:

Zobel says that he was sitting in his office when his secretary came on the line with a surprise message.

"Call on line two for you, Mr. Zobel. It's a man who says he wants to buy the Clipper."

"Are you the man who advertised the trailer for sale in Fortune *last May?"*

"Yes."

"Still available?"

So many false alarms had been sounded that I had given up hope. I might as well play hard to get. "I have a couple of good offers I am considering. Better call me the end of the week."

"I have to see it right away."

The urgency in his voice commanded my interest. I thought fast. The Clipper had been sitting in an open car lot for nearly a year. It surely would be a mess. Probably there was no air in the tires. Perhaps no tires.

"Well, when?" I began.

"This afternoon," the voice stated firmly.

"All right. Meet me at the parking lot at Ninety-first and Broadway at six o'clock." I glanced at my watch. It would be dark by six. The Clipper would look better in the dark.

My prayers were answered. It grew dark outside; but the gleaming lights from within made the Clipper look like a nighttime Pullman diner—vibrant, exotic and alluring.

A bottle of bonded bourbon stood on the bar. The ice cubes came forth like magic. I turned on the automatic record player and sweet music filled the Clipper. No siren of the silent movies ever sprayed her lair with more seduction. Surveying the scene, I felt again that old urge to hit the highway.

My prospect arrived on the dot of six. He was a small, intense man with movements that were quick and birdlike. His keen, flashing eyes took in the whole interior at a glance. Waving aside my proffered old-fashioned without comment, he started, at a jog trot, on a running tour of the Clipper. I couldn't keep up with him. The bath door banged, the galley door slid open and shut, but he moved quicker than the eye could follow. I heard him testing the water pressure in the galley, inspecting the cupboards and slamming the refrigerator door.

Then he flashed past me and up to the flying bridge to check the instruments. The whole inspection tour took two minutes.

"I'll buy it," he announced. They were his first words to me.

My reaction was one of annoyance. The man must be mad. Maybe he thought he was Napoleon Bonaparte.

"You haven't even looked at the truck."

"My client doesn't care what the truck looks like."

"Then you're not buying it for yourself?"

"No."

"Does your client know how much it costs?"

"He probably saw the price in your ad. But," he added grandly, "that's quite unimportant."

Now I was convinced he was a phony. Fourteen thousand dollars not important! I suggested, with some heat, that his client take a look for himself.

"That is impossible. He is out of town."

"When will he be back?"

"Never. He lives abroad. In fact, he's never been to the US. And never intends to come."

The enormity of this situation was too much. Was I supposed to believe that a man wanted to buy our Clipper and never expected to come here to use it!

"I will ship the Clipper to my client," the mysterious little man explained.

"He's a foreign shipowner, then?"

He smiled. "In a way."

I decided to end this pointless game of Twenty Questions. "How about a deposit to bind your purchase? Say, two thousand dollars."

My baffling prospect whipped out his checkbook and wrote a check for that amount. Before the ink was dry, he delivered his instructions.

"The air-conditioned wine cellar and bar come out."

I was convinced that the man was mad and his check was rubber, so I only fought halfheartedly against this heresy.

"Everybody wants a bar," I explained patiently. "I am sure your client will want one too."

"My client does not drink."

"Some of his friends may want a snort now and then."

His face twitched at the suggestion. "My client does not drink and his friends won't want a 'snort,' either!"

Must have pretty dull parties, I thought to myself.

My prospect issued further orders. "The two-way radio is to be reinstalled."

"Why? Is your client a ham?"

"Not exactly," he smiled.

"It doesn't matter. I couldn't put it back anyway. I took it out when we entered the war. All amateur transmissions are prohibited."

"Who prohibits them?"

"The Federal Communications Commission." I breathed those four words in the hushed tones hams reserve for this awesome body.

The little man waved the prohibition aside with a disdainful gesture.

"The transmitter goes back in. My client has his own Federal Communications Commission."

Thereafter, I offered no further opposition to his suggestions, no matter how much they jarred me. It was obvious that this man—who said his name was Hammer—was perfectly crazy. Why argue, since his check was certainly going to bounce?

I presented it next morning, with apologies, to the vice president of my bank. "Undoubtedly phony," I said. "Brought it in to save you the trouble of sending it back."

He looked at the signature. "Good as gold," he assured me. "Hammer owns the Hammer Galleries. Sold the treasures of the Russian Czar. This check's on a special fund some customer set up for him. Even with three more zeros we'd honor it."

The following weeks were busy. Hammer called daily to order extensive and expensive alterations. The new owner had cabled that he wanted the bathroom fixtures gold-plated. In place of the bar and wine cellar, a safe must be installed. Then came an order for a larger motor in the truck. Next was a call for complete reupholstering in silk damask, refinishing of all interior woodwork, exterior repainting, two new sets of balloon tires and twenty new and bigger batteries.

To cover these directives came a rain of checks, all cheerfully accepted by my bank. But our efforts to pump Hammer for information failed utterly. He could have made Calvin Coolidge sound like a chatterbox.

The last cable demanded that I dictate complete details covering the operation of everything to be shipped via air mail, together with all instruction manuals.

The Clipper itself was to follow by fast boat, with metal greased to prevent corrosion and interior padded with cotton wool. The entire truck and trailer were ordered packed in specially constructed wooden crates.

"Put it in a box," sang my wife, "tie it with a ribbon and throw it in the deep blue sea."

"Can you think of anything else?" I asked Hammer's secretary when I finished the required two solid hours of dictation.

I caught her off guard. "How in heck are they going to get those enormous crates from the dock in Alexandria to the Abdin Palace in Cairo?"

Shades of King Tut! We'd sold our Clipper to King Farouk of Egypt!

Fortunately the Clipper was never called upon to give active service in time of war, and Farouk's neck was saved when Field Marshal Bernard Montgomery's Eighth Army threw Rommel back at the battle of El Alamein. After the war, the King tried to make use of the trailer for romantic excursions, and it worked for him about as well as it had worked for Zobel.

Every time he took it out on the road for a grand seduction scene, it blew all its tires and the driver had to radio the palace for a car to come and rescue the King and his companion. He soon tired of it and it was relegated to a garage, along with other discarded toys.

Our sales to Farouk ran into many millions over the years and ended only when Egypt's Society of Free Officers, led by Nasser, forced Farouk's abdication in July 1952. Before that, however, he had sent us two final and completely typical commands. The first was in the form of a cablegram which read simply: BUY ME A BAKELITE FACTORY. The second came in an airmail letter, enclosing a clipping from a movie magazine and a handwritten note. The note said: "Send me Lana Turner." We managed to comply with the first command, but the King's second request was, alas, beyond our powers.

15

An American Emperor in Gimbels

"One thing led to another." That has been my reply whenever I have been asked to explain how I came to be involved in so many different businesses—from pharmaceuticals manufacturing to asbestos mining to pencil manufacturing to merchant banking to department store art sales to distilling to cattle breeding to oil. I always add that I have done my best to ensure that one thing *should* lead successfully to another: "Seize the opportunity by the forelock and see where it leads you" is one of my favorite mottos.

In the case of my department store sales of the Romanov treasures, one big thing led to something even bigger: our successes in disposing of the artistic and domestic properties of the Russian emperors led to my doing the same kind of job for an American emperor—the legendary William Randolph Hearst.

Bizarre as Harry Clifton and Farouk were, the work I did for them was small potatoes compared with selling the contents of William Randolph Hearst's treasure houses. Set beside Hearst, Harry Clifton was a pauper and Farouk was a minor collector of trinkets and baubles. Only the Czars of All the Russias themselves stood comparison with Hearst in the majesty of their spending and the insouciance of their collecting.

Heir to a great American fortune, and himself the creator of one of the country's mightiest and wealthiest publishing empires, William Randolph Hearst had amassed a haul of the world's art treasures which ranked with the state properties of some former empires. However, whereas the British Empire had provided the contents of London museums over hundreds of years, Hearst had assembled his gigantic collection in a single lifetime; and, whereas the museums of Paris still bulge with the booty captured by Napoleon's grand armies, Hearst had pillaged the artistic world with nothing more than a persuasive and ever-open checkbook.

Beginning as a boy, it had been Hearst's regular habit, every year, to spend at least a million dollars (and, frequently, multiples thereof) in the auction houses and art rooms of the world, buying anything and everything which took his fancy. By the end of the thirties it was estimated that he had spent at least fifty million dollars on his collection—close to a billion dollars in today's values. His personal fortune was then figured to be approximately two hundred and twenty million dollars, about four and a half billion today.

It should be remembered, too, that most of Hearst's purchases were made when the art market was deeply depressed. During the early part of this century, when Hearst was at his most active in the market, a million dollars would buy quantities and qualities of work which are beyond dreams today. My own collections of art are estimated to be worth at least one hundred million dollars. Hearst's was worth fifty million nearly half a century ago.

He was the opposite of the discriminating epicure; he was an all-consuming, all-devouring jackdaw. Agents and dealers all over the world knew that they had to do little more to win their commission than find and nominate antiquities or works of art that struck Hearst's fancy and the cash would roll in. He bought everything, from the archeological sweepings of ancient societies—the equivalent of salt and pepper shakers—to its greatest and most glorious masterpieces.

Such was the scale of Hearst's spending that he had, literally, no idea what he owned. Shiploads of treasure would arrive in America to be deposited, uncrated, in his Bronx warehouse or to be dispatched to his castle in San Simeon on the California coast, where they would frequently be consigned to the cellars, unexamined and unidentified. Some years after I became involved with selling the Hearst collection, I was staying in San Simeon, sleeping in a Tudor four-poster bed in a room stuffed with European antiques. Looking for something to read and opening the drawer of my bedside table, I found a photograph of a fine tapestry, across which Hearst himself had scribbled, in thick crayon, "Do I own this? Or is it being offered to me?"

In the mid-thirties Hearst hit a major cash crisis. It was as unimaginable that Hearst might ever be hard up for cash as that the *Titanic* might hit an iceberg and sink. Both events occurred and both titans were holed.

During the later years of the decade, it steadily became apparent that the Hearst empire was a shambles. The details of its disorder are not my concern here. Suffice it to say that by the end of the thirties the wolves were baying at the doors of San Simeon itself, and were about to break down the gates. The banks were pressing him for umpteen millions in cash. Several groups of injured stockholders had carried their complaints to court, demanding a receivership. What may have been Hearst's gloomiest hour came when he learned that his principal California rival in newspaper publishing, Harry Chandler, publisher/owner of the *Los Angeles Times* and grandfather of the present publisher Otis Chandler, was actually the holder of the mortgage on his beloved San Simeon.

Chandler extended the loan on the castle, but other creditors were not so kind. Hearst's executive, Richard Berlin, had to dive and weave like a dolphin to protect his employer when a Canadian newsprint cartel made a concerted bid to shut down Hearst's newspapers and magazines. Berlin also blocked Joseph P. Kennedy's self-serving offer to "help" Hearst by taking all his magazines off his hands for eight million dollars, a fraction of their worth.

When former Under Secretary of the Treasury John W. Hanes was called in by Hearst directors to save the sinking ship, he learned that ninety-four separate Hearst corporations were grouped together under the single leaking umbrella and many of them owed each other mountainous sums of money. Some transactions between these corporations had been curious, to say the least. For instance, American Newspapers, owned by Hearst, had sold their Baltimore, Atlanta and San Antonio papers to Hearst Consolidated for eight million dollars in 1935, when those three newspapers were losing a total of $550,000 a year.

Apart from his vast holdings in real estate—he owned three estate homes in California, ranches in Mexico, St. Donat's castle in Wales and four major hotels in New York, to name but a fraction of the sum— Hearst's most liquid disposable asset was his art collection. The members of his board pleaded frantically and persistently with him to dispose of some large part of it, to ease their difficulties. Hearst, equally persistently, refused for some years. Then the moment came when he had to stump up eleven million dollars or face the certainty of losing his publishing empire, the fruit of his life's work, altogether. In 1938, grudgingly, he agreed to let about half of his collection be sold.

Hearst insisted that his treasures should be disposed of with decorum. He was very anxious not to give the impression that he was acting out of desperation, and he wanted nothing to do with a garage sale of his effects.

The International Studio Art Corporation, a Hearst holding company, was charged with conducting the sale and, in November of 1938, part of the collection went on public display for the first time at New York's Parrish-Watson Galleries, where a four-part auction was held. In the same month, the Parke-Bernet Gallery staged an auction of

Hearst's notable collection of historical literary autographs of manu-scripts, early American furniture and blue Staffordshire china.

The sales were a flop. The international dealers who had filled their coffers with Hearst's cash for decades either spurned his sales or ganged up on him, rigging their prices and driving them down to absurd levels. Then the executives of the International Studio Art Corporation tried to turn their hands to some discreet sales in department stores, emulating my own efforts with the Romanov treasures. They held a trial exercise at Marshall Field's in Chicago. It also bombed. Less than two hundred thousand dollars was raised and considerably more than that was spent in advertising, salaries and expenses. "It would have been cheaper to give it away," grumbled Judge Clarence Shearn, Chair-man of the Hearst trustees.

Finally, Hearst's executives turned to me. On the board of direc-tors of the Hearst Corporation was a friend of mine named Charles B. McCabe, who had been the publisher of the *Daily Mirror* in New York before he joined the board of the parent company. Before that he had been United Press Bureau Chief in Chicago and had witnessed my successful marketing of the Romanov art objects at Marshall Field's. Not only was he a brilliant journalist, but he had one of the best analytical business brains I ever came across.

"There's only one man who can unload this art," Charles McCabe told Martin Huberth, the head of Hearst's real estate division who was overseeing the attempted disposal, "and that's Armand Hammer."

Mr. Huberth was a very solid businessman and, when he called me, he knew that it would be futile to conceal the desperation of their position. He was very frank in saying that they had to raise eleven million dollars immediately. He said that he had heard of my success in department stores with the Czarist art treasures and he was willing to let me handle the Hearst Collection on my own terms. I told him I wanted a free hand and 10 percent of the gross as our compensation. He agreed without reservation and an agreement was drawn up imme-diately.

As soon as the ink was dry, I telephoned Beardsley Ruml, Chair-man of the Board of Macy's and of the Federal Reserve Bank in New York.

"Beardsley," I said, "I've got the greatest department store pro-motion that's ever been pulled off for you. How would you like to merchandise fifty million dollars' worth of art over the counter? You know the success I had with the Romanov treasures. This will eclipse it. This will make department store history."

"Come right down," said Beardsley. "While you're on the way, I'll talk to Jack Strauss." (The Strauss family owned Macy's.)

When I got to Beardsley's office, I found that he had assembled a roomful of the company's top executives to hear my story. It didn't take me long to convince them that this was a unique opportunity. By the time I left, they were all glowing with excitement. That was my best moment with Macy's.

Beardsley and his executives turned the proposal over to Macy's legal department, and, for the next several weeks, while the whole Hearst empire was trembling on the brink of final catastrophe, I was engaged in daily meetings, picking lint with inside lawyers and outside lawyers. I never saw so many lawyers in my life. No lawyer represented me. I didn't need one. I had power of attorney and a free hand from the Hearst Corporation and only had to consult them just before the final agreement was ready for signature.

Macy's lawyers were tied up in a net of terrors and wanted impossible guarantees. They were worried about the authenticity of all the works which were going to be offered for sale. What if they were fakes and the purchaser sued for reimbursement? This apparently reasonable question occupied unreasonable eons of time in negotiation.

The other sticky question between us was in the setting of retail prices for the collection. I insisted that we should have the last word. We knew about this business, Macy's didn't. From the moment that I had signed the agreement with Martin Huberth, Victor had gone to work and done a heroic job inventorying and pricing the objects in the Bronx warehouse of the International Studio Art Corporation.

This astounding edifice at 387 Southern Avenue in the Bronx occupied an entire city block. It was four stories high. Nobody, nobody on earth, knew how many items it contained, but fifty thousand pieces was one guess. A crew of experts retained by Hearst had spent two years cataloguing the collection, and the work had not nearly been completed when the first, failed sales attempts began.

Victor examined all 152 volumes of their catalogue, rummaged through thousands of photographs and compiled price tags and descriptions for more than twenty thousand items.

Finally Macy's lawyers were ready to present their draft of the agreement for signature. It was three inches thick. Mr. Huberth and the Hearst executives signed, but I held back, insisting on the right to cancel if we could not agree on the question of prices. I was beginning to fear that we were riding the wrong horse. I suspected that Macy's wasn't competent to handle the sale and they soon proved it.

I decided to test Macy's "experts" on the pricing of the collection. I arranged with the Bronx warehouse to pull out a big selection of china, lamps and furniture and display them on long tables in the warehouse, all bearing Victor's price tags. Then Macy's buyers came down.

There must have been twenty of them, half men and half women.

They had all been with Macy's for years. They went up and down the tables and made lists of their own suggested prices on each subject.

We didn't agree on anything. Not one object. They were marking objects at the prices they were used to commanding in the store. They had no idea of the value of the objects they were scrutinizing.

In misery and exasperation, Victor and I watched them working. We stood there shaking our heads. The last straw came when they priced a pair of black Chinese Hawthorne vases from the seventeenth century for which Mr. Hearst had originally paid $20,000. The Macy's price was $29.95. For the pair.

Victor protested. "Do you have any idea what was originally paid for these?"

The Macy's buyer was unimpressed. "Doesn't make any difference," she said. "Twenty-nine ninety-five is all our kind of customers will pay for them."

We were disgusted. I went to see Martin Huberth and told him what was going on. "Try somebody else," he said.

Macy's hadn't anticipated trouble with the Hearst Corporation. They figured that, being such big advertisers in Hearst newspapers, they had an unbeatable hand. It was greatly to Martin Huberth's credit that he wasn't going to let his arm be twisted.

At that moment my invaluable colleague Chance intervened again. Fred Gimbel of Gimbels department store in New York had been a small customer of the Hammer Galleries and, liking him at first sight, I had struck up the beginning of a friendship with him, which was to last until he died. One day while I was in the throes of the struggle with Macy's, Fred walked into my office at the Hammer Galleries.

He said that he had heard about my difficulties with Macy's and asked, "Would you consider Gimbels?"

The idea sounded preposterous. Gimbels was best known for its "bargain basement," which contained every second-rate item not sold on any of the other floors, marked at knock-down prices. The store's reputation for quality was, to be polite, less than excellent. It was the least appropriate place to display and sell fifty million dollars' worth of the finest art collection in America.

However, Fred Gimbel had an entrepreneurial spirit which was close to genius and he was immensely persuasive. "I'll clear a whole floor for you," he said, suggesting their fifth floor, which could be reached by elevators as well as by escalators. "We'll bring experts from Hollywood to design the lighting and the sets. We'll put the art treasures of each country in a fitting setting. I'll make a hundred thousand dollars available right away just for that purpose. And you and Victor will have complete control of setting the prices: you'll run the whole show."

I was very taken with Fred's enthusiasm, but I guessed that some opposition might come from within the Hearst group to the idea. I was right. It came from William Randolph himself. When he got word that his great art collection, his pride and joy, was going to land at Gimbels, he said, "Oh, my God. Macy's was bad enough, but Gimbels basement—my God!" He was adamant that the deal should be stopped. Martin Huberth was very apologetic, but he was sure that Hearst's mind was made up. I had to find a way to change it.

I went back to the Gimbel brothers and said, "Look, you own Saks Fifth Avenue, one of the most prestigious names in New York. Let me take some space there, as well as at Gimbels, for the Hearst Collection. I'm certain Mr. Hearst will accept that."

At first they resisted. They said that there was no spare space at Saks; and, more importantly, they had always made sure that the names of Gimbels and Saks were kept completely separate so that the fancy customers at Saks should not feel that their shopping was tainted with a Gimbels connection.

I persuaded them. I only wanted a small space at Saks. If we could put on a small show of some selected pieces, I argued, we could intrigue and encourage the customers at Saks to visit the main exhibition at Gimbels. Fresh money would thus be brought to Gimbels. The key argument, of course, was that if the Gimbel brothers turned me down and refused space at Saks, they would lose the whole deal—on which they stood to make a fortune.

They consented. Hearst was mollified.

Now the way lay clear to stage the show. True to his word, Fred Gimbel brought in the best Hollywood designers to remodel the eighty thousand square feet of the store's fifth floor.

More than twenty thousand items were displayed here, including a regiment of medieval armor (of which Hearst owned one of the world's finest collections), Tudor paneled rooms, Florentine silver, carved Gothic doorways, stained-glass windows and so on. Twenty thousand square feet on the third floor was converted to display the hundreds of paintings in the collection.

In a press release describing the sale, I said that it was like "the contents of the Louvre and the British Museum combined." And, as I told the *New York Times* on December 29, 1940, "The collection ranges from everything to everything. Just imagine walking into the Metropolitan Museum of Art and finding price tags on every piece. That's the only way I can describe it. The prices will be quite reasonable. Everybody will be able to afford to buy something from the Hearst Collection."

One of my pleasures in running the Hammer Galleries had been to entice into its rooms people who would normally feel out of place in snooty art galleries. I felt that the Hammer Galleries did something genuinely useful in giving ordinary people a taste of buying art works of high quality which were easy to appreciate and enjoy. They might then go on with more confidence to browse in other galleries. This "democratizing" instinct also gave me pleasure in staging the Hearst shows. I loved the idea of a housewife from Queens popping into Gimbels to buy a kettle in the basement and then going up to the fifth floor to pick up an Egyptian bead for 99 cents or a figurine for $9.95.

We were offering all kinds of small treasures at prices accessible to wage-earners. For $325, for instance, you could buy a pair of Benjamin Franklin's silver-rimmed spectacles, engraved with his name. Or you might choose a waistcoat worn by George Washington or a small purse once owned by Martha Washington.

We were also offering unprecedented bargains to the most serious and discerning art collectors: pictures by Vestier and Boucher; an agate bowl, adorned with mountings of gold and precious stones, attributed to Benvenuto Cellini; Andrea del Sarto's painting of the Holy Family. Victor put a tag of $12,998 on a picture of the Madonna and Child with the infant John the Baptist and two angels by Raffaelino del Garbo, a fraction of the price paid by Hearst. For a Flemish painting by David Teniers the Younger of a village dancing scene, Victor decided that $998 would be fair. Both those works would be worth at least twenty-five times as much today.

Victor was also in charge of hiring the staff to sell the collection. He assembled an extraordinary crew of art enthusiasts, museum curators, students and professional salespeople to man the counters and advise the customers, and he gave them crash courses of instruction in the provenance and particular interest of the works.

It was my job to bring in the customers. After all my time on the road with the Romanov treasures, I knew that work like the back of my hand.

Robert Lehman, head of the banking firm of Lehman Brothers, and one of Gimbels's directors, wanted to spend one hundred thousand dollars hiring the best public relations company in the country to publicize the event. I told the board that they would be wasting their money. "If Mr. Bernard Gimbel will take me around to meet the publishers of the New York papers, we won't need to hire anybody. We've got the best story in town here, and I know how to sell it."

Somewhat doubtingly, Bernard took me to see Arthur Sulzberger of the *New York Times,* Mrs. Helen Reid of the *Tribune*, Roy Howard of the *World-Telegram* and Dorothy Schiff of the *Post.* I took with me a specially prepared album showing photographs of some of the outstanding Hearst pieces and I gave them the story of each item. The result was a storm of front-page pieces that preceded the opening of the exhibition.

Bernard Gimbel had bet Fred ten dollars that it would be impossible to get any free publicity for the exhibition. Seeing the mass of newspaper stories, he was very glad to pay up, and Bernard said of my efforts, "If we had paid Steve Hannigan [a well-known publicist] a hundred thousand dollars to run the publicity, he couldn't have done a better job." Our satisfaction was short-lived.

The day after the first newspaper stories appeared, Martin Huberth telephoned me and the Gimbels to say, with unmistakable anger, "Please see that no more releases are given out without our approval." He was a very frightened and angry man. He was afraid that his boss's well-known wrath was about to explode all over him.

The cause of Mr. Huberth's distress lay in the press release which I had written. Referring to the works for sale as part of Mr. Hearst's collection, I had said that their total value had been estimated at around fifty million dollars. The statement was true, but Huberth was worried it would both very gravely offend the old man and cause him to cancel the whole deal. Hearst's purpose in commissioning his International Studio Art Corporation to oversee the sale was to put himself at a dignified distance from it.

The last thing Hearst wanted was for the public to think that he was so personally hard up that he had to sell his own property. As for the figure of fifty million, it was hard to see what Mr. Huberth was upset about. I had taken the figure from the International Studio Art Corporation's own publicity when they had launched their failed show and sale at Marshall Field.

Nonetheless, when he called me, Mr. Huberth said, "This fifty-million-dollar story may get us into trouble. Likewise, there must be a clear distinction that this sale does not include Mr. Hearst's personal collection. If we get a blast from the Coast, it is going to embarrass you as well as us."

The Gimbel brothers deeply feared that Hearst would not only pull out of the deal altogether, but sue them for breach of contract, misrepresentation and perhaps even libel. All hell broke loose.

I was terribly depressed, feeling that I had pulled a real boner. I had a really sticky time with the press in a conference on December 28. A reporter from the *Sun* named Heyden had got hold of the story that Hearst himself had tried to kill the Associated Press story based on my release, even though it had been picked up and run by the *Journal,* Hearst's own paper in New York.

I did my best to isolate Mr. Heyden during the press conference and afterward, while champagne and highballs were being served, I took him aside and made friends with him, giving him a glass of champagne and patting his back and reassuring him. At length he departed, saying, "I guess everything is okay," marking the peaceful conclusion to what might have been a disastrous episode.

The next evening Martin Huberth got the series of irate calls he had been dreading from his master in the castle at San Simeon, and he asked me to go and see him at his office at three-thirty P.M. on December 30.

I went with a very heavy heart, expecting the worst, expecting to be told that I was fired. Huberth's expressionless face, as I walked into his room, did not help to lift my spirits. I felt like a sack of lead as I sat down. Then Mr. Huberth began:

"We have had a very narrow escape," he said, "but I have calmed down the old man. The publicity in the *Times* and the other papers was wonderful. We have never seen anything like it in our newspaper experience. However, for God's sake, let's be careful from now on. Control your impetuosity. The old man woke me up the first time at one A.M. I told him we were being blamed for something that had originally been said in connection with the Marshall Field's sale.

"The old man said, 'What imagination to compare the things you have to the British Museum and the Louvre combined.' Then he said, 'I liked the brochure of the Hammer Galleries. That's the kind of publicity to get.'"

I exhaled a long sigh of relief. Huberth went on: "The real reason for the old man being upset is because way down deep he does not want to sell anything. He is irritated and resentful. However, I want to show him we were right. I believe a department store is the best way to sell this. If only you had not said fifty million, there would have been none of this trouble. It was like waving a red flag in front of a bull."

Looking back on this brouhaha, I think I can see more clearly now than I could at the time. Huberth and his colleagues lived in awe and dread of "the old man," and they were excessively nervous of his sensibilities. No doubt William Randolph Hearst did have a wayward and whimsical temper, but I don't believe that he was nearly as thin-skinned and delicate as Mr. Huberth imagined. The understandable fearfulness of the employee toward the boss frequently results in a stifling of executive imagination and an unhealthy degree of conservatism in action.

Anyway, this tempest in a teacup having subsided, we were now ready to go for the grand opening.

To help to bring in the big spenders, I wrote and sent out to Saks Fifth Avenue's one hundred thousand charge account customers a fancy embossed invitation to a three-night black-tie preview and sale at both stores.

No place on earth sees more first nights than New York and, having seen it all, no citizenry is harder to impress. The Hearst collection seemed to dent their complacency a little.

Police had to be called out to control the crowds of guests and rubberneckers on each of the three preview nights. More than thirty thousand people besieged the stores each evening, causing Gimbels to remark, in a triumphant advertisement in the *New York Sun* on February 8, 1941, that it was a greater attendance in an evening than New York's three principal art museums drew in a week!

Edward Alden Jewell, the art critic of the *New York Times,* from whom a guarded response might have been expected, wrote, "Only an experience-toughened specialist wearing blinders could, we cannot but decide, fail to be staggered by the sheer inclusive heterogeneity of this vast congeries of art objects of all periods and from all parts of the world. The impact is amazing."

Once launched in such a firestorm of attention and curiosity, the sale never slackened. The five-million-dollar mark of sales was passed in late fall of 1941, and the items which had been assigned to Saks Fifth Avenue were moved across Manhattan to Gimbels without incident or a sales recession. By this time Mr. Hearst was so contented with the results of the sale that he made no protest.

The department-store democratization of art sales produced some nice moments. A housewife named Klotz wrote a penny postcard to Gimbels, which said, "Dear Sirs, Please Send me a Benvenuto Cellini bowl, as advertised. Kindly choose a good color to go with a blue dining-room." She had seen a newspaper photograph of John D. Rockefeller standing with Bernie Gimbel, examining the Cellini bowl on exhibit. Gimbels replied to Mrs. Klotz that there was, alas, only one such bowl and Victor had put a $25,000 price tag on it.

A reporter from the *Washington Daily News* described:

> The casual way in which average people bought fairly expensive items. . . . A woman fron St. Louis, who was visiting in New York with her son, a lad of about 11, boarded the escalator on the street floor, intending to get off on the sixth and buy him a suit. In changing at the fifth, the pair fell victim to a natural curiosity and began wandering through the Hearst display. In the American section, the boy went into a kind of trance before a case which contained a score or more of Abraham Lincoln autographs. The one the boy fancied was scrawled on a rough slip of paper at the end of a message to a Union general requesting the release of a Confederate prisoner. The note was written on the day Lincoln was assassinated and was quite possibly the last thing he wrote that is still extant. Some of the autographs were priced as low as $40, but the boy wanted this particular one and his mother bought it for him for $304.

A dark, chesty fellow from Brooklyn, who seemed to be in a hurry, asked to see some paintings, any paintings at all, he said. A clerk showed him one marked at $800. "Not enough," said the man, hardly looking at the canvas. He was shown one at $1,200. He frowned, saying reprovingly, "I can go higher than that, pal." The clerk led him to a painting for which $1,500 was asked. "Sold!" said the customer, paying in cash. "Send it to this address. And leave the price tag on. I want to show some of my smart neighbors I can pay a higher price for Hearst stuff than they can."

One of the most perplexing and comic of our transactions was the attempt to sell a complete Spanish Cistercian monastery of the twelfth century, which bowed the floors of the Bronx warehouse in 10,700 crates.

During his 1928 tour of Spain, Hearst's acquisitive eye had fallen on this building, which had stood for almost a thousand years. It had originally been built in 1114 by Alfonso VII, King of Castile. Hearst paid the mystified monks $500,000 for their retreat and, to compensate them even more copiously for their loss, he built them a completely new monastery, which cost him more than the original. He then engaged a team of American architects and engineers to dismantle the entire building, stone by stone, numbering every stone and packing it separately. A three-mile narrow-gauge railroad had to be constructed to move the load to the nearest standard railroad spur.

When the cargo arrived in New York, it was seized by agents of the Department of Agriculture looking for hoof and mouth disease in the straw padding wrapped around the stones to prevent them from chipping en route. Hearst had to pay $53,500 to have the crates opened and inspected. They were all clean.

Victor's first price tag for the monastery—which, naturally, we could display at Gimbels only in an array of photographs—was $100,000. Don't ask me why. No takers. So he knocked it down to $50,000, and it was bought by the proprietors of a Florida cemetery who thought it would grace their grounds; and there it is to this day.

Victor and I were never slow to reassess a price if an item in the collection stubbornly stuck to its plinth or plaque. The Van Dyck portrait of *Queen Henrietta Maria with Her Dwarf* attracted no takers at our original valuation of $175,000, so we cut it to $124,998. Then it sold. It now belongs to the National Gallery in Washington, the gift of the Kress Foundation. If it came up for auction today, I dare say it would fetch a few million dollars.

As with our sales of the Romanov treasures, we were constantly feeling our way with the sale of the Hearst collection, adjusting the prices in response to demand on the shop floor. It was a hand-to-hand and improvised business and some of the results are unfathomable to this day. Who can make sense, for instance, of a price of $17.50 successfully asked for a powder horn used on Nelson's *Victory*? Or the $1995 we demanded for two suits of sixteenth-century Maximilian armor, for which Mr. Hearst had originally paid $4000? A woman from Philadelphia bought for $1895 a high-case clock which had originally belonged to Benjamin Franklin, while two pairs of his spectacles were bought by a Madison Avenue physician for $500 each. A New York building contractor paid $2185—Victor's asking price—for George Washington's hot-water urn.

We sold seventy—the figure gives me pause even today—seventy paneled rooms, including one called Albyn's Room, from a seventeenth-century manor house in Essex, England. It came complete with James I oak paneling and a great ornamental carved chimneypiece, as well as the original plaster ceiling, the whole room measuring 100 feet in length and 22 feet in width. There was also a Tudor room from King's Lodging in England, which had been occupied by King Henry VIII and his daughter, Queen Elizabeth I. For $5985 we sold a room from the ancestral estate in Lancashire, England, of Myles Standish, defender of the *Mayflower* Pilgrims and runner-up for the hand of Priscilla Mullens.

A California oilman breezed onto Gimbels's fifth floor one day and decided that a council chamber of a sixteenth-century Venetian doge, with wall frescoes by Bernardino Parentino depicting the life of Scipio Africanus, was "pretty." He took it for $9495 and went on to spend a further $90,000 in the store in a single day. A New York lawyer dropped by one day and picked up three thirteenth-century stained-glass windows and sent them off to the simple frame church in rural Wyoming where his father had been an itinerant preacher.

Among my efforts to draw attention to the sale, I published an elegant monthly art magazine called *The Compleat Collector,* whose articles gave prominent attention to the items on sale at Gimbels. The editor of this magazine was named Braset Marteau and he contributed many articles. Another frequent contributor was Dnamra Remmah. My readers who know French will readily be able to translate *"bras et marteau"* as arm and hammer, while those who know only English should try reversing the letters of the second name. Both translations produce the same result.

And so it went on, this random dispersal to the domestic homes of Middle America of the civilized world's antiquities, originally garnered by one of the New World's most stupendous plutocrats.

I guess that this wonderful carnival will never be matched or equaled—only if the unlikely day ever dawns when the Norton Simon collection is put up for sale at your neighborhood Neiman-Marcus or J. C. Penney.

Before the end of 1941, less than a year after we had opened, we hit the designated mark of eleven million dollars in sales for Mr. Hearst. The contract was completed and the carnival wrapped its tents for keeps. I was taken out for the biggest celebratory dinner which New York could provide: not by William Randolph Hearst—by his bankers.

"Art over the counter"—Romanov or Hearst—wasn't the only business on my hands during the thirties and forties. One thing had also led to another in quite a different direction, from coopering beer barrels to distilling spirits. One thing led to another so comprehensively, in fact, that by the end of the forties I was operating one of the largest distilling operations in the United States.

As usual with the largest undertakings in my life, this development had a modest beginning. I was simply trying to fill a small gap I had spotted.

One of the first bills to which Franklin Roosevelt signed his name after taking office in 1933 was the repeal of the Volstead Act. For fourteen years, the country had been legally and nominally teetotal while, in fact, it had been awash in illegal hooch. FDR eliminated the conflict between the law and common practice simply by sweeping aside the humbug and acknowledging that people who wanted to drink would drink.

Will Rogers gave perfect expression to FDR's attitude. "Just three words, that's all he [FDR] said: 'Let 'em drink'—that's all he said. And he collected $10 million in the first two weeks. And if'n he'd've had good beer, he'd've paid the National Debt by now."

Good beer was not the only commodity in short supply after the repeal of Prohibition. Even if the brewers could get into production fast enough to meet the nation's demand, they had no barrels for the beer. Not only had all the country's barrel manufacturers gone out of business, so too had all the manufacturers of barrel staves.

The staves had to be made of white oak and, being an inch thick, they had to be air-dried for at least two years. Naturally, none were to be had in the whole of the United States. The Soviet Union, however, produced a huge crop of staves every year, nearly all of which went to the German brewers. I knew that because I had had a hand in exporting Russian staves to Germany through my Moscow trading company. Therefore, when a friend of my brother Harry asked, "Can you get me some Russian staves?" I answered that we probably could.

I sent a telegram to the Foreign Trade Ministry in Moscow inquiring about supplies, and got the reply that yes, they were just about to complete negotiations with the Germans for that year's crop of staves, but the Germans were hesitating about the increased price the Russians were demanding. When the Russians named the price, I quickly calculated that I could produce barrels at approximately five dollars each.

I immediately replied that I would meet their price for the whole year's crop. I went to Anheuser-Busch and told them that I could supply their needs. They gave me a check for $100,000 and an order for 10,000 barrels at $10 apiece. When other brewers heard that I had cornered the Russian staves, they came to me with equally large orders.

I figured I was sitting pretty. I had not anticipated one snag, however. The Russians sold their staves to the Germans in blocks, unshaped. The Germans looked after the shaping themselves.

I hadn't realized that the ships from Russia would be bringing unshaped staves. I could not find a shaping mill in the entire United States to do the work. I was in plenty of trouble. I had paid the Russians with the American brewers' money, which I had received for finished, shaped staves. There was only one solution: I had to create my own stave-shaping plant.

As a temporary measure, just to be able to begin deliveries, I set up a plant right on one of the piers of the New York Dock Company in Brooklyn where the Russian ships berthed. It was easy to find plenty of experienced stave mill operators who had been unemployed during Prohibition and were eager to get jobs in their old trade. At that plant, we worked three eight-hour shifts around the clock and produced a thousand barrels a shift for many months to meet the ever-increasing demand of the American brewers.

Everything looked to be going beautifully when my bank hit me with an outrageous demand. Its timing was extremely deft. If I hadn't acceded to it, I would have been ruined.

The Trust Company of North America was financing my shipments of staves, allowing me to pay the Russians as soon as a ship arrived. One day in 1933, while a consignment was actually on the high seas in a ship named *Albert Ballin,* an Assistant Vice President of the bank came to see me in my office. He had a letter of agreement in his hand, and told me that the bank insisted I establish a line of credit of $100,000 for one year, for which they wanted a $50,000 bonus, payable in advance. If I didn't sign the agreement they had prepared, they would not honor the drafts for the shipment on the *Albert Ballin,* and all my credit at the bank would be withdrawn.

"What about this shipment which is already at sea?" I asked.

"We will have to return the unpaid drafts to *Amtorg,* the seller," he said.

That would mean the cancellation of my valuable contract, and *Amtorg* would be free to sell the staves to someone else. I would be ruined.

I read the letter of agreement through and then I looked at him and said, "You left something out."

"Oh?" he said. "What?"

"The arsenic I might as well take if I sign this," I said.

I signed. I had no choice.

After the *Albert Ballin* shipment had arrived and the Russians had been paid, I immediately went looking for another bank. And I refused to make payment to the Trust Company of North America on the grounds that their letter of agreement had been obtained under duress.

They sued. They wanted $230,000. I resisted. At first the victory was ours, as the New York State Supreme Court in Brooklyn threw their case out entirely. Then the victory was partially theirs, as a Manhattan judge granted them a partial verdict. It was all a lot of nonsense, but it came about in the first place because they recognized how promising the barrel business was going to become. Simply by answering the call of necessity, I had run into a tremendous opportunity. I was in a better position than anybody else to shape staves and make barrels even when the domestic American white oak product became available.

I moved into cooperage full steam. Between 1933 and 1934 I built a full-scale, twenty-thousand-square-foot modern barrel factory in Milltown, New Jersey, called the A. Hammer Cooperage Company. It was large enough to take care of demand for beer barrels throughout the entire United States and, in its first two years alone, it made a profit of about a million dollars. After a time I also started making whiskey barrels in Milltown. When US brewers began to resort to aluminum barrels, toward the end of the thirties, and the distillers started to make their own whiskey barrels, my profits started to taper off and I gradually liquidated the cooperage business as I moved into the distilling business itself, as I shall describe in a moment.

The cooperage business produced a sideline which is itself a little footnote in American social history. The insulating properties of the white-oak staves were so great that I produced an object called the Ice-Saver from whiskey barrels which were sawn in half and fitted with a tight white-oak cover. The Ice-Saver could be used as a cold picnic box or as a cooler in the home. It was made obsolete, of course, by the arrival in every home of refrigerators and plastic picnic boxes, but it was a very popular item for a time.

While my business life was active and my working days full, my personal life was, sad to say, something of a mess. My marriage with Olga was virtually through. We hardly saw each other and our occasional meetings were far from successful. I tended to compensate for my dissatisfaction by working still harder. During the thirties, when I was looking after the Hammer Galleries and the cooperage business, I often worked so late at night that I fell asleep at my desk and woke with a start in the small hours, to drive through the empty streets to my house in Greenwich Village. The gathering success of my businesses was, I am afraid, partly at the expense of my relationship with my young son, Julian.

He would sometimes come down to New York City from his mother's house in Highland Mills to spend a weekend with me. He loved to go to the movies and he had a trying taste for seeing the same movie twice straight through in a single sitting.

I simply didn't have the time or the patience to indulge this enthusiasm. Only my father Julius had the time on his hands to accompany Julian to his five-hour viewings.

One weekend in 1939 Julian was coming to New York with a party from his school to visit the zoo. He called me at my office, very excitedly, to tell me of his plans, and we arranged to meet at the entrance of the zoo on the Saturday afternoon at two P.M.

I arrived a little late. There was no sign of Julian or his party. I was gripped by that terror which every parent knows, fearing that he was lost and feeling that I had let him down. I asked the clerk at the ticket office if she had seen a group of children waiting. No help. I dashed into the zoo and ran around the site, in a lather of anxiety, from one caterwauling cage to another. Finally, I found Julian and his friends calmly moving around the monkey house.

He was thrilled to see me, very proud that I was the only parent who had joined the group. We had a lovely afternoon, visiting all the exhibits, buying souvenirs and hot dogs. We held hands all the time and, in some ways, we were never closer. As the bus left the parking lot, I stood beneath a tree waving to Julian, who waved and waved back, until the bus turned the corner and was out of sight. I remained there, under that tree, for some time with a great weight of sadness on my heart that he and I had had so few close moments together. I made myself a promise that in future we would see more of each other.

It was not to be. Olga decided that she wanted to go to California to live, to resume her singing career and take her chances in Hollywood. Naturally she took Julian with her. They lived together in Los Angeles. I saw Julian even less; and I am sorry to say that he suffered from his divided, difficult circumstances. His adolescence was even more uneasy than most and there were constant worries with his schools. It wasn't Olga's fault: she cared very lovingly for Julian, and, in her way, I believe she loved me. It wasn't really Julian's fault or mine, come to that. It couldn't be helped, that's all.

It didn't make things easier with Julian when I fell in love with Angela Zevely.

She and I met in 1938, shortly after Frances Tolman decided to return to Elmer. I was on the rebound, I guess, but I was mightily smitten when I saw Angela at a literary party in Greenwich Village.

Within a very short time I knew that ours was going to be a serious affair.

She was separated from her husband, who had deserted her—vanished completely, leaving her penniless. Tremendously glamorous, witty and dashing, she was a true socialite—loved parties, dinners, theater trips and horsey society. Her husband's family had bred Thoroughbred racehorses—one of which, called Zev, was the winner of the 1923 Kentucky Derby. When I met Angela, she was dating a prominent book publisher who was proposing marriage, but Angela was still married, hence not free.

The Hammer brothers seemed to have a weakness for singers. Angela was a singer too, and she occasionally appeared on a radio show sponsored by the Canada Dry Ginger Ale Company. It was always a complete mystery to me how she could even whistle a tune, let alone sing a complicated melody in front of a big band, because she was almost stone deaf and had been from birth. However, she did have a fine voice. She fought the handicap very bravely and did everything to conceal it. She could read lips with miraculous fluency, and, being vain as well as brave, she refused all artificial aids because they were unsightly. My father persuaded her to try a hearing aid and took it to Angela's home to show it to her. She ripped it from her head and threw it across the room, saying that the volume of sound was unbearable.

Soon we were living together while she tried to find her husband and get a divorce, and then, after a year in New York, we decided that we both liked the idea of a peaceful life on a farm in the country.

Angela loved to be in the country, surrounded with farm animals and horses and country people. She had always longed to own a farm. A friend of ours who dealt in real estate encouraged us to look at some properties in the area of Red Bank, New Jersey, and we drove there with him one fine winter's day in 1939. Toward the end of the day, when we had seen and rejected several farms, we drove across a causeway to a property on the edge of Shadow Lake. As soon as we saw the place, we were in no doubt that it was for us, even though the house and its surrounding nine acres were badly run-down. It looked exactly like a Currier and Ives print of a typical early-American farmhouse and surrounding barns.

Angela stayed out there at the farm, hiring crews and fixing up the property, while we lived in a couple of rooms. Then Angela got her divorce on grounds of desertion, Olga and I divorced, and Angela and I were married. Among her presents to me were a couple of jolting surprises.

The first occurred on our wedding night, when she made it clear she wanted no children.

I was thunderstruck. More than anything in life, I wanted more children. More than any other single reason, I had married Angela to have children with her.

She never tried to explain herself. I suspected that she believed her deafness to be a congenital defect and she did not want to pass it on to children. I had always made it clear to her that I loved children and wanted to father many more, and she had never demurred.

What was I to do? I could have applied for an annulment of the marriage, I suppose, but I hoped that, if I worked on her, I might be able to change Angela's mind. As the years were to prove, I was mistaken.

Angela's other big surprise—which she revealed early in our marriage—was that she was an alcoholic. I had known that she liked to drink, but her drinking then had seemed part of the general excitement and celebration of our romance.

When I discovered how grave her addiction was, I tried to help her overcome it. I persuaded her to get treatment from special doctors and in clinics and hospitals. Nothing worked. She would go to any lengths to deceive me into thinking that she was dry. She hid bottles on lengths of string hanging out of windows; she concealed little flasks in her clothes and her purses. Anytime that she was in the city alone—on business or shopping—she would make long detours into bars. Few marriages can survive the strains of such constant anxiety and deception. It is a wonder that ours lasted as long as it did.

Apart from the sale of the Hearst Collection, my main business interest and my biggest success during those years was in distilling. Fred Gimbel again played a decisive role in the earliest, small beginnings of my entry into this business.

Fred was my best man when I married Angela. After the ceremony, as we were getting ready to leave for our honeymoon in Mexico, he gave me a stock market tip, though he knew that I had never gambled on Wall Street. The great crash of the stock market impressed upon me a lesson I already knew: I have never believed in easy money.

However, Fred Gimbel was a serious man and he understood everything there is to know about business. If he gave you a tip, you'd be a fool not to listen.

"You should buy some American Distilling stock," Fred told me. "There's no risk to you. They're going to give a barrel of bonded bourbon as a dividend to everybody who buys a share of their stock. We [Gimbels] will buy the whiskey from you, any amount you want to sell us." (The law did not allow retailers to own shares in a distilling company.) I bought 5500 shares at $90 each on the 10 percent margin and left for my honeymoon.

When I got back to New York, a glad tiding awaited me. Stock in American Distilling had jumped to $150. I had made $330,000 while I was on holiday! And I still had 5500 barrels of bonded bourbon to sell to Fred Gimbel.

Or, at least, I should have had my bourbon.

The American Distilling Company had not delivered any of the barrels of bourbon it had promised to new shareholders. Someone had brought suit against the company to prevent them from distributing the whiskey, and the court had appointed a receiver. This receiver had plans of his own for the whiskey: he wanted it for himself and his friends.

I went out to the company's headquarters in Peoria to meet him.

"Why aren't you distributing the whiskey?" I demanded.

"Well," he said, "I am afraid that under the law I would be liable for the tax on the whiskey if I distributed it."

"I see," I said. "All right. You tell me how much the tax will be on my fifty-five hundred barrels."

He gave me a figure.

"Very well," I said. "I will put up a bond for that amount to indemnify you for the taxes."

The man's face turned white at the offer, and then I knew he was up to something.

That same day there was a meeting of all the shareholders, the largest of whom was the state of Virginia, with 20,000 shares. I was among the biggest of the individual shareholders. I proposed a strategy to pry our whiskey out of the hands of the receiver, and we all agreed on it.

I hired the firm of the former Attorney General of the state as our lawyer. Then we went to see the receiver and gave him notice that we would see him in court, where we would hold him personally responsible for our losses and sue him for millions upon millions of dollars. Frightened the hell out of him. He collapsed completely. We got our whiskey.

I commissioned the American Distilling Company to bottle about 2500 barrels of my stock, put up in fifths, 86 proof, and labeled "Cooperage," after my barrel company in Milltown.

Gimbels took full-page advertisements in the New York papers to promote my bourbon and, in a city which liked a drink and was finding it scarce because of the war, lines formed all around the block.

I had very good cause to give thanks to Fred Gimbel for his tip. We had both done extremely well, and no doubt we would have continued to make terrific profits on bottling and selling the remaining 3000 barrels of my bourbon and that would have been the end of my little foray into whiskey baronage—except for a chance encounter which led me still further into the distilling business.

One day at my office at the Hammer Galleries, my secretary announced that a Mr. Eisenberg had come to see me. I was slightly impatient to be interrupted on what I took to be a social call, and then Mr. Eisenberg came in and immediately launched into an excited account of some discovery of his. I hardly paid him any attention, just tried to keep on working at my desk, while I kept half an ear open to his story. Suddenly I seemed to hear him saying, ". . . and, by this means, of course you can stretch whiskey."

Now he had my full attention.

"What are you saying about stretching whiskey?"

"Yes," he said. "You can make alcohol from potatoes just as good as grain alcohol: you can't tell the difference. Then you can blend it with straight whiskey. You could add up to eighty percent of neutral spirits to your bourbon and stretch your stock five times."

Five times! That would produce 15,000 barrels out of my remaining 3000 barrels of bourbon, giving me 9500 more barrels than I had bought in the first place.

"I'm very interested in what you're saying," I told Mr. Eisenberg. "Can you give me a demonstration?"

He had come prepared. He had a sample of neutral spirits made from grain and another sample made from potatoes. I opened a bottle of Cooperage. Eisenberg poured some of my bourbon into two paper cups and added grain spirit to this and potato spirit to that. He invited me to taste.

I couldn't tell the difference between the blends. More than that, I couldn't tell the difference between the blends and the real stuff.

"All right," I said. "Where can I get a good supply of potato alcohol?"

Eisenberg grinned victoriously. "I know where," he said. "There's an abandoned rum distillery in a place called Newmarket, New Hampshire, just over the border from Maine. The people who ran it defaulted on a loan from the Reconstruction Finance Corporation and the RFC has taken it back. They want to get rid of it. You could pick it up for very little money.

"At the same time," he went on, "over the border in Maine there's a terrific glut of potatoes. The government keeps subsidizing the farmers who grow more and more and the market is overloaded. The warehouses are full of them. They're rotting and stinking to high heaven, and about the only thing they'd be good for is making alcohol."

I was going to need some hefty support for this venture. The War Production Board had curtailed the production of alcohol for beverages because it was needed in so many other forms for the war effort. I went to Washington and sought out the Senators from New Hampshire—Styles Bridges—and Maine—Owen Brewster. Both welcomed me with open arms, Bridges because he could see that I would be bringing employment to New Hampshire, and Brewster because he wanted to help the Maine farmers. They arranged for me to see Donald Nelson, head of the War Production Board. He agreed that the mountain of Maine potatoes was "smelling up the countryside" and he gave me a letter of approval permitting me to produce alcohol for beverage purposes. Now I was well set.

I went to the offices of the Reconstruction Finance Corporation in Boston and asked the official in charge of the Newmarket rum plant how much he wanted for it. He said $55,000—the amount of the bad debt for which they had repossessed the distillery. I whipped out my checkbook and wrote a check.

The official smiled. "Well, Doctor Hammer," he said, "you're now the owner of a distillery. It's a good thing you acted so promptly because only yesterday Mr. Joseph Kennedy was in here expressing an interest in this plant. He asked if we would put it on hold for him and we asked for a deposit. He said that he would be in today with a deposit. You've just beaten him to it."

My experience of running my Moscow pencil factory was invaluable now. Just as I had gone to Nuremberg and to Birmingham, England, to hire the best craftsmen in pen and pencil manufacturing, I now went to American Distilleries and hired their top chemist, a German named Hans Meister, who was perhaps the country's leading expert in distilling, and above all had experience in distilling alcohol from potatoes in Germany. I gave him a free hand to hire his own technical staff.

Then I went back to the government and bought thousands of tons of their surplus potatoes from them at the bargain price of 10 cents for each hundred-pound sack. The potatoes were loaded into the warehouses of the Newmarket distillery. I shut down all bottlings of Cooperage at the American Distillery in Peoria and transferred my barrels of bourbon to their bottling lines, where they cut it in the proportion of 20 percent bourbon to 80 percent potato alcohol.

Never has the lowly spud been more completely transmuted into pure gold. Fred Gimbel called my new product Gold Coin when he began to sell it in Gimbels and, again, huge lines formed around the block—despite the fact that every customer was rationed to two bottles of Gold Coin and they each had to buy a bottle of Cuban rum as well.

Gold Coin did good business, but it was also the butt of many jokes and became known as "spuds" whiskey, which did nothing to help its reputation. I decided that it needed a less humble nomenclature.

Potatoes are only vegetables, I thought, so if I can say that Gold Coin is made from vegetable spirits, I will remove the curse of the spud from its name.

Thinking further on these lines, I realized that I could take a leaf out of the manufacturing book of the blended-whiskey distillers who extracted neutral spirits from grain. They didn't have to declare the kinds of grain they used, whether rye, barley or wheat. I went to the alcohol tax unit in Washington and said, "Suppose I were to mix my potatoes with other vegetables. Would I be allowed to call the distillage 'vegetable spirits'?"

"Certainly," they said.

I started taking a carload of potatoes and several bushels of carrots or turnips or other root vegetables, mixing them together, and turning out vegetable spirits. That put me in a tremendously strong position with the traditional distilleries, which had very large whiskey reserves. I offered them a straight swap. For instance, I did a trade with National Distillers of four barrels of my neutral vegetable spirits for one barrel of their four-year-old straight whiskey. Then I stretched the whiskey according to the formula of good old Mr. Eisenberg, and Gold Coin poured in a torrent from the old rum plant in Newmarket. We got fantastic orders. I was set to clean up.

Just when the business seemed to be glittering most promisingly, a big, black cloud lowered over it. I received a telegram from the War Department announcing the declaration of a "grain holiday" from August 1, 1944, until further notice: American distilleries were to be permitted to resume making alcohol for beverages from grain.

When Fred Gimbel heard about the grain holiday, he got straight on the telephone to me. He said, "You might as well shut up shop and come home. Close up. Sell the potatoes. Sell the alcohol."

"You got anybody in mind to buy it?" I asked testily.

"Search me," said Fred.

It looked as if I was ruined. There I was, in Newmarket, up to my neck in rotting potatoes and the canceled orders for Gold Coin began to shower in like a blizzard. The roof was falling in on me.

I called a council of war with Hans Meister and his technical people. Most of them favored throwing in the towel. I decided to ignore them.

"We're going to keep making the alcohol," I said. "We'll fill up all our storage tanks and when they're full we'll build some more. The potatoes are useless to us as rotten garbage but, as alcohol, at least we've got a commodity we can store. *Somebody* will want it, someday."

A tense time began. I was running a large operation with no sales, gambling that the accumulated reserves would find a market somewhere. I hate to gamble on blind faith. The proper exercise of business should be an intelligent calculation based upon known factors and leavened with imagination and foresight. The best kinds of business decisions combine a conservative sense of certainty with the thrill of an imaginative leap. Blind faith is a straight road to catastrophe.

In the case of the potato distillery, however, blind faith paid off. Within a month I received another telegram announcing that the grain holiday was to be terminated forthwith. The orders for Gold Coin instantly began to roar down the telephone lines again and bulge the mailman's sack. We were back in business, bigger than before.

I decided that I would never again allow myself to be threatened with such a complete collapse of my market. I would move into conventional distilleries using grain, so that another grain holiday—if one was declared—would be a nice holiday for me as well, instead of giving me such a dousing that I might almost lose my shirt. I figured that when the government prohibited the use of grain, I could increase production of vegetable spirits; and when the bans on grain were lifted, my distilleries could produce straight whiskies for aging as well as neutral spirits.

I started buying idle grain distilleries, beginning with the Blue Grass Distillery, later called Dant and Head, in Gethsemane, Kentucky. I also got another distillery there, which had a family connection called J. W. Dant. Then I bought a huge former molasses-processing alcohol plant in Gretna, Louisiana, from National Distillers. This plant could be converted to use grain, entitling me to a larger grain quota whenever there was a grain holiday. When the grain holiday ended, it could switch back to molasses. By the end of the war, I owned nine grain distilleries and was second only to Seagram's in the production of bulk whiskey in the United States. All because of a single tip from Fred Gimbel.

I united all my separate distilleries under a single corporate banner called United Distillers of America Ltd., which owned the Baltimore Pure Rye Distilling Company. Ultimately, United Distillers employed about two thousand people and produced some fifty million dollars a year in sales. It was a private company, jointly owned by me and my brother Harry. We never had to issue a single public share or report. In those days I used to feel that shareholders were a nuisance I could do without. That was before I started running a global business with responsibilities for billions of dollars of shareholders' money.

The little J. W. Dant distillery was one of the smallest of my acquisitions, but I remember it fondly because, small as it was, it turned in a whopping performance. When I bought J. W. Dant, it was producing only about twenty thousand cases a year of sour-mash bottled-in-bond bourbon, priced about the same as the much better-known brands like Old Grand-Dad, Old Taylor and I. W. Harper. By the time I sold the company, along with all the companies in the United Distillers group, J. W. Dant was selling a million cases a year.

The transformation was wrought, again, partly in response to government action. After the end of the war, when the government again permitted continuous grain usage for the manufacture of beverages, there was, naturally, an instantaneous slump in demand for my blended brands. The public wanted straight whiskey at least four years old, bottled in bond and bearing an old, established name.

I decided to make J. W. Dant bourbon the flag-bearer in our assault on the new market. The twenty thousand cases of the distillery's normal production retailed at $7 a fifth, which was netting me just under $20 a case. I decided to slash the price to $4.95 and make J. W. Dant's bonded bourbon an irresistible bargain, competing directly with blended brands.

My Vice President, Newt Cook, agreed to this plan reluctantly, and only after I had let him know that it was going to happen, whether he liked it or not.

"Nobody sells bonded Kentucky bourbon so cheap," he said. "Nobody."

"Watch me," I said.

Just as we were about to launch the advertising campaign for the $4.95 Dant, my brother Harry happened to be buying a bottle of bourbon in a New York liquor store. He asked, loyally, for J. W. Dant. The store didn't carry the brand. Instead, the storekeeper reached under the counter and fished up a bottle of something called Heaven Hill, a Kentucky sour-mash bottled in bond. "Have a shot of this," he said. "We only sell it to our best customers."

Harry thought it tasted as good as J. W. Dant.

"How much do you charge for this?" he asked.

The storekeeper whispered, "Four forty-nine"—the same price as Seagram's 7-Crown blended whiskey.

Harry ran home to the telephone and called me.

I called Newt Cook.

"Change all the ads, Newt," I said. "The new price will be four forty-nine."

"You can't do that," he protested.

"Who says I can't?" I replied. "The drinkers will say, 'Hey, if I can get straight whiskey for the price of Seagram's Seven, why the hell should I buy a blend? Why drink something made of sixty-five-percent alcohol when you can get the real aged stuff for the same price?'"

Newt changed the ads.

Profiting from the lessons we had learned with our department store sales of art, we launched a full-blown campaign of publicity for J. W. Dant. We stamped a crown into the shoulder of the bottle and called it "The Crown Jewel of Kentucky Bourbon" in newspaper and magazine advertising. Victor got hold of a Hapsburg crown and some jewels and we sent them out on a publicity tour to promote the whiskey. Exactly as I had done with the Romanov treasures, I organized charity functions with the Hapsburg jewels and invited prominent local ladies to model for photographs in tiaras and crowns. Those pictures always got a good spread in local papers.

In only three years, J. W. Dant jumped from a tiny sale, virtually confined to Kentucky and southern Illinois, to national acceptance. The other distillers were going crazy. When sales of J. W. Dant hit the million-cases mark I had set, I got a call from Louis Rosenstiel, the Chairman of Schenley's. He said that he wanted to talk some friendly business.

I sold him the J. W. Dant distillery and inventory for $6.5 million in cash. What he really wanted was not the inventory but the brand name. For the same property, I had paid $100,000 only a few years before.

Newt Cook graciously acknowledged that he might have been mistaken.

The rapid expansion of United Distillers' business during the war years put a great strain on the offices we were occupying at the Hammer Galleries, and we were in desperate need of new premises. However, office space in New York—especially in prominent and central locations—was as hard to find then as good bourbon. I sent out scouts to hunt all up and down the canyons of central Manhattan, to find a good-sized place for the company. They returned with nothing to show except their morose expressions.

The answer to my problem came literally out of the air, and under most tragic circumstances. On July 28, 1945, a US Army B-25 crashed into the uppermost heights of the Empire State Building during a fog, killing fourteen people and virtually demolishing the seventy-eighth floor. The floor was then occupied by officials of a Catholic charity, who were, of course, forced to evacuate the premises.

I guessed that the former occupants would not be eager to return to the scene of the disaster. On the day after the accident, I called the agent for the Empire State Building and said, "If the tenancy of your seventy-eighth floor should become available, I want it."

I got it.

Restoration and remodeling of the floor took the best part of a year, and it was only in June 1946 that United Distillers of America Inc. was able to throw a big party to warm its new home. For the pleasure of our guests, we had some office furnishings to show which were, for a time, the talk of New York—and, come to that, of London.

In 1945 Victor had received a message from an English art and antiques dealer that a rare treasure was about to become available. It was called the Treaty Room of Uxbridge. Measuring approximately twenty-one feet by eighteen, the room was paneled in oak, eleven feet high from floor to ceiling. Over the centuries, the oak had acquired a deep reddish-brown patina, and the carving upon it suggested that the room had been created during the reign of King James I, not long before it became the setting for one of the most momentous encounters in English history.

In 1645 sixteen commissioners for King Charles I and sixteen for the Nation—Oliver Cromwell's Puritans—met in session in the house of a Mr. Carr in Uxbridge in the county of Middlesex, some twenty miles from central London. Many of the mightiest lords and nobles in England met there. The King's commissioners were led by the Duke of Richmond, the Marquis of Hertford and the Earl of Southampton. Leading the Nation's commissioners were the Earl of Northumberland, the Earl of Pembroke and the Earl of Salisbury. Their business was to settle terms for a truce in the English Civil War.

After three weeks, negotiations broke off in complete failure—Charles was ultimately to lose both the war and his head—but forever after, the room was known as the Treaty Room of Uxbridge. The largest of the neighboring rooms, to which the commissioners had retired for their private conferences, was called the Presence Room. It was also magnificently carved and wainscotted.

I bought both rooms.

The sale of the precious antiquities to an American businessman caused an immense hue and cry of protest in England: heated editorials and indignant questions in the Houses of Parliament. I had not at all expected that. The Treaty Room was installed as my personal office, the Presence Room became the tasting room of United Distillers, and a third room, which had been the Council Chamber from the last of the Medici palaces in San Donato, Italy, which was not far from Florence, became the Board Room of United Distillers—but I was uneasy. I said to my brother Harry, "You know, it would be a nice gesture if someday we could find a way to give the Treaty Room back to England, if ever an appropriate occasion arose."

The right moment came in 1953 with the coronation of Queen Elizabeth II. I offered the rooms as a coronation gift, and they were very graciously accepted by Prime Minister Winston Churchill on behalf of the Queen, who gave instructions for them to be installed at the Victoria and Albert Museum in London. Finally, the old glories made their way back to their ancient and historic home in Uxbridge. The Queen agreed to put them on permanent loan in their original setting. Allied Brewers, which now owned the Olde Treaty House as a public house, arranged very handsomely for their reinstallation and I was thrilled to see the rooms restored to their historic place on one of my visits to England.

My experiences with the Treaty Room taught me a lesson which I have followed ever since. Great works of art should not be held in the private and exclusive property of rich men. They should be shared with and enjoyed by everybody, for the education of the young and the enrichment of the lives of all humans.

In the later part of my life I have been fortunate to acquire many of the world's greatest masterpieces, from which I derive immeasurable personal delight and interest. However, I take as much pleasure and satisfaction from showing my art collections in museums and galleries all around the world, and I feel certain that I can say that nobody's private collections have been exhibited in more places or seen by more people.

But I am getting ahead of myself. In fact, I must backtrack several years. Long before I bought the Treaty Room, long before I became a distilling king, long before I remarried, something happened that dwarfed all business and personal concerns, not just for me, but for the entire globe.

The world went to war.

16

FDR

Throughout the thirties I watched the rise of Hitler's Nazis in Germany with mounting horror, dread and rage. Though I had never been an actively practicing Jew, my ancestry was Jewish, multitudes of my friends were Jewish and, of course, that was where my instinctive sympathies lay.

Like all Jewish children of my parents' immigrant generation, I was brought up on stories of the Czarist pogroms and the institutionalized anti-Semitism of Old Russia. Nobody with that history in their veins could fail to mistake the menace of Hitler's rabid anti-Semitism. As early as 1931, when I was working and living in Paris, the stories I heard from my friends about the rise of the National Socialists across the border in Germany chilled my blood. During the thirties, as New York increasingly became a haven of refuge for German Jews, I became certain that Hitler had to be stopped. The Munich agreement of 1938 appalled me.

Unlike many Americans of that time, I was against an isolationist policy for the United States. I thought it was folly. Hitler's unmistakable ambition was the mastery and enslavement of the whole world. Of course he was insane; of course the Nazis' world picture was unbelievable and grotesque. Many Americans thought that Hitler should not be taken seriously, however, merely because he appeared to be a dotty house painter suffering from a terminal dose of megalomania. I was not one of those.

I joined and gave very active support to every reputable organization and committee I could find which supported the Allies' war effort against Hitler and opposed America's isolationism. Prominent among them, in the early years of the war, was The Committee to Defend America by Aiding the Allies, which had been organized by William Allen White, the distinguished author and political commentator. Another was Bundles for Britain, which, through private hands, supplied immense quantities of essential provisions to Great Britain. Because of my work in the distilling business, I was appointed Chairman of the Wines and Spirits division.

Bundles for Britain came to me for help when J. P. Morgan very generously donated all the fittings of his fabulous yacht *Corsair* for sale for the organization's benefit. I was asked if I would conduct the sale through the Gimbel brothers, with whom the Hammer Galleries had a management contract. The *Corsair,* of course, was best known for Morgan's line when he was asked how much it cost to operate it: "If you have to ask," he replied, "you can't afford it."

In May of 1940 the 343-foot yacht had been turned over to the British and had gone into war service. All the fittings and furnishings had been stripped out of it, and, when we put them on sale at Gimbels, we arranged the exhibit to look like the deck of a yacht. Prices ranged from $7.50 for a chair to $250 for a salon rug, and tens of thousands of dollars were raised for Bundles for Britain.

Irving Berlin and his wife Ellin were very active participants in Bundles for Britain as well, and when Ellin's father, Clarence Mackay, died, Ellin wanted to sell his art collection, which she had inherited, to benefit the British war effort. Berlin, whom I had known since the twenties, asked me if I could arrange this sale through Gimbels too— and over a million dollars more was raised for the British.

Bundles for Britain did good work and certainly helped to keep the British fighting, starved as they were of essential supplies. Britain's plight was so desperate, however, that our effort was little more than that of a finger in a leaky dike.

To hold back Rommel's Panzer divisions and Goering's Luftwaffe, to break the encirclement of Doenitz's U-boat squadrons which were plundering British shipping carrying supplies across the Atlantic, the active involvement of the United States government was essential.

Apart from the isolationist instincts of some of the people, the main obstacles to American aid for Britain were legislative and political. FDR had said that the United States would help Britain in every way short of war itself, but his hands were tied by the Neutrality Act of 1939 and by the 1934 Johnson Act "to prohibit financial transactions with any foreign government in default on its obligations to the United States."

In 1925 Great Britain's debt to the United States from the First World War stood at over five billion dollars. Between 1925 and 1940 nearly $1.5 billion was repaid, leaving a debtor balance of over $3.5 billion. The provisions of the Neutrality and Johnson acts, put together, meant that Britain would have to hand over $3.5 billion in cash before any financial and material aid could be sent to her from America to aid her in her fight against America's future enemies. By a cruel paradox, Britain's war debt had not been favored with the same treatment which had been applied in 1925 to Italy's war debt. Easy terms had nearly halved Italy's original war debt of more than two billion dollars. Thus America had provided generous economic aid to one of the Axis nations which was now threatening the liberty of the world, while similar aid had been denied to the only country left in Europe which was still fighting the fascist dictators.

FDR's political difficulty in providing aid to Britain in 1940 arose because of his tough election fight that year. In that long-ago age before the science of opinion measurement had become as advanced as it is today, nobody could know for sure what the American electorate would feel about financing another war in Europe. On that question, one man's guess was literally as good as another's.

It was understandable, therefore, that FDR should have trodden quietly on this question before the election. He needed the help of his friends and supporters to boost public opinion in favor of aid and to come up with a solution to the statutory impediments.

I had a solution. It was a businessman's solution but none the worse for that.

Britain owed massive cash debts to America. Britain also had possession of capital assets, in the form of colonial territories in the Western Hemisphere, which could be useful to the United States. The disposal of those assets could eliminate the cash debt and allow the President legally and constitutionally to supply some of Britain's war needs. In particular, the British were desperate for destroyers for the protection of Atlantic convoys. In the summer of 1940 William Allen White's Committee to Defend America by Aiding the Allies had launched a campaign named "Destroyers Today or Destruction Tomorrow," which called upon the government to make available to Britain about 60 of the 162 destroyers then on the Navy's lists as "overage," meaning more than sixteen years old. Supporting that campaign, I came up with the idea of trading off Britain's territorial assets against her cash debt.

The British colonial territories of potential interest to America were its islands in the Caribbean Sea, together with British Honduras, the Falkland Islands, British Guiana and the French islands of St. Pierre and Miquelon off the coast of Newfoundland. (When the proposal was originally put forth, it encompassed the French and Dutch possessions in the Western Hemisphere. Since then, France had been conquered and a plan for joint trusteeship of those possessions was adopted at the Pan American meeting in Havana on July 20, 1940.) It had been suggested that the British sell their territories to the Americans in settlement of the outstanding war debt, but that was an impractical proposition. The British government regarded the territories as a trust, and would have considered it morally repugnant to surrender sovereignty over any part of that trust, however dire the material needs of the Mother Country.

My idea was marginally, but crucially, different: I proposed that the British *lease* the islands to the United States for air and naval bases, negotiating joint sovereignty with the US government and the government of Canada.

Raymond Gram Swing, my old fellow-sufferer of the miseries of the Moscow Savoy, by now a very well known radio commentator on foreign affairs, was enthusiastic about the proposal and offered to help me with its drafting and editing so that it could be circulated in Washington.

I got straight to work analyzing the overall extent of Britain's outstanding war debt and the value of the territories which could be leased. First of all, I proposed, the same terms should be applied to the British debt as had been granted to the Italians. That discounting move alone would reduce the British debt to $311 million. If thirteen island bases were leased for ninety-nine years at $25 million each, the debt would be eradicated!

With Raymond Gram Swing's invaluable help, the document was rapidly prepared for the printer. It had one of the snappiest titles in the history of creative writing: "A Proposal for the Immediate Leasing of Military Bases in Certain Territories of Great Britain in the Western Hemisphere, Payment for Which Is to Be Applied in Full Settlement of the War Debts and Any Balance to Be Placed at the Disposal of England for Purchases in This Country." It might not have rolled off the tongue, but it stated its business. On July 1, I sent Raymond a telegram saying: IF THERE IS ONE CHANCE IN A HUNDRED OF GETTING AN IMMEDIATE LOAN FOR THE ALLIES OUT OF THIS, DON'T YOU THINK IT'S WORTH TRYING?

Then I got to work to promote the proposal. It was my first effort ever to influence public affairs, and I found it fascinating, enthralling and exhausting, as I have ever since. To see the proposal given effect, I needed to get the backing of a lobby in Washington and of the British themselves.

William Allen White's committee was the most influential organized group of Americans in favor of aid to Britain, and in that connection I met him many times and we exchanged a lot of letters. A typical letter from my side of this correspondence was written on July 10, 1940.

I wrote:

Your words keep ringing in my ears "something ought to be done to place funds at the disposal of Great Britain." I feel so helpless as day after day goes by and nothing is being done to give England substantial financial assistance.

It is pitiful when one reads in this morning's newspaper that the English Government is asking housewives to surrender their pots and pans to supply the country with much needed aluminum: or to read that the English people are being put on a restricted diet of badly needed fats because of the necessity of economizing on foreign exchange—and these people are fighting our battle. Every day that is lost in supplying them with funds and necessities makes their situation (and incidentally our own) just that much more precarious.

I heard yesterday that one of the reasons more English children are not being sent over here is because of lack of ships. If England had a billion or more dollars from the sale of leases for military bases in her Western Hemisphere possessions, she could utilize the boats taking supplies purchased with this money to carry children to this country on their return trips. If England did not have the boats, she would have enough money to purchase some of ours.

William Allen White gave me invaluable help with introductions in Washington, where I wanted to get the proposal put before Congress as a bill. The British themselves were less positive.

The British Embassy in Washington was in an official dither over American aid: they wanted it, but they didn't want to look desperate for it. The country was scratching at the bottom of its coffers to finance the war, but the proud British didn't want the world to think that they were paupers parading their begging bowls. Any suggestion that the British Empire could not afford to wage war against Hitler was greeted with gleeful triumph by Dr. Goebbels's propaganda machine in Berlin. So obsessed were the British about this question of appearance that they couldn't even be very active behind the scenes in Washington.

During the summer of 1940, I went several times to the British Embassy in Washington to see Mr. G. H. S. Pinsent, Chief Financial and Economic Advisor to Lord Lothian, the British Ambassador. He provided me with essential data in support of my proposal and, generally, gave me discreet encouragement—but his position for the formal record was something else. In a typical letter, he wrote to me on October 18, 1940:

I think I must be completely candid with you on this subject and tell you that we do not feel that any public ventilation of this question at the present time would be of assistance to us; perhaps even the contrary.

We have rather regretted the discussion which has taken place as the result of the introduction of Senator King's bill, and elsewhere, and we would prefer that the question should not be developed until after the Elections at least.

I still find this letter incredible. It expresses the obverse and frustrating side of the British character; the sense of decorum, justice and fair play which finally led them to stand up to Hitler can also produce a self-defeating preoccupation with being "proper." In that hour of direst plight, the British could have done with a healthy injection of brash American assertiveness.

Finally, on September 30, 1940, through the good offices of my old friend Senator William King of Utah, my proposal was introduced as a bill in the US Senate which would authorize the President to enter into negotiations "for the acquisition by lease or otherwise" of Great Britain's island possessions, to make loans or extensions of credit to the British government through the Export-Import Bank in Washington and to apply to Britain's war debt the terms which had been allowed to Italy.

I'd like to say that it breezed through with nary a dissenting vote. That wasn't the case, however. The bill immediately got bottled up in committee, and it never even got to the floor of the Senate for a vote. So much for my proposal.

But I wasn't through. *Somehow* we had to get aid in Britain, and I was determined to demonstrate that the bulk of America agreed. During October 1940 I commissioned a survey of American newspapers to analyze editorial comment and opinion on the question of aid to Britain. A professional clippings bureau was hired to gather all editorial comment published that month and my own office staff did the work of analysis. The results were impressive: 92 percent of editorial comment in newspapers bought by over thirty-four million Americans—and read by probably three times as many—was in favor of aid.

On November 28, 1940, Thanksgiving Day, I was given an appointment to see the President at the White House and present him with the results of my survey. It was only in 1986 that I discovered that FDR shunted his own son aside to see me that day. At a meeting in Toronto in March 1986, Franklin Roosevelt, Jr., laughingly remembered that he had been scheduled to see his father in the Oval Office that afternoon, only to get a call to say that the President had to see Dr. Hammer on urgent business.

There was a long delay before I was ushered into the Oval Office. Also waiting to see the President was John Cudahy, former US Ambassador to Poland and Ireland, whom I knew slightly. We waited in the office of Major General Edwin M. ("Pa") Watson, the President's appointments secretary. On his desk was a pair of oversized wooden dice, a gift to the White House from the builder of the Panama Canal, General G. W. Goethals. The dice were made of lumber taken from railroad ties used in the canal's construction. When I admired the dice, Pa Watson said, "Well, let's have a crap game while we're waiting."

We got down on the rug, pulled out our money and started rolling. After about half an hour, by which time I had won about three hundred dollars, the President's visitors emerged from the Oval Office and Pa Watson led me in.

"Mr. President," he said to FDR, "you should listen carefully to this man. He's really lucky. John Cudahy and I just played craps with him for half an hour and he took us to the cleaners."

FDR threw his head back and let go one of those pealing laughs which were his trademark and said, "Well, I hope he didn't clean you out completely!"

The President's magnetism was irresistible. He listened so keenly to what I had to say: his responses were so incisive and illuminating. The force of his personality drew me immediately into and under his influence. That superb intelligence, allied with vivacious charm and uproarious humor, captivated me completely. I had been a devoted fan before I met him; I was all his once I had been with him in the Oval Office.

I presented my volume of clippings, which he received with great interest (the next day he even brought them with him to a White House press conference). He knew about me and was well aware of my ideas and intentions. On the question of the destroyers-for-bases idea, he pointed out to me a number of serious difficulties, but made it clear that, overall, he was in favor of some such plan and that he wanted me to help to work one out.

He felt, however, that England had not yet exhausted its own extensive financial resources and that the question of active aid should wait until this had happened. I said, "Well, Mr. President, do you think Hitler will wait?"

He smiled wryly and, after a moment's thought, he replied, "Everything in Germany can be bombed. Everything in England can be bombed. But England has something that can't be bombed—the United States."

I pointed out that this was a short-term advantage: if Germany conquered Britain and obtained possession of her Caribbean islands, then Germany would get bases from which they would be able to bomb the Eastern Seaboard of the United States. The President did not contest the point.

He said that my friend Beardsley Ruml had discussed my scheme with Harry Hopkins, the Secretary of Commerce, who was about to be appointed head of the Lend-Lease Administration. FDR said that Harry Hopkins and I should put our heads together and see if we couldn't come up with a joint plan. In the next few months Hopkins came several times to my office at the Hammer Galleries. Ultimately, a version of my proposal was adopted and Britain did receive the fifty surplus destroyers which played a decisive role in keeping her in the war during 1941, while the United States had yet to enter the conflict. I know I was only a very small player in the process that helped provide those vital destroyers—but I am proud of the part I played.

I also did what I could to help FDR's reelection in 1940. Besides donating money, I became involved with an organization called the Writers for Roosevelt Committee, which, under the chairmanship of Robert Sherwood, had created a radio program to dramatize the social benefits of the New Deal. The program, written and directed by the playwright-producer Marc Connelly, presented actual case records derived from the Social Security Board, and the actors were the real recipients of the old age pensions, unemployment insurance and other benefits which were being illustrated. We had had to fight tooth and nail to get the program transmitted—the major radio chains refused to broadcast a "dramatization of a political nature"—but when it finally ran on WOR in New York, paid for by Ellin Berlin and myself, the *New York Post* called it "exceptionally novel and interesting," and Eleanor Roosevelt wrote to me from the White House to say, "What a grand thing you did to help the President!"

I still treasure that letter today, as much as I treasure Mrs. Roosevelt's words on another occasion, eighteen years later.

In 1958, the Internal Revenue Service was demanding $750,000 of me in connection with a tax assessment of the whiskey businesses which I had sold some five years before. I offered to settle for 50 percent, the IRS insisted on at least 75 percent, and we went to court. My lawyer and friend, Arthur Groman, determined that the outcome of the case would turn upon the question of my credibility. He asked me to come up with the best character witness I could name. I said, "Well, who do you want?" and he, apparently thinking he would stump me, said, "I'd like Eleanor Roosevelt best, but I don't suppose you could get her." Next morning at nine o'clock he was interviewing Eleanor Roosevelt.

On the stand, Mrs. Roosevelt was, in Arthur's words, "the greatest witness in my forty years in court." Under his examination, she testified that she knew me socially and in a business way; that her husband knew me and her children knew me and that I had been a guest in their home. She stated that she was familiar with my reputation in the community in which I lived for truth, veracity and honesty and she said that "it is a most excellent reputation."

I won the case hands down.

During his terms of office I sent FDR a number of presents as tokens of my esteem. His fondness for ship models was very well known and, through my business with the Hammer Galleries, several unusual models came my way, one of which, a Dutch war vessel, I sent him for Christmas 1940, and which, he wrote me, he received with delight.

Another ship model, however, not given by me but sold by the Hammer Galleries, caused a piquant incident at the White House.

Early in FDR's first term, a well-known Midwestern entrepreneur in the greeting card business named Bigelow was sentenced to federal prison for tax evasion. There, he was befriended by a fellow inmate named Charlie Ward, who looked after his rich new friend and protected him physically from the other inmates. Mr. Bigelow was so grateful that he promised, when he got out, that he would take care of Charlie for life.

In time, Roosevelt pardoned both men for their separate offenses and Charlie Ward became his rich friend's partner. When Bigelow died, Ward became the sole owner of the business. Feeling beholden to FDR, and wishing to commemorate his generous friend, Charlie searched for a suitable gift for the President's birthday in 1943. He found it at the Hammer Galleries.

It was a twenty-four-inch model of a Volga steamboat. Made of silver, platinum and gold, it had been created in 1913 by Carl Fabergé as a present to the Czarevich Alexis to mark the three hundredth anniversary of the Romanov dynasty. We had bought it from a Moscow commission house in the late twenties and it had been part of the collection at our Brown House.

Victor estimated that the original price received by Fabergé was about $50,000, but we asked $10,000, as we had purchased it for half that amount (its value in gold and silver) and had owned it for some time and had never had any offers. Victor told Charlie, "This is the most expensive toy in the world."

Charlie was delighted with his purchase, and arrangements were made for a formal presentation to FDR at the White House. The President was very taken with the gift, and invited Maxim Litvinov, the first Soviet Ambassador to the United States, to attend the small ceremony in the Oval Office.

Showing the Ambassador his new toy, the President touched the button which turned on the Volga boat's music box. A delicate tinkling melody began, instantly recognizable to everybody in the room and especially to Litvinov, whose features paled. The tune was "God Save the Czar"—the anthem of the Romanovs, whom Litvinov's Bolsheviks had executed.

As always, FDR saw the funny side of the scene and roared with laughter. A hint of color returned to Litvinov's cheeks and he laughed too, albeit mutedly.

*   *   *

By this time, of course, we were deep into our own military involvement in the war. Early on, I became convinced that to complicate the Nazis' efforts on the Russian front, Germany had to be attacked in Europe from the west. Since it was inevitable that the preparations for a massed landing on the mainland of Europe would take years, the only way to get at Hitler directly and immediately was by air.

All my life I have been against war, but since we were in it, and Hitler had to be stopped, I looked for any way to accomplish the job in the shortest possible time and with the least loss of American and Allied lives. The way to do it, it seemed obvious to me, was to bomb the engines of Fascism out of the industrial heart of Germany.

Self-evident though it seemed to me, however, there was deep dissent about the matter in America. It always happens, when war breaks out, that a large body of public and military opinion supposes that the new war will be waged like the last war. Because the American experience of war in Europe came from the Great War of 1914–1918, it was generally assumed that the war against Hitler would again be fought in the bloody trenches of Flanders. This assumption took no account of the massive technological leap which had been made in the intervening twenty years: the airplanes of the First World War had been little more than weavings of string and balsa, glued together by the young pilots' intrepidness. By 1940 the aviation industry had made such strides that the new war was bound to be fought in the air, and won and lost there.

Some pioneers of military thought, such as General Billy Mitchell, had been telling America for nearly twenty years that its future security lay in the skies. After Billy Mitchell's death in 1936, the standard of his ideas was taken up by Major Alexander P. de Seversky and editor/publisher William B. Ziff. The wisdom of these men, spurned during the peacetime decades, was ignored during the first months of America's engagement in the war. I decided to throw whatever weight I could muster behind them.

During the spring and summer of 1942, I put my name and money to a campaign called "Knock Out Germany Now—by Air!" Bill Ziff was an active participant, as were numerous prominent Americans, including my old friend Senator King. The guiding principles of the campaign were expressed in its first publication, a short pamphlet which I edited:

This war can be won quickly.
It can be won by knocking Germany out by air.
Overwhelming air attack can destroy Germany's communication and industrial system.
The war is fundamentally a matter of factory output and superior

industrial economy. The great masses are not in the front line but at their production machines behind it.

Therefore, to strike at key industrial centers and communications systems, *in sufficient force,* will mortally wound our enemies. It will constitute a Second Front.

On May 29, 1942, I wrote to Joe Laurie, my friend from the old days of the Romanov exhibition at Scruggs-Vandervoort-Barney in St. Louis:

I hope that your surmise is correct and there is a chance of the war being over much sooner than the general public thinks. However, I think it would be a mistake to underestimate our enemies. It may be part of their strategy to let us think this while they are preparing something in the nature of a surprise. We are dealing with desperate people who feel they have nothing to lose by taking a chance.

I would feel a lot better if we had permission from Russia to use the Siberian bases so that we could bomb Japanese cities and especially their factories. I also think that Colonel Lord's plan to use England as a land aircraft-carrier and limit England to the production of fighters while we produce all the bombers—sending them over to Germany in waves of a thousand, each carrying 20 tons per bomber—would quickly reduce German cities and transportation lines to rubble. It looks as though our military authorities are going to try something like that, although at present they may be going off half-cocked, without sufficient numbers of the heavy type of bombers Colonel Lord had in mind. . . .

Later in the year, on September 26, 1942, I wrote to Joe Laurie again, in response to questions of his:

Regarding the chance that Germany will be on the road to defeat before the end of 1943, I think it all depends on the use we make of our industrial facilities to construct bombers and cargo planes. Unless Germany's factories and transportation are reduced to a pulp by more intensive combined bombing by America and Great Britain, a second front would probably end in a terrific slaughter and defeat.

This might not only set back the date of the ultimate victory but also mean the loss of our air base, namely Great Britain. Once Great Britain was lost, there would be the danger of Germany doing to us what we want to do to her, that is build fleets of big bombers to destroy our industries. If the Germans join hands with Japan they will probably use the Aleutian Islands as a base unless we have driven them out by that time.

All in all, I think the only hope for victory in 1943 would be the Ziff plan and that is why I am so interested in furthering it.

The Committee to Destroy Germany by Air begat The Committee for a Second Front by Air, which prosecuted identical principles through 1942–1943, until the Allied landings in Sicily and Italy carried the war onto the European mainland. Again, I think we had some part, however small, in converting orthodox military opinion to our cause, and I think we helped to accelerate the building of the gigantic fleet of heavy bombers which pulverized Germany in the later years of the war.

The destruction of Germany's cities by Allied bombing was one of the saddest and most painful aspects of that dreadful war, particularly for me. As a young man, I had known and loved the Hamburg, Berlin and Nuremberg that few Americans had seen, before the Gestapo's jackboots descended upon them. It was misery for me to know that they had to be reduced to rubble. But war calls for intolerable decisions to be taken and unspeakable actions to be committed. War is not "a continuation of political relations by other means"; it is nothing so nice. It is hell on earth.

I was also concerned about what would happen after that hell had subsided. On January 14, 1942, I made a speech to the National Resources and Planning Board, part of the Executive Office of the President in Washington. Part of the board's brief was to prepare America's strategy in the postwar world. At that moment in 1942 it was obvious that the war would last at least another two or three years, so it was prudent and sensible to give some detailed attention then to the world which we wanted to create out of the rubble of war. Most obviously to me, the United States had to take the lead in organizing political and military power and the distribution of wealth, to try to avoid another armed conflict between nation-states. The cardinal errors of the Versailles Treaty after the First World War were to punish the defeated Germans by exacting economic tribute, thereby humiliating and impoverishing them and driving them into the hands of the National Socialists.

As I put it to the board, "Our first goal should be to organize the world so that reason and justice will replace force and violence in settling disputes between nations. Parallel with this objective, we should also strive ultimately to bring about an economic New Deal for all nations and to help to raise the standard of living of all peoples of the world, so that they may achieve social security with freedom from fear and want, as well as the other freedoms enjoyed in a true democracy."

I sketched to the board a plan for a world organization, guided by a Declaration of World Independence and with a new World Constitution. The obvious umbrella organization for this body was the United Nations, to which I suggested that the nation-states of the world should be federated, after the model of our own United States. The central message of my speech was:

> After the war is over we must not return to the old political and economic order. We must not shirk our duty as a member of the family of nations. The world cannot be mismanaged any longer by sixty self-centered and unconnected governments, without any responsibility to the world as a whole. In setting up an international organization, let us restate the fundamental truth contained in the American Declaration of Independence; namely, that just power derives only from the consent of those subject thereto.
>
> Any international decision and the carrying out of such decisions should be in the hands of men who recognize their responsibilities for the general welfare and owe allegiance to the entire community of all nations as well as to their own nations.

In the question-and-answer period afterward I was asked where I saw Stalin fitting into my plan. I answered that he was precisely the kind of man who did not and would not owe allegiance to the entire community of all nations, and that his ambitions for Soviet expansion needed to be firmly checked by the Western powers. I said that our alliance with Stalin—and our sympathies for the dreadful suffering of the Russian people in the war—should not blind us to Stalin's ambition to extend Soviet-style Communism around the world.

The President's uncle, Frederic A. Delano, ran the board, and took me up quite hotly on my warning about Stalin. He said that I was unjustly running down a good and brave ally and that the picture of the Soviet Union's relations with the Western democracies would be very different after a war in which they had fought with us.

I said that my long experience in Russia and my observations since had convinced me that, having secured socialism in the Soviet Union and having enjoyed military success in the war against Hitler, Stalin would not be content to rest his armies and his expansionism on the territorial line which marked the end of hostilities with Germany. Stalin's own ideological dogma showed, as clearly as Hitler's declarations in *Mein Kampf,* that he believed in a kind of manifest destiny of socialism for all industrialized countries. Sadly, in the years to come, he proved the truth of my words.

My thoughts about a world organization to regulate the peace of the world might seem utopian today, now that we have endured a further forty years of conflict, armed and unarmed, between nation-states around the world, but they were not so unusual in those days, when many people felt an idealism for profound change. The idea of a world government was quite widely shared then. In the closing years of the war, when the peoples of the free world were yearning for a new world without war, it might just have been possible to create such an order. If the United States, then the only power on earth in possession of nuclear weapons, had put its might behind such a plan, who knows how the postwar world might have been different?

As it happened, the postwar world was a ghastly mess. Final victory over Germany had left all Europe in a chaos which exceeded even the horrors of 1919. The economies of all the warring nations were in ruins, and governments were unable to provide basic necessities to their people. Refugees and dispossessed homeless people streamed across Europe in millions, jamming temporary camps and creating monstrous administrative confusion.

Early in 1946 I heard Drew Pearson describing these dreadful scenes over the radio and I was very moved. I felt as if I were back on that train running through the Urals in 1921, seeing the bloated bellies of the starving children and hearing their cries.

I immediately sent Pearson a telegram, offering to put up a million pounds of grain from my allocation for my whiskey distilleries—grain was still subject to rationing controls then. It was Pearson's idea that I should make my million pounds of grain available to the United Nations Relief and Rehabilitation Administration (UNRRA), which I promptly did.

Pearson then put me in touch with Fiorello La Guardia, Mayor of New York, who was Director General of UNRRA. La Guardia, who was an irresistible bundle of drive and energy, asked me, "How can we persuade the other distillers of America to do what you have done?"

"I can only think of one way," I said. "You've got to embarrass them into it. Get President Truman to invite the Chairmen and Chief Executives of all the distilling companies to the White House and tell them that there is a need to get one hundred million pounds of grain, and ask each of them to give up a percentage of their grain allocation proportionate to their size in the industry."

That's how it was done. We were all summoned to the White House by Herbert Lehman, a leader of UNRRA, former Governor of New York and former partner in the Lehman Brothers investment banking firm. He put to us exactly the message I had recommended to Fiorello La Guardia. When Lehman was through speaking, I answered him first.

"My company receives six percent of the total distilling allotment of grain for the whole United States," I said. "Therefore, I will give six percent of the total you want—six million pounds." This was in addition to the million pounds I had already contributed.

Stifled choking sounds seemed to come from the throats of some of the other Chief Executives in the room, but they were all over a barrel and they knew it. If any of them refused to cough up their share, they and their companies would look like skinflints. They also ran the risk that their entire allocation might be canceled.

One hundred million pounds of grain was thus made available to UNRRA.

After that, Harry Truman appointed me a member of his Citizens' Food Committee, which was chaired by Charles Luckman, head of the prestigious architectural firm of Luckman Associates. Through the committee, I had a hand in organizing a sixty-day shutdown of distilling production across the nation to release more grain for food production and for the people of Europe. Needless to say, the plan was not well-received by all of my brother distillers or by the members of the labor union movement. Two of the industry's giants, Seagram and Schenley, along with the smaller firm Heaven Hill, stood out against the shutdown, and it took a lot of persuasion and some tough talk to bring them around. But come around they did.

FDR's death did not mark the end of my connection with him and his family. In the years after the war, the President's son, Elliott, took some of his father's personal effects to Victor for sale in the Hammer Galleries. We also sold a collection of books bearing Eleanor Roosevelt's bookplate. We bought a number of items ourselves and returned some of them to the Roosevelt residence at Campobello after I had acquired and restored that house.

FDR's summer holiday home on Campobello Island was as well-known to the world, during his lifetime, as the Kennedy compound at Hyannis Port or the Reagan ranch at Santa Barbara were to become. Lying in the mouth of the Passamaquoddy River off the coast of Maine, the island is actually part of the province of New Brunswick. The thirty-four-room mansion, set in twenty acres of grounds, had been in the Roosevelt family since FDR's boyhood. It was there that he suffered the attack of polio which nearly destroyed his political life in 1921, there he had spent his honeymoon with Eleanor, and it was there that their son Franklin Delano, Jr., was born in 1914. The house formed the backdrop for a stage and screen play by Dore Schary called *Sunrise at Campobello,* starring Ralph Bellamy and Greer Garson. In other words, Campobello was a kind of national shrine to FDR. That, at least, was how I felt about it.

In 1952 Elliott Roosevelt decided to sell the house and grounds. By that time the property had been neglected for eight years and was in a very poor state. Hundreds of thousands of dollars needed to be spent to repair the place. As it stood, the property was worth very little, but I bought Campobello from him.

I wanted to restore the house completely in memory of my great hero, and to make sure that it was always available for Eleanor and her family during her lifetime. We put in a new roof, supports, floors and windows, plumbing and electrical wiring. Then Victor and Eleanor worked together to restore the interior of the house in keeping with its appearance as it had been when Eleanor first visited. We restored to the house many of the personal effects which Elliott and Eleanor had offered to us for sale through the Hammer Galleries, and Victor dug up many more objects of memorabilia from FDR's youth—such as the rowing oars he had used at Harvard. Bit by bit, inch by inch, Campobello became again "my beloved island," as the late President had called it. Soon after we had completed the major work of restoration, a syndicate which wanted to commercialize the place offered me five hundred thousand for the property. I turned them down without a second thought.

The Hammer and Roosevelt families spent many happy summers at Campobello in the fifties. Until I moved to California, in the mid-fifties, I visited the island occasionally for weekends and holidays. My mother, Victor, Harry and their wives always took their holidays there. Eleanor Roosevelt and her sons stayed frequently. Eleanor's feelings about the house and the island are vividly recorded in a little note she wrote to Victor on August 19, 1962:

Dear Victor
On this my last day at Campobello, I want to thank you again for your great kindness in letting me stay in the cottage and for arranging every-thing for my comfort. I had a most delightful time, topped off today with one of the most beautiful days the Island could produce and ending in a glorious sunset.

I am leaving much, much stronger than I came, and I attribute the renewal of my strength to the peace and quiet I have found here.

Words cannot express my gratitude to you and Ir[e]ene [Victor's wife], but I do hope you realize that it is deep and warm.

Looking forward to seeing you both very soon, and hoping you will come to visit at Hyde Park before long.
Affectionately
Eleanor Roosevelt.
P.S. Your couple are wonderful. They could not have been more kind, and, of course, Linnea [the housekeeper] was as good as gold.

She was never to see Campobello again. She died on November 7, 1962.

The death of my old friend caused me to consider anew my stew-ardship of Campobello. I was, by then, completely attached to life in California. The island was underused and deserted most of the time. The time had come to make a change.

During the same month of August 1962, when Eleanor had been

enjoying Campobello for the last time, President Kennedy had arrived in Maine to dedicate a short causeway-bridge to the island. In his speech, JFK said that he thought a park in the vicinity of FDR's old haunts would "further strengthen the bond of friendship between the two countries."

The idea stuck in the back of my mind that winter and popped up, fully grown, the following May when I overheard a radio news report of a meeting at Hyannis Port between President Kennedy and Canadian Prime Minister Lester Pearson. According to the radio, the President had mentioned his idea for a park to the Prime Minister.

I promptly called the Senator from Maine, Edmund Muskie, and told him that I wanted to give Campobello to the people of the United States and Canada, and create an international park in memory of FDR. Mr. Muskie was all for the idea.

Then I called Jimmy Roosevelt, who was not only my best friend among the children of FDR but also my congressman, and asked him what he thought. He was very enthusiastic, and said that he would relay my offer to the President. For confirmation, I wrote the offer out in a telegram which I sent to Jimmy.

I heard almost immediately from the White House that President Kennedy wanted to discuss my offer in person, and that he would be calling me at my home early next morning, a Sunday. It was a great and historic moment for me and my household and, to treat the occasion with its due ceremony, I arranged to have the President's call put on loudspeakers so that it could be heard by my family and staff and be recorded. The equipment was set up in the library of our home in Westwood and, just before nine A.M. (twelve noon EST), we all assembled.

The call came. The President was speaking from Hyannis Port.

JFK said that he was calling to check that my offer, relayed by Jimmy Roosevelt, was true.

"Yes, I meant it," I said.

"That's a very generous gift, Doctor. The Prime Minister is here with me at Hyannis Port. We wanted to get your confirmation before we released it to the press."

"Have you received the telegram I sent to Jimmy Roosevelt last night to show to you?" I asked.

Mr. Kennedy said that he had not; evidently there had been a delay in transmission.

"Would you mind holding the phone while I get a copy of it to read to you?" I said. He said that he would hold on.

I ran out of the library up the stairs to my bedroom to search for the paper.

Now, I pride myself on being a man of reasonably orderly mind and habits. It is impossible to run a business of any size, especially a great corporation, without establishing and respecting a system for the flow and retrieval of information. My office is, I think, a model of systematic arrangement: my bedroom is something less than perfect in this regard.

Many of my most personal papers and records are kept in my bedroom, filed under a system which is my own invention and which would make no sense to anybody else. The room also contains thousands of books, hundreds of current journals and newspapers, four television sets and racks of recorded films and TV programs. Nobody ever lays a hand on these papers except me. It is not, I must admit, the most highly organized and efficiently run archive imaginable. Sometimes, to tell the truth, papers go astray (occasionally they turn up under my bed).

The telegram to Jimmy Roosevelt had vanished. I turned over piles of papers in my bedroom, but I couldn't put my hand on it. I looked under the bed. Nothing. The minutes were ticking by and Mr. Kennedy was still hanging on the telephone. Finally, I ran downstairs to the library again. I can still hear the sound of my slippers flip-flopping on the hardwood floors and the voice of my wife Frances as she scolded me: "Do you realize that you've kept the President of the United States waiting on the phone?"

I apologized to Mr. Kennedy and said, "This is what I said in my telegram, Mr. President." Then I repeated my words to Jimmy Roosevelt from memory, writing them down as I spoke. When I later compared this note with the copy of my original telegram, I found that, luckily, I'd managed to get it completely right.

On May 12, 1963, the President directed the State and Interior departments to enter into negotiations with their counterparts in the Canadian government to implement the Campobello memorial. Two days later, the Senate and House of the State of Maine passed a resolution commending the Hammer family's generosity. The following January, two months after Mr. Kennedy was assassinated, President Lyndon Johnson invited Harry, Victor and me to lunch at the White House for the signing of the intergovernment agreement.

On August 20, 1964, after Queen Elizabeth II had added her signature to the agreement, the First Ladies of the United States and of Canada, Mrs. Lyndon Johnson and Mrs. Lester Pearson, officially opened the Roosevelt Campobello International Park.

It was a glittering, gusty, glorious day typical of the rugged beauties of the place: a very good day for me and one of my proudest. In her short speech, Lady Bird Johnson spoke well when she said, "Both Franklin and Eleanor Roosevelt knew the meaning of courage sustained by compassion in every day of their lives. This landmark is an inspiration for all future generations. This island off the northeastern coast of our continent will always turn its face towards the sunrise of world events—the sunrise at Campobello."

She kindly went on to praise my family for the gift.

Campobello is often in my mind, and it fills a powerful place in my emotions. It is my permanent connection with FDR, and my permanent memorial in honor of the greatest man of my time, whom I am proud to have known and to have served.

The Campobello connection continues. Only last year, on October 22, 1985, President Reagan appointed Frances Hammer to be an Alternate Member on the Roosevelt Campobello International Park Commission. I hope that my family will sustain our connection with Campobello forever.

The Tough Years

My middle age was tough going. Many accounts of my life make it look as if it was roses all the way—and to some extent that is my own fault. When I put on my public face, I try to brush off yesterday's troubles as if they never happened. In private, I try not to dwell upon dark thoughts. What's the use? Regrets and recriminations only hurt your soul.

Nonetheless, the full list of my woes in those years of my middle age makes a sorry catalogue. Apart from my business life, nearly everything possible went wrong. My father died. My second marriage broke up in very public and embarrassing circumstances. My son got into deep trouble and narrowly missed going to prison. My health was rocky. It wasn't, to say the least, the best of times.

After all the tumult, turmoil and difficulty of his life, my father's last years were relatively calm and easy. Though his intellectual devotion to socialism never slackened, he became much less active in his political pursuits after he and my mother left Russia. The truth is that he was disillusioned.

During his years in Moscow, he had witnessed the beginning of Stalin's Terror at first hand. Friends of my father's, loyal old Bolsheviks who had fought alongside Lenin, were removed from office, publicly humiliated in show trials and executed. Some were brutally murdered without trial. Many others disappeared to long exile in Siberia. The full horror of Stalin's regime was not acknowledged in Russia until Khrushchev made his secret denunciation at the Communist Party Congress in Moscow in February 1956. As early as the beginning of the thirties, however, my father understood exactly what "Uncle Joe" was doing and he was shaken to the core. Witnessing Stalin's perversion and corruption of the dreams and ideas of socialism, my father was shattered and depressed.

Relations between my father and the Soviets were far from friendly during the thirties. As a critic of Stalin, he was not considered a friend of the state, and the animosity felt toward him spread to other members of our family, even to my brother Victor and to my mother.

Victor was still trying to arrange to bring his son, Armasha, to America, but the Soviets were icily uncooperative. Even though Armasha had been registered as an American citizen at the American Consulate in Berlin on August 2, 1929, the Soviet authorities refused to allow him an exit visa. They even made it impossible for Victor and my mother to get visas to go to Moscow to visit the boy. Victor finally saw his son only after Stalin was dead and the boy was grown up.

When the United States entered the war, and for the first time since his imprisonment in 1920, my father felt very strongly that he ought to practice medicine again. He felt that it was his duty to help free younger doctors for military service.

Even though he had been pardoned by Governor Alfred E. Smith of New York in 1924, my father had never applied for the restoration of his license to practice. During his years in Moscow he had written articles on medical matters for the English-language *Moscow Daily News* and, after his return to America, he worked voluntarily with my old friend Maxie Rosenzweig, who had become an associate in gynecology at the Jewish Hospital in Brooklyn—together they helped to develop the Aschheim-Zondek test for pregnancy. So my father had kept up-to-date on medical matters and was perfectly competent to resume practice.

The last hint of a stain on his name would be removed if his license were restored by the Board of Regents. In May 1943 they heard the case. Some exceptional documents were placed in evidence and some unusual witnesses were heard. Lawyer Smyth, who had made such a mess of my father's defense, wrote a letter to say that he should have applied for a mistrial when copies of the newspaper reporting the alleged bribery of a juror were seen by the jury. Former Governor Al Smith wrote a letter to the Regents which explained the full circumstances of his pardon and said, "An examination quite clearly showed that he had no criminal intent. . . . I feel perfectly free and safe in recommending that he be reinstated to the practice of medicine."

A unique contribution was made by James W. Gerard, formerly Ambassador to Germany and, before that, the partner of Judge Francis M. Scott, who had argued my father's appeal in 1921. Judge Scott was dead by 1943, but Mr. Gerard remembered that, "When Judge Scott had been retained to argue this appeal, I happened to ask him why he had taken up this case which, as it was a criminal case, was not in our line of general practice. He told me that he had done so because, after examining the case, he felt that there had been no guilty intent on the part of Dr. Hammer, the defendant, and that he felt that an innocent man had been convicted. He asked me to look over the papers, which I did, and came to the same conclusion.

"The restoration of Dr. Hammer to practice would be of great benefit at this time when there is such a need of skilled medical work," he concluded.

I myself appeared before the Board of Regents to testify to the quality of my father's work and his compassion. By the time the hearings were over, the decision was plain: my father's license to practice medicine was restored to him. He established an office in the Wellington Hotel on West Fifty-fourth Street in Manhattan and became a general practitioner, like an old country doctor. He once calculated that he had delivered more than five thousand babies during his medical career.

On October 17, 1948, he died. He was operated on for a prostate condition, which disturbed his long-standing heart complaint. Then, after leaving the hospital, he contracted pneumonia, which further weakened him. While reading a newspaper in the apartment he and my mother had taken at the Barbizon-Plaza, he slid off his chair unconscious and died of a cerebral hemorrhage.

My diary, with its patchy and inadequate entries, records nothing of my feelings then. There is, however, an entry for my fifty-first birthday on May 21, 1949:

My whole family got together for a cruise up the East River, and the next evening we all had dinner at Jack Madden's, a famous restaurant in New York. Mama Rose got up to make a toast, and said: "I want you children to know that I'm going to Europe tomorrow because I have some obligations to people there who were good to me when I needed them. I hate to leave you, my children, because I love you dearly. These moments mean so much to me, because I am an old lady of seventy-four [she lived to be nearly ninety]. *Your dad played a trick on me by leaving me at this time, so I must make the trip alone. I shall miss him, because he was a wonderful traveling companion. He was my secretary and wrote all my letters. He was a great man and a wonderful person. You children can be proud of having had such a father."*

One of my father's most precious legacies to me was spiritual. I learned from him the value of courage and the strength of will. He taught me that despondency and despair can be overcome by determination. During those middle years of my life, when I was often acutely unhappy at home in my marriage and when my business life was so hectic and strenuous that I often felt I had bitten off more than I could chew, I was frequently subject to bouts of despondency. My usual optimism would give way to dark pessimism, hope would be replaced by despair, daring by uncertainty, and courage by defeatism and fear.

At those times, I would try to remember the maxims by which my father had sustained his own courage through his troubles. I would try to remember that if I allowed myself to be discouraged, I made myself my own worst enemy. I would tell myself that the only way to defeat those invasions of gloom was to fight back, inch by inch. Every action taken against troubles, no matter how small, may help to roll them back. Kipling's poem "If" was a great help to me, as were Dale Carnegie's recommendations for self-improvement—I was thrilled when Mr. Carnegie became a customer of the Hammer Galleries and I was able to tell him how influential he had been in my life.

For very many years I also carried a small leather pocket-size copy of the sayings of the Emperor Marcus Aurelius, whose philosophy of life gave me strength. I even suspect that Dale Carnegie himself drew from Marcus Aurelius for some of his prescriptions for success.

Sophisticated people might jeer at these old-fashioned remedies for unhappiness, and, of course, I am not suggesting that a serious condition of depression can be relieved by will and determination alone. However, for the ordinary states of unhappiness which enter every life, we often need to remind ourselves that we are not powerless to act: our lives are our own responsibility. By acting, by doing, by gathering up all our resources of courage and will, we can make a difference in our circumstances and make a dent in our miseries. Every dent counts.

It didn't help in my fight against unhappiness that I was usually tired and always in pain with gallbladder and kidney stone disease. There was little I could do to relieve either condition. The work that I had taken on simply had to be attended to: there was no ducking or dodging it. I had responsibilities for the members of my extended family and for hundreds of employees. I slept badly at night and my daytime naps were restless. People who need rest get a form of the blues which only rest will cure. It was not available to me.

A terrific pain developed and stayed in my right leg. For months on end in the early forties the pain persisted, almost paralyzing my leg. I had to hobble on crutches for much of the time, and my car was specially adapted so that I could drive using hand controls instead of my feet.

My doctors couldn't explain the paralysis. They suspected it was caused by an infection, but they could not find the site of the nuisance. Finally, I went to a urologist who found the focus of the infection in my prostate, which he massaged, and at last the pain and paralysis disappeared. The urologist felt that he should perform a urethral prostatectomy to make sure that the problem would not recur, and an operation was successfully conducted.

The scar tissue which formed after this operation was to come close to killing me more than forty years later. Gradually, over the decades, the scar tissue formed an obstruction, requiring another operation in 1973 to remove a kidney stone impacted in my left ureter. Twelve years later, in the summer of 1985, my doctors came to the conclusion—mistakenly as it subsequently emerged—that I was in danger of death from uremic poisoning, and a major operation was performed at UCLA to implant the ureters to bypass the obstruction.

As for the gallbladder disease, I depended so much on Seidlitz powders that I was practically living on them. The nagging discomfort troubled me on and off for nearly thirty years, until it exploded in 1968.

One night in that year I was in Washington, having attended a long session at the Securities and Exchange Commission. Suddenly, in my hotel room, I was gripped by a savage and crippling pain in my abdomen. With the help of my attorney, Arthur Groman, I was able to get to a doctor in a building near the White House. He gave me a painkilling injection, and somehow I got onto my plane and rested in bed during the flight to Los Angeles.

Next day the pain had disappeared but, nonetheless, I went to see Dr. William Longmire, past President of the American College of Surgeons, at the UCLA Medical School. The X rays Dr. Longmire took revealed nothing, but even so he felt that he should conduct an exploratory operation. He left the decision up to me. I said, "Go ahead. Let's see what's there."

In a five-hour operation, Dr. Longmire and his colleagues found a large, walled-off abscess full of pus and gallstones.It could have burst into my abdomen at any time and would have caused instant peritonitis.

The pains in my kidneys went on. In December 1970 Dr. Longmire operated again with Dr. Willard Goodwin, UCLA's Professor of Urology. This time they discovered a huge stone, too big to pass, in the duct leading from my kidney to my bladder and a diverticulum in my bladder. This second operation took six hours. Once I had been sewed back together again, my torso was covered with crisscross scars like the frame for a game of tic-tac-toe.

Other people's operations can be a very tedious subject for a reader or a listener, and I am not giving all these grisly details of my illnesses just to show off my scars. My point is that ill health and pain have to be faced and fought like despondency and despair. If you let them get you down, they will flatten you. Some pain has to be expected in every life. There is nothing unusual about it and there is nothing very interesting or rewarding about it. I've had my share and I know what I'm talking about.

I also had my share of marital trouble and I know very well what misery a bad marriage can bring. On the whole, if I had to choose between a decade of ill health or a decade of marital infighting, I would choose the sickness. In the decade from the early forties to the early fifties, I had them both.

My life with Angela wasn't all bad all the time. She gave me a lot of encouragement when I was involved in wartime activities. She wrote me notes then, saying that she believed I could be a great man and make a real difference to the world if only I could believe in myself.

When she was sober she was capable, intelligent, industrious and a delightful companion. If she could have kept away from drink, I think our marriage would have survived, despite my disappointment about children. Unfortunately, that was never to be.

She used to say that drinking kept her energies running, which was a sad travesty of the truth. In fact, she was a naturally energetic and highly strung woman who took alcohol, I think, as a kind of anesthetic to ease her nervousness and suppress her energies. She was a steady, day-long drinker, and by the end of the day, she would have drunk herself out of control, and in those hours she might say and do anything. I often caught the wrong side of Angela's tongue, especially when we were together in company. When we were with friends, it gave her a perverse pleasure to deride my origins and my family. When she was in the depths of her cups, it wasn't unusual for her to sneer at me and say that I was a filthy Jew.

The time came when I realized that she would never stay sober and that I had the choice between saving some chance of happiness for myself or submitting to an endless misery. That understanding came slowly and, for the sake of our marriage, I suppressed it as long as I could. One night in 1953 it exploded.

I had returned to our home in Red Bank after a long business trip to Florida. I was whipped with fatigue, looking forward to a homecoming and a nice dinner. Angela started in on me. Drumming up the usual ritual frenzy of jeers, she added one or two new touches, accusing me of various infidelities and then letting go with a string of anti-Semitic insults.

My patience snapped. I turned on my heel and left the house, and spent the night in one of the cottages on the farm. Next day I sent for some of my belongings from the house. I was to live in that cottage for nearly two years, until our divorce was finalized. Angela and I hardly ever saw or spoke to each other again. When the break came between us, it was complete and irrevocable.

The break was clean, but the divorce was a grisly mess. I was ready to make a fair and generous settlement to provide for Angela as long as she lived, as long as it was effected as quickly and quietly as possible. Angela and her lawyers, however, had other ideas. She decided to go for broke and launched a huge and carefully orchestrated action against me claiming ten million dollars, to include interests in the Hammer Galleries and United Distillers.

A ten-million-dollar divorce action was almost unprecedented at that time. The size of the figure and my own prominence made major news stories all over the country. Soon there were to be more headlines, when Angela filed a suit for temporary alimony while we were waiting for the divorce action to be heard. To support her in the manner to which she had become accustomed, Angela asked for $158,000 a year!

Her motion included monthly sums of $2500 for clothing, $1000 for entertainment and $500 "for her hobby of collecting antiques"—a hobby of which I had, up to that time, been unaware. She wanted a total of $11,525 in cash each month and $20,000 annually for "necessary repairs" to the house at Red Bank, which could, effectively, have been rebuilt from top to bottom for that amount.

The media, understandably, reacted to Angela's claims with glee. People couldn't hear enough about this high-flying scandal between "the socialite and the multimillionaire," as it was billed. Angela and her lawyers piled on every allegation they could dream up, even claiming that my son Julian had kept watch on us in our bedroom and observed events in our marital bed through binoculars, reporting the details to his mother, Olga. That fantasy had the intended effect of upsetting Julian and Olga and further complicating my relations with them.

J. Paul Getty, who had as much experience of ex-wives as King Henry VIII of England, liked to repeat a rueful line about alimony which he had borrowed from John Barrymore: "I know you're supposed to pay the piper," Paul would say, "but I feel like I'm subsidizing a whole orchestra." During the divorce proceedings with Angela, I came to know how Paul felt.

To get a crack at my business holdings in New York, Angela sought to have the case heard there. Even though I felt she had not the faintest whisper of a fair claim, the fortune I had worked to accumulate over thirty years was in real danger. It was then I had the great and abiding good luck to engage the legal services of Louis Nizer.

By that time Louis Nizer was already one of the most famous trial lawyers in America, a fighter for rich and poor alike, and well on the way to becoming the doyen of American attorneys and one of the most admired men in the history of the American bar. I had first met him when he was the opposing attorney against me in a small business matter, and I immediately recognized his outstanding ability. My first consultation with him about my divorce was to form the basis for an enduring friendship and business association. Scarcely a week has elapsed in nearly thirty-five years that I have not profited from the wisdom of Louis's judgment and the profundity of his knowledge, always delivered with eloquence and conciseness.

Louis had not studied my case for long when he came up with a remarkable suggestion. He said, "In view of the tortures and humiliations you have endured at your wife's hands, and the patience with which you have suffered her alcoholism, I believe that you could yourself file for divorce on the grounds of her cruelty."

That recommendation was startling not only because it was a new idea, but because it was going to cost Louis a profitable case. The laws of New York did not provide for a husband to divorce his wife for cruelty, but the laws of New Jersey did—though no such action had ever been fought there. Louis's idea put the initiative back into my hands, put Angela's lawyers on the defensive and removed the case from New York, much to her chagrin.

An interminable rigamarole of court hearings, stays and delays ensued, each attended with more publicity. Angela's lawyers were repeatedly unable to produce her in court because she was confined to bed with what they described as "a fairly chronic" liver disease—the onset of cirrhosis.

Finally the papers declared, IT'S ALL OVER. A compromise had been struck between my attorneys and Angela's. She agreed to settle for reasonable compensation and alimony and, in return, I dropped my own cruelty action. To avoid "further heartache and agony," as I explained to the court, I agreed not to contest her suit for desertion. The explanation was truthful, but I also had other, urgent reasons to expedite my divorce from Angela. They came in the form of Mrs. Frances Tolman.

Frances, from whom I had been divided for all the years since our first meeting in New York but whom I had never forgotten, reentered my life during the long agony of my divorce from Angela. It was not, however, the divorce which was the first cause of our reuniting; it was an even more serious court action in California.

My son, Julian, was charged with manslaughter.

Julian's adolescence had been difficult. His mother, Olga, was deeply devoted to him, as was everybody in my family, but he suffered from the lack of a father's constant care, love and discipline. The pleasures of California, where Olga and Julian were living, have turned many a young boy's head and, without having me to keep him in check, Julian enjoyed them all, perhaps too well.

Whenever we were able to be together we had good times. We once had a great fishing trip to Canada together, canoeing the lakes and rivers and carrying the canoes on our backs over land, sleeping in tents and cooking our catch. In 1950 Julian and Angela came with me in my Beechcraft on a business trip to the Caribbean Islands, where I made deals for rum and molasses for United Distillers. We combined my business with family pleasure and had long days fishing for tarpon off the Florida Keys and sailing in the seas around the West Indies.

Julian even gave me valuable business assistance on that trip. When we arrived in the Dominican Republic, Julian called a close friend of his, a classmate who was the son of the Dominican dictator, Rafael Trujillo. We all got the red-carpet treatment during our stay on the island, and it was quite a help in my negotiations that my son was the friend of the dictator's son.

Julian wrote a long and frequently hilarious account of this trip called "Caribbean Diary—Being a factual account of the way a business trip should really be taken." The diary's dedication read:

To Dad and Angela, not only for making this trip possible, but for interspersing it with their peculiar brand of adventure and misadventure, which makes any trip with them a delightful experience not soon to be forgotten.

The shame is that we could not share more delightful experiences together and that our adventures and misadventures were so rare.

Julian went to Golden State University, was graduated in 1953, then joined the Army. During his Army years, we naturally saw very little of each other. After his discharge he went to live in California, where he met his wife, Sue, who soon became pregnant. He seemed to have settled down quietly when, suddenly, in early May of 1955, I got the terrible message from his mother that our son had been arrested for manslaughter.

I took the first plane to the West Coast. The headlines which greeted us in Los Angeles recalled those grim days, thirty-six years before, when my own father had been arrested. This time, however, it was not MILLIONAIRE DOCTOR ARRESTED, but MILLIONAIRE'S SON KILLS GI.

I quickly got the details of the awful story from Julian and established that, while he had actually killed a man, he had acted to defend his pregnant wife and himself.

The dead man had been Julian's buddy at boot camp when they

were both recruits. Julian had been assigned stateside duty while his friend—who was a former Golden Gloves fighter—was sent to Korea. The war separated the young friends and they lost touch with each other, until the buddy turned up in California in 1955. The two men enjoyed a celebratory reunion in a Los Angeles bar, and then Julian took his friend home to meet his young wife, whose first pregnancy was far advanced. Julian's friend drank a lot more.

He began to make passes at Sue. A menacing argument started and the ex-fighter grew violent. He threatened to attack Julian with a beer bottle and moved toward him. Julian reached into a drawer and took out a loaded pistol. He warned the man to stand back, but he kept coming forward. Julian shot him.

I contacted my friend Jimmy Roosevelt, who put me in touch with Mendel Silberberg, senior partner of Mitchell, Silberberg and Knupp, one of the most prominent law firms in California. Silberberg said his firm did not handle criminal cases, but, as a favor to me and Jimmy Roosevelt, and in view of Julian's obvious innocence of murder, he would assign his junior partner, Arthur Groman, to the case.

Having just met Louis Nizer, I now met a second attorney whose counsel and friendship I have depended upon ever since. Both men were to become Directors on the board of Occidental Petroleum and, as with Louis, the wisdom I found in Arthur Groman was to be a vital asset in the years to come.

Arthur disposed of Julian's case with startling speed and efficiency. Julian's wife fully corroborated his story. An autopsy report showed an extremely high level of alcohol in the dead man's blood. Arthur showed that the prosecutor had used Julian as his witness, contravening two rulings of the Supreme Court of California that the prosecutor cannot impeach his own witness.

The case was dismissed without trial. Julian was set free.

Between that and the divorce case, however, the hares of the press had kept running, and my name was being bandied about in headlines from coast to coast. The *Police Gazette* carried one especially lurid story—but from the publication of that unpleasant article came one of the most fortunate twists of fate in my life.

Sitting in a Los Angeles beauty parlor, a wealthy widow was idly turning the pages of the *Police Gazette* while her hair was drying. Suddenly she came to the story about my divorce case, sat bolt upright and began reading with electric concentration. Later, she picked up the Los Angeles papers and read about Julian's arrest.

The woman was Frances Tolman. She had been living alone for years since the death of her husband, Elmer. She was lonely, she was free and she had never forgotten me. The article in the *Police Gazette* and the story about Julian galvanized her. Rushing home, she quickly composed a telegram which she sent to me at the Hammer Galleries. She said that she was sorry to hear about my troubles and offered to help me if there was anything she could do.

Reading this telegram in New York, I chuckled and said to myself, "Yes, Frances, there is something you could do: you could marry me."

The telegram did not give her telephone number. There was nothing for me to do but to go and see her. Next morning Frances looked out her study window onto the lush and sunny gardens of her Los Angeles home and saw me running up the steps to her front door. Ever since that morning, we have always been together, and her home in California has been mine also.

At last, nearly twenty years after our first meeting, there was no impediment between us. Frances was single. I was in the throes of my divorce from Angela. Frances was childless, and my only child, Julian, was grown. I was more than ready to liquidate my business interests on the East Coast and retire to the eternal spring of California to be with Frances. In fact, I couldn't wait.

I had just turned fifty-seven years of age—four years more than Frances—when we were reunited. I was ready to ease up in my business life. Elmer Tolman had left Frances with a substantial fortune and, together with my millions, we had far more money than we would ever need or want to spend. The distilling business had been good to me, but it had really ceased to hold my interest. I was ready to quit.

There was nothing to keep me on the East Coast, as I had decided to sell my Aberdeen-Angus herd. For the past seven years, I had developed yet another sideline, very lucrative and extremely satisfying, which was the breeding of Aberdeen-Angus cattle. I had become genuinely fascinated by my new occupation: it was a challenge both to my business acumen and my intellect. The study of bloodlines and the task of keeping the animals healthy or curing them when they fell ill reawakened a division of my mind which had lain fallow for nearly thirty years, since my medical days.

It began this way: toward the end of the war one day, I took a fancy for a steak. Nothing very exceptional in that, but this was a time of shortages, and a good hunk of prime steak was as hard to come by as a two-pound tin of the best Beluga caviar.

Henry, our man at the farm, suggested that I should buy a steer for slaughtering and he would store the cuts in a freezing locker. I told him to go ahead.

Next weekend I found an Aberdeen Black Angus tethered in the yard. "I couldn't find a steer," Henry said, "so I bought this cow instead."

"That's fine by me," I said. "When do we eat?"

He looked embarrassed and coughed nervously. "She's been bred, Doc," he said. "She's going to have a calf pretty soon."

"Good God," I said, "I can't kill a cow that's going to have a calf! I don't need a steak that bad. Don't kill her. Let her stay here on the farm and we'll treat her nice and see what happens."

A calf happened, a good, strong, handsome female creature to whom I grew attached, as I had to the mother, who soon calved again. The three of them might have remained on the farm as superannuated pets if I hadn't had a business brainwave.

A small but highly profitable by-product of my distilling businesses was in the nutritious residue of the mash. Cattle breeders bought all of the residue from my distilleries to feed their herds. We had never made much of this business, being very pleased simply to get any kind of price for what we considered as little more than the garbage left at the end of the distilling process. One day I realized that this so-called dross might be transmuted, if not into gold, then into its dollar equivalent.

It was in 1947. One of Angela's friends, an authority on Black Angus, invited us to go with him to an exhibition, competition and sale. A cow from the herd of Seymour Knox of Buffalo won the top ribbon that day and was offered at auction.

The bidding was stuck at around $500 when I began raising my hand. The animal was graveled down to me at $1000.

Knox's manager, Mr. Baker, came over to see me after the sale and said, "I don't seem to recognize you. Have you got a big herd?"

I burst out laughing and told him about my three pets at home. He was very puzzled. "Well," he said, "what are you doing buying a champion animal?"

I told him about our residue mash feed, and then said, "I think I'm going to raise the best purebred herd in this country to show how good our feed is."

This idea must have been germinating in a dark room at the back of my mind for some time, but I had been unaware of it until that afternoon, when it seemed to burst into full bloom in my consciousness. I could see exactly where I wanted to go and how I should proceed.

Baker seemed to be intrigued by my idea. He asked me a string of questions. I was impressed by his curiosity.

"Would you like to come and work for me?" I said.

He thought for a moment. Then he said, "Mr. Knox really isn't that interested in my work. He didn't show up to see me win the championship. If you're really sincere about wanting to go to the top, I'll do my best to help you get there. How do you want to go about it? Fast or slow?"

"Fast."

"Well, then," he said, "you're just going to have to buy the best bull in the country. As it happens, he's coming up for sale in a few weeks at Chillicothe, Missouri. His name is Prince Eric. If you can get him, I'll create the best herd in the country for you."

"How high do you think I'll have to go?" I asked cheerfully.

"How high do you want to go?"

"Well, what do you say to fifteen thousand?"

He didn't say anything. He just gave me a wide-eyed stare and sucked in his breath in a whistle over his gums. I didn't know if he thought the sum was far too much or far too little, and I was too much on my dignity to ask. I soon found out.

The bidding for Prince Eric reached $15,000 before I was able to get my hand up. When Prince Eric was led into the ring, the opening bid was more than $5000 and it roared up to $30,000 in $1000 jumps. At that stage only two contenders were left in the competition: a Chicago hosiery manufacturer named Leslie L. O'Bryan and me. The bids had now slowed to raises of $100, but I was sweating.

I was risking a huge sum of cash in a venture in which I was a complete novice, which went against all my instincts and my business experience. I had always learned a new business from the bottom up, slowly, cautiously and conservatively, taking the next risky step only when I was sure of the foundations I had built. Here I was risking a very hefty pile of cash to enter a business at the top with no foundation of experience.

Worse than that: just before going to the sale at Chillicothe, I had completed negotiations with the ultraconservative Chase Manhattan Bank for a loan of ten million dollars to finance some expansions of my whiskey business. It made me very uneasy to imagine the face of Bill Dubois, Executive Vice President of the bank, as he perused the morning newspaper next day and read that his customer Dr. Armand Hammer, who knew nothing about the cattle business, had purchased the most expensive Black Angus bull on earth.

Torn between desire and anxiety, I hung on in the auction and bid $35,000.

"Thirty-five thousand, one hundred," replied O'Bryan with the ease of a man who was ready to go double.

That was the end. I stopped. But even before I had left the ring, I was cursing myself black and blue for a fool. I abhor indecision. I had always figured that if you enter a competition you must be prepared to pay the necessary price for victory. If you can't pay, stay away. I vowed to myself that it would never happen again: nobody would ever outbid me on something I had decided to buy. Nobody has.

I had lost the best bull in the world, so I had to settle for the second-best, called Prince Barbarian of Sunbeam. With Prince Barbarian, the Shadow Isle herd expanded, and sales of Shadow Isle feed grew very healthily. By the end of the forties, the two annual public auctions at Shadow Isle were each grossing about $500,000, and private sales were raising more hundreds of thousands of dollars every year. Nonetheless, the knowledge gnawed at my mind that I would never be better than second-best without Prince Eric.

Then Dr. Mac Cropsey, an itinerant veterinarian from Crystal Lake, Illinois, who came periodically to Shadow Isle to check my herd, gave me some extraordinary news: Prince Eric had become impotent.

"What on earth could have happened to make an eight-year-old bull impotent?" I asked.

"My guess is that Mr. O'Bryan overdid him," Mac said. "He let him run with about fifty cows and that's just too much for any bull. The way I look at it, he screwed himself almost to death."

"And what made it worse for poor Prince Eric," Mac went on, "was that a handler on O'Bryan's farm would beat him with a bullwhip if he hesitated about mounting a cow. So he began to associate intercourse with agony, and now every time he's given a cow, he looks the other way.

"My guess is that his problem is psychological, not physiological. I have a hunch this bull's semen would prove as vital as ever if it could just be extracted from him."

I went straight to the telephone and reached O'Bryan in Chicago. He said he'd be more than happy to sell me Prince Eric.

"Great," I said. "You've got a sale. How much do you want for him?"

"One hundred thousand dollars," came the immediate reply.

I felt as if my heart would stop. "Are you crazy?" I shouted. "I just heard that your bull is a nonbreeder."

"So why do you want to buy him?" O'Bryan asked calmly. He went on: "I know what you want to try. I've been told that this bull might be made to breed artificially."

"So why the hell don't you do it?"

"I'm too busy with my hosiery business to pay proper attention to my herd. I'd just as soon sell him, if the price was right."

"Well, now, Les, I'll tell you what I'll do," I said, settling to business. "You paid thirty-five thousand, one hundred dollars for him three years ago. I'll give you what you paid: I'll give you your money back. After all, there's no guarantee that artificial insemination will work. I'll be taking a chance."

"One hundred thousand dollars," he said.

"Now look, I'll give you fifty thousand, but . . ."

"One hundred thousand."

"Let's split the difference, Les," I said. "I'll give you seventy-five thousand, providing I can make a test and it checks out."

There was a moment's silence on the line and then he said, "All right. Come on out."

Next morning I flew to Chicago with Mac Cropsey. As we landed on O'Bryan's fields, he came out of a barn to greet us and led us to a paddock where Prince Eric was standing.

The memory of that moment is still vivid in my mind. I was on the verge of capturing at last a creature of incomparable beauty. It may sound absurd, but when I saw Prince Eric in O'Bryan's paddock and thought that he might soon be mine, I felt a charge of excitement which has never been surpassed by any of the great pictures I have bought in the world's auction rooms. I just stood there gaping at him and mentally thrashing myself for having missed the chance to have owned him three years before. By this time, offspring of Prince Eric were selling for at least $5000 each.

Mac Cropsey went to work the bull, fitting him with a condom like the *Graf Zeppelin,* took a specimen on glass and focused his microscope. Then he turned it over to me.

Thousands upon thousands upon thousands of sperm were thrashing in a mass under the lens. I saw them all as five-thousand-dollar bills. I turned to O'Bryan and said:

"I'm satisfied. Here's my check for seventy-five thousand dollars. I accept all your conditions. You don't guarantee him as a breeder. If he drops dead five minutes from now, that's my tough luck."

O'Bryan took the check and held it in his hand for a second, then he gave it back to me.

"It's not enough," he said. "I told you I wanted one hundred thousand dollars."

"No, you didn't!" I roared. "I told you I'd split the difference at seventy-five thousand and you said, 'All right. Come on out.'"

"Sure I said, 'Come on out,'" O'Bryan answered. "But I didn't say I'd take seventy-five thousand. It's not enough."

"You son of a bitch!" I shouted. "I wouldn't buy that bull now if he was the last bull in the world." I turned to the other men in my party and said, "Come on. Let's get out of here," and we marched off to the plane without a backward look.

Prince Eric was not to be mine, or so it seemed. At the next Chicago International Livestock Exposition, I knew I had a world's champion. It was a young cow by Prince Eric which I had bought as a calf—but when the champion was led out, it wasn't my cow at all: it was the most magnificent beast I had ever seen, and it was also by Prince Eric, a full sister to my cow out of the same mother. My own came second, but it was no consolation. I flew out of town on a quick business deal and then came back. I lay on my hotel bed, but I couldn't sleep. The image of that big, beautiful bull kept me tossing and turning: Prince Eric was making a fool out of me.

I got up and called Leslie O'Bryan.

"Do you still want to sell Prince Eric?" I said.

"Yes, I do."

"What's your price now?"

"Still a hundred thousand," he said.

"If you'll come straight over to this hotel," I said, "I'll meet your price in full."

And that's what we did. In the remaining three years of his life, Prince Eric earned two million dollars for Shadow Isle. He produced a thousand calves, including six international champions. I was never happier.

One night in August 1953, Prince Eric was overcome by a wholly unexpected burst of amatory passion which must have puzzled him profoundly. A heifer was in heat on the other side of a high, barbed-wire fence. Poor Prince Eric gamely mounted the fence in his efforts to reach the heifer, and his stomach was fatally torn by the barbs. He crashed on his own side of the fence and was found in the morning, dead in a huge pool of blood.

The day Prince Eric died, my heart went out of the breeding business. He was my champion and my pride and he was irreplaceable. I continued halfheartedly for a further year, and then, as another casualty of the divorce, tax duties made it imperative I dissolve the herd, and so, in what was billed as "the Sale of the Century," I had them all auctioned off. They brought in a million dollars.

(Later, I entered the business again when I became head of Occidental Petroleum. At the Shadow Isle Ranch outside Scottsbluff, Nebraska, Occidental now owns and runs the biggest herd of purebred Black Angus cattle in the world, numbering over four thousand head.)

Having disposed of the Shadow Isle herd, it remained for me only to liquidate my remaining interests in United Distillers. I would never have let go of the Hammer Galleries. I was bound to the gallery, both by sentimental ties and because it was my brother Victor's main work and interest in life.

Before the J. W. Dant distillery was sold to Schenley's for $6.5 million in cash, my manager, Newt Cook, had pleaded with me not to sell but to take the company public. "The underwriting will produce at least as many millions for you as you'll raise by selling the company privately," he told me, "and you'll still own fifty percent."

I'll admit that I was tempted by Newt's reasoning, but I had no experience of running public companies, and didn't relish the prospect of dealing with dissenting shareholders and a bureaucratic SEC. I didn't feel any reluctance in rejecting Newt's advice, though his theory was perfectly sound and would have made me a very much richer man.

But it wasn't my intention to cash in and to keep a hand in the distilling business. I wanted out—out to California and to Frances.

I headed West as fast as wings could fly me. In my mind, my business life was largely finished. Ahead, I thought, lay the marriage I had wanted for twenty years and a tranquil retirement among California's palm trees and bougainvillea.

As soon as I got word that my divorce from Angela was final, Frances and I drove to Pomona to get married at the home of a local judge. We chose Pomona because Mendel Silberberg had said that we could avoid publicity there, since the announcement would appear only in the local newspaper and there was little chance that it would be picked up by Los Angeles papers or any other.

It was January 25, 1956, one of the rainiest days of Southern California's rainy season. The judge's wife, who acted as witness, put on her best dress for the ceremony before the fireplace. I had purchased two diamond rings, a ten-karat square-cut solitaire and a wedding band, neither of which Frances has removed from her fingers since then.

If a fortune teller had told me then that the most hectic, adventurous and successful decades of my life were only just about to begin, my laughter would have shattered the crystal ball.

As though to prophesy the happy years ahead I would share with Frances, we returned from our honeymoon to discover I had made an extraordinary buy in a great painting.

To celebrate the wedding, I had wanted to buy a picture to hang above the fireplace in my Greenwich Village house, in place of a Russian painting by the museum director who had faked the Rembrandt *Circumcision of Christ.* Just before the wedding, the Metropolitan Museum of Art had a sale, in which they included a picture called *The Best Children,* described in the catalogue as being "of the school of Sir Thomas Lawrence." Lawrence was the Court Painter to George III.

All the circumstances of this sale suggested that *The Best Children* was of little value. The Metropolitan does not put its masterpieces up for sale, and the words "of the school of . . ." frequently mean that the vendors think poorly of a picture.

Still, I liked the picture, a very handsomely painted study of two little girls, on a huge canvas, about ten feet by six feet. I liked the subject and the size, since the picture would fit exactly in the space above my fireplace. I was determined to have it, despite the experts' doubts.

Even my brother Victor tried to talk me out of bidding for the picture. He said: "At best, this is a copy. If it was genuine, all the dealers from all over America and from Europe would be after it and offering more than you would want to pay. But if it was genuine, the Met wouldn't be putting it up for sale. Forget it, Armand."

Well, it's a weakness and a strength of my character that I don't take anybody's word without doing my own checking. I went to the Metropolitan Museum, and, explaining that I was conducting some research, asked the archivist there for all his records on Sir Thomas Lawrence. He sat me at a large table and brought me a mass of files.

Among the documents about *The Best Children* I found letters from a Mr. Pratt to the Metropolitan Museum. Mr. Pratt, it turned out, had originally acquired the picture in England and he had given it to the Met. An ancient, worn and grubby newspaper clipping recorded that Mr. Pratt had acquired *The Best Children* for the highest price ever paid for a Lawrence.

This was telling information. I knew that Mr. Pratt was a partner of John D. Rockefeller's, a millionaire in his own right, a serious collector of pictures and nobody's fool. If he had paid a large sum of money for *The Best Children,* he must have had good reason to believe that it was authentic.

Armed with this information, I was even more determined to get the picture. I went to the auction with a dealer and we sat side by side, high in the balcony. I didn't want anybody to know that I was bidding or that he was representing me. I simply tapped his foot with mine to raise my bid.

The picture was gaveled down to my agent for a ridiculous $2100. Then somebody protested that the auctioneer had not taken his bid and the sale resumed. This time it was gaveled down to us at $2700.

I was very pleased. I didn't even care if it was a copy, because it was a good colorful picture and I looked forward to seeing it in my living room. I arranged for the picture to be delivered to Victor so that he could supervise its cleaning.

Victor met Frances and me upon our return. Our spirits were soaring, and Victor's news only put the icing on the cake. "Congratulations," he said. "You've bought one of the best of all Lawrence's pictures."

When the picture was cleaned, a third figure—a small boy sitting on a step and dressed in a velvet suit and a high hat—was revealed. Checking into the mystery on a visit to England, Victor had contacted descendants of the Best family and been told that the boy was painted out of the picture after his premature death. His grieving parents could not bear to see his image and had called in a painter of Lawrence's school to paint a pillow in the boy's place. That was why the painting looked badly proportioned and was presumed to be a copy.

Above my fireplace, where I had hung the work of the Rembrandt faker, I now hung my genuine Lawrence; it is still there today. The fake Rembrandt had issued a silent message counseling caution in the tricky world of art sales. *The Best Children* also emits a powerful message, which I have always kept in my mind: the experts aren't always right.

A Little Company Called Occidental

I should have known myself better than to think I could retire.

All my friends knew better. When I told them that I was going to put my feet up and take it easy in California, they all said, "It will never work, Armand—but you will."

I had been working hard for forty years. Business meant much more to me than the creation of wealth: making money for its own sake was never my main purpose. I cared about business for its challenge and difficulty and drama. I cared about it because it is an endless puzzle, demanding constant attention to the smallest detail and the biggest plan. I cared about it because business made America and, in a vital sense, the American way of life *is* business.

My error, when I left the East Coast for California in 1955, was to mistake a temporary fatigue for a permanent exhaustion. After all my problems with my health, my family and my marriage, I was—for the first and only time in my life—feeling my years. Nearing sixty, I began to think that I was getting old and needed a rest. It's funny to remember those feelings now, when I am over eighty-eight years of age, in fine health, full of energy and still as busy as I have ever been.

I spent most of the fall of 1955 in California, with interruptions for forays into the divorce battlefield in New Jersey, and the winding up of my business affairs in New York.

Frances and I took a long, leisurely honeymoon. We spent our days quietly together. We looked after our stocks and shares, laid plans for the house and garden, and pored over travel catalogues, planning trips and vacations around the world. We lived just exactly the way retired people are supposed to. Within a few months I was bored to death.

I began to dread each new day with nothing to do, no place of work to go to, no appointments to keep, no decisions to make. For forty years I had been used to a daily schedule in which tasks, meetings, calls and trips were tightly jammed in against each other. I had lived, seven days a week, with all the personnel and administrative problems of running big concerns. My adrenaline was hooked to the telephone and I was used to picking it up, night and day, to receive news and give instructions.

Now the telephone rang infrequently in our house and the day's mail might only be a handful of letters instead of the hundreds I was used to receiving. I became restless and depressed. Despite my happiness with Frances, I knew that I had made a serious mistake.

I told her, "Unless I can find something to do out here, I think we'll have to go back East. I can't stay here if I'm going to be idle. I'll go crazy."

Frances was very concerned and very encouraging. She didn't want to prevent me from working, but I knew that she didn't want to live on the East Coast again. After all her winters in Chicago and Mundelein, she was happily addicted to the Southern California sunshine.

It looked as if we were in trouble, when we had only just begun together.

Then I happened to meet Sam Shapiro and my life changed. Again.

My life changed in 1921, when I had the idea of going to Russia to help in the famine. It changed again the same year when I offered grain to the Ekaterinburg Soviet and Lenin took notice of me. The change which followed my meeting with Sam Shapiro was as big as either of those.

Sam was a distant relative, and a well-known accountant in Los Angeles. We met one evening at a cocktail party and, as accountants will, he started probing me about my tax arrangements—a subject in which I had a painful interest, Frances and I being inextricably stuck in the highest bracket.

"Why don't you take advantage of oil shelters?" asked Sam.

I didn't know what he was talking about.

He explained. Investment in oil drilling provided a very neat tax deduction, he said. All money invested in dry wells could be written off against tax. Meanwhile, of course, if a well came in, an investor had better go looking for another tax shelter. Fast.

He had my full attention as he went on and said that he knew of a little company which would be an ideal candidate for such investment. It was called Occidental Petroleum, a California corporation which had been struggling since its birth in the early 1920s. Sam knew a small group of people who had joined up to take over Occidental and he offered to put me in touch with them. Their names were Dave Harris, Roy Roberts and John Sullivan.

The company's outstanding 600,000 shares were then trading at 18 cents a share on the Los Angeles Stock Exchange. The takeover group offered to sell me a further 600,000 shares at 20 cents a share, to put $120,000 in their treasury and give me 50 percent of the company. I looked at their balance sheet and quickly determined that the shares weren't even worth 18 cents.

The company had total assets of only $78,000, including $14,000 cash at the bank. It was trading at a loss: its income from all sources was just over $50,000 and its expenses were $93,000. I calculated that the true worth of the company was actually only $34,000. I said, "Judging from this balance sheet, the stock isn't worth its market value. I think it'll have to go into bankruptcy." I turned down the offer of the 600,000 shares.

Then they said, "Well, we have two leases where we think there may be oil, and we want to explore. If you will lend us the money to drill, we'll give you a half interest in the wells."

On July 30, 1956, petroleum engineers had advised Occidental that there might be an oil and gas accumulation covering approximately thirteen hundred acres on those two leases, and estimated a gross recovery of oil from the acreage to be in excess of seven million barrels.

The first of the leases was in Burrel, in Fresno County, about 200 miles north of Los Angeles; the other was in Mountain View, near Bakersfield in Kern County, California. The group wanted a total of $100,000 to drill the two leases. Thinking that we had nothing to lose except tax dollars, Frances and I each lent Occidental $50,000.

Both wells came in. The Burrel well, called Burrel Number One, brought in a field with production of about two hundred and fifty barrels per day. Frances and I had struck a puddle of black gold at our first attempt. Many people never have such luck in a lifetime of investment with independent oil companies.

Neither of us knew anything at all about the oil business. Neither of us had ever even seen a modern oil well close-up. Frances was so excited about our finds that she even thought of buying a mobile home in which we could go and sleep on our field, among the nodding donkeys and the pumps. I didn't want to go quite that far, but I was thrilled, too.

Frances and I put more of our cash into the company toward the end of 1956 to purchase and renovate an antiquated property called the Amber Lease in the McKittrick Field, west of Bakersfield, California. There were thirteen producing wells in this lease, but most of them were producing only two or three barrels a day of low-gravity oil. Some of the wells had been drilled during World War I and the production setup mainly dated from the 1920s.

On the other hand, it had been estimated that the reserves on this lease ran into hundreds of millions of barrels.

Frances and I again put up $100,000, and a full remedial program was undertaken. We drilled some new wells, cleaned out the best of the old wells and installed "bottom hole heaters"—a new technology of the time which heated the very heavy oil in place and made it flow more easily.

Twenty-eight years later, in 1984, Frances and I, together with Occidental, sold our holdings in the Amber Lease. She received $6.2 million and I received $5.3 million—all from an original investment of $100,000!

Fired up by these acquisitions and finds, I wanted to press on with Occidental and encourage the company's expansion. In those days there was no shortage of leases and fields being offered to us by experienced oilmen who thought we were an easy touch. The only shortage was of cash in Occidental's coffers. It was up to me to fill that deficiency.

In November 1956 I again agreed to partner Occidental in joint financing to buy another small field. The vendor was J. K. Wadley.

"J. K.," as he was always called, was a very famous old-time wildcatter and speculator from Texarkana, Arkansas, where he was also a noted philanthropist. He owned a small field with nine wells producing an average of one thousand barrels a day each and several undrilled locations in Dominguez, a suburb of Los Angeles. In November 1956, J. K. wanted to raise $1.25 million and he offered the Dominguez field for sale. Occidental and I went for it.

With Arthur Groman, I rushed over to J. K.'s hotel, the Beverly Hilton in Beverly Hills. The deal was done in the hotel lobby. Arthur picked up a piece of hotel stationery and scribbled out a note of agreement with J. K. and I signed.

He was to receive $1 million in cash and a three-year Occidental note with interest for $250,000. I offered him Occidental stock instead of the note, but he turned me down. Fifteen years later I reminded him that if he had taken the shares they would then be worth over four million dollars! But I didn't blame him—at the time, the stock wasn't even worth the four dollars we were getting.

The day after J. K. and I signed our deal, I picked up Arthur Groman again and we drove out to Dominguez to look at the field. On the way, I suddenly stopped the car at a drugstore, telling Arthur that I wanted to buy a Polaroid camera.

"Why?" he asked.

"Because I've never seen a modern producing field close up and I want to get some snaps for Frances of our new wells!"

I was beginning to get hooked on the oil business. It was simply more exciting, more interesting, more complex, riskier and more rewarding than any other business I had encountered.

After the company's first successes at Burrel and Mountain View, Occidental's stock jumped to one dollar a share, and I started buying it on the open market until I became the largest stockholder. I was then invited to join the board of the corporation and, in July 1957, I was elected President and CEO.

However, I was not yet ready to commit myself to the business or to Occidental. The company was a frail and sickly infant whose growth could easily be snuffed out by the mildest sneeze. I wasn't going to put all my eggs into that basket. In any case, some of my eggs were in an entirely different basket back East: broadcasting. I had just taken control of the Mutual Broadcasting System, the largest radio network in the United States. Throughout 1957, I commuted between New York and California, watching over my new interests and undecided whether I wanted to be an oilman or a media tycoon.

Mutual had come my way as a result of the happy law that one good turn deserves another. It was suggested to me by a lady called Frieda Hennock, who felt that she owed me a favor.

I had known Frieda in New York for some years. She was a lawyer and her ambition was to become a member of the Federal Communications Commission. A mutual friend, Paul Fitzpatrick, who was Democratic State Chairman in New York, asked me if I could help put Frieda on the Commission. I spoke to my friend Senator Robert Taft, the Republican leader, and he and Senator Barkley, the Democratic Senate Minority Leader, sank their differences to recommend Frieda to the President and she was appointed.

Shortly after I became President of Occidental, Frieda called me from New York to say, "I've never forgotten how kind you were to me and I want to throw something your way. I think I can recommend something that will interest you."

The Mutual Broadcasting System was about to come up for sale. It was then owned by the O'Neill family, which had interests in the growing television industry and in the General Tire Company. After the assumption of its operating liabilities, it cost only $750,000. I bought it for Occidental, to spread the company's interests. Frances and I also purchased a minority interest in the deal, so that Occidental would not have to come up with all the cash.

MBS was cheap because it was in plenty of trouble. It supplied program material to hundreds of radio stations throughout the country, but it owned not a single station in its own right. The growth of television had punched a hole in demand for its products like a shell from a Sherman tank. Meanwhile, the costs of the operation were excruciating. All of MBS's output was transmitted to its client stations over the telephone wires. The company's telephone bill ran into millions of dollars. And a goodly slab of its revenues was going straight into the pockets of its President.

This man was making secret deals with the company's advertisers, quoting them cut prices for air time and taking a personal bonus under the table. I discovered what was going on when an advertiser turned down his offer and reported it to me. As soon as I found out, I had myself elected President and called a meeting of the Directors. He was not invited. We all went into his office at night and searched through his desk. Sheaves of letters in the drawers incontestably incriminated him. When he appeared in his office next morning, he found a couple of Burns detectives waiting for him. They brought him to me.

I gave him a choice: he could resign quietly or face prosecution. He resigned.

Now I set to work to reorganize the company. The big job was to adapt and modernize its output in harmony with the changing times. The radio audience was no longer the families of America gathered by the hearth to spend an evening together listening to comedy shows and big-band concerts. Instead, it was fast becoming an audience of housewives and motorists, cocking half an ear at the radio for music and the latest news. MBS needed hard news and big names. So I signed up Walter Winchell and Kate Smith.

In June 1986, while this book was being written, Kate Smith died. Though she had been out of the public eye for many years, her passing made the front page of the *New York Times,* in an article which accurately recaptured the scale of her popularity: "Everything about Kate Smith was outsized, including Miss Smith herself. She recorded almost 3,000 songs—more than any other popular performer. She introduced more songs than any other performer—over a thousand, of which 600 or more made the hit parade.

President Roosevelt once introduced her to King George VI of England, saying: "This is Kate Smith. Miss Smith is America."

If Kate Smith was the singing voice of America, Walter Winchell was its spoken voice. Winchell was one of the great pioneer figures of American broadcasting and journalism, a character straight from the pages of Damon Runyon's Broadway menagerie and one of the most recognizable voices of the American midcentury. He could inject an urgent, cliff-hanging suspense into a reading of the stock market report. Every tidbit of news was a treat for Walter to devour, and he was insatiable for more.

I have sometimes been asked whether it wasn't strange for me to be dealing with artistically and journalistically creative people at MBS instead of with the business executives to whom I was accustomed. My answer has always been that I really found no difference. The challenge for the Chief Executive of any enterprise is always the same: you have to find out what people want from their work and then you have to find a way to give it to them. Walter Winchell, for instance, was not solely interested in money. What he cared about was to be known to the biggest possible audience and to have a major influence on the news. The offer I made him—apart from giving him much more money—was tailor-made to suit his ambitions, and he found it irresistible, as I intended. I gave him the prime Sunday evening spot; which had the ears of all America.

The fortunes of MBS revived very sharply during the year of 1957–1958. During that time we revolutionized the network radio field by introducing advertiser time buying.

We realized that the traditional concept of network radio—spectacular shows and razzle-dazzle promotions and exploitations—were a thing of the past. The television set had captured the living room and, to a marked degree, the entertainment field. Radiomen began writing off radio—and did so too soon. The viewers themselves knew the limitations of the TV screen. They still listened to the radio for news of the moment, special events, sports programs and good music.

We were fully aware of that situation and set ourselves to one basic goal: to provide the kind of network service that would be most compatible with our affiliates' local programming requirements and to provide that service in such a way as to enhance affiliates' positions in their marketing areas. The new concept did just that. We provided news programs on the hour and half hour, plus sports, special events, good music and specialized features. They provided pre-cleared time periods that served national advertisers' needs.

Sound familiar? Well, it wasn't then. I don't claim to have been a revolutionary innovator of a media style. I was simply responding to a visibly changing market by supplying its new essential needs—but I can certainly claim to have been among the first to recognize those new needs.

Running Mutual Broadcasting was a lot of fun, but in the end it wasn't right for me. I didn't want to be in New York, especially in winter. I wanted to be warm and tanned in Los Angeles with Frances. Moreover, I was much more excited about Occidental and the potential of the oil business than I was about radio and media enterprises. When the time came in 1958 to make a choice, there really was no contest. It was Frances, L.A. and Oxy for me. I sold Mutual for a profit of $1.3 million.

Before I left New York, however, I had a job to do. My friend for thirty-seven years, Mike Brignole, who had delivered groceries from his father's store next door and had looked after my Greenwich Village house, was in a jam. His life was being threatened by gangsters.

Mike's father had died in the early fifties, and Mike and his sisters each inherited a tidy amount of money. A distant relative immediately fastened on to him and lured him into investing his inheritance in the over-the-counter stock of a company which was building diners. Mike was told that the company was growing quickly, that it was about to become very important, and that Mike, with all his stockholdings, could become an executive in this company and would be able to retire from his grocery business.

Sure enough, shortly after Mike bought the stock, the price started to move up on the over-the-counter exchange, and it looked as if Mike were in for good profits. But the relative who had introduced him to the principals told Mike that he mustn't sell unless they did. The stock kept moving up, and pretty soon Mike's $50,000 investment was worth $150,000. He wanted to sell. He was very firmly told not to. In fact, he was told that if he got out of line, his partners would make him a present of a nice concrete coffin in a good site at the bottom of the East River.

To say the least, this threat alerted Mike's suspicions; obviously the stock was being rigged. He came to me and asked my advice.

I drew a report on the company and discovered to my surprise that one of the Directors was a partner in a law firm which I was using, headed by Congressman Emanuel Celler, whose New York partner was a very reputable attorney and a friend of mine. I invited him to lunch and began, gently, to quiz him about the company, saying that a close friend of mine had bought a big block of stock and was concerned about the character of the company.

The attorney butted in: Was my friend an Italian? he asked. I replied that he was. "I know all about this company," he said. "As a matter of fact, I have resigned from it. Your friend is quite right. These people are criminals, they're dangerous and, with any luck, they'll wind up in jail pretty soon."

"Well, that's all very well," I said. "But what is my friend supposed to do? The fifty-thousand dollars he has invested is his life's fortune. It's a huge amount of money to him."

We drew up a plan to save Mike. He should start to sell his shares, one thousand dollars' worth at a time. The crooks would be watching every sale, and they would know where the selling was coming from. They would then threaten Mike again and he should say, "Listen, I've written up a full account of this entire transaction and it's in my safe deposit box. A member of my family has the key. If anything happens to me, I have instructed my relative to open the box, take the letter to the District Attorney and tell him the whole story."

Mike followed this plan to the letter. When he sold his first slice of one thousand dollars' worth of stock, he got $3000. He was elated. He was trebling his money. Then he got his expected visit from the gang, who came to Mike's store on my street and invited him to take a little ride with them in their big car.

Mike was scared, but he stood his ground. "I know what you intend to do," he said, "but you'd better be careful." He then repeated exactly the lines we had rehearsed. Crestfallen and angry, the gangsters got back in their car and drove away. After a while they came around again and said to Mike, "Now let's settle this thing. We'll give you back the balance of the fifty-thousand dollars you've invested." Again, Mike was ready for them. As we had planned, he told them, "I want full market value or nothing."

He got it. They paid him $150,000.

All that happened at about the time that I first got involved with Occidental Petroleum Corporation, which was then struggling to survive. As a mark of faith in me, and by way of thanks, Mike invested $30,000 in Occidental stock.

In January 1968, when Occidental shares were selling at $150, the stock was split three-for-one and Mike's shares were worth more than three million dollars.

At that point I suggested that he sell off a million dollars' worth of his stock, put it in a bank at good interest and live happily ever after. He refused. He said: "If you're not selling your stock, why should I? I'm with you all the way." As he was from 1931 to February 5, 1987, when sadly he died of a heart attack.

Not since I took over my father's Good Laboratories had I been involved with such a two-bit, one-horse company as Occidental was in the early days. I felt like a kid again. At least I could no longer complain of having nothing to do. There was everything to do.

I moved Occidental into a suite of offices at 8255 Beverly Boulevard in Los Angeles. I recruited a staff of three. Paul Hebner was the Secretary: he is still the Secretary of Occidental Petroleum today. Gladys Louden (since deceased) was the bookkeeper and Dorothy Prell was my secretary. Frank Barton was our attorney, but he had his own office downtown. Our office furniture was rented.

The landlord of the building refused to give me a lease on more than a month-to-month basis because, he said, "I've had too much experience with fly-by-night companies and I've no reason to think that you will last any longer than the others."

I don't know if that man is still alive, but, if he is, he owes himself a kick or two. Thirty years later, in 1986, Occidental is the eighth-biggest energy concern in the United States and the twelfth-biggest industrial corporation. Its gross revenues in 1986 were approximately $16 billion, and it employs 45,000 people. Its stock is owned by 350,000 share-holders and its interests and activities loop the world.

Somebody recently calculated that $10,000 invested in Occidental when I started to finance the company in 1956 would be worth about $4.5 million today. If that landlord had invested only $1000 in the company in which he had so little faith, he would now be sitting on almost half a million dollars in return. Not bad for a fly-by-night company.

The story of "the most expensive Porsche in the world" makes the same kind of point. That Porsche was bought by the son of Albert J. Brown, a very prominent lawyer in San Francisco, who did a lot of indispensable legal work for Occidental in the early days. We couldn't begin to afford to pay Mr. Brown's fees, so he generously agreed to take ten thousand dollars' worth of stock when it was priced at one dollar a share. He gave one thousand dollars' worth to his son. When the stock hit four dollars a share, the son sold out and bought a Porsche. Forever after, especially when the stock went as high as $150 a share before it was split three-for-one, Albert would look at that car and say to his son, "I hope you're pleased with yourself, boy. You own the most expensive Porsche in the world."

Nobody could have blamed the boy or our landlord for their lack of confidence, however. At first, the company's books exuded a decid-edly unpromising air.

Occidental did make a profit in 1957, my first year as President. The profit was $36,000. I had sometimes made nearly as much as that in a single day when I was running Allied Drug and Chemical nearly forty years before. For several years, I worked as Occidental's CEO without a salary or expense account (to this very day, I pay most of my own expenses).

You will not be surprised to learn that Occidental did not declare a dividend in 1957. In fact, Paul Hebner didn't know the procedure for issuing a dividend in those days, and he didn't need to find out for a few years to come.

The first annual meeting of my presidency was held in our office corridor, as there was no room large enough for the few dozen share-holders who attended. We weren't eager to see many of our share-holders at our annual meetings so, in subsequent years, we made it as difficult as we could for them to attend. For the first few years of my presidency, we held the annual meeting in a restaurant in Bakersfield, California. The meeting was not a protracted affair.

Turning Occidental around was not the miracle of alchemy which has sometimes been suggested in the press. I simply applied to my new interest all the lessons I had learned in my forty years of business. To make any business succeed, you need to find out what the competition is doing and beat them to it. You need to get the best men and women in the business to join you and share their skill and experience. And you need the help of friends.

Many of my friends invested in Occidental when I took over. The New York builder Louis Abrons took half of the 50-percent investment which Frances and I had staked in the Dominguez field. Mr. and Mrs. Randolph Hearst, Mr. Morrie Moss, Dr. Myron Prinzmetal, the famous cardiologist, and his assistant, Dr. Rex Kennamer, all joined with me and Frances in investments in our oil drilling leases. J. Paul Getty, who took ten thousand shares, was among the legion of friends, and friends of friends, who bought hundreds of thousands of shares to help me fund new exploration and development.

Friends also joined the board of directors, including Arthur Groman and Fred Gimbel. Through Frances I gained another friend and another Director of the Board: Professor Neil Jacoby, then Dean of the Graduate School of Business Administration at UCLA. My friends at the Chase Manhattan Bank in New York introduced me to the Bank of America in Los Angeles, and, through them, I met and made friends with Professor Nico van Wingen, Professor of Petroleum Engineering at the University of Southern California. He was a former Shell engineer and one of the best brains in the oil business. Having been elected to the board, he introduced me to the engineer who undoubtedly made the biggest single difference to Occidental in the early days. That man was Gene Reid.

When I joined Occidental, I found that the company's chief drilling engineer, a part-time employee, was a hopeless drunk. Obviously he had to go, but where was I to find a replacement? Having only just learned to recognize an oil rig, I was not in the best position to interview and assess prospective chief engineers. On top of that, the company couldn't afford to pay the salary of a good engineer: those men have always been able to command small fortunes in pay; Occidental hardly had two nickels to rub together.

I consulted Nico van Wingen and asked his opinion. He told me, "When the majors have drilling problems, they always say, 'Send for Gene Reid.'"—just as they always send for Red Adair whenever there is a fire at a well today. Nico warned me that Gene Reid was an independent and feisty kind of man who went his own way and didn't care what he said to anybody. I wasn't interested in his manners. All I cared about was to get the best man for the job.

I went to see Gene Reid for lunch in his little office at the Gene Reid Drilling Company in Bakersfield. He looked and spoke like Will

Rogers. His long, lanky frame folded awkwardly into his chair and under his desk. While we talked he smoked incessantly, rolling his cigarettes with papers into which he tipped a line of tobacco from a bag of Bull Durham. His big fingers and thumbs neatly rolled the cigarette and he sealed it with a good dab of spit which he had ruminatively prepared.

My eye kept drifting out of the window, drawn by the amazing spectacle in his yard, which was jammed full of old oil-drilling machinery. There must have been about thirteen full rigs scattered in a million pieces around the place. All these rigs were for sale because Gene needed money, was near broke, having bought out a former partner with borrowed money.

Selling his rigs was the only way that Gene could stave off bankruptcy, and he had gained a few inches of breathing space by selling a portable rig to J. Paul Getty.

Gene's big trouble was that, despite being one of the best and highest-paid drillers in the oil business, he was a terrible judge of an oil field. He would take the huge fees he earned from the majors for drilling and sink them in his own drillings, on his own account. The wells were always dry. Drilling for himself, he had never once hit oil. The man who was one of the nation's biggest successes in the drilling side of the oil business was an abject failure in discovering oil. When I asked him to explain this paradox, he very grumpily replied, "Damned geologists, that's the answer. I've never met a good one yet. 'Damned mud-smellers,' I call them. I got so mad with them always failing me, always giving me dry holes, that I took a pack of them into a field one day and I pointed to the ground, and I said, 'To hell with all of you, we're going to drill right here.' That one was dry, too." He shook his head ruefully. "Can't win. Just can't win."

When I met Gene in 1959, he was going to set up a partnership with the one geologist he did trust, his own son Bud, who had just graduated from Stanford University. He was going to capitalize the new company out of the sale of the rigs in his yard. The banks were heavily on his back and his total assets amounted to four hundred thousand dollars, little of it liquid.

I had been warming to him more and more while we talked and, suddenly, my mind was made up: "I want us to work together," I said. "I think we'll make a great team. Instead of going into business yourself, why don't you come in with me and Occidental? We've got a public company here. I can go out and sell shares and raise enough money for you to go ahead and drill. I couldn't pay you any kind of salary which would approach your true worth, so what I propose is that we become partners. You take stock in the company and join the board, and we'll make you Vice President in Charge of Exploration and Development. What do you say?"

He looked at me for a moment with a half-smile on his lips and then he said, "All my life I've wanted to be a millionaire and I've never come close. But I've got a feeling that, with you, I might make it."

He decided that he would take half of his capital and invest it in Occidental, merging his Gene Reid Drilling Company with us. However, when he consulted his tax attorneys, he was told that he couldn't effect a tax-free merger without investing all of his capital. He barely hesitated before he said, "Okay, I'll put in everything I've got."

Only a few years later, Gene had achieved his lifelong ambition and his shares in Occidental were worth three million dollars. At that time, a friend of his who was head of the United California Bank said, "Gene, why don't you sell off a third of your shares and then you'll have your million dollars cash safely in the bank and you can gamble with the rest?"

"Not at these prices, I won't," said Gene.

He held on to his Occidental stock until he died. By that time I would guess that he was worth thirty million dollars.

Bud Reid joined Occidental along with Gene and became Vice President and Manager of Exploration. Bud also brought with him one of the brightest geologists in his Stanford class, a young man named Dick Vaughn, who became Chief Geologist.

Again, we couldn't afford to pay Bud or Dick an adequate salary, and so I offered them stock options, which quite soon made them both millionaires. Another young geologist who joined us about that time was David R. Martin. Twenty-five years later, he is now Executive Vice President of Occidental Petroleum Corporation and President of Occidental Oil and Gas Corporation, chiefly responsible for the company's global drilling operations.

When Dave Martin joined us, the geological and engineering departments were working out of a tiny building in Bakersfield which would not accommodate the janitors in our undertakings there today. These days he spends his time zooming from Bakersfield to the farthest-flung oil fields in our interests—one day Pakistan, the next Peru or Colombia.

Occidental's exploration program for 1961 was just about exhausted when our geologists convinced Gene Reid and me that we should drill a lease called Lathrop in the Sacramento Valley, east of San Francisco.

I went round the usual circle of friends and supporters, beginning with Frances, asking for funds to let us drill the Lathrop lease. To raise $320,000 for a half interest, I offered to sell ten units at $32,000 apiece.

I bought half a unit myself. Frances bought one, Morrie Moss bought three, and so on.

The company was so strapped for cash then that we couldn't even borrow money from the banks at fair interest. Shortly after we started drilling at Lathrop, Paul Hebner went to a bank in New York to try to borrow $400,000 for the program.

The bank insisted that Paul borrow $440,000, the additional $40,000 to remain on deposit. In other words we were going to have to pay interest on $440,000 in order to borrow $400,000.

Paul was very anxious when he called me to relay those terms. I told him to forget all about the deal, come home and quit worrying. "We'll be all right," I said. "They'll soon be sorry they weren't more accommodating." I don't know if my whistling in the dark made Paul feel better, but I wasn't fooling myself. We were in trouble.

Texaco had quit-claimed the Lathrop lease when the last well drilled was still dry at 5600 feet. A geologist friend of Dick Vaughn's, Bob Teitsworth, left Amerada and agreed to join us if we would pick up this lease and drill about 600 feet away from that last Texaco well and to be prepared to go a lot deeper.

Every foot of drilling then felt like a dentist's drill on Occidental's nerves. We sat in Los Angeles, desperate for news from Lathrop, knowing that failure there would almost certainly knock a big hole in the value of the company's shares. When Gene called to say that he had drilled below 8000 feet and the well was still dry, I began to feel decidedly edgy.

We bit the bullet till our teeth were clenched. At 8600 feet, a full 3000 feet deeper than Texaco had gone, Gene Reid's bit punctured the second-largest gas field ever discovered in the history of California, a two-hundred-million-dollar lode.

Occidental's stock jumped like a jack-in-the-box from about four dollars a share to seven dollars. Offers of a million dollars each were made for the $32,000 units I had sold in the Lathrop exploration. I went home and told Frances she could get a million dollars for her unit, and at first she didn't believe me.

Next morning I asked her whether or not she had decided to sell, and she said that she had called Morrie Moss overnight to find out what he intended to do. Morrie had said, "I'm not selling. I think they're worth a lot more than that." So Frances said, "I've decided that I'm not going to sell either." A few years ago we all decided to sell. By that time, however, the units were worth several million dollars each, and we had received very substantial dividends in the meantime. Nobody was ever smarter than Morrie Moss, and nobody ever went far wrong by following his advice.

A few months after Gene Reid brought in the Lathrop Field, he hit another gas bonanza in the Brentwood Field nearby.

With these immense finds of gas, I went confidently to see executives of the Pacific Gas and Electric Company, prepared, in my own mind at least, to sign twenty-year contracts to supply them with gas. They rapidly deflated my optimism, saying, in effect, "We have no need of your gas."

They had just gone to the heavy expense of building a pipeline from Alberta, Canada, to the San Francisco Bay Area. They thought they had the territory locked up. I was crestfallen for a moment.

Then I went to the city of Los Angeles and declared that Oxy would build a pipeline from Lathrop to L.A. and undercut Pacific Gas, or any other bidder, to supply the city's needs. Hearing that, Pacific Gas immediately caved in and signed long-term contracts to buy our gas.

We had hit the jackpot.

Now the company was secure. Now it could start paying dividends. Now I could go looking for still richer fields and bigger targets on equal terms with the serious principal oil companies. Now I might even be able to ruffle the petticoats of the Seven Sisters themselves.

Mister K and Mister JFK

Just as Oxy was getting set to expand into the national and international oil business, I myself took on a new role in the world. For the first time in thirty-one years, I went back to Moscow, at the request of the President of the United States.

I first met John Kennedy in Washington, while he was still Senator from Massachusetts. We were introduced by our mutual friend Senator Albert Gore, Sr. JFK had just finished a committee meeting and we all three stood together in a corridor chatting for about twenty minutes. He was intrigued when Albert Gore told him that I had been the first American concessionaire in the Soviet Union, and he said that he would look for an opportunity to hear about my experiences there.

When he was campaigning for the presidency, Frances and I attended a fund-raising dinner in Los Angeles, during which he came to sit beside me for ten minutes as he was table-hopping. We were not to get the chance for a proper conversation, however, until the winter of 1960, after he had been elected.

The young President-elect was taking a few days in the Palm Beach sunshine to recharge his batteries after the campaign and prepare himself for the rigors of his new job. He was relaxing on the deck of his boat, the *Honey Fitz,* when my seventy-eight-foot yacht came knifing through the waters at close to thirty knots, and set the *Honey Fitz* tossing and jouncing all over the place. He jumped up to watch us pass and called out to his captain, "Who the —— was that?" That evening he asked his host, Colonel Michael Paul, if he knew the owner of an extraordinarily powerful yacht called *Shadow Isle.* Colonel Paul and I had known each other for many years and he was a large shareholder in Occidental. He offered to bring Mr. Kennedy aboard *Shadow Isle* before lunchtime the next day.

As the visit was arranged with no notice, my steward George had no time to prepare, and he was thrown into confusion by the prospect of entertaining the man who was in the eye of the whole world at that moment. I had heard that Mr. Kennedy liked to drink Bloody Marys and told George to mix up a pitcher. Poor George's heart nearly gave out when he discovered that there wasn't a bottle of vodka on board. Mr. Kennedy was expected imminently. There wasn't time for George to go ashore. He jumped into a dinghy and rowed over to a neighboring boat to scrounge a bottle. The owners were more than ready to help when they learned who it was for. Even then, George was in a terrible state of nerves. "Relax," I said. "Just do the best you can."

Sure enough, when I offered Mr. Kennedy a drink, he asked for a Bloody Mary. George was trembling so much when he brought the tray that he could hardly set it down. Mr. Kennedy took a sip of his drink and his big eyes dilated. "I think I'd better treat this with care," he said, and congratulated George. George was walking on air as he backed out of the salon.

After I had shown him over *Shadow Isle* and answered all his questions about the engines and the boat's capacities, we had a long talk about the work of the administration he was forming. He returned to the topic of my years in Moscow and quizzed me closely for my opinions on dealing with the Soviets. He told me that he wanted to improve relations and get the negotiating process moving toward a summit conference, but he was aware that real and serious distrust existed on both sides and it was vital, he said, that he should not appear to be a weak President to the Russians.

I told him that, from my experience and certain knowledge, the Russians respected and admired strength, that they were firm, tough and smart in their negotiations, but they invariably honored their obligations and kept their word. Smoking one of his favorite Havana cigars and keeping his eyes trained on mine, Mr. Kennedy listened thoughtfully.

He asked me about the Soviet leadership. I had never met Khrushchev, I said, but I had known Mikoyan pretty well, and said that I had never met a smarter man at any level of political office, anywhere.

(Khrushchev had met my brother Victor briefly, though, when he visited the United States in 1959 and went to see Eleanor Roosevelt at Hyde Park. Eleanor had kindly offered to speak to Khrushchev about Victor's son, Armasha, whom he had not seen for more than a quarter of a century. Khrushchev agreed to help get permission for Armasha to come to the US to visit his father, and he kept his word.)

As he rose to go, Mr. Kennedy said that we should keep in touch. I, naturally, assured him that I would always be available to him if there was ever anything I could do to help.

I next saw him at the inauguration in Washington on January 20, 1961. In that brilliant snow scene which was made radiant by the verve and glamour of the new President and his First Lady, Frances and I had seats close behind the swearing-in podium. Along with all Americans, I was inspired by the most stirring inaugural address of the postwar era, especially when Mr. Kennedy told us, "Ask not what your country can do for you: ask what you can do for your country." Even when he declared that ". . . the torch has been passed to a new generation . . . born in this century," I did not feel excluded from the new age of energy and hope which was being inaugurated. I told Albert Gore that I was eager to play my part.

Shortly afterward the Gores attended a small dinner party at the White House. The conversation turned to Russia, and President Kennedy mentioned a current charge that Russia was using "slave labor" in producing crabmeat for export, which had resulted in a longtime ban on the product by the US, but which had been emphatically denied by the Soviets. Whereupon Gore suggested that I, a son of emigrés from Russia, should go to the Soviet Union to ascertain its truth or falsehood. The President asked Gore to talk to Secretary of Commerce Luther Hodges about it; Hodges promptly got in touch with me, and the trip was set. I was then planning a round-the-world trip with Frances anyway, and nothing could suit me better than a chance to revisit Moscow and show her some of the sights and scenes of my earlier life. If I could also do something to ease tensions between East and West, that would make it perfect.

At the beginning of JFK's administration, relations between America and Russia were veering perilously toward confrontation. In the last months of the Eisenhower administration, Gary Powers had been shot down in his U-2 spy aircraft over Sverdlovsk, Khrushchev had angrily withdrawn from the scheduled four-power summit meeting in Paris and canceled his invitation to Eisenhower to visit Moscow and address the Soviet people on radio and television. The new administration urgently needed to know whether Khrushchev would keep up his belligerent stance over the U-2 incident or be willing to make a fresh start with the new President.

Luther Hodges also suggested that I should turn other stages of my coming trip to the government's advantage: he wanted me to investigate and report to him on means to improve trade, not only with the Soviet Union, but with many other of the countries which lay upon my intended route.

I was to be traveling entirely as a private citizen, with no formal status as a representative of the US, and I would be paying all my own expenses. Nonetheless, Luther offered to draw up an itinerary for me and Frances and to arrange introductions at the highest levels for the countries we were to visit. He decided that I should take a look at the United Kingdom, France, West Germany, Italy, Libya, the Soviet Union, India and Japan. Eleanor Roosevelt very kindly wrote letters to introduce me to Khrushchev and Indian Prime Minister Nehru.

We left Los Angeles only days after the inauguration, swung quickly through Europe and touched down briefly in Libya, where I paid very close attention to the possibility of future business. My Libyan adventures come in the next chapter. On February 11, 1961, we arrived in Moscow.

Driving from the airport, we passed through hilly woods of silver birch and tall firs where hundreds of young people were skating and skiing, their long student scarves flying behind them. Frances was instantly charmed by the colorful, jubilant spectacle, and she said, "Well, if this is Russia, I think I'm going to like it." Her cheerfulness was to be short-lived.

The date of our arrival in Moscow was only five months shy of the fortieth anniversary of my first visit there. Naturally, very much was new to my eyes, but it was even more surprising to me how much had remained the same.

In place of the huddled masses of crumbling shacks which I had known stood great municipal housing developments in Moscow's suburbs, their tower blocks ranged like huge dominoes to the horizon. Also new to me were the monumental "wedding-cake" edifices of Stalin's efforts to rival New York's skyscrapers—the absurdly colossal and clumsy hotels and government offices he had created. I had never seen the magnificent subway system, developed by Khrushchev himself in the thirties on Stalin's orders. Great strides had obviously been made in the development of heavy industries, and vast plants belched steam and smoke right in the heart of the city.

The *droshki*, the horse-drawn sleighs of my earliest days in Moscow, had, of course, all vanished by 1961, but the cabdrivers in their beat-up, Soviet-made vehicles remained as wily and cunning as their enterprising forebears. No children dressed in rags were running the streets, as they had been in 1921; nor were there adults to be seen with rags for shoes.

However, the drab uniformity which had settled over Moscow during my last years there in the twenties was still present. Everybody now wore serviceable clothes, but the garments were, for the most part, lacking in variety and style, and the expressions on the faces of the people on the street were for the most part marked by hardship, as they had been when I left. They still had to wait hours in line to buy even the most basic foods and household necessities. A roll of smooth lavatory paper was still difficult to find in 1961, just as it had been in 1921; and the trifling contents of one's pockets—a fountain pen, an automatic pencil—were still invaluable as tips in restaurants and shops.

We stayed in the Sovietskaya Hotel, formerly a lavish club. Legend said that, in the pre-Revolutionary days, Rasputin, the "mad monk" of the Czarist court, had entertained the many ladies of his fancy in there.

I naturally wanted very much to revisit my old pencil factory and show it to Frances. The Soviet officials to whom I put this request were discouraging and said that it was undergoing repairs and not available to be visited.

My first interview with senior Soviet officials did not go well. On February 14 I went to the Ministry of Trade to meet V. M. Vinogradov, chief of the Administration of Trade with Western Countries, and M. N. Gribkov, chief of the American Trade Section.

Both of these gentlemen had been in knee-pants when I left Moscow thirty-one years before. The magic of Lenin's name and my association with him was still powerful, even with these officials, but I was a remote and shadowy figure of history to them and they were cautious and circumspect toward me.

I opened the meeting by describing my previous experiences in the Soviet Union and my American business activities during the past thirty years. In the course of those remarks it was emphasized that improvements in US-Soviet trade would take time, but that it would be helpful to make some small beginnings. Changes which require administrative action probably could be effected more easily than those requiring legislation. As a businessman, I studiously avoided political questions and sought only to explore areas which offered some promise for improved trade.

I recognized a number of Soviet misstatements, propaganda points and old arguments, but I felt it would be inappropriate in this kind of exploratory discussion to argue or belabor those points. Rather, I was seeking to find some areas of agreement which—under appropriate political conditions—might lead to an improvement in trade relations.

The next day, when I was visiting the US Embassy, I was shown a list of other Soviet officials with whom I might meet. As politely as I could, I pushed it aside. "All these men were boys when I left here," I protested mildly. The moment had come to swing some of my clout.

"I want to see Mikoyan," I said.

The embassy aide looked at me as if I had lost my mind.

"That's impossible," he said. "Mikoyan is the Deputy Prime Minister . . ."

"I'm aware of that," I said.

". . . He doesn't see *anybody*—especially not American busi-nessmen. You must be joking, Doctor Hammer." The aide's expres-sion settled into a patronizing complacency.

I spoke deliberately and carefully: "I met Mr. Mikoyan in 1923," I said, "the day I brought the Fordson tractors into Rostov. He was Secretary of the local Soviet at the time. He was quite keen to meet me. I knew Lenin, he didn't. Later, in Moscow, I came to know him very well when he was Minister of Foreign Trade and handling the sale of pictures from the Hermitage Museum in Leningrad. I think he'll see me. I'm going to send him a note right now, tell him why I'm here in Moscow, and that I want to see him. I'd be grateful if you could arrange for the note to be delivered."

That seemed to take some of the wind out of the aide's sails, but, even so, he took my note and arranged to send it with a barely con-cealed air of skepticism.

He and his colleagues could not disguise their astonishment when, two hours later, Mikoyan's office called the Embassy to say that it was sending a car immediately to collect me and bring me to see the Deputy Prime Minister.

A broad grin lit up Mikoyan's face when he embraced me. "I never thought that I would see you again," he said. "What have you been doing all these years?"

We had a long personal chat in which he was delightfully warm and relaxed. He looked much older, of course, his black hair liberally mixed with gray, but he was still very bright, very alert and quick in his movements. Though an interpreter was present, our conversation was conducted almost entirely in Russian. He soon led it around to the subject of the US ban on Russian crabmeat and the question of "slave labor." I quickly realized that I had been underestimating the impor-tance of this matter. I had supposed that it was as inconsequential as it sounded—crabmeat exports to the US had been worth about seven million dollars a year before they were banned.

Anastas Mikoyan made it very clear that the Soviets were seriously vexed by the ban, which had been in existence for nearly ten years. It was an affront to their dignity and, he felt, to common sense. "Do you think we'd eat this crabmeat ourselves if it were produced by slave or forced labor?" he asked sardonically. "That would be unsanitary and dangerous. Why don't the Americans ask their Japanese friends for the truth? Their vessels crab side by side with ours. They would surely know—and they would tell you—if you were using forced labor."

It was obvious to me that if he could settle this apparently futile quarrel, President Kennedy could make an easy political gain of good-will and ease the Russians' feelings of affronted dignity.

The conversation with Mikoyan turned to more general political and economic questions. He certainly welcomed the recent change in administration. He was critical of former Acting Secretary of Commerce Strauss, who only wanted to discuss religious issues in the USSR, and of former Secretary Mueller. In his opinion, neither of these Secretaries was interested in any way in improving trade between the US and the USSR. He had never met Mr. Hodges, but intimated that he would be glad to meet with him and hoped the new Secretary would have a more constructive approach.

The outstanding unresolved questions of the day were the Soviet Union's unpaid Lend-Lease debt to the US and the refusal of the US to grant "most favored nation" status or credits to the USSR. Mikoyan stated that major problems such as a Lend-Lease settlement, credits and the granting of most favored nation treatment required legislation and would take time. He believed that before he died, even John Foster Dulles favored the granting of credits, settlement of Lend-Lease and the expansion of trade between the two countries.

If Lend-Lease could be settled and credits arranged, the USSR could place orders in the US in the amount of one billion dollars. Mikoyan said that these orders would not include military items. In his words: "After all, we can make these better than you can. For example, we are ahead of you in rocket development."

He added that only a few days previously the USSR placed an order with Sweden for delivery of 135,000 tons of wide-gauge steel pipe, and with the Italians for 240,000 tons. No long credits were involved. "Orders like these," he said, "could have been placed in the US and would have helped to solve the US unemployment problem, when the US steel industry was operating at only fifty percent of capacity."

I gained the impression that the Soviets were eager to improve relations and that they were clearly anxious to expand US-Soviet trade. However, I pointed out to Mr. Mikoyan that it was my opinion the USSR would have to create a better atmosphere in the US before the new administration would have any chance for success in getting Congress to pass the necessary legislation to permit most favored nation treatment for the USSR and the granting of credits.

I told him that goodwill among the American people, which had reached its peak following Mr. Mikoyan's visit to the US in early 1959 and by Mr. Khrushchev's visit in the fall of 1959, had considerably deteriorated. I did not want to get into a controversy over the rights and wrongs of the USSR or US position in regard to the U-2 incident, but the fact remained that if Russian trade were to be expanded to any considerable extent, an attempt had to be made to obtain the support of American public opinion. That would have to be a slow process, and there had to be evidence of goodwill and good faith on both sides.

I pointed out that, in my opinion, settlement of the Lend-Lease debt would go a long way toward creating the proper atmosphere for changing the situation, and Mikoyan vowed that Khrushchev had given orders to settle the Lend-Lease debt when he was in Washington, but the Russians wanted the assurance they would be treated the same way as the English had been in that regard. Mr. Mikoyan said, "How can we make our payments under a Lend-Lease debt settlement, and pay for the orders we would want to place, if we did not receive credits and if we could not sell our goods on the same conditions as other countries which sell to the US?"

I said that improved relations could be assisted by increasing tourist trade both ways and by cultural exchanges, and suggested that Russia send a representative collection of their art treasures from their leading museums to the United States. The impact of a representative group of paintings from the Hermitage Museum in Leningrad, for example, would be enormous.

In order to make it strictly noncommercial and nonpolitical, I suggested that Eleanor Roosevelt be appointed chairman of a committee to supervise the undertaking and that any benefits from admission should go to the Eleanor Roosevelt Cancer Foundation. I said that I believed the first exhibition could be held at the National Gallery of Art in Washington, D.C., and then in the larger cities of the US such as New York, Chicago and Los Angeles. Mr. Mikoyan said he thought it was a very good idea and he would speak to the proper authorities.

I showed Mr. Mikoyan the sales catalogue of my last cattle sale, which was the only Angus cattle sale that ever ran over a million dollars. He was extremely interested in the development of the pure-bred cattle business in the US and wanted to know its significance in respect to meat production and commercial cattle-raising.

I explained to him that thanks to the pure-breeders in the US, there had been an upgrading in the quality and a reduction in the meat cost to the American people. With the same amount of feed and care, farmers could now produce much more meat at no greater cost. I offered to send him one of my bulls as a gift which they could use for experimenting. He wanted to know if there was an expert in the US available who could come over and teach them how to use the methods that had been successful in the US, and I told him that I knew of several such experts, and that I would be glad to talk to them when I got back to the United States.

After that meeting I felt I had made as much progress as I could in Moscow, and Frances and I started to pack our bags for a flight next day to New Delhi, where I had an appointment with Prime Minister Nehru.

Next morning we were just about to leave our hotel when a call came through for me from Acting Ambassador Freers (Ambassador Thompson was in Washington). "Hold everything," he said. "It looks like the Big Boss wants to see you."

Evidently Mikoyan had spoken to Khrushchev about me, and the General Secretary had decided that he wanted to see me in person. An appointment was arranged for the following day, February 17, 1961, in Khrushchev's office in the Kremlin. I sent my apologies to Mr. Nehru and made plans to extend our stay in Moscow.

Waiting for me in the General Secretary's office was a tall, portly and jovial man whom I had never met before, but with whom I was to build a friendship which continues to this day. He was Anatoliy F. Dobrynin, then chief of the American Countries Division of the Ministry of Foreign Affairs, later to become Ambassador to the US, until, in 1986, he was recalled to Moscow as a Secretary of the Central Committee of the Communist Party.

At that moment, however, Anatoliy was very much the junior counsel to General Secretary Khrushchev, who was at the height of his confidence and his powers. Robust in his squat peasant body and rough in his intelligence, Khrushchev greeted me warmly and got briskly down to business.

Khrushchev felt that my Russian was sufficiently clear to permit the entire conversation to be held in Russian. He had in his hands the copy of my Angus sale catalogue I had left with Mikoyan two days before, and stated that he had spent last evening reading it with the help of an English-speaking member of his staff. He said that meat was a major problem facing the USSR and indicated that Soviet cattle were yielding only about 50 percent of their gross weight in usable meat. In the US, on the other hand, he understood that we were getting 65 to 70 percent. He also said that, from his personal experience, the quality of US meat was better. "When I was in the States, I enjoyed your large steaks. I ate every bit of them. I'm not going to be happy until the Russian people have steaks like that." He had received a Black Angus heifer from President Eisenhower and one from former Acting Secretary of Commerce Strauss. I said, "You can't do much with two heifers. I'll send you an Angus bull, a son of my famous Prince Eric."

Khrushchev indicated that his country had learned much from the US and was eager to learn more in the fields where we excelled. Ford, for example, had taught them how to make automobiles. He thanked me for bringing Ford to Russia and enabling the first modern plant to be completed. He continued that although the USSR had made a lot of mistakes, and its workers had broken a lot of machines through ignorance or otherwise, his country excelled over the US in several fields.

He said that a group of American engineers had expressed admiration, even envy, of Soviet hydroelectric installations, that his country could now make synthetic rubber directly from gas without first making synthetic alcohol, that the USSR had produced 65 million tons of steel in 1960, would produce 71 million tons in 1961 and from 76 to 78 million in 1962. In 1965, he predicted, they would produce from 86 to 95 million tons, and in 1970, "we will beat you in steel output and in 1980 we will produce double what you will be producing."

The wisdom of hindsight shows us that Khrushchev was wildly overoptimistic. Far from doubling US steel production by 1980, the USSR managed to exceed it by only about one third—nonetheless a notable achievement in itself.

He continued: "Now we want to put more into agriculture than in the past, because we are no longer afraid of the United States. We want to improve the conditions of our people. We want to strengthen our chemical industry in order to provide more clothing for our people. Other countries in Western Europe have no hesitancy in selling us this equipment and giving us credits. If some people in the US think that by not trading with us they can crush us, they are mistaken. We now turn out three times the number of engineers you do. We don't want you to sell to us unless it is profitable for you to do so, and profitable for us. We'll buy what we need. Your man Dillon"—C. Douglas Dillon, Eisenhower's Under Secretary of State—"spoke about selling us shoes. I showed him my shoes and said they were better than his, and made in Russia. There are many things we want to buy—if we can get them, we don't have to develop our own industries.

"If we work together, our economies will thus be tied in together. If you give us credit, you should do so because it is to your benefit and not as a favor. You will earn interest, you will make a profit on the goods you sell, and it will keep your plants busy. There has never been a case when we have failed to pay our commercial obligations and there never will. We will not buy on credit, even for five years, unless we know we can pay for it."

I repeated to him substantially what I had told Mikoyan, namely that there had been a deterioration of goodwill toward the USSR, both in Congressional circles and among the American public, since the collapse of the Paris Summit. As a consequence, prospects for improved trade relations had worsened. The process of regaining the support of American public opinion would be slow. Before any new legislation could be enacted, I thought that Lend-Lease must be settled. Khrushchev said, "I gave orders to settle it, but US authorities did not wish to treat us as well as they had treated the British; just treat us as you did the British and we will be satisfied."

Khrushchev brought up the subject of the U-2 incident. He stated that US authorities had sent a U-2 across Russia in April of 1960. It was not shot down and the man responsible for that failure was punished.

Khrushchev then said, "I was awakened early in the morning, May 1, when the second plane was sighted, and was told. I personally gave the orders to shoot it down. This was done with our rockets. I also laid a trap by withholding the announcement to see what the US authorities would say. When they lied, I exposed them. We caught them as you would a thief with his hand in your pocket." He said Eisenhower later admitted that they had lied, but would continue to send U-2s over Russia. "This was too much for us to stomach," Khrushchev said. "Remember that Mr. Eisenhower had an invitation to be our guest. It was as if a guest in your home were saying, 'I'm going to destroy you.'"

Khrushchev continued: "I believe that while Mr. Eisenhower may have been consulted, and approved the general plan for the U-2, and had known of the flight in April, he was not consulted in advance about the May 1 flight. That was authorized by Allen Dulles or those under him in your CIA. I think their purpose was to embarrass me by showing Mr. Eisenhower that we were unable to defend ourselves. I tried to give Mr. Eisenhower an opportunity to apologize, but when he refused, I would not speak to him in Paris. Mr. Kennedy said, during the campaign, that he would have apologized. This shows that he is an honorable and clever man. However, the matter is now forgotten and we do not require any apology. Both Senator Fulbright and Mr. Stevenson took an attitude similar to that of Senator Kennedy." He added, "I also like your ambassador, Thompson. In our talks, Thompson presents the capitalist view, of course, but I understand him and he understands me. We get along as representatives of two great powers should."

Khrushchev volunteered the statement that he still had a high regard for Eisenhower who, he remarked, was a noble and dedicated man who sincerely wanted to bring about peace in the world. However, he thought Eisenhower delegated too much authority to others and was "lazy."

I told Mr. Khrushchev that there should be more cultural exchanges between our two countries and made the same suggestion I had previously made to Mikoyan regarding increases in tourist trade by both countries and the desirability of an art exchange. He said it was an excellent idea and that he would give orders to Mr. Yuri Zhukov, Minister of Culture, to work with the Cultural Counselor of the American Embassy on the proposal, and he asked me to prepare a plan for carrying this out.

When I suggested that it might be desirable for Mr. Mikoyan to consult with the new Secretary of Commerce in light of Mr. Mikoyan's statement to me that he was not able to accomplish anything with previous Secretaries of Commerce, I got the definite impression that it would be welcomed as a step toward improved economic relations.

When we touched on the vexing question of the banned crabmeat exports, I saw Khrushchev's famous belligerence for the first time. He was almost shouting when he said, "There is no slave labor anymore in Russia! Not since Stalin died! There are no slave camps anymore. They've been disbanded since Stalin."

I shrugged and tried to calm him with a suggestion: "All you have to do," I said, "is let us send an inspection team or a representative to check on this and bring back a report that what you say is true. After that, there will be no problem. The ban will be removed."

Again, Khrushchev's dignity was affronted. He said, "Your CIA wanted to send spies, but I'll let you go and look for yourself."

I replied that I was leaving Russia and would not be available.

He then said I could suggest other "people" who might do this, to which I remarked that I would communicate that to appropriate persons and asked how I might get word to him. He suggested it might be done through Ambassador Menshikov.

Mr. Khrushchev said, "If we cannot give our people the same standard of living that you give your people under the capitalist system, we know that Communism cannot succeed. However, we are convinced that we can, and our performance over recent years is proof of this; and we are perfectly willing to leave it to history as to which system is the better for mankind and which will survive."

I pointed out to him that in my opinion it was necessary to establish peace and order in the world by strengthening the UN and noted that Adlai Stevenson, who represented the US in that body, was well-disposed toward settling disputes with the USSR within this framework. Khrushchev replied that he had a high regard for Mr. Stevenson and remarked, "We shall see. We too want to settle all matters in dispute in a peaceful way."

He invited me to return in the summer when the weather is nice—which I assured him I would be happy to do. From his desk, he picked up an engraved gold automatic pencil, topped with a ruby in the shape of a star, and gave it to me, saying, "This is in return for what you have done in establishing the first pencil factory in the USSR."

As I was leaving, I told Mr. Khrushchev that I had tried unsuccessfully to visit my old pencil factory. He turned to Mr. Dobrynin and said, "Arrange it at once."

Looking back at the record of this meeting twenty-five years later, what strikes me most vividly is the continuity of history. Many of the topics I discussed with Khrushchev had been raised in my conversations with Lenin, and they recur today in my talks with Gorbachev and the present Soviet leadership. Khrushchev, needless to say, was not Lenin—beside whose brilliance and charm Khrushchev's peasant qualities of pugnacity and craftiness were relatively dim—but Khrushchev repeated many of the points Lenin had made to me when he drew his chair near to mine in 1921 and spoke of the Soviet need for trade with America.

Like Lenin, Khrushchev admired American technology and our inventiveness. Like Lenin, he believed that American industry could profit from trade with the USSR and he emphasized that the Russians were willing and able to pay fully and on time for their purchases.

The main difference between the two men and between the two interviews, forty years apart, was in the clarity of their understanding. Lenin knew and recognized unswervingly that a vast gulf of economic and material achievement separated the USSR from the USA. He knew that Communism was not working and he ordered a retreat to State Socialism.

Khrushchev could never have made the admission that State Socialism was not working either. Whether for reasons of pride or fear, his aggressive bullishness led him into foolishly combative and rhetorical declarations. Remember, this was the man who had spoken one of the most chilling and provocative lines of the Cold War, when he told then Vice President Nixon, "We will bury you." Now he was telling me that Russia would humble America in industrial production before the end of the century, and that Communism would equal the material benefits of capitalism.

Well, as former President Nixon recently pointed out, Khrushchev's style of Soviet Communism has lost that battle. We don't have to wait for the verdict of history: the verdict is in. In the years since I met Khrushchev, the Russians have been unable to meet the test he set for them: they have not been able to give their people, as he said, "the same standard of living that you give your people under the capitalist system"; and the failures of the system in Russia have been many times worse in those satellites, such as Poland and Czechoslovakia, where the Soviet system has been most rigidly applied. Only in the more "liberal" socialist states like Hungary and Yugoslavia, where a degree of free enterprise has been encouraged, has the general standard of living been remotely close to that of the West.

Mr. Gorbachev has shown some positive signs of recognizing the urgent need for change in the Soviet economic system and, in calling for studies of Lenin's NEP policy, he may be compelled to follow Lenin's lead and allow an injection of capitalist methods and competition. We will have to wait and see, however, if he will ever allow a relaxation such as was permitted the twenties, when an American businessman was encouraged to set up a factory in Moscow, employing capitalist methods and paying piece rates. At present Gorbachev has advocated setting up joint ventures between foreign companies and Soviet institutions. He has also decided to decentralize foreign trade,

permitting some seventy Soviet industrial organizations to seek partners abroad and to do their own trading without going through the
bureaucratic Foreign Trade Monopoly. In this way he hopes to modernize the present Russian economy without going as far as Hungary or
China have gone.

Anatoliy Dobrynin acted fast on Khrushchev's instructions. That
same evening, while I was at the US Embassy reporting on my interview with the General Secretary, a call came from the Kremlin to say
that a car was on its way to take me and Frances to my old pencil
factory.

When I created the factory, it had been on the outskirts of the city.
By 1961 Moscow had grown up all around it. Even so, I found it just
as I had left it, thirty years before. The only new thing was the name
over the gate—THE MOSCOW WRITING APPLIANCES PLANT SACCO-
VANZETTI. Apart from this leaden touch, everything was pure romance.

Snow was falling heavily when we arrived, falling on the factory,
on the schoolhouse, the recreation hall and all the little cottages I had
built there for my German workers. The white birches which had been
saplings when I left had grown tall and thick. The whole scene was
bathed in soft, glowing lights—the most romantic and stirring setting
imaginable. I could hardly speak as we walked in. I held Frances's hand
tight.

We walked in on the night shift. All the smells and noises were
freshly familiar to me. Except for several new machines, they were still
using some of the machines I had picked up in Germany all those years
before. The executives who met us led us through one division after the
other and I saw that the production process was almost unchanged. We
toured the factory floor for almost an hour and came, finally, to the
executives' offices. When I entered my old office, I could hardly believe
that my desk was still in place, almost as if I had just risen from it to
drive Will Rogers and Victor across Moscow. I was all choked up and
all I could do was shake my head and say, "I can't believe this, I just
can't believe it."

The boardroom had been all set up for a party, with caviar, champagne, vodka—the works. All the executives of the factory had been
invited, and about half a dozen of the workers who had been there in
my time. This was the most emotional moment of the evening. I had to
look into those worn and lined faces for some time before the years fell
away, and I saw and recognized them as the young men and women I
had employed. One little old lady came up to me with tears in her eyes,
sad because Frances and I had not been brought through her section of
the plant.

"Armand Yulevitch," she said, "I am Anna Ivanovna. When your brother Victor Yulevitch came to work in this plant, I was the one who saw to it that he learned to operate every machine."

Now I recognized her and we embraced and hugged each other. She stepped back and looked at me appraisingly and not altogether flatteringly.

"My," she said, "but you've changed!"

I'm not the only one, I thought, remembering her as a pretty and flighty girl who turned so many heads that she could practically stop production by sashaying through the factory. But I said nothing and smiled at her.

The evening went on and more people came into the room. In the end, there must have been about fifty people seated at the table, raising toast after toast of vodka, wine, champagne and, finally, cognac. The prodigal son's reception was cool by comparison. It was a great, great night—never to be equaled.

Next day, slightly pink in the eye and sore in the head, I saw Khrushchev again briefly at Party Headquarters in Moscow, where he was giving a reception to high-level Communists from the Soviet Union's satellite countries. At that reception I introduced Khrushchev to Frances. He grinned toothily and said, "Now I understand why you have been hiding her away from me. You were afraid I would steal her from you." We managed to smile.

We watched Khrushchev while he moved along the table laden with buffet dishes, and grazed with an intense contentment. He dropped a strawberry as he was eating and nonchalantly kicked it under the table.

Later, in a speech which was reported in *Pravda,* Khrushchev made reference to my visit to the pencil factory. He gave a muddled account of my concession for pencils, saying that I had discussed it with Lenin when, in fact, Lenin had been dead for some years before I got the idea of manufacturing pencils.

Khrushchev said:

Hammer went to V. I. Lenin and said that he had decided to apply for a concession for the manufacture of pencils. V. I. Lenin looked at him with surprise and said, "Why do you want to take a concession for the manufacture of pencils?"

"Mr. Lenin," said Hammer, "you have set a goal that everybody should learn to read and write and you haven't any pencils. Therefore, I will manufacture pencils!" [Noisy applause in the hall]

Some of the old employees were still there to greet Hammer. "See how pleased our old boss is with our progress," they said. [Laughter and applause]

So, you see, V. I. Lenin went even further than we by granting concessions to foreigners.

Khrushchev had arrived in Moscow, as a junior party apparatchik, in 1929, and it was one of the great disappointments of his life that he had never met Lenin, whom he idolized. My connection with Lenin made me a very important figure of history in Khrushchev's eyes, as he intimated when he autographed a photograph of the two of us together and dedicated it: *To Mr. Armand Hammer—first foreign concessionaire who conferred with V. I. Lenin —N. Khrushchev.*

I now felt that the news I had for Washington was so important that I should cancel the rest of my trip and hurry back to report to Luther Hodges. India would have to wait.

We arrived in Washington on February 23, 1961, and I went to see Luther Hodges the next day. I gave him a full report of my meetings with Mikoyan and Khrushchev and he relayed a digest of points to President Kennedy. Kennedy asked Secretary of the Treasury Dillon to inquire, as Mikoyan had suggested, as to whether the Japanese knew of slave labor being used by the Soviet crab fleet in Kamchatka.

On March 10, 1961, the *New York Times* carried this news headline: U.S. DUE TO ADMIT SOVIET CRABMEAT—TEN-YEAR BAN TO BE LIFTED. As Senator Gore wrote me, Hodges had called him, said he had personally reported my conversation with Premier Khrushchev to President Kennedy, with emphasis on the crabmeat ban, and thereupon Kennedy had contacted the Treasury Department to remove the ban.

"In the broad spectrum of the struggle to find a way for the East and the West to live in peace on one planet," the Senator wrote, "this may not appear to some as a major item, but when one considers the dangers to mankind involved in war today, any step that moves towards better understanding and peaceful relations is important. Just as Rome was not built in a day, peace will not be achieved in one cataclysmic event, one major conference or one international concert. Instead, it will come step by step, little by little."

In September 1961 I saw President Kennedy in the White House. Congressman Jimmy Roosevelt and I met him in the private sitting room connected with his bedroom in the family quarters. Luther Hodges had, of course, already relayed my full report of my meeting with Mikoyan and Khrushchev to the President and he had thanked me. He now thanked me again for my help in trying to improve relations with the USSR.

He was intrigued when I repeated to him Khrushchev's admission that Soviet Communism must fail if they failed to provide their people with the same standard of living as America. I said to JFK, "In my opinion, since they do not give their people enough incentives, and their bureaucratic ways and lack of competition stifle progress, they will never be able to compete with us in the long run."

In my informal mission for President Kennedy, I may have placed a small stone in the foundations of a better relationship between the White House and the Kremlin, a relationship which improved, piece by piece, through the sixties and culminated in the détente of the seventies.

Terrible strains and conflicts still lay ahead—the Cuban missile crisis, the Vietnam War, the Russian invasion of Czechoslovakia—but still, through all the changes of administration on both sides, the decades of the sixties and the seventies were to see the steadiest peacetime growth in trust, trade and communication between the two superpowers since the Bolshevik Revolution. By the middle of the seventies I began to feel confident that the close of the twentieth century would also close the age of nuclear terror and end the childish belligerence on both sides which threatened to blow the world into oblivion. And then came Afghanistan.

I had a part to play, too, in trying to settle that appalling crisis. Two full decades were to elapse, however, between my quiet mission to Moscow for President Kennedy and the frenzied shuttling between Washington, Moscow, Warsaw, Paris, London and Islamabad that happened then. They were to be decades full of renewed business with Russia, full of art and oil, political intrigue and some skulduggery, travel and travail, as Occidental and I extended our interests around the world.

The story of those decades lies ahead.

20

Occidental in
the Big World

I was full of pep when I got back to Los Angeles. My brain was swarming with big ideas for Occidental, and a vision of the company's future on the other side of the world, in North African deserts and Ukrainian wheatfields.

The oil developments I had seen in Libya were rich in promise. My conversations in Moscow, especially with Khrushchev, had given me ideas for the diversification and development of Occidental. I wanted the corporation to develop broadly into the extraction of natural resources to supply the burgeoning demand for fertilizers both in Libya and in Russia. I couldn't wait to tell the board and executives and get them to share my visions.

They would have looked more cheerful if I had told them I was going to pull out their fingernails one at a time.

Many of them were more than satisfied with Oxy's growth in the four years since I had assumed control, and they didn't want to push their luck. They felt that we should stick to a steady development of domestic operations and be content with a fair chunk of change as a small independent oil company.

Chief of these conservatives was Gene Reid. Having achieved his lifetime ambition of becoming a millionaire, Gene was nervous about seeing Oxy's new prosperity blown on faraway projects in foreign fields, and on business ventures which he knew nothing about from his own experience. He didn't like the sound of oil in Libya or of fertilizers anywhere. I had to fight hard to win Gene over to my ideas. He had already succeeded in talking me out of a venture into gold mining.

Not long before, a group of mining engineers had approached me with what seemed like an ingenious idea. They wanted to reopen a number of mines in northern California which had remained abandoned since the old Gold Rush days. Their proposal was perfectly sound, in theory. They said that the old claims had been worked with primitive methods, like panning in streams. Modern methods and machinery, they figured, would expose a wealth of gold which the old prospectors had been unable to unearth.

I got very excited about this idea. Something about gold mining touches a nerve of romance and daring, and I was not the first to succumb to "gold fever." The engineers gave me a phial of gold dust which they had extracted from their prospective workings, and I rushed off to New York to present it to a meeting of security analysts. Gene Reid came with me. He agreed that the mining idea was sound in theory—it was practice that worried him.

I made an enthusiastic speech to the analysts, pulling out all the stops and waving the glittering phial in front of their faces. Gene got up to speak after me. "I've listened closely to what Doctor Hammer has told you," he said, "and I just want to remind you and him that there's an awful lot of gravel between those specks of gold he's shown you."

Gene's cold water doused my gold fever like a soggy match. And that was the end of that venture.

I was willing to bow to Gene Reid's skepticism over gold mining, but I had to get him to see things my way over fertilizers, Libya and Russia. In those fields, I knew more than he. I knew for sure that the Russian demand for fertilizers was going to be gigantic, and I was pretty sure that fertilizers would be the key to success in negotiations for oil contracts in Libya. Gene bowed to my greater experience and acumen, but he watched with apprehension and unease as I moved Occidental forward.

Oxy's first major acquisition in that direction was the largest marketer of fertilizer in the world, the International Ore and Fertilizer Corporation, or INTERORE. With branches in twenty-three countries and operations in fifty-nine, INTERORE's sales amounted to more than 50 percent of all US exports of fertilizer.

A white Rolls-Royce made all the difference. Without that car, I might not have got the company.

INTERORE was owned and controlled by Henry Leir, an outstanding businessman. Once we had determined that we wanted to take over his company, I started working on the best means by which to approach Leir and win him over. I did some research, asked questions of some mutual friends and read the newspaper clippings about him. What emerged from these researches was that Leir was a terrific snob. I decided to find a way to play on it.

Henry was spending the fall of 1962 in Montecatini, Italy's world-famous watering hole, where he was hobnobbing with European grandees and retired millionaires. I arranged an appointment to see him there and flew to London.

As soon as I got to Claridge's in London, I walked the short distance to Berkeley Square and went into the showrooms of Jack Barclay, the most famous Rolls-Royce dealer in the world. I told the salesman that I wanted to see the most beautiful and desirable Rolls-Royce in the place.

Jack Barclay didn't let me down. I was shown a magnificent white Rolls-Royce Silver Cloud Mark II convertible, a two-door coupé with red leather upholstery and coachwork custom-built by Park Ward. I decided to buy it on the spot. I don't remember the price. I only know that it was the most expensive car in the showroom, and new Rolls-Royces are never cheap. Frances was with me and said, "I'm giving it to you as my gift."

Then I hired a liveried driver and made arrangements for the car to be shipped to Paris to meet Frances and me. From Paris, we set off for Italy, taking our time and enjoying the car.

We arrived in Montecatini just before lunchtime on a Friday. I had telegraphed ahead to Henry, who was waiting to give us lunch. The white Rolls-Royce caused such a sensation as we drew up in the forecourt of the hotel that one of the guests interrupted his pre-lunch drinks and came out to look at the car. It was Olav V, King of Norway!

Arriving in such style and attracting the King's attention made my job with Henry Leir a lot easier. Walking in the hotel gardens with Henry after lunch, I was able to tie up most of the major points for our deal, which we concluded quickly during the rest of the weekend. I couldn't offer him cash. In those days Occidental never had any spare cash, and all its acquisitions were negotiated in exchange for stock.

After we had agreed on the main elements of the deal, Henry and I had a leisurely chat, turning over some imaginary plans for Occidental's expansion. "You must never be too familiar with your employees, you know," Henry informed me. "My philosophy is, 'Familiarity breeds contempt.' You and I should think of ourselves as emperors and our employees are there to serve us." I had a job hiding my chuckles.

INTERORE was an even bigger bargain for Occidental than the Rolls-Royce was for me. If we hadn't had INTERORE, we might not have been able to offer fertilizers as part of our application for Libyan oil leases. If we hadn't offered fertilizers, our tender might not have succeeded. And if we hadn't gotten Libyan oil, Occidental would probably have remained a relatively small company, dwarfed by the majors.

INTERORE alone wasn't going to be enough for the job, though, and we immediately set out to increase our fertilizer holdings. In 1963 we bought Best Fertilizers in California, with its ammonia plants, and in March 1964, the Jefferson Lake Sulphur Company in Texas, the third largest sulphur company in the United States.

Jefferson Lake was a steal. The price of sulphur was very low and the company was in a weak trading position, chiefly because it was pouring money into an unproductive asbestos subsidiary in Canada. We offered Occidental stock worth fifteen million dollars to complete the merger and sold the asbestos subsidiary for one million. The big boon of the acquisition was in the 70 percent holding we also received in Jefferson Lake Petro-Chemicals, a Canada-based company listed on the American Stock Exchange with a market value of about twelve and a half million dollars. Very soon after the merger was completed, the market price of sulphur went into a climb which quadrupled the value of Jefferson Lake.

We now had gas, ammonia and sulphur—three essential ingredients for making fertilizer. We still needed potash and phosphates. Potash we purchased from huge low-cost mines in Canada. Phosphates were a problem.

The phosphate industry was run as a tight monopoly by a small group of producers in the south Florida area around Tampa. They believed they had a lock on the only significant reserves in North America. If you wanted phosphates, you paid their prices or you went without.

A young geologist under contract to Occidental told me that in his opinion great untapped reserves of phosphates still existed in north Florida. The only reason they had never been found, he said, was that nobody had ever looked hard enough. Most of the land in that region was controlled by the Continental Can Company, which was solely interested in the timber on the land.

Our geologist organized crews to dig exploratory holes along the roadsides in the area, in the few feet of ground which belonged to the county rather than to the can company. Sure enough, they lifted samples which suggested rich reserves of phosphates there. Armed with the geological reports, I got in touch with Continental Can and arranged to take options for drilling on thirty-thousand acres of their lands. The explorations turned up fantastic reserves, calculated at one hundred million tons of high-grade phosphate rock.

We were in business—except that the *production* of those reserves called for major industrial developments, developments that over the years amounted to about $750 million in costs. Reproducing that sum in cold print conveys none of the anxiety and excitement which was involved in raising and investing it. A corporation which had trouble raising $100,000 in 1956 was investing three-quarters of a billion dollars in industrial plant less than ten years later. No wonder Gene Reid was nervous. I wasn't altogether calm myself.

As we leaped up the league of natural-resources companies, we also jumped to the big board of the New York Stock Exchange. In the last couple of years we had moved from the Los Angeles Stock Exchange to the American Stock Exchange, and now I decided we were mature enough to go for the big board itself. Trading in our stock began on March 2, 1964, the week after we acquired Jefferson Lake. This was a very big day for us, and Keith Funston, President of the New York Stock Exchange, threw us a thank-you party, attended by all the Directors of the company, all three Hammer brothers and, of course, Frances. When our quote first appeared, under the ticker symbol OXY at 28½ (before the split of three-for-one, after the Libyan discoveries), Frances bought the first 200 shares.

All Occidental's ventures in diversification and the fertilizer business made good business sense in themselves as independent ventures. Put together, however, they gave Occidental the ace-in-the-hole in the poker game for oil concessions in Libya. That was the biggest game in town and the pot was unimaginable.

Libya made all the difference in the world to Occidental, and the world itself was changed by Occidental's success in Libya. Some long-term effects of that change are being felt even as of this writing. In April 1986 US aircraft attacked and bombed targets in Tripoli and Benghazi in retaliation for acts of terrorism said to have been sponsored by Libya. In the summer of 1986 OPEC ministers met in concert and agreed on oil-production limitations to control the price of oil, in an attempt to reexert their almost unrestricted powers of the seventies. Both of these scenes of major import for the world result indirectly from the discovery of oil in Libya in the sixties, in which Occidental had a big hand. If I'd known what a heap of trouble I was bringing on my head by getting involved in Libya, I would have thought twice before beginning. Having thought twice, I still would have gone ahead.

Libya was always different, always a special case. Its approach to the development and production of its oil resources was always revolutionary, even before political revolution overtook the country and threw Colonel Muammar el-Qaddafi onto the center of the world stage.

Oil was first discovered in Libya in 1959. Before then, the only explorations for oil had been conducted by Mussolini's army of occupation, which drilled a few shallow wells. They were all dry and the venture was abandoned. One trembles to think what difference it might have made to the Axis powers if the Italians had persevered and hit the mother lode of oil which lay beneath the Libyan sands.

Geological surveys conducted in the fifties indicated plainly that the country contained recoverable reserves on a gigantic scale, potentially comparable with some of the major oil-producing states of the Middle East. The Europeans and Americans went crazy at the prospect of Libyan oil—mainly because of the country's geographical location. It was a thousand miles closer to the main markets than the oil states of the Gulf and, better yet, oil from Libya would not have to pass through the strategically vulnerable Suez Canal.

The major oil companies went for the Libyan prospect like dogs for a bone. I wanted to get in this game from the moment I caught sight of it: in January 1961 Occidental incorporated OXYLIBYA, a wholly owned subsidiary, to develop our interests there.

The Libyans were determined to break with tradition in the development of their resources. They were not content to become prisoners of the major oil companies as Saudi Arabia and Iran had. In those countries, exclusive concessions had been granted to one major company or to a consortium of majors. The Seven Sisters had thus been able to control prices with absolute efficiency.

The Libyans refused to grant exclusive concessions to the majors. Instead, they threw open the land, block by block, to all bidders, inviting tenders. At one stroke the monopoly of the Seven Sisters was smashed.

When oil was first discovered in Libya, the country was ruled by King Idris, whose full title was Emir Mohammed Idris El Senussi. He was the absolute monarch of his tribal lands which, both in their style of governance and in their way of life, remained very much as they had been for thousands of years. The discovery of oil and the arrival of the oil companies slammed Libya in the twentieth century with traumatic abruptness.

Over the years King Idris has been described as corrupt, gullible and near-senile. I must say that picture bears no relation to the King Idris I knew. I always saw him as a typical Arab of the old world, deeply devout in his religious observances, modest and abstemious in his way of life, and fatherly in his care for his subjects. I don't believe that he filled his own bank accounts at the expense of his people and I know for certain that he wasn't an old fool. No man who was a fool could have made the Seven Sisters dance to his own tune as Idris did.

It is perfectly true, however, that some strange and exotic characters were crowded in the wings of the Libyan stage, trying to shuffle into the limelight and the money. Many of them claimed either to be related to Idris or to have special access to him. One such fantasist came my way. He liked to be known as the Black Prince because of his family connection to the King, largely imagined I think. He was a giant of at least six feet six, weighing I guess about three hundred pounds. Swathed in a turban and silks, burdened with a gold dagger in a jeweled belt, he came to visit me in my hotel room when I first visited Libya in 1961, saying that he would get me a concession if I would give him a couple of million dollars up front. He tried to convince me that this was the going rate of "baksheesh" for the job. When I refused, the Black Prince vanished in a large puff of hot air.

By opening his oil lands to bidders, Idris created a commercial pandemonium which was without equal in modern times, comparable with the California and Alaska gold rushes and the oil mania of the old days in Texas and Oklahoma. In the early and mid sixties, Benghazi and Tripoli became cockpits of what *Fortune* magazine correctly called "the biggest floating bazaar and crap game anywhere."

Those cities were jammed with oilmen, consultants, bankers, con men, politicians, all scrambling for a piece of the action. After the first round of concessions, it looked as if all the gamblers were going to get their fingers burned.

The first concessions in Libya were taken by the majors, and they all struck out. Shell sunk about fifty million dollars in noncommercial wells, as did the French National Oil Company. Esso-Libya, a subsidiary of Esso Standard of New Jersey, had also spent many millions, with no sign of encouragement, and they were about to pull out when they hit on their last exploratory well.

All the majors had gone to drill in western Libya, up by the Algerian border. They were drawn in that direction because huge quantities of oil had already been discovered in Algeria. The wells sunk there were all dry. Then some wild geologist at Esso came up with the idea that all the majors had been drilling in the wrong part of Libya: he suggested that Esso go east and look in the direction of Egypt, where nobody had thought of drilling.

That guess brought Esso-Libya its bonanza at Zelten, where the "C1-6" well tested at seventeen thousand barrels per day. The Zelten field of some fifty wells was producing about five hundred thousand barrels a day by the time bidding began for the second round of concessions. That was where we came in.

If the first round of negotiations had been a muddle, the second was like visiting day at the Tower of Babel. There never was a more exotic, mixed-up and complicated business carnival. More than forty companies from nine countries entered the bidding. Hordes of dealers occupied Libya, all tripping over each other, trying to find the key to a successful bid. The single figure at the center of all this palaver was, of course, old King Idris himself; his signature was the only one that counted.

If Idris had been as corrupt as legend suggests, it should have been possible to get a concession by bribing the King. I'm sure that method was attempted by other companies, but the Occidental bid succeeded because it appealed to the King's patriotic instincts for the welfare of his people rather than to any mercenary side of his character.

Having been in Libya prior to my mission to Russia in 1961, I had a pretty good idea what the Libyans wanted and what they cared about. I knew that the King and his Ministers were determined to make sure that Libya as a whole would benefit from its new oil prosperity. When the oil was all extracted and the dollars no longer flowed, Libya should not return to the abject poverty of former times—that was their ambition.

I personally supervised the preparation of our bid and went to Libya to lead the team which presented our tender. We flew in a beat-up converted A-26 bomber, our first overseas aircraft.

In his outstanding book *The Seven Sisters*, Anthony Sampson gives a good account of the Libyan concessions and calls my bid "[one] of exceptional generosity." He also refers to me personally as "an extraordinary old walnut of a man [who] had a combination of imagination and ruthlessness that made him in some ways more disrupting to the sisters than Getty or Mattei." I don't know whether to feel flattered or aggrieved by this description. In any case, "generosity" is not, I think, the best word to use about our bid. I would prefer "ingenuity."

Our bidding documents were prepared in the traditional Arab way, on sheepskin manuscripts, rolled and bound with silk ribbons of red, black and green—the Libyan national colors. The terms of the bid also differed dramatically from the conventional offers of the other companies. For instance, we offered to conduct a feasibility study for an ammonia plant in Libya and to build it jointly with the government if oil were struck.

More importantly, we promised to search, without charge, for water. We offered to explore near the desert village of Kufra—the birthplace of the King and Queen and the site of the King's father's tomb. The absence of water, more than the lack of oil or foreign exchange, had imprisoned Libya in its medieval poverty and condemned its people to nomadic lives. Idris undoubtedly cared as much that we might bring his country water as that we might find oil. On top of the normal division of profits, I offered the Libyans an extra 5 percent of pre-tax profits to be used for agricultural developments.

When the bids were opened, the Oil Minister, Fuad Kabazi, complimented Occidental on its bid. The head of one of the majors who was present turned to his local representative and was heard to whisper accusingly, "Why didn't we think of that?"

In February 1966 Occidental was granted two concessions. Our major competitors were astonished and far from enchanted by our success. Anthony Sampson records a remark made by the American Ambassador, David Newsom, which gives the majors' response with marvelous understatement: "I think it's fair to say," said Ambassador Newsom, "that the advent of Occidental on the scene was not warmly welcomed by the other companies."

One of our concessions had been given up as hopeless, after the first round, by a consortium consisting of Shell, Amerada, Marathon and Continental. Oxy had been one of seventeen bidders for this concession in the second round. The other block we won attracted only seven bids in the second round—it had been relinquished by Mobil after millions of dollars had been sunk in dry wells. Our geologic reports on both blocks were very encouraging. I believed that we just needed some luck, plenty of patience and a lot of nerve to commit ourselves to a full drilling program.

All of Gene Reid's senses rebelled against what seemed to be a huge and potentially catastrophic gamble. "We don't belong in Libya, Doctor," he told me during a board meeting. "Only the majors can make it there. It's just no place for a small company like Oxy. We ought never to have got involved and we ought to pull out before we're ruined."

In the first stages of the Libyan exploration, Gene's words echoed ominously loud in my memory. The first three holes we drilled were all bone-dry. They cost a million dollars each—on top of $2 million we had already spent on seismic research. A dead loss of $5 million was a whale-sized bite out of a company whose net worth, as attested in a letter from the Chase Manhattan Bank, was $48 million. Other members of the board began to side with Gene and, apparently, they started calling our Libyan operation "Hammer's Folly." After seven months of expensive failure, I faced the real danger of uncontrollable boardroom revolt.

In November 1966, however, the gamble paid off. We struck oil on the 610-square-mile Concession 102, with a well which tested at 14,860 barrels per day, making it the second-largest discovery well in Libya's history. Within a few months eight additional wells had been drilled on this concession, which was named the Augila Field. They tested at an aggregate rate of 97,500 barrels per day.

To give an idea of the value of this field, I need only say that the total oil output of the entire State of California at that time was only 900,000 barrels per day. We had hit not big but huge.

The crude oil from this field was of an exceptionally high quality, with a sulphur content of less than one quarter of one percent. At that time, the industrialized countries were just beginning to become concerned about pollution from exhaust emissions. Our "sweet oil," as it was called, would reduce smog, and it was obviously going to be sweetly prized in Europe and the US.

The spectacular find at Augila was to be overshadowed by developments on our second block at Concession 103, nearby and to the southwest. New seismic techniques, with which we began to explore in November 1966, strongly suggested that Mobil had missed extensive reserves at 103. With the Augila wells beginning to produce, I found no opposition on the Oxy board to a crash program of exploratory drilling on 103. I ordered it in March 1967. Within six weeks the first well drilled there—right on the site of the abandoned Mobil camp—discovered a new field which spouted in excess of 43,000 barrels a day.

We had hit what the oil industry calls a "reef"—a concentration of oil so bountiful that it will flow without the use of pumps. This was the first reef to be discovered in Libya. We were about to hit a second. And then a third. The second flowed at a stabilized rate of 17,600 barrels per day. The third was to be by far the biggest well ever hit in Libya, officially tested at a stabilized completion rate of 74,867 barrels per day.

Crude oil was then selling at three dollars a barrel. As of November 1967, it was estimated by the engineering firm of De Golyer and MacNaughton that the four fields discovered by Occidental would yield producible reserves in excess of *three billion barrels*. Occidental was no longer a small fish, nor even a big fish in a small pool. We were right in there with the big fish in the main pool.

One of those big fish had already come gliding out of the depths looking to gobble us up. After our discoveries in the Augila Field, I received a visit from the President of Esso-Libya, Hugh Wynne. He came bearing commercial instruments in the forms of a stick and a carrot.

He congratulated me on Occidental's discoveries in the Augila Field and smiled over Mobil's embarrassment. Then he asked me— here was the stick—how I proposed to market the oil. "You have no pipeline and no terminals for shipping, no refineries and no retail outlets," he said. "You are at the mercy of the majors, who have surplus of their own to sell."

Even though he was speaking as one of those very majors, his facts were undeniable. Then, to show his magnanimity, the carrot was proffered.

Esso-Libya would offer $100 million for half of Oxy's Libyan operation and take all of our production into their refining and retailing system.

I was of two minds about this offer. On the one hand, I was reluctant to step into the embrace of one of the majors, especially when we had battled on our own against overpowering odds to succeed in Libya. My instincts told me that we were better off to keep going it alone. On the other hand, $100 million in cash represented a mountainous profit for an independent company of Oxy's size, more than twice our total net worth at the time. I obviously had to refer this bid to my board.

They were all for it, without reservation. Negotiations went ahead. The deal was done.

Then it was undone. The President of Esso-Libya took the deal to the board of Standard of New Jersey for the approval which, he had told me, was a formality. Without discussion or apology, that board threw the deal out. I suspect that they wanted to teach the upstart little independent a lesson: they must have thought that they had us over a barrel—or three billion barrels—of unmarketable oil. It was reported to me that one of their executives said, "We tried to make a deal with Armand Hammer. The trouble was that he doesn't understand the oil business."

The big fish sank again to the bottom of the pool.

After our discoveries at the Concession 103, it surfaced again for another bite.

This time I received a visit from Siro Vazquez, a Director of the parent company, Standard of New Jersey, itself. He was not alone. He came out to Los Angeles with a full crew of executives and attorneys, some seventeen in all. They took a floor of the Hilton Hotel in Beverly Hills. I was, understandably, reluctant to take them seriously. Mr. Vazquez assured me that these negotiations would be different: he had the full authority and confidence of his board.

Negotiations were extensive and arduous, consuming many a vat of midnight oil. The original offer for the Augila operation having been $100 million, I was now demanding $200 million for 50 percent of Augila plus the new Idris Field. That sum was, at length, agreed upon. Everybody was very happy. The Directors of Occidental were jubilant. The lawyers were relieved and exhausted. We had a long and rowdy party at the Hilton to celebrate.

There was only one small hitch: as before, the deal had to be approved at a meeting of the full board of Standard of New Jersey. "No problem, Doctor Hammer," said Siro Vazquez. "Don't give it a thought. The deal will go through on the nod. My fellow Directors on the board have never failed to approve my deals." He and his men went back East and I went home to my bed, counting Oxy's prospective hundreds of millions.

Their board threw it out again. They must have figured, again, that we would have to go crawling to them and accept any terms they dictated, as long as we were without a pipeline and a marketing setup of our own.

We had been left with no choice. We had to create or obtain that marketing organization. My original instinct, to shun the majors and go it alone in the distribution of our Libyan crude, now became, by force of circumstance, a necessity.

I took the problem to my friend Steve Bechtel of the giant engineering group Bechtel of San Francisco. I told him that I had potential producible reserves of three billion barrels of crude in the ground and nowhere to take it. I said that I needed to build a pipeline system more than 130 miles long to the nearest suitable port, at Zueitina on the Mediterranean coast, and build a terminal and port facility there. For the time being, however, I couldn't afford to pay for those developments, and I didn't yet have any customers for the crude even when it did reach the coast.

I've always had a soft spot for Steve Bechtel because of the response he gave me that day. "We'll do the whole job for you on credit," he said. "I believe in you and I'm sure you'll find a way to market this oil." Sometimes big business decisions really are taken on the basis of personal trust and confidence. The human factor in business relations can sometimes be as significant as the dollars and cents in the profit and loss account. Steve Bechtel effectively granted me a $150-million credit that day because he trusted me.

(In later years Steve's trust and confidence were to be rewarded more than ten times over in business with Occidental, when we gave him the multibillion-dollar development of our North Sea discoveries.)

The main pipeline was to be the largest in Libya, forty inches in diameter and capable of transporting a million barrels a day from the Idris Field to Zueitina on the coast. A secondary pipeline, twenty-four inches in diameter, was to be built along a forty-mile connection between the Augila Field and the Idris Field. Bechtel also had to create gathering, separating and metering facilities in the field and build new terminal facilities at Zueitina, including vast holding tanks and docking facilities for tankers capable of carrying a million barrels of crude. The total cost of all those developments was to be $300 million. The banks were willing to finance the development to the tune of $150 million once we started shipping oil.

I went to the desert several times to oversee the construction workers in person and drive them on. The work went on through the most blistering days of heat, when the temperature often touched 120 degrees Fahrenheit and it continued all night, too. I ordered a system of special lights, strung along poles set at fifty-foot intervals in the desert, so that work could continue through every minute of every twenty-four hours. Field construction work began in August 1967. Oil began flowing into the pipeline on February 5, 1968, and arrived at the terminal on February 16. We gave it quite a welcome. King Idris himself was the guest of honor at the royal reception we threw in the desert.

Fortune magazine reported: "Red, green and black national flags snapped in the breeze. Camel troops patrolled the dunes around the installation, scarlet-coated bandsmen stood in formation with their instruments shining in the midday sun and the blood of sacrificial lambs stained the desert sand. Some 800 cabinet ministers, robed local chieftains, religious dignitaries, diplomats, a U.S. Senator [Albert Gore] and other assorted guests and attendants filled a splendid pavilion erected solely to house a half-hour ceremony."

The party cost a million dollars. I thought we all deserved a good celebration, but perhaps not *that* good. I looked into the books and found all kinds of financial weevils and grubs, including a virtual blank check handed over to the contractor for the celebration. I believe in charity, but not that kind!

While the pipeline system was under construction, I had solved the problem of refining and marketing the oil.

One morning at my home in Los Angeles, I read an item in *Oil Daily*—the industry's Bible—about Signal Oil, an international marketing organization with a huge European operation. They had oil tankers and terminals. They had an 85,000-barrels-per-day refinery located by deep water in Antwerp Harbor and a 15,000-barrels-per-day refinery on the Rhine-Herne Canal in the heart of the Ruhr Valley of West Germany. They had marketing outlets under the VIP brand in the UK and Belgium, and they had established sales to wholesale and industrial consumers right across Europe. Best of all, they were short of oil and thinking of selling out.

I made some urgent inquiries and found out that the Director in charge of Signal's entire marketing operation was a Frenchman named Claude Geismar, who was considered to be one of the smartest marketers of oil in the world. I got in touch with him and said, "Why don't you take our oil? We've got plenty. We can fill your terminals, tankers, refineries and retail outlets. We'll pay you a commission on every barrel of oil you sell."

He said, directly, that he would be glad to recommend to the Signal board that they should act as agents for our oil. I then negotiated with Forrest Shumway, President of Signal. Negotiations went very smoothly and our arrangement was agreed upon when I surprised Forrest by saying, "I hear you've put a price tag of one hundred and five million dollars on your whole marketing setup, to include all your refineries, tankers, terminals and retail outlets. Well, I want you to give me an option to buy. I'll offer you half in preferred stock and half in five-year notes."

He said, "I will give you an option, on one condition—you'll have to exercise it on or before the day the first barrel of oil is loaded at Zueitina."

I then got down to work with Claude Geismar, making sales contracts for our crude through the Signal network. By the middle of November 1967, Signal announced that it had already entered into sales contracts for Occidental crude in excess of one billion barrels over and above the 800 million barrels Signal needed for its own use.

By the time the first barrel of oil was ready to be loaded at Zueitina, the commissions payable on those contracts amounted to nearly two hundred million dollars.

Of course I then exercised Occidental's option, and we became overnight the owners of the whole Signal setup. I appointed Claude Geismar to run the operation for us and he joined the Occidental board.

Without investing a penny, we had acquired the means to refine and market our entire Libyan production which, very soon after, was to edge close to 800,000 barrels a day. That acquisition didn't make us the Eighth Sister of the oil industry, but it legitimized us in the family, albeit as a black sheep—this, from somebody who "didn't understand the oil business." Sometimes I wonder what might have happened if I had understood it!

The majors got their revenge when they effectively prevented Occidental from building a refinery in Machiasport, Maine, to process 300,000 barrels of Libyan oil a day.

New England was subject to one of the most idiotic restrictions of the oil import quota system of the time. Oil shipped from Africa and the Middle East to Portland, Maine, had to be piped to Canada, where it sold for 3 cents a gallon less than the oil from the Gulf to which Maine was restricted.

It made obvious sense to build a refinery in Maine for Libyan crude and supply New Englanders with cheap foreign oil. I asked Washington to establish a "free trade zone" for customs and trade purposes in return for which I offered 10-percent cheaper oil for defense, gasoline and home heating.

As Robert Sherrill has commented in his book *The Oil Follies of 1970–1980,* "That sort of free enterprise was highly objectionable to all the major oil companies and most of the independents. Almost as one man, they rose against the Machiasport proposition. Some of these honest gentlemen went so far as to accuse Hammer of trying to bribe his way to success." Permission was denied.

Oil was not the only liquid which Occidental caused to flow from the sands of the Libyan desert. We also delivered on our promise to look for water. Professor Neil H. Jacoby of UCLA, member of the Occidental board, told this story well:

It was about a million dollar gamble, I'd say. We took a drilling rig and crews five hundred miles inland across the burning desert to Kufra, started the drilling and found an underground reservoir estimated to be as big as the flow of the Nile for two hundred years! It was beautiful, clear spring water. The people couldn't believe it and I don't think we could either. We found it at only two hundred and fifty feet below the surface. The doctor flew in some San Joaquin Valley farming experts, ordered miles of aluminum irrigation pipes, sprinklers and chemical fertilizers, and we taught those people how to make the desert bloom. We planted alfalfa and it sprang up from the sand as if it had taken root in the richest soil on earth.

King Idris was so delighted by our discovery that he said to me, "Allah sent you to Libya!" He offered to rename his birthplace and call it "Hammer." I told him this was too great an honor for me to accept. That was when I asked him if he would consent to a renaming of our field on Concession 103: I wanted to call it the Idris Field.

I had already discussed this idea with the Prime Minister, Mustaba Halim. Throwing up his hands in horror, he had warned me not, at any cost, to suggest it. "The King is a holy man and he would never consent to this," the Prime Minister said. "He will only ever agree—and then with reluctance—for his name to be given to a mosque or a university. But an oil field? Never!"

However, when Idris said that I had been sent by Allah, I thought to myself, "Well, if Allah sent me, then I ought to be able to ask the King to give his name to the oil field."

I told the King what I wanted. Idris laughed and said, "What have I done to be honored in this way?"

I said, "Because what you have done for Libya will make you immortal."

"Not if Nasser gets his way," he answered.

Those were prophetic words. Our great oil field in Libya was not to be called Idris for long. Gamal Abdel Nasser, who had become President of Egypt by overthrowing my old customer King Farouk, and who had become the guiding star of Arab nationalism in the postwar world, made no secret of his hopes for revolution in Libya.

Nasser lived just long enough to see it happen. He died in 1970. Idris was overthrown on September 1, 1969. Paradoxically, Idris lived out his remaining years in Cairo, under the protection of Nasser's successor, Sadat.

The coup against Idris was led by a young Army officer who idolized Nasser and who was a proud disciple of Nasser's peculiar ideology which blended Arabism, socialism and nationalism. He was a communications officer, only twenty-eight years old at the time. After the Revolutionary Command Council had deposed Idris and declared the Libyan Arab Republic, some days elapsed before we came to know his name as the leader of the revolution.

He needs no introduction from me. For seventeen years, the world has known and feared Muammar el-Qaddafi's name. When you remember that Libya's population is barely more than two million people, it is amazing that Qaddafi has been able to hold such sway over the world's affairs and its imagination. Without oil, Libya would have remained an undeveloped third-world country. Without oil, Qaddafi would have been unknown to the world and, even if he had ever risen to power there, would have been no more than another obscure dictator.

One of the earliest acts of the new government was to require the renaming of our oil field. It ceased to be called Idris and became Intisar, as it remains today.

Because his own idea of himself is so lurid and dramatic, we tend to think that Qaddafi owes nothing to Libya's earlier regime, from which he likes to say that he made a clean break. In fact, however, Qaddafi quite smoothly and logically succeeded Idris to the leadership of the country, and some of his policies differed from the old King's not in substance but in style. There, admittedly, the difference was immense.

For instance, Idris's Ministers had always wanted 30 cents more per barrel than the producers were willing to pay. They always felt that Libya was being short-changed and they said so repeatedly. The producers pretty well ignored them, thinking that their King was effectively powerless.

Qaddafi also believed that Libya was not being fairly paid for the oil. He, similarly, wanted between 30 and 40 cents more per barrel. The difference was that, if he didn't get more money, Qaddafi was willing to nationalize the oil fields and boot the companies out of the country. That, you might say, is a difference of style.

Qaddafi put the writing on the wall for the whole world to see very soon after his coup. In January 1970, less than five months after his takeover, he organized a meeting of oil producers in Libya, at which he told representatives of the companies that he was determined to get 40 cents more per barrel. It is worth noting that James E. Akins of the State Department, formerly US Ambassador to Saudi Arabia, later said that this figure was "not outrageous" and he also calculated that the Libyans could, fairly, have demanded more.

The companies, understandably, did not see Qaddafi's demand in the same light. They wanted to offer no more than an increase of 10 cents per barrel. They were concerned that acquiescence in Libya would lead to a domino effect throughout the world, and that they would be held to ransom in every other oil-producing country. They wanted to hold the line in Libya.

That was all right for them to say, they *had* large interests in other countries. Occidental did not. We were totally dependent on our Libyan production which, in 1969, amounted to more than 90 percent of the corporation's total oil production. Naturally, Qaddafi and his Min-

isters fully recognized the scale of Occidental's dependence and, early
on in their campaign, marked us out as the most vulnerable target for
attack.

All through the early months of 1970, I heard rumblings from
Libya about threats that our production would be cut back or curtailed.
The formal reason given for these threats was, the Libyans claimed,
that the 800,000 barrels per day we were producing was much more
than should have been allowed by a good conservation practice. That
claim was a guise. The real reason the Libyans were threatening cut-
backs in our production was to soften us up. Our vulnerability made us
the ripest fruit on their tree, and the company most apt to negotiate an
increase in the price per barrel. In the worsening atmosphere of the
time, it was imperative that we should reduce our commitments in
Libya, and my first response to the Libyans' threats was to cut back on
construction of a giant liquefied petroleum gas installation at Zueitina
on which we had already spent sixty million dollars. Soon after, I closed
it down altogether.

On June 12, 1970, the Libyans told us that our production would
be reduced from 800,000 to 500,000 barrels per day. Two months later,
on August 19, they announced a further reduction to 440,000 barrels
per day. Though cuts were also imposed on other companies, nobody
suffered as severely as Occidental.

Between those two dates in the summer of 1970, I had tried to
strengthen Occidental's hand against the growing threat in Libya. On
July 10, 1970, I went to New York to see Ken Jamieson, the new Chief
Executive at Esso.

Whisked to the fifty-first floor of the Esso building on the Avenue
of the Americas, I was ushered into the large room—more like a state
receiving room—which Ken Jamieson called his office. He—tall, cool,
reserved—was not warmly welcoming.

I put my cards straight on the table, face up. Having nothing to
play with, I had nothing to hide. I told him that I could not hold out
much longer against Qaddafi. With Occidental's Libyan production
already so savagely restricted, I was having serious difficulty in fulfilling
contracts for delivery of oil. I would shortly be unable to complete
those contracts, and my corporation was in danger of being wiped out. I
reminded him—though it was surely unnecessary—that if I was forced
to give in to Qaddafi, all the oil companies in Libya would be forced to
follow suit.

"I will be willing to hold the line," I said, "if you will sell me the oil
I need—at cost, plus a reasonable profit such as ten percent."

Mr. Jamieson received my offer in silence and then he said that he
would need time to consider it. I left the building without any indication of how Esso might respond. They took two weeks to decide—two

weeks during which Occidental was, no doubt to their delight, twisting in the wind on the rope which Muammar el-Qaddafi had tied around our neck. Then came the Esso decision: they would sell us the oil we wanted—but only at the going market price. No rebuff could have been more studied. We could do without friends like that: we would have to!

The full consequences of Esso's shortsightedness were about to break upon us. One evening late in August, I got a call at my home from George Williamson, our Executive Vice President and Manager in Libya, that we were about to be nationalized. This act was apparently being planned for the celebrations to mark the first anniversary of the revolution.

I decided that I must immediately go to Libya in person. I placed a call to my pilot, Fred Gross, and asked him how long he would need to prepare our aircraft for the flight to North Africa. By that time, I was traveling in a Gulfstream II jet.

"A couple of hours," he said.

"I'll see you at the airport," I said.

I asked Frances to help me pack some clothes. She urged me not to go. She said that I was out of my mind.

"Qaddafi will have you arrested," she said. "You're an old friend of the King's, and in their eyes you're a guilty man. They'll probably put you on trial and they might even have you shot. If anybody has to go, why can't it be a younger man?"

"I have to go," I said. "The shareholders would never forgive me if I allowed us to be nationalized in Libya without doing everything possible myself."

"Well," she said, "this is one trip I'm not going on."

It was the first and only time she has ever refused to travel with me.

We flew all night. In Turin, Claude Geismar met me. We decided to charter a French Falcon jet for the trip to Tripoli for fear the Libyans would confiscate our plane.

When the plane came to a standstill, just before dawn, we looked nervously out the windows, half expecting to see squads of police and soldiers sent to arrest us. The airport was deserted, however. Only one man was waiting to meet us—George Williamson, our own colleague. He told me that Prime Minister Abdul Salam Ahmed Jalloud had been told of my arrival and was waiting to see me in his office.

When I walked into Jalloud's immense room, he jumped up from his desk and came forward to greet me, smiling broadly.

"Welcome, Doctor Hammer," he said. "You're the first Chairman and Chief Executive Officer of any of the oil companies who has come to see us since the revolution. Please be at your ease here as the guest of the government. Quarters have been prepared for you at the ex-

King's palace, which, of course, you know from your previous visits. Have you had your breakfast? We have hot rolls here for you, and coffee. Please, sit."

I was momentarily thrown by the warmth of this welcome and further disoriented by Jalloud's first act before we sat down together, side by side on a sofa. He unbuckled the broad leather belt around his waist and placed it on the low table in front of us. Suspended from the belt was a holster containing a very large and purposeful-looking revolver. He smiled. I smiled. Then I tried to compose myself. I had conducted business negotiations in some strange circumstances before, but never over the dully gleaming barrel of a .45!

Then we began. I assured him that I had come to negotiate in good faith, that I was open to all reasonable proposals and that my principal concern was to protect the interests of my hundreds of thousands of shareholders. He replied that the Libyans, too, were men of reason. All he wanted, he said, was a 40-cent-per-barrel tax increase. The alternative, he said charmingly, was simple: we would be taken over completely.

I negotiated with the Libyans for most of a week. I chose not to accept their offer of hospitality. I didn't feel safe in Tripoli. The risk of trouble and possible arrest was constantly in my mind.

Instead of staying in Idris's old palace, I flew every night to Paris, usually arriving there about two A.M., and taking off again for Libya at about six A.M. After the first trip, I used my own plane. This routine was terribly hard on Fred Gross, but he didn't complain. He wasn't eager to sleep nights in Tripoli, either.

Finally a compromise was reached at an increase of 30 cents per barrel and an agreement was prepared for signature. I was to sign for Occidental. Mr. Mabruk, the Oil Minister, was to sign for Libya. When George Williamson, Claude Geismar and I arrived in Mr. Mabruk's office for the signing, I asked him if he had a resolution from the Libyan government authorizing him to sign.

"I have," he replied. "It's here in my desk."

"I would like to see it, please," I said. "I want to make a copy of it and attach it to our agreement."

"I'm sorry," he said. "That's quite impossible. It is a private government document."

That reply made me very uneasy. I suspected a trick. Without a formal resolution, any agreement I signed would be unenforceable, worthless.

I told Mr. Mabruk that I was unwilling to sign in those circumstances. I asked him to speak to Mr. Jalloud. He left the room, saying that he would call Jalloud from another office. I don't know whether he placed the call or not, but, after a few minutes, he returned to say that

Jalloud had agreed that I might see the resolution. He insisted, however, that I should neither make a copy nor attach it to the agreement.

"I'm going to have to think this over," I said. "I am afraid I'm not willing to sign right now. You'll have to give me time to consider this development."

I left the office. As soon as we got outside, I said to George Williamson, "This is very ominous. I don't like it at all. I'm going to leave directly. You have my full authority to sign the agreement in my name if—and only if—they will let you attach the resolution to it. Otherwise, you are not to sign. Let hell freeze over first."

Claude and I drove directly to the airport. It was late at night. The place was deserted. Fred Gross was asleep in our aircraft. I woke him up and said, "Freddie, wake up. We've got to get out of here right away. Just start your engines and let's go."

"But I'll need to get permission to take off," he said.

"Don't ask," I said. "Don't wait for anything. Don't stop if they tell you to. Let's go. Right now."

Nobody's got more guts than Fred Gross, and nobody enjoys a touch of adventure more than he does. He grinned and said, "That's fine with me, Doctor, but I've got to tell you the risk you're taking. They could start shooting the minute we begin to taxi. They might even send up fighters after us, but, if we get off the ground, we'll clear their airspace very fast."

"Let's take the chance," I said. "They're all asleep now. We'll be gone before they know."

Fred taxied the plane to the runway as if it were a sports car and gunned it down the runway. One of the advantages of the Gulfstream II is that it will take off at a rate of climb like a fighter aircraft. After a few minutes Fred spoke on the intercom and said, "Clear of Libyan airspace now, Doctor. Next stop Paris."

Safe at the Ritz Hotel in Paris, I got a call next day from George Williamson in Tripoli. The Libyans had been so startled by my sudden departure, he said, that Mr. Jalloud had relented and agreed that the resolution should be attached to the agreement.

"In that case," I said, "go ahead and sign."

The immediate crisis was over. We agreed to pay 30 cents more per barrel at once and a further 2 cents a year for five years. We also accepted a rise in the tax rate from 50 to 58 percent. Occidental was saved. Our Libyan production was secure. Now, all hell was let loose.

As soon as the details of our agreement in Libya were made public, the other oil companies with interests there went into paroxysms of rage, claiming that I had sold them out and betrayed them. "From that point on," one Shell man was reported as saying, "it was either a retreat or a rout."

The very companies which had refused to come to Occidental's aid were now gnashing their teeth and wailing, knowing that they were next in line for the Tripoli treatment.

Belatedly, the companies began to think of defending themselves. On September 7, 1970, John J. McCloy, counsel and spokesman for the majors, led a delegation of oil company chief executives to Washington for a conference with Secretary of State William Rogers, Under Secretary Alexis Johnson and Mr. James Akins. It was agreed at this meeting that the situation in Libya was very serious, but no decision was made.

The major British companies, Shell and BP, now tried to lead the organization of resistance. Their respective Chairmen, Sir David Barran and Sir Eric Drake, visited all the majors in the US and called upon the Seven Sisters to "stand together" in Libya. However, Socal and Texaco were not willing to face a fight, and they soon caved in to the Libyans on much the same terms that I had negotiated for Occidental.

The dominoes now began to fall with a vengeance. As the companies fell into line in Libya, what the oilmen had always feared happened: the other producing countries followed Libya's lead. In quick succession, Iran, Algeria, Kuwait and Iraq all demanded and got 55-percent increases in their tax rates. On December 9 the OPEC countries met in Caracas, Venezuela, and issued a series of saber-rattling statements, threatening to demand still further tax increases.

On December 10 I was on the operating table at UCLA, having kidney stones removed. The very next day, December 11, when I was barely recovered from the anesthetic, a call came through to my hospital bed from Sir David Barran.

"Armand," he said, "there's good reason to think that the Libyans are about to start all over again, and this time they'll go for a further dollar a barrel. It looks as if they'll pick on you again, because they think you are in the weakest position. I hope that you will resist them."

"Well," I said, "it's very nice of you to call, but I'd like to know who's going to take care of my company if I do resist them, and they then turn around and nationalize us? Will you supply me with oil at cost so that I can complete my contracts and meet my commitments?"

"I think that's a perfectly reasonable request," he said. "Let me discuss it with the other companies and see what we might be able to come up with." Of course he meant that he would talk to the other Sisters.

Next day Sir David called again to say that he was ready to work out a deal. He asked me to send a representative to negotiate with him in London. I sent him John Tigrett, an American consultant whom I retained on contract. John dropped everything and flew immediately to London.

During the days just before and after Christmas 1970, John and Sir

David discussed a "safety-net" proposal to protect companies in Libya. Sir David then wrote a "New Year's Letter" to all the companies, proposing a meeting in New York.

On January 11, 1971, all twenty-three of us met in John J. Mc-Cloy's offices in New York. The safety net was stitched together there. Essentially, we agreed that we would all support any company which was cut back or nationalized in Libya. Each company would supply oil to the victimized company in amounts according to its Libyan production. Companies operating in the Persian Gulf would make up the oil lost by Libyan companies which were supporting Qaddafi's victim.

The big questions about this agreement were: "Will it work?" and "Is it legal?" John J. McCloy was quick to point out that our agreement constituted an apparently obvious breach of the antitrust laws. We asked him to approach the Justice Department to explain our dilemma and seek an assurance that we would not be subjected to antitrust action. The Department of Justice replied in typically ambiguous terms, saying that it did not intend action at that moment, but that it reserved the right to act on the same issue in future. Thanks a lot, men.

At the same time that we were creating this safety net, the companies were also drawing up a Libyan Producers' Agreement, which was an attempt to prevent the Libyans from splitting off any one company for attack. The agreement proposed that "an all-embracing negotiation should be commenced between representatives of ourselves . . . and OPEC, as representing all its member countries . . . under which an overall and durable settlement could be achieved."

As to the question "Will it work?," the answer is, "It might have, if anybody had tried it." The producing countries, not surprisingly, were dead set against our proposals and they were determined not to bargain with us collectively. The Libyans saw clearly that they would lose all the advantages of their position by joint negotiation. For different reasons, the more moderate Iranians took the same position. In the face of this opposition, the major oil companies abandoned our agreed collective strategy and caved in again, accepting individual negotiations with the producing governments.

The result of these vacillations was to bring nearer the threat of nationalization in Libya.

It didn't happen overnight; we had plenty of time to prepare. Occidental's production in Libya was curtailed further—to 423,000 barrels per day in 1972 and 354,000 in 1973. The writing was plainly on the wall in those years, and after the first restriction was imposed, I announced that we would henceforth "reduce our Libyan operation considerably."

The Libyans didn't have things all their own way. They were as tough as nuts over their general principles, but they left some slack in the fine mesh of our business operations. I was able to haul in some of this slack with a catch, on one occasion, of half a billion dollars.

In raising taxes and cutting our production, the Libyans were in open violation of our contracts. Of course we complained. Of course they took no notice. I decided that it would be prudent to make preparations to clear out of Libya altogether. As provided by our agreement, I wanted to take them to international arbitration in Paris, to recover at least our assets, then reckoned at $275 million, but I wanted to have a hold on some of their assets to give us leverage at that arbitration. A means was at hand.

We were paying the Libyans for our crude on sixty days' credit. We were collecting from our own customers on thirty days' credit. We were piling up a huge credit balance. When the amount of cash we were holding equaled the assets we might lose in Libya, we wrote to the Libyans giving notice of our intention to go to arbitration and saying that we expected them to show up. The letter caused as much of a flurry in Tripoli as a fly landing on a rhinoceros. They didn't answer it. We went right on shipping oil and holding their money.

The cash piled up until we were holding $550 million. Some of our directors started getting nervous, thinking that Qaddafi might send his hit men after us and have us kidnapped and held until the money was released. Arthur Groman anxiously counseled me to wear a bulletproof vest, and our security people got a price for an armor-plated car for me. I wouldn't consent to either proposal. Once you let fears of that order get a hold, you're in danger of ending up like Howard Hughes, in living dread of every moment and every human being. (Any would-be kidnappers reading this, however, should note that I do take sensible precautions to protect myself and my family.)

Finally the Libyans came to their senses. Jalloud sent a delegation to see me in Los Angeles.

"Mr. Jalloud hears that you are hot," the leader of the delegation told me. "He suggests that you take a shower and cool off. We want to settle this dispute."

"I'm ready," I said.

"Well, then, you must give us our money back."

"I'm willing to give you back two hundred seventy-five million dollars," I said, "but I'm going to hold on to the other two hundred seventy-five million as an insurance against any further violation of our agreement or the threat of outright confiscation of our assets."

"Fair enough," they said.

I was rather taken aback. I hadn't expected to be made a present of $275 million quite so easily.

We kept their $275 million for a couple of years, enjoying the use of it without interest until, finally, Jalloud sent for George Williamson in Tripoli and said, "Look, this is preposterous. Doctor Hammer has to give us back our two hundred seventy-five million dollars." So we returned it, gradually, over a number of years, until our accumulated profits exceeded the $275 million of our assets.

In the middle of this time, when my dealings with the Libyans were at their tensest, a stroke of mischance delivered me physically into their hands.

I was flying overnight from Nigeria to Europe when a generator began to fail in my plane. We were over the Sahara. Fred Gross told me that he was going to have to put the plane down at the nearest strip that could take the plane. That was Tripoli.

"Oh, my God," I said. "If the Libyans get word that we've landed, they'll put us all behind bars. I'm not their favorite man right now."

With his previous experience of Tripoli airport, Fred thought that he could get in and out quietly, without the Libyans learning the identity of the plane and its passengers.

We limped in and Fred parked the plane way out in the back reaches of the airport. Then we got in touch with our Libyan offices and had them send out their best mechanics on the double. Fred and his boys worked with the mechanics through the night to repair the engine. I lay hidden. Finally we were ready to go. For the second time, Fred took the plane screaming off the runway without clearance from the tower.

The Libyans' present to me for my seventy-fifth birthday was the threat of outright nationalization. I celebrated that birthday in Malta in May of 1973, with John Tigrett and George Williamson, working out a proposition for the Libyans which would allow us to keep producing there.

John and I had jetted out to Malta as fast as we could go, once we heard from George that full-scale nationalization was immediately in the cards. The elaborate plans which had been made for my birthday celebrations in Los Angeles had to be postponed. If we lost Libya altogether, there wouldn't be much to celebrate.

I believed I understood the Libyans. I said to John and George, "I don't think the Libyans want to run the oil fields. I think they just want control. Even though they would have a fifty-one-percent interest in the operation, we will still keep forty-nine percent, which will allow us to supply our contracts."

That was the way we played it. The Libyans agreed to pay $136 million in cash for 51 percent of our operation. Other companies in Libya were then forced to follow suit, but I believe we were the only company to receive compensation in cash. The others were paid with their own oil. Some were not even that lucky. Bunker Hunt and others were nationalized outright.

Oxy makes it to the Big Board, March 2, 1964. Victor is on the extreme right, Harry on the extreme left, I'm in the middle next to Keith Funston, President of the New York Stock Exchange. The others are members of the board and staff of Oxy.

With King Idris of Libya at the dedication of Oxy's completed pipeline and facilities, April 23, 1968. Prime Minister Abdul Hamid Bakkush is at the left of King Idris.

With President Lyndon Johnson in the Oval Office, 1968.

Fruits of the cultural exchange: Russian Minister of Culture Furtseva and Hermitage Museum Director Piatrovski examine my collection on tour at the Hermitage, October 1972.

With Leonid Brezhnev in 1973 and 1980. The interpreters were never needed, although Victor Sukhodrev was present.

To my good friend Armand Hammer
Jimmy Carter 5-78

With President Jimmy Carter in the Oval Office, May 1978.

With Anwar Sadat in Cairo, 19
His tragic assassination ended a
plan for a joint American-
Egyptian-Israeli industrial proj

With Menachem Begin, 1981.

To my dear friend, Dr. Armand Hammer — M. Begi

A dinner conference with Prince Charles. (Bryson)

With Margaret Thatcher talking to reporters after touring one of our North Sea installations, September 1980.

A North Sea platform,
with me at lower right.
(Bryson)

Opening up China for Occidental,
with Deng Xiaoping, 1981.

With old friend Anatoliy Dobrynin,
September 22, 1982.

French President Mitterrand presents me
with the Commander's Cross of the Legion
of Honor, 1983.

With Indira Gandhi in Moscow. (Bryson)

Reading a eulogy at Brezhnev's funeral, 1982. Senator Robert Dole is at left.
(Bryson)

My second meeting with Konstantin Chernenko, December 4, 1984. Andrei
Alexandrov-Agentov at right. (AP)

March 13, 1985—Chernenko's funeral. (Bryson)

The funeral provided me with my first chance to meet the new leader of Russia, Mikhail Gorbachev. (Bryson)

My first extended talk with General Secretary Gorbachev, June 17, 1985. (Bryson)

Reporting back to President Reagan in the Oval Office, June 24, 1985.

"Hammer House"—the international trade center and hotel we built in the heart of Moscow. (Bryson)

Revisiting the "Sugar King's Palace," now the British Embassy, Moscow. (Bryson)

In Lenin's office. The bronze statuette on the desk was my gift to Lenin in 1922. (Bryson)

At Hospital No. 6 in the aftermath of Chernobyl. From left to right: hospital chief Dr. Angelina Guskova, Dr. Nicholai Fetisov, Deputy Minister of Health Oleg Shchepin, me, Dr. Robert Gale, Dr. Alexander Baranov.

With Dr. David Goldfarb aboard Oxy One en route from Moscow to New York, October 16, 1986.

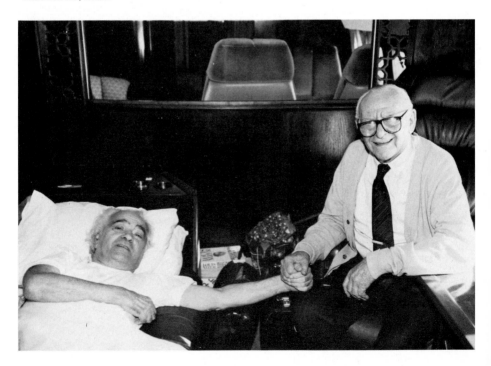

With Metropolitan Museum of Art Director
Philippe de Montebello (left), Soviet
Ambassador Dubinin (right), and Met
President William Luers (far right) at the
opening of the Russian exhibition of French
Impressionists at the Met, August 21, 1986.

With Jonas Salk of the
Salk Institute, 1982. (Bryson)

A student, Anna Leander of Sweden, from the
first graduating class of the Armand Hammer
United World College, 1984.

The Board of Directors of Occidental Petroleum Corporation, seated from left to right: Morrie A. Moss, Louis Nizer, Dr. Armand Hammer, Dr. Ray R. Irani, Rosemary Tomich, and Arthur Groman. Standing, left to right, are: Paul C. Hebner, C. Erwin Piper, Albert Gore, Arthur B. Krim, Robert L. Peterson, Aziz D. Syriani, George O. Nolley, and John W. Kluge.

In my office at Occidental. (Wallace Seawell)

With son Julian, grandson Michael, and great-grandson Armand Douglas Hammer.

few of my well-worn passports. (Bryson)

As I look today. The portrait, by Chinese artist Yao You Xin, is in the boardroom at Occidental Petroleum Corporation.

During the decade following that deal, I worked continually to reduce Occidental's dependence on Libyan oil. It was just too dangerous for the corporation's health that more than 90 percent of our oil should come from a country which was so constantly at odds with the rest of the world, especially America. Our people went looking for oil all over the world, and we were to gamble gigantic sums on exploration and development in the North Sea, Peru, Colombia, Pakistan, Oman, the South China Sea and elsewhere. Luck smiled on many of these efforts and on our moves to strengthen our position as oil producers at home in the USA.

As a result of those moves, which I will describe in more detail later, Occidental was not threatened with extinction when Ronald Reagan, after his election in 1980, went head-to-head with Muammar el-Qaddafi. When diplomatic relations were broken between the US and Libya in 1981, we abided by the President's instructions to withdraw all our American nationals from Libya, and our operations there were continued by employees from other countries, chiefly Great Britain. In June 1985 we announced that the Austrian state oil company, OMV AG, had acquired for cash 25 percent of our remaining interests in Libya.

When President Reagan announced a ban on all US trade with Libya in January 1986, following the terrorist bombings by the Abu Nidal group at Rome and Vienna airports in December 1985, Occidental was able to comply effortlessly. At that moment, thanks to all our previous efforts, our Libyan operation represented just under 1 percent of the total value of the corporation's business worldwide.

In less than twenty years we had gone from absolute dependence on Libya to complete independence. The "whale-sized bite" out of a struggling little California corporation in 1966, when we began exploration there, had become a fleabite out of a giant multinational corporation.

Over those twenty years I have often been attacked by executives of other oil companies for my role in Libya. My answer to those critics is simple: I survived, they didn't. Occidental was many times in danger of complete extinction because of our Libyan operation and the problems it posed. My responsibility was plain and unmistakable: I had to protect the investment of our shareholders. They would have been the ones to suffer from failure in Libya.

Because Qaddafi's regime excites such interest in America, some stupendous nonsense has been written and rumored about my dealings there. The most menacing of the myths—which nearly provoked a full-scale crisis—was that Occidental had secretly offered the CIA millions of dollars to help overthrow Qaddafi.

The first we knew of this invention was on a Saturday noon in the mid-seventies. Larry Stern, then Assistant Editor of the *Washington Post,* delivered the bombshell in a call to the home of Bill McSweeny, President of Occidental International and my main man in Washington.

Larry told Bill that he had the story on good authority and intended to run with it. Apparently his source was a disgruntled former Occidental executive who had told the Los Angeles field agent of the CIA that twenty-four million dollars—who knows where he got the sum?—could be raised from the oil companies in Libya to help depose Qaddafi. Occidental was top of the list of supposed contributors. This story had been relayed to a reporter at the *Washington Post.*

I was in the air en route to New York when Bill got the call from Larry Stern, who agreed to put the story on hold until I could respond. Bill McSweeny reached me with word of the story when my plane touched down in Newark. Using pay phones at the airport, I tried to get to the bottom of the nonsense, while Bill McSweeny contacted William Colby, then head of the CIA.

Colby issued a statement disowning the story and reducing it to a state which not even the Libyans could possibly take seriously. Thus we squeaked out of the vise. If the Libyans had been given reason to think we were trying to subvert their government, we would have been thrown out of the country like a used Kleenex.

Not all the press was as responsible as the *Post,* however. One magazine even alleged that Qaddafi had granted me specially favorable treatment in Libya at the behest of the *Soviets.* The writer's only evidence for this nonsense was that the CIA had detected an increase in coded communications between Libya and Moscow during the week of my negotiations in Tripoli. Since that week was also the first anniversary of the Libyan Revolution, and since Qaddafi was threatening to take on all the major oil companies of the developed world as an anniversary celebration, it is scarcely surprising that the Russians might have had a word or two to say to the Colonel.

The Soviet Union has never had anything to do with our success in Libya. That we had to earn for ourselves. Of course, as of this writing, we are not doing any business at all with Libya. Occidental has stopped all its activities in accordance with President Reagan's request that all US companies cease doing any business with them as of June 30, 1986. We will still retain our property rights, however, and I believe that either Qaddafi will make some offer of a settlement or, if he is replaced by a democratic government, we will someday recover our property.

21

Boardroom Pirates and the Perfidious Shah

Business, in one of its dimensions, is battle. Competitive capitalism inevitably places individuals, companies and corporations in conflict with each other. It is a harsh and bruising system, unkind and unforgiving to the weak and the timid, but it is also, as President Kennedy said, the most durable system we know for the creation of wealth and material progress.

Along with its benefits, my business life has brought me a full share of battles, in boardrooms and in courts. My back has been against the wall so often that I suspect it has left a permanent impression on the bricks. I do not go looking for fights—but when I enter a fight, I fight to win. Here is an account of five of those battles, of widely different natures. The first takes us back to the oil fields of Libya. . . .

Occidental's venture into Libya brought many difficulties and conflicts, but one of them deserves to be described in detail. It was one of the most momentous litigation wars I ever entered, fought before fourteen federal judges, and waged not only in America but in Italy, Switzerland, England, Germany and Belgium. If the ultimate verdict had gone against Occidental, it would have cost us hundreds of millions of dollars, and I would also have lost my good name in the business world and on Wall Street. In this great clash I was fighting not only for business reasons but also for my honor.

As Louis Nizer later wrote in *Reflections Without Mirrors,* "The author of the Arabian Nights could not have provided a more engrossing scenario. We were engaged in a fascinating struggle, filled with mystery, intrigue, forged documents, and miracles, such as the discovery of an ocean of water beneath the Libyan desert. Naturally, then, Hammer enjoyed the drama while hiding his anxiety, while I, as lawyer, shared the anxiety without appreciating the drama."

The story begins in 1964 in England. The highly regarded Allen brothers, Charles and Herbert, heads of the Wall Street investment company which bears their name, suggested to me that a friend of theirs, one Ferdinand Galic, could be very helpful in obtaining oil concessions about to be granted in Libya. Galic was a Czech, married to an American woman and a well-known figure in Parisian society. He claimed to be a friend of a man called General de Rovin who, in his turn, was supposed to be in the good graces of King Idris's Libyan government.

At that time I was still searching around for the most effective approach to the Libyans and, if I gave some of my time to "the Black Prince," I would certainly see men who were introduced and recommended by the Allens.

A meeting was arranged at Claridge's hotel in London. A draft of a letter agreement between Occidental and the Allens was drawn, granting them a 25-percent interest in any concession which "Galic turned up." Costs and profits were to be shared in the same proportion. After the word "costs," however, the Allens then inserted the phrase "to be mutually agreed upon." They did not wish to subject themselves to costs which might run to millions of dollars and wind up with nothing but dry holes. This allowed them to be let out if they so chose. I accepted and, in signing, also took the burden for Occidental alone of millions of dollars for seismograph and other expenses, and later enormous drilling costs, without assurance that there would be a barrel of oil.

Then came the first melodramatic incident. A routine check by a firm of private detectives disclosed that "General de Rovin" was an impostor. He was no general. He was a notorious crook with a long criminal record. He had been a swindler in Paris, Berlin, Vienna and elsewhere before World War II. He had had dealings with the Nazis during the war, for which a French court later sentenced him to death in absentia. In the postwar period he had traveled about South America and Canada passing bad checks. He had returned to France from Argentina under the phony name de Rovin, where he was employed by a firm whose assets he promptly squandered. He was not, in short, the kind of character you would welcome in your home or your boardroom. In the wake of this discovery, we also learned that Galic, too, had no real standing in Libya.

By that time, in any case, I knew that the concessions were not to be granted by negotiation. They were to be awarded on sealed competitive bids.

I decided to cut all links with these men and, early in July 1965, terminated their representation. Since Galic would therefore no longer be in the picture, he could not "turn up" any concessions, and the letter agreement with the Allens also fell. I so wrote them, and they never protested. Not until eighteen months later, when one of the greatest oil gushers in the world's history flooded the sands and floated Occidental's stock upward, did the Allens decide that they were 25-percent partners—although they had not put up a cent of risk capital.

The Allens could not resist the temptation to lay claim to some of Occidental's Libyan wealth, and brought suit in Federal Court in New York. At stake was a quarter interest in Occidental's Libyan operation. The damages sought against Occidental were "in excess of 100 million dollars" and an accounting which might well increase the claim to a quarter of a billion dollars.

A defeat would have been a crippling blow to Occidental—but I refused to settle. I had, in effect, been accused of welshing on a written contract. All of Wall Street and the whole commercial world was watching this case. If I agreed to settle, it would have been tantamount to an admission of guilt, and my word and Occidental's probity would be so disfigured as to be worthless. I was determined to fight, to win, and to be vindicated.

In all its ramifications and complexities, the case was to stretch from September 1967 to September 1974.

In the beginning our position seemed invulnerable. The Allens had avoided the risk of investment. They had not protested Occidental's cancellation notice until a year and a half had elapsed, by which time we had made our tremendous discoveries in Libya. My cancellation of our agreement had not been frivolous. Notorious crooks had been proposed as agents and I had had the right to get rid of them.

All looked well for a victorious defense. But, as Louis Nizer wrote, "was there ever a suit in which a surprise witness or document didn't suddenly appear to upset all calculations?"

The Allens produced such a document. It detonated in our midst and almost drove us to surrender. It was nothing less than a letter from King Idris's Minister of Petroleum Affairs, Fuad Kabazi, on the official stationery of the Libyan government, addressed to Ferdinand Galic, and indicating their intimate relationship and Kabazi's reliance on the Allens' financial ability. In this letter, Kabazi advised Galic that Occidental would receive two concessions. The letter could not have served the Allens better if it had been prepared by them to create a perfect claim against me and Occidental. That was the trouble with it. It was too pat.

When we had recovered our breath, we launched a counterattack to demonstrate what we suspected: that Kabazi, who was no longer a

Minister, had backdated his letter to aid in winning the suit.

The Allens' counsel sought to take Kabazi's testimony in advance of trial. We welcomed a chance to get at him. We might as well know whether we could survive his damaging testimony.

The examination took place in the American Embassy building in London, so that the American Consul could swear in the witness and preside, if necessary, over formal matters, acting as an extension of the United States courts.

Kabazi was a handsome, academically bearded man, with eyes which could have qualified him as a hypnotist. He prided himself on being a poet, which he announced frequently to offset his difficulties with the commercial issues. He had not the slightest idea of Anglo-Saxon judicial procedure. He did not understand the function of cross-examination and considered Louis Nizer's questions an insult to his integrity.

Louis's subtle and skillful cross-examination led Kabazi into trap after trap which he dug for himself. He testified that he was in Tripoli when he typed the letter to Galic—and later, unaware of any contradiction, testified that he had attended council meetings in Beida, seven hundred miles from Tripoli, on dates which included the very day of the letter's date. He said that he had always communicated with Galic in Italian, addressing him as "Dear Ferdo," and received replies in French. English was never used. He overlooked the fact that the questioned letter was in English and addressed, "Dear Sir—"

He conceded that neither Galic's name nor the Allens' was mentioned in Occidental's tender for leases, and that we had attached a letter from the Chase Manhattan Bank showing satisfactory financial support—yet Kabazi's letter claimed he was relying on Allens' financial standing. Again, the contradictions escaped him. And there was an even more subtle contradiction. His testimony was in broken English, the kind one speaks when one is mentally translating into a language and grammar of which one is unsure, but the letter, which he claimed he personally typed, was in perfect English.

When the cross-examination became really cross, and Louis confronted him with a section of the Libyan criminal law which would send him to jail for six months for leaking the grant of concessions in advance, as he had done in his letter, Kabazi rose in mighty indignation at the insult to his honor and stormed out of the room.

Louis moved to strike his entire testimony if he did not return to complete his examination in accordance with the court order, which caused the Allens' lawyers to join with the American Consul in pleading with Kabazi to continue. He finally returned, sulking in his chair as if it were a tent. He continued to make speeches about his being an artist and resenting the insinuations against his honor. But as admissions were wrung from him, his protestations of a poet's honor began to sound more and more hollow.

The contradictions continued. He claimed that he typed the letter on his portable Olivetti typewriter. Where was the typewriter? He fumbled around, resentful of the probing questions, and finally said he had given it as a gift to a friend in Rome, whose name he could not remember. We retained an expert who provided objective evidence that the type on the letter was not even that of an Olivetti—which even the plaintiffs' experts conceded.

Kabazi claimed that he had made a copy of his letter and filed it in the Ministry of Petroleum Affairs. We obtained an authenticated statement from the ministry that no such copy was found in its files and, furthermore, challenged his statement that he had made a carbon copy at all. The original letter was submitted to experts for microscopic and ultraviolet-ray tests to determine whether any traces of carbon could be detected in the indentations caused by the keys striking the paper—and there were none.

Thus the legal contest raged to overcome the surprise Kabazi document presented by the Allens. But the shock of newly discovered documents was not ended. This time it was Occidental which provided the surprise.

A rumor had reached us that "General de Rovin" and Galic had split: the thieves had fallen out. Galic, we learned, had obtained a 10-percent interest in any judgment the Allens recovered in the suit. De Rovin apparently felt he was entitled to part of the loot, but it had been denied to him and the betrayer felt betrayed. Louis Nizer asked his partner, Neil Pollio, to visit de Rovin in Italy to find out whether his bitterness could be turned to our advantage.

De Rovin was so eager to do Galic in that he delivered to us his personal file of correspondence. When we read its contents, we could not believe our eyes. There, set forth in Galic's own handwriting, was a detailed description of the fraudulent arrangement to make it appear that Galic had "turned up" the concessions through his association with Kabazi, and thus give substance to the Allens' suit.

It began to become clear to me. The letter was a scheme purely cooked up by Galic, de Rovin and Kabazi. The Allens were not participants in the scam. They had had blind faith in their personal friend Galic, and he deceived them too.

We laid a deep trap for Galic. Armed with his letters, Louis Nizer deposed him for days without disclosing that we had his writings hidden, like explosives, under the table. He felt free to paint a fictitious picture of his intimacy with Kabazi and the way he was responsible for everything good which had happened to Occidental. Louis led him on, each question phrased closer and closer to the contradictions in his own handwriting, which Louis had memorized.

Then, when the examination seemed to have been exhausted, and opposing counsel asked whether we would be through in an hour or so, Louis began all over again. But this time, after quoting Galic's previous days' answers from transcripts, Louis confronted Galic with his letters to de Rovin. His own words gave the lie to almost every answer he had made. Instead of "palship" with Kabazi while he was Minister, he wrote to de Rovin that he had tried to arrange a meeting with Kabazi twice, but that Kabazi would not see him.

Instead of learning in advance from Kabazi that concessions would be awarded to Occidental, he confessed knowing nothing and suggesting that perhaps someone else might find out for him.

At one point he wrote ruefully, "I wanted to be the first to announce to Dr. Hammer, but I see he is informed before everybody. I do not know from where. . . . He is always in advance of anybody."

In another letter he said he had learned that "Kabazi did nothing at all" to obtain the concessions.

The most embarrassing of all was Galic's letter to de Rovin, revealing the Allens' predicament. Galic wrote, "I relied on your [de Rovin's] statement that the concessions could be obtained by negotiation and then it was by tough bidding. This is what Mr. Allen reproached me yesterday. You could have avoided that. That will be the weak point in my lawsuit."

As he was confronted with these devastating letters, Galic's face seemed to turn the colors of the Libyan flag. Then, in order to salvage his prior testimony, he condemned his own letters as lies, "all lies." After a while he got tired of calling himself a liar and shifted to "baloney." He stuttered and fumed as the contradictions in his own words struck him.

More revealing than Galic's disintegration was the conduct of the Allens' lawyer. He put a wood pencil in his mouth and, as the letters unfolded, he actually bit it in half. Meanwhile, as the devastating details emerged, Herbert Allen pushed his chair back, foot by foot, from the table where he had been sitting with Galic, as if to separate himself as far as possible from Galic's disgrace.

The Allens approached Louis Nizer and Arthur Groman, asking for a relatively small settlement to end the case. At lunch in my Greenwich Village house, Arthur said, "Armand, why not settle now? The amount they want is peanuts—less than your legal bills will be if you go on to win the case."

"No," I said. "Those bastards called me a liar and I'll see them in hell before I'll settle. We will win this case. Let's go to trial."

The trial lasted three weeks. At its conclusion, the judge ripped into Galic's "perfidious conduct," proclaimed his testimony "utterly lacking in credibility," and Kabazi's replete "with inherent contradictions and implausibilities" and condemned the Kabazi letter as "deliberately contrived and written some time after the awards were announced, predated, and sent to Galic in an effort to aid Galic in a contemplated lawsuit against Occidental."

The Allens, meanwhile, suffered not only from the Galic-Kabazi debacle, but also from their own inconsistent conduct. After the cancellation of the agreement, Occidental had floated a sixty-one-million-dollar debenture issue, and the Allens had been one of the underwriters. As such, Allen & Company, Inc., had to sign a statement to reveal whether it had any financial interest in Occidental. Had they believed that they had a 25-percent interest in Occidental's Libyan concessions, they would have said so—but they answered that they had no "material relationship" with Occidental, which, we argued, demonstrated that they had accepted my cancellation letter and did not consider themselves partners.

The court agreed. The proof, it said, was "overwhelming."

Louis Nizer commented wisely on the conclusion of the case: "As in every case," Louis wrote, "there was an equitable principle at the core. Can one lie in wait to see how a risky enterprise turns out and then announce that he was a partner all the time? The courts have dealt with many such cases, particularly in mining, where millions may be lost or won. One judge expressed this age-old principle in colloquial terms: 'Heads I win and tails you lose, cannot, I fancy, be the basis of an equity.' Judge Weinfeld put it another way: The Allens 'sought the best of two worlds. If oil was struck they could claim a twenty-five-percent profit in the joint venture; if it turned out to be a dry hole, they could disavow liability for twenty-five percent of the loss, pointing to Occidental's termination letter. The Allens cannot have it both ways.'"

I was vindicated. I had saved my name, my honor—and a quarter of a billion dollars.

The second battle concerns a little place called Umm Al Qaywayn. When I die, the name of Umm Al Qaywayn may be found stamped on my heart in indelible bruises. I'll bet that not one in a thousand of my readers will even be able to pronounce the name, let alone say where it is in the world, yet that obscure sheikhdom in the Persian Gulf caused me almost as much trouble, worry, expense in lawyers' fees and legal conflict than the rest of Occidental's worldwide interests put together. It was a thorn in my flesh for years on end.

My good friend the late John Mecom introduced me to the idea of exploring for oil in Umm Al Qaywayn. He thought that he was doing me a kindness.

John Mecom's company had been drilling for oil off the shores of Umm Al Qaywayn in the late sixties. Geologists' reports on the concessions very powerfully suggested the presence of large reserves, but John was unable to carry the drilling work through to its conclusion before his lease expired. He suggested that Occidental try to take over his concession.

I got in touch with the Sheikh Sultan, the absolute ruler of Umm Al Qaywayn, and arranged to meet his son, the Crown Prince, at Claridge's in 1969.

The titles "Sheikh Sultan" and "Crown Prince" carry automatic associations in Western minds, especially since the explosive growth of Arab oil wealth in the last twenty years. They conjure images of cultivated and sophisticated Muslim potentates like the Saudi Arabian kings and princes, deftly managing the multibillion-dollar interests of their countries in all the complexities of their dealings with the developed world. These images do not apply to the rulers of Umm Al Qaywayn.

For more than a century, until it became one of the United Arab Emirates, Umm Al Qaywayn had been one of the Trucial sheikhdoms of the Persian Gulf under the protection of the United Kingdom. The British government was in charge of Umm Al Qaywayn's international relations, defense and the jurisdiction of the territories, including territorial waters.

Those responsibilities cannot have caused many sleepless nights for the Queen and her ministers. Administering Umm Al Qaywayn's affairs would have called for less effort than running a remote rural county. The territory stretched about twenty miles inland from a fifteen-mile coastland. The population of the sheikhdom in the late sixties was about four thousand (nobody had ever counted every head). The *total* income of the state, before the discovery of oil, was estimated to be about twenty-two thousand dollars a year, mainly from the export of dried fish. There was one school and one paved road. Occasionally, a transient doctor would visit the place, but otherwise no health care facilities existed. In 1968 water and electricity arrived for the first time in the village which was called the capital of the sheikhdom but, by the end of that year, only ninety applications had been made for service connections. The royal household was the first to be connected.

The royal household was not, however, housed in a palace or even much of a house. When John Mecom's people conducted their early negotiations for the offshore lease, they reported that they "attended several meetings which took place in a building in the form of a glorified tent."

The ruler of Umm Al Qaywayn was little more than the undisputed head of an extended family. He had all the power and nobody could or would oppose him. He had no cabinet, no independent civil service and no judiciary. All the revenues of the state were his to spend as he liked. When the sheikh sold concessions for oil exploration in his territory, the payment he received was his own personal property. As he chose, he could spend the money on schools, roads and hospitals for his people or he could stash it in bank accounts in Switzerland.

The Crown Prince demanded a million dollars for the Sheikh Sultan. We gave it to him. Sometime later the SEC wanted to know if the million wasn't really an under-the-table bribe by which we unfairly obtained favorable treatment.

The answer was: it couldn't possibly be. You couldn't possibly bribe the Sheikh to influence himself. He wasn't employed by anybody and he had no superior. Payments made to the Sheikh through his son the Crown Prince were simply part of the payments for a concession. If any other oil company had offered a larger payment to the ruler, they could have received the concession.

I often wish they had.

On November 18, 1969, the Crown Prince and I signed a concession agreement by which Oxy was granted, for a period of forty years, the exclusive rights to explore for and recover oil within all territorial and offshore waters of Umm Al Qaywayn. The British Foreign Office approved the concession agreement.

Frances and I flew out to Umm Al Qaywayn to join the Sheikh and his family in celebration of the contract. It was an unusual party. We sat on the floor of the Sheikh's palatial tent and feasted from an array of delicacies offered by deeply attentive servants. Frances was curious about one of these treats, which she couldn't identify. She was sorry she asked: as a special mark of favor, she had been offered the sheep's eyes.

Anyway, we left Umm Al Qaywayn feeling very happy and hoping that we might have similar success in the neighboring sheikhdoms of Ajman and Sharjah. One of our Bakersfield geologists quickly signed a concession agreement with the Sheikh of Ajman, but for some reason turned down a similar deal offered by the Ruler of Sharjah. I never knew why, but that geologist is no longer at Occidental. Shortly thereafter the Ruler of Sharjah announced that he had granted a concession to a small oil company from Bakersfield, California, called Buttes.

I felt the Sharjah concession had been filched from under our noses—but we didn't cry. We got on with testing our concession area in the waters of Umm Al Qaywayn, and spent millions of dollars on seismic surveys. The tests indicated the prospect of oil and gas in very large quantities in strata wholly within our concession area, and we began drilling.

Then it happened. Late in March 1970 Buttes announced that, operating under the terms of its Sharjah concession, it intended to commence drilling *precisely* on the spot where we had conducted our successful tests and had begun our drilling work.

By this time I had been in the oil business for nearly fifteen years, and I thought I had seen most of its wildest and wooliest behavior, but this was the most outrageous act I had ever witnessed. I assumed, however, that Buttes's action would be legally indefensible and that they would be shooed off our concession back where they belonged. I had a surprise in store.

The Ruler of Sharjah declared that on September 10, 1969, he had issued a decree extending the territorial waters of Sharjah from *three* to *twelve* miles, to include the island of Abu Musa off the coast of Umm Al Qaywayn. Conveniently for Buttes, this "extension" brought the exact spot where we were preparing to drill for oil within territorial waters claimed by Sharjah.

Nobody had ever heard of this decree before then. On all the maps furnished to us by the British Foreign Office, on which we had based our negotiations with the Sheikh of Umm Al Qaywayn, the territorial limit of Sharjah's waters was plainly shown to be three miles. A distinctive odor hung over the whole affair. I made the obvious assumption that the Ruler's "decree" had been backdated. When he was asked why he hadn't published the decree and where it might be, the Ruler of Sharjah answered that he had put it in his pocket and forgotten all about it. I am not joking. That is what he said.

It fell to the British government to try to make sense of this fantastic tangle. The Foreign Office, hoping to avoid conflict between the sheikhdoms, instructed both Occidental and Buttes to stop drilling.

I would not accept this instruction. We had acted honestly, we had made a very large investment and we were entitled to proceed. It took the presence of a Royal Navy frigate—and Royal Air Force planes—to stop us from sending our drilling barge into the waters.

Faced with this display of force, we had no choice but to back off and await a fair adjudication by the British, but the British were in no hurry to give a ruling. Their responsibilities for the Trucial States were scheduled to expire on November 30, 1971, when the United Arab Emirates would come into being. If the British could hold the problem in abeyance until that date, it would be off their hands. A power vacuum was created.

On the other side of the Persian Gulf, in Tehran, the Shah of Iran was poised to fill that vacuum.

In May of 1970, Iran declared that the island of Abu Musa, far from belonging to Sharjah, was actually the property of Iran. The

National Iranian Oil Company, on the Shah's behalf, claimed that ancient title established Iran's right to the island.

Curiously enough, Iran had never bothered to make this claim before. Now, however, with the scent of oil in his nostrils, the Shah threatened to invade Sharjah to claim this dot of land which had suddenly become so vital to his imperial prestige.

The entrance of the Shah into this drama lifted the action out of the obscurity of a tiny and unimportant theater and onto the big stage of world politics. Now we really were dealing with a sophisticated Muslim potentate, one of the biggest of all the big players.

I flew to Tehran and was received by the Shah at the Gulistan Palace. No royal personage was ever more conscious than he of the dignity of majesty. He had cultivated a manner of almost inhuman suavity and self-control, as if to distance himself from the rest of humanity.

Like many other human beings, however, the Shah was not altogether trustworthy. In the course of this visit to Tehran, he set me up for a two-fisted drubbing of regal double-dealing. The Shah was the opposite of the Sheikh of Umm Al Qaywayn. Faintly but discernibly contemptuous of big business as a vulgar game played by lesser forms of human life, the Shah made it clear that he had higher things on his mind than the discussion of major deals which reached into billions of dollars. Far from being intimidated by American businessmen, the Shah felt perfectly at liberty to cheat them.

I had gone to Tehran with a massive international proposal which would have far-reaching effects on the US economy and the balance of power in the Middle East. Inspired by Lyndon Johnson, I had offered to act as an intermediary in a huge deal between the Shah and the aerospace giant McDonnell-Douglas.

I should double back for a moment and explain how this proposal emerged out of my relationship with President Johnson and his wife, Lady Bird.

With Lyndon Johnson, I had one of the easiest and most open relationships I have enjoyed with any President. While we saw each other infrequently, we exchanged many letters on issues of domestic and foreign policy. You could say anything you thought to Lyndon Johnson, for he relished candor, directness and open argument. He appointed me a member of the Public Advisory Committee on US Trade Policy, and I worked closely with him on his efforts to reduce the likelihood of nuclear war. During his term of office, he pulled off an historic coup in the signing of his Nuclear Non-Proliferation Treaty, which he called "the most important international agreement in the field of disarmament since the nuclear age began." After the signing of this treaty, I received a letter from James Jones, LBJ's Special Assistant at the White House, dated July 25, 1968. He wrote: "He [the President] is grateful for your partnership in helping to achieve it and is proud to know that your leadership will assist this nation's efforts to move beyond this historical and hopeful hour."

On May 22, 1970, Frances and I flew from New York to Washington in my plane to pick up LBJ and Lady Bird and take them on to a weekend at the LBJ ranch. The Johnsons put on a movie show for us on the first evening. I was sitting between the President and James McDonnell, the boss of McDonnell-Douglas. LBJ turned to me and said, "Mr. McDonnell has a proposal to make which I think might interest you."

"What is it?"

"Well," he said, "we have the chance to get a big order for fighter planes from the Shah—a couple of hundred planes worth several hundred million dollars."

"Congratulations," I said.

"Yes, thank you, it's great, but there's a catch," he said. "The Shah wants to pay us in oil. I don't know what to do with oil. I was thinking maybe you would like to take the oil and pay us in cash."

"I certainly would," I said. Oil supplies from the Shah might allow me to keep supplying Occidental's European customers while the Libyans were being so rough. Moreover, if I did the Shah a favor in this regard, he might be more inclined to act reasonably toward Occidental over the question of Umm Al Qaywayn.

My meeting with the Shah at the Gulistan Palace was meant to settle those two points. He told me that he saw a chance in the McDonnell-Douglas deal to break the monopoly of the Seven Sisters and he thanked me for offering to help.

He also thanked me for having benefited all the oil-producing nations in my recent settlement with Libya. This, he said, had relegated the Seven Sisters from their position of absolute power and had obliged them to pay him more for the oil they purchased from Iran. Considering the amount of trouble I had got into for my Libyan settlement, the Shah's compliment was, at best, backhanded and I accepted it with a somewhat rueful effort at a smile. The smile grew harder to maintain as the Shah went on and said, "So long as the world demand for oil keeps growing and you in America do not have a substitute, we shall continue to raise and raise the price."

On the question of Occidental's thwarted drillings in Umm Al Qaywayn, the Shah very grandly told me to set my mind at ease. It was simply a matter of a local misunderstanding, he said. He would prevail on the Ruler of Sharjah to be reasonable and restore Occidental's legitimate rights, he assured me.

I left Tehran feeling confident that justice would be done, and that I was about to do a magnificent deal for Occidental in getting the Shah's oil and lifting the Libyan gorilla off my back. The Shah promptly reneged on both his undertakings, and Occidental's position, on all sides, grew ten times worse.

First he tricked me over the fighters-for-oil deal. After brief negotiations with the National Iranian Oil Company, the contract for the deal was to be signed in Athens in July 1970. I flew there and joined up with Bill Bellano, my then-President and Chief Operating Officer, Claude Geismar, and John Tigrett, our consultant. NIOC sent a troop of negotiators.

When the contract was all finished, I signed it. That's what you do with a finished agreement—you sign it. The Iranians, however, said that before they signed it, they would like to read it over again.

"All right," I said. "It seems odd to me, seeing as we've just been going over it in every detail and I've already signed it. Why don't you read it again while I go to the bathroom?"

I was out of the room for not more than five minutes. When I returned, the Iranians had vanished.

"Where are they?" I asked Bellano and Geismar.

"They left," they said.

"Did they sign the agreement?"

"No," they said.

"What!" I exploded. "You let them go without signing!"

"They said they wanted to show it to the Shah. They said that they'd sign it as soon as they got to Tehran," they answered weakly.

"You fools!" I shouted. "How could you let them get away with that? They were supposed to have full authority to sign. That was the basis of the meeting, that's why we're here. Don't you see what they're going to do? The Shah will show the agreement to the Seven Sisters with my name on it and then they'll sing his tune. They'll do anything to keep us out of Iran."

That's what the Shah did. The Seven Sisters took the Shah's oil, paying him more than had been agreed on with Occidental and taking the loss to keep us out. Shortly afterward the price of oil rose steeply. Without the contract we lost several hundred million dollars.

This display of chicanery wasn't enough for the Shah. Next, he gave it to us over Umm Al Qaywayn.

Four days before the British Protectorate treaty expired, under threat of forcible occupation by Iran, the Ruler of Sharjah surrendered to the Shah and agreed that Iranian troops should occupy Abu Musa and fly the Iranian flag there. The agreement further provided that the territorial waters of Abu Musa should be extended to twelve miles, to include the concession area granted by Sharjah to Buttes.

In other words the concession originally granted to Occidental by Umm Al Qaywayn and invaded by Buttes as a result of Sharjah's fraudulent action had now been annexed by Iran through an extension of the territorial waters of the island of Abu Musa. I realize that sentence is hard to follow. To put it in simple terms, we were robbed.

Our concession area was farmed out by Buttes to other oil companies, including Cities Service and Ashland. They eventually developed an important oil field. The total loss to Occidental, including development costs, legal expenses and lost revenues, amounted to hundreds of millions of dollars. No legal remedy was available.

We tried to bring suit for compensation, arguing our case in United States courts and in the Royal Courts of Justice in the Strand in London. We got nowhere and we got nothing. The essential obstacle was that the laws of sovereign states do not provide for other sovereign states to be sued for commercial misconduct. If a sovereign state chooses to annex a corporation's rights and properties, and can get away with it, there is no recourse in law. That, of course, is how wars get started.

One benefit came out of the general fiasco of Umm Al Qaywayn. The legal adviser to Umm Al Qaywayn on behalf of the British government had been Sir John Foster KBE, a fellow of All Souls, Oxford, and one of the most distinguished men in Britain. I was enchanted by his mind and dazzled by his abilities and I had the good luck to be able to persuade him to become my attorney and join the board of Occidental. For the rest of his life, until his untimely death in February 1982, Sir John brought wisdom, charm and gaiety to the councils of the Occidental board. I wish I had him beside me today.

The last consequence of the Umm Al Qaywayn imbroglio was the most bizarre. The Shah of Iran tried to buy Occidental.

When I saw him in Tehran, the Shah had toyed lightly with ideas of mutual ventures between Occidental and the National Iranian Oil Company. We had supertankers on our inventory then, with which we could freight crude from Iran's Kharg Island; and there were other commercial possibilities between us. Nothing came of these notions, however, and after the Shah's perfidy over the matter of Umm Al Qaywayn, I was not in much of a mood to follow them up with him. Then, with no notice or warning, on May 5, 1976, I received a baffling telex from A. A. Hoveyda, the Shah's Prime Minister.

He informed me that a Mr. Cyrus Ansary—brother, it turned out, of Iran's Minister of Economics and Finance, Hushang Ansary—was on his way to meet me. Why, he didn't say. Cyrus Ansary duly came to see me at my office in Los Angeles. He did not beat about the bush.

"Doctor Hammer," he said, "I am empowered to inform you that the Shah would like to buy shares in Occidental Petroleum."

"Well," I said, "the Shah is quite welcome to buy shares in Occidental. In fact, there is nothing to prevent him. Shares are available on the stock market."

"No," he said. "The Shah wishes to buy a block of shares directly from Occidental."

"How much of a block has he in mind?" I asked.

"He would like to obtain ten percent of the company's shares now, with an option to purchase a further ten percent."

I controlled my expression. A 10-percent holding in the company's shares would make the Shah by far the biggest stockholder. It would also cost him at least $125 million in cash.

At that moment the corporation was strong in cash and had no urgent need for more, but the Shah was leading a drive for modernization in Iran, which opened immense opportunities there for us in the manufacturing and sale of chemical fertilizers. On the other hand, 10 percent of the company would give the Shah a commanding position from which to take over Occidental or mount a raid.

Mr. Ansary assured me that the Shah's motives were wholly friendly. He wanted to benefit from the company's present management, not to replace it. As a mark of good faith, he wanted only one nominated Director to be included on Occidental's board. I let Mr. Ansary know that we were willing to discuss the offer and take it further. He relayed that message to Tehran and the instructions came by return that the deal should be consummated with all speed.

Crews of lawyers were hired by both sides and convened in New York. There may have been as many as thirty lawyers working for weeks on end to refine the draft agreement which, by mid-August, was nearly an inch thick and ready for signing. I had insisted on one immovable point: if the Iranians ever wanted to sell their block of shares, they had to offer them first to us and they should not be allowed to sell to anybody else until and unless we had turned them down. That point was acceptable to the Iranians throughout the negotiations.

Finally, word came that Hushang Ansary would meet me in Paris to sign the deal on behalf of his government. All the lawyers on both sides promptly loaded themselves into a plane and took off for Paris, while I left from Los Angeles with Arthur Groman in my own plane.

When Fred Gross put the plane down in Newfoundland to refuel, he was told that there was no fuel. The airport was clean out of gas. Fred came to me with the news and a long face.

"When will they get some more?" I asked.

"In two weeks," he replied, his face growing longer.

"Two weeks!" I cried. "Is this a joke?"

I went to the pay phones and called Pierre Trudeau, Prime Minister of Canada—no, I *did* know him. Within two hours we were on our way to Paris.

Our team occupied the Ritz Hotel and the Iranians took a floor in the Meurice Hotel.

The last details of the deal were being stitched into the agreement when I received a call from Hushang Ansary asking me to visit him in his hotel suite. He said that it was vital that I should go alone, without a lawyer.

I was suspicious. I had an urgent conference with Arthur Groman and he said, "I don't like the sound of this, Armand. I think I'd better come along with you, regardless of what they say."

When we got into the Minister's suite, he and his brother Cyrus received us with emollient charm. Nothing was wrong, they assured us; the deal was fine and Hushang was ready to sign.

"There is just one small detail which the Shah would like to modify," he added.

"Which detail is that?" I asked.

"The Shah does not approve of the stipulation that he can't sell the stock to anybody else without offering it to you first. He would like that clause deleted from the agreement."

I got out of my chair and said, "The deal is off."

"You can't mean that," exclaimed the dumbfounded Minister.

"I certainly do," I said. "The deal is off. Come on, Arthur. Let's go."

Arthur and I marched right out of the room, got in our car and were driven to the Ritz. There we assembled all our lawyers and told them to pack. Within an hour and a half we had flown out of Paris.

The perfidy of the Shah would be hard to beat. That was the third time he had tried to stick it to me. I was insulted that he could think I would fall for such a crude tactic. It wouldn't have deceived me when I started out in business as a boy with my Hupmobile delivering candy.

If the Shah had been entitled to sell his block of stock where he chose, he could have overturned the existing management of Occidental with a takeover tender at slightly above the market value of our shares. Or he could have delivered us, chained and bound, into the hands of one of the Seven Sisters, which could have done the same and we wouldn't have had a chance of a fight.

In view of the Shah's ultimate fate and the tragic fate of Iran at the hands of the mullahs, it was a mighty good thing for Occidental that he blew the deal by being so devious. Desperately complicated and exacting as it has been to manage our Libyan interests, I count myself fortunate that I never had to try to bargain with the Ayatollah Khomeini.

*   *   *

I might have been able to fend off a possible takeover attempt by the Shah, but he wasn't the only shark in the waters. In the mid-seventies the corporate raiders were out in full force. The one I had to repel was mounted by Standard Oil of Indiana, one of the mightiest of the majors. I guess they must have thought of themselves as a full-scale battleship and of Occidental as a single-masted tub. When the Chairman of Standard, John Swearingen, came swinging aboard Occidental with his corporate cutlass in his teeth, he probably thought he was going to capture us without a fight.

He called from Chicago on November 13, 1974, and asked if he could see me in my office in Los Angeles the next day. I thought he probably wanted to talk about our oil shale operations in Colorado, where we had recently been attracting a lot of publicity because we had successfully experimented with extracting oil from shale underground. I guessed that he might want to mount a joint venture. That would have been very welcome as a topic for negotiation. I invited him to come along.

He arrived in the company of Robert Greenhill, a senior executive of Morgan Stanley. Our preliminary exchanges were very courteous. I told them all about the latest development in our shale venture. They were politely attentive.

It was obvious, however, that they had not come to talk about shale. John Swearingen shifted in his chair and said, "I've come here, Doctor Hammer, to make you an offer for your company."

My answer was direct. "The company's not for sale," I said.

"Well," he said, smiling patiently, "I think you'd be wise to listen to my offer before you turn it down. We will pay you seventeen dollars a share for all your shares and take care of the preferred as well."

That day Occidental stock was trading at $14 a share on the New York Stock Exchange. Fifty-five million shares of common stock and fifteen million shares of preferred were outstanding. Swearingen's offer was thus for $1.35 billion.

"Naturally," he went on, "we'll take care of key Occidental personnel, including, of course, yourself. We'd encourage your exploration program in the North Sea and elsewhere and provide fresh capital for your oil shale experiments in Colorado. The merged company would be one of the top ten industrial companies in America. Our joint sales in 1974 would be nearly seventeen billion dollars."

He must have thought that I would be unable to resist the temptation of the twenty-million-dollar profit which I would personally make on my shares in Occidental. I disabused him.

"I'm willing to discuss this offer with members of our board," I said, "but I can tell you now that I will not recommend this. The company is worth more than seventeen dollars a share."

"Think it over," he said. "I'm going to my hotel now. I'll call you tomorrow."

As soon as they had gone, I called a meeting in my office of all the company's top executives and those directors who lived in Los Angeles. "We're about to go to war," I told them. What had particularly gotten under my skin was that Swearingen had more or less *told* me that Indiana Standard was taking over. He hadn't *asked*.

He was about to push even harder. He called me the same afternoon and said, "In accordance with the SEC rules governing disclosure, I'm issuing a press release to say that we have had talks about a possible merger."

I couldn't believe my ears.

"I can't stop you putting out a release," I said, "but I will absolutely deny that we have shown any interest in your offer."

The release was published. I instructed our lawyers to issue a denial of any interest in their offer, which was grossly inadequate, and to bring suit against Morgan Stanley for conflict of interest in representing Standard of Indiana—they had only just been representing us in a major real estate acquisition.

I kicked up a storm all over Washington, complaining to the Federal Trade Commission that Standard Indiana was in violation of antitrust regulations, and on December 3 I appeared before a Senate subcommittee on the oil industry. I opened my remarks by saying:

> I believe these hearings are of greater national importance than any in which I have previously participated. The freedom and independence of Occidental Petroleum is at stake. This is a matter of vital importance to our three hundred thousand shareholders, to our thirty-two thousand employees and to the many companies, large and small, with whom we deal in the free marketplace.
>
> If Occidental falls into the hands of one of the major oil companies, then the American people will have lost the largest independent oil company and, with it, a strong champion of competition in the world of oil, coal, chemicals, fertilizers and international trade.
>
> What Standard is embarked on is conquest, plain and simple; conquest insidious to its anticompetitive consequences and overwhelming in its economic implications, a conquest which is an unprecedented challenge to the antitrust policies of the United States. If Standard succeeds, it will accomplish the largest corporate seizure ever consummated in the United States—and a message will reverberate through every competitive zone of American business: Free enterprise and independence are dead!
>
> If Standard can so arrogantly pull this off, then how can any businessman consider himself safe? Standard apparently believes that

they can accomplish their monopolistic drive because no power can stop them. I say this time they can be stopped. I say that Occidental's management and shareholders will stop them. I say that our government will stop them, not because it defends Occidental but because I believe the laws of our land are designed to prevent rapacious takeovers!

John Swearingen acted as if he were pained and mystified by the vehemence of my attack. He said he found it difficult to understand my—or anybody else's—fear of bigness. Those who took this position, he said, displayed "economic know-nothingism on a par with Chairman Mao's injunction to the Chinese to make steel in backyard furnaces."

The Senators listened, however, and referred the takeover bid to the Federal Trade Commission, which immediately prepared for lengthy hearings and a possible antitrust action.

We had subpoenaed all of Standard Indiana's records and had subjected them to minute scrutiny by our lawyers. In those records, our attorneys dug up a document which had the explosive power of a blockbuster. It was a report, prepared by an executive of Standard, which gave details of a plan to put some of their independent competitors out of business. It proposed, for example, that in the Chicago area, Standard should open its own filling station opposite the filling stations of every independent. They should then cut prices at their pumps well below the price any independent could afford to sell at—even though it would mean a loss to Standard Indiana—and thus drive the independents to the wall.

No document could more vividly have illustrated Standard's monopolistic drive, and it would have created a scandal if we could have published it. We were bound, however, by the conditions under which we had obtained the document, which swore us to confidentiality. My attorneys warned me that I must not divulge the information to anybody.

The dilemma drove me nearly crazy with frustration. Here I was with the weapon in my hand to kill the Standard Indiana takeover bid, and I was stayed from executing the fatal blow.

The FTC investigators appointed to examine the takeover bid came first to Occidental's offices in Los Angeles. We met them in our boardroom and I sat in on the preliminary discussions. They said that they were going, next day, to Standard of Indiana's offices in Chicago.

"When you get there," I said, "may I recommend that you be sure to look very carefully through their files in connection with competition from independents? That question, after all, is the nub of our opposition to this takeover bid."

The FTC investigators must have taken the bait, because immediately after their visit to Standard Indiana headquarters in Chicago, UPI carried a wire-story headlined STANDARD OF INDIANA DROPS OCCIDENTAL BID. As *Forbes* magazine put it, "Hammer in the first round by knockout."

No major ever attempted a serious bid again—although, just to make sure, we asked Joe Flom—the greatest expert in takeovers—to devise a series of legal measures which would safeguard our independence. He came up with a detailed plan which will make it decidedly impractical for any hostile takeover to be attempted in the future.

There are other kinds of takeover attempts, however—the kind that come from within. Most of the Directors on my board have been loyal to me through the years, but there have been times when dissident groups formed, usually around the figurehead of the incumbent President, with the ambition of bringing me down. It's a common enough occurrence in business, and it keeps you on your toes, to say the least.

The last two battles I have to describe have to do with exactly those circumstances, though in vastly different ways.

The first is the story of Joe Baird. In 1973 I nominated Joe Baird, an investment banker who had been with Smith Barney and had formed a bank of his own in London, to be the President of Occidental. It was a time of worldwide oil crisis; Oxy was threatened with nationalization in Libya; the stock had slumped to as little as seven dollars; the banks were pressing us very hard; and I thought we should have a banker as President to deal with them. Everything was fine through most of the seventies. Until he got the idea that we should take over the Mead Corporation.

He led me to understand that James McSwiney, the Chairman of Mead, would welcome a bid, and that was good news. With its extensive interests and resources in lumber and the manufacture of paper products, Mead looked to have an ideal fit with Occidental. I hastened to meet Mr. McSwiney at the Mead headquarters in Dayton, Ohio. Joe Baird came with me. Our reception was less than enthusiastic.

Mr. McSwiney looked at me coldly across his desk and said, "Let it be plainly understood, Doctor Hammer, that this company is not for sale. I have nothing more to say. You will be hearing from our attorney, Mr. Joe Flom."

I was surprised, since Joe Flom had already represented us in a proposed acquisition of a Canadian-American company. He was the outstanding corporate attorney on takeovers in America. It is a great comfort to have Joe on your side and a sore distress to have him against you.

We left the room in confusion. I turned to Baird and said, "What have you got me into here? I thought this was going to be a friendly takeover."

"Take no notice of McSwiney," Joe said. "If we go on with our bid, he won't be able to carry his shareholders with him. We've made them a very generous offer and they'll have to accept it. We'll win, you'll see."

However, I pointed out to him, since Joe Flom had represented us previously, he knew a lot about our company. There was an obvious conflict of interest, and I told Baird to call him and get him to withdraw as Mead's attorney.

Flom said he hadn't really done much for Occidental, and so didn't know much about our business, but if Oxy insisted, then of course he'd withdraw. Joe Baird never insisted. He said, "We'll let him continue to handle Mead's case."

The next thing I knew, I was walking into my office and found the corridors almost blocked with packing cases piled almost to the ceiling. Joe Flom had subpoenaed all of Occidental's corporate records *for years*. A whole warehouseful of documents had been emptied for him.

My attorneys tried to calm me down. "Don't worry," they said, "we've given him so much that he'll never be able to get through it."

You don't know Joe Flom, I thought.

Joe hired a team of twenty top-flight attorneys to examine our records. They worked in shifts, day and night, minutely scrutinizing every document in Occidental's twenty-year history. They were looking for any material which might embarrass us and make the Mead shareholders less willing to accept our bid. They found it.

Joe Flom assembled a raft of allegations against Occidental, many of which resulted in SEC complaints, and though we took care of them all, he had achieved his purpose. No acquisition was worth this battery of problems. I told Joe Baird that we had to pull out. To my astonishment he disagreed and said that he would oppose me. Now it had become more than a ghastly messed-up takeover bid—now it was a fight to see who was CEO of Occidental.

"All right," I said, "we'll go before the board and see who they support."

He made his speech to the board. I made mine. The vote was taken, and only three hands were raised in Joe's favor. That was the end of Joe Baird's presidency.

I had survived that internal takeover attempt without much difficulty. The one that followed, however, was much worse—the most bruising and bloodiest round of all.

David Murdock, the prominent California financier and developer, began his attack on my job from a position of natural advantage: his office was and remains above me. When we first met, he had offices, formerly occupied by Howard Hughes, on the sixteenth floor of Occidental's building. My office was then directly beneath his on the fifteenth floor. At that time he was constructing Murdock Plaza, a tower of some eighteen stories, on the corner diagonally across the street from our building. When David topped out his building and moved his own office across the street, I took over the sixteenth floor of our building and installed my office there.

David Murdock is one smart man, and he may be characterized as a business barracuda. Gifted with a sharp intelligence, he is a street fighter who got his start in business slinging hash to customers in his own diner. The combination makes him a deadly adversary.

He is also capable of an ingratiating charm one day and a steely abruptness the next. It took some time for this picture of his character to form clearly in my mind. By the time it had come into focus, it was almost too late: he was poised to strike and get the company in his jaws. My place in his plans was in the trash can.

I had met Murdock occasionally in the elevators at our building, but I did not know him at all well before he called me one day and invited me to lunch. The invitation was not purely companionable. He wanted my help.

He had already made a name for himself as one of America's leading breeders of Arabian horses. At his spread in Ventura, he had dozens of the most magnificent specimens in the Western world. He drew me a very enthusiastic and convincing picture of his Arabians' business, presenting me with figures which showed terrific appreciations in value on his investments.

Like everybody involved in breeding Arabian horses, Murdock knew that many of the greatest Arabians were in the Soviet Union. He wanted to buy horses from the Russians, but he had no experience of dealing with Soviets. He asked me to help him, make introductions, smooth the bureaucratic formalities and generally support him with my name.

For providing these favors, my reward was to be in heaven, I guess, because nothing was offered on earth.

I said, "Look, I'll be glad to help you, but I want you to take me in as a partner, and I'll put up my money to bring in these Russian horses."

He said, "I already have a partner."

"So why don't you have a partnership of three, with me as the third?" I said.

He looked doubtful. "I don't know."

"Well, think it over," I said. "If you want my help, that's what it will take."

It didn't take long. Murdock talked to his partners. They said that they would welcome me. We drew up an agreement and set off for Moscow on June 20, 1981.

The trip was highly successful and a lot of fun. Murdock was very attentive to me and Frances, a delightful companion, witty, warm and charming. His business brain was indisputably first-rate and I found his conversation very interesting.

We wanted to acquire Pesniar, the greatest of the Russian Arabian stallions. The Soviets didn't want to discuss a sale. They froze us out. I used my contacts and took the matter all the way to the top, persuading the Minister of Agriculture to look favorably on our proposition. We got Pesniar for a million dollars. I became a partner with David Murdock. I also created a division of Occidental called Oxy Arabians to develop an independent interest in this fascinating business.

During one of our talks on the trip, Murdock interested me in the Iowa Beef Processors, Inc., in which he was the controlling stockholder. He talked the company up very well, telling me that it had 25 percent of the whole boxed-beef market and praising Iowa Beef's Chief Executive, Bob Peterson. We made a deal. Iowa Beef merged with Occidental, and David Murdock exchanged his 20-percent stake in that company for $135 million in Occidental stock, which made him the biggest shareholder, with about 5 percent.

I told him that we were under no obligation to put him on Occidental's board of directors. He said he accepted that position. "I just want to be an investor," he said.

He wasn't content to remain on the sidelines for long. One day shortly after the acquisition of Iowa Beef had been completed, he told me that he had changed his mind and now wanted to join the board and be elected to the executive committee. He wasn't sticking to our bargain, but I couldn't very well refuse him and, in any case, I didn't want to provoke a fight. I did, however, get Joe Flom to draw up an ironclad agreement, putting a ceiling of 5 percent on the amount of stock David could own.

As soon as he got on the inside, David Murdock began to throw his weight around, opposing most of our corporate strategies and, in particular, criticizing me in board meetings. Murdock even had one of his own men constantly in Occidental's President's offices as his representative. I did not object, as we had nothing to hide. During the frequently stormy board meetings, Bob Abboud, our President and Chief Operating Officer, generally maintained a neutral silence, neither opposing me nor supporting Murdock.

Nevertheless, it was getting nasty.

After he had been on the board for several months, David Murdock called one day to invite me to lunch again, this time in his Regency Club at the top of his new building. There was to be an executive committee meeting that afternoon and he said he wanted to discuss some details in advance. He sounded friendly, conciliatory. I took the short walk across the street, little suspecting that he was going to try to cut off my legs.

We had our lunch in a private room. It was an enjoyable, relaxed meal. As we finished our dessert, he said, "I want to be elected Chairman of the executive committee at this afternoon's meeting."

Just like that.

I took a moment to compose myself before I replied. "I am the Chairman of the executive committee."

"Yes," he said, "but I think you should resign. I think you're too old to be running Occidental."

Very few people on earth would have the nerve to speak to me like that. David Murdock was as cool as a cucumber.

I answered quietly. "You may think I'm too old, but I don't. And the directors and stockholders don't either. I'm going to finish my term."

"In that case," he said, "you and I are at war."

He paused as he looked levelly at me and added, "And I never lose."

I got out of my seat and looked straight back at him. "I never lose either," I said. "If we're at war, we're at war."

I walked out.

Murdock came to the executive committee meeting and acted as if nothing had happened. He didn't ask to be elected Chairman; he didn't make an open declaration of war between us. Nonetheless, I knew that he was in earnest and I started organizing my forces. Evidently he thought that there must have been ways to break our contract.

He wouldn't sell. He refused, several times, to consider any offer for his shares. He let it be known that he was determined to fight me to the finish.

A stand-off began which lasted some weeks. Then, suddenly and without warning, he collapsed. He called me and said, "Does Oxy want to buy my stock? The price is forty dollars a share."

Occidental stock had reached 35¾ two weeks earlier, and was selling at that moment for around thirty-one or thirty-two dollars. His demand was in the range of acceptability for a block of stock that size. I decided to go for it. I told him I would be over to see him.

I drove to Murdock's extremely grand house in Bel Air. Inside the house, Murdock and I sat around for a while with drinks, and then he said, "I am ready to close if you are ready to pay my price of forty dollars."

"Well, then," I said, "let's close tonight. You send for your lawyer and I'll send for mine."

I was joined by my Executive Vice President and Senior General Counsel, Jerry Stern, my legal right hand within Occidental. Max Mesmer was Murdock's lawyer. We all four stayed up far into the night, and by the early hours of the morning we had completed the agreement, which was approved by the Oxy board the next day.

The war was over.

Robert Abboud resigned. In came Dr. Ray Irani as President and Chief Operating Officer. Ray had been the highly successful President of the Olin Chemical Company before I engaged him as Chairman of our Chemical Division and as Executive Vice President of Occidental. Thus he was well suited for the job—and he has since proved to be exactly the man I have been seeking to be President and Chief Operating Officer ever since I started with Occidental.

I don't want to leave the impression that I feel any enmity toward David Murdock. He, who is a gifted and imaginative businessman, fought me in the only way he knows how to fight, hard and tough. As he once said about himself, "I'm pushy about everything. I'm aggressive about everything. All my life I've had one desire—to be Number One."

Anywhere but Occidental, David.

I am always being asked when I am going to retire, and this is my answer: when Occidental stock hits 100, then I'll leave it to the directors to decide if they wish me to carry on. As must be obvious by now—I don't believe in premature retirement.

22

The Eighth Sister

In the spring of 1968, J. Paul Getty wrote to me from Sutton Place, his country seat in England. I had sent him a copy of Occidental's annual report for 1967 and, unknown to him, he was about to play a big role in Occidental's development. As for Occidental's development now, he wrote, "It is an amazing story of what one man can do today. We all know there were Titans in the past, but most of the present generation believes that conditions today do not permit a small independent to become a great major oil company. You have proved that it is still possible."

His flattery aside, Paul squarely hit a truth. The conventional wisdom of that time—and of this—decrees that the great monopolies of American capitalism are too broadly entrenched in their powers to be challenged, that they will always gobble up or erase any minnow enterprise which threatens their hegemony.

The skeptics insisted that Occidental could never grow big enough to challenge the Seven Sisters. If I had listened to all the people who have told me, "It can't be done," I would never have done anything. I always say, "Don't tell me it can't be done: tell me *how* I can do it."

This is the story of how we did it.

The annual report which so impressed Paul Getty did not even include the first real flood of financial benefits from our Libyan successes during the reign of King Idris. Even so, it recorded that, for the first time, Occidental's gross revenues were in sight of a billion dollars for the year. Like all windfalls, our Libyan revenues posed a happy dilemma for me and the management of Occidental: how best to invest the proceeds.

Like lucky gamblers at the one-armed bandits, we could simply have been happy to stash the cash in the bank and distribute dividends on the interest. Few of our shareholders would have complained, I expect. But I feared that the Libyan bonanza could not last. The whole of the Middle East was as explosively volatile as a box of fireworks. The old Arab monarchies—like King Idris's—were toppling like dead trees before the advance of the new Muslim zealots like Qaddafi.

You did not have to be a seer to predict the renewal of armed hostilities between the Arab states and Israel, and to see that American companies in the Middle East would be treated unfavorably when, as was inevitable, the United States supported Israel.

It was as dangerous for Occidental to sit complacently on our Libyan profits as it was for Humpty-Dumpty to sit on the wall. "A house built upon sand cannot stand." Our house was built upon the sands of the Libyan desert. We had to shift the foundations elsewhere, so that the collapse of the Libyan wing would not bring down the whole edifice.

The Libyan riches had supercharged Oxy's stock which, after the three-for-one split, was valued at fifty to fifty-five dollars a share. That stock provided me with the currency for one of the fastest and most extensive drives of corporate acquisition in the American twentieth century. If Occidental were to be impregnable to takeover, I had to make it too big for the majors to swallow.

In quick succession we acquired the Permian Corporation and the McWood Corporation, both of which marketed crude oil (McWood also owned and operated natural-gas processing plants); the Island Creek Coal Company, the third-largest coal company in the United States; and the Hooker Chemical Company, which got us into the field of chemicals and plastics and provided Occidental with an immediate market dominance in the field of petrochemicals.

The acquisition of Hooker, as important as it was, and is, though, also brought us considerable grief, for, with its assets, we also purchased problems we never would have expected. From 1941 to 1952 Hooker had buried chemical waste products in land adjoining their plant in Niagara Falls, New York, until the city of Niagara Falls had taken the land over for itself. The city had agreed not to disturb the surface—but then it had allowed a contractor to build a road which removed the clay cover. When we bought the company in 1968, we had no idea what had transpired: of the problem that had already been sown, nor of the vast emotions that would become attached to the words "Love Canal" as a symbol of chemical pollution nationwide.

When, in the late seventies, the scope of the damage became clear, Occidental moved as quickly and expeditiously as possible, under the complex circumstances, to ameliorate the situation, even though Occidental itself had had nothing to do with the cause of the trouble. In all, twenty million dollars was distributed, largely through our insurance companies—and Occidental took care to see that never again would such a disaster befall any of our sites. We believe that corporate responsibility demands we guard the public health and safety, and to that end have spent many millions of dollars on environmental protection. We will never cease doing so.

Such unhappy events still lay several years in the future, however. For now, we were still looking to expand, and though the chemical, coal and marketing operations we had acquired were highly welcome, the history of Occidental has always been, above all, a history of successful exploration for oil and gas. What we needed most of all, in the late sixties, was a really major find of oil to supplant the threatened supplies from Libya. If Colonel Qaddafi and his men were to nationalize our Libyan fields, we would need a strike elsewhere which would supply us with hundreds of thousands of barrels a day. If we couldn't get such a strike, we would need to buy crude to supply our existing contracts and orders; and we knew, from the hardest experience, that the majors would rather cut off their own noses than sell us their crude at a reasonable price.

The need for such a strike was a very tall order indeed. It was supplied in the North Sea.

Nowhere would have seemed less promising as a site for major oil fields than the seas between Great Britain and Scandinavia. Up to that time everyone had grown accustomed to thinking of great oil fields as lying in burning deserts and icy wastes, in remote and uncultivated outposts of the world. Great Britain, sliding politely into post-Imperial and post-industrial decline, seemed the least likely candidate on earth for membership among the great oil-producing nations.

Denis Healey, Chancellor of the Exchequer in Harold Wilson's Labour government, put it well when he said that the discovery of oil in the North Sea was "Britain's first major stroke of luck in the twentieth century."

The problem for Britain—and, secondarily for me and Occidental—was that the British were ill-prepared to make the most of their gigantic good luck. In the far-flung dominions and dependencies of the British Empire, the Foreign Office had been dealing with oil companies and the management of concessions for fifty years. All that experience counted for nothing, however, when the prospect of oil in domestic waters first arose in the early sixties. The British government treated the potential bonanza as carelessly and complacently as any untutored sheikh and, in those early days, practically threw it away into the hands of the Seven Sisters.

It was not until 1971, seven years after the first round of North Sea concessions was granted, that the British Parliament finally awoke to the full extent of its self-inflicted impoverishment at the hands of the majors. A fresh policy was then inaugurated for another round—following the early Libyan example—to encourage both British companies and smaller independent consortia.

That was the signal I needed to get busy in London.

I decided to put together a consortium to bid for blocks in the fields which were later called Piper and Claymore, in waters east of Aberdeen and the north of Scotland. It was obvious that, in awarding concessions in this new round, the British government was going to be looking for special qualities. They wanted, first, a proven capacity to produce oil, which we could certainly demonstrate, and, second, evidence of a definite UK interest, preferably in Scotland.

Tremendously passionate political argument had been provoked in Scotland over the discovery of North Sea oil. Scottish nationalism, latent but keen for centuries, had been explosively ignited by the thought that the North Sea oil revenues would be funneled directly into the Treasury in London. Scots angrily suspected that they would receive no benefit from the bonanza, while they continued to suffer from economic depression and high unemployment, due largely to the decline of their traditional heavy industries. So hot were these feelings that a popular movement had gathered strength in Scotland, calling for separate regional powers and control of the North Sea revenues.

It was, partly, in an effort to still the anger in Scotland that the British government would favor bidding consortia which included a Scottish element.

I knew only one man with a Scottish connection. He was my old friend Roy Thomson, Lord Thomson of Fleet. Roy owned many newspapers, including the *Times* and the *Sunday Times* of London. More to the point, he also owned *The Scotsman*—Scotland's most important newspaper—and a major share in STV, the Scottish commercial television station.

Roy had very kindly tried to help me with my Libyan headache in 1970 by accompanying me to see Gamal Abdel Nasser, whom he knew, to see if Nasser would speak to Qaddafi and ask him to treat me and Occidental fairly. Nasser agreed, though I don't know if it ever ended up doing any good.

Roy Thomson was one of the nicest men I ever knew—unfailingly courteous, cheerful and good-natured. He was also an astute businessman, as was shown by his early entry into commercial television, which he correctly described as "a license to print money." After he got into our North Sea consortium, he had plenty of money to spread around.

When I went to see him to invite him to join the consortium, he laughed and said, "I've always wanted to be a billionaire and never came close. God knows I'll never get there with my newspapers. But maybe this will give me my chance."

For one of our earliest meetings about the consortium, I went to see him at his penthouse above the *Sunday Times,* off Fleet Street. The meeting stretched on through the morning, and Roy said, "Come on, I'll take you out to lunch." We went down into the street and climbed into Roy's Rolls-Royce and he started fiddling through his pockets, finally drawing out a single, crumpled pound note. "It's going to have to be a cheap lunch," he said. "This is the only money I've got."

I wasn't carrying any British cash, either. It was a ludicrous situation. Two of the richest men in the world were discussing a deal potentially worth many billions of dollars, and they couldn't raise the price of a pub lunch. In the end, my consultant, John Tigrett, intervened and took us to the Claremont Club, where he could charge the check.

Having secured Roy's participation, I then put together the rest of the consortium. Occidental was to be the operating partner in the bid, with 36.5 percent; Thomson Enterprises and Allied Chemical took a 20-percent participating interest each; and Paul Getty, who already owned quite a large chunk of Oxy stock, took the remaining 23.5 percent.

The initial development cost of our concessions was going to run to two hundred fifty million dollars (in the last fifteen years we have spent more than three billion dollars on our North Sea operations). Roy couldn't put up the cash for his 20-percent share in the consortium, so we struck a deal which allowed him to pay for it out of future oil. That saddled him with a big obligation and a hefty risk, which troubled him for a time. Then, one day when I was in London, he again invited me for lunch in his penthouse. As soon as I arrived, I could see that he was obviously in a very merry mood, even more cheerful than usual.

"Well, Armand," he said, beaming, "at last I'm feeling pretty good about my investment."

"Listen, Roy," I said anxiously, "it's too early to be feeling any confidence or optimism. The seismic looks terrific, I'll grant you, but we haven't lifted a pint of oil yet."

"I know that," he said, "but just last week Paul Getty invited me to lunch. And, Armand, *he paid.* Well, you know Paul, if he pays for lunch, you'd better be on your guard."

"What did Paul say?" I asked, warming to the idea of this unprecedented Getty largesse.

Roy could hardly stop chuckling. He pulled a long, hangdog face and tried to imitate Paul Getty's lugubrious features and tone of voice.

"Paul said, 'You know, Roy, I'm worried about your role in this consortium. I feel that Armand talked you into it without your properly understanding the risks. I don't think you realize that these wells will cost millions of dollars each and, if they're dry, you don't get a cent for your investment. Even if we hit oil, I don't think you understand what a huge investment will be required to develop it. I'm just speaking to you as a friend, you understand.'"

Roy went on. "I sat there and tried to contain myself and didn't say anything. I was waiting for him to come round to the point. Finally Paul pulled this face of the deepest concern, and he said, 'Roy, why don't you let me take you out of this?'" Roy let out a great roar of laughter. "That was the first time I knew for sure that I had a great investment. I said, 'Thank you for your concern, Paul, but I think I'll stick with Armand.'"

Paul Getty was a rascal, but he was the most fun in the world to deal with. There was no secrecy in his deviousness; he was openhandedly underhanded and for that reason it was impossible ever to get cross with him or to feel double-crossed. He once tried to fleece me in the most outrageous style, which I would never have forgiven if it had been any other man but Paul.

That was when he was trying to inveigle me into partnership with him in his exploration in Algiers. He collared me on this proposition once when Frances and I were staying with him at Sutton Place. He made it sound like a very good thing and painted the rosiest picture of the concession's potential.

I instructed my executives and attorneys in Los Angeles to open urgent negotiations with Getty's people there and wrap the deal up with all speed. They got to work and ran straight into trouble. Getty's people were playing the hardest of hardball, demanding thirty million dollars up front for participation in the exploration. Rosy as Paul's picture had been, nothing in it warranted this extortionate demand.

While we were having dinner one evening, I told Paul about the trouble our negotiations had hit in Los Angeles and I said that unless his people changed their tune, I would have to pull out. Shortly after— perhaps as the result of a secret signal Paul had given—a servant came into the room to say that Paul was wanted on the telephone to take a call from California. I suspect that he had given instruction for the call to be made. He left the dining room, leaving Frances and me alone.

I needed to go to the bathroom. I left the table and walked along a stately corridor in search of relief. Passing an open door, I heard Paul shouting into the telephone.

"You damned fool!" he was roaring. "You're going to wreck the whole deal if you go on like this, and you'll cost *me* thirty million dollars. We have no chance of striking oil there, in my judgment."

There it was: he had no faith in the project himself. He was expecting to hit dry wells and he wanted to shunt his prospective losses onto me!

Paul and I returned separately to the dining room and I quietly finished my dinner. After dessert I said, "Will you excuse me for a moment? I've got to make an urgent call."

I went upstairs to our rooms and placed a call, collect of course, to my office in Los Angeles.

"The deal is off," I said quietly. "Pull out now and don't go back."

I never told Paul the true reason for Occidental's withdrawal. I let him stew in his misunderstanding. It was good for him to be bested for once.

I suppose the unfortunate creature who had been on the receiving end of Paul's wrath on the telephone must have been his son, George, his nominated heir apparent. Getty loved George immeasurably, but he gave him a hell of a time and always let him know that the boy could never measure up to the father.

According to Robert Lenzner's book *The Great Getty,* Paul once mused about me as his possible successor as head of Getty Oil. Naturally, George was seen as the logical heir, but Paul wrote, "It would seem that if GOC [Getty Oil Company] cannot do better than predicted by its present management, I should ask Dr. Hammer or Mr. Robert Anderson [Chairman of Atlantic Richfield] to replace me."

Paul never discussed this notion—which I am sure he never seriously entertained—with me, but we did recognize in each other some kindred traits. I wouldn't like to be compared exactly with that tight old weasel, but I did love his zest for business and his entrepreneurial drive, his eagerness to get on and do something with every minute of every day. I also enjoyed the regal independence of his spirit. Regarding himself as equal to any human and few as equal to him, Paul never kowtowed or bent his knee to another man in his life.

Women were another matter. Paul bent his knees to a never-ending succession of women, but not in supplication. They were his to enjoy and to discard. As in business, I think he made his dishonorable intentions completely clear, and a woman would have had to have been a fool to misread them. Many women, however, deluded themselves that they could capture the true heart of the old rogue of Sutton Place, and Getty impishly goaded them on in their efforts, relishing every second.

Frances and I were once witnesses to a farcical scene at Sutton Place, when a pitched battle occurred between female rivals for the Getty favors. Two of his mistresses were in the house, and one of them had brought her mother along for support.

She retired upstairs to sulk in her room, feigning a twisted ankle, while her mother berated the other mistress, calling her a whore and telling Paul that he should marry her daughter.

Paul was enjoying this fight enormously, his smile widening and widening as the accusations flew and the tears streamed. Finally he rose and said, "Well, I hate to tear myself away but it's time for *Upstairs, Downstairs*"—his favorite television program, which he never missed. He asked me to go upstairs and give a medical opinion on the condition of the injured mistress. I found her crying on her bed and insisting that she *wasn't* his whore.

Paul contributed occasional articles to *Playboy* magazine. I suspect his motive was to encourage Hugh Hefner to invite him to the Playboy mansion so that Paul could play around with some of Hefner's bunnies. Roy Thomson once asked Paul directly whether he was still sexually capable at his great age, and Paul very definitely asserted that his virility was not in question. He depended, he said, on aphrodisiacs.

In the last years of his life, when he was stricken with illnesses, Paul wanted nothing more than to end his days in the land of his birth and his beloved home in Malibu, California. He had always been phobic about air travel, however, and he couldn't make himself get on a plane, even for the homecoming he so desperately wanted.

I was saddened by Paul's plight, which seemed to be troubling him more and more every time I saw him at Sutton Place. I urged him to use my plane. I said, "You can take a heavy sleeping pill and we'll have you carried onto the plane and put into my bed. You won't even notice the plane taking off. Next thing you know, you'll be in Malibu."

He was tempted by the offer and recorded it in an entry in his diary, noting his intention to accept. Letters he wrote me on business just before his demise were used after his death to prove that he was mentally competent up to the end (which was later contested by some members of his family who wanted more out of his estate). The diary entry proved immensely valuable to the Getty family fortunes, since it enabled the estate to escape the confiscatory death duties which Britain would have imposed if Paul could have been shown to be a permanent resident of Britain with no intention of ever returning to the US.

Those somber matters were far away in the early seventies when I was taking the plunge into the North Sea. What with Roy Thomson's irrepressible good humor and Paul Getty's habitual skulduggery, our North Sea oil consortium was a constant delight for me to organize and, to my pleasure, I was very frequently in and out of London in those years. Frances and I kept an almost permanent suite at Claridge's and came to be on almost family terms with many of the staff.

Other aspects of the North Sea development were less enjoyable. The concession, which we were awarded in December 1972, was embedded in a mare's nest of political complications and tangled in the cobwebs of age-old disputes between labor unions. In some ways, making the deal in the United Kingdom and getting the oil to flow combined the worst headaches of trying to do business in Russia and Libya. In Britain at that time the impediments of a heavy-handed bureaucracy were magnified by zealotry on the fringes of political power.

It was very odd, in old England of all places, to be even remotely threatened with nationalization, as we were in Libya. The call for nationalization in Britain came from groups far to the left of the political spectrum which, naturally, had no influence on government during the Conservative administration of Edward Heath.

However, when Heath was defeated in two General Elections in 1974 and Harold Wilson led his Labour Party into office, the balance of power moved markedly left. Then the idea of nationalization of the North Sea fields gained a measure of political respectability, particularly when it was combined with the nationalistic mood then sweeping Scotland.

The possibility of nationalization in the UK was never strong enough to cause serious worry in our consortium, but we certainly kept a wary eye on political developments there. We drew confidence from the obvious pragmatic good sense of Harold Wilson and his most senior colleagues, James Callaghan and Denis Healey. The worst we expected from them was that they would make very stiff demands for taxation on revenue; and this they did—so stringently that they actually restricted commercial developments of the fields, to the detriment of the operating companies and the Queen's Exchequer.

We might have expected most official obstruction from Tony Benn, Wilson's Secretary of State for Energy, who was notorious as the "wild man" of Labour's left. Mr. Benn had been steadily lopping off the names and titles of his noble birthright as his political inclinations moved left. Born the Honorable Anthony Wedgwood Benn and heir to the title Viscount Stansgate, he had first disowned his title and then amputated the aristocratic limbs of his name, to make democratic cause with the common people. We were advised that Mr. Benn was unlikely to look kindly on a consortium composed of California oil magnates and one of the "press barons" his Labour group so much hated and feared.

However, I liked Tony Benn and I think he liked me. We got on extremely well together and established a good understanding and quite a warm personal friendship. He was very interested in my recollections of Bolshevik Russia and my friendship with Lenin, and I think he figured that if I was good enough for Lenin, I was good enough for him!

I found his eyes disconcerting: with their very bright and distinct separations of white and blue, they reminded me of Daniel De Leon's and of Trotsky's hard, bright eyes. Their eyes were not the same colors as Mr. Benn's, but all shared the same intensity of focus. I usually feel that eyes like those are the windows to a fanatical soul.

It was also a little disconcerting to see the scale of Mr. Benn's addictions to tea and tobacco. He was a dedicated and complete abstainer from alcohol, I believe, but whatever gains there might have been to his health from that abstention, he erased them all with his pipes and his tea. A fuming, noxious pipe was eternally clenched in his teeth, removed only when he opened his mouth to pour in some tea—of which he was supposed to drink up to seventeen large cups a day.

The combined stimulations of these addictions made Tony Benn's mind—and, no doubt, his heart—run at the speed of an express train. I feared that one day he would run himself off the track and, when I heard that he had suffered a serious illness toward the end of the seventies, I felt pretty sure that my fears had, sadly, been confirmed.

The possibility of nationalization in the United Kingdom was never a grave worry, but the combination of abominable weather and suicidally obstructive labor unions threatened, it not to blow us out of the water, then at least to undermine and imperil our venture.

The waters of the North Sea in which our concession blocks were located were among the fiercest in the world. Rising in the Arctic and storming across the open sea from Scandinavia, winds up to one hundred mph drove waves up to seventy feet high in battering torrents. Hailstones the size of children's glass marbles and withering sheets of icy sleet whipped across the waves like machine-gun fire. The water itself was so cold for most of the year that divers could remain below the surface only for forty minutes, after which they had to spend days in a decompression chamber to avoid death from the bends. Not even on the North Slope of Alaska was the weather less hospitable for oil exploration than in the North Sea.

As for the engineering challenge—nothing like the North Sea explorations had ever been attempted in the world. Our blocks, which covered about three hundred thousand acres, were in more than 450 feet of water, and the seismic indicated the oil-bearing strata to be between 8000 and 12,000 feet. To explore the field, we had to hire a self-propelled semi-submersible drilling rig called *Ocean Victory*. This monstrosity of marine engineering stood as high as a twenty-nine-story building, twice as tall as Niagara Falls. Twelve huge anchors were needed to hold the vessel steady while she was drilling. It cost us forty thousand dollars a day to operate *Ocean Victory*. She repaid the investment a million times.

In January 1973, less than two months after the concession had been awarded, *Ocean Victory* bit into the Piper Field, one of the biggest finds in the North Sea. The independent engineering consultant De Golyer and MacNaughton estimated that the field contained nearly 925 million barrels of oil, for which they calculated a 65-percent recovery.

Piper made Occidental safe from Qaddafi. Even if he shut us down altogether, we could still supply our customers with our own crude. The discovery called for some heady celebrations in Aberdeen, London and Los Angeles. I imagine it might even have raised a smile on the lugubrious face of the master of Sutton Place.

The discovery also called for the immediate commission of gigantic engineering works and facilities. We needed a drilling platform to extract the oil, a pipeline to carry it to land and a terminal at which to process the oil and gas, store it and move it to tankers for transportation.

Compared with the problems of building the platform, the pipeline and the terminal were a breeze.

The nearest land to our block was the Orkney Islands, just a few miles north of mainland Scotland and 135 miles due west of Piper. Getting his just deserts at last for the credit he had given us in Libya, Steve Bechtel came in to lay a thirty-inch pipe on the seabed from Piper to the isle of Flotta, where we would build our terminal.

Flotta is a wild and beautiful place, populated by hosts of cormorants and oyster-catchers and hardly any humans. The few people who live there are descended from the Picts of old Scotland, their blood mingled with the genes of the Norsemen who arrived in their Viking longships as they sailed to colonize Iceland and Greenland.

The low-lying, forbidding islands are littered with the remains of earlier societies—Pictish burial chambers, mysterious stones covered with runic inscriptions, and a vast castellated cathedral originally built by a Norse earl. The strangest of all these remains lie at the bottom of Scapa Flow, the magnificent deep-water harbor naturally created and protected by a ring of the islands. Into Scapa Flow, after the cease-fire ending the First World War, sailed all the ships remaining in the German Atlantic Fleet. The Royal Navy received the German Fleet's surrender there. In 1919, on the command of their Admiral, the captains of all those battleships opened their sea cocks and sent their ships to the bottom. Many were subsequently salvaged, but some remain, resting on the floor of Scapa Flow, and their hulks can clearly be seen from a small boat as it passes above them on a still day.

In a setting of such extreme natural beauty and deep historical interest it was natural that some people would get upset at the proposed intrusion of an oil pipeline and the creation of a huge terminal.

We completely understood the fears of local people that our work might spoil that extraordinary place. The people of Flotta and the surrounding Orkney Islands were, however, mighty impressive in their good sense. While they were determined to protect the age-old beauties of their islands, they welcomed the cash that we would be bringing into their economy and the opportunities for employment we would offer. In fact, once the construction of the terminal had begun, large numbers of Flotta men and women returned to their native isle, from which they had previously been driven by unemployment and economic necessity.

The finished terminal would employ almost three hundred people, of whom about 90 percent would be local Orcadians.

The terminal site would cover 385 acres, or more than a tenth of the entire island of Flotta. It would be dominated by oil storage tanks capable of containing four and a half million barrels. The gas processing plant we needed would process up to twenty-two million cubic feet of propane and ethane. We needed a jetty which would accommodate crude tankers up to 150,000 tons; and supply lines to moorings in Scapa Flow where even larger ships, up to 200,000 tons, could receive our oil.

We had been told that there was absolutely no chance of getting permission to build such a huge facility in such a treasured spot and that we might as well not bother to try. We tried. We succeeded.

We employed the best design teams in Britain to come up with aesthetic schemes to blend the terminal as far as possible with the surrounding countryside. I remember that very elaborate and prolonged tests were conducted before the designers finally decided on the exact shades of paint which would best match the terminal to the surrounding colors of nature.

Seeing how diligent we were, the Flotta people warmed to us and we all became good friends. I made a contribution to their local museum in Kirkwall and sent a selection of pictures from my collection for exhibition there. In return, the Orcadian people threw a party for Frances and me in Kirkwall.

The terminal has won a great number of prizes, both for its design and for its safety record. In nearly ten years since the first barrel of oil came through the pipeline, there has been not a single accident at Flotta, though more than a billion barrels of oil have arrived there. The terminal has received an award from the Association for the Protection of Rural Scotland and a Premier Award from the Business Panel for Industry and the Environment. The Royal Society for the Prevention of Accidents and the British Safety Council have both awarded the terminal many gold prizes and, in 1983, the Oxy consortium was awarded the Sir George Earle Trophy, the Premier Award of the Royal Society for the Prevention of Accidents, "for outstanding performance in health and safety at the Flotta terminal."

Tony Benn came with me in my plane when we flew up to Flotta to open the terminal on January 11, 1977, and to see the first shipment of Piper oil loaded. That was one of the best days of the North Sea development and Flotta was far and away the best part of it. At the other end of the pipeline, the Piper platform had given me a brow-busting headache.

Though we had been one of the last major consortia to enter the North Sea, we wanted to be among the first to produce. Contracts for elements of the gigantic platform—495 feet tall and weighing over 14,000 tons—went out to major constructors all over the world. We put those constructors under the lash and they all delivered promptly—all, that is, except the British themselves.

Chiefly because it was close to the field, but also because we wanted to benefit the United Kingdom economy, we chose to have the platform assembled at Ardersier in Scotland by a subsidiary of the prime contractor, J. Ray McDermott and Company of New Orleans. Fabrication work began in late 1973. We wanted the platform to be on station and producing in June 1974. However, it was not until June 1975 that it was finally towed out to the field and uprighted there. We lost a whole year's production because of a futile dispute between labor unions at Ardersier.

Eric Jacobs, the Labour Editor of Roy Thomson's *Sunday Times* in London, wrote a good article about this dispute in June 1974. He said, "Essentially, the dispute . . . is a classic power play between two traditional shipyard unions, the Boilermakers and the Engineers. It could mean a return to the kind of inter-union struggle reminiscent of the old who-does-what rows that characterised the shipbuilding industry a decade ago. It would be hard to imagine a greater disincentive to the international oil companies placing new orders in Britain than that."

The Engineers were claiming exclusive right to the work. Much of that work, however, was welding—a task traditionally performed by Boilermakers. Victory or defeat in this fight would matter a lot to the coffers of the respective unions. As a senior union official said, "It is also basically a fight for membership."

A strike was called, resulting in a general paralysis of our work. The subcontractors' boilermakers, like our United States Boiler-makers, would not cross their brothers' picket lines at Ardersier. The strike lasted for most of a month, by which time we had missed the very small "weather-window" which would have allowed us to get the platform in place before the storms resumed in September.

I despatched sheaves of telegrams and telexes to London to urge a quick settlement of this damaging fight. Roy Thomson called privately on the Prime Minister to tell him about the seriousness of the delay, and the Minister of Employment and the bosses of the trade union movement were all badgered for their support. Nothing helped, nothing changed. The Ardersier unions went on growling and glaring at each other, and we missed our chance to get the platform away to sea.

The United Kingdom economy suffered a loss to its balance of payments of about three hundred eighty million pounds at a time when it could barely afford to lose three hundred eighty cents. Our confidence in the capacity of British industry to delivery the goods also took a jarring knock.

Concluding his survey of this sorry tale, Eric Jacobs of the *Sunday Times* wrote, "Occidental must order a new platform soon. The question must be whether, after what has happened in the last month at Ardersier, it or any other company will be in a hurry to place their next order in Britain."

Mr. Jacobs was either very well informed or very astute. We were, at that moment, about to award contracts for the fabrication of a platform for the second North Sea field we had discovered. In May 1974 *Ocean Victory* had bit into the Claymore Field, twenty miles to the west of Piper. Claymore had recoverable reserves estimated at four hundred million barrels and would require a platform identical to the Piper platform.

With the dispute raging at Ardersier, I gave orders that we should look elsewhere for yards in which to fabricate the Claymore platform. Very quickly an excellent tender came in from Union Industrielle d'Entreprise [UIE] in Cherbourg, France, and the contract was awarded there. The only disadvantage of UIE was that the platform would have to be towed across the English Channel and up the full length of the British Isles in North Sea waters to reach the Claymore Field, risking a shipping accident en route. That danger was more than offset, however, by the advantage of quick work in France and prompt delivery. Our new French-built platform commenced production at Claymore on time, in November 1977.

On February 24, 1978, I stood bundled up on the rain-lashed Claymore platform, peering into the scudding gray clouds and listening into the wind for the clatter of helicopter blades. Finally, through the gloom, came a bright-red helicopter which landed neatly on the platform's pad. Out stepped the grinning pilot, the Prince of Wales himself, making his first official visit to an offshore North Sea installation.

I had first met Prince Charles in London on May 4, 1977, when the Knoedler Galleries staged an exhibition of paintings and drawings by Sir Winston Churchill as one of the opening events in celebration of the Queen's Silver Jubilee. Prince Charles, then of course a dashing bachelor, visited the exhibition and, with his keen practitioner's interest in drawing and painting, had a very long talk with me and grilled me extensively about the exhibits. I had heard that, while his mother owned a Churchill painting, he had none. His enthusiasm for the pictures was so engaging that I offered him one I owned as a present. He demurred, saying that he could not accept it personally, so I offered it to the Queen's Jubilee Fund, and he very enthusiastically accepted.

That was the beginning of a deeply cherished and wide-ranging friendship. The next steps in our acquaintanceship both involved North Sea oil.

In Los Angeles on October 26, 1977, Prince Charles was to speak at a lunch in his honor given by the World Affairs Council. The day before, the British Consul General gave a garden party, at which Prince Charles again turned his inquisitive mind upon me. He had read, he said, all about our North Sea discoveries and he wanted my assessment of their importance for Britain.

"Is there any chance of Britain becoming self-sufficient in oil, do you think?" he asked me.

"Not only self-sufficient," I answered. "Britain will become a major exporter of oil."

Next day, at the lunch, I was seated beside the Prince. He was scribbling feverishly on the pages of his prepared speech. When he rose to speak, he repeated exactly what I had said to him, surprising his audience with my opinion of Britain's oil prospects.

The Prince's visit to the Claymore platform followed from that Los Angeles encounter.

He spent half a day on the platform, insisting on peering into every corner and under every pipe, determined to understand everything. He talked at length and in detail to many of the workingmen, quizzing them about their jobs and their conditions.

"Are they paying you well?" I heard him ask one man.

"Oh, very well, sir," he answered, "but the trouble is that we lose fifty percent of it in taxes."

"That's bloody hell," the Prince royally exclaimed.

On February 7, 1980, Prince Charles's father, Prince Philip, the Duke of Edinburgh, honored us with a visit to another of our North Sea facilities, attending the flag-raising ceremony on the MSV *Tharos*. This astounding vessel, which cost us one hundred million dollars to build, looks like a conventional semisubmersible drilling rig, but is actually a multifunction firefighter and wild-well killer. The famed Red Adair consulted closely with us on the *Tharos* design and on her equipment, such as the water cannon which can throw forty thousand US gallons of water per minute over a horizontal distance of two hundred and forty feet.

During our helicopter flight to the vessel, the Prince told me about his work on behalf of the World Wildlife Fund, of which he is President, to save the world's whales. I lightly undertook to support this effort, a promise which the Prince did not forget.

On September 5, 1980, we got another important visitor, that majestic lady, Mrs. Margaret Thatcher, Prime Minister of Great Britain.

By that time, of course, power had changed hands again in Britain, returning to Mrs. Thatcher's Conservatives. All thoughts of nationalization vaporized when that white-hot advocate of free-market capitalism entered Number Ten Downing Street. Indeed, she upended the restrictive taxation policies of the previous administration, with the direct result that we were able to embark on fresh explorations on our concessions, bringing extended life to our fields.

Mrs. Thatcher's enthusiasm for enterprise and initiative bubbled all over us when she came to Flotta. Like the Prince of Wales, she was into every corner of the terminal, scurrying from one employee to the next, firing questions and concentrating like a laser gun on the answers. When she and I went out to meet the press, she gave one of her most characteristic performances, declaiming—at dictation speed—"Eight hundred thousand man-hours have been worked here without a single accident. Have you got that? Eight hundred thousand. That's a magnificent record."

North Sea oil didn't exactly save Occidental's bacon; we were never that much at risk. But, when we jumped out of the Libyan frying pan, we certainly landed on our feet in the United Kingdom.

We had also benefited from tremendous good luck in Peru, Venezuela and Nigeria, though politically speaking, we did jump out of the fat and into the fire with our South American explorations. During the sixties and seventies, almost every one of the governments Occidental dealt with in South America was unstable and many of them were less than savory. Those were the ones which were in power, though, and so those were the ones with whom we did business.

Texaco and Gulf had taken successful concessions in Ecuador, next to Peru. I wanted us to get a territory in similar terrain, just across the border, but the military junta in Peru had passed a law forbidding foreign firms to work within fifty miles of the border. I managed to persuade the Peruvian generals to waive this law.

We took a 2.9-million-acre tract of Amazonian jungle right by the border, and we entered into a development agreement with Petroperu, the Peruvian national oil company. We offered to build a six-hundred-mile pipeline across the Andes. However, Petroperu preferred to build and own it themselves, in anticipation of large discoveries of their own and by other firms which would need to pay transportation fees through the pipeline. In any event, neither they nor the other companies came up with large discoveries, and Petroperu had to carry the whole cost of the program, from which we benefited.

By 1973 the first five structures drilled in Peru by Occidental had all resulted in new oil field discoveries of up to three thousand barrels per day each. Despite enduring political difficulties, threats of guerrilla attack and of nationalization, Occidental has continued to produce oil in Peru to this day.

Occidental has had its share of disasters in South America, however. In Venezuela, our successful developments on Lake Maracaibo were expropriated by the government in December 1975 after trumped-up charges of bribery were alleged against Occidental. We received no compensation, and we were forced to write off our entire investment there, which amounted to $73.5 million.

We brought suit in Venezuela to recover our investment and we're still hoping to recoup our losses, since the Venezuelan court has found us not guilty.

You win some, you lose some. When you win in the oil business, you win big; when you lose, you lose plenty.

In 1967, foreseeing the problem of dwindling oil reserves in the US, I became interested in new sources to supply America's domestic requirements for liquid fuels. I found the answer in shale oil. By far the richest deposits in the world occur in the United States in three states, Colorado, Wyoming and Utah, and there is more oil in these three states than in the entire Arabian peninsula.

Oxy acquired a piece of this precious property in 1971, and in 1972 secured the first US patent on a process known as Modified In Situ (MIS). We built an underground cavern filled with rubblized shale, ignited it, and the oil flowed as from a well. Some of it is of such high quality that it can be used as diesel fuel without further refining. This ingenious process proved not only to be an enormous success for retrieving oil from shale, but also provided an answer to the environmental problems of mining shale.

With the steep increase in oil prices in the seventies, our process for extracting oil from shale started to become an economic reality. The US government began to see the strategic value of the shale oil potential for military and civilian use. For instance, Brigadier General Anthony J. Farrington of the Headquarters San Antonio Air Logistics Center at Kelly Air Force Base in Texas wrote us about the Air Force's test flights, "We plan to convert from conventional to shale-derived [fuel] . . . as soon as sufficient quantities are available."

However, we needed government help to "scale up" to commercial levels. When oil prices dropped, the government decided to stop funding alternative-energy research. With the abolition of the United

States Synthetic Fuels Corporation by Congress in 1985, I had no other choice but to put our oil shale operations on hold—but only temporarily.

I am convinced that oil shale will have a new day, will protect us from the disaster of depleted reserves and rationing. There is more than enough oil right in our own backyard, locked in the strata of the mighty Rocky Mountains, to see us through with all our demands well into the middle of next century. And with only seven years of proven reserves of oil in the US, we may be back to shale oil sooner than later.

Throughout the seventies and into the eighties, we went ahead with worldwide explorations, bidding for concessions in Bolivia, Ecuador, Colombia, Pakistan, Oman, Madagascar and the South China Sea. Some of these ventures have been disappointing. For instance, the South China Sea, where all the major oil companies held very high hopes, has yet to yield a single discovery of any size. However, largely because of our good relations with the Chinese government, we have, at the time of this writing, drilled in an extension to our block to the north, where we recently made an important discovery, suggesting the presence of a large field.

In other territories, Occidental has brought in relatively small fields which have made a tremendous difference to the economies of the host nation. In Pakistan, for instance, we have successfully developed fields where other companies had previously failed. In terms of Occidental's worldwide production, or even in terms of a major field like the North Sea or Libya, our Pakistan discoveries are small. However, when I first went to Pakistan, I promised President Zia Ul-Haq that we would make his country self-sufficient in oil. That's exactly what we are near to achieving.

Domestic demand for oil is very low in Pakistan, but the difference made to the country's balance of trade by achieving near self-sufficiency in oil is immense. The per capita GNP of Pakistan is about two hundred seventy dollars per year. In that context, the production of more than 20,000 barrels of oil a day, which we have achieved in our fields, represents a major economic breakthrough.

The discovery of our Cañon Limón field in northern Colombia did more than affect Colombia's struggling domestic economy. As *The Wall Street Journal* wrote in a headline on May 13, 1985: DISCOVERY IN COLOMBIA POINTS UP BIG CHANGE IN WORLD OIL PICTURE.

The Cañon Limón field was and is a monster, comparable with the "elephant" fields of Mexico and the North Sea. Its discovery followed a pattern which had become well-established in Occidental's history. Only after a extended run of failures did we find oil where other companies such as Exxon and BP had given up.

After our successes in Peru, Venezuela and Bolivia, our Bakersfield geologists had considered it logical to explore in Colombia. Starting work in 1980, we spent $50 million on seismic and exploration on our block beneath the vast savannah east of the Andes foothills, and hit nothing but dry holes. We tried to farm out our block to seventy-five companies which could earn one-half interest by drilling a single well, but there were no takers. A lot of pressure was put on me to cancel the Colombian program, but by now I had acquired over twenty years' experience in the oil business, and I knew that you had to play out every card in your hand before you walked away from the table.

In June of 1984 we hit a discovery well named the Layuca which seemed to indicate that we had a field of perhaps 100 million barrels. During the late summer and fall, further wells were drilled which suggested reserves of up to a billion barrels, allowing production of about 250,000 barrels a day. I ordered a crash program to build a pipeline capable of carrying up to 250,000 barrels a day, and the other major companies stepped up their exploration programs, spending about $500 million a year to the benefit of the Colombian economy.

The discovery of Cañon Limón also marked a major turning point in Occidental's fortunes. It allowed us to discharge much of the debt we had incurred when we acquired the Cities Service Company, unquestionably the most important acquisition I ever made.

Following our long-term successes in foreign exploration, we faced the choice of investing further in foreign fields or attempting to acquire a domestic company which already owned extensive reserves. From all points of view, it made the best sense to go for a domestic acquisition. Cities was the ideal choice.

Cities Service had been negotiating a merger with Gulf. When that fell through—in acrimony which led to Cities' suing Gulf for breach of contract—a scramble was on for a company to replace Gulf. Nearly four billion dollars would be needed to make the acquisition, plus the assumption of three billion dollars of Cities' debt.

The investment bankers representing Cities—First Boston Corporation and Goldman Sachs—looked down their noses at Occidental when we entered the field. "This is like Jonah trying to swallow the whale," I was told.

I recognized that the key to the deal was to win over Cities' Chief Executive Officer, Charles (Chuck) Waidelich. I went to see him and explained how our companies made a perfect fit. With the Permian Corporation in our control, we had access to huge volumes of crude oil through twenty thousand leaseholders who were dependent upon our transmission system of pipelines. I showed Mr. Waidelich that we could guarantee cheaper crude for Cities' refineries. I also assured him that he and his top executives would all be kept in the management of the merged corporation unless, after a reasonable time, they wanted to retire. Then they could activate their golden parachutes which Cities had granted them to allow them to bail out in comfort.

Chuck Waidelich was attracted by my proposition, but he was opposed by his investment bankers. One day at Cities' offices in New York, I was in one room with Chuck Waidelich, while representatives of First Boston and Lehman Brothers were in another, frantically scouring the world of commerce by telephone, trying to find a bidder to improve on Occidental's offer. Finally I made a deal with Chuck, who asked me to appear before his board of directors and make my case. I could sense that my speech was being well received—and soon after we had the green light.

That deal, finalized on December 3, 1982, made Occidental the nation's twelfth-largest industrial concern and the eighth-largest oil company, nudging the Seven Sisters. More significantly, it accomplished my long-term goal of guaranteeing Occidental's future with a sound domestic base in the USA, reducing the corporation's dependence on uncertain foreign ventures. We sold off enough assets that we didn't need, so that as of this writing we have paid off the banks and redeemed the preferred stock we issued, leaving us with the domestic oil and gas properties which we wanted.

And that's the story of how, in J. Paul Getty's words, we achieved the transformation from a small independent to a major international oil company. The skeptics said it couldn't be done. We proved them wrong. They still say it can't be done today. Somebody else will prove them wrong again.

23

Business with Brezhnev

Leonid Brezhnev was the Soviet leader I knew best. From the early seventies until his death in November 1982, I saw him many times for extended interviews. We met in his office in the Kremlin, at state functions in Moscow, at his holiday palace in the Crimea and when he visited America for his summit conference with President Nixon. We also exchanged dozens of personal letters which, in turn, produced a mountain of correspondence between my offices and bureaus of the Soviet state.

To the extent that a working relationship with a head of state can ever be more than functional, Leonid Brezhnev and I were friends. Our characters were cut from very different bolts of cloth, but we developed a warm understanding. I didn't find him altogether easy—especially in his emotional impulsiveness and his enormous capacity for drink—but I liked him very much and I believed in the sincerity of his efforts to improve Russia's relations with America.

In 1973 Brezhnev appeared in an hour-long NBC program about me, made by Lucy Jarvis and Ed Newman and called *The Russian Connection.* He emerged in the finale of the program, hugely grinning and bearishly booming as ever, to speak about my business efforts in the USSR and his relationship with me. He said, "Armand Hammer has expended considerable effort. I help him, he helps me. It is mutual. We do not discuss secrets—just business."

Almost the truth—but not quite.

During Brezhnev's years I negotiated huge deals with the Soviets for Occidental, including one which was, at that time, the biggest business deal ever done between the Soviet Union and a foreign corporation—worth, in total, some twenty billion dollars. Those deals called for constant discussion and revision between Brezhnev and me and, during these meetings, we invariably got around to more general questions of trade between the US and the USSR.

So it is perfectly true that we did discuss business.

But we also discussed arms control, détente, the position of Soviet Jewry and the refuseniks, the plight of American businessmen who had tangled with the KGB, the Soviet invasion of Afghanistan, the position of Soviet defectors in America and a host of other questions.

My connection with the Soviet Union, more or less dormant since Khrushchev's fall from power, flourished afresh in the early seventies. Under the umbrella of a growing rapprochement between President Nixon and General Secretary Brezhnev, conditions for trade between the two countries, in which I played a prominent role, improved dramatically. (In 1978 the Soviet government honored me with the Order of Friendship Between Peoples for my efforts to establish friendly relations and economic cooperation between the two countries—it had never been given to a foreign businessman before.)

Prompted by Henry Kissinger, Nixon wanted to achieve a major shift in United States global relations during his second term. Having settled the Vietnam war, he wanted to open a new era with the Communist superpowers—Russia and China. He wanted to let the bygones of the cold war be bygones and to remodel his own reputation as the McCarthyite scourge of the Reds. With his eye lifted to the judgment of history, Nixon wanted to be remembered as the President who had brought peace between East and West.

The political and economic reasons for this polar swing in US foreign policy were pretty clear. The Japanese and South Korean economies were exploding like starshells, not only over the Pacific rim but around the world. More or less open trade war had been declared between the industrialized states of the West. To hold anything approaching its economic supremacy, the United States had to beat the Japanese in major new markets, especially in China. And Russia.

The triangulations of Henry Kissinger's design called for both the other corners to be locked up at the same time. Nixon had to get rapprochement with both China *and* Russia—simultaneously. Otherwise, whichever power was excluded would feel doubly suspicious of the new coziness between the US and its rival. If Nixon and Kissinger had opened negotiations for détente with Brezhnev without entering into a new understanding with Mao Zhedong and Zhou Enlai, China would have been cast into a menacing isolation, and vice versa.

The greatest diplomatic benefit of the Nixon/Kissinger strategy was that it made the US the critical junction between the Soviet Union and China. America entered the Sino-Soviet split not as a hyphen, but as a partner of each of those antagonistic powers.

The greatest benefit to the world at large was that it called for peaceful and tolerant relations between and among the three most powerful nations on earth. Nixon and Kissinger plainly saw that *trade* had to be opened up with Russia and China. Trade was the key—not only to a new era of political relations, but also to the defense and enlargement of America's interests.

Naturally I watched the development of this strategy with the sharpest interest and enthusiasm. No policy could have been framed closer to my own beliefs and attitudes. By the time of the 1972 presidential election, there was no doubt whatsoever in my mind that Nixon was framing the most imaginative foreign policy initiative of my lifetime.

I wanted Occidental to take a lead in the new policy of détente and to lend its weight to my own ideas of "détente-through-trade." The corporation was better placed for this role than any in America.

All the ingredients were coming together for the fertilizer deal which I had carried in my mind and prepared for so many years. In July 1972 Occidental and the Soviets signed a five-year scientific and technical cooperation agreement covering many areas, including fertilizers, but I knew there was still a long way to go between an agreement and its fulfillment. If I wanted this plan to succeed, I needed the help of one man: Leonid Brezhnev.

During this period, Brezhnev had kept himself aloof and apart from the business end of détente. He did not see any individual American businessmen, nor did he give more than a cursory nod of acquiescence to our efforts in Moscow. If my seventy years' business experience have taught me anything, however, they have taught me this: deal with the man at the top, the boss. That's the way to get things done. When the bosses of corporations get together, they can quickly decide whether or not a deal can be made, and they can then leave the details to be arranged between their executives.

With all its enterprises and offices under the control of the government, the Soviet Union is, in a sense, a giant corporation—and the ultimate boss of this vast conglomerate is, therefore, the General Secretary of the Communist Party of the Soviet Union. If you want to get things done there, if you want to smash through the maze of bureaucratic complications which exist in a corporate state, it helps to have access to the Chairman of the Board.

I kept trying to figure a way to make a connection with Leonid Brezhnev. For a long time it eluded me, and then finally it came about in a curious way and more or less by chance.

In the middle of 1972, when the earliest stages of the fertilizer agreement were under way, I received a call from an art dealer named Otto Kallir, the owner of Galerie St. Etienne of New York. He claimed that two original letters written in Lenin's hand had come into his possession, and he had a proposition to make.

He would give me the Lenin letters, to give to the Russians, if I would persuade them, in exchange, to give *him* several masterpiece paintings from their collections at the Hermitage in Leningrad or the Pushkin Museum in Moscow.

Some deal! It was a preposterous idea. Kallir was effectively asking the Russians to hold themselves up for ransom. That, in my experience, is not the best possible way to get their cooperation. Nonetheless, if he was telling the truth, Kallir had documents of great historical importance and value in his hands. Hoping that I might be able to reason with him, I arranged a meeting.

As a precaution I took along several photostated copies of letters Lenin had written to me, to make sure there was no fraud. Peering through a magnifying glass, I scrutinized the dealer's letters as minutely as I could, comparing the form of each character with my originals. They seemed to check out completely.

One letter, written in French in 1919, was addressed to "Comrade Loriot and all French Friends of the Third International." The other was in German, written in 1921, to Clara Zetkin and Comrade Levi. Clara Zetkin was a German feminist and Communist who later became a senior member of the Reichstag during the Weimar regime, and who died in Russia in 1933.

I insisted that I would need expert authentication, and Kallir agreed that I could send photostats to show to scholars at the Lenin Institute in Moscow. Word came back by cable that the letters on offer were indeed genuine.

Now I had to persuade Kallir to see reason. Since he wanted pictures in exchange for the letters, I offered him a number of works from the Hammer Galleries, and since he also wanted cash, I offered him a lot of cash. The haggling was protracted over several months, but at last, in October 1972, the letters were mine.

I was going to Moscow in that month. I took the Lenin letters with me.

My main contact in Moscow at that time was Jermen Gvishiani, son-in-law of Premier Kosygin and Deputy Chairman of the Committee for Science and Technology of the USSR Council of Ministers. I delivered the letters to Gvishiani, with a separate letter addressed to Leonid Brezhnev, in which I declared the Lenin documents "my unconditional gift to the government and people of the USSR."

The response was immediate.

Frances and I were staying in the old National Hotel opposite Red

Square, in the suite Lenin himself had occupied when he first came to Moscow during the Revolution of October 1917. A few days after I had sent the letters to Brezhnev, Gvishiani visited me in my suite and told me that Brezhnev being out of town, the Lenin letters had been turned over to Mikhail Andreevich Suslov, the second most powerful man in the Soviet Union. And Suslov wanted to see me.

That was astonishing news. Suslov, the Politburo's chief ideologist, was the Soviet leader least likely to want to make friends with an American capitalist. One of the last major figures from Stalin's era to survive in power, Suslov might easily have become General Secretary when Khrushchev had been toppled, but apparently he had preferred a lesser office, which allowed him to concentrate on maintaining the purity of Marxist-Leninist ideology in Soviet practice. His reputation gave him out as an austere, unbending and forbidding man.

On first sight, when we met, that reputation was confirmed. Suslov was extremely tall, well over six feet, with a gaunt high-cheekboned face and stern gray-blue eyes behind thick lenses. His manner seemed to be intimidatingly grave and impassive.

I quickly saw that Suslov's appearance disguised his true character. His impassiveness hid a deep shyness. The scholarliness of his rather tousled gray hair was genuine and the intelligence of his features was unmistakable. But he was modest rather than stern and, far from being cold, his smile was kindly. His face positively lit up when he spoke of Lenin.

On his desk were several volumes of Lenin's published correspondence. I could see slips of paper, as markers, sticking out from many pages. Suslov had been doing his homework on me and had read all the letters and memos Lenin had written to and about me.

Suslov read aloud to me a resolution of the Central Committee of the Communist Party thanking me for my gift of the Lenin letters. And he presented me with a beautifully engraved portrait of Lenin made of silver and other metals found in the Urals. Then, escorting me through his secretary's outer office, Mr. Suslov pointed to a door which opened into the same secretariat. It was Brezhnev's office. Suslov said, "General Secretary Brezhnev regrets he could not be here, but he will write you on his return to Moscow and will also receive and thank you personally on your next visit to the USSR."

That was the breakthrough I had been seeking for months on end—and within a matter of weeks, I did indeed receive a letter from Brezhnev himself, thanking me:

It is unnecessary for me to tell you at length how dear to the Soviet people is everything that is directly related to the life and activities of the great founder of our Party and the Soviet State.

And continuing on:

The leadership of the Soviet Union attaches great importance to the present positive turn in the Soviet-American relations. The development of contracts and mutually beneficial peaceful cooperation between our peoples in different spheres is considered by us a matter of great importance. A highly significant role in that belongs to the economic relations and you, Dr. Hammer, are making an active contribution to their development.

I was walking on air. In early February 1973, I received word that the General Secretary himself would see me. I flew to Moscow on February 11, and on February 15, 1973, the closed door which Suslov had pointed out opened to me.

Brezhnev and I spent two and a half hours together. The only other man in the room was Viktor Sukhodrev, the official interpreter. Sukhodrev didn't have much work to do. Soon after Brezhnev began speaking, I started replying to him in Russian before Sukhodrev had completed the translation. Brezhnev said, "Well, Doctor Hammer, you apparently can understand my Russian very well."

"Yes," I said, "but it's more important to know whether you can understand *my* Russian."

He laughed and said that I was doing all right, and we went on with our business without much more of Sukhodrev's assistance.

I found Mr. Brezhnev to be a man of great humanism and vast warmth. Brezhnev's emotions were deep and his eyes quickly filled with tears when his sentiments were stirred. As a sign of his emotional character, Brezhnev was embarrassed that no gift had been prepared for me, and, standing up, he whipped the gold watch and chain from his vest and handed it to me. I carried it with me for years, and liked to tease Americans with it as an example of Soviet technology. "Keeps pretty good time, you know."

Brezhnev was eager to open up Soviet trade with the West and particularly with the United States. He liked my formulation "détente through trade," and he was ready to put his weight and muscle behind the deals I wanted to make for Occidental.

They were:

• For Occidental to ship one half-billion dollars' worth of fertilizer to Russia annually in exchange for urea and ammonia of equivalent value which we could sell in the United States.

• For the building of an international trade center and hotel in the heart of Moscow to service the growing number of American and international companies which would need office space and hotel accommodations there.*

• For an incredibly ambitious plan to supply Soviet gas from eastern Siberia to West Coast states of America.

• For the export of Russian nickel in exchange for American nickel-plating machinery to process Soviet metals.

I went over the details of all these proposals with Brezhnev. He approved them all. The breakthrough I made with him was, in its way, as significant as Lenin's offer that I should become the first American concessionaire of the USSR.

The deals would make Occidental the number-one American corporation in the Soviet Union until close to the end of the twentieth century. The twenty-year fertilizer deal, scheduled to commence in 1978, would conclude in the year of my one hundredth birthday. I told Brezhnev that I intended to be there to celebrate the occasion, and I hoped he would be there to raise a glass with me.

He might have made it to that date, too, but for his huge indulgence in food, drink and tobacco. At our first meeting he told me that he needed to lose a lot of weight, but he got bored with the tasteless rigors of all the diets he had tried. I recommended that he should try *Dr. Atkins' Diet Revolution*, the program which was helping me to lose a troublesome twenty surplus pounds while still allowing me to eat well and enjoy my food. I gave him a copy of the Atkins book, which I understand he had translated into Russian. I also told him he should quit smoking cigarettes. This conversation about diet and health was to be a standard feature of all our meetings in coming years. I think his efforts to follow the Atkins Diet were defeated by his appetites. I kept nagging him about his cigarettes. At one time he did try to switch to using a cigarette holder with a filter, but that didn't make a lot of difference. It wasn't until shortly before his death that he gave up smoking altogether.

His drinking was far beyond moderation or any sensible control. Every time I saw him in the evening, during the coming years, he was lacing into vodka at a terrifying rate. Especially at his holiday home near Yalta on the Black Sea where Frances and I visited him, he drank so heavily that he had to be supported from the room. I couldn't have kept up with this flood of vodka even if I had wanted to. As surreptitiously as possible, when no one was looking, I would pour some of

---

*Opened in 1980, it is now often referred to in Moscow as "The Hammer House": more than 600 office suites, 600 apartments and 600 hotel rooms—besides conference rooms, multinational restaurants and shops—a lasting monument to the decade of détente.

my glass under the table or take small sips for every one of his "bottoms-up."

The only one who could trade drink for drink with Brezhnev was, apparently, Konstantin Chernenko—for whom the medical consequences were to be equally fatal. When Chernenko died—only two years after Brezhnev—it was widely rumored in Moscow that he had cirrhosis of the liver, among other serious illnesses.

This excessive drinking among the Russians, I believe, was undoubtedly one of the main reasons why Mikhail Gorbachev made it an early priority to crack down on vodka consumption, launching a nationwide drive for restraint and forbidding the serving of vodka at official functions or the sale of vodka until the afternoon, when the working day is nearly finished.

Back to 1973, however. At that first meeting, Brezhnev said that the only major obstacle in his mind to "détente through trade" was the political climate in America. The Watergate crisis was only just beginning to make itself felt at that moment. It did not appear to worry Brezhnev: he was certain that an affair which seemed to him so trivial would not interfere with the momentous political interests at stake in Nixon's new global strategy. The key question to Brezhnev was whether or not Nixon truly wanted a new era of détente with Russia, and whether he could carry it off with Congress and the American people.

Political memory is very long in Russia, and slights and insults are never forgotten or quickly forgiven. Nixon's long-standing hostility to the Soviet Union and his aggressive anti-Communism within the US had all been minutely recorded in the Kremlin's ledgers. His eyeball-to-eyeball confrontation with Khrushchev, when Nixon visited Moscow as Eisenhower's Vice President, had left an indelible impression of belligerence.

I tried to reassure Brezhnev. I was certain, I said, that Nixon's change of heart was sincere. He had realized that, through détente, he could leave his mark in history as one of America's greatest Presidents; and the judgment of history was, as everyone knew, Nixon's outstanding preoccupation for his second term.

As for the President's capacity to carry the American people with him, I asserted that it was not in doubt. Nixon had won one of the greatest electoral victories of all time. His standing with the people was at a record high. In the post-Vietnam atmosphere, America was looking for a new role in the world and a new age of reconciliation. All the political constituents, I assured Brezhnev, were right for the new deal which he wanted with the West; and for the deals I wanted to make for Occidental in Russia.

Brezhnev took my word and believed me. He guaranteed that he would give his personal support to our deals and keep a close eye on their development. He told me to get in touch with him directly if we ran into any major problems or if I thought that his intervention would be helpful.

That was the bonus that, above all, I had wanted. The seal of the General Secretary's approval would guarantee the success of Occidental's new ventures in Russia. Open access to Brezhnev, "the Chairman of the Board," would let me leapfrog the tangled fences of bureaucracy which would undoubtedly stand in our way.

Finalizing the fertilizer and trade center deals took a further full year from the date of my Brezhnev meeting. Business with the Russians is not done quickly. They move very methodically through a routine of steps, at each of which they make sure that they can change their minds, withdraw or close a deal with somebody else. They never open negotiations without getting competitive bids. They start negotiations with a protocol, without which you can't get visas and you can't get any official access for discussions. The protocol lets you in. Next they move to writing a letter of intent, followed by a global agreement which sets forth the principal terms of understanding. This paves the way for the last step, which is the implementing agreements.

Dealing with the Russians takes a lot of patience, competitive sense and keen watchfulness. Asked by the Society of American Business Writers once for advice to American businessmen, I said:

> I would sum it up in this fashion: Draw your contract carefully because, once you sign it, the Soviets will make sure you live up to it, just as they intend to live up to their commitment. . . . Their Chairman of the State Bank, Mr. Alkhimov, tells a story about the Russian press that you may find instructive. In Russia, the word for "however" is *vsyahtekey*. Mr. Alkhimov says the best way to read *Izvestia* and *Pravda* is to follow the story to the sentence which you will find beginning with the word *vsyahtekey*. And then, from that point on, pay *very close attention*. The same tip applies to contracts.

Any American businessman who entered negotiations with the Russians expecting them to be naive in the drawing of contracts and the exaction of the last kopek would be making a horrible mistake. Once when I met him in his office, Brezhnev laughingly said, "I trust Komarov [the First Deputy Foreign Trade Minister] is squeezing you." I truthfully answered that we were being squeezed plenty.

On the other hand, American go-getting can occasionally cause a surprise in the Soviet bureaucracy. One day during my first visit to Moscow after the Nixon/Brezhnev summit there in July 1972, I dumbfounded Jermen Gvishiani with our informal style of decision-making.

He had called me to his office to show me a draft of our proposed five-point agreement. It was written in Russian, of course. I looked it over and it seemed all right. So I took a pen, struck out the word "draft," signed it and handed it back to him. He was nonplussed.

"Don't you want to show it to your lawyer?" he said.

"No," I said. "I don't need a lawyer to tell me that it's all right as it stands."

"Don't you at least want to think it over?"

"Look," I said, "this is your draft, not mine. I haven't changed one word of it and I've signed it. So we're in business, aren't we?"

He stood there for a moment, holding the document and obviously not knowing what to do. Then he said he needed to take advice. He left the room. I have always thought he went to telephone his father-in-law, Premier Kosygin. After a while he came back into the room and said, "Okay." Then he took the pen and signed his own draft, still acting as if I had put one over on him.

Before the final stages of the negotiations, I saw Brezhnev twice. When he was in Washington in June 1973 for his summit conference with Richard Nixon, I met him for lunch at Blair House, the diplomatic residence for visiting heads of state across from the White House. That evening, as Frances and I were entering the White House for Nixon's state dinner, the President, the General Secretary and I had an impromptu meeting. Seeing us coming along the receiving line, Brezhnev held me up for a few minutes, talking to me in Russian while I translated for the President.

On November 17, 1973, I saw Brezhnev again in his Kremlin office.

By this time Brezhnev had looked closely into the Pandora's box of Watergate, and the full extent of Nixon's plight was beginning to dawn on him. Even though he had a painfully sore throat on the day we met and had been told not to talk, he insisted on seeing me because, as he said, "one of my greatest needs is to get your ideas." Most of all, he wanted my opinions on Nixon's Watergate troubles.

At that point I still believed Nixon would survive. I told Brezhnev that the President's fighting spirit would see him through. Brezhnev said that he was baffled by all the fuss being made about Watergate. He said, "You have your own ways and, speaking confidentially, I must confess I don't understand them." He said, "I worry about Nixon. A man can only stand so much and then he's bound to break down." He said that he was being very careful not to take advantage of Nixon's troubles and "not to jump on him, as others are." He had sent Nixon a warm personal letter which, Dobrynin had told him, Nixon had greatly appreciated.

Declaring that Nixon was "the only true statesman in the United

States—even Pompidou thinks so," Brezhnev said he wanted to do everything possible to help Nixon settle his political problems, especially in the Middle East. Brezhnev was startlingly undogmatic and pragmatic about the position of Israel. He said that there should be a settlement which would provide security for Israel and "good neighbor relations." He went on, "The United States is more interested in this than we are. After all, we don't buy any oil from the Middle East."

He felt that Nixon had to deal with an almost impossible problem with American Zionists who would allow no compromise on Israel's position. "They cannot live long this way," he said. "Both Arabs and Israelis will have to compromise."

Despite his bad throat, Brezhnev was in high spirits that day. He asked about the progress of the fertilizer deal and then launched into a long reminiscence of his own farming days on one of the largest communes in Khazakstan, where "nothing would grow without chemical fertilizers." He said that he had always enjoyed work and abhorred red tape. "I like to speak my mind and get on with things," he said.

He asked me to let Nixon know that he was truly "confident of détente as a workable premise," and that he believed in Nixon, but was worried about his health. I relayed this message to the President in a letter.

Along with my letter, I enclosed a quotation from Abraham Lincoln which has always meant a lot to me. Lincoln said, "If I were to try to read, much less answer, all the attacks made on me, this shop might as well be closed for any other business. I do the very best I can; and I mean to keep doing so until the end. If the end brings me out all right, what is said against me won't amount to anything. If the end brings me out wrong, ten angels swearing I was right would make no difference."

I was particularly sympathetic to President Nixon's plight, because I was having Watergate troubles of my own.

In late March and early April of 1972, I had made a contribution to Nixon's campaign fund—anonymously, and from my own funds, as I had been accustomed to doing since Roosevelt ran in 1932. Because I had the ill luck to put my contribution into the hands of a trusted executive who turned out to be a rascal, however, my contribution was to entangle me in a fight which threatened to destroy my reputation, my work, my health and even, at one moment, my life itself.

Richard Nixon's 1972 campaign was organized almost as if he were an unknown with an outside shot at the White House, rather than an incumbent President running against a weak Democratic candidate. With maximum efficiency, the Committee to Re-Elect the President combed the nation for every possible dollar of financial support, so it came as no surprise to me when Maurice Stans, Chairman of the Finance Committee, came looking to me for "a substantial contribution."

"Substantial" to me meant $50,000, and that's what I packed when I went to see Stans in Washington on March 30, 1972. Stans had something slightly bigger in mind, however: he suggested that I might like to give $250,000. I managed to smile, and demurred.

"Well," he said, "at least I think you should contribute a hundred thousand dollars and be a member of The One Hundred Thousand Club. It contains many of your friends." Without great enthusiasm, but with a sense of resignation, I agreed, though, I told him, I still insisted on anonymity.

"In that case, as you know," Stans said, "you will have to make your contribution in full before April seventh. On that date the Federal Election Campaign Act becomes effective and contributions will have to be declared."

I knew all about it, told him he could have $50,000 right away, and promised to get the balance to him within the next seven days. As it was, I could give him only $46,000 at that time—$4000 was needed for tickets to a political dinner—but I said he'd have the outstanding $54,000 within a week. On April 3, back in Los Angeles, I took out $54,000 from my bank, flew to Reno, where I had an appointment to see *Manchester Union Leader* publisher Bill Loeb, and, on April 5, I gave the money to my associate, Tim Babcock, to give to Stans, impressing upon him the necessity of delivering it before April 7. He said it was no problem.

Tim Babcock was a very trusted member of my staff, the Executive Vice President of Occidental International, my Washington division, and a former Governor of Montana, from 1962 to 1968. I believed in him implicitly.

Two and a half months later, on July 20, I met with President Nixon in the Oval Office. I had just returned from the Soviet Union, where I had signed the first trade agreement since the Nixon/Brezhnev summit, and Nixon naturally wanted to hear all about it. He was jovial, friendly, at the peak of his powers and sky-high with confidence. "I've done my duty," I told him. "I'm in The Hundred Thousand Club with Maurice Stans."

We both laughed.

A year later I wasn't laughing anymore.

As it turned out, Tim Babcock had *not* delivered the $54,000 to Stans by April 7. In fact, incredibly, he had not even begun to give the money to Stans until September 14, when he visited Stans's office and handed over $15,000. Stans, naturally, said that the sum would be recorded as a donation from Armand Hammer. Oh no, said Babcock, the contribution was not from me, but from several individuals whose names and addresses he would supply soon. That's what Stans wrote.

On November 3 Stans received an additional $25,000 through Babcock's attorney, again attributed to various, soon-to-be-named donors. And on January 17, 1973, he got a final $14,000, with the same proviso.

There was my $54,000, to which Babcock had helped himself and which he had then replaced from some other sources—but why had he done this? A strong clue was provided by a later investigation which, unfortunately, came too late to help my cause.

Apparently Babcock was in severe financial difficulty in April 1972, and sorely pressed for cash. He had borrowed $2 million to build a hotel in Helena, Montana, and then a further $600,000 to furnish and equip it. He was restoring a historic mansion as a luxurious home for himself and was running a loss-making radio station. It seems reasonable to suppose that during the summer of 1972 he might have found it convenient to have access to $54,000.

Meanwhile I sailed on, blithely unaware of the storm that was about to break. By April 1973 events were unfolding so quickly and dramatically in the Watergate scandal that it was clear that Maurice Stans's Finance Committee would be formally investigated. In June, Stans made a full disclosure of the funds which he had received, and informed me that my contribution had been $46,000.

Forty-six thousand dollars? To say that I hit the ceiling would not be going far enough. I called Babcock to my house and he lied, saying that I had given him the money in "July or August, I can't remember which." It was patently untrue, but from then on Babcock was caught in his lies. And so was I.

Shortly thereafter the Senate Select Committee headed by Sam Ervin sent a questionnaire to all donors, requiring a statement of their campaign contributions. I asked Louis Nizer what I should do. His answer was unequivocal: I had not been asked how much money I had given to be delivered as a contribution, I had simply been asked how much I had contributed, and that amount was $46,000. Whatever had happened to the money given to Babcock was a matter between Babcock and myself.

That's what I answered—but it did not end there. The Watergate special prosecutor didn't believe it. First he prosecuted Babcock for "aiding and abetting" me in the making of an illegal contribution. Babcock was convicted and sentenced to four months in jail (which was later reduced to a one-thousand-dollar fine on appeal after I was sentenced to a fine), but note that it was for aiding and abetting *me*. Babcock was committed to a story which blamed me for his wrongdoing. He alleged, and the Special Prosecutor so charged, that I had given him the $54,000 on or about September 6, 1972, with instructions to deliver the money to the Finance Committee in the names of other people. It was further alleged and charged that I had conspired with Babcock to conceal the making of campaign contributions as they were delivered to the Finance Committee on September 14, November 3 and January 17.

How was I to prove my innocence? I had no receipts, no witnesses, no documentary proof of when I had given the money to Babcock. Furthermore, at the time, I had even forgotten about the trip to Reno—the whole thing had happened eighteen months previously— and so the only date I could think of for the day I had handed the money to Babcock was April 3, the day I had taken it out of the bank— and Babcock could prove that he wasn't in Los Angeles that day.

Nevertheless, I knew that if I could appear before the grand jury and tell my story, that I would convince them. I knew that talking to them face-to-face would persuade them that I was innocent of wrong-doing. My attorneys argued against it, but I was ready for the fray.

Or at least my brain and my soul were ready; my heart wasn't. At the moment of the greatest personal crisis in my life, my health disintegrated.

I was seventy-six years old, had suffered intermittent bad health for more than twenty years and had twice submitted to major surgery within the previous three years. In addition I was under immense strain in my business life, between boardroom battles, the crazy menace of Oxy's Libyan connection and the fathomless complications of doing business with the Soviets. To be confronted at such a time with the threat of a criminal conviction was more than my heart could stand. It didn't quite give out, but it gave notice of a desire to quit.

Under no circumstances, said my doctors, was I to go through the strain of a trial. It could, quite literally, kill me. As Louis Nizer was to write in his book *Reflections Without Mirrors,* "It was desirable to have a vindicated client, but only if he was alive."

I had no alternative: swallowing my pride, and in agreement with the prosecutor, I entered a guilty plea to three misdemeanors and determined to put the whole ugly mess behind me. I presumed that the worst was over. But it was yet to come.

In a way it was my fault. The probation officer in Los Angeles invited me to open my heart and mind and set forth fully all the circumstances surrounding the events which led to the misdemeanor plea, and I accepted the invitation. I wrote a letter in which I acknowledged a measure of guilt for having failed to give close supervision to the money I had placed in Babcock's hands, and concluded that in pleading guilty I was willing to resolve all doubts in favor of the prosecutor.

When the judge read that, he hit the roof. He read it—correctly, I must admit—as a protestation of innocence inconsistent with a plea of guilty, then, on his own motion, vacated the guilty plea, entered a not-guilty plea for me and set the case down for trial. The prosecutor, hearing that, proceeded to announce that, the plea bargaining having been set aside, he was convening a grand jury and would indict me on two felonies, to be added to the misdemeanors which had been set down for trial.

Now I had the worst of all possible worlds: felonies, a trial, all of my worst nightmares had come to life. Fortunately, the judge's action was reversed on appeal, and the original guilty plea to misdemeanors reinstated, but this latest development almost stopped my heart for keeps.

At ten o'clock one evening, at my home in California, my heart failed. I thought I was going to die. I was rushed to the Los Angeles Hospital, where my condition was diagnosed as preinfarction angina, congestive heart failure and disturbance of the cardiac rhythm. When in late March 1976 I appeared in Los Angeles for sentencing—the case had been transferred from Washington for my health—I was invisibly wired with telemetered electrocardiographic equipment so that I could be monitored by doctors and medical aides in an adjoining room.

I have never felt closer to death. All my life I had tried to live decently and act honestly. Nothing in life meant more to me than my good name and reputation. And now here I was about to be sentenced.

I was given a fine of $3000 and one year's probation. I could go, I was told; I was free.

But, once convicted, a human being can never be free again. Guilt and innocence are more than legal terms. Guilt lives on in the mind of the criminal and in the society in which he moves, where he will always be suspected and distrusted. Innocence is a state of grace, conferred and confirmed in trusting relations between people in all their dealings with each other. The innocent man cannot be free until the world acknowledges his innocence.

I set out to clear my name.

Gradually, my health recovered, and I began to make headway. The first breakthrough came when my memory suddenly cleared and I remembered that I had given Babcock the money in Reno on April 5— a day for which he had no alibi. The second came in 1985, when some extraordinary information came my way. This is what I learned:

When Babcock had gone to Stans's office on January 17, 1973, with his final parcel of $14,000, the election, of course, had long been over. Stans had explained to Babcock that the Finance Committee had more than enough money to pay for campaign expenses but that money was needed for noncampaign expenses such as the compilation of voter profile records at the White House. Stans had asked Babcock if his fictional contributors would mind applying both the current $14,000 and the previous $25,000 to those purposes. Babcock had replied that it was no problem.

That meant that the $39,000 had not gone for campaign expenses after all—and thus they could not possibly have been illegal campaign contributions! I was technically innocent even of the technical offense which had been laid against me. And as for the first $15,000 Babcock had given them on September 14—the statute of limitations had expired on that contribution by the time my case was heard.

In truth, I should not have been called to answer for any of those contributions, and the prosecutor must have known it. Why hadn't he informed us? When my attorneys heard about it, they immediately swore in a deposition that they would never have advised me to plead guilty if they had known the facts.

In addition we discovered that a case similar to mine had come up at the same time, and the man had never been prosecuted because the prosecutor had no case. Dwayne Andreas, head of Archer-Daniels-Midland Co., the agricultural-processing giant, had promised Stans $25,000, and, in good faith, had made every possible effort to complete his contribution before April 7. However, the contribution hadn't been lodged with the committee until after that date.

When the Justice Department investigated the Andreas contribution, they concluded that, even though the money had been received after April 7, it was not governed by the new law because it had been pledged before that date—exactly my case! Not only was I innocent of what I had been charged, but I never should have been charged in the first place.

Needless to say, the discovery of all this information has been extremely heartening, and, as I write these words, my case is again before the government, with all the exonerating evidence intact. Eventually I hope to be vindicated.

Meanwhile, back to Russia. As my health improved, once the stress on my heart had been removed, I began to shuttle back and forth from Moscow again, and, by the middle of the decade, Frances had been to Moscow as many times as she cared to for the rest of her life. One evening, when we were in the Lenin Suite at the National Hotel, she put her foot down.

"Listen, Armand," she said, "I've really had enough of this place and I'm never coming here again unless there are some changes made. I don't like this hotel. I don't feel safe in the elevators, because they're always breaking down. The plumbing doesn't work most of the time. The room is either too hot or too cold. You can't open the window to get any fresh air. The charm of these rooms has completely evaporated for me. Unless we can be more comfortable here, I don't want to come back."

Next evening we had to attend a banquet at the Kremlin. I was sitting beside Brezhnev's assistant, Alexandrov. Brezhnev himself was a few seats away. Suddenly Alexandrov turned to me and said, "I understand Mrs. Hammer is not happy with her accommodations at the National Hotel. Since you have to visit Moscow so frequently, perhaps it would suit you better to have an apartment here. Please allow us to make the necessary arrangements. I'm sure we could find you an apartment to Mrs. Hammer's satisfaction in the diplomatic quarter."

How, I wonder, could they have known that Frances was not happy with her accommodations?

In any case, they found a five-room apartment at Lavrushensky Perulok, with a view of the Kremlin, which had been occupied by five families. I had it completely rebuilt and elegantly furnished on a turn-key job by a West German contractor working under the supervision of MacDonald Becket, the architect who built the Moscow Trade Center. The walls were decorated with beautiful paintings by famous Russian artists which I had repatriated.

Without a word to Frances until the day the apartment was finished, I rode with her to the building, took her upstairs, opened the door, and there stood a Russian maid in uniform welcoming us to our new home. Needless to say, France was flabbergasted.

As we got to know Brezhnev better, we also had to get used to his unusual style of greeting special friends. Though I could have lived without the experience, I have been kissed by thousands of Russian men—but always on the cheek. It was Brezhnev's mark of special esteem to impose enthusiastic kisses on the lips. I seemed to find this marginally easier to take than Frances.

Presidents came and went in the White House, but only death would dislodge Brezhnev from the General Secretary's office in the Kremlin. As Gerald Ford took over from Richard Nixon, only to be defeated by Jimmy Carter, I became one of the few Americans providing continuity to the policy of détente. My usefulness as a contact between the Kremlin and the White House consequently increased.

Jimmy Carter's ascendancy took me by surprise. I was among those who figured he didn't stand a chance.

I had first met Jimmy Carter during his campaign at a party in Los Angeles at Lew Wasserman's home. At that time I barely knew and hardly cared who Jimmy Carter was. Frances happened to be sitting next to Mr. Carter at dinner, however, and as we were going home she said, "You'd better watch that man. He's going to be President."

Because Carter had no previous experience in foreign relations and was a completely unknown quantity for the Russians, I was in a position to be a useful intermediary between them.

For instance, in September 1976, I carried a message to Carter from Brezhnev's Foreign Minister, Andrei Gromyko. Having seen

Gromyko in New York at a meeting arranged by Ambassador Dobrynin, I was going to a party in Georgia at the home of Miss Lillian, Jimmy Carter's mother. Hearing this, Gromyko wanted to be sure Carter had the same information on the Soviet arms position as Kissinger did. He asked if I would carry a message to Mr. Carter.

Fred Gross had to land our plane at Americus, the nearest airport capable of taking the plane. When we went back to the airport after the party, a sizable crowd had gathered on the tarmac.

"Is somebody famous coming in, Fred?" I said.

"No, Doctor," he said. "They're here because no plane like this has ever taken off from this strip, and they're all making bets about whether we make it over those trees at the end of the runway."

We trimmed a few inches off the treetops.

On December 9, 1976, I met Jimmy Carter for lunch at Blair House and gave him an up-to-date account of our dealings with the Russians. At the meeting I urged him to arrange a summit meeting with Leonid Brezhnev as one of his earliest priorities. Toward the end of his administration, President Carter told me that he wished he had acted on my advice and not delayed as long as he did. Like most American Presidents, however, Jimmy Carter had to deal with a powerful anti-Soviet lobby in his own White House. Carter's was led by Zbigniew Brzezinski, whose family property in Poland had been expropriated by the Communists, and who hated the Russians.

A worldwide campaign in defense of human rights was obviously going to be a strong plank in Carter's administration. A powerful thread of moral-reforming zeal ran through Jimmy Carter's character, and he regarded it as part of America's mission in the world to give a lead to less enlightened countries.

In general terms I approved of this stance—except that I think it's asking for trouble for any individual or nation to be a moral exemplar to others. As far as the administration's attitude affected America's relations with the Soviet Union, however, it made me uneasy. The position of the Russian Jews was the most prominent and volatile issue of human rights between the USA and the USSR. Being a true dilemma, this question needed very careful handling.

Essentially the Soviet authorities have always indignantly denied that Jews in their country suffer any disadvantages or restrictions on their freedom. The Soviets insist that their constitution guarantees rights of religious freedom to all groups.

The theory is fine. The practice is different. The Soviet authorities say that most of those Jews who are forbidden exit visas have had access through their work to confidential or secret information. Some violated their laws by "hooliganism" or "anti-Soviet slander" and have been sentenced to prison in Siberia. The authorities seem to think that one or other of these situations fits nearly every Jew in Russia who wants to emigrate.

As a Jew I feel the most powerful bond with the State of Israel, and Israel's interests beat in my heart. Many of my Jewish friends in Israel and in America have come to me for help in aiding the Jews in Soviet Russia, and I have done everything I could to help them.

I believed that the best way to help the Soviet Jews, however, was through discreet and quiet work both on individual cases and on larger principles. I feared that vague and ill-defined sentiments were going to interfere with the absolutely essential progress of détente between the USA and the USSR.

After the Nixon/Brezhnev summit meetings of 1972 and 1973, Jewish emigration from Russia proceeded at an average rate of more than 20,000 a year. In some years, such as 1973 and 1978, numbers exceeded 30,000. In 1979, 50,000 Jews left Russia. In 1980—the year of the Afghanistan crisis—the figure was down to 20,000, which it has never since approached. In the last four years, up to 1986, only 1000 Jews a year have been permitted to leave.

I tried to encourage the growth of emigration in the seventies and urged the Soviets to look again at their policies. In a letter written on December 9, 1976, for instance, I pleaded with Brezhnev to reexamine the so-called security dimension of the problem. "Surely," I wrote, "some of these citizens have now been away from sensitive matters long enough that their emigration will have no detrimental effect on the USSR?"

On individual cases, I worked closely with Jewish friends in America, notably Harry Simon-Levi, one of our attorneys, who was closely involved in Jewish and Israeli affairs. Before he had come to the United States, Harry had fought in the Irgun with his close friend Menachem Begin, and he retained close connections in Tel Aviv and Jerusalem. We managed to get the Soviet authorities to relent on a number of cases.

My biggest success in that field came at the prompting, not of private Jews in America, but of Golda Meir herself.

On September 5, 1972, she wrote to me:

> I am sure you have heard of the plight of Jewish academicians who wish to come to Israel. The matter is of such significance that I would do anything to be able to meet you and discuss with you this matter which may become one more great tragedy in Jewish life.
>
> It seems to me that you, because you have done so much for Russia, more than others can help avert disaster for the Russian Jews.

Please forgive me for writing about this to you whom I have never had the privilege of meeting. Believe me it is due to my great anxiety as to what is already taking place and what the future may be.

Please let me know if you are prepared to suggest some way in which we might meet for a discussion of this matter, or if you are prepared to meet with somebody whom I would send to you.

Of course I agreed to go see her. Shortly after I received her letter, I got a message from Zvi Dinstein, Deputy Finance Minister and the brother of a member of Golda's cabinet, that she wanted to talk to me in person in Jerusalem. If I would go to see her, she would send a plane for me to carry me there in secret. I knew I might be risking my life because there were new terrorist attacks under way, but the urgency of the request impelled me to go.

Leaving Frances in Paris, I told Fred Gross I wanted to go to the Da Vinci airport in Rome. On arrival, I advised Fred I would be tied up a few days and he should stand by to leave at a moment's notice.

Then I got in a taxi and told the driver to drive me out of the airport.

Once we were through the airport perimeter, I told the driver to turn around and go to another, remote part of the airport.

An unmarked Boeing 707 was waiting for me there, its engines running. Armed guards with drawn machine guns stood around the steps. As soon as I entered the plane, the steps were lifted and the plane taxied for takeoff. Zvi Dinstein and I were the only passengers, attended by a full cabin crew of stewards and stewardesses.

When the plane touched down at Jerusalem airport, Golda Meir's car was waiting to meet me. I was driven straight to the state guest house, where dinner was ready to be served. Golda and I dined together; Dr. Dinstein was also present.

Golda wanted me to persuade Leonid Brezhnev to lift the Education Tax.

The Education Tax was an additional penalty which the Soviets had levied upon all Jews who wished to emigrate. Claiming that the state should be recompensed for the education which they had enjoyed in the Soviet Union, the authorities demanded an average of 12,500 gold rubles—about $15,000—before an exit visa would be issued.

Golda said that this crippling tax made emigration impossible for all but a tiny handful. It imprisoned would-be emigrants in Russia as surely as if they were bound in chains. The financial benefit of this tax to the Soviet Union was trivial. Golda believed that Brezhnev might respond to a direct appeal from me. She wanted me to tell Brezhnev that the Education Tax was a cruel measure unworthy of a great country like the Soviet Union, that it damaged the Soviet Union's standing in the world and disqualified the Soviet Union from leading Israel toward any compromise settlement with its Arab neighbors.

I told her that I was hoping to see Brezhnev early in the new year of 1973. I said that I would raise the question with him then and do everything I could to stress the strength of Golda's feelings, giving her request my utmost support.

Golda's 707 flew me back to Rome, where I returned to my plane and told Fred that I wanted to return to Paris to pick up Frances. Imperturbable as ever, Fred got on with the job. After all our years together, I don't think he'd turn a hair if I told him that my destination was the dark side of the moon. Frances was still under the impression that I had simply gone to Rome on business.

At my meeting with Brezhnev on February 15, 1973, I gave him the message from Mrs. Meir and then I added my own arguments. I said that the continued imposition of the Education Tax would undoubtedly bring powerful pressures on the White House from Jewish groups and détente might be seriously damaged. On the other hand, I argued, the lifting of the Education Tax would be seen by the world as an act of great magnanimity and goodwill. The Soviet Union's prestige would rise out of all proportion to the tiny financial loss it would incur from dropping the tax. I assured Brezhnev that the entire community of world leaders would be grateful to him for such a statesmanlike step.

After a few days, before I left Moscow, the tax was lifted.

I was elated, but my efforts did not stop there, of course. For instance, with the help of Austrian Chancellor Bruno Kreisky and Rumanian President Nicolae Ceausescu, I tried to solve one of the logistical impediments to the emigration of Russian Jews, which was also raised by Golda Meir at our meeting. Those Jews who were granted exit visas were being taken first to Vienna, where they were accommodated in transit camps. In these camps, many of them took the opportunity to change their minds about their chosen destination and applied for United States visas rather than going on to Israel. That practice was irritating to the Soviets, who felt that they were being taken for a ride. It also defeated Israel's goal of increasing the number of immigrating Jews. Perhaps, it was felt, if there were direct flights to Israel, with only a stop in Bucharest, there would be a better chance of persuading the would-be immigrants to settle there.

At my suggestion Ceausescu offered to take the emigrants into transit camps in Bucharest, from whence they could transfer to El Al flights to Israel. This plan went down, with so many other high hopes and good intentions, when détente hit the reef of the Afghanistan crisis.

Arms control agreements were delayed; possible trade deals were shelved; cultural exchanges were canceled. The ball which Richard Nixon had passed down the line through Gerald Ford was dropped by Jimmy Carter.

The ultimate collapse of détente had a lot to do with Carter's belief that America had to teach the Soviet Union a moral lesson. He seemed to expect the Russians to do public penance for the faults of their system and their society. That is not the best way to get cooperation from such proud, stubborn and defensive people as the Russians.

If only he could have dealt with the Russians privately and without the intervention of Brzezinski on this question, they would not have felt that they were being publicly chastised, and they might have been more malleable. This view is supported by the one example I know of first hand—the case of Francis Jay Crawford.

Mr. Crawford, a Moscow-based senior executive of the International Harvester Corporation, got into trouble with the Soviet police in 1978. He was accused of profiteering in black market currency swindles, which he fervently denied.

There was an almost boring banality about Mr. Crawford's position—though I don't imagine he thought so. Black market dealings is a charge with which the KGB can easily embarrass foreigners. Many foreign businessmen have fallen into this mantrap—none, I am happy to say, from Occidental—and Mr. Crawford was merely another in a very long line.

His arrest came—not by coincidence—at a bad moment for US/USSR relations. The FBI had just arrested two Russian members of the UN delegation for spying, and the Russians wanted to retaliate. And, at the time, the Carter administration was belaboring the Soviets over the Moscow trials of dissidents. Mr. Crawford's case gave the Russians a small stick with which to beat the Americans in return, as if to say, "Who do you think you are to give us lessons in morality when your people behave like this?"—kid stuff, of course, but international relations all too often descend to the level of juvenile street games.

International Harvester was, understandably, deeply upset over their man's fate and they kicked up a storm in US business circles. Potential deals with the Soviet Union were stalled and American businessmen put pressure on the White House to flex its muscles at the Kremlin.

At this moment the Carter administration asked me to intervene.

I believed in the SALT agreements, and still do. I thought they were the best fruit of the détente decade, even though SALT II went unratified by Congress. I thought they pointed the way to a rational and progressive disarmament by the superpowers and to the end of the nuclear nightmare. I would have done anything possible to encourage the SALT talks.

A message was relayed to me by Dr. Marshall Shulman, the Special Adviser to the Secretary of State. Apparently he had called Bill McSweeny, President of Occidental International in Washington, to say, "I have just had a call from Secretary Vance, who was talking to the President. With the approval of the President, Secretary Vance suggested I get in touch with Armand Hammer to see if he could lend influence in explaining to Brezhnev the harmful effects of the Crawford case."

I got word from Dr. Shulman as I was landing in a helicopter at our shale oil works in Colorado. I told Marshall that I would write directly to Brezhnev about Mr. Crawford. I was also planning to be in Russia in late August, and perhaps I might be able to discuss the case with Brezhnev then. Marshall Shulman said that anything I could do would be appreciated.

I wrote to Brezhnev on July 6, 1978, expressing my view that

> *The Crawford matter is an irritant which should be quickly resolved, lest it create a problem which could cause serious injury to the growth of trade we all seek.*
>
> *I am not raising a question about the guilt or innocence of Mr. Crawford, since I do not know the facts. . . . I believe very sincerely that it would establish a good precedent and help future economic relations if Mr. Crawford was asked to leave the country and was not subjected to trial, with all the unfavorable and volatile publicity which would result, and which would be seized upon by those who oppose détente.*
>
> *The Crawford matter is a small annoyance in the larger framework of successful trade and mutual understanding and, in my opinion, should be treated as such and resolved very swiftly. Otherwise it could grow like a tumor and seriously poison relations with other companies and with the Congress of the United States.*

Our ammonia and SPA facilities at Odessa were due to be commissioned on August 22, 1978. The occasion also had sentimental significance for me—it was my first visit to my father's hometown. Brezhnev made arrangements for us to meet after the Odessa celebrations.

Brezhnev was on vacation at the General Secretary's Black Sea dacha near Yalta. After the commissioning of the works at Odessa, I had to fly back to Moscow, carrying the press corps who had attended the opening. Brezhnev sent his plane to Moscow to collect Frances and me and fly us out to Yalta.

We were accommodated for the night in some of the most sumptuous quarters I have ever occupied—a former Czarist summer palace, the Alexander Palace. We were alone there and the entire staff was at our disposal. The palace had its own switchboard with tied-lines direct to Brezhnev's own dacha and to Moscow. In the morning a ZIL was waiting to carry me to my interview with Brezhnev.

He was in a very relaxed, holiday-making mood, which he expressed by drinking even more vodka than usual. When we began to talk, his geniality did not, however, extend to Mr. Crawford.

"We've caught this man in the act," he said. "His Russian girlfriend was working for us. We have examined his expense accounts and we've got documentary proof that he was working a currency swindle. We're completely within our rights to prosecute him and we want to expose him."

"Well," I said, "I don't want to get involved in the specific rights and wrongs of the case. I just want to point out that you don't stand to gain anything by making a big public example of this man. If you send him to prison for a long time, you'll do untold damage to relations with the United States. American companies just won't come here."

"We can't simply let him off. He has to stand trial," Brezhnev protested.

"Maybe so," I said, "but you could just fine him and expel him from the country. That way you could carry out the full process of your laws."

"That's a pretty good idea," Brezhnev said. "That's what we'll do."

That's what they did.

As for the two Russian spies, they were found guilty and sentenced to fifty years' imprisonment, but after serving a short time in prison, they were exchanged for several dissidents languishing in Russian prisons. Marshall Shulman wrote me, speaking of President Carter, Secretary Vance and himself, "All of us were appreciative of what you were able to do."

When he visited Washington in 1973, Brezhnev said that he expected trade between the US and the USSR to rise from $100 million in 1974 to $1000 million in 1980. Led by Occidental, there *was* a boom in trade during the seventies, but by the end of 1980, Occidental's much-reduced business in Russia represented almost the sum total of trade between the two countries. The reason was Afghanistan.

Détente ended with the Soviet invasion of Afghanistan and Jimmy Carter's subsequent economic and cultural reprisals. One of the most imaginative and original political initiatives was shot to pieces in the hostile exchanges between Moscow and Washington.

I did not believe at the time that the Afghanistan crisis was a good enough reason to abandon détente. I thought the crisis could be solved by political negotiation. I still think so today.

Whispering over Jimmy Carter's shoulder, urging him to cast the die, was Zbigniew Brzezinski, the leading anti-Soviet in the administration. Brzezinski's mentality was perfectly pictured when he posed for photographs in the Khyber Pass and was seen aiming a machine gun into Afghanistan, like a little boy with a popgun chasing the baddies.

The Carter administration took the Afghanistan crisis as its chance to finally teach the Soviets a moral lesson.

One of Mr. Carter's first acts was to embargo exports of grains and phosphates to the USSR. Under Secretary of State David Newsom called me personally to warn me that the President would announce this embargo in a televised Address to the Nation. I gave immediate instructions effecting this presidential edict throughout Occidental, and wrote to the President that we would, of course, support his decision. "However," I added, "I do not think that suspension of shipments or any unilateral modification of the existing contracts will have a significant effect on the Russians." I was right.

At first the crisis seemed to threaten much more than mere diplomatic and economic relations. It seemed to threaten war between the superpowers.

On January 23, 1980, I wrote to Brezhnev, asking for a meeting.

I am addressing myself to you at a time when, I believe, I can make a positive contribution to the easing of the tension which has arisen in relations between our two countries. The situation is so volatile and indeed critical that it is strongly reminiscent of the worst days in relations between the United States and the USSR in the 1950s. My greatest concern is, of course, that the edifice of US-Soviet détente which has been erected through such heavy efforts on both sides is listing precariously.

It is to enable me to be of help in this time of crisis that I am kindly asking for an appointment with you as soon as possible.

Brezhnev received me in his Kremlin office at the end of February 1980.

Describing the Soviet military presence in Afghanistan as a police action, Brezhnev said that he had been amazed by the intemperance of Carter's response. He claimed that the Soviets had sound evidence that the CIA had been subverting the Afghan government, especially by providing arms through Pakistan, and was plotting to set up an anti-Soviet government there. Considering the instability of Khomeini's Iran, Brezhnev said that the Soviets could not allow the imposition of such a regime in Afghanistan, right on Russia's southern border. Flanked by NATO's forces in the west and China's to the east, the Soviet Union's land borders were in danger of being surrounded by hostile governments. He said that he would immediately pull Soviet troops out of Afghanistan if he got a guarantee from the US and from Afghanistan's neighbors that they would not interfere with the pro-Soviet government there.

I said that he should make it an urgent priority to get his Foreign Minister, Andrei Gromyko, together with Carter's Secretary of State, Cyrus Vance. I promised to do everything possible to bring the two sides together.

For most of the rest of 1980 I shuttled around the world trying to pull together a political settlement of the crisis. This globe-trotting was greatly facilitated by the recent acquisition of our customized Boeing 727, Oxy One. It was fitted out with a paneled suite of rooms for me and Frances, including a double-bedded bedroom and an office, with salons forward and aft containing chairs and couches which could be converted into full-length beds for my passengers. Even more importantly, the plane was equipped with the most advanced air-to-ground communications, enabling me to make and receive calls to most places around the world.

My shuttling took me to see President Giscard d'Estaing of France; Chancellor Bruno Kreisky of Austria and his Foreign Minister, Willibald Pahr; Nicolae Ceausescu of Rumania; Edward Gierek of Poland; President Zia Ul-Haq of Pakistan; the Aga Khan; and President Jimmy Carter himself.

I talked to anybody who had a good idea about how to settle the crisis, and carried messages between them.

Giscard and his wife joined Frances and me at a private lunch on April 3, 1980, hosted by Edgar Faure. He was very despondent about the crisis and held no real hope for a solution. He said that it would not be resolved quickly.

I said, "Well, we can't afford to let it stay like this indefinitely. We've got to get talks started. You're about to have Andrei Gromyko visit you here in Paris. Why don't you get Secretary Vance here at the same time?"

"I don't know," he said. "Do you think Gromyko has a lot of influence these days?"

"Yes, I do," I said. "But Brezhnev's still the boss."

"Well, why don't you try to get Gierek to invite Brezhnev to meet me in Warsaw, and perhaps France could act as a mediating force?"

I tried this line, but Gierek lost his job in Poland before the meeting could be fixed.

Bruno Kreisky and Willibald Pahr believed that the crisis could be solved by a peacekeeping force drawn from nonaligned countries. I gave that line a shot when I met Jimmy Carter in the Oval Office on June 5, 1980.

I suggested to Carter that a peacekeeping force could remain in

Afghanistan for five years, at the end of which free elections could be held. Carter said, "I don't think we can wait that long." He said that he would never understand why the Russians had moved into Afghanistan with such massive forces so suddenly. The only solution, he said, was for the Russians to pull out. I said that this was an unrealistic demand—it practically demanded a public apology from the Russians—but he said that there could be no negotiations before a Russian withdrawal. He felt personally betrayed and bitter because Brezhnev had lied to him about the movement of troops into Afghanistan.

President Zia of Pakistan seemed to me to be a pivotal figure. When he received Frances and me at his home in Rawalpindi, he told me that he would consent to a pro-Soviet government in Kabul and give an undertaking of noninterference. In return, the Soviets should withdraw their troops and permit the millions of Afghan refugees in Pakistan to go home without reprisals.

I thought this offer was so important that I flew directly to Moscow to present it to Brezhnev. He agreed, so long as China and India would also give guarantees of noninterference, backing up Zia. The Carter administration was not persuaded.

A stalemate developed. The machinery of détente rusted and some of its best opportunities were foregone. The Moscow Olympics were reduced by the absence of the United States to a stunted celebration for the Soviet bloc. Frances and I were two of the very few Americans who attended the opening ceremonies of the Games. A real despondency was in my heart that day. All the progress toward peace which had been made so painfully during the previous decade now seemed obliterated—almost as if it had never happened at all.

Brezhnev died along with détente. As the new age he had done so much to create faded into another cold war, his own vigor seeped out of him. Rumors of his ill health and imminent death had begun to circulate in the West even as early as August 1979, when I was asked to stand by to join a massive television obituary being organized by one of the networks. I refused. I said—as I was to say later when Konstantin Chernenko's health preoccupied the Western media—that you can't write off a Russian leader until you have seen him in his coffin.

I last saw Leonid Brezhnev on December 16, 1981, eleven months before his death. Age was certainly taking a severe toll on him, and the massive vitality of earlier years was fading pitifully fast—but there was no doubt that day that he was still the man in charge and the undisputed "Chairman of the Board." Almost the last words I ever said to him were to remind him that our fertilizer agreement was well on course for its final conclusion in 1998, when I would be one hundred years old. I repeated that I wanted to see him on that day.

His weak smile seemed to say that he knew better.

*   *   *

I cannot close this chapter without making mention of another remarkable world leader—a man to whom I became very close during the late 1970s, and with whom a personal friendship flourishes to this very day.

As noted before, one of our attorneys was Harry Simon-Levi, a former comrade-in-arms of the man who would become Prime Minister of Israel in 1977, Menachem Begin. Harry believed I could be useful to Begin in his historic efforts to reach political accommodation with Egypt, and thus it was that I found myself introduced to that man of great intellect, one of the most passionately driven human beings I have ever known.

We hit it off right away. Believing as I did that business is the best peacemaker, because trading partners seldom make war, I was full of ideas for industrial developments in Israel and joint ventures with Egypt. Begin saw their potential immediately, and before I knew it, I was off on another round of shuttle diplomacy.

The plan that he, and Anwar Sadat, liked best was for a multi-billion-dollar fertilizer project which would have involved American capital, Egyptian phosphates and natural gas and Israeli potash. It would have provided thousands of jobs for the Egyptian economy and shown the world that Egypt and Israel really did intend to cooperate. Tragically, Sadat's horrific assassination and Begin's incapacitation due to his wife's death and his own illness put an end to that plan. Had they both remained in power, I believe that it would be a reality today.

I remember one meeting with Begin in particular. It was on June 10, 1980. At Camp David, the Israelis reluctantly agreed to hand over to Egypt an Israeli air base in the Sinai. In return the US agreed to provide funds for the construction of a new air base for Israel in the Negev. In our meeting of June 5, 1980, I suggested to Jimmy Carter that the US lease the base in the Sinai instead of building a new air base. I felt it would be added protection for Israel and help ensure peace in the Middle East. Jimmy Carter said, "We tried this at Camp David, but Sadat wouldn't buy it. You are so persuasive, why don't you try it?"

When I talked with Sadat in Cairo, he said, "I would do anything for my friend Jimmy, but I could not live with my Arab neighbors. Why don't you ask Begin to let the US take over the lease of the new air base which they agreed to build for Israel?" I jetted off to Tel Aviv right away.

Frances and I were driven directly to Begin's house, where Alisa Begin, Menachem's devoted wife, made a little supper for us all and we sat up until near midnight discussing the proposal. Begin liked the idea and said he would take it up with the cabinet and would sound out the

US about my idea. Later I heard that Brzezinski talked Carter out of the plan.

I was disturbed to notice that Menachem was frequently distracted with concern for Alisa's health. It was obvious that she was having a lot of respiratory problems, likely due to her incessant cigarette-smoking. Menachem and Alisa had been married for many decades; she had been his staunchest and fiercest defender all through the years when he was in the political wilderness, and they were joined by indissoluble bonds of love and loyalty. It was painful to see how tenderly and apprehensively Menachem watched over Alisa's obviously declining health.

I brought two prominent doctors from America and they offered to see her and to arrange to take her to American hospitals for further treatment, but Alisa politely spurned all offers of help; she was not interested in her health; she was only interested in supporting her husband in his great work. In a typical letter written to me in late 1981, she said, "It was very generous of you to offer me the facilities of the hospital in the States. I just couldn't do it. After a rather stormy 42 years of marriage, when the only time we were separated was that of the Russian prison, I find it not fair to leave Menachem on his own now. As you no doubt follow the events in the Middle East, you will understand that I must spare him any private worry and anxiety."

Her death almost destroyed Menachem. His grief was crushing and unbearable. He wanted only to step down from office and retire into seclusion. Along with his friends in Israel, I tried everything possible to encourage him to stay in office, but in September 1983, he resigned.

Before he left office, however, he did one very good deed for me. One day in 1981, I was sitting in my office in Los Angeles when the phone rang. It was Menachem himself, calling from Washington.

"Armand," he said. "Something very important just happened which I wanted to tell you about immediately."

"What is it?" I asked.

He was very agitated and spoke quickly. "I've just been talking here with President Reagan and your name came up. I told him that he really ought to make more use of you, because you understand the Russians so well. He said, 'But I am told that Armand Hammer is a Communist.' I was appalled. I said, 'Armand Hammer is not a Communist. He's a pure capitalist, through and through. Everybody knows that. The Russians know it perfectly well.'

"'Well,' President Reagan said, 'Armand Hammer's father was a Communist.'

"'Yes, he was,' I said, 'but that doesn't mean that Armand is a

Communist. I'm afraid I think your supporters have been seriously misinformed, Mr. President, and I urge you to check him out more thoroughly. I know you'll find that Armand is a completely loyal American.'"

I was dismayed to find that such ludicrous assertions—apparently based on an anonymous memo someone with an ax to grind had circulated in Washington claiming that Israeli Intelligence actually had "proof" I was a Communist!—had taken a hold in the President's mind, but Begin told me not to worry. He would take care of it.

Shortly thereafter the Israeli Ambassador in Washington, Ephraim Evron, wrote to Secretary of State Alexander Haig, vigorously defending me, and concluding, "The Prime Minister asked me to tell you that there is no truth to these allegations, and that we consider Dr. Hammer a good and trusted friend."

I have always believed that by speaking and acting as he did, Menachem Begin changed Ronald Reagan's mind about me. My appointment as Chairman of the President's Cancer Panel—which required a full investigation of my record and FBI clearance—followed soon after.

In September 1984 I made my first public trip to Israel—all the others had been made secretly, with Israel's help, to protect me from the possible menace of Muammar el-Quaddafi's wrath. This time I was in Israel to attend the opening of my Five Centuries of Masterpieces collection—and to try to save Menachem Begin's life.

Begin was suffering from an acute urological problem, easily correctable, but he refused to have surgery. He had still not recovered from his wife's death, and he was withdrawn, nearly reclusive. On my plane with me was Dr. Willard Goodwin, one of America's most eminent urologists, and I hoped that, in collaboration with Begin's doctors, we could somehow convince Menachem that something had to be done.

We drove to Shaare Zedek Medical Center. The building was large and open, typical of Israeli architecture, complete with stained-glass windows in the lobby. We went up to Begin's room, where there was a great flurry of activity. It turned out that his doctor was a Hungarian-born physician named Amicur Farkas, whose mentor had been none other than Willard Goodwin, so he was delighted to see us. After extensive consultations both doctors concluded that surgery was absolutely necessary to save Begin's life, and after much cajoling from them, and me, he finally agreed to the surgery. Today, he leads a healthy life, and I like to think that if he ever writes his memoirs, I had something to do with there being an extra chapter or two.

While I was in Israel, I also visited Hadassah Hospital at Ein

Kerem, where, on the good advice of Dr. Robert Gale, I pledged a donation of $250,000 to their Cancer Research Program, to be used in their work in bone-marrow transplantation.

I also met for an hour with Prime Minister Shimon Peres to discuss the economic health of his small country, and that very day pledged to develop at least one hundred million dollars in business ventures to boost the Israeli economy. The first fruits of that pledge began to develop immediately.

By chance, during my visit, I ran into a former Occidental geologist named Jerry Williams in the lobby of the King David Hotel. Jerry had worked for us in the North Sea and in Libya, and was now working with a small company in Israel trying to find oil. It stuck in my mind, and when I returned to Los Angeles, I asked Dave Martin in Bakersfield to find Jerry Williams; Jerry came to Los Angeles, and we discussed the possibility of looking for oil in Israel. Soon a scheme grew to raise over $18 million for drilling in the Negev in Israel. By June 1985 I had raised $12 million from some of my friends, which was matched by $4 million from the Israeli government and $2 million from our Israeli partners. Occidental could not take the job on itself, due to our connection with Libya and other parts of the Arab world, but the board agreed that I could take it on privately without causing a conflict of interest.

Today we have nearly half the State of Israel under license, and for the first time in the country's history, systematic seismic work has been carried out. By January 1987 we will have begun drilling and we will discover whether God put oil into the substrata of Israel, just as he did with her neighboring countries. The seismic work looks very encouraging—and our geologists are optimistic.

John Kluge, an investor in the Israeli oil venture and a longtime friend of mine, asked that I give him at least one week's notice before any drilling takes place. A Jewish friend of his will make a special prayer for our success in finding oil. It is certainly worth a try!

On another front, Occidental is working with Israel Chemical, Ltd., the Israeli chemical conglomerate, on several notions, and while nothing has been consummated yet, it looks likely that we will reach an agreement soon.

If we can find oil in Israel, and help increase the base of Israel Chemical's economy, we can transform Israel into a self-sufficient state much less exposed to the vicissitudes of world politics. Muammar el-Qaddafi may not think that a very admirable ambition, but the prospect fills me with joy.

One last note about Israel: I sometimes find that my business relations have a way of bridging borders where diplomacy has failed. In

1986 the Israeli government asked me to help obtain some documentation crucial to their case against the Nazi war criminal known as Ivan the Terrible, who operated the gas chambers at Treblinka, the notorious death camp, and murdered countless thousands of Jews. The Israelis requested and were granted the extradition of the accused perpetrator of these crimes from the US so that he could stand trial in Israel. His name was John Demjanjuk, but he claimed not to be the same Ivan the Terrible sought by the Israelis.

The Israeli government needed proof that Demjanjuk was Ivan the Terrible. The Soviets had the documentation—the original SS identification card of "I.N. Demjanjuk"—but would not release it to the Israelis. I explained the situation to Anatoliy Dobrynin, and in December 1986 he presented me with the document the Israelis needed for the prosecution. When I forwarded it to Vice Premier and Deputy Foreign Minister Shimon Peres, he and the entire government were elated.

Besides thanking me personally for my "tireless efforts on behalf of the State of Israel, the Jewish people and the cause of justice and human rights the world over," he wrote: "Please convey our appreciation to the Soviet authorities for their cooperation in the effort to bring Nazi war criminals to justice."

I will be sure that this message of appreciation reaches Dobrynin and Gorbachev. Perhaps it will be an opening wedge for further cooperation between the two governments.

24

Of Men and Masterpieces

I believe in the power of great art to transcend geographical boundaries, political differences and even the restrictions of time. The greatest works of Rembrandt, Leonardo da Vinci, Raphael, Michelangelo, Rubens, Gauguin, Renoir, van Gogh and a host of others work on the minds and emotions of their beholders as tellingly today as when they were painted. And whether those beholders be in Beijing or Novosibirsk, in Washington, Los Angeles, Caracas or London, they can look upon the canvases as they were first seen in Holland or Italy or France centuries ago. The greatest of all works of art tell us that humankind never fundamentally alters, that we are all, forever, the same creatures with the same longings, passions and pains. The greatest art reduces and elevates us all to the point of our common humanity.

Since I was first introduced to the world of art, when Victor and I began buying pictures in Moscow in the twenties, I have been educating myself in this most fruitful branch of human understanding. For nearly thirty years I have also been dedicated to using art as a tool to encourage tolerance and understanding between nations and peoples. I believe I can claim to have been more influential than any man today in arranging art and cultural exchanges between the West and the East.

The first of these efforts began after my meeting with Nikita Khrushchev in 1961. When I suggested that exchanges of art works might help to lift the US and the USSR out of the doldrums of the fifties, Khrushchev promised to relay the suggestion to his Minister of Culture, Yuri Zhukov, the former editor of *Pravda*. Nothing came of it.

Toward the end of Khrushchev's era, however, the idea was given wings by Zhukov's successor, Mme. Yekaterina Furtseva, the first woman to become a member of the Politburo. I met her on June 10, 1964, and immediately took to her. She was a very attractive, bright and energetic woman in her fifties whose only failing was a too strong taste for vodka. Whispers around Moscow also suggested that she lived too well, and she was ultimately removed from office in some disgrace for having exceeded the Soviets' very rigid lines of public propriety. She should be remembered, nonetheless, as the Soviet official who did most to encourage art exchanges before the Nixon/Brezhnev détente made everything easier in the seventies.

When I first met her, Furtseva had just returned from Copenhagen, where she had seen an exhibition of the American primitive painter Grandma Moses. It happened that I had had a hand in that exhibition and in the world tour of Grandma Moses's works which was just then concluding.

When Furtseva had finished enthusing about the exhibition, I said, "Why don't you let me bring it to Moscow?"

"Can you do that?" she said.

"All it takes is your invitation," I replied.

"Consider it offered," she said.

We took the exhibition to the Pushkin Museum on November 12, 1964. It was a hugely encouraging success. Lines of Muscovites stood around the museum in fiercely subzero temperatures waiting their turn to see the works of "Babushka Moses," as they called her. It was enchanting to see their enthusiasm for pictures which are as American as Kentucky bourbon, and as easily appreciated. Grandma Moses's scenes of domestic life and the emotional power of her attachment to the countryside speak the most universal of all languages. I was only sorry that she couldn't have been there herself to enjoy her success. She had died in December 1961, at the age of 101, painting up to the time of her death.

The Soviet side of this first exchange was not so easy to arrange. Mme. Furtseva wanted to send the Red Army Chorus to America, but the State Department refused to allow fully uniformed soldiers from the USSR on United States soil. Furtseva was boiling mad about this ruling.

"The chorus has appeared, to great acclaim, in Britain, all over Europe and is now being invited to make a second tour of Canada," she said. "Canada is not so strong as the United States, yet Canadians are not afraid of Red Army uniforms. If you wanted to send your famous Navy Band here, we would have no objection to their performing in their uniforms."

I promised to speak to President Lyndon Johnson about this absurd dispute, but then I came up with a better idea. I suggested to Furtseva that she send instead the works of a Russian artist of similar standing to Grandma Moses. I suggested Pavel Korin, the most honored Russian painter of the time, whose works were deeply influenced by the icon tradition in which he had been schooled as a child. Korin's work was technically unsurpassed, and reflected age-old themes in Russian religious life and art. He was a safe, if unexciting, choice for the first Soviet offering in art exchanges. There would be no criticism from the Bolshevik-haters in America who feared Soviet propaganda.

My brother Victor was asked to make the selections from Korin's works for a show at the Hammer Galleries in New York. Pavel Korin, a stately old man, and his wife both came to the Hammer Galleries as our guests for the opening of the show on April 5, 1965. The exhibition was respectfully received, though Pavel Korin's work was never likely to arouse great excitement in New York, the art capital of the world.

However, the exchange was a good start. It put Furtseva and me on a footing of mutual respect and trust; and it led to exchanges which did thrill even the sophisticates of New York, Washington and Los Angeles.

In 1971 Furtseva came to Los Angeles on a leg of her United States tour. I invited her to an exhibition of my collection which was just then reaching its full maturity. The collection was scheduled to travel to the Royal Academy in London in June and July of 1972, to be followed by an exhibition at the National Gallery in Dublin from August to October. Furtseva asked me to send it on to Russia for an extended tour. The collection arrived in Leningrad in mid-October 1972, and remained in the Soviet Union for nearly a year. It was seen by millions of people at the Hermitage in Leningrad, at the Pushkin in Moscow and in Kiev, Odessa, Minsk and Riga.

The exhibition included one picture of which I was particularly proud, a Goya portrait of Doña Antonia Zarate, an actress friend of the artist's. When Furtseva had talked to me in Los Angeles the previous year, she had said rather wistfully that there was not a single Goya in the USSR.

"As it happens," I said, "I have two Goyas. I'd be happy to make a gift of one of them to the Russian people." And so I did.

Now it was Furtseva's turn, again, to offer Soviet works for a show in America. There was to be no talk, this time, of military choruses or works of uncertain quality. Having sent Furtseva my own collection of masterpieces, I wanted masterpieces in return. I was in a stronger position to make this demand because the Hammer Galleries had recently purchased the Knoedler Galleries, the oldest gallery in the United States. That acquisition transformed the position of the Hammer Galleries and put us among the leading art dealers in the world.

It happened this way: In October 1971, I was flying to New York with my friend and associate Dr. Maury Leibovitz. We were investigating some oil deal. Maury, who is an outstanding CPA as well as a highly innovative businessman, always examined the books of any company I wanted to acquire, and invariably delivered an absolutely reliable assessment of the company's standing and value. On this night in October 1971, he was given an opportunity to exercise his skills which neither of us had been expecting.

We stopped the plane in Joplin, Missouri, to pick up my brother Victor. He had been visiting the Joplin Museum, looking in their basement at paintings which they wanted to sell. Victor came onto the plane with hot news.

He said, "I hear Knoedler's has given up its lease on Fifty-seventh Street and is planning to move to a building they've acquired on Seventieth Street. More than that, the company is for sale."

I turned to Maury and said, "This sounds interesting. Why don't you check it out?"

In New York, Maury went straight to visit the owners of Knoedler's: Jacques Lindon, who was the Paris partner, and Roland Balay, nephew of Charles Henschel, who had been President of the company from 1905 until his death on October 2, 1956. After a quick examination of their books, Maury rushed down to see me at my little house in the Village. I had never seen him so excited. Come to think of it, I had never seen him excited at all.

He said, "Many times, Armand, you've invited me to go into business with you, to take a position in Occidental or even to be President and Chief Operating Officer. I've always said that I'm not interested because I'm happy with a few accounts, including your own. I cherish my freedom. I'm not interested in business. I'm more interested in teaching psychology in my free time [he actually taught courses at USC]. But, if you'll buy Knoedler's, I want to take a small piece of it. It's that good."

Knoedler's was asking three million dollars for its whole business. Maury declared this price one of the most outstanding bargains of his entire business experience.

He had discovered that while Knoedler's carried its inventory on its books at cost, as is customary, any item which hadn't sold in ten years was written off as worthless. "This so-called worthless inventory alone is worth many, many times the asking price for the whole company!" Maury exclaimed.

Maury and I picked up two of our attorneys, Sam Harris and Herbert Hirsch, and went zipping off to see Lindon and Balay. I wanted to close the deal that night because I was afraid that they might change their minds and the price. There was no need to worry. Their

minds were at ease. They wanted out. Lindon just wanted to retire and
walk his dogs in the Bois de Boulogne; and Balay, who had a great eye
for paintings, had an equally alert eye for ladies and was interested in
indulging the latter.

I pushed them to close the deal. The night wore on. Maury
Leibovitz was exhausted after the flight from Los Angeles, and kept
falling asleep. To keep him alert, Sam Harris and I went out to Reu-
ben's delicatessen and bought coffee and cheesecake. Herbert Hirsch
had forgotten to tell his wife where he was going and, by the small
hours of the morning, she became frantic that he wasn't home. She
called the police, who started searches all over New York.

By dawn of October 18, 1971, the deal was done. Knoedler's was
ours. The cost was three million dollars, for which Hammer Galleries
put up the cash. Later we restructured Hammer Galleries so that I
received preferred stock for my investment and 75 percent of the common shares, which were set up with a nominal value of one hundred
thousand dollars. Maury bought 25 percent of the common shares; I
bought 75 percent.

Then we almost lost Knoedler's entire stable of distinguished con-
temporary artists.

We took possession of the building on East Seventieth Street on
December 10, 1971. When Maury Leibovitz and I arrived, we found
the manager, Xavier Foucade, in an extremely unwelcoming mood.
Knowing the true value of the inventory, he had wanted to buy the
business himself. To try to drive the price down, he had spread the
rumor that Knoedler's was bankrupt. That rumor had reached the ears
of the great artists represented by Knoedler's, many of whom had
demanded the withdrawal of their works.

Trucks had been backed up to the building to take away works by
Henry Moore, Salvador Dali, Willem de Kooning and others of equal
prominence. The gallery was practically empty of everything except the
previous old inventory. I had to work like a maniac, calling all the
artists and reassuring them that the gallery was safer than ever and that
their works would be properly represented. Willem de Kooning always
speaks about the day I flew to see him, met him on my plane at the
airport at East Hampton and persuaded him to leave some of his works
with Knoedler.

Anyway, that's how we got Knoedler's, and that's why I was in
such a strong position to demand masterpieces from Furtseva for exhibition in New York. I knew exactly what I wanted. Victor and I and
an official of Knoedler's had written out a shopping list. We wanted
thirty-six Impressionist and Post-Impressionist masterpieces from the
Hermitage and Pushkin museums. It included works by Matisse,
Gauguin, Picasso, Cézanne, van Gogh, Rousseau, Renoir, Monet, De-

rain, Braque, Sisley, Léger, Vlaminck and Pissarro. They had been seen by only a handful of Western art critics and connoisseurs who had traveled to Russia. The art world knew them only through photographs.

They had formerly belonged to—and in some cases been commissioned by—two of Czarist Russia's richest merchants and rival collectors, Ivan Morozov (brother of Savva) and Sergei Shchukin. Each of these men had turned his mansion into a personal museum to which the public was invited each Sunday. Morozov, for instance, owned 430 Russian and 240 French works. After the Bolshevik Revolution, the paintings were nationalized as public property. During Stalin's decades they lay hidden in museum basements because Stalin regarded Impressionism and Post-Impressionism as decadent. More modern paintings, such as the works of Kasimir Malevich, Kandinsky and others, excited torrents of his contemptuous abuse.

In 1955, two years after Stalin's death, Furtseva arranged for a modest showing of the paintings in Moscow. Huge crowds appeared to see them. Thereafter, they were divided between the Hermitage and the Pushkin. Western art lovers, as well as sophisticated Soviet citizens, were longing to see them.

J. Carter Brown, Director of the National Gallery in Washington, pleaded with me to ask for the pictures to be shown there as well as at Knoedler's.

I decided I might as well go for broke. I asked Furtseva to consent to an extensive tour of the United States, with showings at the National Gallery of Art, the Los Angeles County Museum of Art, the Art Institute of Chicago and the Kimbell Art Museum in Fort Worth, Texas.

In late March of 1973 the forty-one pictures arrived in Washington for exhibition at the National Gallery from April 1 to 29. They were to go on to Knoedler's in New York in May. The *Washington Evening Star* correctly described the collection as priceless, though it was insured for twenty-five million dollars. "I'd very much like to buy them for twenty-five million dollars," I said.

Newsweek and *Time* both carried full-page previews of the show and were carried away into the hyperbole of "legendary," "stupendous" and "miraculous" in their efforts to describe it. Record crowds attended the exhibition wherever it was shown. Both President Nixon and General Secretary Brezhnev contributed letters to the exhibition catalogue, describing it in similar terms as an important step on the road to mutual understanding.

Those words make the exhibition sound like a ritual exchange in the United Nations. It was not; it was a festival. The joy the pictures gave to the millions who saw them discernibly shifted, for a moment, the standard American image of the Russians as a joyless people.

The traffic in gifts of paintings was not all one way, from me to Russia. The Soviets very handsomely reciprocated my gift of the Goya.

One day when I was in Moscow, Mme. Furtseva called me to say, "We understand you don't have a Kasimir Malevich painting in your collection. We have selected what the curators at the Tretiakovsky Gallery consider his finest Suprematist-period work, and the Soviet government wishes you to have it as a gift." Some gift! It was valued by Knoedler's John Richardson as being worth at least a million dollars. Since I do not collect modern paintings, I traded it years later for a group of French Impressionists.

They entered one of my present collections, of which there are now five in all. I will describe them in a moment, but first I'd like to say this: Most private collectors of great art have had the interests of the public somewhere in their minds when they created their collections— usually at the backs of their minds. Most of them arranged to bequeath their collections to the great museums and galleries. In the meanwhile they kept their collections to themselves.

The main difference between my collections and others is that I created mine with the interests of the public in the front of my mind. I always intended, from the first, that my collections should be put on show in museums and that they should travel the world. No collection in private hands has ever traveled more than mine or been seen by more people.

Few people in the world can afford to travel to all the great museums. Most cities of most countries have meager collections and their citizens never get a chance to see great works of art where they live.

Just as I got a big kick out of selling Hearst's art collection over the counter at Gimbels, to people who might never have set foot in an art gallery, so it gives me terrific pleasure to send my collections to cities of the world whose people otherwise might never see a masterpiece.

For instance, a selection of paintings from my masterpiece collection was once exhibited in Moultrie, Georgia—the tiny hometown of Tom Beard, one of President Carter's aides and a good friend of mine. He implored me to send my exhibition there. It was housed in the town hall. An old farmer drove all day from the deepest countryside to bring his grandson to the exhibition. He couldn't write, he signed the visitors' book with an X, but he said that it was one of the biggest days of his life to be able to introduce his grandson to beauties and pleasures which otherwise he might never know.

Great artists speak the same language to all men and women, and their works belong to all people. They were not made for rich men to hide away in their vaults or to conceal in their mansions.

In the late sixties I decided that I wanted to create a great collection, and I was told then that it was impossible. The greatest works, it was said, had already passed out of circulation and into the hands of the great museums.

The collection that I began establishing then was, in fact, the third of my life. I have described how my first collection was assembled in the Soviet Union with the assistance of my brother Victor, when we found that we could buy works of art for the price of ordinary household furnishings.

My second collection was assembled when I was in the whiskey-distilling business, to reflect my growing interest in sixteenth- and seventeenth-century Dutch and Flemish paintings. Again, I chose each of the pictures with the help of my brother Victor, and of a great picture restorer named Anthony Reyre, who had been responsible for discovering many masterpieces now hanging in the world's great museums.

I formed a partnership with Anthony. Every picture we bought was authenticated by Professor W. R. Valentiner, former Director of the Detroit and Los Angeles museums, and author of several books and articles on Flemish and Dutch paintings. The collection we built up consisted of some fifty paintings, including works by Jan Steen, Gerard Terborch, Adriaen van de Velde, Jacob van Ruysdael, Frans van Mieris and Gerard Dou. It also included paintings by the Breughels (Younger and Elder), Frans Hals, Anthony Van Dyck and Rembrandt.

One of my prized paintings discovered by Reyre was entitled *The Letter,* by Gabriel Metsu. Dr. Valentiner, after first accepting the authenticity, gave me the sad news that my painting was a copy and the original was hanging in the Walters Art Gallery in Baltimore. I asked the Walters Gallery to send me a photograph of their painting. When I compared the two, I was convinced that my picture was far superior to theirs. I took my painting to the Walters Art Gallery, and after the Director and his staff compared the two paintings, they acknowledged that I had the original and they had the copy. Dr. Valentiner was much relieved to find that his original opinion was correct. I understand the picture is no longer displayed at the Walters.

This collection gave great beauty and charm to my working life when it decorated my offices in the Empire State Building after I bought out Reyre's interest. However, I always felt that the collection should be seen by a wider public than the employees and clients of my distilling companies.

At about the time of my move to California, and after the works had been on indefinite loan to the Virginia Museum of Fine Arts, the collection was mounted for travel and toured to eighteen locations in the US and Canada between 1957 and 1960. Professor Valentiner wrote the catalogue for the collection, and it was reprinted wherever the collection was shown. In 1965, I selected the Fisher Galleries of the University of Southern California to be the permanent home for the collection and gave it to USC as an unconditional gift.

Shortly after making that gift, I became a member of the Board of Trustees of the Los Angeles County Museum of Art (LACMA), and it was about that time that I dedicated myself to the building of a new, third collection that would be unexcelled—contrary to the predictions of art "experts," collectors and dealers, who scoffed at the idea. Proving experts wrong has always been one of my most enjoyable recreations. The pace at which this collection was assembled was so rapid that, by late 1969, eighty-two works had been acquired and were loaned to the Brooks Museum in Memphis, Tennessee, for a special exhibition . . . of a collection in its formative phase.

The list of works presented in Memphis suggests the ambition and scope of the third collection: Rembrandt, Rubens, Fragonard and Goya through the Post-Impressionist work of Rouault, Bonnard and Gauguin. Included in the Memphis showing were three works which had been acquired by the Los Angeles County Museum of Art through funds provided by a million-dollar Frances and Armand Hammer Purchase Fund.

These three works are extraordinary examples of each artist and would be welcomed by any first-rank museum in the world. The first was Rembrandt's *Portrait of a Man from the Ramon Family,* later discovered to be the *Portrait of Dirck Jansz Pesser.* Next came Rubens's oil sketch *Israelites Gathering Manna in the Desert* and Sargent's *Portrait of Mrs. Edward L. Davis and Her Son, Livingston Davis.*

Also included in the Memphis showing were two works which I had recently acquired and had already given to the Los Angeles County Museum: Renoir's *Two Girls Reading* and Modigliani's *Woman of the People.* The former had been on loan at the Metropolitan Museum for many years until the owner, a client of Hammer Galleries, decided to sell it to me, to the dismay of the Metropolitan, which hoped to inherit it some day. Kenneth Donahue, the former Director of the Los Angeles County Museum of Art, predicted it would someday be one of the most popular paintings at LACMA. The Modigliani, for which I paid in excess of three hundred thousand dollars, is one of the artist's greatest works. Modigliani was too poor to pay for a model, hence his landlady's daughter sat for the painting, which Modigliani gave to the landlady in lieu of rent. I venture to guess that these five works would bring a total in excess of ten million dollars on today's market—ten times what I paid for them.

I was building a close connection with the Los Angeles County Museum, beginning with a leadership gift to the museum's construction fund. The museum very handsomely recognized this million-dollar gift by naming the wing of the museum which houses many of its important traveling exhibitions after Frances and me. The Frances and Armand Hammer Wing was later renamed the Frances and Armand Hammer Building, and its entrance is directly opposite the grand entry created by the museum's current expansion program.

The Armand Hammer Foundation also donated approximately $2.5 million to pay for construction work to join the Hammer Wing with the Ahmanson Wing, allowing the public to move from one building to the other without leaving either. I saw that an escalator was needed to carry the public to the second floor, the existing elevators being overburdened and causing long lines to form. I was told that the installation of an escalator would be impossible because the entire façade of the building would have to be remodeled. I consulted a well-known architect. He solved the problem. I paid for the reconstruction as well as the escalator. The escalator was installed.

(The Los Angeles County Museum was not the only museum to receive such help. In 1979 I donated $1.25 million to the Corcoran Gallery of Art in Washington, D.C., so that they could continue to operate every day without charging admission fees. The Corcoran was so pleased that it surprised me with an official "Armand Hammer Day," attended by Washington Mayor Marion Barry and complete with marching bands! They also placed a marble bust of me by a celebrated Russian sculptor in the entrance opposite the bust of William Corcoran, the founder of the museum. The only other time I was so surprised was when the Chairman of Washington's National Symphony, Leonard Silverstein, invited me to a performance on my eighty-fourth birthday. I thought it would be a small postperformance party. To my astonishment, the Concert Hall was filled with Washington friends waiting to surprise me. Isaac Stern had flown in to be the guest soloist, Robert Merrill sang "Happy Birthday" and Mstislav Rostropovich conducted. At the end he called me down, and I found myself conducting the Symphony in "The Stars and Stripes Forever"!)

The inaugural exhibition of the third collection at the Los Angeles County Museum of Art was exceedingly well received. In addition to the works already mentioned, no less than eighteen works by Corot, three by Boudin, two by Pissarro, three by Fantin-Latour, two by Monet, four by Renoir, three by Bonnard, two by Matisse and two by Rouault were included. The success of the exhibition came to the attention of the Smithsonian Institution's Traveling Exhibition Service and I was asked if I would allow the collection to travel throughout the United States. I very gladly agreed.

Some criticism by the *Washington Post* of certain "weak" paintings in the collection, however (to which the *Post* graciously allowed me the right of an unprecedented reply much longer than the original review), made me determined to do more, to build a collection which would be critically irreproachable. I asked John Walker, my fellow trustee of the Los Angeles County Museum of Art, to work with me on improving it. I told him exactly what the test should be for any new work I might acquire. The collection, I said, should "include only works capable of being hung in the permanent collections of the finest museums in the world, such as the Metropolitan Museum in New York and the National Gallery in Washington."

At first Walker demurred. He had recently retired as Director of the National Gallery and was reluctant to provide opinions on the quality of paintings in a private collection—something he had studiously avoided as a museum director. When I got John's letter of refusal, I immediately flew to Washington to present my arguments in person.

I convinced him.

John agreed to survey the collection and write a report on the works he believed met my test, and to list those he recommended be sold or traded. Prior to writing his report, Walker warned that his recommendation might oust up to half of the works he had viewed at the Smithsonian. When the report was finished and the Walker recommendations implemented by the including of new acquisitions, as well as the elimination of the lesser works, the collection was readied for showing at the Los Angeles County Museum of Art in late 1971. At the same time I announced that I would leave the paintings in this collection to the LACMA in my will.

That presentation is the foundation of the Armand Hammer Collection of today.

This time there were no slighting reviews. Forty-six drawings and paintings remained in the collection following the Smithsonian showing. At John Walker's suggestion, a further twenty oil paintings and a superb group of thirty drawings, pastels and watercolors had been acquired, which brought the total number of works to over one hundred. The fifty new works had been added in only eighteen months.

The acquisition of the drawings proved most timely. In 1970 and 1971 it was possible for a collector to purchase important drawings for reasonable prices, compared to the millions spent today for comparable works. They weren't cheap—I paid hundreds of thousands of dollars for the *Sheet of Studies* by Leonardo da Vinci, the *Study for a Fresco of the Prophets Hosea and Jonah* by Raphael and the two drawings by Watteau, *Couple Seated on a Bank* and *Young Girl*—but if these same drawings were to be auctioned today, they would bring winning bids ten times their original purchase price.

I agreed to give my drawing collection to the National Gallery of Art in Washington, D.C. The Gallery wants to increase its holdings of drawings, and so was quite pleased to receive my drawings, designating a special gallery to be known as the Armand Hammer Collection. This gallery will also include a Chapel for the exhibition of the Raphael Cartoon (drawn in 1504–1508), the sketch from which he painted his famous *La Belle Jardinière* (which hangs in the Louvre). I donated $1.2 million for the cartoon, allowing the National Gallery to purchase it from Lord Leicester at Holkum House in England, where it had reposed since Thomas Coke, first Earl of Leicester, acquired it in 1713.

The oil paintings added during this period met the quality standard I had set and pointed the direction of future acquisitions. Numerous important American paintings were added to the collection, such as *Summertime* by Mary Cassatt, *Still Life* by William Harnett, *Portrait of George Washington* by Gilbert Stuart, *On the Beach* by Maurice Prendergast, *Portrait of Sebastiano Cardinal Martinelli* by Thomas Eakins and *Dr. Pozzi at Home* by John Singer Sargent. In addition, works purchased provided an important context for the Impressionist and Post-Impressionist works: Géricault's *Portrait of a Gentleman,* Moreau's *Salome Dancing Before Herod* and *King David.* Many of the drawings served this same context-setting purpose: four splendidly finished drawings by Fragonard and a preliminary study by this same artist for the previously purchased painting, *The Education of the Virgin,* as well as a drawing by Ingres and a charcoal by Manet.

The rapid pace of acquisition also brought two superb Corots *(Portrait of a Young Girl* and *Pleasures of Evening),* Renoir's *Coastline at Antibes,* Caillebotte's *Square at Argenteuil,* and the Monet *View of Bordighera.* The collection rapidly became a survey of Western European art from the Renaissance to the twentieth century, with a special emphasis on French and American art.

It was altogether fitting and proper that the collection be filled out in this way, for it was about to be launched on a tour previously unequaled by any collection in art history. The Los Angeles showing was the first location on a tour which has not yet stopped.

The first stop was the Royal Academy in London, followed by a showing at the National Gallery of Ireland in Dublin. In 1972–1973 the collection visited six cities in the Soviet Union. It visited Lima and Caracas in 1975 and four locations in Japan in 1975–1976. As of the spring of 1986, the collection had visited fifty different cities in eighteen countries, and been viewed by nearly four million people.

In my view the collection is largely complete—but this has not stopped me from adding to it when the time was right: in 1976 a drawing by Michelangelo and the spectacular and important *Juno* by Rembrandt; in 1977 a rare drawing by Andrea del Sarto, a drawing by

Greuze and paintings by Morisot and Soutine; in 1979 Rembrandt's *Portrait of a Man Holding a Black Hat* and the first English picture, *Caller Herrin* by Millais.

In 1980 came two drawings by Cassatt and paintings by two of America's artists of the West, Remington and Russell. From 1981 through 1984 we enriched the collection with paintings by Andrew Wyeth, Manet, Ensor, Gilbert Stuart, Titian and Watteau.

I bought my first work by Honoré Daumier in 1970. The watercolor, *Pleading Lawyer,* was destined to become the first work in the largest collection of works by that artist ever to be amassed by a private individual. As is my custom for every new artist that joins my collection, I began to read about Daumier. The more I read, the more I became fascinated by Daumier's productivity, obvious compassion for the human condition, and his courage to stand up to authority. Soon, additional works by Daumier were added to the collection, and in 1975—with the help of Martha Wade Kaufman, then curator of the Armand Hammer Foundation—I made arrangements to purchase the George Longstreet Collection of more than six thousand Daumier lithographs.

The Longstreet Collection had been built up over a period of fifty-one years to a point where it was the most comprehensive private collection in the United States. With an eye to making the Armand Hammer Daumier Collection the most comprehensive public *or* private collection in the world, I added paintings and drawings to it. For a time it seemed that nobody else could successfully bid for a Daumier work at auction. After setting two world record prices for Daumier works—one for an oil painting (since surpassed) and one for a watercolor—the acquisition pace slackened, but not before the Longstreet Collection of works by Daumier's contemporaries—more than three thousand five hundred prints and a significant group of drawings—was added in 1980; and in 1983 the Andrea Rothe Collection of over three thousand prints.

With so many prints on hand, it was possible for me to make two gifts of Daumier prints—over two thousand in all—to the Corcoran Gallery of Art in Washington, D.C. The Armand Hammer Daumier Collection now numbers in excess of ten thousand objects, including paintings, drawings, watercolors, sculpture and associated works.

The Daumier Collection followed the master paintings and drawings on the road, and has been seen in eighteen different cities in seven countries by more than one million people. Like the paintings in the collection of traveling masterworks, the entire Daumier Collection is an intended gift to the Los Angeles County Museum of Art, where it will eventually create a Daumier Study Center—a deep resource for scholars to study the popular arts of France during its most turbulent era.

Prior to December 12, 1980, I visited several galleries in London to view works by Chardin for possible inclusion in my collection. The asking price for most of the desirable paintings was a few million each and I passed them all up. At eleven o'clock in the morning an important sale of old master paintings began at Christie's Auction house. Frances and I were present at the sale when a Chardin still life, *The Attributes of Painting,* was presented for bidding. The picture needed skilled conservation work, but I could see that there was a fine painting to be recovered if the proper conservator could be found to do the work. When the bidding for the Chardin stalled well below the price I was prepared to pay, I made a successful bid of $105,000.

Now properly restored to its original condition, the Chardin travels with the collection of master drawings and paintings. If it came up at auction today, it would easily bring a million dollars or more.

However, it was not whim that brought me to Christie's that day. It was the sale of an object that followed the sale of the old master paintings. The object was the so-called Leicester Codex by Leonardo da Vinci, a 470-year-old compilation of Leonardo's handwritten notes and sketches, in his famous reverse mirror-writing, on the nature of water in its many forms and other scientific matters: the color of the sky, how the moon is lit, canals, dams, the drainage of swamps, astronomy, cosmology, geology, the effect of tides and the principles of evaporation and condensation, bubbles, the theory of the siphon, snorkels and the concepts of steam power and submarine warfare. Almost a complete collection of works in itself, the Codex consists of eighteen double-sided sheets, with four pages on each sheet, including approximately three hundred sixty drawings by the greatest of all the masters. The Codex was well known to Leonardo scholars, but as it had been the private property of the Earls of Leicester since 1717, and had been shown only once at exhibition, in 1952 at the Royal Academy, it was relatively unknown to the public.

The sale of the Codex had provoked great excitement, for here was the only manuscript by Leonardo remaining in private hands. Pre-sale estimates of the final sale price ranged as high as fourteen million dollars, and it was rumored that the Italian government, by special appropriation, was prepared to bid at least that much to return the manuscript to Italy. The British press and museum community were keenly interested in the bidding, fearing that if the manuscript were purchased by someone outside the United Kingdom, it would be yet another example of what they perceived as a loss of the nation's cultural heritage.

I sat quietly in the front row after the purchase of the Chardin. Only I knew my reason to be at the sale: I intended to purchase the Codex. As I told the press later, "Not even Mrs. Hammer knew why we were there." When the gavel fell on the final bid, I had won the Codex. With the Christie's commission included, I had spent nearly six million dollars to get what is now not only the last Leonardo manuscript in private hands, but the only one in the Western Hemisphere.

In those press interviews I admitted that I had been prepared to bid much higher. Luck had been with me. The Italian government had dropped out of the bidding weeks earlier after a disastrous earthquake had occurred and an expensive relief effort had been required. British museums had not been able to mount a concerted effort to bid for the Codex, and no other private bidder even attempted to bid against me.

I promised to return the Codex to the United Kingdom regularly, however—a promise which has been kept with showings in London, Edinburgh and Aberdeen.

The Codex was carried to Los Angeles on a commercial flight by one of my aides. He took a first-class seat for the masterpiece next to his own. It's a long way from London to Los Angeles, and nobody could make the flight without visiting the bathroom a few times. My man was so terrified of leaving the Leonardo Codex alone that he took it with him on each visit. Emerging from the bathroom on the last occasion, he found himself confronting the massed ranks of the plane's cabin crew, who had been summoned because a passenger had been seen entering a bathroom with a large package which looked suspiciously like an infernal device.

To make a tour of the Codex possible, I had it restored to its original "loose sheet" configuration under the supervision of my Leonardo adviser, the scholar Carlo Pedretti. Then, following the procedure used for the mounting and display of the many Leonardo sheets in the Queen's collection at Windsor Castle, the Codex was ready for public viewing. Mounted in its freestanding exhibition modules, the Codex sheets seen singly make a presentation which is almost overwhelming in its power and detail—almost a complete collection in itself.

The Codex has now traveled the world, following the example of the other Hammer collections, and has visited fifteen different cities in nine countries, attracting a total audience of one and a half million. But it was the return of the Codex to Italy that produced the most heartwarming reception of all.

Renamed the Codex Hammer by Pedretti, Leonardo's work was scheduled for exhibition in Florence in 1982. I took the Codex on my plane, flying to Pisa, for it was the only nearby airport large enough to accommodate Oxy One. When I left the plane, I was followed by security guards armed with sawed-off shotguns and Uzi machine guns; they carried the Codex to Italian soil after an absence of 265 years.

Although coverage of the event had to be limited for security reasons, spontaneous applause greeted the Codex Hammer's return to its country of origin.

Four hundred thousand people viewed the Codex in Florence. I was made an honorary citizen of Vinci, and I was honored by the presence of the President of Italy, Sandro Pertini, at the exhibition's opening ceremony. He also presented me with Italy's highest honor to a foreigner, the Order of Grand Officer to the Merit of the Republic. I promised to return the Codex for exhibition and study no less than every five years; a promise I have already kept by a showing in Bologna in 1985.

The acquisition and tour of the Codex Hammer have been complemented by the commissioning of Carlo Pedretti to produce a facsimile of it with a complete transliteration, translation and notes with tables which relate the manuscript to all prior studies. Through an endowment of one million dollars established by me and at the initiative of Franklin Murphy, an Armand Hammer Center for Leonardo Studies has been created at the University of California at Los Angeles to advance work on the understanding of this great genius of the Italian Renaissance.

The Armand Hammer Collections were created for the public—to share the love of art and to promote international peace and goodwill. Those are the true motives—but I have to admit that there is another one as well.

Collecting pictures is also one of the best games in the world. It combines the satisfactions of detailed scholarship with the thrill of the hunt and the excitement of business. It is an ideal recreation for me. The art world is a jungle, echoing to the calls of vicious jealousies and ruthless combat between dealers and collectors; but I have been walking in the jungles of business all my life, and fighting tooth and nail for pictures comes as a form of relaxation to me.

There is a good story connected with the acquisition of almost every work in my collections—stories of auction-room intrigue, of pell-mell flights to remote places to close last-minute deals, of deceit and skulduggery. This chapter would go on forever if I listed them all. I'll simply give a few choice examples.

The acquisition of Gauguin's *Bonjour Monsieur Gauguin* was a classic case.

I heard that the picture was coming up for sale in Geneva on November 6, 1969. I flew there and landed in a snowstorm. The airport authorities told Fred Gross that ours was the last plane cleared to land that Thursday afternoon. All following planes would be redirected elsewhere.

The sale began in Geneva's Hotel Richmond in the early evening. Bidding for the Gauguin was spirited, to say the least. Finally, it was knocked down to me for just over $329,000. As soon as I left the auction room, I was confronted by one of the most plutocratic of the Greek shipowners, who offered me a huge profit if I would sell him the picture. His plane had followed mine to Geneva and had been forbidden to land in the snowstorm. He had rushed by car from a nearby city, only to find the painting sold to me.

"The picture's not for sale," I said.

I then had to clear up some uncertainty about the picture's provenance, which was complicated by the circumstances of the artist's difficult and penurious life. When he was living in Le Pouldu, a fishermen's hamlet in Brittany, Gauguin had been too poor to pay his rent. He had given *Bonjour Monsieur Gauguin* to his landlady to settle his bill. Later, when he had a little money from an inheritance, he asked the landlady to return the painting to him for what he had owed her. She refused. Gauguin then painted another version of the picture from memory. Both versions survived. The question was, which of them had I bought?

The other picture was in the Prague Museum. I made an appointment to see the museum director and flew there with Peter Nathan, a famous dealer and Gauguin expert from Zurich. We hung the pictures side by side and examined them. After a moment the Director of the museum and his staff of curators said to me, "There's no doubt about it. Yours is the original."

Many of my hunts for pictures brought me into rivalry with other outstanding collectors, such as Norton Simon and Paul Getty, both tough customers and accustomed to getting their own way. Once or twice I managed to beat them to the punch and, as was their way, they did not take their defeats lightly.

Norton Simon was not delighted when I acquired the Rubens *Girl with Curly Hair*. That wonderful picture, one of my greatest favorites, came my way in London.

While I was staying at Claridge's in March 1971, I got a call from Knoedler's man in London, Ernest Johns. We did not own Knoedler's at that time.

"We've got an exceptional Rubens I want to show you," he said.

"Bring it over," I said.

I sent for my good friend Michael Jaffe, a Cambridge professor who keeps a home in London. He arrived at Claridge's just after the man from Knoedler's had gone, leaving the painting on approval. When Michael saw the Rubens, he flipped.

"At last," he said. "I see the original. There are six copies of this picture in various museums around the world, Armand, but this is the original. You must buy it."

I didn't need a lot of prompting: I had fallen in love with the picture on first sight.

The girl in the picture had been a servant in Rubens's home. Legend had it that she had become his mistress after the death of his wife, and that he had considered marrying her but never did. The expression in the girl's eyes seemed to say, "Is this man going to marry me or not?" Or, at least, that's how I have always read it. Some women who have seen the picture tell me that the girl's eyes tell a much more directly erotic tale.

Rubens never sold the picture. It was found in his studio after he died, along with a companion self-portrait.

I did the deal with Knoedler's on the spot. I paid nearly a quarter million dollars.

When I got home to Los Angeles, Norton Simon called me, fishing for news, as always.

"Well, Armand," he said, "did you buy any interesting pictures in Europe?"

"As a matter of fact," I said, "I did. I bought the loveliest Rubens I've ever seen."

There was a pause on the line. Then Norton quietly asked, "It wasn't a girl with curly hair, was it?"

"That's the very one," I answered.

I could hear Norton sucking in his breath through clenched teeth.

"Knoedler's offered that to me," he finally said. "They wanted a quarter of a million dollars. I had it hanging on my wall for six months on trial. Finally I told them that they wanted too much for it and sent it back. But I wanted it so much I couldn't get it out of my mind. Just yesterday I called them up and said, 'Okay, if you won't reduce the price, send me the picture back and I'll give you what you want.' And they said, 'Sorry, the picture's been sold.' I guessed it had to be you."

The story of my acquisition of Rembrandt's *Juno,* in which I managed to put one over on Paul Getty, followed a similar pattern.

The *Juno*—Rembrandt's regal portrait of the Queen of Gods—is one of the finest and best-documented late masterworks of Holland's greatest artist. John Walker believes it to be the finest Rembrandt in the world in private hands.

It had been on loan for years from an anonymous collector at the Metropolitan Museum in New York, hanging next to *Aristotle Contemplating the Bust of Homer,* in the Rembrandt room, and considered of almost equal importance. The Metropolitan believed that someday the owner would give it to them or leave it to them in his will. It came up for sale in June 1976, when the owner wanted to raise some cash. He was Bill Middendorf, former investment banker, Secretary of the

Navy, Ambassador to the Netherlands, artist, musician and composer—and art collector.

He called me and asked whether Knoedler's would be willing to take the picture on consignment.

"Sure," I said. "How much do you want for it?"

"Five million dollars," he said.

"Okay," I said, "but I want you to give me first refusal on the picture if it fails to bring five million. If you become willing to accept a lower offer, I want to be the first to know."

He sent me the letter of agreement on those terms. Knoedler's put the picture up for sale at five million dollars. No takers.

A few months later I was having dinner at Ed and Hannah Carter's house. Ed is one of the greatest benefactors of the LACMA and is himself a great collector, with an outstanding collection of Dutch landscapes. During dinner, I was summoned to the telephone. Bill Middendorf was on the line. Sensing that this was going to be about the *Juno*, I asked Ed to listen in on the extension. Bill said, "Armand, I'm selling the *Juno* to the Getty Museum."

"How much are you selling it for?"

"Three million dollars," he said.

"I'll buy it for three million dollars," I said.

"Well, I don't know," he said. "I'll need to speak to Mr. Getty, because I've already indicated his offer is acceptable."

"Have you closed the deal?"

"No, not yet."

"Well, if you look at our agreement, you'll see that you're bound to offer me first refusal. You've just told me that you're willing to sell the picture for three million and I'm telling you that I'll buy it for three million."

I let Bill sweat through one of the longest silences I can ever remember in a telephone call. Finally he said, "Well, I guess it's yours." Thus I spoiled Bill's hopes of running a private auction between me and the richest man in the world. There is no telling who would have paid the most and ended up with the picture. Not owning a late Rembrandt, I would have gone to ten million dollars. The picture is worth it.

I told Bill I wanted to close the deal before midnight. I called Bill McSweeny in Washington and dictated the terms of the contract to him. He had the papers drawn up and rushed over to Bill Middendorf's house, where Middendorf signed them in his pajamas.

A few days later, on September 28, 1976, Middendorf delivered the picture to Bill McSweeny in the back of a little Toyota pickup truck, driven by his daughter. The temperature in Washington was about ninety-eight degrees. Bill McSweeny felt that he would faint when he saw the *Juno,* half-wrapped and exposed to the sun in the back of the truck.

Bill had arrived at the rendezvous with his driver Sylvester in one of the corporation's limousines. The *Juno* wouldn't fit in the car. One of the men with McSweeny climbed into the back of the truck and accompanied it on its journey to the National Gallery, where it was to be temporarily hung on loan. Carter Brown, who loves to get the upper hand on the Metropolitan, was ecstatic.

Bill McSweeny was in living dread of a tree falling across the pickup or of an accident in the five o'clock traffic. He told me later that he sat in the car thinking, "If anything happens, I'm going to owe Hammer three million dollars." I called him on his car telephone to make sure that the exchange had been accomplished and he smoothly told me that everything was okay.

Paul Getty raised hell with me ever afterward. He could never see me without chiding, "You do know that you stole that Rembrandt from me, don't you?"

When Norton Simon heard of my coup from Ed Carter, he phoned me immediately.

"How much do you want for *Juno*?" he asked.

"It's not for sale," I replied.

"How about five million dollars?" he offered.

"It's not for sale."

"Everything has a price," he said.

"Not *Juno,*" I replied.

"If you change your mind, call me," he said, and hung up the phone angrily.

The Hammer Galleries, as I have said, brought us some business, in the persons of Harry Clifton and King Farouk, which would have been more fitting in Alice's Wonderland than a distinguished gallery; but nothing more incredible ever happened to me in the art world than the arrival of the building wrecker with the 110 Pissarros.

There I was, sitting in my office in the Hammer Galleries, when Victor rushed in and said, "There's a man downstairs who has a hundred and ten Pissarros to sell."

"Ridiculous," I said. "How could anybody have a hundred and ten Pissarros?"

"All I'm telling you is what he's telling me," Victor replied exasperatedly. "He's got the pictures here. I've glanced at them and they look as if they might be authentic."

"Well, where did he get them?" I asked.

"He's a wrecking contractor from Chicago," Victor explained. "He had the contract to tear down the house which belonged to the man who founded International Harvester, a Mr. McCormick. The whole property and everything in it belongs to him. In the walls of the building, he found a hidden safe containing a huge portfolio of watercolors. He has dragged it all over town looking for a buyer, but nobody believes his story."

"Can you blame them?" I said. "How much does he want for the portfolio?"

"Ten thousand dollars," said Victor.

"Ten thousand dollars for a hundred and ten Pissarros! Less than a hundred dollars each!" I nearly yelled. "This is the craziest thing I ever heard in my life."

If the pictures were genuine, the portfolio had to be worth at least a million dollars.

"Let's check this out," I said. "You keep him downstairs and I'll get hold of John Rewald and ask him to come over and look at them."

John was probably the greatest authority in the world on Pissarro and the author of a string of renowned books on Impressionism. I got him on the telephone.

"What do the pictures portray?" John asked.

"Apparently," I answered, "they're mostly South American scenes, flamenco dancers, some jungle scenes."

"This sounds promising," said John. "Pissarro was born in the Virgin Islands and lived for a time in Venezuela. Those places were a strong influence on his early work."

"Can you come over and take a look at this portfolio?" I asked.

"I'm on my way," he said.

Looking over the portfolio, John declared the majority of the paintings to be authentic Pissarros. The remainder were almost as interesting: they were by Pissarro's tutor, a Danish painter named Melbye.

"This is a tremendous coup," John whispered to me.

The wrecker had peddled the pictures to almost every dealer in New York, none of whom believed they were genuine because they were unsigned. If I hadn't purchased them, he would have given them away for nothing, I learned later. I gave the wrecker his ten thousand dollars and he went away whistling like a songbird. Victor and I practically danced around the gallery.

Just about that time, I was negotiating for an oil concession on Venezuela's Lake Maracaibo. It did no harm to my standing with the Venezuelan authorities when I took the Pissarros down to Caracas and mounted an exhibition in the Presidential Suite of one of the city's leading hotels. Alfredo Boulton, one of the country's leading businessmen, and himself a great art connoisseur, got the Central Bank of Venezuela and other contributors to purchase the entire collection, and it was transferred to the walls of the bank, where it remains on exhibition.

I was glad to sell the collection, feeling that it properly belonged in Venezuela. The price we agreed on was many times less than I might have gotten if the collection had been broken up and sold in single lots, but it was, nonetheless, over a hundred thousand dollars.

We also got our oil concession.

Part of the fun of collecting art is in giving it away. There is an old Chinese proverb which says that you never fully own anything until you have given it away. My art collections are constantly being shown on their exhibition tours and I have made arrangements to bequeath them all to museums. The paintings and the Leonardo Codex will go to the Los Angeles County Museum of Art, to reside permanently in the Frances and Armand Hammer Wing, and the drawings to the National Gallery. In those senses, I have given away the great bulk of my art collections. But I have also had a lot of pleasure in giving works of art to American Presidents and to the White House.

I have shared with a succession of recent Presidents an interest in and love of America's own artistic traditions. Lyndon Johnson was particularly fond of the frontier art of Charles Russell, whose works I had been steadily collecting over many years.

In 1967 I was at a state dinner for the Shah of Iran, chatting with LBJ and Senate Majority Leader Mike Mansfield. LBJ was talking very proudly about a fine bronze by Frederic Remington which had been presented to the White House by Amon Carter, the Fort Worth publisher. Knowing that I had one of the best collections of Russell sculptures, Mike said longingly to the President, "Wouldn't it be nice if somebody gave you a good Charlie Russell bronze to match the Remington?" The Senator from Montana was naturally very proud of the work of Charles Russell, one of Montana's most distinguished sons.

I stepped into the gap Mike had opened. "I would be very glad to give you one of Russell's greatest pieces, the *Meat for Wild Men* bronze, if you would like it, Mr. President."

LBJ was as thrilled by the offer as a kid who's been promised a new bike. He said that Lady Bird would make all the necessary arrangements to receive the piece, under the auspices of the Committee for the Preservation of the White House.

Lady Bird duly organized a big tea party to receive the bronze in the White House on November 8, 1967. She walked around and around the piece, gazing at it with the happiest of smiles when it was put in place. She herself had chosen the place so that it would be seen by the 1.8 million people who visit the White House in an average year.

It would be hard for anybody to miss. Set on a revolving stand, the sculpture is three feet long, two feet wide and one foot high. Only ten bronzes were cast from the original wax model, which is in Montana's Historical Museum. Depicting Indians on horseback attacking a buffalo herd, it is a perfect example of Charlie Russell's meticulous faithfulness to the authentic details of life on the Western frontier and, like his glorious paintings, it surges with life and drama. At the time I gave it to the White House, it was valued at $100,000. Today it would bring many times that amount. It has a prominent place in the ground-floor corridor of the White House by the doors leading from the White House to the East Wing.

The sculpture was such a hit with the Johnsons and gave LBJ such pleasure that I gave him two more. Remington's giant-sized *Bronco Buster* was placed in the Lyndon Johnson Library in Austin, Texas, after LBJ's retirement, and, to mark the dedication of the LBJ Library, I gave him a little Russell bronze called *The Best of the String*.

I recently learned that LBJ was not the only President who admired Russell's work. In August 1986 I received word that one of President Reagan's favorite paintings, which was on loan to the White House, was about to be removed. The Hammer Galleries handled the painting, but the owner had died and the estate wanted to sell it. I was told that the President saw the painting every day, as it hung outside the Oval Office.

This Charles Marion Russell masterpiece, *Fording the Horse Herd,* painted in 1900, had to be left in the White House, but the estate wanted nearly $700,000 dollars for it. I immediately made some phone calls and raised the money from my friends Ray and Joan Irani, Michael and Lori Milken, Carl and Edyth Lindner and the Armand Hammer Foundation. It is now in the permanent collection of the White House, where President Reagan and future generations of American leaders can enjoy it.

My personal favorite among the works of art I have given to American Presidents is William Harnett's *The Cincinnati Enquirer,* which I bought for $400,000 dollars from Bill Middendorf and presented to Jimmy Carter for the White House Collection. The picture was also, plainly, a particular favorite of the President himself. Once Rosalynn Carter was asked which objects the President would save if there was a fire at the White House. She answered that he would pick up a picture under each arm. One of them would be William Merritt Chase's *Back of a Nude,* the other *The Cincinnati Enquirer.*

The picture was certainly one of the finest of all Harnetts, and the Carters received it with obvious and touching pleasure. As Lady Bird had done for the Russell bronze, Rosalynn Carter threw a big tea party to welcome the picture in the Blue Room of the White House. I flew in from Bolivia for the party.

Victor and I shared an enthusiasm for Harnett's still-life pictures. In the discipline of their detailed realism and the skillfullness of Harnett's trompe l'oeil techniques, they transcend mere photographic duplication. They speak with the tenderest melancholy of the transience of the moment and the impermanence of all things.

The *Still Life* in my collection was one of Victor's greatest delights. He returned to look at it again and again, wherever it was shown. I think the last time he saw it may have been at the exhibition we staged at the National Gallery in Washington as part of the Inaugural festivities for Ronald Reagan's second term in January 1985. I can still see him standing in front of the picture, resting on his cane and on the arm of a friend, smiling in rapture at Harnett's masterwork.

Victor's lifelong enthrallment with the world of art and his measureless happiness in great pictures was one of the deepest sources of my own interest in collecting. The happiness he derived from helping me to assemble my collections he more than amply returned to me. My collections are, in one vital sense, a memorial to Victor, and the pleasure they give to people all around the world is his most fitting and lasting tribute.

25

Through the Gates of the Forbidden City

The first words of the book I wrote in 1932 about my years in Russia were: "Business is business but Russia is romance." The same goes for China today.

When relations between the US and China began to improve in the seventies, and the prospect of more open trade appeared, I wanted to be among the first American businessmen to enter Beijing. It was not only the allure of vast new territories and commercial opportunities which galvanized me. I also wanted to contribute to one of the most exciting political and economic shifts of our century. The romantic ideal which led me to knock on the gates of the Imperial Palace in T'ien An Men Square in Beijing was the ideal of peaceful coexistence and trade between East and West.

Jimmy Carter deserves much credit for having continued and enlarged the policy of rapprochement with China which Richard Nixon, Henry Kissinger and Gerald Ford began. His administration was not, however, eager to open the doors to China for me. Mindful of my long-standing connections with the Soviet Union, the administration was afraid that I would be persona non grata with the Chinese. When the Chinese Vice Chairman, Deng Xiaoping, visited America in 1979, Carter's advisers did everything possible to keep me away. I was not invited to any of the occasions Deng attended in Washington.

I kept drumming on the closed door until, finally, when my insistence grew too embarrassing—and since I was one of Carter's more prominent supporters—my Washington office was told by Bob Strauss, the President's Special Trade Representative, that tickets would be made available for me and Frances at a function for Deng in Texas.

The oilmen of Texas were to give Deng and his delegation a big barbecue dinner and rodeo show at the Rodeo Arena in Simonton, near Houston. When our car pulled up to the Arena, we found the place swarming with security guards and the entrance protected by stewardesses checking off the guests. The girl recognized my name when I gave it to her, and then she ran her eyes up and down her list of guests. She looked very concerned as she said, "Well, I'm sorry, Doctor Hammer, but your name isn't here."

I suspected Brzezinski's hand in this.

"Never mind," I said, "there's obviously been a mistake. Where is the dinner itself being held?"

"In the club inside," she said.

"Then obviously my name will be on the list there," I said.

She let us through. Now we were inside.

Secret Service men guarded the door to the club. I gave my name again and repeated the story, saying, "My name has been left off the list at the main door by mistake. The girl there said that it must be on the list inside the club."

The Secret Service men said we could go through and check with the list inside, but if our names weren't there, we would have to come out.

Now we were inside the club itself. The lady holding the master list scrutinized it ruefully and shook her head. "I'm sorry, Doctor Hammer," she said. "Your name is not on the list."

"Would you mind if I looked over that list?" I said.

She handed it over. I ran my eye down the list until I saw the name Robert McGee.

"Ah!" I exclaimed. "Now I understand what has happened. Bob McGee is a senior executive in our Washington office. He arranged with the White House that I should be here. My tickets must have been issued in his name by mistake."

"Oh," she said, greatly relieved. "That explains it. Well, then, you're seated at table number five."

Nothing would hold us back now. We made our way to the table. The room was filling up. Some people were already seated at "our" table. I had never seen them before. They introduced themselves. They were Mr. and Mrs. Robert McGee.

Frances was petrified. "Come on, Armand," she said. "Let's get out of here."

"Nothing doing," I said. "They're not going to get me out of here now."

We sat down at the table and started a friendly chat with Mr. and Mrs. McGee. Mr. McGee was in charge of a large oil-supply company which did business with Occidental. My name was well-known to him. As more and more Texas oilmen came into the room and took their places, I saw the look of surprise on some of their faces to see an invader from California in their midst.

A receiving line was formed to greet the Chinese delegation. Fifty executives, some with their wives, joined the line. I got in there too, with Frances.

Deng led the delegation down the line. He was a tiny man with a wonderful smile, which he kept flashing as he worked his way down the line. He was accompanied by an interpreter, who gave each executive's name in turn and spoke some words of introduction. When he reached me, Deng said, "You don't need to introduce Doctor Hammer." Then he smiled at me, shaking my hand and saying, "We all know you. You're the man who helped Lenin when Russia needed help. Now you must come to China and help us."

"I'd love to," I replied, "but I understand that you don't allow private aircraft to enter China, and I'm too old to fly commercial."

"Oh," he said, waving his hand as if to dismiss the problem, "that can be arranged. Just send me a telegram telling me when you want to come and I'll make all the necessary arrangements."

Then we went back to "our" table. A member of the Chinese delegation was seated at each table. Sitting with us was Zhang Wenjin, the Chinese Ambassador to Canada, who later became the Ambassador to Washington. He said, "You shouldn't be sitting here. You should be with Deng Xiaoping." He took my hand and led me over to Deng's table, where the Vice Chairman told me to sit down next to him.

James Schlesinger, Secretary of Energy, was sitting there looking daggers at me, but there wasn't much he could do. Seeing the warmth of Deng's greeting, Schlesinger could hardly say, "This man's a gate-crasher and we ought to throw him out." Bob Strauss arrived a little late to take a seat somewhat removed from Deng's table and looked at me quizzically.

Deng talked to me through his interpreter all through dinner. He wanted to know all about my meetings with Lenin and my experiences of Lenin's New Economic Policy.

He was very quick, very intelligent and, as I later found, possessed of a great memory—each time I would meet him, he would remember exactly what he talked about the last time, and he never needed notes or had to turn to an aide for an answer: he always knew the answer.

After dinner Deng took me to sit beside him in his box for the rodeo which was put on for him. We got along famously. At the end of the evening he very firmly reiterated his invitation. I told him that I would see him in Beijing just as soon as I could put together some firm proposals and a team of executives.

After a brief exchange of letters during the next two months, a telex arrived at my office in Los Angeles, saying, COME IMMEDIATELY. BRING AS MANY PEOPLE AS YOU LIKE.

In mid-May 1979, I took sixteen executives from our oil, gas, coal, chemical, mining, agriculture, research and engineering divisions to China. Four of them went ahead by commercial flights and twelve came with me—one of the first flights into Chinese airspace by a private aircraft since the Revolution of 1948. Even Fred Gross was impressed.

Frances and I were instantly charmed by the Chinese. They were all exhilaratingly buoyant, busy, laughing people. China under Mao was given out as a dour and unsmiling land, gripped by a repressive uniformity. The China we found under Deng's leadership was as friendly a place as I have ever entered. We were welcomed with a smiling exuberance which made us all feel ten years younger.

On this first trip we stayed in the Beijing Hotel. On subsequent trips, we have been accommodated in the most sumptuous style in the Diao-yu-tai State Guest House, near the center of Beijing, on the grounds of an ancient Imperial fishing palace. President and Mrs. Reagan stayed here on their visits to China, as did Henry Kissinger and Richard Nixon.

Every day a fleet of immense black limousines waited to ferry us to our meetings with government officials. The cars were recent models, but with their bulbous wings and convolutions of chrome, they looked more like American Packards and Cadillacs of the forties. Lace doilies adorned the cushions within and curtains could be drawn to shield the occupants from the curious gaze of pedestrians. We kept the curtains open, the better to see the transfixing spectacle of Beijing in change from the isolated frigidity of Mao's era to the modernization being attempted by Deng.

In 1979 the streets of Beijing were almost empty of motorized traffic apart from trams, buses and trucks. Countless thousands of bicyclists wheeled along the wide boulevards. There were no big billboards then advertising Japanese electronic wizardry, as there are today, but on every side there was a frenzy of activity on construction sites, with apartment buildings, offices and factories taking shape in steel and concrete while hordes of blue-jacketed workers swarmed upon them.

In a single week in Beijing, we signed four preliminary agreements for oil exploration, coal mining, hybrid-rice seeds and chemical fertilizers.

One month after our visit to China, Kang Shien, then Vice Premier and Chairman of the State Economic Commission, was invited to the United States by James Schlesinger. Again, I was not asked to any of the official functions in Washington, but this time nothing could prevent me from throwing my own party for Kang. I hosted a reception for him and his delegation in Houston.

At this reception, Kang reiterated his government's invitation to Occidental to participate in seismic studies of seven of the eight areas of the South China Sea which had been set aside for exploration by foreign companies. He also asked Occidental to be the first foreign oil company to visit China's inland basins. Mel Fischer, our Vice President in Charge of Exploration in the Eastern Hemisphere, made the trip with a team of geologists.

Thus began a long series of contacts between Occidental and the Chinese government. They concluded in two offshore oil exploration and development contracts for the South China Sea and an agreement for joint development of the An Tai Bao surface mine, one of the biggest coal mines in the world, with a projected annual raw coal production capacity, in the first phase, of 15.33 million tons. On successful completion of this phase, we projected that the second and third phases would increase production to some 45 million tons a year. As recorded in the minutes of our meetings and reported in the Chinese press, Deng himself gave his approval to this agreement.

The joint venture contract for the An Tai Bao mine was as hard to create as a Stradivarius. It took endless patience, application and dedication from Occidental's staff, and we had to steel ourselves against skepticism in the foreign press and to carry some faint-hearted partners who dropped out.

As finally concluded, it was a thirty-year contract calling for a total investment of $650 million, of which Occidental's share in project financing with a syndicate of international banks would be about $200 million. When construction is completed and the mine reaches full production, the banks will take over the financial risk in full. Peter Kiewit Sons, a construction company in Omaha, Nebraska, signed a letter of intent to be our partners, but when they dropped out, leaving me holding the bag, I was able to get the Bank of China to replace them through its subsidiary, the Bank of China Trust and Consultancy Company. Quite a coup. This effectively left the China National Coal Development Corporation with 42.5 percent of the venture, and the China International Trust and Investment Corporation with 7.5 percent, and Oxy and the Bank of China held 25 percent each.

The Chinese government was to make a substantial investment in the mine's infrastructure, providing railroads, highways and waterways to serve the plant and homes, schools and other facilities, in a village for some seventeen thousand construction workers and their families.

This village will ultimately house about one thousand eight hundred mineworkers and expatriate managers and their families, together with several thousand additional workers, paid by the government, who will service and maintain the hospital, schools and other facilities.

Occidental took primary management control in operating the An Tai Bao mine. We are not just sending in advanced equipment and handing it over to inexperienced managers and workers. We take responsibility for operational supervision.

This is something new in China and a considerable breakthrough. In the early years of their open policy, the Chinese tended to think that all they needed to do was to purchase some new equipment and, operating it themselves, create their own modern enterprises. Harsh lessons of reality changed their ideas. Several of their ventures languished or failed because they could not effectively operate the equipment they had purchased at great expense. When he visited the United States, Deng saw the need for China to take advantage of Western managerial skills. By the time we concluded our deal over the mine, the Chinese had realized that skilled management counts as much as modern equipment, and they agreed to have us provide managers and supervisors.

The Chinese were very smart bargainers but, being inexperienced, they created obstacles and difficulties for themselves which frequently drove our people near to distraction. In 1982 I wrote an article for China's official newspaper, *China Daily*, in which I pointed out some of the shortcomings in the Chinese system and encouraged them to improve their laws and wages policies.

I asked for

> . . . a more complete and comprehensive set of laws and regulations regarding administrative management and industrial operation, in addition to the tax laws and regulations for foreign enterprises and individuals which have already been promulgated. There should also be a statewide standard for different levels of wages, salaries, service charges, methods and terms of depreciations, material fees, etc., for joint ventures. At present, these issues are discussed and solved item by item. Specific negotiations have to be held for each single problem. It is time-consuming and confusing.

Today, most of these suggestions have been acted upon or are in the pipeline. One of the major causes of difficulty was a shortage of Chinese lawyers—there simply weren't very many of them. For our early negotiations over the coal project, the Chinese engaged Shearman and Sterling, a prominent New York law firm, to represent them. Deng has been undecided for some years as to whether or not he wants to encourage the training of a large corps of lawyers. He recognizes the need, but on the other hand he doesn't want to see Chinese society become hidebound by legalistic procedures. As one who has chafed against lawyers all my life, I have some sympathy with Deng's dilemma.

The Chinese negotiated very smartly over the oil leases in the South China Sea. They made all the bidding companies conduct their own seismic surveys and give them the results before they awarded the plots.

The leases were then assigned to partnerships nominated by the Chinese themselves. They were thus able to balance out the distribution of plots very judiciously and keep a substantial measure of control. A large number of multinational companies entered the rush into the South China Sea. A bonanza on the Saudi Arabian or Alaskan scale was widely hoped for and expected.

It hasn't materialized. To date Arco's gas field near Hainan Island has been the only major discovery—Arco made an agreement to sell this gas to the Chinese government, which in turn has sold it to Hong Kong. Chevron and Texaco have made noncommercial discoveries. In an extension to our block, we have made three small discoveries amounting to a total production of four thousand barrels per day. All the other companies have pretty well struck out. This initial failure has caused despondency in many of the companies and a deep disappointment in Beijing. I am not discouraged. The examples of Occidental's successes in Libya, Peru, Colombia and Pakistan keep my confidence alive that we shall find oil in the South China Sea where other companies fold their tents and withdraw.

Western businessmen are very excited by Deng's policies of encouraging trade, but when they talk to me, they always ask nervously whether his free-market practices will survive his death or be overturned by his successor.

In my judgment Deng has made provisions to ensure continuity. Recently there has been considerable unrest among some of the students in the universities and many public demonstrations in opposition to some of the government policies. However, Deng has a majority in the Politburo and if this does not change, I believe Deng will see that the line of succession makes his policies irreversible.

I have met Deng nearly every year since we began business in China, at ceremonial occasions and in private discussions. We have been at banquets together in the Great Hall of the People and at the Diao-yu-tai State Guest House. I saw him after the opening of the Armand Hammer Collection in Beijing and briefed him at length after my first meeting with Mr. Gorbachev when I went to Beijing in June 1985. He has always impressed me as the most astute and smartest of politicians who unswervingly follows the line of his country's best interests.

Naturally Deng confronts immense social, political and economic problems. Some Communists have frankly opposed his open policy and have slightly hindered the growth Deng is seeking. The old hard-line Maoist lobby still has influence in the corridors of power and cannot be discounted. Resentments between the cities and the countryside seem to be growing as the prosperity of farmers increases faster than that of city-dwellers. The national economy is running into a balance-of-trade deficit which could become serious. And it has been estimated that even if China achieves all of Deng's growth targets by the year 2000, per capita income of the Chinese, now about $300 a year, will still be less than $1000 a year—far less than projected per capita income for that year in Taiwan.

This network of problems poses serious challenges for Deng's leadership and for his successors. I am confident that they will succeed. A people which tackles its problems with such effervescent enthusiasm and is so hectically busy with the business of improving itself is capable of defying dry economic statistics and prognostications. China will come through: I am sure of it.

The opening of our Chinese operations took me on a series of looping flights around the world, and Fred Gross and his crew were frequently making flight plans from Los Angeles to Beijing; from Beijing to Moscow; from Moscow to a European capital; from Europe to Washington or New York and then on home to Los Angeles. Our time in the air increased so much that Frances complained of a permanent case of jet lag.

With my long-cultivated ability to take catnaps, I suffered less than Frances or other companions. My friend Jerry Weintraub ruefully remembers one trip we took together with staging posts in Beijing and Moscow—Jerry and I had created a joint venture called Hammer-Weintraub Productions to promote entertainment industry projects like movie productions in China and Russia.

After several days of serious business in Beijing, we left to fly to Moscow overnight. Jerry and his wife, Jane Morgan Weintraub, were trying to catch up on some sleep on beds in the front salon. Frances was asleep in our bedroom. I was working in my office on the plane.

Jerry remembers that, at about three A.M., he realized that he was being shaken awake. Now, Jerry is a very big man, who combines the sophistication of the top businessman with some of the attributes of a street fighter. He is not a man who reacts kindly to having his rest disturbed. He came out of his sleep with his fists up. Then he saw that the culprit was me.

"We've got to have a meeting," I said. "Come to my office, would you?"

Jerry got up, put on his robe and sleepily followed me through to my desk.

"What's up?" he said.

"I've been looking over these contracts," I said, "and I want some changes made. They cover only four years. I want ten."

Jerry looked at me in astonishment for a moment and then he said, "At this point, Armand, you can have anything you want. If an eighty-four-year-old is going to wake me up in the middle of the night to say that he wants a contract extended to ten years, all I can say is, 'Have it and let me get back to sleep.'"

In April 1984 Fred Gross had to fly a tight schedule eastward to get Frances and me to a party in London with Queen Elizabeth, the Queen Mother, followed by dinner in Beijing with Ronald Reagan. In China I was to announce project agreement for the An Tai Bao mine. For this flight Fred asked the Russians for clearance to fly clear across their airspace and the Russians consented.

The schedule was so tight that we had to get to Heathrow, London's major airport, precisely on time after the party to take off before the night's curfew on air traffic. The party, however, was good and the Queen Mother, always convivial, was enjoying herself and staying on. Protocol forbade Frances and me from leaving before the Queen Mother. I nervously watched the minutes ticking away on my watch, knowing that I was in danger of missing my date in China with the President. Finally I walked up to Queen Elizabeth and explained my predicament. She immediately said, "Oh, well, I don't want to cause you any embarrassment. I will leave straightaway." Thus she saved the day.

I arrived in Beijing in time for two dinners with Ronald Reagan, the first a state banquet given by Premier Zhao and the second a return dinner given by the President at the Great Wall Hotel. At the state banquet I approached Premier Zhao and the President with a glass of white wine in my hand and, in accordance with custom, offered to toast them. Premier Zhao said, "White wine isn't strong enough to symbolize the strength of connection between China and Occidental. We must toast with mao-tai," their 106-proof liquor, which is stronger than vodka. He said that we should go bottoms up with our glasses and asked Ronald Reagan to join us, which the President gamely did.

I also helped my friend Malcolm Forbes to make one of his own idiosyncratic flights in China. Malcolm, publisher of *Forbes* magazine and one of the most unabashed hedonists and capitalists in the world, has traveled the world in or upon the two conveyances which he prizes above all—motorbikes and hot-air balloons. You wouldn't get me into or onto either of those things for all the Fabergé eggs in Malcolm's splendid collection.

Nonetheless, Malcolm is an ardent advocate of the principle that people should get their fun in life any way they choose. He chooses motorbikes and hot-air balloons. Who am I to argue?

In 1980, when Malcolm wanted to take a party of motorcyclists on a tour through Russia, I helped him to get permission and visas. In 1982 he conceived a yet more implausible fantasy, to take a motorcycle gang, equipped with hot-air balloons, across China. He couldn't get the Chinese to take him seriously—can you blame them? Richard Nixon wrote a personal appeal to Deng Xiaoping. Nothing happened. Malcolm asked former Secretary of State Henry Kissinger to see what he could do. Again, nothing.

Finally Malcolm brought his notion to me. I didn't bother to try to talk him out of it. Reason didn't enter into it. As a personal favor to me, the Chinese agreed to let Malcolm have his way. However, I had to go all the way to Deng Xiaoping.

When Malcolm arrived with his oily crew in Beijing, I hosted a dinner for him at the Beijing Hotel, where seventeen courses were served to hundreds of guests and Malcolm gave presents to Premier Zhao Ziyang. These included a motorcyclist's vest and a scarf inscribed with Malcolm's motto, CAPITALIST TOOL. Zhao smiled gracefully through his bemusement.

When I got back to the State Guest House after that dinner, a message was waiting for me from President Zia of Pakistan. He was in Beijing for meetings with Deng. He wanted to see me. Even though it was late at night, I called him back and he asked if I would come to his guest house. I thought Malcolm might like to come and meet Zia, Pakistan being just about the last territory on earth over which Malcolm has not wafted or ridden. Given the faintest chance to float through the air down the Khyber Pass or gun his engines in the streets of Peshawar, I knew he'd jump at it. He did. We set off together in my limousine.

The car broke down on a deserted street, well past eleven P.M. We might have been there for hours if rescue had not come in the shape of an old bus rattling along with a load of night workers. I jumped out in the road and flagged the bus down. Our interpreter explained our position and asked the driver to make a diversion and take us to Zia's guest house.

We climbed aboard, easing ourselves into the cramped spaces between the tightly packed standing passengers. I hadn't ridden in a bus for more than sixty years. I thought it made an interesting change in Beijing, in the middle of the night, on the way to see a President. Malcolm and President Zia hit it off, and Malcolm got an invitation to bring his motorcycles and balloon to Pakistan.

Deng Xiaoping also helped me to make arrangements for the flight of some creatures even more exotic than Malcolm Forbes, when he cleared the way for me to bring Chinese pandas to the Los Angeles Olympics in 1984.

I had first mentioned this thought to Deng on March 26, 1982, when I met him in Beijing after the opening of my art collection there. I told him that the presence of the pandas, accompanying the first team of athletes from Communist China ever to enter the Olympics, would delight Los Angeles and be an immeasurable aid to goodwill between the USA and China. Various committees and delegations from America had been dickering with the Chinese, asking them to send the pandas to the Games, but the answer had always been nothing doing. The Chinese always said that their law specifically forbade the export of pandas—only a handful of whom live in captivity in all China. When I took it up with Deng, he immediately saw the value of the idea and said that he would give instructions for the pandas to come.

Quite soon thereafter, Quing Jianhua, Director of the China Wildlife Conservation Association, was surprised when he got a call at his office in Beijing telling him to make preparations to send the pandas to California. "But this is against the law!" Quing cried.

"Deng Xiaoping has just made a new law," he was told.

Staff at the Los Angeles Zoo were simultaneously thrilled and daunted when they discovered that the pandas were definitely coming for a ninety-day stay. A special pavilion had to be built for them and extensive arrangements made to ensure their safety and health. Their dietary needs alone presented a complicated challenge. Each animal needed to eat twenty-five to thirty pounds a day of bamboo, including leaves and stems. They also needed daily helpings of milk, rice porridge with raw eggs, steamed black bread, apples and ground beef. Twice a week, on Tuesdays and Saturdays, they were to have two pounds each of roast spareribs.

I paid to fly the pandas and their keepers from China to California aboard a 747 of CAAC, the PRC airline. I also paid for the maintenance of the group in Los Angeles. The total cost was $150,000. I met that cost as my contribution to the occasion. The animals were greeted with all the pomp and attention of visiting heads of state when they arrived in Los Angeles, and we held a magnificent reception in their honor before the Games opened.

My joy on that occasion, however, was lessened by the knowledge that something very important was missing from those Olympics. The sadness I had felt at the Moscow Games over the absence of the American athletes was matched on opening day in Los Angeles by the absence of the Russians. Once again, a major opportunity to improve relations between the USA and the USSR had gone by the boards. It was a symptom of the worsening relations between the two nations, and I resolved to do what I could to alter it.

During the weeks and months immediately preceding the Los Angeles Olympics, I had been working hard to arrange a meeting in Moscow with Konstantin Chernenko, who had been keeping a very low profile since his accession to power on the death of Yuri Andropov. I wanted to talk to Chernenko about even bigger issues than the Olympic Games. I wanted to urge him to meet Ronald Reagan in a summit conference and I had some specific proposals for diminishing international tension.

It took the rest of the year to arrange the meeting with Chernenko. It happened only in December 1984 and it comes first in the last chapter of this book.

26

Pushing Toward
the Summit

One advantage of living to be eighty-eight years old, if you are fortunate enough to keep your wits and senses, is that the focus of your interests becomes pinpoint-precise. It is possible to see with absolute clarity what matters and what is unimportant. I know very clearly what I want to achieve in the time remaining to me, and if my ambitions are larger than many people's, that just means I have to try harder. I can't think of anything better to do with a life than to wear it out in efforts to be useful to the world.

What follows is the story of how I pursued two of the greatest goals I can imagine—world peace and a cure for cancer—during the year from November 1984 to December 1985, the last full year which I can include in this book. By the end, both had crept just a little bit closer.

The year began gloomily in a forbidding atmosphere of suspicion and fear between the superpowers. Near its end my year was dazzlingly lit by the presence of the Prince and Princess of Wales at a Palm Beach gala given in my honor by the United World Colleges. Tough start, fair end.

PART ONE

Andropov and Chernenko

(I seem, in recent years, to have elected myself as unofficial physician to the world's leaders: perhaps the frustrated doctor in me is coming out. I have described how I tried to help Menachem Begin and his wife, Alisa. I offered similar medical help to Yuri Andropov.

I never met Mr. Andropov, although we exchanged cordial letters. His health was so poor during his brief tenure of office in the Kremlin that he had to postpone several meetings with me. Hearing that Andropov's kidneys were failing, I consulted my old friend Bruno Kreisky, who had also suffered from the same malady and had benefited greatly from treatments on a dialysis machine and a kidney transplant. Bruno's life had been saved, he said, by Dr. Kurt Mengele, head of the Rudolf Stiftung Hospital in Vienna. I offered to take Dr. Mengele to Moscow for Andropov's benefit. Since the Kremlin would not publicly acknowledge the seriousness of the nature of Andropov's illness, my offer was not taken up.

After Andropov's hospitalization from September 1983 until February 1984—a period of almost six months—Dusko Doder, the brilliant head of the *Washington Post*'s Moscow Bureau, scooped the world on February 9 with the news that Andropov had died, deducing this from several indications including the playing of classical selections on Moscow TV by musicians in formal tails, replacing the usual program. This was similar to what occurred on the day of Brezhnev's death fifteen months earlier and before the announcement. Not wanting to miss Andropov's funeral, I flew to Moscow with John Bryson, who was photographing my visits to the Soviet Union. It was on this occasion that I met Konstantin Chernenko, who had been chosen by the Politburo to head the funeral commission. The commission informed me that Chernenko would be chosen by the Politburo as the new Soviet Leader. This must have been a disappointment to Gorbachev, who had been groomed by Andropov to succeed him.)

On November 23, 1984, it was announced that Secretary of State George Shultz and Soviet Foreign Minister Andrei Gromyko would meet in Geneva the following January 7 to discuss a schedule for new arms control negotiations. That meeting would at least open a channel of direct communication between the countries, but there was a serious risk that the session would amount to little more than talks about talks.

It was vital that President Reagan and General Secretary Chernenko themselves get together for a summit meeting, but both sides had spoken very discouragingly about the prospects for such a thing. I hoped to be able to bring it closer.

Several meetings with Anatoliy Dobrynin brought only noncommittal responses, but finally the answer came that I had been waiting for. On December 4, only ten months after we had met briefly in Moscow at the funeral of Yuri Andropov, ten months during which there had been minimal personal contact between the leaders of the United States and the Soviet Union, I was to see Konstantin Chernenko.

A series of briefings with the State Department followed, and then, on December 2, Oxy One taxied away from the company's private hangar at Los Angeles International Airport. Frances was with me as usual. Not so usual was one of our other passengers, Daniel Simmons, a Professor of Pulmonary Medicine at UCLA and one of the world's leading specialists in lung disorders. His mission to Moscow, which was kept secret even from his wife and my closest associates, was to offer his expertise and brilliance to the Soviet leader and his doctors, it having been widely rumored that Chernenko was suffering seriously from emphysema. I didn't rate the chances high that Danny would be allowed to see Chernenko, but, in talking with the Soviet leader's physicians, he might at least be able to make suggestions for treatment which might lengthen Chernenko's life. Dobrynin had encouraged me in this. He must have known the true seriousness of Chernenko's illness.

As darkness fell across the northern world, we stopped to refuel at Goose Bay in Newfoundland. While we slept in our beds, the plane roared on through the night to London, where we again refueled and picked up the two Russian pilots who were always assigned to navigate the plane through Soviet airspace. When we landed at Sheremetyevo II Airport in Moscow, we were taken to the VIP lounge, where we waited while one of my Russian staff arranged for our passports to be checked and another saw our baggage cleared through customs. It took an hour, but anybody who has suffered the attentions of Soviet officials in their most bureaucratic moods will know that a single hour's delay represents something like lightning service.

The cold of night in Moscow's midwinter is always amazing—even to me, though I first encountered it over sixty years ago. It hits you with the force of a body blow, and its shock ripples in chilling waves through even the thickest and warmest clothes. I wear undershirts and long-johns made of 90-percent cashmere and 10-percent nylon. I cover my head with a fur hat, my body with a full-length mink coat and my feet with wool-lined galoshes, but even so, any prolonged exposure to the cold makes me feel as if I have dressed in paper bags.

We hurried to our car and were transported into Moscow to our apartment near the Kremlin, had supper and immediately went to bed. I had a big day ahead of me.

My appointment had been set for noon. I was intensely keyed up. Fate had delivered me an opportunity which I must not mishandle. In the ten months since Mr. Andropov's death, when Chernenko had had a brief meeting with Vice President Bush after the funeral, no Americans other than Dusko Doder and journalists from NBC had been invited to meet the new General Secretary; and their exchanges had been confined principally to twenty-minute discussions mostly of written questions and answers. Chernenko had met no Americans at all since President Reagan's landslide victory in the November election.

Meanwhile relations between America and the USSR were as bad as I had ever known them in the sixty-three years since I had first gone to Russia. Each derided the other's "evil empire." The two sides had to begin talking to each other again. It was vital that Reagan and Chernenko hold a summit meeting without delay, in which the public hostilities between the two countries might melt a little in the private warmth which they might generate. They had to start a dialogue face to face.

I knew, however, that neither side would be willing to go to the summit table without the prospect of some concrete achievements there. A few cozy, fireside chats and some exchanges of rosy platitudes about peace would satisfy neither side—although neither side at that moment had any substantial proposal to make for the other's consideration. All prospects for negotiations had become inextricably snarled up in acrimonious bickering over the details of each other's weaponry, and an endless and fruitless head count of warheads had driven both sides into a dead end.

I felt that I had something to offer. I had come with three concrete proposals, the first of which—though perhaps the most daring—was actually the simplest. Knowing how interminable and complicated any negotiations on arms control were, with their detailed accounting of warheads and throw weights, my idea was for a basic agreement which would help the world sleep easier at nights while the two sides worked through the years of talks which arms reduction and the elimination of nuclear weapons would demand:

If both sides could agree that neither of them would be the first to use force of *any* kind—nuclear *or* conventional—then the military superiorities and disadvantages between them would be nullified.

The Russians fear the Americans' nuclear superiority. The Americans and NATO fear the mass of Warsaw Pact conventional forces mustered on the east bank of the Elbe. A properly verifiable agreement not to be the first to use either nuclear or conventional weapons would, therefore, ease the fears of both sides, and the people of the world would not feel they were living on the brink of extinction.

My other proposals were for an annual summit—a meeting between the two leaders year after year every year, to keep the progress going—and for a new cultural agreement, such as had not existed since the end of 1979.

All this was in my mind as I left my apartment to keep my appointment.

At noon the light of day was dim and murky. The early snows of winter were already packed deep and dirty on the sidewalks. A hard wind cut along the streets, bearing fresh snow. Though it was only a few yards from the curtained warmth of my ZIL limousine to the doors of the office building we were visiting, my companions and I were chilled by the move.

They were Vladimir Rachmanin, protocol officer of the Foreign Trade Ministry, and Michael Bruk, my extraordinary Moscow aide, a full member of the Communist Party whom the Soviets had seconded to my staff and who has worked for me in Moscow for nearly twenty years.

The building we were entering was the offices of the Central Committee of the Communist Party of the USSR at No. 1 Staraya Ploshad, which means Old Square, one of central Moscow's busiest thoroughfares. The passersby on the pavement paid no attention to the fact that the most powerful man in Russia was working behind its doors. We pushed through those double doors into a lobby like that of a large and thriving corporation, quietly thrumming with activity. No ranks of armed soldiers stood guard demanding passes, as they do at the Kremlin. No Secret Service men were visible.

From Lenin to Brezhnev, my meetings with the Russian leaders had been held in the General Secretary's office in the Kremlin, so it was something of an honor, I felt, that Chernenko should have decided to meet me at his place of work rather than at the more ceremonial offices in the Kremlin.

Chernenko's assistant, Andrei Alexandrov-Argentov, known as Alexandrov, was waiting to greet me in the anteroom outside Chernenko's office. It was good to see him again.

His friendly face had become one of the regular features of my encounters with the Russian leaders. He had been present the last time I met Brezhnev and he was at the side of the successive General Secretaries for fourteen years, making him a very important and powerful man in the Soviet hierarchy—he was, himself, a member of the Central

Committee. He was chief aide to the General Secretary on all matters relating to the English-speaking Western world in general and the United States in particular, and he was as close to the General Secretary as the National Security Adviser is to the President—with the difference, of course, that National Security Advisers come and go, but Alexandrov remained through all changes, up to the accession of Mikhail Gorbachev—who retired Alexandrov on a "pension," just prior to the Twenty-seventh Congress of the Soviets in February and March 1986. (Even now, he serves as adviser to Foreign Minister Eduard Shevardnadze.)

We walked together to Mr. Chernenko's room. As the door swung open, I searched the huge room eagerly and curiously for my first glimpse of the new Soviet leader, one of the two most powerful men on earth. Naturally, I wanted to see if he was, indeed, desperately and terminally sick as he had been portrayed.

He rose easily from his desk at the other end of the room and strode purposefully toward me, smiling and extending his hand for a warm, strong and confident handshake. His slightly flushed face and confident manner contrasted vividly with the pale, feeble figure we had seen on television. The set of his shoulders, however, was as square as if he had a hanger in his coat, like a caricature of a military man. This suggested that he had to hold himself erect to breathe more easily, and I could faintly hear his lungs wheezing as he moved and spoke.

We stood together for a moment, posing for a photographer from TASS, the Soviet news agency, who also took pictures of us as we sat opposite each other at the long table in the middle of the room. Then the photographer left.

The room was austere in its decorations. Only two large portraits of Marx and Lenin hung on the walls. The furnishings and carpets were very plain. From a distance I could see that Chernenko's desk was tidy and uncluttered. Several telephones stood on a table to the side of the desk, but nowhere near as many as the battery of a dozen or so instruments at the side of his secretary's desk in the outer office.

Michael Bruk sat beside me, Alexandrov sat on one side of Chernenko, and the interpreter, Grachikov, sat on his other side. Though I usually speak my imperfect Russian with Soviet leaders, Chernenko began our meeting by speaking through his interpreter, possibly to give him room for maneuver and time for thought.

I had come bearing a gift—a letter bound in leather which had been written in London in July 1871 by Karl Marx to Lord Aberdare, then Home Secretary of Great Britain. The letter was one of the documents which Marx had submitted to the Home Secretary as part of his formal application to establish the headquarters of the Socialist International in London. Having been hounded in France, Marx was eager to be granted refuge in England. The letter referred to correspondence between Marx and Abraham Lincoln, in which Marx had congratulated Lincoln on his reelection and on his freeing of the slaves. I had had the good luck to acquire the letter at an auction at Sotheby's in London in May 1984.

I now presented the letter to Chernenko. He had been given notice to expect the gift, and he was also aware of the subjects I wanted to discuss with him, as set out in two written questions which I had submitted. He had prepared a general statement which, having put on his glasses, he began to read, with long pauses for translation.

He praised my efforts "aimed at promoting cooperation between our countries in various fields" and then he said, "The most important task today is to find practical ways of saving the world from a nuclear catastrophe. I stress practical ways. The world does not lack general statements of goodwill: they are to be heard in abundance from Western statesmen. But no words, even the most eloquent, can put a halt to the arms race. In that matter, everybody should roll up their sleeves and get down to business by preparing concrete agreements on limiting and reducing armaments."

That was my cue: I had a practical suggestion to make. When he had finished reading his statement, Chernenko took off his glasses and pushed the paper aside. Now it was my turn. I referred to the written questions I had previously submitted and read the first of them. Speaking in Russian, I said, "Mr. General Secretary, in your interview with the *Washington Post* newspaper earlier this year, you said that the Soviet Union has more than once called on Washington to follow your example and make a commitment not to be the first to use nuclear weapons. . . . If Washington would agree to the commitment you asked for . . . and if the NATO countries would likewise make such a commitment with the Warsaw Pact countries not to be the first to use nuclear weapons, would this be what you consider desirable?"

He paused for a long moment before he spoke. Then he said, "As you know, we made that proposal two years ago. I repeated it in my interview with the *Washington Post* and with NBC. But every time we suggest it, we get no from your country, from your President."

I cut across the interpreter's translation into English and, again in Russian, I said, "Well, Mr. General Secretary, it's obvious that America will always take that position because such a proposal gives you a great advantage with your preponderance of conventional forces . . ."

He interrupted me, saying, "Well, suppose it was the other way around? Suppose the United States said to the Russians, 'We're willing to be the first not to use nuclear weapons,' and we said, 'No, it doesn't suit us.' The whole world would say, 'You see, the Russians obviously do intend to be the first to use nuclear weapons.'"

Now the interpreter was redundant. Our conversation was spontaneous and immediate. I said, "I understand your point, Mr. General Secretary, but let me make another suggestion. Would you consider an agreement by which both sides would agree not to be the first to use either nuclear *or* conventional force and submit to verifiable on-site inspection on both sides? That form of agreement would, I think, satisfy the fears and suspicions of the United States. And it would create a climate of understanding in which the detailed arms negotiations which we need to have can be conducted steadily and calmly."

"Well, I would need to think about that," Chernenko answered. "My first response is that such an agreement might leave us open to trickery and sabotage by which war could be provoked. The Russian people well remember the duplicity of the Nazis when they dressed their own men in Polish uniforms and photographed them on German territory to pretend that they had been attacked first. Under this pretext the Nazis declared war on Poland."

I answered that in the nuclear age it would be an insane act for any nation to provoke a war in the way he feared, since they would be inviting certain nuclear retaliation and annihilation on their own heads.

Chernenko smiled slightly and opened his hand in a little gesture of apparent assent. "Perhaps this might be open to negotiation," he said.

I read him the second of my prepared questions, asking whether the chances for an early summit might be improved if the United States would make a declaration that they did not intend to be the first to use force. "Yes," he said.

I was warming to my task now and speaking without restraint; all inhibitions had slipped away. I urged him to make arrangements to meet Mr. Reagan without delay, not to be hindered by the inevitable and interminable wranglings over the arithmetic of disarmament. "Leave it to the committees," I said, "to decide how many warheads each side should have and when their dismantling should begin and how verifiable inspection should be conducted. Leave it to the committees to draft an agreement restricting nuclear weapons tests in space. These are technical problems. They're not going to be solved overnight or at a two-day summit conference between the two leaders."

"But there will be no point in a summit unless something concrete emerges," he answered.

"Well," I said, "don't you think it would be a sufficiently concrete achievement if you were to make this agreement that neither side would be the first to use force of any kind?"

"Yes," he said. "I think it might. But how would President Reagan react to that proposal?"

I could not answer him. I had been firmly instructed by the White

House that my visit was purely personal and that my proposals were to be presented only as my own private ideas.

"I do not know," I told him, "but I believe that President Reagan is open to ideas. I know that he genuinely wants peace and that, having won his enormous and historic victory in the recent election, it must now be his overpowering ambition to make a place for himself in history as one of the great peacemaking Presidents."

Chernenko listened to me intently; he did not interrupt or contradict. "Well," he said, "I shall be interested to learn President Reagan's response." I took this as a sign that the window was open, that the way to an early summit was being cleared if advantage could be taken of the opportunity.

Our discussion turned to business matters, including an export license I had been granted for a coal slurry pipeline we were tendering to build for the Russians in Siberia. I said the license was an important breakthrough because it would never have been granted before, under President Carter's trade sanctions.

Chernenko made a gesture as if of weary resignation and answered that the American policy of denying trade with the Soviet Union couldn't possibly benefit American businessmen and was, in any case, futile. "We have lively trade with the rest of the world," he said, "and it continues to flourish. If we can't get what we need from America, we will get it elsewhere."

The interview had now lasted well over an hour, and there was no sign of Chernenko's attention slackening or of impatience in him to return to his desk. I had almost completed the list of points I wanted to raise with him. I told him briefly about my hopes for a resumption of cultural exchanges between the USA and the USSR, and said that I was still hoping to sponsor an exhibition of paintings from the Hermitage and Pushkin museums in Washington, New York and Los Angeles, for which I asked his help. He agreed to look into it.

Finally, I told him about Dr. Daniel Simmons, the UCLA professor I had brought with me.

"This man is one of the greatest doctors in his field in the world," I said. "He may be able to suggest remedies and treatment which won't have occurred to your doctors."

I was slightly apprehensive about making this offer, which could easily have been taken as an unwelcome intrusion. Fortunately, Chernenko seemed pleased and said, "I will make arrangements immediately for Doctor Simmons to meet my doctors."

It was time to leave. I thanked him for granting me the great privilege of this interview and assured him that I would report fully on our conversation to the White House. "I am always ready, at a moment's notice," I said, "to come to Moscow if ever you feel that I can be of use."

"Now I have a gift for you," Chernenko said. He walked around the table and presented me with a huge package, half as big as me. I grappled with its ribbons and wrapping papers until, at length, the box was open. It contained a magnificent vase, decorated gloriously with a hand-painted pastoral scene. The vase was a replica of one commissioned by Czar Nicholas I from the Imperial Russian Porcelain Works, many of whose pieces I had acquired in Moscow in the twenties.

Seeing my pleasure, Chernenko beamed and embraced me. A warmth had grown between us which felt like the beginning of a real friendship. I sensed that I could come to like him very much and I also felt that if he and Ronald Reagan could meet—both men in their early seventies, both warm and generous-hearted men—they might find that they liked each other and had much in common. I could not have known then that this meeting with Konstantin Chernenko would be my last, and that he and President Reagan were destined never to meet.

Alexandrov escorted me from the room and, as the door closed behind us, he turned to me and said, "Well, Doctor Hammer, I am completely astonished. Do you realize that you have been with Mr. Chernenko for one hour and thirty-five minutes? He has not granted an interview of such length to any foreigner, even heads of state."

I quickly said goodbye and hurried to my car. I had a press conference waiting for me, and after that I was booked to appear live by satellite on the morning news programs of three American networks— NBC's *Today* show, the *CBS Morning News,* and CNN. To catch the satellite in position, I had to be at the studios of *Gosteleradio,* the state TV station, by three P.M., local Moscow time. As it happened, the reporters did not let me begin to wrap up the news conference until two-forty. We were tight for time as we again hurried away to our cars.

There were no cars. The street outside the *Sovincenter,* where our drivers were supposed to be waiting, was completely deserted. While the daylight dimmed around us and the snow in the wind flecked our coats and hats, we stood on the pavement for a moment in bewilderment close to despair. Then one of my party dashed away around the corner of the building. In moments he returned, sprinting beside a Volvo station wagon belonging to a Danish TV crew which had been at the news conference.

"Do you know the way to *Gosteleradio*?" my colleague had bellowed.

"Of course," they said.

"Will you take Doctor Hammer there?"

"Delighted!" they shouted.

We bundled into the car, which took off in a slide and a scream of rubber. The car swerved in and out of the traffic, running lights and risks at every junction. The driver was enjoying himself no end, and so was I.

Within moments of arriving at the studio I was saying "Good morning" to John Palmer on NBC's *Today* show, reporting on my meeting with Chernenko and saying that the prospects for a summit were good if the two leaders would seize the opportunity which had arisen. No sooner had the NBC transmission ended than CBS's Bob Schieffer began interviewing me. Then it was time for Stuart Loory of CNN. In the space of less than twenty minutes, without moving from my seat or adjusting my position, I had spoken live from Moscow into the homes of millions of Americans.

As the sun was coming up across America, night was falling in Moscow and my day was ending. For a moment I had bridged the divide between the two countries and, I hoped, brought them closer together. It seemed like a satisfactory day's work.

In the evening I went to the American Embassy for dinner and to await the response from the White House. When it came, it was dispiriting. Larry Speakes dismissed the idea of a no-first-use agreement, saying that nuclear weapons were a critical element in deterring Soviet aggression in Europe, "where the Warsaw Pact has superiority in conventional forces."

In my talks with the press, I had suppressed the part of my conversation with Chernenko about conventional forces. Since he had not given a definite reply to my idea, I had not wanted to complicate matters, and perhaps embarrass him. But now I was beginning to regret my caution. A special effort was going to be called for to pry open this obstinately sticking window of opportunity . . . and a good moment to speak was coming my way.

First, however, I was to have an extraordinary meeting with Chernenko's doctors. Alexandrov had promptly followed Chernenko's instructions, had summoned the doctors to meet Dr. Daniel Simmons in the very early morning at the Kremlin Hospital, just outside the walls of the Kremlin on Kalininsky Prospekt.

I can't say the gentlemen looked very pleased to see us, which was understandable: we were invading their turf, after all. Their greetings were peremptory and edgy; a tense atmosphere filled the room.

The Russians gave us a brief account of Chernenko's condition, describing a typical case of emphysema which was being treated in conventional ways. Opening a large case that he had brought from California, Simmons tried to offer a selection of his medicines and equipment; the Russians waved them away, saying that their own products were superior.

Simmons tried to ask some investigative questions, but he received only cagey or soothing replies. The overall message was: "There's nothing terribly serious about Mr. Chernenko's condition, and in any case we've got it under control." They said that it was unnecessary for Danny to examine their patient. Danny asked if there was any question of heart trouble and they replied that there was none. That answer puzzled us both. If it was true, why were the two top cardiologists in the country attending Chernenko, while his lung specialist obviously could not match them or Dr. Simmons for experience?

The uneasy interview continued for a short time and then, to the obvious relief of the Russians, we decided that there was nothing to be gained from continuing our questions and rose to go. Then they became much more friendly, and invited Danny to take advantage of his time in Moscow to visit the All-Russian Institute of Cardiology. They even picked up the bottles of medicine and boxes of equipment which Danny had offered them and said that they would examine them.

I suppose we can easily understand the difficult dilemma those doctors faced: they had something very serious to hide. As was soon to become evident to the world, Chernenko's condition was far graver than his doctors would admit to us.

P A R T   T W O

Opening the Window

The next day I was on my way to Madrid, to open the Armand Hammer Conference on Peace and Human Rights, which was to be held in the Chamber of Deputies in the Spanish Cortes, its Parliament. On the plane, I decided that as soon as I got the chance I would tell the whole story of my discussion with Chernenko. I had to take the risk of embarrassing him. If I could say that the Russians were willing to consider an agreement not to be the first to use conventional *or* nuclear weapons, I might be able to show the White House that a genuinely new mood of conciliation existed in the Kremlin. In any case, I could reduce the risk of embarrassment if I emphasized that the idea was mine alone, and that Chernenko had not made any clear commitment on the question.

The conference in Madrid was the sixth held under my name and with my sponsorship. These conferences have attracted the presence of men and women from all parts of the globe—former Prime Ministers and Foreign Ministers, parliamentarians, jurists, lawyers, judges, professors of law—all dedicated to a common resolve.

At these conferences, delegates from Russia and the Warsaw Pact countries have frequently been challenged with great rigor and sharp criticism on their countries' records in the field of human rights. In no other convention that I know about, not even the United Nations, have these Eastern countries been held so publicly accountable for their repressive laws and practices.

Opening day I decided to set aside my prepared remarks and speak straight from my heart. The delegates didn't want to hear me recite a catalogue of clichés. They wanted to know what I had said to Chernenko and what he had said to me.

"As you have heard," I said, "I had the privilege and the honor of meeting with President Chernenko for more than an hour and a half the day before yesterday. I would like to say that I think it is relevant that I came directly from that meeting to this conference. This is advertised as a conference on human rights, and I think the most important human right is the right to peace. And I feel optimistic after my meeting with Mr. Chernenko that . . . we have an opportunity before us to have peace if we are able to take advantage of it."

I spoke for about twenty minutes, giving a full account of my interview with Chernenko. I have never addressed a more attentive audience. The emotional atmosphere in the chamber lifted me. "I'm interested in survival for my family, for my children and my grandchildren," I said, "and I'm interested in trying to find a solution. . . . I can tell you, ladies and gentlemen, we have a solution; and it's so simple, we wonder why it hasn't been thought of before. The solution is for both sides to meet and agree not to use weapons *of any kind* on a first strike.

"Now is the time to talk to the Russians as equals," I went on. "Now is the time to say to the Russians, 'Let's stop spending hundreds of billions of dollars on worthless nuclear weapons which will never be used and never should be used, unless we want to commit suicide.'"

I ended with a call for action: "I urge every member of this delegation to use his influence with his own government and with Washington to see that Mr. Shultz and Mr. Gromyko, when they meet next month in Geneva, place, as the first article on the agenda, the avoidance of the first use of weapons of any kind. Then let's take our time about determining how many missiles each side should have, whether we should militarize space or not. This may take years. But if we wait until we get agreement on all those points, there will never be a summit meeting and we'll expose ourselves to the risk of utter destruction.''

The reaction of the delegates was truly astonishing. Those sophisticated and accomplished men and women rose together in applause which lifted me as though I were surfing on a huge rolling wave of feeling. I think it was my words about future generations which struck home so forcibly with them. We all care most for the children, and dread to think that nuclear holocaust will be the legacy we will leave them and our grandchildren.

In my suite at the Ritz in Madrid, I urgently composed a letter to the President with copies to Robert McFarlane, his National Security Adviser, and to Michael Armacost and Mark Palmer of the State Department, describing the scene at the Cortes and the delegates' response to my speech, and urging him to consider my proposal.

Was I going too far? Was I pushing too hard? Among my staff there was unease about the approaches I was making to the White House. They felt I was in danger of provoking an adverse reaction in Washington by seeming to interfere in delicate political business. I was convinced, though, that on a matter so transcendent as the future of human life itself, fine distinctions of protocol should not prevent the responsible citizen from attempting to make his voice heard.

I also wanted to reach the President himself, without having to go through the wall of suspicion that surrounded him. In my meetings with Ronald Reagan, I had found him intelligent and lucid in expounding his own views and inquisitive and attentive in asking questions and listening to new opinions. I had come to the conclusion that he was not being fully informed by some members of his circle, who were almost as suspicious of the Soviet Union as some members of the Politburo were of the USA. Somehow I had to find a way past Reagan's advisers and touch the warm heart of the man himself. That was my task: it wouldn't be accomplished if I succumbed meekly to sending messages through "proper channels."

I wasn't back in the United States for long before Washington and the Western world were humming with renewed rumors about the health of Konstantin Chernenko, who was reported to be confined to a sanitorium, in critical condition. I was getting conflicting messages from my staff in Moscow: Chernenko had certainly disappeared from public view, but my informants believed that he was merely refusing to waste his time on formal engagements with insignificant visitors.

I went to the studios of ABC in Washington to record an interview for *Nightline* about the Soviet leadership. Mikhail Gorbachev and his wife were then in the middle of their triumphant visit to Great Britain, and the world press was in a frenzy of excitement at the sudden appearance of this magnetic man—of whom the British Prime Minister, Mrs. Margaret Thatcher, had cheerfully declared, "I like Mr. Gorbachev. He and I can do business together."

In the absence of hard information, I counseled caution. It was very important, I said, that we should face reality and not dream our opportunities away. For the time being at least, Chernenko was the man we had to learn to deal with, and it was fruitless to speculate on his successor while he was still in power.

I acknowledged that Gorbachev was an interesting and powerful figure, but I suggested that we had more vital business on the international agenda right then than the cut of Mr. Gorbachev's suits and the charm of his wife's smile.

There was no denying, however, that death was advancing on Russia's aged Politburo. One after another of its septuagenarians was passing away, causing changes in the Kremlin which even the best-informed Westerner could only guess at.

Even while I was sitting in that Washington studio, discussing Konstantin Chernenko's health, Marshal Dmitri Ustinov, the Soviet Union's Defense Minister and one of its most implacable hard-liners, was on his deathbed. Along with the rest of the world, I watched with fascination when pictures of Ustinov's funeral rites were transmitted on television; and we saw Mikhail Gorbachev apparently relegated to obscurity in the line of mourners, while Chernenko appeared barely able to catch his breath in the vicious cold of that Moscow day.

As the new year began, I felt frustrated. My efforts appeared to be producing little change or progress. No word had been published from Moscow to develop my proposals, and despite my constant knocking, the door to the Oval Office in the White House remained jammed.

Meanwhile I was back in Washington to attend Ronald Reagan's second presidential inaugural. The day of the Inauguration itself was one of the most bitterly freezing Washington mornings in living memory. The wind-chill factor was so extreme that the grip of frostbite began to tighten around one's mouth and jaw after about fifteen minutes' exposure to the wind. The organizers had no choice but to cancel the open-air ceremonies and conduct the swearing-in in the warmth of the Capitol.

Invitations to witness the ceremony in the Rotunda were few and far between, and several of my political friends pulled my leg when they saw me. "I might have known you'd be here," said Bob Dole, Majority Leader of the Senate. Edward Kennedy reminded me that when Ronald Reagan was first sworn in as President in January 1981, I had sat beside him on the platform reserved for Senators, immediately behind the podium. "Meet the one-hundred-and-first Senator of the

United States," was how Teddy introduced me to his surprised colleagues.

After the ceremonies, as we left central Washington to drive to Dulles Airport to meet my plane, it struck me again, as it has so often in the past, how much Washington and Moscow resemble each other. The similarity starts with the weather. That morning in Washington, lit by sunshine of crystalline brilliance, with a ripping wind whisking flurries of snow into the air, was like a typical January morning in Moscow. The resemblance goes further, in the mighty frozen rivers of both cities and the countryside which surrounds them—rolling hills, densely wooded with larch and spruce.

Both cities are the grand architectural expression of mighty political power and aspiration, and it should not be forgotten that they are both the capitals of revolutionary republicanism (small rs)—though the revolution produced government by democracy in one capital and government by oligarchy in the other. Even the fur hats worn by the traffic cops, with their deep earmuffs and flat peaks, are identical in Moscow and Washington. As this thought ran through my mind, I was saddened all over again by the knowledge that the people of those great cities have no idea how much they share in common.

January wore on, and I continued to be frustrated. What could I *do* to force a break in the wall of indifference and complacency which was blocking the road to the summit?

Then, on January 29, late in the afternoon, while I was working at my desk in Los Angeles, came one of the most exciting and rewarding moments of the year. One of my colleagues in the building came through an internal line to ask if I had seen an Associated Press dispatch from Stockholm which had been collected in that day's briefing assembled by Occidental's News Bureau. I had not yet gone through the briefing.

"Well, Doctor," he said, "I think it's terribly important. Shall I read it to you?"

"Go ahead," I said.

"It's by David Mason, AP's Chief European Correspondent, and it's datelined today," he said. "It begins: 'The Soviet Union opened this year's session of the thirty-five-nation European Security Conference today by proposing a treaty that would commit nations not to be the first to use military force . . .'"

"What?" I said.

"Wait a minute, Doctor," he said. "There's more. It goes on: 'Soviet Ambassador Oleg A. Grinevsky, Moscow's delegate, outlined the proposal to the conference, which includes the United States and Canada, the Soviet Union and all European countries except Albania.

The treaty outlined by Grinevsky would impose on all Soviet-led War-saw Pact and US-led NATO forces an obligation not to be the first to use either nuclear or conventional arms against each other, and hence not to use military force against each other at all.'

"That's your proposal, Doctor," said my colleague. "Chernenko has actually put it on the table and made it official."

There was no doubt about it—a policy development of this impor-tance could come only from the Politburo and on the direct instructions of Chernenko himself. "Now maybe we're getting someplace," I said.

PART THREE

Nearing a Cure for Cancer

Meanwhile I continued to pursue my other great goal—a cure for cancer.

Over the years I have given many tens of millions of dollars to important causes, but of them all, only two have really occupied my heart and my mind: the search for world peace and the search for a cure for cancer. That hasn't stopped a lot of people from writing in and asking me for money, though.

Recently I pulled out a bunch of letters at random, representative of the crop I get every day of every year. A man from Syracuse in Italy wrote to ask "to obtain within limits of absolute legality and honesty a financing or donation of $20 million, to form a productive activity for the purpose of to help the people in condition of vital necessity. It is very urgent."

My correspondent thoughtfully did not trouble me with the details of this proposal. He asked only that I credit the money to his account in Lugano or in New York. In return he offered to give me "my life, my blood. I give to you total assistance humane and effective as brother or as father: can you adopt me as brother or father?"

The next correspondent displayed a touching concern for my well-being. He wrote: "Last night I had a very unusual dream. It was about you. I saw your financial Empire collapsing, with considerable losses to you. In the *Dream* I wanted some way to help you but there was nothing I could do. Then a *Voice* said that if you would help me your losses would be overturned and your *Life Span Increased.*"

This kindly soul requested only that I give him the money to buy his house. He thoughtfully attached a savings deposit slip made out to his account at the Valley National Bank in the amount of one hundred thousand dollars. I should think he must be a well-known customer there: he signed himself "The King of Israel and The Messiah of all Israel."

The next letter, from a dentist in Geneva, was similarly considerate: "Dear Sir," he wrote, "Your time is precious so I will be short. I want to ask if you can rent to me 650,000 US dollars for 13 years. I can give back to you 50,000 US dollars a year. This would give me the possibility to change profession and so I can continue to work for my family."

What, I wonder, is so bad about being a dentist in Geneva?

The next letter was very unusual, almost unique in my experience. It offered me money. My correspondent told me that he had recently read an article about me in a German Sunday newspaper.

"According to that article," he said, "you live in a 20-room house in Los Angeles. It so happens that my family and myself will spend a part of our this year's vacation in the United States and arrive by plane in Los Angeles on July 3, 1986. Reading that article, I got the startling idea to ask you whether it would be possible to spend one night in one of your 20 rooms before we continue to Oceanside. It goes without saying that we are willing to pay a reasonable amount of money for the overnight stay."

. It goes very much with saying, in my book. Nobody has ever demanded bed and breakfast from me and Frances before.

I don't know exactly what it is about Germany. A great number of weird requests come from there. Perhaps things are tougher than we suppose in the land of the miracle economy. There was, for instance, a really impressive communication, embossed with a magnificent coat of arms, from a hustler in Essen.

The letter was exquisitely word-processed, with a justified right-margin, set on the kind of stationery you could use to make big bills of currency. It began:

"This letter contains an exceptional and indeed unique offer which is not without a certain delicacy.

"A member of the German High Aristocracy asked me to find a person who would be interested in assuming his titles and to bear his name for society reasons or for business purposes.

"The member of the High Aristocracy is———, Prince, Duke and Count.

"The assumption of the three titles is possible by adoption or marriage, or by contract at the use for business purposes."

What could this man have been thinking of? Did he imagine that I was going to marry his daughter? Or be adopted by him? So delicate was this "unique" offer that no charge was mentioned. My guess is probably better than yours: I'd say, not less than ten million.

Nearer to home, from Salt Lake City, came a simple little request: "I would like to ask you for 4 to 5 million dollars," wrote a thirty-one-year-old who described himself as a yuppie. The inexactitude of the sum he wanted was very charming: four million, five million—who's counting? He went on:

"Although this amount is insignificant when viewed in the context of your entire fortune, a gift of this magnitude would have a dramatic impact on the quality of my life and enhance the lives of others."

It's comforting to know that four or five million dollars would improve his life-style. I feel tempted to answer that four or five million dollars would have a dramatic impact on Adnan Khashoggi's "quality of life"; and he works for his money. Mr. Salt Lake City disarmed this reply, however. He continues:

"While I have done nothing to deserve such generosity, my determination motivates me to solicit your support."

All I can say is, "You're not the only one, brother."

So it went. My very favorite among recently received requests was from The Ambassador of the Galactic Alliance, whose headquarters are in London. This man—if human being he is—appears to be the sole repository of the Unifying Truths of the Universe (strange how letters from KOOKS always come in capitals). For a sum yet to be disclosed, but likely to equal Occidental's total net worth, I could myself be appointed an Ambassador of the Galactic Alliance and, presumably, live forever.

You've got to admit it's imaginative.

Needless to say, none of these "causes" ever got any money. But about the search for a cure for cancer, I was perfectly serious—there has never been any equivocation. The search for that cure has cost me an average of several million dollars a year for many years, and I have never regretted a penny.

My passion on this subject came about as a kind of living memorial to the medical work of my father. I have never forgotten the misery and sense of hopelessness my father felt as he battled the polio epidemics in the early decades of this century. He felt a cure for that dreadful scourge would never be discovered—and yet it was, by Dr. Jonas Salk in 1955. Several generations have now grown to adulthood free from the menace of that mutilating and killing sickness.

My father considered polio to be as incurable then as many people suppose cancer to be today—as if it were a rogue development of nature which is beyond the powers of human beings to control or defeat. I have never shared that pessimism—yet we have been miserably deficient in applying adequate resources to the defeat of cancer. As Chairman of the President's Cancer Panel, I, along with my colleagues, have charge over the one billion dollars of federal funding which is allotted to the National Cancer Institute, headed by the brilliant Dr. Vincent De Vita. A billion dollars sounds like a lot of money, but it's not enough.

Over four hundred thousand Americans die of cancer every year. Divide that number into a billion and you see that we're spending the grand sum of $2500 on cancer research for every victim. Compare that amount with some other items of federal expenditure and it begins to look like a nominal gesture. For instance, a new nuclear-powered aircraft carrier, with all its weaponry and aircraft, costs four to five billion dollars—for the price of a single aircraft carrier, we could spend $10,000 a head for the present victims of cancer.

I first got involved in cancer research on a Sunday in May 1968. I was at home watching Walter Cronkite on a program called *21st Century,* and Cronkite was interviewing Jonas Salk, who was explaining the purposes of his new Salk Institute, then being built in La Jolla. He said they were short of funds to complete the institute.

I called him immediately and made an appointment to go and see him in La Jolla. I said, "Can you possibly tackle cancer the same way you beat polio?"

"Theoretically," he said, "it ought to be possible to develop a vaccine. But it would cost a tremendous amount of money."

"How much?"

"Five million dollars, for a start," he answered.

"All right," I said. "I'll give you five million dollars. Go to work."

Jonas created the Armand Hammer Cancer Center at La Jolla, a wing of his building containing laboratories, library, offices and conference rooms. He also inaugurated a series of symposia, drawing together many of the world's top medical scientists to pool their findings on cancer research.

It was at one of these symposia that I first met Dr. Ronald Levy, whose astonishing work I had read about in an article in *The Wall Street Journal.* Using techniques derived from research into monoclonal antibodies, Dr. Levy had relieved a cancer victim of all his tumors; and others of his patients were showing some signs of improvement.

Having met Dr. Levy at La Jolla, I went to see him at his laboratories at Stanford University. He and his assistants were jammed together and bumping into each other in about a thousand square feet of space. Cages filled with mice and other animals were hanging from the ceiling. I was appalled.

"How can you work in these conditions?" I said.

"It's not easy," Dr. Levy said ruefully. "I need about four times the space I've got here, but I can't get any money from Stanford for construction and remodeling."

"Well, how much would it cost to remodel the floor?" I asked.

"I should think about five hundred thousand dollars," he said.

"You've got it."

I also gave Ronald Levy a half share in the first Hammer Cancer Prize, which was awarded in 1982. In that year, I created the Hammer Prize Foundation, pledged to give $100,000 a year for ten years to the scientists deemed to have made the greatest contribution in each respective year toward a cure for cancer. At the same time I announced that the Foundation would award one million dollars to the scientist or scientists who achieve a cure for cancer similar to Jonas Salk's vaccine for polio.

Sharing the prize with Dr. Levy in 1982 was Dr. George Stevenson, Director of the Tenovus Research Laboratory in Southampton, England. Dr. Levy joined the Selection Committee for the Hammer Prize, along with myself, Dr. Vincent De Vita and Nobel Prize–winner Dr. Renato Dulbecco.

In 1983 we gave the prize to four American scientists for their discoveries about oncogenes. Oncogenes are normally "silent" or inactive cells, present in the bodies of all humans. As our prizewinners had demonstrated, they cause cancer when activated.

The prizewinners were Dr. J. Michael Bishop and Dr. Harold E. Varmus, of the Department of Microbiology and Immunology at the University of California in San Francisco; Dr. Raymond L. Erickson, of the Department of Cellular and Developmental Biology at Harvard University; and Dr. Robert A. Weinberg, of the Massachusetts Institute of Technology and the Whitehead Institute.

My other major contribution to cancer research was the donation of five million dollars to Columbia University in 1975 for the creation of the Julius and Armand Hammer Medical Center. I was very proud that they elected to name the center after their Hammer alumni, and especially touched that my father should be commemorated in this way. At the ceremony to open the center, I was presented with a bound volume containing the record of my father's achievements in his classes from 1898 to 1902.

I felt that a circle drew near to completion that day. It will finally be linked on the day that a cure for cancer is announced. I hope to see that day, and I know that the spirit of Julius Hammer will rejoice then with all the world.

On February 11, 1985, I presented the fourth annual Hammer

Prize of $100,000. This time, three Japanese scientists—Yorio Hinuma, Isao Miyoshi and Kiyoshi Takatsuki—shared $50,000; and a further $50,000 went to Dr. Robert Gallo of the National Cancer Institute's Division of Cancer Treatment. All these men had been working on related fields of research and had made connected discoveries about the nature and growth of adult T-cell leukemia viruses.

It was Dr. Gallo who isolated the first human leukemia cancer virus and discovered Interleukin, a biological growth substance produced by the body which enhances the ability of lymphocytes to fight disease. He also discovered the virus which causes AIDS and is working on a vaccine.

During the lunch, Dr. Vincent De Vita, who is a member of the panel which chooses the prizewinners, told me about the work being done at the National Cancer Institute at Bethesda, Maryland, by Dr. Steven Rosenberg. Vincent said that Rosenberg was applying Gallo's discoveries in clinical practice and getting astounding results in reversing the progress of cancerous tumors.

I almost jumped off my chair. That could be the beginning of a new approach to a cure for cancer. Vincent De Vita had some trouble restraining me from blurting out the news to my guests right there in the Beverly Wilshire Hotel. "The research is at a very early stage," he said, "and we must be careful not to raise people's hopes unduly. If word of this gets out too early, Rosenberg will be besieged from all over the world and his work may actually be hampered."

I could see the sense in what Dr. De Vita was saying. What I did was to go and see Rosenberg as fast as Oxy One could carry me. Within three days I was in his laboratories and wards on his medical floor at the NCI in Washington. Accompanying me was a very exceptional aide— film producer Sherry Lansing. Sherry's own mother had suffered from cancer and, having cared for her mother during her terrible illness, Sherry swore after her mother's death that she would do everything in her power to help find a cure for cancer. She came to me and volunteered to help in any way. Without any previous medical training, but with her great gifts of drive and application, she very quickly familiarized herself with all the latest developments in cancer research, and she became my eyes and ears in this field, traveling the country to meet research scientists in their laboratories and doctors in their surgeries. It is greatly to the credit of this talented and highly successful woman that she vigorously and selflessly gives so much of her valuable time to this effort, where it would be so easy for her simply to write a big check and let it go at that.

So there we were, Sherry and I and one of my Washington assistants, Eleanor Connors, driving up to the National Cancer Institute, just as darkness fell on a freezing Washington afternoon. Dr. Steven Rosenberg was waiting to meet us for one of the most thrilling moments of my life.

He had the classic appearance of the scientific scholar—slightly worn clothes, curly hair carelessly combed, a bright and healthy face whose earnestness was emphasized by rimless glasses. His eyes looked tired, faintly bloodshot with fatigue. He looked like a man who was working himself like a dog.

There was no weariness or weakness, however, in his presentation of his work. Eagerly and quickly, he explained the principles of his research: his enthusiasm caught us up and brought us to the edges of our seats as he spoke.

Since approximately 1976, he said, he had been working on techniques for the development of "adoptive immunotherapy," to enhance the activity of cells in the body's own immune system which have a capacity to recognize and kill tumor cells. Because of the extreme technical difficulties of obtaining these cells, Dr. Rosenberg's research had for many years been chiefly concentrated on efforts to enhance T-cells and find ways to reincorporate them in a body.

Finally, through "the serendipitous coincidence," as he called it, of Dr. Gallo's discoveries on T-cell growth, Dr. Rosenberg and his team had been able to develop a system for administering the cells together with Interleukin 2.

He moved to a light-box to show us X rays of his experiments. The pictures he clipped to the box made us gasp. First he showed an X ray taken from the lung of a mouse with tumors which had metastasized (spread). The X ray was heavy with the fatal black spots of tumor. Then he showed a photograph of tissue cross-section from the lungs of the same mouse after the treatment he had described. The black spots were gone. The lung was clear. Sherry and I almost cheered.

He showed us more evidence of the results of his animal experiments. They were all similarly dramatic.

"Have you attempted to apply this treatment to humans?" we asked.

"We've just begun," he answered.

"Can you tell us the results?"

"They're encouraging," he said quietly. The treatment had been given to two patients. In both patients the tumors were now receding.

Dr. Rosenberg took us on a tour of his wards and introduced us to the very brave people who had offered themselves to be experimented upon for his treatment. One of them was a man who told us he had quite a chunk of Occidental stock. He was particularly delighted to meet me.

Back in Dr. Rosenberg's office, I tried to tell him how excited I was by his report. "I believe we're on the verge of something tremendously important here," I said. "Something which could make a difference to the whole world."

Steve Rosenberg counseled caution. The experiments were at a very early stage, he said. It was too soon to tell whether the process actually worked; he had suffered too many reverses and disappointments over the years to be overly optimistic now. "I need at least another month to get more results from these two patients and start the process on another two before I'll begin to feel confident."

"I understand your caution, Doctor," I said, "but a month's delay could cause hundreds of people to die who otherwise wouldn't. Is there anything—anything at all—which can be done to facilitate this process? Is there anything you need?"

He seemed mildly embarrassed for a moment and reluctant to speak. Then he said, "The main problem we have is that the process of cell extraction is extremely laborious, and if we had a few more assistants to help in that process, we could immediately double the number of patients under treatment. If I had a hundred thousand dollars additional appropriation, we could work with four patients instead of two."

"You've got 'em," I said. He seemed about to protest. "We're not talking about money in a business way here," I said. "We're talking about life and death." I've never met a man more reluctant to take money than Steven Rosenberg, but he consented at last that I make my contribution through NCI.

Rosenberg was able to start treating an extra two patients. Soon after, with the help of Dr. De Vita, he was able to double the number of his patients again, to eight.

After I returned from seeing Steve Rosenberg, at the suggestion of Dr. William Longmire, my colleague on President Reagan's Cancer Panel, I went to see the cancer group at UCLA headed by Drs. Carmack Holmes and Sidney Golub. I reported Dr. Rosenberg's findings to the UCLA group and encouraged them to contact him and see if they could pool their efforts. The UCLA group also needed funds, so I provided them with $100,000. I then linked Steven Rosenberg with Dr. John Lloyd Old's group at Sloan-Kettering, where one of his doctors, Roland Mertelsmann, was working along similar lines. I gave $200,000 to Sloan-Kettering to further the work of Dr. Old's group.

While Steven Rosenberg was attending to the regeneration of life in Washington, the world had been thrown on its ear yet again and I was attending a funeral in Moscow—the third such occasion in three years for which I had made a sudden flight into Russia for the state

funeral of a Soviet leader. My journey to Moscow for the funeral of
Konstantin Chernenko was, however, among the more dramatic flights
of my life.

PART FOUR

The Old Order Changeth—
Enter Gorbachev

The first intimation that death had struck again in the Kremlin came
obliquely. I was packing my bags for a business trip to West Germany
when the news came on the radio that Vladimir Shcherbitsky, the
Ukrainian party leader and Politburo member, who was then in the
US, had suddenly interrupted his tour to return at once to Moscow. It
was also reported that Moscow Radio was playing solemn music—a
sure sign of a death in the Soviet hierarchy. I said to Frances, "You'd
better pack my galoshes and my fur hat and give my mink coat to Andy
[my driver]."

"What for?" she said.

"Because I think I may wind up in Moscow," I said.

No definite news was available when I left Los Angeles in Oxy
One. I was asleep in my bedroom when the plane touched down at two
A.M. to refuel in Newfoundland. My principal personal aide, Rick
Jacobs, went to a telephone in the airport buildings and called the
offices of CBS News in New York. Then he ran back to the plane to
wake me up.

"Doctor," he said, "it's been confirmed that Chernenko has died.
It has already been announced that Gorbachev will be in charge of the
funeral, which is tantamount to naming him as Chernenko's successor.
President Reagan is asleep and he has not yet been informed."

I immediately wrote a telegram to Mikhail Gorbachev, expressing
condolences on Chernenko's death and asking permission to attend the
funeral. We sent the telegram to Los Angeles, to be relayed to our
Moscow office and thence to Gorbachev.

Then the plane took off again to continue the flight to Germany.
In Düsseldorf, on a morning of glittering brilliance which lit the

frozen fields and forests of Germany with the colors of spring, I made arrangements to go to Moscow.

No reply to my telegram to Mr. Gorbachev had yet arrived. Obviously I could not instruct Fred Gross to fly my plane into Soviet airspace without permission. The funeral was scheduled for Wednesday, March 13. Time was getting short.

I decided to take a chance. Though we might have to wait to get permission for my plane to enter Russia, there was nothing to prevent me from taking a scheduled commercial flight to Moscow. I didn't have a visa, but my people in Moscow could fix that. I would leave the plane behind in Düsseldorf to await the arrival of three of my close associates, who were coming posthaste from Los Angeles, and Fred could bring them in once clearance had been obtained.

I hadn't flown on a commercial plane for some twenty years. Lufthansa had flights from Düsseldorf to Frankfurt and thence to Moscow. The first-class cabin was full, but I made friends with one of the very kind stewardesses on the plane and asked if she would let me stretch out and sleep on three seats if by any chance they became available. My luck: three passengers did not turn up and, with blankets and pillows, I was able to make myself a cramped and uncomfortable bed for an hour's sleep.

Michael Bruk had been busy in Moscow while I was sleeping in the air. My telegram to Mr. Gorbachev had been well-received and acknowledged. Bruk had contacted my good friend Vladimir Promyslov, the Mayor of Moscow, who had obtained entry visas for me and Rick Jacobs. They were waiting for us at Sheremetyevo Airport when the Lufthansa plane touched down.

I went directly to the Hall of Columns near the Kremlin, where Chernenko was lying in state on a bier. As we drew up outside, I could see a line of people stretching blocks and blocks—ordinary people lined up side by side in the cold and the dark as far as the eye could see. I was escorted up a huge, wide flight of stairs, and at the top was a beautiful chandelier completely enclosed with black crepe, and all around the stairs were more people lined up to go in. A military escort brought me into the room itself. There were banks of flowers and the casket was up high and open so that people could see. The room was darkened except for the television floodlights and the spotlights over the casket. An elegant honor guard stood watch over the bier, changing guard in a solemn, slow motion goose-step. They let me stand alone in front of the casket after they placed my wreath. The sorrow of that moment, while I stood there before his open casket, was very painful. I felt that he and I could have become friends and that if he had lived, he might have done real good in the world. I also felt thwarted that the progress we had made toward a summit meeting and a no-first-use agreement had been halted, and that I now had to begin all over again with his successor.

Next day I called on Mayor Promyslov to thank him for helping me. "Soviet airspace is always open to you," he said. Our friendship went back a long way. He and I had worked together on "The Hammer House," and Promyslov had personally arranged to have the urgent last stages of the building completed with the help of the Red Army.

The Mayor of Moscow has extraordinary powers which far exceed those of his counterparts in America. He is in charge of all the utilities and the bulk of industrial production in that city, operates all the bakeries and supplies dairy products to the city and all its restaurants. It is as if the Mayor of New York were also the Chairman of General Motors, General Foods, AT&T, U.S. Steel and most of the Fortune 500 list.

Promyslov and I discussed the likely effects of Gorbachev's succession, which had been confirmed. He very guardedly hinted that a new age might be about to dawn and that big changes could be expected. He seemed genuinely depressed by the attitude of the American administration to arms reduction negotiations with the USSR. He thought there was no chance of progress unless the Americans could begin to believe that the Russians negotiated in good faith and genuinely wanted peace.

(Promyslov, who was in his late seventies, subsequently retired with honors.)

After the funeral of Yuri Andropov in February 1984, Konstantin Chernenko said that I must have been the only man there who had also stood in a favored spot in Red Square on the day that Lenin was buried. On Wednesday, March 13, 1985, I stood on almost the very spot where I had stood for Lenin while the Politburo buried Konstantin Chernenko. Images of those earlier occasions flooded my mind.

As the funeral procession shuffled mournfully into Red Square, creeping along to the strains of Chopin's Funeral March, I was struck again by the similarities of the new Russia and the old. The funeral of a Communist leader of the USSR is almost exactly the same as the funeral of a Czar, except for the absence of priests. The portraits of the deceased which are borne aloft in front of the casket merely substitute for the portraits of the saints in an Orthodox funeral. The casket is open. Members of the mourning family throw themselves upon the corpse in a last, racking farewell. In some ways this century has changed Russia less than she likes to think.

I had plenty of time for such thoughts. I was standing for three hours. The temperature was murderously low. If I hadn't had my full winter gear on, including packets of self-heating chemicals in my boots, I would have been a basket case.

Mikhail Gorbachev spoke the eulogy from the top of the Kremlin Mausoleum on behalf of the Central Committee of the Communist Party. Gromyko stood beside him, impassive and enigmatic as ever. Gorbachev's speech was harsh with aggressive attacks on the US, and while I listened to it I felt a foreboding that perhaps the changes which had been predicted might not be so sweeping and dramatic. Gorbachev's public voice, that day, was the voice of the old Politburo.

His private face and manner, however, were something else. When I was introduced to him in the receiving line in the great Kremlin Hall of St. George, his face brightened with charming warmth, his handshake was firm and friendly and his gaze direct and open. "I received your telegram and acted immediately," he said. "I'm very glad you were able to be here."

I said that I was looking forward to coming back to Moscow soon and that I hoped we might be able to meet then. He said that he would be glad to see me and told me to let him know when I was coming.

I moved on to shake the hands of Nikolai Tikhonov and Andrei Gromyko, standing in their accustomed places at the right hand of power. Little did any of us know, at that moment, that their occupancy of that prime spot in Russian life was about to end. Both of their positions would change in a matter of months.

Gromyko certainly gave no sign of being affected by it. He greeted me jovially with the almost imperceptible pursing of the mouth and wrinkling of the eyes which passes for a grin on Gromyko's face. "We've taken many teas together," he said, "and I hope we'll have many more."

Leaving the hall, I met President Zia of Pakistan. He said, "Remember, we're expecting you for dinner at the end of the month." Margaret Thatcher said, "I expected that you would be here." And George Bush, who was talking to Senator Howard Baker, looked up and said, "Armand, what are you doing near the back of the line? I thought you'd be at the head!" As we had all met together in the same place after the funeral of Yuri Andropov, there was something curiously informal and unsolemn about these moments. It seems absurd to say that the atmosphere was like a family occasion, but it certainly felt like the meeting of an intimate club to bury one of its members.

The mood of Moscow itself, on the day after the funeral, was also unexpectedly light. All the flags of mourning which had been flying at half mast had been removed. The people on the sidewalks seemed to be moving buoyantly; many were even smiling, a rare sight in Moscow. A distinct touch of spring was in the air, and as I drove to the airport to meet my plane, I noticed that the pipes and gutters on buildings, which had been blocked with ice only yesterday, were now gently dripping in the thaw. I took that as a good omen.

A dramatic change also occurred that day in the behavior of the police and customs authorities at the airport. In a magical transformation, their usual hindrances disappeared. As the cars of my party approached the airport's perimeter fence, a jeep swung in front of us, surmounted with a large sign saying, FOLLOW ME. It led us directly onto the airport's tarmac and to the steps of my plane, whose engines were running and was ready to go. An Army officer at the foot of the steps briefly inspected our passports and visas and glanced at our bags as they were carried aboard. Then the doors of the plane were closed and we were on our way. In sixty-five years' experience of Soviet customs officials, I have never seen anything like that.

PART FIVE

Shuttling

The road back to Moscow was long and winding. Before June 1985 came, and I finally went to Moscow to see Mikhail Gorbachev, I had many matters to attend to, chief among them being Steven Rosenberg's research.

At the Cancer Ball in Washington, D.C., on May 11, I introduced Rosenberg to Dr. George Keyworth, then President Reagan's science adviser. I urged Keyworth to go to the President and ask for an additional appropriation for the National Cancer Institute to launch Rosenberg's work all across the nation. He said that he would ask the President for a twenty-million-dollar supplemental appropriation as soon as Steven Rosenberg could report successful treatment of twenty patients. That day was coming fast.

On June 11, 1985, at eleven A.M., I finally departed from Los Angeles in the direction of Russia to see Mikhail Gorbachev. Like Konstantin Chernenko, Mr. Gorbachev chose to see me in his office at the Central Committee building, the very same room in which Chernenko had received me on December 4, 1984. Andrei Alexandrov met me and Michael Bruk when we arrived in the anteroom and, exactly as he had done when I visited Chernenko, warned me that I was likely to have only a very short meeting with Mr. Gorbachev, who had to see a number of heads of state that day. "It may be as little as twenty minutes or half an hour," Alexandrov said.

As I entered the office, Mikhail Gorbachev came quickly toward me, shook my hand, and said how glad he was to see me again. He then guided me toward a seat opposite him on a long table covered with a green cloth while two TASS photographers snapped pictures. The General Secretary and I began to talk. No interpreter was present. Mr. Gorbachev preferred to speak in Russian, though I had the impression that he had some, less than fluent, understanding of English. Occasionally Michael Bruk or Alexandrov would help me out with a word or two, but our talk was free-flowing, spontaneous and informal.

Gorbachev had not prepared a speech or any notes. He spoke off the cuff, with unmistakable authority, understanding and knowledge. From the first moment it was obvious that he was entirely his own man and very much in charge of himself. He made an extremely effective first impression and I had to search my mind to think of another Soviet leader whose presence was so immediately commanding. Khrushchev, Brezhnev and Chernenko were all dominant characters in their different ways, but Gorbachev's bearing had upon it the stamp of leadership—the sense that he was cut from an extraordinary cloth of humanity—which I had encountered previously only in Lenin. I kept this thought to myself, watching the General Secretary closely and thinking, as our interview progressed, "Ronald Reagan will need to be on his best mettle if ever he meets this man in a summit, because he's obviously going to be a formidable negotiating adversary."

The conversation began with a brief business discussion, then the talk turned to politics. Anatoliy Dobrynin had already told me that Gorbachev would definitely not be attending the General Assembly of the United Nations in New York in September, as had been rumored. I therefore urged Mr. Gorbachev to make alternative arrangements for the earliest possible summit meeting with Ronald Reagan.

"I am in contact with the President," he replied. "We are communicating on this question and we are willing to have a summit meeting, but we have yet to fix a date and a place."

I realized that I had been given a startling item of news: the chances that there *would* be a summit looked favorable. I beamed with pleasure at Mr. Gorbachev. He looked less excited.

"I don't feel much optimism about it," he said. "I don't think that it will be worth doing unless some good comes from it, and there is not much chance of that as long as the Americans keep up the arms race and insist on going ahead with their Star Wars program."

I told him about my meeting with Mr. Chernenko—how I had proposed a no-first-use agreement and Chernenko had been noncommittal.

"When the same proposal was made by the Soviet representative at the Stockholm Conference in January," I said, "I felt sure that instructions must have been given by the Politburo."

Gorbachev smiled and said nothing.

"Since my meeting with Mr. Chernenko," I said, "I have had discussions with senior people at the State Department in Washington and I have the impression that if the Warsaw Pact nations really will agree to no-first-use of conventional or nuclear weapons, President Reagan might go along with it."

"Well, we've tried to get him to agree to this before . . ." he started to say.

"I think the United States really will eventually agree to it," I went on, "because otherwise it will look as if the United States is really interested in a first strike, which is not true."

"There I must disagree with you," he said. "I believe that the United States is very interested in having and maintaining a first-strike capability, and we think that this proposed Star Wars development is part of that ambition. The SDI can be of advantage only to a power that is seeking to preserve a first-strike capability and, in that sense, it is an aggressive plan. I doubt your President's sincerity, I'm afraid. I do not believe that he is genuinely seeking peace."

I was very disturbed to hear Mr. Gorbachev speaking like that, and I was reminded of the stern and inflexible impression he had made when speaking from Lenin's tomb at Chernenko's funeral.

"I am in no doubt whatever of Mr. Reagan's desire for peace," I said, "but if you doubt his sincerity, why don't you test it?"

"By what means do you suggest?" he asked.

"Two ways," I replied. "First, you could repeat the proposal for no-first-use of nuclear or conventional weapons; second, if you are so disturbed about the Star Wars development, why don't you propose that you share in the research immediately and conduct the research not in space but on land?"

"They would never agree," he said.

"I don't see why not," I replied. "President Reagan has already said that if the system is successfully developed, he will offer it to the world at cost so that everybody can share its benefits. In that case what's to prevent a sharing right away?"

Now came the most disturbing moment in our interview. Mr. Gorbachev said that President Reagan would never be allowed to make such an offer. "The President is a prisoner of the American manufacturers of armaments who control the White House," he said. He quoted President Eisenhower who, he said, had warned the people of the US, on his retirement, to beware of the influence of the military-industrial complex.

I was shocked. "The President of the United States is nobody's prisoner," I said. "He is supported by a freely elected Congress and a free press which would never tolerate the domination of the presidency by any interest group. Naturally, there are powerful interest and pressure groups in the United States, and the arms manufacturers certainly do represent a powerful lobby. But it is a great mistake to suppose that they can control the President. His powers make him completely independent."

Mr. Gorbachev said, "I'm sorry, but I must disagree with you, Doctor Hammer."

This exchange made me very uneasy. Gorbachev's opinion of the presidency was not original, but I had never heard it expressed before by a General Secretary of the Communist Party of the USSR.

I began to see Mr. Gorbachev's character more clearly. He was obviously a man of enormous intelligence and strength, whose attitudes toward domestic policy and to his country's economic needs were acutely pragmatic. At the same time, no doubt because he had never visited the United States, his view of our country seemed disturbingly limited. I saw a very striking example of that when I showed him a copy of Occidental's annual report for the year of 1984. Alexandrov had to explain to him the concept of a corporation's net worth.

I had an opportunity to eliminate a basic misconception. I had to do everything I could to ensure he met Mr. Reagan as soon as possible, so he could learn that the President was not the tool of any group, and I had to talk to Ronald Reagan personally, to let him know about this disturbing feature of the new General Secretary's thinking.

My interview with Mr. Gorbachev had now lasted nearly an hour and a half, despite Mr. Alexandrov's earlier warning, and I think that it would have continued even longer if I had not risen to leave. Accompanying me to the door of his room, Mr. Gorbachev said, "I know that America can live without Russia, and Russia can live without America, but this is not good for either side or for the rest of the world. The West must realize that it will never destroy socialism: I don't believe that your people understand that."

"Well, I don't believe that's our aim," I said. "We have something to learn from socialism, but you don't get things done the way we do in America. Ours may sometimes be a demanding system, but it motivates people and that's why we have the highest standard of living. Maybe someday we'll have a system of peaceful coexistence where the good things in socialism are mixed with the good in capitalism." Gorbachev made no comment.

He invited me to return to Moscow and see him again. I said that I was always willing to come.

Newspapers all over the world carried reports of my meeting with Mr. Gorbachev. As had happened after my meeting with Chernenko in December 1984, I was besieged by reporters and television crews, and again I appeared in live broadcasts to America. I was circumspect and cautious in my remarks, however. I wanted to report to the President first.

On June 23, 1985, I had two appointments. At noon that day I met Anatoliy Dobrynin. At four I was due in the Oval Office.

I found Anatoliy in an uncertain state of mind. The Americans, he said, were fumbling the chance to fix a time and place for the summit and were not advancing any concrete proposals for discussion. He said, again, that the President's insistence on the development of the Strategic Defense Initiative—Star Wars—was bound to stymie any chance of real progress. He said that Gorbachev had already invited Reagan to go to Russia for a summit, but that the White House had refused. I promised to bring all that up with the President.

Quite a group was waiting for me at the White House. Along with the President was Jack Svahn, the President's Domestic Policy Adviser, Chief of Staff Donald Regan and representatives from the State Department and the office of the National Security Adviser, Robert McFarlane.

The President looked fine, in good health and spirits, and it was amazing that he appeared to be bearing up so well with the TWA hijacking drama unfolding right then. I apologized for taking his time during such a crisis, and took the opportunity to start the meeting with a description of the work that Dr. Rosenberg and Dr. Old were doing to fight cancer, and recommending the money for national clinical trials that I had discussed with George Keyworth.

The President seemed very interested, but it was the question of the summit meeting that was uppermost in his mind. He told me very emphatically that they had already gotten agreement from Gorbachev to have a summit meeting; that a meeting would take place before the end of the year, in a neutral place, and that they were trying to determine where that should be. When I asked when the date might be, Don Regan interrupted to say, "Before the end of the year," but he would not specify any date, which led me to believe they had not agreed on either the date or the place.

I then urged the President to accept the Russians' invitation to visit Russia. Before he could answer, Don Regan interrupted again to shout, "No, Mr. President, it is the Russians' turn to visit the US. We sent them an invitation and they refused. So there is no reason for the President to go to their country." The last summit between a US President and the Russians, he went on, had been when the President went there—I presumed he meant when Ford went to Vladivostok to meet Brezhnev—and now it was their turn.

"What is important," I interrupted, "is to get results and not to stand on ceremony." I said to President Reagan, "You're too big a man to stand on pride. You are the President of the most powerful country on earth and the most powerful man in the world." I said that he should show how magnanimous and generous he was by accepting the invitation and going to Russia, that he could appear on Russian television and make friends with the Russian people, who would see that he wanted peace as much as they did.

Don Regan tried several times to throw cold water on my proposals. The President said, "We have made all kinds of proposals to them. They have never answered for several months." I said that Gorbachev had only been in office for three months. Don Regan interrupted and said, "We made these proposals to him right from the start."

I replied that I thought it was vital that the President should sit down with Mr. Gorbachev face to face, and the President agreed. I said that Gorbachev was under disturbing misapprehensions about America and the presidency, and that he was surrounded, still, by men giving him hard-line advice—but if the two men could meet, things could be different. He could go down as the greatest President since Franklin Roosevelt; it was the opportunity of a lifetime.

The meeting had been scheduled for fifteen minutes—half an hour had already gone by, and people were waiting outside. I felt that the President would have kept me longer if he could. He thanked me warmly and rose to show me out. The atmosphere in the room seemed different, better, as I left. Even Don Regan seemed much softer.

It is almost eerie for me to remember how suddenly so many points in my conversation with Mr. Reagan became active issues commanding worldwide attention. Within three weeks the President himself became a patient of Dr. Steven Rosenberg, undergoing surgery for cancer. Gromyko was removed from his apparently impregnable position as Soviet Foreign Minister and was transferred upstairs to the presidency. And a firm date and place were announced for the summit.

Meanwhile, I was in China with Deng Xiaoping, signing the agreement to develop the An Tai Bao mine in the Ping Shuo mining area of Shanxi Province. As I have described many, many times over the years, it looked as if the project would fall through, and as one of my men remarked after the signing, "It never *would* have happened but for the determination of two pretty tough old birds—Hammer and Deng Xiaoping. When those two octogenarians make up their minds, things tend to get done."

Deng and I get on splendidly. Of course he's a young man compared with me, and I keep telling him that if he'd quit chain-smoking cigarettes he might live to a ripe old age. He laughs and says that, having reached his eighties, he doesn't believe that the habit can do him much more harm now. He always has a spittoon at his feet for his cigarette butts.

Deng must be one of the smartest men in the world. His very survival of the Maoist excesses of the Cultural Revolution, when he was publicly disgraced and humiliated and his son was murdered, is a kind of miracle in itself. Yet he seems to feel no vengefulness toward his former enemies. He just wants to get things done. He wants to ensure that the impetus of China's massive leap forward into the modern age will be sustained, and that the progress made in the last few years will not be reversed even after his death. He is a man possessed of an active vision who knows that he has little time left in which to see it come true, so he is a little whirlwind of ideas and actions, an inspiration to elderly people everywhere. Deng Xiaoping is the living proof that a person can rise to the peak of his powers, making his most valuable contribution when others of his age are passively nodding off in their senescence. He sets a wonderful example to the world—which could only be improved if he would throw away those filthy cigarettes!

There is nothing more delightful than a political discussion with the Chinese leaders. Their perceptions are so acute, their judgments so deft, their words so delicate and allusive that a conversation with them is like one of their banquets—an array of exquisite pleasures. Deng and Vice Premier Li Peng all quizzed me closely on my meetings with Gorbachev and Reagan. They agreed with me that Gorbachev would take control of Soviet foreign policy and that the days of the old Kremlin hard-liners were numbered. They hinted that a rapprochement was in the cards between the USSR and China, so long as Russia did not attempt—as Li Peng put it—"to embrace" China, a very witty way of saying that the Russians had better mind their own business.

Like me, the Chinese leaders were vexed by the posturings of the Kremlin and the White House and the exchanges of recriminations between them, occupying energies which should have been directed toward the peace process. Ideological dicta would never be allowed to dominate the policies of the current Chinese leaders. Their overriding political principle is always to act in the best interests of China and her people: ideology comes a very minor second.

I told them about the impending announcement that Reagan and Gorbachev would meet in a neutral country in November. They knew it, too. None of us knew, however, that two stupendously important announcements would be made after I had left China and had not yet even landed in the United States.

In Moscow it was announced that Andrei Gromyko would cease to be Foreign Minister and would be "promoted" to the largely ceremonial position of President of the state; and that his replacement as Foreign Minister would be Gorbachev's close ally, Eduard Shevardnadze. From the same announcement, we learned that Grigori Romanov—Gorbachev's main rival in the Politburo—had stepped down, "for reasons of ill health." No clearer sign could have been given of Gorbachev's driving determination to be complete master in his own house.

Next day, July 2, 1985, administration officials in Washington announced that the two leaders would meet in a Geneva summit from November 19 to November 21. At last! Like everybody in the world, I felt my spirits lift, but I was disheartened by the downbeat prognostications which issued from the White House, where every spokesman was at pains to say that no great progress should be expected from the summit. It was as if they were saying in advance that the occasion was bound to be a failure. I couldn't understand such negativism. What was the point in creating an opportunity and scuppering it in advance?

On July 5, 1985, Viktor Afanasyev, Editor in Chief of *Pravda*, told a group of American editors visiting Moscow that I "had played a significant role" in bringing about the agreement to hold a summit meeting. He said that Mr. Gorbachev's decision to meet President Reagan had been based in part on the desires of Western European leaders and that I had done a lot to facilitate the negotiations. When the Editor of *Pravda* speaks, he is repeating official truths. One of the main differences between American and Russian journalists is that the Americans say more than they know and the Russians say less than they know.

PART SIX

Time Out

Shortly thereafter I went into the hospital at UCLA to undergo an operation for ureter implantations. While I was recovering, Ronald Reagan was on the operating table at the National Cancer Institute at

Bethesda, Maryland. To my great surprise, one of the surgeons called into consultation to assist the operation to remove a cancerous tumor from the President's colon was Steven Rosenberg, who found himself plucked from the scientific isolation of his research laboratories and thrust into the glare of the world's attention as he led the press conference on the President's condition. Reportedly, when they first met, Mr. Reagan said, "You are the doctor who is doing all the research." "You must have been talking to Doctor Hammer!" Steven Rosenberg replied, which the President smilingly confirmed.

Though the President and I were spared in that month of July, my brother Victor was not. Toward the end of the month Victor suffered a stroke at his home in Florida and died a few days later. He was buried in Los Angeles, in the family crypt in Westwood, where I will also be buried when my time comes.

Apart from Frances and my brother Harry, Victor had been my truest and dearest friend all my life. I benefited from his artistic judgment in a hundred and one art purchases, and my daily contact with him always brightened and enlivened my life with his effervescent wit and his overfilled quiver of gags and stories.

Louis Nizer spoke with the beauty of truth at the funeral, saying of Victor, "If everyone who was a beneficiary of his goodness would place a petal on his bier, he would lie in a forest of blossoms. The only time—the only time—that Victor made anyone sad was the day he died."*

With Victor's passing, the last surviving member of my parents' family had departed, leaving me alone. His loss was a heavy blow to me, especially coming suddenly as it did and while I was weak from the aftereffects of my operation. The last days of July and the first days of August were very bleak.

---

*There was one unfortunate aftereffect to Victor's death, though. After he died, I began taking care of his widow, Ireene, who was confined to a nursing home, unaware of her situation. Relations with Victor's adult, adopted stepdaughter deteriorated. I had put in a claim against Victor's estate for money I had lent him—he had issued me notes—but she attempted to have me removed as one of the executors of Victor's will. The courts ruled in my favor—but it was a sad sendoff for my beloved brother.

PART SEVEN

Star Wars

Throughout August, while I was still recuperating from my illness, I could do little more than keep an uneasy eye on political affairs, and the shaky and stumbling progress which both sides were making to the scheduled summit in Geneva. To my deep despondency, they seemed to be going out of their way to make sure that it would fail.

An absurd and damaging propaganda battle had been joined, with each side trying to outdo the other in painting itself whiter than white and the other side blacker than hell. The Soviets took out a half-page advertisement in the *New York Times* praising their own peacemaking intentions and deploring the ways of the United States. The Americans countered by making a fuss about "spy dust," a powder supposedly sprinkled by the Soviets on the steering wheels and doorknobs of American diplomatic employees in Moscow which allowed the employees to be tracked and theoretically had the potential to cause cancer. If there were any truth to the allegation, it had to have been something the Americans had known about for a long time. They were making a fuss about it now only to score a propaganda point.

As a private citizen, I felt that I had gone as far as I could go. There remained little more for me to say or do.

I had one last card to play before the summit, however, and it turned out to be the most influential card in my hand. I believed I had the solution to the conflict over the Strategic Defense Initiative—Star Wars. Star Wars was the biggest stumbling-block on the road to the Geneva Summit. Both sides were implacable. The Russians stated that nothing would result from the Geneva meeting unless the Americans were willing to abandon the arms race in space. They said they had no desire to waste the billions of dollars required to create a system of their own, but if we proceeded with our own system, they would certainly have to adopt measures to counteract it.

The President, meanwhile, declared that research and development of SDI would go ahead—but he repeated his offer to let the Russians and the world benefit from the system's advantages if it proved to work.

As I had suggested to Mikhail Gorbachev, I had a possible answer to this impasse. If the Americans were willing to share a finished SDI system with the Russians, why not an SDI system in progress? Why couldn't they offer a mutual partnership—with verifiable on-site inspection on both sides—to research and develop the system together, from the start?

Gorbachev's first response to the idea had been the same as most people's. "Your government would never agree to it," he said. American friends with whom I discussed the idea said, "We can't let the Russians play freely in our high-tech backyard."

Others were less polite. "It's the screwiest idea I've ever heard," was one reaction reported to me, not said to my face. Everybody thought that it was impossible—that's often a hallmark of a good idea.

It seemed to make simple good sense to me. If the Americans were going to give the Russians the fruits of their research after the system had been perfected, then the Russians would be able to deduce any high-level secrets involved in the system, anyway. They are not dumb. And there was precedent for such a program: the 1975 space linkup between American Apollo astronauts and Russian Soyuz cosmonauts had required just such cooperation.

If the Russians and Americans could be encouraged even to consider a joint development of SDI, the way to success at Geneva could be cleared of its biggest obstacle.

On Sunday, September 22, 1985, the *New York Times* printed my idea in its editorial pages. The timing couldn't have been better. The General Assembly of the United Nations was about to open in New York for its fortieth anniversary, and Manhattan was jammed with world leaders. Eduard Shevardnadze, the Soviet Union's new Foreign Minister, had just arrived and was preparing to make a big speech during the week. The President was coming in any day. I made arrangements to have my article distributed to every leader who had come for the UN General Assembly, to every member of Congress and a host of politicians around the world.

The results were extraordinary. I have never written or said anything which met such wide approval. Letters flooded in from Senators and Congressmen supporting the idea, and when the article was reprinted in the *International Herald Tribune,* from foreign leaders as well, including two former Prime Ministers of England, Edward Heath and James Callaghan.

Less than a week after the article's publication in the *New York Times,* I was in Washington to discuss it in person with Eduard Shevardnadze. He had made a surprising speech at the UN, impressing everybody with his seriousness and strength while suggesting, in the intellectual flexibility of his speech, that a genuinely new order might have come to power in the Kremlin, replacing the dreary old days of wooden dogmatism.

He impressed me greatly. At first his manner was cautious and quiet, even reserved. He let me do all the talking for quite a long time and seemed to be sizing me up. Our interview lasted a little more than an hour, and by the time it concluded, he was holding my hand while we sat beside each other on a sofa. As we walked to the door together, Anatoliy Dobrynin—who was also present—summoned his photographer and we were photographed together, all three of us with our arms around each other's shoulders.

Shevardnadze and Dobrynin were still skeptical about the President's willingness to share any form of Star Wars, let alone Star Wars-in-progress. I said that in my opinion the President had made the offer in full sincerity and furthermore that he had genuinely undergone a change of heart in his attitude to the Russians and definitely wanted peace with them. They nodded their heads.

Shevardnadze said that he had come to America with a long letter to Reagan from Gorbachev, listing a complete set of firm proposals for the summit, but the Americans, he said, seemed determined to avoid specific business and to ensure that the summit produced only generalities. If the leaders went home from Geneva with nothing more to show than a sheaf of goodwill clichés, he said, the meeting would have failed and the opportunity would have been lost. This time it was my turn to nod.

Shortly thereafter I heard from one of my friends in the State Department who had been sitting in on deliberations with the President over the summit that Mr. Reagan had considered my Star Wars proposal, but had been fearful that if we shared SDI research now with the Russians, we might provide them with the means to get ahead and deploy before us. Then they would have the huge advantage over America which they now feared we were going to create for ourselves. "Surely," I said, "it can't be beyond the powers of imagination to devise a treaty and terms of verifiable on-site inspection which would obviate that risk?"

"I'm just telling you what he's afraid of," said my friend. "I'm not saying that it makes sense." He went on. "There is one thing I have impressed on the President when quoting you, namely that only one person makes the final decision in the Politburo and that is General Secretary Gorbachev; therefore it is vital that the President should concentrate on meeting him alone."

As events were to prove, this message got through.

PART EIGHT

Palm Beach

I had plenty to occupy me while we waited for Geneva. Also looming in the immediate future was the visit to America of the Prince and Princess of Wales and the grand gala I was organizing for them, for the benefit of one of my other favorite causes—the United World Colleges.

Nothing in my recent life has given me more pleasure and pride than to be asked to help the Prince of Wales and to be close enough to observe this remarkable young man as he has grown to full manhood. More than that, I have seen him emerge completely from the chrysalis of his late youth as a man who stands ready to impress the stamp of his character upon the world.

It is said that Prince Charles was inhibited by shyness and uncertainties in his adolescence. I never knew him then, but there remained, when I first met him in the late seventies, some subtle but obvious signs of uneasiness in his attitude to himself. His manner was unfailingly warm, his sense of humor keen and his intelligence as shining as a beacon. But his constant fiddling with his cuff links and with the signet ring on the little finger of his right hand and his curious sudden gestures of hand and arm suggested that he was not fully comfortable with himself. Perhaps—I am guessing—he seemed less than sure that he was entirely worthy of the immense prestige and privilege of his birth; perhaps he did not know exactly what he should be doing with himself while he remained heir to the throne.

Over the last eight years a friendship has grown between me and Prince Charles. Many stages of that friendship must of course remain private, but I see no harm in writing about a few moments which might give a peek into his extraordinary world.

On one occasion, when Frances and I were visiting him at Buckingham Palace, we asked if he would show us his own paintings. Prince Charles was reticent at first. He said that he wasn't much of an artist and that he wasn't very proud of his pictures. We pressed him, and finally he went off to another room and came back with a few watercolors under his arm.

I thought they were pretty good. They showed a strong control of line and color and had considerable emotional power. I said, "Why don't you let me organize an exhibition of your work at Knoedler's? It would be a tremendous success."

"Oh, I don't know about that," he said. "I don't think I'm good enough to have a show."

I tried to talk him round, but he wouldn't budge; his technique, he said, was much too rough and amateurish. He really needed to practice a lot more, he said, and perhaps get a good tutor.

"I know one of the best watercolorists in America," I said. "His name is Bob Timberlake. Why don't you let me bring him over here and give you some lessons?"

"Do you think he'd do it?" asked Prince Charles.

"I think so," I said.

When I got back to the States, I contacted Bob Timberlake, who was represented by the Hammer Galleries, and he, of course, said that he would be honored to give Prince Charles some lessons. Next time I flew to London, Bob came along.

It was his first trip outside the United States. He comes from a little bit of a town, with a population of some eight hundred, in North Carolina. And here he was, on his first trip abroad, going to Buckingham Palace to coach the heir to the throne of England.

Bob was in awe when we drove past the bear-skinned guards and through the palace gates. He was speechless when Prince Charles emerged from a room, dressed in a flowing ceremonial robe with the star of a noble order pinned to its breast. Prince Charles explained that he was sitting for a portrait. Bob was mightily relieved. He thought Prince Charles always dressed like that around the house.

Then Prince Charles said, "So you've come over to give me some painting lessons?"

"Yes, sir," said Bob.

"Well, what I want to know," said Prince Charles, "is, how do you do clouds?"

"Oh," said Bob, "that's the easiest thing in the world. You just soak a Kleenex in paint and dab it all over your sky. That's the best way to get clouds."

"But that's cheating!" said Prince Charles, aghast.

Then I told Prince Charles that Bob had never been out of the United States and he said, "Perhaps you might like to see the Palace. The Queen is away today, so I can get my secretary to show you through all the private apartments."

So there was Bob Timberlake, from a dot of a place in North Carolina, walking through the private quarters of the Queen of England, studying her private collection of pictures and admiring the wonderful furniture and decorations. Bob turned to me at one point and said, "Where I come from, this is what we call walking in tall cotton."

Frances and I once had a delightful lunch with Prince Charles at his new home, Highgrove, in the Cotswolds. He was tremendously proud that everything we ate that day—fruit, vegetables, meat, dairy products—had been grown or prepared in his gardens and on his farm. We ate at a table set out on the lawn, and Prince Charles was at his most informal and unregal.

After lunch he and I took a walk around his farm, while his little boy, Prince William, scampered with us or was carried in his father's arms. "I couldn't afford this farm myself," he told me, "but my mother lent me the money to buy it."

When we were about to leave, Prince Charles suddenly disappeared and returned to present us with several boxes of the plump, sweet strawberries which he had picked himself as a present to us. I think his pleasure in those strawberries tells you all you need to know about him. He was more delighted to give us berries he had grown, and picked with his own hands, than if they had been jewels from the family vault.

As I came to know Prince Charles well, he inspired me with his enthusiasm for a multitude of projects. One night I was sitting next to Princess Diana at dinner and said, "You know, I can't say no to him, whatever he asks me to do. I have so much confidence in him that if he asked me to jump through that window there, I think I'd jump through the window." She smiled and replied, "Well, I'd jump right after you."

Every time I saw him, he would have some new project buzzing in his brain that he wanted to discuss with me or for which he wanted to solicit my aid. He enlisted my support in the successful raising of the *Mary Rose* in 1982, the flagship of the fleet of Henry VIII that sank before the King's eyes in 1545, carrying with it an archeological treasure trove of Tudor artifacts. Because of the Prince, I became involved in the organizations that saved two of the loveliest buildings in the world, the cathedrals of Wells in Somerset and Salisbury in Wiltshire, both of which had been threatened with severe decay, and made large donations to the Royal Opera House in Covent Garden, London, and the Royal Academy.

Perhaps the oddest of Prince Charles's enthusiasms for which he lassoed my support was the Transglobe Expedition of 1979–1982, the first longitudinal—pole-to-pole—circumnavigation of the world by land, sea and ice. This cavalier display of derring-do was being led by a friend of his, a polar explorer who gloried under the name of Sir Ranulph Twisleton-Wickham-Fiennes, better known to everybody as Ran. When he was once asked how he managed to endure all the tortures and deprivations he had imposed upon himself in his adventuring career, he answered, "With this damn stupid name I've got, I learned to be tough quite early in life."

When Prince Charles told me about this expedition, he said, "Of course, it's completely insane, but it's rather gloriously insane"—and glorious it was, as well as entirely successful.

The project that always meant the most to Charles, however, and which cemented our friendship, was the United World Colleges.

On November 8, 1978, Prince Charles invited Frances and me to attend a reception at Buckingham Palace for Friends of the United World Colleges. I didn't know much about UWC then, except that it was an international education movement and one of his favorite causes. At the reception Prince Charles promptly steered me into a corner with his beloved great-uncle Lord Louis, Earl Mountbatten of Burma and Britain's last Viceroy of India. Lord Louis had been the first President of the International Council of United World Colleges, and it was largely to honor and serve his uncle that Prince Charles had become so vigorously committed to the movement.

Lord Louis was the perfect model of the English aristocrat—tall, erect, startlingly handsome, naturally dignified yet easy and approachable in his manner and speech. Explaining his own interest in UWC, Lord Louis spoke some of the most memorable and inspiring words which have ever been addressed to me. He said, "I witnessed the horrors of two world wars and I came to the conclusion that, if we were ever to have peace in the world, we would have to start with young people of an impressionable age who would learn to live together, regardless of their nationality or religion or their ideology."

I have been a citizen of the world all my adult life. I have lived abroad and traveled so much in the world that I know, with the certainty of long experience, that people are the same wherever you go; and that they are divided from each other only by ignorance, misunderstanding and prejudice. Lord Louis could hardly have found a more sympathetic ear. Even in 1978 there weren't so many people left in the world with clear memories of both world wars. Lord Louis and I were two of them. He had seen the horror of war at first hand in many battle actions. I had seen them from a distance, but I had lived through them and, even as early as 1915, when I was seventeen, been possessed by a dream of a world without war.

If seventeen-year-olds all around the world could share that dream and act upon it in their adult lives, they might become the ushers to an age of peace on earth. Lord Louis explained that this was precisely the object of the United World Colleges.

Founded in 1962 by a group of five men, the UWC movement was mainly inspired by Dr. Kurt Hahn, the founder of Prince Charles's old school, Gordonstoun, and of the Outward Bound survival programs. Dr. Hahn held that the education of young people should involve nonacademic experiences—mountain survival, service to others, a mixture of all kinds of adversity and instruction in how to overcome it—as well as a top-flight academic education. The United World Colleges was formed to provide this style of education for the brightest of the world's young citizens, in the belief and hope that in their later lives, when they assumed positions of influence in their own countries, they would be influenced by an education which had brought them in touch with the cultures, beliefs and ideologies of other people and countries.

The first of the United World Colleges had been opened in 1962 in William Randolph Hearst's old castle at St. Donat's in Wales. Earl Mountbatten had traveled the world, forming committees of educators to choose the students, most of whom received scholarship grants and subsidies for their fees. No student was to be excluded from UWC by reason of poverty.

Since then colleges had opened in Victoria, Canada, and in Singapore; and plans were well advanced for more colleges in Trieste and Waterford Kamhlaba in Swaziland.

At the Buckingham Palace reception, Lord Louis said, "It has always been my dream that there should be a United World College in the United States. We have tried several times to establish one, but I am sorry to say that we have failed completely."

Prince Charles smiled and deftly put the hook on me. He said, "I don't know why you don't turn this over to Doctor Hammer and see what he might be able to do."

"I'd be delighted to," said Lord Louis, "but I don't see why he should succeed where others have failed."

"Well, in my opinion," Prince Charles replied, "if anybody can do it, Doctor Hammer can."

They had no sooner thrown down the gauntlet than I picked it up. "I'll be happy to help you," I said.

Within two years of the original conversation, the purchase was completed of a million-dollar property (formerly occupied by the Catholic Church as a training center for young priests) for the new United World College in America. Two years later, on September 14, 1982, the Armand Hammer United World College opened its doors to 102 students from forty-six countries.

It was in a place called Montezuma, in the foothills of the Sangre de Cristo mountains in New Mexico, sixty miles from Santa Fe and just outside Las Vegas, New Mexico. There we found the historic and abandoned buildings of an old hot springs resort. The main building was a romantic castle, with Gothic towers and turrets, dating back to the days when the Santa Fe railroad had opened the Southwest territories of the United States. The wild beauty of the area and the location of the buildings at six thousand five hundred feet in crystalline mountain air made it a perfect spot for a college, allowing us to develop a range of wilderness programs for the students.

When I had first visited the site in 1981, I had been immediately enchanted with the place but daunted by its dereliction. The buildings were almost in ruins. Every window was broken. The castle's roof was a maze of holes. The grounds were completely overgrown, and we walked around them through mud up to our ankles. Nonetheless, my mind was made up immediately. This was the place.

We renovated five buildings to create residence halls, a dining room, library and academic facilities. The grounds were landscaped, tennis courts built and roads and walkways laid or improved. Many of my best friends gave their support, their time and their money—and the college flourishes today.

We still need money, though, and that was why I was so delighted that the Prince and Princess of Wales had agreed to make one of their few stops in America a benefit for the colleges. One million dollars of the hoped-for money was to go to establish an endowment fund for the UWC world headquarters in London. The rest we would use as scholarships for my College of the American West. It costs about $15,000 a year to provide for tuition and living expenses for one student at the college, and although the tuition is $10,000, the great majority of the students pay nothing at all.

Needless to say, to raise that kind of money, we weren't running a hundred-dollar-blueplate special. Invitations to the party did not come cheaply. Nobody could give less than $10,000 a couple, which provided for one scholarship at the college. For $50,000 per couple you could be a benefactor of the occasion, with the chance to meet the Royal Couple and be photographed shaking hands with them.

I don't know that any charitable occasion has ever been priced so high and been sold out! From all over the country, from all over the world, the checks came in, and it was exhilarating to see how willingly and warmly people pitched in to help out.

Naturally, at those prices, the occasion was within the reach only of the super-affluent, and, equally to be expected, there were those who claimed the whole affair was elitist and ridiculous. Prince Charles himself took on those charges, however, when he gave an after-dinner speech that positively raised the roof.

"What is wrong with being elite, for God's sake?" he said. "How on earth does anyone expect anything to get done in life unless there is some effort to educate people's characters as well as their minds? How are we to have any hope of balanced and civilized leadership in the future unless there are some people who have learned about service to others, about compassion; about understanding, as far as possible, the other man's religion, the other man's customs and his history; about courage to stand up for things that are noble and for things that are true? After all, there's so much to be done in this world—so much famine exists, so much disease, so much poverty, so much conflict, bigotry and prejudice, and there are so many people who are crying out for help, for their own simple dreams to come true.

"So what the hell can the United World Colleges do about it? We have six thousand ex-students after twenty-one years of operation. Now that, ladies and gentlemen, is a veritable army of potential talent, energy and initiative . . . we have an ultimate ambition . . . and that is that the ex-students . . . when they are in their fifties or even their sixties might be in influential positions in their own countries. They might then have some role to play in terms of trying to bring about some degree of understanding.

"And how on earth do they expect to get anything done without money? How do you actually achieve what Doctor Hammer has achieved, what these colleges try to achieve . . . without some form of finance? . . . There is money needed constantly for scholarships. They cost twelve thousand dollars, fifteen thousand dollars—you name it. There is no other way to obtain funds: you're certainly not going to get them from governments. That is why we rely on your generosity and your enthusiasm and, ultimately, on your sympathy. And we are extremely grateful. Thank you."

Whew! An almost audible exhalation seemed to run around the room. The guests had come expecting to look with interest and, perhaps, some skepticism on two pampered creatures of fairyland. They had not expected to have their socks knocked off by as forceful a speaker as any of them had ever heard.

The evening served all its purposes triumphantly. That very evening I was able to present a check for one million dollars to Sir Ian Gourlay, Director General of the UWC. The remaining three million dollars raised would provide approximately three hundred scholarships at the UWC College in Montezuma, New Mexico.

The Prince and Princess of Wales flew away from Palm Beach to hasten back to their children for a family celebration of the Prince's birthday. I flew to Washington, where I had a day of business meetings to conduct before I headed for home in Los Angeles.

PART NINE

Finales

At the end of the first week in December 1985, exactly a year after I had met with Konstantin Chernenko, I took that long, long haul back to Moscow again. I went to attend meetings of the US/USSR Trade and Economic Council—the first such meetings in Moscow since the Russian invasion of Afghanistan—and I went to put the new cultural agreement to work.

I felt confident that, with the cultural agreement signed, I could now persuade the Russians to send to America their Hermitage and Pushkin traveling collection of Impressionist and Post-Impressionist masterpieces which had been loaned to Baron Thyssen for exhibition in Lugano in 1983. Not many other people shared my confidence and, as it happened, it took all my sixty years' experience of doing business with the Russians to pull off the deal.

On December 9, 1985, the day after I arrived in Moscow, I had a meeting with Pyotr N. Demichev, then Minister of Culture of the USSR. I opened up with a big appeal: "Since the one agreement signed at the summit was the cultural agreement," I said, "we should attempt to accomplish something great and memorable in this field." I encouraged him to think that Mr. Gorbachev's visit to the US in 1986 would be boosted by a great popular triumph in the cultural field.

In exchange, I offered my own collection, Five Centuries of Masterpieces. It had been shown in Moscow in 1973, but since that time the collection had been greatly augmented.

Michael Bruk read to Mr. Demichev a list of the twenty-six pictures which had been added to my collection. Demichev said, "Those twenty-six would make a great exhibition on their own." He smiled. "Let's implement this exchange. The Hermitage and Pushkin collections could go to the National Gallery in Washington from, say, May to August 1986 and then, maybe, it could be seen in Los Angeles and at your Knoedler Galleries in New York. Meanwhile we can prepare to get your own collection exhibited in Leningrad and Moscow next summer."

I said that my collection could open in Leningrad as early as March 25 and could then go to Moscow to be shown at the Pushkin. I then gave Mr. Demichev a list and transparencies of forty Impressionist and Post-Impressionist pictures which Carter Brown, Director of the National Gallery in Washington, was willing to make available for loan to the Russians from February to June 1. "This could be the subject of a special exchange," Demichev said.

When I said that I would like to see the Hermitage and Pushkin collections shown at the Metropolitan Museum in New York, he said, "Why not Knoedler's? That is your own gallery and we are doing this for you."

We settled on the bones of this agreement. We said that we would draw up a letter of agreement and sign it toward the end of the week. We shook hands.

You might suppose that if the Soviet Minister of Culture decides that a deal will be done, it will be done. Not so. Every arrangement made in Moscow is tangled with as many obstacles and complications as an octopus has limbs. Mr. Demichev wanted to make the exchange. Some of the lesser officials in the Ministry had other ideas.

When I followed up my meeting with negotiators for the agreed contract, they said, "There are many difficulties. . . ." This is a standard line of Moscow maneuvering, and it amounts to a call to sharpen your wits.

They took this tack: the Pushkin Museum had already agreed to lend another collection of forty Impressionists to Baron Thyssen for the summer of 1986. If, at the same time, the Lugano pictures were to be in America, the Pushkin Museum would be virtually bare of its most essential treasures. They could not allow this to happen.

"It would not happen," I replied. "You will have my collection and the National Gallery's pictures to exhibit. I am confident that the Soviet people will be eager to see these works, which have never before been exhibited in Russia."

They asked if I would get in touch with Baron Thyssen and ask if he would be willing to postpone his exhibition until 1987—which I did, and to which he generously agreed. Well, that should take care of it, I thought. Wrong again.

The agreement was supposed to be ready for signing at the end of the week. As the days ticked by, however, I got messages saying that complications and difficulties had arisen, and final agreement could not be guaranteed. I replied that, a deal being a deal, I was not going to leave Moscow without a signed agreement.

On my last day in Moscow, Friday, December 13, I went down to the Ministry of Culture. I was told that Mr. Demichev was attending a writers' congress, was unavailable, and that therefore the agreement could not be signed. I refused to budge. "Somebody here must be empowered to sign," I said.

I sat in the offices of the Ministry for about two hours while discomforted and embarrassed officials tried to edge me out. Finally, Mr.

Zeitsev, a Deputy Minister, invited me into his office and agreed to sign for the Minister. The Lugano collection would go to the National Gallery in Washington and to the Frances and Armand Hammer Wing of the County Museum in Los Angeles. The forty pictures from the National Gallery would be shown in Leningrad and in Moscow from February to May. My collection would be shown in Leningrad after the National Gallery collection, then in Moscow, Novosibirsk, Kiev, Odessa and finally Tbilisi, Georgia, until January 1987.

We signed.

I immediately held a press conference to announce that the first fruits of the summit's cultural agreement had materialized, and left for London. No sooner had I got there, though, than I got a call from the *New York Times*. They were extremely disappointed that New York had been excluded from the venues for the Soviet collection and they could not understand why such a major exhibition was going to bypass the largest city in the US. I agreed with them. I, too, was disappointed, but said that we had done well to get agreement for Washington and Los Angeles.

Still, it nagged at me. I decided that the moment had come to appeal directly to Mr. Gorbachev. I quickly dictated a letter to him, which was telexed to my Moscow office, translated into Russian and delivered by courier to the offices of Mr. Demichev and Mr. Gorbachev.

"It is important for the collection to appear in New York City," I wrote. "New York is not only the largest city in America, it is the center of opinion formation in this nation."

The letter was sent from London on Saturday, December 14. On Monday, December 16, while I was flying home to Los Angeles, I received a telex aboard my plane from Michael Bruk in Moscow: the Lugano pictures would be shown at the Metropolitan Museum.

As I always say, if you want to get something done, you'd better talk to the boss.

No better example of the benefits of dealing directly with the boss could be given than the deal which I concluded right in the last dying days of the year. Lost in the suburbs of Chicago, seated in a family car, I hacked out an agreement with Mr. Cliff Davis, the CEO of MidCon Corporation. I don't suppose that a three-billion-dollar deal has ever been done in odder circumstances.

Just after Christmas, on Friday, December 27, 1985, the First Boston Corporation approached Occidental to ask if we might be interested in being a white knight to MidCon, to save them from a hostile takeover. Were we ever!

MidCon, based in Lombard, Illinois, operated approximately thirty thousand miles of interstate and intrastate gas pipelines, one of the largest and most flexible pipeline-marketing systems in the nation. Their resources were exactly what Occidental needed. The appearance of MidCon as a potential acquisition was like the arrival of the Christmas fairy.

I had a conference with Ray Irani. Other companies were also interested in being white knight to MidCon. I said, "The only way we'll make this deal is if we go to Chicago ourselves and meet them and convince them that we'll let them continue to run their own company."

MidCon's executives said that they would be happy to see us for lunch in Chicago on Monday, December 30.

I had to get up in Los Angeles at four A.M. that day for a six o'clock takeoff in Oxy One. A whole retinue of Occidental's top staff went with me, including the President, Controller, two Vice Presidents, and Occidental's chief lawyer, Jerry Stern. In Chicago we were to be met by lawyers from Skadden Arps in New York and by representatives of First Boston. The heavy crews were in the field!

Cliff Davis was at the airport to meet my plane. There was a rank of limousines waiting to ferry my staff to MidCon's offices, but Cliff Davis was driving a vintage Cadillac sedan, and he invited me to get in beside him in the front seat while Ray Irani slid into the back. The limousines set off in one direction. Cliff drove away in the opposite direction. I presumed he knew where he was going—it was his town, after all.

I took to him right away. I liked his lack of ceremony and his open manner. He was a big, burly Midwesterner, about five feet eleven and two hundred pounds, just turned sixty-six years of age and justifiably proud of the corporation he had built up.

Sitting in the car, while I, naturally, took no notice of where we were headed, we got right down to business. The hostile raiders on MidCon had indicated they were willing to pay shareholders $70 a share. Our advisers had calculated that we, as white knights, should offer $72 to beat off the hostile takeover. MidCon's own valuation of the company's worth was $75 a share.

I told Mr. Davis, "Look, I'm not going to haggle with you. I want this acquisition to be on the best and friendliest terms on both sides. We'll give you seventy-five dollars, half cash and half stock. What do you say?"

He stuck out his hand. "You've got a deal," he said. We both shook hands.

The lawyers and financial officers could work out the details, but we had struck a deal in the best way possible. We were all very relaxed, jovial and happy as we drove along. We were also lost.

Cliff Davis had been so absorbed in our business that he hadn't noticed where he was driving. Suddenly he said, "I'm sorry to tell you this, but I don't know where the hell I am." It took us an age to find our way back to MidCon's offices, where all our highly paid executives had been twiddling their thumbs for over an hour while we did our deal in the car.

The boards of both corporations were summoned to meet at the same time on the next day, New Year's Eve. My board unanimously approved the deal and we waited to hear from Chicago. Time passed— an hour, two hours, two and a half. I began to get uneasy—but finally the deal came through. Cliff Davis had had trouble with some dissident Directors, but he had stuck to his word, and after three hours, the MidCon board endorsed the deal and it was done.

In the last hours of 1985, I announced that Occidental Petroleum had become the nation's twelfth-largest industrial concern, with total estimated annual sales of approximately sixteen billion dollars.

There are worse ways to end a year.

At the beginning of this chapter, in November 1984, the peace of the world and a cure for cancer were as far from reality as they had ever been. By the end of 1985, both these dreams of humanity had drawn just a little bit closer. The summit conference in Geneva seemed to make the world a safer place—and the publication of Steven Rosenberg's paper in *The New England Journal of Medicine* heralded a new approach in the fight against cancer.

He reported that he had treated twenty-five patients who had not been cured by standard therapies. Objective regression—greater than 50 percent in volume—had been seen in eleven of the patients. One patient had undergone complete tumor regression. Ten partial responses had been seen.

Steven Rosenberg's more recent results, too new to be reported in his paper, on more than one hundred patients, substantiated his earlier findings. As you might expect, it was decided that Rosenberg should be the recipient of the 1986 Hammer Prize. On January 30, 1986, the $100,000 prize was presented to him and to Dr. Tadatsugu Taniguchi of Osaka University—who had succeeded in isolating the gene for IL-2, cloning it and making it possible to produce large amounts of the substance artificially. As of that date, in addition to his earlier reported successes, Dr. Rosenberg had treated ten patients suffering from kidney cancer and had obtained nine out of ten successes with them—a phenomenal result in the treatment of a type of cancer which has hitherto been incurable.

One of my lifelong ambitions is drawing within reach while the other—world peace—may be dimly spied as a distant prospect over the horizon.

I believe the Geneva Summit was a limited success. It produced little of substance, but that was never very likely. Both sides could easily have come away wringing their empty hands and denouncing each other. Just before the summit began, I heard from one of my friends in the State Department in Washington that it was proving impossible to frame the terms for a joint communiqué which could be issued at the end of the meetings. Hearing this, I feared the worst.

Ronald Reagan very intelligently and nimbly hurdled the bureaucratic obstruction between him and Mr. Gorbachev. He sat down, one-on-one, with the General Secretary, for five of the fifteen hours available to them, and, just as I had always predicted and hoped, when the two men met face to face, they found that they could do business with each other. They warmed to each other. Neither man was ever going to surrender any important article of his political beliefs: Ronald Reagan was not going to come away from Geneva a Communist convert, nor was Mikhail Gorbachev likely to return to the Kremlin to preach the benefits of capitalism. However, in talking to each other at such length, they found that they were able to knock out some essential compromises by which our two systems may be able to live together in the future.

The first and most important of their agreements was to continue the peacemaking process begun in Geneva, with annual summits in the next two years. One cheer for that development.

Another cheer for the progress they made in Geneva on the question of arms reduction and Star Wars. Though no agreement was made, the President took up and endorsed the Russians' plan for a 50-percent reduction in strategic nuclear weapons, and he offered to let Russian scientists inspect America's Star Wars laboratories to see for themselves that the SDI is genuinely not an offensive system. Neither of these points is, in itself, a great breakthrough, but they both mark essential beginnings. If Russian scientists are to be allowed to inspect research laboratories working on SDI, the logical next step will be to go the whole distance and begin a joint development, pooling the research and knowledge of both sides. When I proposed that in my *New York Times* piece in September 1985, some people said that it was an impossible fantasy. The Geneva Summit put a joint development of SDI firmly on the agenda for future business.

And a third cheer for the cultural agreement, which was exactly what I and everybody else had hoped for. It opened the way for the peoples of both countries to see and experience each other's best artistic creations.

So three good, rousing cheers were deserved for the Geneva Summit. Mr. Reagan and Mr. Gorbachev amply earned the heroes' welcomes they received on returning to their countries. It was particularly notable that the Politburo promptly endorsed Mr. Gorbachev's report of the summit and the proposals arising from it.

The world was not made safe by the Geneva Summit. It is still a hauntingly dangerous place. A single misjudgment in the maintenance of the balance of terror, a single human error in the working of the Doomsday machines, can still destroy us all and our planet. But I believe that we can sleep a little easier for the beginning made in Geneva; and we must press on until the menace of the nuclear holocaust is completely removed from our and our children's lives.

And I plan to live to see it happen!

Epilogue

These must be my parting words. The moment has come to end this book, two years after it was begun. During these two years an unprecedented opportunity has emerged for the creation of peace. It has emerged unexpectedly; none of us could have predicted it; few of us can see it even at this moment.

With one decisive step, with one great gesture of trust and goodwill, the world might now end the insanities of the nuclear menace. We could set aside the death-laden doctrine of Mutually Assured Destruction (appropriately known as MAD) and embrace the opportunities of a new doctrine, which I want to call Mutually Assured Defense. Which doctrine sounds more rational? Which is more inviting?

The opportunity arises out of an impasse; the brightest hope for the future of the world comes from an apparently hopeless deadlock.

The Reykjavik Summit of October 1986, which seemed to promise such unexpected steps toward a nuclear-free world, foundered on a single obstacle, was riven by equal and opposite intransigency between President Reagan and General Secretary Gorbachev. The obstacle, of course, was the Strategic Defense Initiative, or Star Wars. The Soviets went to Reykjavik prepared to make immense concessions in missile disarmament. Their proposals were so far-reaching, offering such deep cuts, that the President and his advisers were caught off guard. The Soviets' offers were conditional, however: they required the Americans to abandon testing of Star Wars in space and confine themselves to laboratory research.

President Reagan, rejecting this demand and calling it intolerable, said, on leaving Iceland, that no President of the United States could surrender the right to develop defense systems to protect our people and our freedoms. He had made a counteroffer to Mr. Gorbachev, which was rejected on the Soviets' part. Mr. Reagan repeated to Mr. Gorbachev his previous promise to share SDI technology with the Soviets if it were successfully developed. To this offer Mr. Gorbachev had responded with characteristic bluntness: "I cannot take this idea of yours seriously, the idea that you will share SDI results with us. You don't even want to share computers for dairy plants with us at this point."

Nobody could deny that Mr. Gorbachev has a point. Knowing how deep is Soviet distrust of the United States, and our distrust of them, can he reasonably be expected to sit on his hands for ten years, watching us develop Star Wars in the hope that we might hand it over to him as a present once we have made sure the system works?

We have to consider this problem rationally, assessing the difficulties and then trying to arrive at a mutually beneficial solution. In other words let's try to frame the conditions for a deal.

The Soviets must understand that, despite their complaints and their rhetoric, President Reagan seems determined to proceed with SDI development, just as they themselves seem to be doing their best to perfect such a system. That much is obvious. Whether Mr. Reagan will be able to get all the funding he has asked for from Congress is open to question, especially now that he no longer has a Republican-controlled Senate. As of this writing, the President has funding only for research in the amount of a few billion dollars. Before proceeding to development and production, authorization from Congress must be for hundreds of billions of dollars. Nonetheless, it is possible to suppose that SDI may be developed by a future President with the approval of Congress at some point before the end of the century, or beyond, if, for instance, the number of warheads on each side were to be drastically reduced by successive agreement from the present approximately ten thousand each to perhaps one to two hundred each. We would still have a nuclear deterrent against the present superior conventional forces of the Warsaw Pact nations as compared to the NATO forces. Hopefully, both sides will reduce the size of their conventional forces as they come to see no need for them. The history of the world teaches us infallibly that mankind always proceeds toward the consummation of potential progress: it is essential to human nature that we should. Therefore, despite the objections of the skeptics who say that it will never work, we can assume that the US will try to develop SDI. (We should remember that the skeptics also said that man would never walk on the moon. In earlier times, the same skeptics said the earth was flat and that Columbus would fall off its edge into the crack of doom. So much for them.)

So the problem we have to solve is in two parts. First of all, the Soviets may fear that the technological and scientific capacities of the West ensure that, if it proves feasible, we will develop SDI before them. Consequently they fear that we may attain an immense advantage which could guarantee our survival in a nuclear exchange. This advantage, they point out, would negate the deterrence philosophy of Mutually Assured Destruction upon which arms control has rested during these last decades.

The second part of the problem is not stated by the Soviets, but we may reasonably assume it: Star Wars research will be so expensive that it could be an intolerable burden on the Soviet economy. If they are driven to make the sacrifice, we may be certain that they will make it: the history of their society in this century leaves no room for doubt that they will do whatever they feel to be necessary to protect themselves. But the cost, they recognize, is far greater than they can bear without imposing a cruel scale of material privation upon their people. Our problem will be similar—inability to get rid of huge deficits while spending billions on Star Wars. There is the problem. Here is one proposed solution.

During the summer of 1985, as I have described, I proposed, subject to adequate verification, that SDI should be jointly and mutually researched and developed by America and the Soviet Union in a common US research facility with both sides sharing information and costs. The proposal was met with widespread approbation, but the time was clearly not right for it. At that moment President Reagan and Mr. Gorbachev had yet to meet for the first time in Geneva and, being new to office, Mr. Gorbachev had barely had the chance to frame the policies of his administration.

Now the moment has truly arrived for the proposal to be given effect. I believe it is a genuinely workable solution. And, more than that, it can point the way to an entirely new order in relations between the superpowers.

I believe that President Reagan truly intends for the US to provide the Soviets with SDI technology when it is successfully developed. Therefore—why not invite the Soviets to share with us in the system's research and development from the start? We have a new age and a new world to gain. A cooperative endeavor of this scale would set aside more than a half century of distrust and fear. If Soviet scientists and military experts worked side by side with their American counterparts on a joint enterprise of such importance, with such mutually desirable ends, our societies would be drawn closer than we might ever have imagined.

It is natural that the first objection to this idea should be, as Mrs. Thatcher wrote me, that our potential enemies might learn the innermost secrets of our defense plans, or that they might cheat us. This anxiety can be allayed. Rational, adult planning—the framing of a grown-up deal—could take account of this danger and avert it.

What it takes is the creation of full and mutual verification procedures. The Soviets would have to be open with us about the quality and extent of their own research, and we would have to be open with them. Mr. Gorbachev is the first leader of the Soviet Union who has offered this. Why not test him? Both sides would need to be sure that the other was being fully candid. Ignorance, not knowledge, is the source of fear.

Such inspection and verification procedures are not unprecedented. The joint US-Soviet space effort which resulted in the Apollo/Soyuz linkup gives us the model we seek, proving that we can happily and successfully exchange information at the highest level.

The joint French-Soviet development of fast-breeder nuclear reactors also points the way. This project was originally set up in three stages, reflecting the mutual distrust with which both sides approached each other, but at the same time to be competitive with the US. The first two stages involved preliminary exchanges of information by which the partners could test each other's trustworthiness. The third stage called for full, active cooperation. The French and the Russians moved smoothly and quickly to a full completion of the third stage.

Our first step toward Mutually Assured Defense should be the creation of a study group, or "think-tank," to examine and evaluate the possibility of sharing SDI. Discreet signals have already been given from Moscow that a preliminary exchange of information might not be spurned. We need to establish some elementary ground-rules upon which we might proceed. It is not good enough for either side to say that the idea would never work. We must try; we must push at the limits of the impossible and create the possible. Given the remotest chance of Mutually Assured Defense in place of Mutually Assured Destruction, we must go for it. After the failure of the November 5–6, 1986, meetings and the bitter exchange of views by Secretary Shultz and Foreign Minister Shevardnadze at Vienna, it seems unlikely that another summit between Reagan and Gorbachev will be held unless we find some acceptable compromise.

Mr. Dobrynin indicated to me at one of my recent meetings with him that the Russians are ready to be flexible over the term "laboratory research." By "laboratory" they do not necessarily mean a building with four walls and a roof.

My proposal is not, of course, the only route to such a compromise; plenty of intelligent and less drastic suggestions have been aired.

My friend Senator Al Gore, Jr., has come up with the imaginative and practical proposal that arms reductions should be effected by the elimination of multiple warheads and a bilateral agreement on single-warhead mobile missiles. This idea would at least reduce the insanity of the present situation, in which both sides are assured of each other's destruction not once but ten or twenty times each (as if it were possible for a person or a planet to be killed more than once). Again, an imposing group of commentators, led by McGeorge Bundy, Robert McNamara, George Kennan and Gerard Smith, believes that the dispute over SDI development could be contained within modifications to the existing ABM Treaty.

Both of these approaches provide practical and pragmatic compromise solutions to the immediate problems of peace negotiations. If implemented, they would not, in themselves, rule out further progress toward my own proposal for joint and mutual development of SDI. These ideas could all mesh together, bringing us nearer to a balanced and mutual elimination of the nuclear menace. We *must* find a way to protect ourselves and future generations from that final and cataclysmic nuclear disaster. Our responsibilities for the planet and the future of the human race demand no less.

INDEX